J. Ross Eshleman

APPALACHIAN STATE UNIVERSITY

The Family
AN INTRODUCTION

Fifth Edition

ALLYN AND BACON, INC.

Boston · London · Sydney · Toronto

Library of Congress Cataloging-in-Publication Data

Eshleman, J. Ross.
  The family.

  Includes bibliographies and indexes.
    1. Family. 2. Marriage. 3. Family—United States.
I. Title.
HQ515.E83 1988   306.8'5   87–33273
ISBN 0–205–11182–3

Printed in the United States of America

10 9 8 7 6 5 4 3 2 1 92 91 90 89 88 87

CONTENTS

iv   *Contents*

PREFACE

What should an introductory family textbook try to do? First, I believe it should provide a thorough and objective coverage of the basic concepts and ideas in marriage and the family. These ideas should be presented clearly and intelligibly. The coverage should include specific factual data as well as abstract principles, empirically supported findings as well as hypotheses for testing. Since many students will find this introduction to the family to be their terminal course as well, the text should arouse a curiosity toward, and include tools for, an ongoing processes of observation, understanding, and analysis of marital and family relationships and organizations.

Second, and equally important, I believe an introductory family textbook should capture the interest of the student. This should not be done at the expense of accuracy but should convey realistically the processes and organization of marital and family behavior in an understandable, readable, and interesting way. From this, the student should be able to relate personal and familial values and behaviors to differing life-styles and patterns both within his or her own society and in relation to others. In other words, the student should be made to see more clearly his or her place in the United States or in the world picture.

I have tried with this book to write a text that was both interesting and highly readable, to be relatively comprehensive in the coverage of topics, to emphasize the family in the United States and supplement it heavily with historical and cross-cultural referents, and to be accurate, yet contemporary—including nontraditional marital and family life-styles, yet keeping them in a realistic perspective relative to the more common traditional family forms. I have tried to document extensively in presenting the study of the family as a scholarly discipline and have tried to encourage further thought and reading by concluding each chapter with questions for discussion and an annotated bibliography for further reading. Extensive use of the latest census material has been made and illustrative selections have been inserted (note the boxed panels).

Each of these attempts was an outgrowth of several major objectives: (1) to present an objective description and analysis of contemporary U.S. families within a world perspective, (2) to examine without condemnation or praise nontraditional family and marital life-styles, (3) to apply general theoretical schemes and frames of reference to family issues, (4) to present basic concepts and descriptive materials clearly and intelligibly, (5) to suggest questions and supplemental sources to stimulate discussion and reading beyond the textual materials, and (6) to cultivate in the student an increased awareness of his or her particular niche in the family and general social order.

The Family basically follows a sociological and social-psychological approach. Part I deals with understanding the family irrespective of time or place. It summarizes basic issues in families in the United States; examines approaches to the study of families; establishes five basic frames of reference or theories central to understanding family groups and systems; illustrates the boundaries of marital, family, and kinship organization; and looks at the linkages between the family and other institutions with a major focus on marriage as related to the world of work. Part II looks at cultural and subcultural variations in family life-styles: between traditional and contemporary mainland Chinese families, among Black families in the United States, and, finally, by social class. Part III brings structure and process to the creation of a marital and family status by examining the who, why, and how of mate selection in contemporary U.S. society. Part IV singles out sexual norms and relationships as a major and significant social fact of the premarital, marital, and family system. Part V deals with the family life cycle: marriage, parenthood, child rearing or socialization, and middle and later years, including dying, death, and the post-marital family. Part IV examines the nature of crisis, domestic violence, divorce, and remarriage, and concludes the book with a chapter on the family and social policy.

As a result of an extensive review of the literature, as well as sleceted feedback from faculty and students who used previous editions, various changes and additions appear in this fifth edition. Considerable changes in reorganization have occurred within chapters. Chapter 5 from the previous edition on nontraditional marital and family life-styles has, for the most part, been integrated into other chapters as appropriate. For example, commuter marriages can be found in Chapter 4, which focuses on work; childless marriage in Chapter 13, which discusses family size; and remarried couples as well as those with stepchildren in Chapter 17 on divorce and remarriage. Gender identity and sex-role socialization, previously in Chapter 4, can now be found in Chapter 14 on parent-child interaction and socialization. The discussion of single parents previously in Chapter 14 is now included in a section of Chapter 7 on the feminization of poverty.

Extensive new and updated material will be evident throughout the text: there are more recent census data, many new inserts, and significant new research findings and theoretical explanations on topics ranging from the husband's participation (or lack of it) in domestic housework and child care to sexualization and sexual scripts. Chapter 17 in the previous edition has been expanded into a new Chapter 16 on family crisis and domestic violence and Chapter 17 on divorce and remarriage. As in the previous edition, five basic frames of reference (structural-functional, interactional, developmental, exchange, and conflict) are described and applied at various points throughout, extensive use is made of recent census data and research findings, and selected inserts (boxed panels) are provided to supplement the basic textual material. All chapters end with a summary, key terms and topics, discussion questions, and annotated further readings.

It is my hope that you will find the ideas stimulating and clearly explained. Where you find errors, where you disagree with particular points, when you can supply supplemental material or observations, please inform me. I hope the book will be readable and interesting, will present an accurate portrayal of family systems, will be flexible in its use, will stimulate thought and discussion, and, perhaps most important, will change behavior by expanding our awareness of, and sensitivity to, self and others.

It is difficult to know where to begin or end in expressing a deeply felt sense of gratitude and appreciation to many people. Surely, the most sacrifices were made by my wife Janet, my daughter Jill, and my son Sidney, who gave up various family activities to allow Dad to write. I also want to acknowledge my Ph.D. advisor, A. R. Mangus, and my department chairman for the nine years I was at Western Michigan University, the late Leonard Kercher. Both these men had a major influence on my life, my interest in the family, and my professional achievement.

To single out others would require a lengthy list. But several should be mentioned. My daughter Jill and my secretary Joyce Rhymer typed sections of the manuscript. Professionals in the field (some unknown to me) who were users of the last edition and the reviewers for this edition's manuscript—Jill Quadagno, University of Kansas; Karen Wilkenson, University of Michigan—Flint; and Laura Workman Eells, Wichita State University—provided valuable reactions, comments, and suggestions for changes in this edition. Friends and colleagues who provided encouragement and support in areas other than textbook writing should be acknowledged as well. Finally, individuals such as Karen Hanson and Alicia Riley at Allyn and Bacon, each fulfilling his or her professional tasks, were influential in getting this book into its final form. Beverly Miller and Judith Gimple of Bywater Production Services provided excellent editorial assistance. To each of these individuals I extend my thanks and appreciation.

J. Ross Eshleman

I

UNDERSTANDING MARRIAGE AND THE FAMILY

Photo: © John Pearson/Freelance Photographer's Guild

1

An Introduction to the Family: Issues and Change

The Family? What is this family? Is *the* family the one with one female legally married to one male? Does this couple have two children (one of each sex, of course) born within wedlock, a husband employed full time serving as the primary provider and ultimate authority, a wife as a full-time mother and housewife, and a cohesive, loving, sexually exclusive unit bound until death do they part? Or is *the* family one with a single parent who has a child born outside of wedlock? Does *the* family include a wife who is employed full time, a husband who chooses to be the primary child rearer, a childless couple, or a less than cohesive, conflict-ridden, abusive unit that experiences divorce?

This book, although titled, *The Family*, recognizes the family as having a plurality of forms and behaviors. A key goal is to examine the wide range of family patterns that exists in North America and around the world. An attempt is made to incorporate current research findings in an effort to understand the uniformities, regularities, and consistencies as well as the differences, irregularities, and changes that exist in family norms, values, and behaviors. These similarities and differences are reflected in the organization and life-styles of people in diverse social and cultural contexts.

Similarities and most differences in attitudes, behaviors, and organization create little conflict or controversy. Most of these similarities and differences are not even obvious to the majority of persons who never undertake a systematic study of the family. Do parents, teachers, or businesspeople get disturbed over higher divorce rates in the West, employment rates of mothers, or the failure of Amish-Americans to use electricity or drive automobiles? Generally not. However, social controversy does arise when Amish buggies present a highway danger to fast-moving automobiles, when children of working mothers are not provided adequate care, and when property settlements and child placements cannot be agreed upon by divorced couples. This introductory chapter alerts us to selected major issues brought about by social change and to selected characteristics of families in the United States. Chapter 2 discusses approaches used to examine issues such as these.

IDEAL-TYPE CONSTRUCTS

Many concepts, illustrations, and ideas used in this book are treated in "ideal-type" terms. Ideal types are *not* what are implied in the common usage of the word: that which is ideal, good, best, valuable, perfect, or desirable. Rather, ideal types are hypothetical constructs based on "pure" characteristics.

Ideal types always represent the end, the extreme, or the pole of a continuum. Created hypothetically, they provide contrasting points with which to compare any social phenomenon. Patriarchal/matriarchal, nuclear/extended, primary/secondary, individualism/familism, or rural/urban are examples of ideal types. The "pure" characteristics of rural might include geographical and social isolation, homogeneity, agricultural employment, sparse population, and a subsistence economy. Characteristics of urban are likely to include social heterogeneity, industrial employment, dense population, and impersonality. Any community in the world could be placed along this ideal-type continuum, but none is likely to include all characteristics to their maximum degree. These terms accentuate, even exaggerate, reality rather than describe it accurately. On a rural/urban construct, Chicago would fall toward the urban end of the continuum. However, New York may be more characteristic of urban than Chicago, and Tokyo more characteristic than either. Few would argue against the residents of Rough Creek, Arizona, or Mud Lick, Kentucky, being classified as rural, but compared to the Tasaday tribe on the island of Mindanao in the Philippines, both are quite urban.

The concept "ideal type" was systematically developed by the German sociologist Max Weber.[1] He was careful to point out that, first, value connotations should be avoided. The prefix *ideal* denotes a constructed model, not evaluation or approval. It makes no suggestion as to what ought to be or what norm of conduct is approved or disapproved. Second, an ideal type or ideal construct is not an average or model characteristic. An average denotes a central tendency, whereas an ideal type is a representation derived from the extreme instances. Third, as mentioned, the ideal type is not reality. It is an abstraction, a logical construct, and by its very nature is not found in reality in its pure form.

The functions of ideal-type constructs

An ideal-type construct performs several basic functions: (1) it provides a limiting case with which concrete phenomena may be contrasted; (2) it

---

1. Max Weber, *The Methodology of the Social Sciences*, trans. and ed. Edward H. Shils and Henry A. Finch (New York: The Free Press, 1949).

provides for the analysis and measurement of social reality; and (3) it facilitates classification and comparison. In short, the ideal type provides a means to clarify what any phenomenon would be if it always or ever conformed to its own definition. Thus, ideal types enable social scientists to make valid and precise comparisons between societies, institutions, or families separated in time and place. It enables us in a sociology of the family to have a methodological tool that provides assistance in examining the upper or lower classes, black or white families, or arranged or free-choice mate selection. At this point, it is used to examine selected issues in the American family.

ISSUES IN THE U.S. FAMILY

There is little dispute that the family in United States society is changing. Change per se is not necessarily disruptive, nor does it always present a conflict of interest between groups or persons. However, not all changes occur at an equal rate, nor do all segments of a society adjust equally to the changes taking place. Thus it would be possible to deal with nearly any issue in the family by noting what predominant patterns existed at some point in the past and then comparing them with present patterns. Similarly, it would be possible to establish a series of ideal-type constructs (extended family/conjugal family, patriarchal family/matriarchal family, arranged marriages/free choice of mate, homogamy/heterogamy), place any aspect of a given family system at different points of time on the continuum, and observe the changes or trends that seem to be taking place.

The selected issues in the family that will be discussed in this chapter follow this procedure. Using polar extremes as ideal types, changes are shown that have occurred in the family primarily within this century. Thus a comparison is made between traditional and emergent (nontraditional) family forms. A comparison is made between the ideal norms (traditional patterns) and the real norms (emergent patterns).

Issues (that is, unresolved conflicts) exist because both a traditional and an emergent set of norms exist simultaneously. In other words, certain groups and individuals resist the emergent norms and cling vehemently to the more traditional patterns; other individuals and groups find the traditional patterns unacceptable and adhere to a different set of norms and values. The result is that major issues (conflicts) occur primarily because of social change. If no change occurs and everyone accepts the traditional patterns of behavior, no issue or conflict results; similarly, if everyone adopts an emergent set of norms, no conflict exists.

Several ideal-type constructs are developed here to illustrate the conflicts that result when emergent sets of marital and family values

TABLE 1–1
Traditional families and nontraditional family alternatives

The "traditional" way	The "nontraditional" alternative
Legally married	Never-married singlehood; nonmarital cohabitation
With children	Voluntary childlessness
Two-parent	Single-parent (never-married; once-married)
Permanent	Divorce and remarriage (including joint custody and binuclear family; the stepfamily)
Male as primary provider and ultimate authority	Androgynous marriage (including open marriage, dual-career marriage, and commuter marriage)
Sexually exclusive	Extramarital relationships (including sexually open marriage, swinging, and intimate friendships)
Heterosexual	Same-sex intimate relationships
Two-adult household	Multi-adult households (including multilateral marriage, communal living, affiliated families, and expanded families)

Source: Eleanor D. Macklin, "Nontraditional Family Forms: A Decade of Research," *Journal of Marriage and the Family* 42 (November 1980): 906.

coexist with traditional social values inherited from the past. It is in pluralistic societies that both the traditional and a multiple number of emergent family patterns exist simultaneously. This results in conflict, confusion, and an unsettled state in the family system.

The issues that follow are not listed in any order of importance with the exception of the first. It is my belief that all other issues relate to or basically stem from the meaning given to marriage and the family itself.

The meaning of marriage and the family

The most basic issue presented here centers around the meaning and the purpose of marriage and the family. It questions the sources of authority in marital and family decisions. It questions whether marriage is itself necessary.

The most traditional social norm, which represents one polar extreme of our ideal-type construct, views marriage as a *sacred* phenomenon. That is to say, the family and marriage are divine and holy institutions. They are created and maintained by God, Yahweh, or some supreme being greater than men and women. The phrase "marriages are made in heaven" is in many ways consistent with this perspective. This traditional social norm was perhaps most widely prevalent prior to the turn of the century.

In its extreme form, marriage is not only sacred, but it is in itself a sacrament. The Catholic church today views marriage as one of the seven sacraments. This implies that human beings and their personal wishes or wants are of secondary importance to that which is God-created and God-given. Basic to this idea is the source of authority on all family and religious matters as stemming from God or his connecting links (prophets, popes, cardinals, bishops, or priests) in the hierarchy of human-God positions.

A second traditional norm, one in widespread existence at the turn of the century and the first several decades thereafter, views the meaning of marriage and the family as centering primarily around *social* obligations. The social meaning of marriage, like the sacred meaning, represents traditional norms. But rather than the source of authority being God, authority becomes centered in human beings as represented by the kin group, community, church as a social institution, and society in general. Primary values within this meaning of marriage are to maintain social respectability, conform to kin and community wishes, and maintain a "proper image" within society. Thus, within this meaning of marriage, what other people think is very important. Divorce, premarital pregnancy, black-white intermarriage, and so forth are not undesirable per se but

Beliefs and practices of priests differ from church teachings

Differences exist between what the church teaches officially and what priests believe privately. Differences exist as well in what priests say publicly and privately about the teachings of the church. These findings come from a survey conducted by the Association of Chicago Priests of 140 priests in the Chicago Archdiocese.

The official teachings of the church place a ban on artificial birth control. Yet, 73 percent of the priests said they do not publicly support this ban. Even more, 87 percent, did not support the ban in their private counseling.

The official teaching of the church opposes masturbation, premarital sex, and homosexuality. Yet, in regard to masturbation, 60 percent of the priests did not back the stand publicly and 78 percent did not support it in private counseling. On premarital sex, nearly one-fourth didn't back the stand publicly and nearly two in five didn't do so privately. And on homosexuality, 39 percent of the priests didn't publicly support the stand of the Vatican and 44 percent didn't support it privately.

Other areas of considerable difference between the stand of the church and the views or practices of the priests centered on divorce and remarriage and on giving communion to those whose previous marriages had not been judged invalid. Surprisingly, only one priest in ten claimed he was bothered by the gap between the position of the church and his public or private stance.

because "society" (friends, community, kin group, and others), in word and in action, disapproves.

A third meaning of marriage suggests that families and the marital relationship exist for the *individual*. Thus, the concern is not with God or with society but with "me." If I choose to marry outside of my race, religion, ethnic group, social class, and educational level, that is "my business." After all, I am not marrying my family, my church, my community, or American society. If I am happy in my marriage, then it is a successful one. If I am unhappy, neither God nor society can dictate my behavior nor can they force the endurance of an unsuccessful marriage. Within this meaning, the source of authority is the person alone; each individual is responsible for his or her own success or failure without regard to the community structure or the social conditions in which he or she operates.

Thus, there are at least three basic meanings of marriage, all of which exist today. To some persons and groups, marriage is sacred or sacramental; with others, marriage is a social contract and success is viewed in terms of conformity to societal demands; to a third group, marriage is a highly personal, highly individualistic concern. The lack of uniformity in the source of authority on the meaning of marriage is basic to most issues and conflicts that exist in the marital and family system today in our society.

Family organization

Closely related to the basic meaning of marriage is the "proper" form of marital and family organization. Traditionally, in the United States and in much of the world, the extended-family form was most common and most highly desired. Power resided in the elders, and they in turn were responsible for caring for other members of the kin group. Kin-group members were located in geographical proximity to one another. They followed and married those with a similar set of norms and rules, maintained intimate emotional ties to one another, and were isolated from outside contacts. This type of family organization resulted in behavior patterns and values that remained constant from one generation to the next, in children being socialized to be basically duplicates of their parents in thought and in action, and, in Bernard Farber's terms, in having an **orderly replacement**[2] among successive generations.

In contrast to the orderly-replacement concept is the idea of pluralism: many and varied forms of marital and family organization. The family organization that is preferred will vary both over time and from one individual

---

2. Bernard Farber, *Family Organization and Interaction* (San Francisco: Chandler, 1964), Chapter 4.

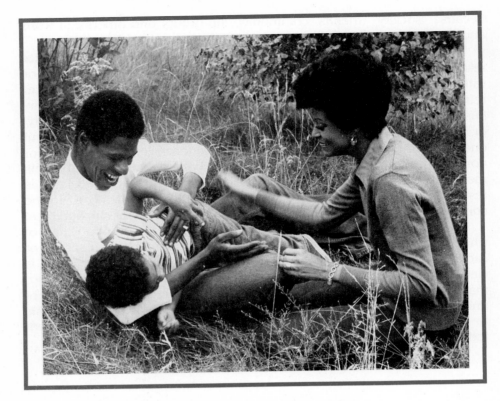

How families are organized and how they function varies widely by age, class, ethnicity, and size, for example, but family units are a central component of every society in the world. (Photo: © Camerique Stock Photos/E. P. Jones, Co.)

to another. Some individuals may prefer to eliminate the marriage contract and simply live together. Others may desire some form of communal family where, at least economically, labor and goods are shared equally among all members. A limited number of persons may desire a group marriage where three or four persons all recognize each other as spouse. Certain members may choose not to marry at all. Some of those who choose not to marry may choose to be parents. The point is that emergent forms of family organization will not be uniform among families nor necessarily within the same family over time. Again in Farber's terms, the result would be **universal permanent availability**.[3]

The universal-permanent-availability concept suggests that individuals are available for marriage with anyone at any time. Homogamous social characteristics decline in importance, and marriage becomes a personal rather than a kinship problem. Thus, love marriages rather than arranged

3. Ibid, p. 105.

marriages become prevalent, the rates of divorce and remarriage increase, the number of children declines, less emphasis is placed on premarital chastity and marital fidelity, emphasis is placed on competence and interpersonal relations, more married women enter the work force, and youth and glamour are emphasized. Thus polygyny, polyandry, homosexual marriages, nonlegal voluntary associations, progressive monogamy, trial marriages, group marriages, communal families, single-parent families, or no marriage at all have a place within emergent forms of family organization.

A basic issue exists today over the "proper" form of family organization. Those who view marriage as sacred, those who view marriage as a monogamous lifelong relationship, and those who insist on two-parent permanent relationships will find difficulty in accepting and adjusting to emergent forms of family organization that are becoming increasingly public. It is not that these forms are totally new; rather, it is that these forms are occurring with an increasing frequency, are being given an increasing amount of publicity, or are resulting in meaningful and realistic alternatives in the form of marital and family organization of thousands of persons in the United States today. A multiple number of acceptable forms of marriage and family life are part of the pluralistic scene of our society.

Family functions

Many critics of the American family have included in their argument for the "breakdown" of the family the loss of functions which has taken place. Throughout written history, the family has been the major social institution. With changes that have occurred, particularly within the functions that a family has performed, the increasing specialization and complexity of modern society has led to a dehumanizing and fragmentizing process.

This issue is by no means a recent one. In the 1930s, William Ogburn argued that the dilemma of the modern family was due to its loss of functions.[4] It was his belief that prior to modern times the power and prestige of the family was due to the seven functions it performed.

1. Foremost was the *economic* function. The family was a self-sufficient unit in which the members of the family consumed primarily that which they produced. Thus banks, stores, and factories were not needed.
2. The family served the basic function of giving *prestige* and *status* to its members. The family name was important, and a member of the family was less an individual and more a member of the family.
3. The family performed the basic function of *education*, not only of

---

4. William F. Ogburn, "The Changing Family," *The Family* (1938): 139–143.

Changes in family life are altering family law

> Prof. Homer H. Clarke Jr. of the University of Colorado Law School recently set out to revise his textbook, "Domestic Relations in the United States," only to find that he had to rewrite it.
>
> "In the 15 years since that book came out, very little of family law remains unchanged," he said. "There's been a complete revolution."
>
> A similar problem confronted Prof. Harry D. Krause of the University of Illinois Law School, when he decided to update his study guides in family law, published in 1976. "After only seven years," he said, "I'm throwing out practically everything. It's not a revision, it's almost a complete redo."
>
> *New themes are emerging*
>
> Changes in the once-stable field of family law have been so vast and so profound that legal scholars now refer to them as revolutionary. Concepts unheard of a decade ago—joint custody of children, for example, visiting rights for grandparents and so-called cohabitation contracts between those not married but living together—have become commonplace in the courts.
>
> Emerging are new themes such as divorce mediation, adoptions of babies borne by surrogate mothers and "wrongful birth" lawsuits in which parents of healthy babies accuse doctors of failing to sterilize them.
>
> While California has pioneered in the changes in family law, both in its legislation and in court decisions, the reverberations have been felt in New York, New Jersey, Connecticut and virtually every other state, according to Dr. Doris Jonas Freed, a family law scholar.

infants and children, but also of youths for their vocational education, physical education, domestic science, and so on.

4. The family provided the function of *protecting its members*. Not only did the father provide physical protection for his family, but children provided social and economic protection against economic and psychological needs in old age.

5. The family exercised a *religious* function, as was evidenced by grace at meals, family prayers, and reading together passages in the Bible.

6. The *recreation* function was performed at the homestead of some family or within the family rather than at recreation centers outside the home provided by the school, community, or industry.

7. The final function was that of providing *affection* between mates and the procreation of children.

Many people in our society today are committed to the idea that these traditional functions of the family should be maintained. That is, families should be relatively self-sufficient, familism should have priority

"One of the big changes in New York and New Jersey," she said, "is that pensions earned during marriage are now considered deferred compensation and dividable on divorce. As a result of this expanded definition of property, wives are getting part of the action."

The family law reforms have come in response to major social transformations, most notably the women's movement, the campaign for equal custody rights for fathers and the rise in the divorce rate, which doubled between 1966 and 1976. Although the increase has slowed somewhat since then, there were one million divorces in the United States last year. As Professor Clark put it: "All the old notions of how families ought to work and how people ought to behave had completely broken down. The only thing left to provide some kind of structure was law."

Paralleling the creation of new laws and new legal presumptions has been an explosion of litigation. Surveys show that roughly half the cases on civil court dockets are family law cases, largely as a result of the higher divorce rate. Moreover, people are far more likely to go to court over post-divorce disputes than over other kinds of disputes, according to a recent national study of 5,000 households directed by Prof. David Trubek of the University of Wisconsin Law School. The study found that 60 percent of those with post-divorce problems went to court, as against 20 percent for accidents and 3 percent for consumer complaints.

"Unless you get a traffic ticket, this may be your only exposure to the courts," said Prof. Carol Bruch of the University of California at Davis. "Doing it right in family law is important to tremendous numbers of people."

Source: Georgia Dullea, *The New York Times*, February 3, 1983, pp. 1 and 12. Copyright © 1983/1984 by The New York Times Company. Reprinted by permission.

over individualism, education should be centered in the home, children should care for their aging parents, prayer and religious rituals should be a basic part of the daily life of the family, recreation should be engaged in by the family as a unit, and affection should be received relatively exclusively within the family unit.

Emergent norms suggest that many of these traditional family functions are being performed by other agencies. The economic function has gone to the factory, store, and office. The prestige and status function is increasingly centering around a family member rather than the family name. Teachers have become substitute parents and are basically responsible for the education of the child. Police, reform schools, social security, medicare and medicaid, unemployment compensation, and other types of social legislation provided by the state have replaced the traditional protective function. The professional priest, rabbi, or clergyman has assumed the responsibility for fulfilling the religious function. Little league baseball, industrial bowling teams, TV-watching, or women's tennis groups have replaced the family as a source of recreation. And, although many would argue that the family still remains the center of the affectional life and is the only recognized place for producing children, one does not have to engage in an intensive investigation to discover the extent to which these two are sought and found outside the boundaries of the family and its members.

Not all writers agree that only losses have taken place in family functions. Talcott Parsons, for example, has emphasized that the shift in functions has produced gains as well.[5] He indicated that when functions are "lost" by one unit, that unit may thereby be freer to concentrate on other functions. It is not merely a matter of "loss," therefore, but also a matter of what one is "freed for." Certain groups have come to specialize more now than in the past upon certain of the functions that mass-society critics fear have been lost. The family and the peer group, for example, have gained in importance as sources of emotional support. Within these primary group boundaries, its members may increasingly find a therapeutic milieu for personal and physical health problems. Also, families may increasingly be responsible for the development of family members' competence in the use of community and nonfamily resources. Existence in complex, highly specialized societies requires a knowledge of the range of options, an ability to make sound choices, and a flexibility toward new technologies and ideologies. Thus a major "new" family function is one of socialization for competence in a changing complex society and world. A further discussion of the concept and use of "function" as well as family functions is presented in Chapter 2.

Marital- and gender-role differentiation

Marital and gender roles need to include masculine-feminine and man-woman roles as well. The confusion and uncertainty over "proper" role definitions for the sexes became very evident to me when a group of students was asked to define and list characteristics of masculinity. Extreme difficulty existed, first, in listing characteristics, and second, in securing agreement. Traditionally, no such difficulty was likely to exist. The male, husband, and father was the head of the family, its main economic support, and its representative in the community. The father was the boss, the breadwinner, and the aggressive partner.

---

5. Hyman Rodman, "Talcott Parsons' View of the Changing American Family," *Merrill-Palmer Quarterly of Behavior and Development* 11 (July 1965): 209–227.

The apostle Paul in his letters to the Ephesians and the Colossians made his views clearly known on husband-wife roles. To the Ephesians he said:

> Wives submit yourselves unto your husbands . . . for the husband is the head of the wife . . . therefore as the church is subject unto Christ so let the wives be to their own husbands in everything.[6]

To the Colossians, Paul was very clear on the "proper" hierarchy of power and authority within the family. To them he wrote:

> Wives submit yourselves unto your own husbands, as it is fit in the Lord. Husbands, love your wives and be not bitter against them. Children, obey your parents in all things: for this is well pleasing unto the Lord. Fathers, provoke not your children to anger, lest they be discouraged. Servants, obey in all things your masters according to the flesh, not with eye service, as men pleasers; but in singleness of heart, fear in God: and whatsoever ye do, do it heartily, as to the Lord, and not unto men.[7]

This traditional role pattern is consistent with the sacred meaning of marriage. The source of authority is not human beings, and the obligations are not fulfilled for men and women but for a supreme being.

The traditional expectations of appropriate marital and gender roles are clear and unmistakable. Women are expected to have marriage, home, and children as their primary concerns. The wife takes the husband's name, shares his income, and relies on him for status and identity. Women should be sympathetic, caring, loving, compassionate, gentle, and submissive, which in turn makes them excellent wives, mothers, nurses, and teachers of young children. To be feminine, the skin must be smooth and soft and the body slim and erotic. Of course, the "lady" or "nice girl,"[8] is chaste, gracious, good, clean, kind, virtuous, noncontroversial, and above suspicion and reproach.

In contrast, men earn livings to support their wives and children. To be masculine is to be self-reliant, strong, verbally and physically aggressive, dominant, tall, and muscular. Men are risk takers, decision makers, and protectors of those around them. The "ideal male" is thus hard working, responsible, achieving, and reliable. In addition, heterosexuality is greatly stressed in interests and activities, and departures from this, particularly as related to sexual desires and conduct, are strongly condemned.

This type of gender-role differentiation has benefits for both sexes, but it has great costs as well.[9] For females, satisfaction may be derived

---

6. Ephesians 5:22–24.

7. Colossians 3:18–23.

8. *See* Greer Litton Fox, "Nice Girl: Social Control of Women Through A Value Construct," *Signs: Journal of Women in Culture and Society* 2 (Summer 1977): 805–817.

9. For an excellent treatment of this, *see* Suzanne Keller, "Male and Female: A Sociological View," University Programs Modular Studies (Morristown, N. J.: General Learning Press, 1975).

> The book of Genesis says:
> "Man and Woman Created He Them"
> The book of Genesis also says:
> "God Created Man in His own Image"
> Taken literally, this means:
> "God is a ManWoman God"

from the stress on beauty, the lack of pressure to achieve, the wide range of emotional expression and intimacy, and the right to claim support. For males, satisfaction may be derived from the access to power, the ideology of male supremacy, the opportunities to develop skills and talents, the exercise of autonomy and independence, and the ability to be self-supporting. On the other hand, it is often at great cost to females that restrictions are placed on self-development, on training to cope with an increasingly complicated world, and on ability to obtain a loan, open a business, and be economically equal or superior to men. It is often at great cost to men that they are pressured to achieve, to assume responsibility for family members, to be in constant competition to excel, and to be unable to shed tears and express themselves emotionally.

The traditional differentiation of male-female roles has come into serious question. While *androgyny,* or a society with no gender-role differentiation, has not been achieved in full, pressures exist in this direction. Nonfamilial roles available to women, an increasing egalitarian emphasis in intimate family and nonfamily relationships, changing beliefs in both work and play, and changes in patterns of socialization and education are leading to increased alternatives for males and females as to appropriate attitudes and behavior. While the labels may vary—*androgyny, unisex, desegregation, new neuter*—the message is similar: men and women are increasingly pursuing their similarities, experiencing the thrill of escaping from traditional gender-role stereotypes, and choosing to behave as persons rather than as males or females. Both sexes are increasingly behaving in ways that are instrumental as well as expressive, assertive as well as yielding, and masculine as well as feminine.

It has been suggested that contemporary American marriages are shifting from the *complementary* type to the *parallel* type based on the kinds of work husbands and wives do every day.[10] In complementary marriages, the husband and the wife perform interdependent but different

---

10. Catherine E. Ross, John Mirowsky, and Joan Huber, "Dividing Work, Sharing Work, and In-Between: Marriage Patterns and Depression," *American Sociological Review* 48 (December 1983): 809–823.

tasks. He is employed outside the home and she does the domestic work. In parallel marriages the husband and the wife perform the same tasks on an equitable or at least negotiable and mutually acceptable basis. Both spouses are employed and both are responsible for child care and housework.

The transition from gender-role differentiation to androgyny or from complementary to parallel type marriage is far from complete. But women's participation in the world of paid employment is increasing, household responsibilities increasingly are shared by husbands and wives, and both sexes increasingly are thinking and behaving in ways traditionally linked to the opposite sex. These changes are more fully described, particularly in Chapters 4, 5, 9, 12, 14, 15 and 17.

Social mobility

The issue of social mobility centers around the extent to which it is possible—or desirable—to move from one status to another. The issue includes the American Dream of going from the log cabin to the White House, from rags to riches, from being a nobody to a Supreme Court judge.

The polar extremes of an ideal-type construct would include an open class society, where anyone could move up or down in the social structure strictly on the basis of personal effort and ability, versus a closed class society, where everyone remains in the position to which they were born with no change in position possible through individual achievement or any other means. The classic representation of the closed system is that of the caste system of ancient India. There, position was based on ancestry and was sustained by strict rules of same-caste marriage (endogamy), by religious beliefs, and by rigidly enforced legal and normative expectations.

No society has an absolutely open or a completely closed class system. In our own society, family position exerts a major influence on one's chances for getting an education, for exposure to literature, travel, and the arts, for inheritance, for marriage choices, and the like. On the other hand, factors such as educational achievement, marriage possibilities, or business successes do provide opportunities for upward social mobility.

Traditionally, factors such as the extended family system, the predominantly rural farming economy, the authority held by elders, and religious and ethnic ties appeared to make personal upward mobility extremely difficult. Likewise today, the lack of opportunity and resources of the poor makes planning for the future and social climbing exceedingly difficult if not impossible. Yet the dream of upward social mobility, of "doing better than my parents," of economic success, and of obtaining a new and superior life-style remains widespread. A further discussion of this issue and of the meaning and consequence of social class position is presented in Chapter 7.

Mate selection

The issue of mate selection centers around two questions: who chooses and who is chosen. The polar extremes of an ideal-type construct would include arranged marriages with no voice given to the mates involved versus absolute free choice where decisions are made solely by the mates involved. Around the world and traditionally in the United States the most prevalent position falls toward the former (arranged) rather than the latter (free choice).

In our society, the traditional norms suggest that parents in particular, if not doing the choosing, should give their approval to the mate chosen. It is not uncommon today to find men in the fifty-and-older age group who formally and directly requested the girl's parents' permission for her hand in marriage. Although mates are not chosen by the parents, as in much of the Eastern world, they are chosen with a clear consciousness of the extent to which the spouse would meet the approval of the parents. And to marry without the future spouse having been known, not only by the parents, but within the kin group and community, is unthinkable. Thus who did the choosing? The emerging norm, in the polar extreme, is to have "absolute free choice" of mate with a total absence of approval by parents, friends, or others.

Closely related to who chooses is a question of who is chosen. Traditionally, in-group (endogamous) selection was extremely important. The ideal spouse was a person from one's own ethnic, social-class, religious, racial, or neighborhood group. Outsiders were viewed with much suspicion, and marriage to an outsider was a sure sign of future marital problems. That the traditional norm still exists today is very obvious when one looks at the type of material taught in marriage preparation classes within our education system, the position taken by most religious groups, or the advice of parents or columnists.

An emergent norm suggests that mate selection is increasingly coming under the control of youths themselves and that out-group selection (exogamous marriages) is increasingly common. Ask yourself if you would

"Marry women of your choice,
Two, or three, or four;
But if ye fear that ye shall not
Be able to deal justly (with them),
Then only one . . ."

Source: The Holy Koran, Sura IV, Verse 3.

be willing to have your spouse chosen for you by your parents, relatives, or friends. Would you marry someone of a different religious background, of a different ethnic affiliation, or of a higher or lower social class? If you want to have the ultimate say in whom you choose to marry or if you are willing to marry outside of your religious, ethnic, or class grouping, you fail to conform to the most traditional mate selection norms. You might find it interesting to inquire of your married friends whether the husband asked the wife' parents for permission to marry or, perhaps today, a more realistic question is whether either set of parents knew about their unmarried cohabitation instead of, or prior to, their marriage. Consistent with the individualistic meaning of marriage is the idea that since it is "my spouse," I should choose any person with whom I am "in love" or with whom I choose to live. That the mate comes from a different community, social class, religion, or race is not the concern of relatives or church groups. These issues focusing on mate selection are discussed in detail in Chapters 8 and 9.

Love

The issue of love as related to marriage centers around questions such as whether it is even necessary, to what degree of intensity, and to what extent of exclusiveness? On an ideal-type continuum, the polar extremes would be represented by: (1) love as not even a factor for consideration in marriage versus love as the sole and prime factor for marriage, (2) zero percent or no feelings of love versus 100 percent feelings of love (whatever that is), and (3) love with one other person only versus many loves.

You can quickly note the linkage between this issue and both the previous one of mate selection and the next one of sexual relationships. Traditionally in North America and today in much of the world, kin, economic, and status considerations are still the key determinants for marriage. After marriage, not before, love is expected to develop. In contrast is the emergent idea that marriage without love is unthinkable. After all, does not "love make the world go round" and cannot "love conquer all"?

Closely related to whether or not love is necessary is the problem of the intensity of love feelings. Clearly feelings are subjective and the question is how intense must these subjective feelings be before they are "real"? Thus reference is made to "puppy love" or "infatuation" as feelings that are superficial and not the type upon which lasting relationships are built. Other descriptions such as romantic love, conjugal love, spiritual love (agape), or sexual love (eros) have been used to clarify different types of love or love conditions. In any case, attempts at understanding what love is, measuring how genuine or "real" it is, and analyzing its intensity have been basic problems for centuries and still engender debate and conflict today.

Finally, the issue of love—particularly as it relates to marriage—centers on the exclusiveness or nonexclusiveness of love relationships. Can two people be loved at once? Does love with one's spouse eliminate the possibility of loving someone else's spouse? The traditional view of conjugal love demands a devotion exclusively to one person—in sickness and in health, for richer, for poorer, and so forth. This traditional relationship is all-absorbing and all-encompassing.

A conflicting view is that one's spouse and/or lover neither can nor need meet all of one's intimacy needs.[11] That is, individuals who are personally growing, developing, and changing find differing needs fulfilled by different individuals. Thus, the fulfillment of various intimacy needs can be met outside of marriage without diminishing the love for one's spouse. If one is to grow and develop, it becomes difficult to imagine one other person fulfilling all intimacy needs of that individual. This type of relationship allows both self and other the right to new experiences and growth possibilities, both sexual and nonsexual. The result is a more enriched relationship with one's spouse, with a drastic reduction in feelings of possessiveness, rigidity of role expectations, or feelings of confinement.

As with the other issues, the traditional and the emergent views of love are in conflict. One cannot be both exclusive in love relationships and at the same time open to other relationships.

Sexual relationships

The central question surrounding the issue of sexual relationships is whether sexual relations (coitus) should be limited to marriage. Are there conditions or circumstances under which premarital, extramarital, or postmarital intercourse is legitimate? In addition, are there rational arguments for a double standard, differentiating the sexual norms for men and women?

The traditional sacred norm is quite clear. Prior to the turn of the century, premarital, extramarital, postmarital, and even sexual relations for the purposes of pleasure within marriage were considered taboo. Officially, the mores allowed little deviation from this norm. Unofficially, a double standard existed whereby sexual deviation by men, although not sanctioned, was understandable. On the other hand, women were socialized to believe that the husband was the one to whom sex was important, that sex should remain solely within the marital relationship, and that a good wife "submits" because she "owes this duty" to her husband.

---

11. A treatment of this idea can be found in Carolynne Kieffer, "New Depths in Intimacy," in *Marriage and Alternatives: Exploring Intimate Relationships,* by Roger W. Libby and Robert N. Whitehurst (Glenview, Ill.: Scott, Foresman, 1977): 267–293.

Various changes took place when the social meaning of marriage began to emerge. As with the sacred meaning, sexual relationships outside of marriage were basically taboo except among unmarried couples who were marriage-oriented or were "in love." The second traditional view of sex primarily limited intercourse to marriage, but it increasingly separated sex from reproduction and allowed it to become a source of pleasure for both sexes. Anything occurring within the marital relationship was perfectly normal and satisfactory as long as it was agreeable and unharmful to the couple involved. Although a double standard remains in effect, this latter view is likely the predominant position today.

The trend has been away from these traditional norms to an emergent sexual norm that questions the double standard and the necessity of limiting sexual relationships to marriage. If sex is fun (to which many agree), why should it be limited to a spouse, someone whom you intend to marry, or even someone with whom you are in love? If maturity and adulthood imply independence and the capacity to make one's own decisions, then two individuals, whether married or single, male or female, should have the choice as to when, where, and with whom sexual relationships will take place. The publicity given to premarital cohabitation and same-sex liaisons presents some documentation of the emergence of this sexual norm. As women seek equality with men, as increasingly it is possible to separate sex from parenthood, and as primary informal means of control lessen, sexual independence and permissiveness are likely to result.

The implications of this issue are far-reaching. It has affected and will continue to affect the family, the educational system, other social institutions, and legislative processes, as well as personal behavior. The conflict is again obvious. One cannot adhere to both polar extremes of sexual relationships—within marriage primarily for reproductive purposes or "sex as fun" in or out of marriage. These issues involving sexual relationships are discussed in premarital contexts in Chapter 10 and in marital contexts in Chapter 11.

Family size and family planning

Closely related and directly limited to the issues of sexual relationships and marital and gender roles is the threefold issue of (1) limiting the number of children, (2) determining when and if to have them, and (3) selecting the appropriate means to accomplish these ends. In the 1960s and 1970s extensive publicity on zero population growth and on the population explosion focused attention on family size. More recently, controversies over abortion and whether public funds (tax money) should be used to pay for them, test-tube babies, surrogate parenting, and the long-

In the United States Thanksgiving day is often a time when the entire family unit gets together for food and sharing. (Photo: © Mark Antman/The Image Works)

term effects of various contraceptives such as the pill have raised new questions about how to have or prevent having children.

The most traditional norm—one highly consistent with the sacred meaning of marriage—suggests that the primary purpose of sex is reproduction and the only approved context for reproduction is within marriage. (One biblical admonition is that families should be fruitful and multiply.) One-child family situations were not viewed as the ideal, and a mother who only had one or two children was an issue of community concern. Even more problematic was pregnancy apart from a marital relationship. Premarital pregnancies forced hasty marriages. Nonmarital pregnancies and birth brought shame to the family unit.

Since, traditionally, large families were an economic asset and contributed to security in old age, children within marriage were highly valued. Few were the families that consciously and successfully controlled family size. Many mothers took pride in proclaiming that they had produced and raised ten or fifteen healthy children. The spacing of children may have raised concern if pregnancy occurred very soon after a previous childbirth, but the concern centered more on the health of the mother than on the additional "blessing."

As the social norms changed, so did the view of large families. As population shifts removed families from farms, children became less of an economic asset. Increasingly, sex came to be viewed as being for pleasure as well as for reproduction. Children became a matter of choice rather than chance. And the emerging norm pertaining to family size now suggests that the maximum number of children should be two. For couples to have only one child or no children is granted social acceptability, to have four or six is to have too many, and to have ten or fourteen is disastrous.

The means of controlling the number of children has shifted as well. Again, the most traditional norm suggests that anything nonartificial or "God given" is appropriate. Since God has provided within each female a period of time each month when conception cannot occur, rhythm as a method of limiting family size is appropriate and consistent with the "will of God." The traditional sex-role norm maintains that women are responsible for the prevention of pregnancy. The timing of sexual relationships around the menstrual cycle is consistent with the sacred meaning attached to marriage.

The social meaning of marriage, and perhaps the one most widely adhered to by couples in our society today, suggests that any means of fertility control that works, is nonharmful, and is agreeable to both spouses is legitimate. As a result, the majority of both Catholics and non-Catholics in the United States today are using some form of "artificial" contraceptive

Beliefs prohibit student from attending and professor from teaching

Only days apart in August of 1986, two events made headlines. In Toledo, eleven-year-old Sarabeth Eason was told by the pastor of St. Agnes parish that she could not re-enroll in the church school unless she disavowed her public support for abortion. Her mother operates a clinic in Toledo, The Center for Choice, where Sarabeth did some volunteer work. On two occasions Sarabeth spoke out publicly, once at a television rally and another time in a signed newspaper advertisement supporting abortion. The diocese spokesman who appeared on several network shows with Sarabeth said it's a cut-and-dried issue of a child and her family defying the stated precepts of their church.

The second event centered around a priest, the Rev. Charles E. Curran, a popular lecturer and theologian at Catholic University in Washington, D.C. The Vatican, in a letter to Father Curran, notified him that "you will no longer be considered suitable nor eligible to exercise the function of a Professor of Catholic Theology." The reason for this action was a result of his publishing and teaching that the church's opposition to divorce, birth control, homosexual acts, and abortion should not be absolute. Father Curran endorsed the morality of contraception, said that divorce should sometimes be permitted, and that abortion, masturbation, premarital sex, and homosexual acts are not always immoral.

or birth-control method, and wide-spread legalization of abortion has occurred in the last decade. The social norm in regard to family planning agrees with the sacred meaning in that the planning should be limited to the marital relationship, but it differs in the reliance on means that relate to the menstrual cycle.

The emergent norm pertaining to family size, family planning, and childbirth in or out of the marital context suggests that family limitation is an individual choice and the methods used (condoms, pills, diaphragm, jellies, abortion, sterilization) should not be limited by laws or measures that prevent couples from preventing pregnancy or childbirth. The emergent social norm places the responsibility for preventing conception on men as well as women, single as well as married. These issues of parenthood, family size, and unwed parenthood are presented in Chapter 13. Less attention is focused on methods of birth control and means of family planning.

Old age

The traditional norms concerning the role of the aged strongly suggest that these persons should be given deference, respect, and recognition. Traditionally, it was the eldest person who had the most prestige, the widest experience in living, and thus the greatest amount of wisdom. The aging family member had various important roles to fulfill, particularly in consulting and managerial positions in addition to those centering around the enjoyment and care of children and grandchildren.

The changing social scene has also changed the role of the aged person in the American family. The number of persons over the age of sixty-five in our population has increased steadily through the twentieth century. Most men and women of this age are no longer employed at their full-time jobs and, for many, retirement is an abrupt event; for most families it means a lowered income, and for the husband it means the destruction of his major role as a productive worker. The ascribed status of age per se no longer brings prestige. The emergent norm suggests that play must be substituted for work. This means a drastic shift in activities, in self-definitions, and in role performance. The basic issue and conflict of the aged centers around providing a meaningful way of life, which includes being able to make a contribution to life and to the society in which the aged live. The role of older people, their marital patterns, retirement, and postmarital family styles are discussed in Chapter 15.

Family reorganization

The issue of family reorganization raises the question as to whether marriage should be a permanent or temporary arrangement. If viewed as temporary, what structural arrangements should be made to end one relationship and begin another, and what criteria should be used to determine when one relationship should end and another begin? Thus our ideal-type constructs might consist of models that include divorce/limited divorce/no divorce, total separation/partial separation/no separation, or any reason/no reason.

A sacred view of marriage suggests that marriage is for keeps. This most traditional view of dealing with marital conflict does not include the option of reorganizing the marital/family structure by means of divorce. Marriage is accepted as a lifelong permanent contract and exists until "death do us part" (unless one happens to be a Mormon who marries in the temple where the celestial marriage is for time and eternity). Marriage exists and remains legally intact irrespective of conflict in the relationship or personal unhappiness. This traditional norm was especially prevalent prior to 1920 or 1930. Even today this is the model used when divorce is viewed as marital or family "disorganization" rather than as a reorganization of structure to new forms such as single-parent or the reconstituted family involving at least one spouse who was previously married and divorced.[12]

Less extreme than the idea of marriage as a permanent relationship irrespective of persons or circumstances is a second traditional norm that suggests certain conditions or reasons are legitimate for ending marital and family commitments. Adultery has long been a socially acceptable reason for ending a legal marital contract. Even the Catholic church, which takes a sacramental view of marriage relationships, accepts the ending of the marriage if it is due to conditions that existed prior to the start of that marriage. This structural form of ending a relationship (annulment) is a legally recognized type of marital dissolution.

The most common means for ending a marital relationship (other than death) is divorce. Since the legal grounds for divorce are determined by individual states, the reasons for permitting divorce vary widely. Traditionally, there was general agreement that one party had to be guilty. With time, several states made legal changes and most states interpreted the existing laws more leniently. Whereas many people believe that a major reason for the increasing divorce rates has been a change in the law, it is likely that the greater change has been in the increased tolerance toward divorce. Thus the changing social norm has been toward a greater acceptance of divorce, although a widely held social norm maintains that divorce should come only as a last resort after all other options have

---

12. Margrit Eichler and others make this point in their argument of the inappropriateness of a monolithic model of the family. *See* Margrit Eichler, "The Inadequacy of the Monolithic Model of the Family," *Canadian Journal of Sociology* 6 (1981): 367–388; and Barrie Thorne with Marilyn Yalom, *Rethinking the Family: Some Feminist Questions* (New York: Longman, 1982): 2–6.

been considered. In any case, the 1970s witnessed a major increase in divorce rates, reaching levels in the 1980s unexceeded in U.S. history.

An emergent idea concerning family reorganization suggests that in many instances marriage is a trial. This norm maintains that marital success stems less from existence and permanence and more from a meaningful dynamic interaction of persons even if the partners may change. Immorality stems not from getting a divorce but from maintaining a relationship that is for all practical purposes broken. Thus divorce, rather than being a social problem, may be viewed as a solution for other types of problems. The end result is that marriages become more "vital and successful" than ever before in our history. Marriages exist out of personal desire rather than out of social or sacred obligations.

The same issues exist in regard to remarriage. Prior to the Civil War, remarriage was a right only of the innocent party. Many clergy would refuse to marry divorced persons. In certain fundamentalist denominations this is still the situation today. Within the Catholic church as well, canon law prohibits the remarriage of divorced persons previously married in the church. In actual practice some priests do perform marriage ceremonies for divorced persons. And remarriage among the majority of divorced persons is high. Divorcees have a higher rate of marriage, age for age, than have single persons entering their first marriage or the widowed.

The basic nature of this issue of marital and family reorganization should be quite evident. Conflicts exist between those who adhere to a sacred meaning of marriage, accepting no reasons for ending a marriage, and those who grant social approval to a temporary marital relationship. The shift toward the greater acceptability of divorce may be seen in legal changes in several states which permit divorce to whomever desires it and in the passage of "no-fault" divorce bills. Unless the day comes when divorce in U.S. society is granted full social approval, conflict on the basic issue of marital reorganization will remain. These issues of divorce, separation, remarriage, and the like are further discussed in Chapter 17. Our attention is now directed toward selected characteristics of families in the United States.

CHARACTERISTICS OF FAMILIES IN THE UNITED STATES

The United States Bureau of the Census is the primary source of national numerical data about families in this country. To provide an introduction to the American family, a summary of various characteristics as portrayed by census material is presented. More specific characteristics, statements of relationships, and research findings are presented throughout the book in the chapters appropriate to their discussion.

In 1985 the total resident population of the United States was estimated at 239 million.[13] This included approximately 116 million males and 123 million females.

The U.S. population by race included 202.8 million classified as white (84.9 percent), 28.9 million classified as black (12.1 percent), and 7.1 million classified as other races (3.0 percent).[14] "Other races" as used by the census bureau does not denote any scientific definition of biological stock. It is based on the self-identification of respondents into one of fifteen groups that, in addition to white and black, includes American Indian, Eskimo, Aleut, Japanese, Chinese, Filipino, Hawaiian, Samoan, Asian Indian, Korean, Vietnamese, Guamanian, and other. Persons of Spanish origin (who may be of any race) maintained 6 percent of all households.

The U.S. population in 1985 had a median age of 31.5; whites had a median age of 32.4, and blacks had a median age of 26.6.[15] Approximately one-fifth of our population (21.8 percent) was under fifteen years of age, one-fourth was fifteen to twenty-nine (25.7 percent), one-fifth was thirty to forty-four (21.8 percent), one-fifth was forty-five to sixty-four (18.8 percent), and roughly one-eighth of all persons (11.9 percent) was sixty-five years or over.[16] Our changing age distribution shows a decrease since 1970 of about 9 percent in the proportion of the population under age twenty, an increase of 54 percent in the twenty to thirty-nine age group (the baby boomers), an increase of 10 percent in the age group of forty to sixty-four, and a 43 percent increase in the proportion of those age sixty-five or over. In other words, the United States experienced a decrease in the proportion of children and adolescents and a huge increase in the proportion of persons we might term young adults and senior citizens or the aged.

The number of families and households

The term **family,** as used in census reporting, refers to a group of two or more persons related by birth or "blood," marriage, or adoption, and who reside together in a houshold.

In 1986, there were 63.6 million families in the United States. Of these, 50.9 million were considered to be married couples, that is, husband-wife families, 2.4 million were families with a male householder, no wife present, and 10.2 million were families with a female householder, no

---

13. U.S. Bureau of the Census, *Statistical Abstract of the United States: 1987,* 107th ed. (Washington, D.C.: U.S. Government Printing Office, 1986), Table 20, p. 18.

14. Ibid., Table 17, p. 17.

15. Ibid., Table 20, p. 18.

16. Ibid., Table 20, p. 18.

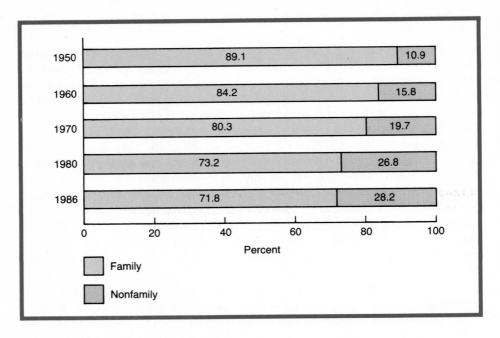

FIGURE 1–1
Family and nonfamily households as a percent of all households: 1950 to
1986. (*Source:* U.S. Bureau of the Census, *General Population Characteristics:
United States Summary* [Washington, D.C.: U.S. Government Printing Office,
1983], Figure 18, p. 15; Statistical Abstract, Table 55, p. 42.)

husband present.[17] Beginning with the 1980 Current Population Survey,
the Bureau of the Census discontinued the use of the term "head" of the
family or household, substituting the terms "householder" and "family
householder." This change resulted from a recognition that household
or family responsibilities are frequently shared among the adult members
of either sex. This significant classification shift discontinues a longtime
practice of always classifying the husband as the reference person (head)
when he and his wife are living together. Today's "head of family," that
is "family householder," is legitimately recognized as either female or
male.

A family is different from a **household.** A household consists of all
persons who occupy a housing unit. A house, an apartment or other group
of rooms, or a single room are regarded as a housing unit when they are
occupied or intended for occupancy as separate living quarters. A household
includes the related family members and all other unrelated persons, if
any, such as lodgers, foster children, wards, or employees who share the
housing unit. A person living alone in a housing unit, or a group of

17. Ibid., Table 55, p. 42.

unrelated persons sharing a housing unit as partners, are also counted as a household. Thus, not all households contain a family. In 1986, there were 88.5 million households[18] and as can be seen in Figure 1–1 the proportion of nonfamily households is increasing. In 1950 only about one in ten households were of the nonfamily type but by 1986 more than one in four were nonfamily units. In other words, more people are living alone or with a nonfamily member.

The size of families and households

Family size refers to the number of persons who are living together and are related to each other by birth, marriage, or adoption. The average size of all families was 3.21 in 1986. Data from the previous year showed that the average size of husband-wife families was 3.28, compared to 2.77 for families with a male householder and 3.05 for families with a female householder. The average size of white families was 3.16, compared to an average black family size of 3.60 and an average of 3.88 for Spanish-origin families.[19]

Households had fewer persons per unit than did families in 1986. The average number of persons per household was 2.67 compared to the 3.21 average size of all families.[20] The number of persons per household has decreased considerably since the earliest census reports were taken. The average size of a household was 5.4 in 1790, 4.2 in 1900, 3.3 in 1940, and, as shown, 2.67 in 1986. Thus, the average household has 2.8 fewer persons today than at the end of the eighteenth century. This decrease in the average size may have some positive influence on the interaction of its members and the social connectedness with others outside the household. While many households can adjust to a higher density, others report increased instances of aggression, disagreements, frustration, and general dissatisfaction.

One national study found that a shortage of household space affected parental attitudes negatively regarding their ability to control their children's actions, in the number of health complaints, and in their satisfaction with leisure time.[21] Another national survey concluded that persons living alone don't feel they are isolated and living alone against their will, but prefer this arrangement, provided that they have attachments outside the house-

---

18. Ibid., Table 55, p. 42.

19. U.S. Bureau of the Census, *Current Population Reports* Series P-20, No. 411, "Household and Family Characteristics: March 1985" (Washington, D.C.: U.S. Government Printing Office, 1986), Tables 1 and 2, pp. 13–19.

20. *Statistical Abstract: 1987*, Table 55, p. 42.

21. Mark Baldassare, "The Effects of Household Density on Subgroups," *American Sociological Review* 46 (February 1981): 110–118.

hold; they frequently have higher levels of social contact and integration than those living with others.[22] The smaller household size and even the large increase in persons living alone (mentioned toward the end of this chapter) suggests an active preference made possible by rising affluence and the greater desire for autonomy among all age groups in society.

Marital status

Census marital-status classification identifies four major categories: single, married, widowed, and divorced. A married couple is husband and wife who are enumerated as members of the same household and who may or may not have children living with them.

As can be seen in Table 1–2, approximately 81.5 million men and 89.9 million women were age eighteen or over in 1985. For men, 65.7 percent were married, 25.2 percent were single, 2.6 percent were widowed and 6.5 percent were divorced. For women, 60.4 percent were married, 18.2 percent were single, 12.6 percent were widowed, and 8.7 percent were divorced. Thus, ignoring age differences, men are more likely than women to be married or single, and women are more likely than men to be widowed or divorced.

Marriage is popular. More than 80 percent of the men between the ages of thirty-five and seventy-four and more than 73 percent of the women between the ages of thirty and fifty-four are currently married. That only about 5 percent of both men and women are listed as single at a specific age would suggest that at least 95 percent (19 out of 20 persons) of both sexes marry at some point in their lives.

The large numbers of nonmarried males and females at the younger and older ends of the age spectrum reflect a premarital status for young single persons and a postmarital status (widowed or divorced) for older persons. Note the vast differences between widowed men and women after age sixty-five (38.9 percent women versus 9.3 percent men) and after age seventy-five (67.7 percent women versus 22.7 percent men). The percentage of men and women who are divorced in a given year holds fairly constant for both men and women between the ages of twenty-five and sixty-four (6.0 percent to 10.3 percent for men; 7.9 to 14.0 percent for women). Even at the maximum age category, only 14 percent of women and about 10 percent of men are divorced. Thus, in spite of all the talk and concern about "easy divorce," "marital breakdown," and "family decay," most of the United States adult population at any given time is married, and when divorced, most remarry.

---

22. Duane F. Alwin, Philip E. Converse, and Steven S. Martin, "Living Arrangements and Social Integration," *Journal of Marriage and the Family* 47 (May 1985):319–334.

TABLE 1–2
Marital status of the population, by sex and age, 1985 (persons 18 years old and over)

Sex and age	Number of persons (1,000)					Percent distribution				
	Total	Single	Married	Widowed	Divorced	Total	Single	Married	Widowed	Divorced
Male	**81,452**	**20,543**	**53,536**	**2,109**	**5,264**	**100.0**	**25.2**	**65.7**	**2.6**	**6.5**
18–19 years	3,640	3,534	106	—	—	100.0	97.1	2.9	—	—
20–24 years	10,055	7,605	2,310	3	138	100.0	75.6	23.0	—	1.4
25–29 years	10,420	4,037	5,751	3	629	100.0	38.7	55.2	—	6.0
30–34 years	9,764	2,027	6,804	7	926	100.0	20.8	69.7	.1	9.5
35–44 years	15,333	1,444	12,254	54	1,581	100.0	9.4	79.9	.4	10.3
45–54 years	10,848	682	9,096	131	939	100.0	6.3	83.8	1.2	8.7
55–64 years	10,377	633	8,711	388	644	100.0	6.1	83.9	3.7	6.2
65–74 years	7,259	380	5,899	672	307	100.0	5.2	81.3	9.3	4.2
75 years old and over	3,755	200	2,604	851	100	100.0	5.3	69.3	22.7	2.7
Female	**89,917**	**16,377**	**54,354**	**11,372**	**7,814**	**100.0**	**18.2**	**60.4**	**12.6**	**8.7**
18–19 years	3,738	3,240	468	2	28	100.0	86.7	12.5	.1	.7
20–24 years	10,411	6,091	3,953	20	347	100.0	58.5	38.0	.2	3.3
25–29 years	10,686	2,824	6,963	57	843	100.0	26.4	65.2	.5	7.9
30–34 years	9,987	1,351	7,299	104	1,234	100.0	13.5	73.1	1.0	12.4
35–44 years	15,966	1,091	12,312	323	2,242	100.0	6.8	77.1	2.0	14.0
45–54 years	11,550	529	8,812	809	1,401	100.0	4.6	76.3	7.0	12.1
55–64 years	11,774	440	8,240	2,047	1,047	100.0	3.7	70.0	17.4	8.9
65–74 years	9,317	412	4,764	3,622	519	100.0	4.4	51.1	38.9	5.6
75 years old and over	6,487	400	1,543	4,390	154	100.0	6.2	23.8	67.7	2.4

— Represents zero or rounds to zero.
Source: U.S. Bureau of the Census, *Statistical Abstract of the United States: 1987,* 107th ed. (Washington, D.C.: U.S. Government Printing Office, 1986), no. 46, p. 39.

Family income

Family income refers to the total amount reported by related persons who were members of the family at the time of enumeration. In the census, each family member fifteen years of age and over was asked the amount of income received in the preceding calendar year from sources such as wages or salary, self-employment, social security, dividends, interest, rental income, public assistance or welfare payments, or other periodic income. It did not include amounts from sources such as the sale of property (stocks, bonds, a house, or a car), nor did it include borrowed money, tax refunds, gifts, or lump-sum inheritance or insurance payments. The total income of a family is the algebraic sum of the amounts received by all income recipients in the family.

Family income appears to have increased considerably since 1970. The median family income in 1985 was $27,735 compared to $9,867 in 1970. This 281 percent increase appears impressive until the figures are adjusted for the change in consumer prices and inflation. Adjusting this for the previous year (1984), the median family income of $26,433 in constant 1984 dollars compared to a 1970 value of $26,394, an increase of $39 in actual purchasing power. In addition, the failure to index income tax against inflation compounds the dismal financial picture even more since greater proportions of earnings go to taxes as workers move into higher tax brackets.

As might be expected, rates of growth as well as median income for families varied widely by social categories. For example, in 1985 the median income of white families was $29,152, compared to $16,786 for black families and $19,027 for Spanish families. Families with a male householder with no wife present had a median income much higher than those with a female householder with no husband present ($22,622 versus $13,360). Married couples with a wife in the paid labor force had a median family income of $36,431, while couples where the wife was not in the paid labor force had an income of $24,565. Families with householders who had a college education of four years or more had a median income of $46,423, compared to $27,472 for high-school graduates and $13,539 for householders with less than an eighth-grade education.[23] Many other examples could be given to illustrate the wide range of median incomes that exists for families in the United States. In any case, it should be clear that family incomes differ dramatically by sex, race, marital status, employment of one or both spouses, educational attainment, and other factors.

TODAY'S FAMILIES: SIGNIFICANT CHANGES

Dramatic changes over time and diversity at any given point are illustrated by noting various demographic characteristics. Consider factors such as the following, which are supported by data from the Bureau of the Census.

The United States in the 1980s had one of the highest marriage and divorce rates among the world's industrialized countries.

---

23. All figures in this paragraph and the section that follows were taken from U.S. Bureau of the Census, *Current Population Reports*, Series P-60, No. 154, "Money Income and Poverty Status of Families and Persons in the United States: 1985" (Washington, D.C.: U.S. Government Printing Office, 1986); *Statistical Abstract of the United States: 1987*; and *Current Population Reports*, Series P-20, Nos. 410 and 411.

About 2.0 million unmarried couples lived together in 1985, nearly four times the 523,000 who lived together unmarried in 1970.

By 1985, the median age of first marriage had advanced more than two years since 1970, from 23.2 to 25.5 for men and 20.8 to 23.3 for women. About one year of this advance occurred since 1980.

By 1985, 58.5 percent of the women age twenty to twenty-four were single (never married), compared to 35.8 percent in 1970. For men of similar age, 75.6 percent were single, compared to 54.7 percent in 1970.

The number of divorced persons per thousand married persons in 1985 had increased two and one-half times since 1970 (from 47 in 1970 to 128 in 1985).

Less than one-half (47.4 percent) of the nation's 51.1 million married couples in 1985 had children under age eighteen in the home. In 1970, 56 percent of married couples had them.

One-parent families accounted for 23.4 percent of all families with children under age eighteen in 1985, up from 11.4 percent in 1970.

In 1985, the most common household size was two persons (31.6 percent), but the next most common size was the one-person household (23.7 percent). The average size had decreased to 2.69 from 3.14 in 1970.

The number of persons living alone had increased from 10.8 million in 1970 to 20.6 million in 1985.

The number of interracial married couples among the fifteen groups listed in the race item on the census questionnaire had increased more than two and one-half times (from 310,000 to 792,000) between 1970 and 1985 but still comprised only about 1.5 percent of all married couples. Black-white interracial married couples increased from 65,000 to 164,000 but comprised only 0.3 percent of the total.

Only about 5 percent of the people over age forty had never married. Statistics showed that most men and women marry at some time in their lives.

Approximately 20.3 percent of ever-married women aged fifteen to forty-four were childless in 1985, up from 16.4 percent in 1970.

Approximately 14.4 million single women in 1985 had given birth to children, 6.4 million more than in 1970.

Children born in 1984 had a life expectancy of about 75 years (78 for females; 71 for males). This is up from 70.8 in 1970, 68.2 in 1950, and 54 in 1920.

The number of persons below the poverty level was 33.1 million in 1985, comprising 14.0 percent of the population. This is up from 25.4 million in 1970 or 12.6 percent of the population that year.

The number of families below the poverty level in 1985 was 7.2 million or 11.4 percent of the total. This includes 9.1 percent of white families, 28.7 percent of black families, and 25.5 percent of Spanish-origin families.

Need more illustrations be given? Census data alone, apart from the countless number of completed research studies, illustrate quite clearly the pluralistic, diversified, and changing nature of U.S. families. More detailed breakdowns of characteristics such as these are presented at appropriate places in the text.

SUMMARY

1. This first chapter is intended to introduce some basic issues and characteristics of U.S. families. While all family systems adhere to similar basic general norms and values, great diversity exists in family structure, attitudes, and behavior.

2. Ideal-type constructs were introduced as a way to provide a range of perspectives between two polar extremes. It was the tool used to examine major issues in the U.S. family. Each issue was brought about by or was a result of social change; that is, traditional patterns coexist with emergent patterns. Were there no change or were there total change, no conflicts or issues would exist.

3. In my view, the most important issue to which all other issues are related centers on the meaning given to marriage and the family. The most traditional social norm holds that marriage and the family are sacred phenomena created and maintained by factors that are beyond human beings. Less traditional is the norm that suggests that marriage is created and maintained by society or by kin, by community, or by social institutions. The emergent norm suggests that marriage is created and maintained by the individual for the individual. Thus at least three meanings that are basically incompatible exist simultaneously. Only when individual meanings are identical to social meanings that are identical to sacred meanings, can there be no conflict.

4. Related issues include the "proper" form of marital and family organization, the functions of the family, social mobility, the choice of a mate and the authority to choose, the degree of or need for love, the limiting of sexual relationships to marriage, husband-wife and male-female roles in relation to each other, the choice of the number and spacing of children and the means to fulfill that choice, the role of the aged in society, and the permanent or temporary nature of marriage.

5. It is impossible to state that one issue is more important than another. For young single people, primary issues may focus on mate selection and sexual relationships. For married couples the primary issues may focus on children, birth control, and marital roles. For elderly

persons, the primary issues may focus on the functions of the family and their place in society. The meaning given to marriage, if maintained consistently from one issue to another, will influence whether one is for divorce or against it, for abortion or opposed to it, for extramarital coitus or opposed to it, or for accepting parental authority in selecting a mate or in personal choice irrespective of parental wishes.

6. This chapter, while highly descriptive, presents an overview of issues and changes in the family within the United States. The next chapter focuses on disciplinary and theoretical approaches to family study.

KEY TERMS AND TOPICS

DISCUSSION QUESTIONS

1. How many "ideal types" of polar constructs can you list that describe issues in families?

2. Check with five married adults as to their perceptions of the most important issues in the U.S. family today. Do the same with five single students. Compare results.

3. Which issue (of those listed or others) do you perceive as the most significant or serious today? Why? How can the conflict or issue be resolved?

4. Why do marriages exist today? What is their purpose? What or who should be the ultimate authority?

5. If conflicts exist between traditional and emergent marital and family norms, do the adherents of either position have a right to impose their position on the other? Take for example the couple that wants an abortion versus those who argue that abortion is wrong.

6. Can a person "love" more than one person simultaneously? Can intimate relationships with someone other than one's spouse enrich a relationship with the spouse?

7. Has there been a greater change in sexual norms for men or for women? Why is this so? Is this issue or conflict primarily a thing of the past or will it be an issue ten years from now?

8. List the characteristics of "true" masculinity and femininity. Include behavioral as well as attitudinal characteristics.

9. Is an increase in divorce rates primarily indicative of a breakdown or a strengthening of the marital system in the United States? How about the increase in premarital and extramarital sexual relations, out of wedlock births, and interracial marriage? Why?

10. If a student from Nigeria asked you to describe the typical family in the United States, how would you respond?

11. In what ways are families different in your community? Identify as many variables as you can.

12. To what extent is your family "typical"? How is it similar to or different from other families in our pluralistic society?

FURTHER READINGS

Adams, Bert N., and John L. Campbell, eds. *Framing the Family: Contemporary Portraits*. Prospect Heights, Ill.: Waveland Press, Inc., 1984. A collection of twenty-eight readings covering numerous issues raised in this first chapter.

Caplow, Theodore; Bahr, Howard M.; Chadwick, Bruce A.; Hill, Reuben; and Williamson, Margaret Holmes. *Middletown Families: Fifty Years of Change and Continuity*. New York: Bantam Books, 1982. Middletown, a fictitious name given to Muncie, Indiana, was immortalized in two classic studies by Robert and Helen Lynd in 1929 and 1937. In the late 1970s a team of sociologists returned to Middletown for an extensive look at families in this community.

Crosby, John F. *Reply to Myth: Perspectives in Intimacy*. New York: John Wiley, 1985. A listing of ten myths about sex, love, marriage, and the family with selected readings that address each myth.

Farber, J. Bernard. *Family Organization and Interaction*. San Francisco: Chandler, 1964. A book that concentrates on the explanation of stability and change in the family. Chapter 4 presents the orderly replacement and universal permanent availability models of change.

Feldman, Harold and Margaret Feldman. *Current Controversies in Marriage and the Family*. Beverly Hills: Sage Publications, 1985. Fourteen chapters brought together to illumine current controversies revolving around marriage and the family by using sets of paired comparisons.

Gordon, Michael, ed. *The American Family in Social–Historical Perspective*. 3d ed. New York: St. Martin's Press, 1983. A collection of readings reflecting on family subjects in an historical context.

Kammeyer, Kenneth C. W., ed. *Confronting the Issues: Sex Roles, Marriage and the Family*, 2d ed. Boston: Allyn and Bacon, 1981. A book of readings built around controversies relating to marriage, love, childbearing, child rearing, the women's movement, and sexual behavior.

Levitan, Sar A. and Babous, Richard S. *What's Happening to the American Family*. Baltimore: The Johns Hopkins University Press, 1981. A review of various changes in American families with a look at selected programs and policies that have influenced them.

Olson, David H. and Miller, Brent C., eds. *Family Studies Review Yearbook*. Vol. 2. Beverly Hills: Sage Publications, 1984. A collection of forty-four previously-published articles covering theoretical and methodological advances and substantive issues such as parent-child relations, sex roles, divorce, and marital-family therapy.

Scott, Donald, M. and Wishy, Bernard, eds. *America's Families: A Documentary History*. New York: Harper & Row, Publishers, 1982. An extensive collection of historical materials that contain the story of families in America, beginning in the European world of the early seventeenth century and ending with contemporary controversies over the future of the family.

Skolnick, Arlene S., and Skolnick, Jerome H., eds. *Families in Transition*. 5th ed. Boston: Little, Brown and Company, 1986. A book of thirty-six readings, with major sections on the changing family, gender and sex, couples, parents and children, and a wider perspective that includes varieties of family experience and debating the future of the family.

Sussman, Marvin B., and Steinmetz, Suzanne K., eds. *Handbook of Marriage and the Family*. New York: Plenum Publishing Company, 1987. A primary source-book covering family perspectives and analysis, diversity in family life, life cycle processes, and family dynamics and transformation.

U.S. Bureau of the Census. *Current Population Reports*, Series P-23, No. 104, "American Families and Living Arrangements." Washington, D.C.: U.S. Government Printing Office, May 1980. An eighteen-page chartbook originally prepared by the Bureau of the Census for the 1980 White House Conference on Families, providing a graphic overview of recent family trends in the life-styles of many Americans.

Wells, J. Gipson, ed. *Current Issues in Marriage and the Family*. 3d ed. New York: Macmillan, 1983. An examination of eight issues of central importance to the U.S. family system. Many of the twenty-seven articles covering these issues provide excellent supplements to the issues discussed in Chapter 1.

Zimmerman, Carle C. *Family and Civilization*. New York: Harper, 1947. An examination of the role of the family in Western civilization; of trustee, domestic, and atomistic typologies of families; and social change. It presents an interesting discussion model for contemporary families.

Photo: © Ewing Galloway/E. P. Jones, Co.

2

Disciplinary and Theoretical Approaches to Family Study

Chapter 1 was devoted to a general introduction to the family, particularly the family in the United States. It provided some descriptive material on families, and then examined selected major issues in the American family by use of ideal-type constructs. This general overview was intended to set the general stage and introduce various issues, topics, and themes that follow throughout the book. There are many disciplines, approaches, and frames of reference used to study these family-related issues. These are examined in this chapter, with an emphasis given to the basic approaches and orientations emphasized in this book.

DISCIPLINES INVOLVED IN FAMILY STUDY

The area of marriage and the family touches upon a wide range of topics, lends itself to many types of research, and uses the results of the research in various ways. The orientation used in dealing with families will, in large part, determine the areas to investigate, the questions to ask about those areas, the research and theoretical approaches to apply, and the results that are derived. Since no single discipline is asking all the questions, obviously none has all the answers. Note in Table 2–1, for example, the wide range of disciplines that are concerned with families or family-related topics, and the examples of illustrative studies within each discipline.

Interdisciplinary approaches and concerns

No one discipline or occupation has a corner on the marriage and family market. The subject itself is highly interdisciplinary. The problem of disciplinary isolation is strikingly persistent. Anthropologists who focus on families and family structures often overlook emotional dynamics of family life. Psychologists, focusing on child development and personal adjustment, often overlook cultural variation and social organizational aspects. Sociologists, focusing on the social order, often overlook historical and personal developmental factors.

Since the late 1960s, major changes have taken place in the extent to which one discipline has challenged and/or incorporated ideas and

TABLE 2–1

Selected disciplines involved in areas of family study

Disciplines	Illustrative topics
Anthropology	Families in developing societies: cross-cultural studies; evolution; kinship
Biology	Human growth: genetics; conception and reproduction
Child Development	Infant growth; learning; personality formation
Counseling	Family therapy; interpersonal relationships; vocational guidance
Demography	Marriage; birth; divorce rates; mobility patterns
Economics	Family finance; consumer behavior; standards of living
Education	Family life; marriage preparation; child development; sex education
English	The family through literature, poetry, novels, and mass media
Gerontology	Family life of the elderly; intergenerational links; kin support systems
History	Family origins, trends, and patterns over time
Home Economics	Housing; nutrition; ecology; child development
Law	Marriage; divorce; abuse; adoption; welfare; child custody
Psychology	Interpersonal relationships; learning; human development
Public Health	Venereal disease; maternal and infant care; preventive medicine
Religion	Morality; marriage vows; love; sex; religious training
Social Work	Family, child, maternal, and aging assistance
Sociology	Family systems; interpersonal relationships; social change

theoretical frameworks of another discipline. Arlene Skolnick claims that old social science theories are in a state of decline and that the family seems to be in a process of being rediscovered.[1] Variations in family systems are emerging as distinct cultural phenomena rather than the abstraction and universalism of "the family" being focused on. The idea of the natural state of the family being one of harmony is being replaced by notions that conflict and violence are equally natural. Treatment of individual persons has expanded to a focus on interaction and the whole family group. It is Skolnick's contention that today we know both more and less about the family than we thought we did a decade ago. In her words:

---

1. Arlene Skolnick, "The Family Revisited: Themes in Recent Social Science Research," *Journal of Interdisciplinary History* 4 (Spring 1975): 703–719.

Some theories of human behavior are based on assumptions and inferences derived from the study of animals. (Photo: © Allan Rose/Freelance Photographer's Guild)

We know that there is no uniform type of family, no Family that is everywhere and at all times the same. We know that there is great variation in family size, in extent of kinship, in residence patterns, in the organization of domestic functions, in the cognitive meanings of family, and in affective styles. We know that these features may vary not only from one culture to another, but also from one family to another in the same culture. We also know that we cannot extrapolate from family ideals and norms to behavior, or vice versa, but rather that behavior, norm, and symbol represent dimensions of family life that need to be analyzed separately. Finally, we know that there has been more physical and emotional conflict in families than anyone had acknowledged, and that somehow most families have coped with these strains and children have grown up amidst them without society's "falling apart."[2]

2. Ibid., p. 718.

The orientation of specific disciplines

New interdisciplinary approaches may lead toward closing some of the gaps that separate disciplines and may bring forth new concepts and thus new meanings; yet each discipline will continue to focus attention in specific directions. The anthropologist will focus on family patterns in a cross-cultural and national context. The counsellor, usually in an applied context, will attempt to assist individuals, couples, or groups in resolving conflicts or modifying attitude or behavioral problems. The educator will attempt to convey ideas and elicit thought on child development, preparation for marriage, sexual concerns, or parental functioning. The historian will examine family patterns, events, and change in the past and over time. The politician will formulate policy and enact laws to deal with child care, marriage age, parental duties and responsibilities, or divorce. The social worker will direct knowledge and skills toward assisting families and family members in coping with problems of income, health, or behavior.

Neither the disciplines described nor the illustrative studies in Table 2–1 present an exhaustive listing of approaches to family study. The humanities have long been interested in the family.[3] Poets have been writing about love, marriage, and family matters for centuries. Theologists, philosophers, artists, musicians, and linguists have not been immune from dealing with areas pertinent to the family. Biology, genetics, anatomy, and other biological sciences are interested in many facts that affect families. In fact, it may well be the biosocial science area that will provide the next major revolution, replacing the industrial one and having an impact on families far greater than anything experienced or known at this time.

The point is that a student could take a large number of family courses and encounter different ideas, approaches, and interests. Some courses would include theories and findings from other disciplines; others would have no interdisciplinary focus. The question becomes less "Which is better or correct?" than "Which fulfills the objectives or purposes desired?" The student interested in the portrayal of mothers in the mass media may not find much satisfaction in a course on child growth and development. Neither may the student interested in sex education care much about insurance plans or marketing behavior of nineteenth century English households.

Textbooks, like disciplines or courses, approach the family with a particular focus and orientation. That this book gives minimal attention to human anatomy, childhood diseases, and family nutrition is not meant

---

3. An excellent illustration of fiction writings related to marriage and the family can be found in Rose M. Somerville, *Intimate Relationships: Marriage, Family and Lifestyles Through Literature* (Englewood Cliffs, N.J.: Prentice-Hall, 1975).

to indicate a lack of importance of these areas. Rather, the orientation and frame of reference of this book basically follows that of the social sciences and more specifically that of sociology.

A SOCIAL SCIENCE APPROACH TO THE FAMILY

As with the other areas mentioned, and perhaps to a greater extent, the social sciences have a primary interest in the family. Generally, the social sciences include sociology, anthropology, psychology, economics, and political science. Sometimes history, geography, and linguistics are added to this list. Each examines the same subject matter—the behavior of human beings—employs the same body of general explanatory principles, and shares similar aims and methods. Science is determined by its aims and methods, not by its results.

Regardless of the topic that is studied, be it the family or the economy, the social scientist is obligated to follow certain standards of inquiry. These include:

1. Objectivity. The personal biases and values of the people doing the research must never influence the data reported or the interpretation of results.
2. Replication. Research should be conducted and reported in such a way that someone else can duplicate it.
3. Precision of measurement. The phenomenon being studied should be measured in precise, reliable, and valid ways.[4]

All phenomena, including social phenomena, have certain regularities and uniformities that operate independently of the researcher or observer. These patterns or regularities can be discovered through objective observation. Science is predicated upon the assumption that there is a "real world," that something exists "out there"—something that is divorced from the individuals themselves and is empirically knowable.

The aims and goals of a social science approach to the family are to establish more-or-less general relationships, to require that they be based on empirical observation, and to view findings as tentative and open to multiple interpretations. Within the social science framework, let us examine the sociological approach to the family.

---

4. J. Ross Eshleman, Barbara G. Cashion and Laurence Basirico, *Sociology: An Introduction* 3rd ed. (Boston: Little, Brown and Co., 1988).

The sociology of the family

Sociology per se is devoted to the study of how society is organized, its social structure, and its social processes. The primary units of investigation include human groups, social systems, and institutions.

A sociology of the family seeks to explain the nature of the social order and disorder of the family. The attempt is to discover, describe, and explain the order of family systems and family groups. A sociology of the family is interested in the organization of the family: its structures, functions, and changes. It is interested in how the family as a social system is sustained and modified. It is interested in how family relationships are formed and changed, how the components within the family are interrelated, and how the family as a unit is interdependent with other groups or systems.

A sociology of the family differs from either psychological or social-psychological approaches to the family. Whereas both of these are primarily concerned with the behavior of individuals, sociology is interested in the social forms and structures within which this behavior takes place. Sociology has no primary interest in the individual, his or her personality, or his or her behavior, but rather with the nature of the groups to which the individual belongs and the society in which he or she lives. The separation of psychology, social psychology, and sociology is not always distinct, but each of the three branches of social science has different emphases. According to Eshleman and Cashion, and Basirico:

> Psychology is concerned with individuals. Social psychology is the study of how an individual influences his or her social interactions with other individuals or with groups, and of how social behavior influences the individual. Sociology deals primarily with groups and social systems.[5]

A sociology of the family will not focus on the motivation, drives, or perceptions of individuals. Technically speaking, a major segment of this book is a social psychology of marriage and the family. The sections that deal with interpersonal relationships (mate-selection processes, sexual behavior, parental interaction) focus on explaining how the structure and function of the family group influence the behavior of the members within that group and, reciprocally, how the behavior of each member modifies or shapes the family organization and its functioning.

A sociology of the family, operating within the social science framework, does not have as its major intent the direct application or utilization of the knowledge gained by the "pure," "concrete," or "basic"disciplines. On

---

5. Ibid., p. 16.

a pure-applied ideal-type continuum, and operating within an ideal-type construct (*see* Chapter 1), persons involved in the acquisition of knowledge do not devote their time and attention to the direct, day-to-day application of the knowledge. Thus the "basic" psychologist does not counsel family members, the sociologist does not work in adoption agencies, nor does the economist assist a family member in obtaining a job. The psychologist, sociologist, or economist might, however, provide theoretical orientations, evaluation skills, research findings, data interpretations, policy suggestions, and the like to counsellors, teachers, social workers, politicians, or others. In this sense they too, as social scientists, become applied sociologists, psychologists, or economists.

Hopefully, this book will increase our knowledge about existing situations, present frameworks for analysis and/or action, and suggest alternate life-styles and directives. Based on the available knowledge and various interpretations of that knowledge, based on various theoretical explanations and methodological approaches, based on the presentation of multiple structures and various alternatives, I hope you, the reader, will be in a better position to make your own choices of action and make sound judgments on social policy and social action.

HISTORICAL APPROACHES TO FAMILY STUDIES

It was only after the middle of the nineteenth century that a systematic study of the family began. Prior to that time, thinking about the family had been based on emotion and superstition and was expressed by means of folklore, proverbs, and moralisms. Bert N. Adams says that the beginning of the movement toward systematic understanding rather than reliance on folklore can be traced roughly to the time of the appearance of Charles Darwin's *The Origin of Species* in 1859.[6] Adams subdivides the years from 1860 to the present into four thirty-year periods: social Darwinism (1860–1890), social reform (1890–1920), scientific study (1920–1950), and attention to family theory (1950–present).

Prior to the mid-1980s, family guidelines took the form of philosophical speculations, religious pronouncements, and often contradictory generalizations (such as today's "out of sight, out of mind" and "absence makes the heart grow fonder"). Although these types of speculation continue today, and many untested assumptions regarding the family are rigidly defended, various shifts have taken place in the development of the study of the family. In the middle of the nineteenth century, several writers

---

6. Bert N. Adams, *The Family: A Sociological Interpretation*, 4th ed. (Chicago: Harcourt Brace Jovanovich, 1986): 7–9.

began to apply Darwin's biological evolutionary scheme to changes within the family. Based on "primitive" peoples, these macroanthropological schemes traced the evolution of the family through a series of "natural" and "progressive" stages. For example, one series of stages might suggest the earliest relationship between men and women to be promiscuous, followed by a maternal (mother-child) family, and then by an original pair marriage. These schemes, which are often intuitive, raised questions such as how monogamy came to be and whether wife-capture or group marriage were earlier forms in a patterned sequence of stages.

Toward the end of the nineteenth century and the beginning of the twentieth, especially in the United States, social problems led to a concern for social reform. Many of these problems were closely related to the family: poverty, child labor, prostitution, illegitimacy, divorce, and the like. These problems were intensified by industrialization and urbanization, both of which disrupted kin ties.

The first half of the twentieth century emphasized large-scale comparative studies, aimed at attacking some of the social problems but emphasizing more of a value-free position and a more rigorous methodology. Various statistical techniques were developed and certain social psychologists and sociologists began to focus on individual personality

Filipino marriage folk beliefs

If you awaken at 12:00 midnight and look at the mirror, you will see your future partner or sweetheart.

A person with dimples will marry someone from a place far away from his place.

It is not good for a girl or woman to sit at the head of the table because she won't get married and will eventually end up as an old maid.

A layman who goes through life without being married will not be admitted in heaven. He lacks the sacrament of matrimony and fails to comply with the commandment of God.

If a man marries a woman who is one year older than him their whole married life always meets problems and difficulties.

A girl who is always fainting should get married and she will be cured.

Marriage should be held at a date when the moon is getting big—half moon or full moon—for abundance of children.

If a husband can cut a banana plant with just one stroke of the blade (bolo), he is the master of the house. If he cannot, he is a henpecked husband.

Source: Francisco Demetrio y Radaza, S. J., ed., *Dictionary of Philippine Folk Beliefs and Customs*, Book III (Cagayan de Ora City, The Philippines: Xavier University, 1970): 619–622, 624–625.

adjustment, the family as a major factor in this adjustment, and the relationship between certain family problems and social problems in general.

A social-psychological orientation replaced the macroanthropological approaches of the earlier periods. Characteristic of this period of family study was an emphasis upon the internal relationship of family members. Charles Cooley, Robert Park, George Mead, W. I. Thomas, and others contributed to this emphasis, but it was Ernest W. Burgess who did most to both conceptualize and assist in the development of family studies. In 1926 he referred to the family as "the unity of interacting personalities," a definition that is still in wide use today. This was basically the beginning of the scientific orientation to family study, and by 1950 it was perhaps accurate to speak of the scientific study of marriage and the family.

Adams prefers to describe the 1950–1970 decades as a period of summarization of findings, of conceptual frameworks, of complaint about the lack of comprehensive theory, and of tentative theoretical attempts. He argues that it is instructive to view the 1960s as dominated by conceptual frameworks and the 1970s as oriented toward codification and theory building.[7] Research does appear to increasingly turn to cross-cultural and comparative studies, not purely for descriptive purposes but to discover relationships that are generalizable beyond a given societal context. Much evidence of this can be found in a two-volume work dealing with contemporary theories about the family that brought the 1970s to a close.[8]

What about the 1980s? Thomas Holman and Wesley Burr[9] suggest that we seem no closer to the general theory of the family many have called for, but argue that such a theory may be not only an impossible dream, but also unnecessary. Instead they urge theorists to continue to improve existing theory, to develop metatheory (new and different forms of theory) and methodologies of building theory, to refine and validate theory with cross-cultural research, and to develop a reciprocal interaction with practitioners. Related to this latter point is the view of Greer Fox that one of the most interesting challenges facing the field in this decade concerns our role as family specialists in the public arena.[10] Since most readers of this book will be or are family practitioners as children, spouses, parents, or as a family-related professional, one goal of this chapter and those that follow will be to present major theories and frames of reference and show how they are relevant to everyday life.

---

7. Adams, *The Family*, p. 9.

8. Wesley R. Burr, Reuben Hill, F. Ivan Nye, and Ira L. Reiss, *Contemporary Theories About the Family*, vols. 1 and 2 (New York: The Free Press, 1979).

9. Thomas B. Holman and Wesley R. Burr, "Beyond the Beyond: The Growth of Family Theories in the 1970's," *Journal of Marriage and the Family* 42 (November 1980): 729–741.

10. Greer Litton Fox, "Family Research, Theory, and Politics: Challenges of the Eighties," *Journal of Marriage and the Family* 43 (May 1981): 260.

THE NATURE OF THEORIES AND FRAMES OF REFERENCE

Like the theoreticians in most other fields, family scholars are increasingly attempting to organize their accumulated knowledge in the form of concepts, generalizations, and theories. Specialists in the family area have been conscious of the need to organize concepts, develop hypotheses and propositions, and interrelate these propositions in a meaningful fashion in order to explain a particular aspect of marital or family organization and behavior. Concepts, conceptual frameworks, frames of reference, and theories are important in that they tell scholars where to focus their attention.

Family theories are neither right nor wrong but are basically ways of looking at and rationally explaining phenomena related to the family. An understanding of the most widely used frames of reference can enable the student to study and analyze family behavior in a way that is organized and logical. Rather than behavior within the family context being idiosyncratic and inconsistent, it becomes patterned, consistent, and predictable under certain given conditions.

Concepts and variables

Basic to all theory and to all sociological research tools are **concepts**. A family concept, as in any area, is a miniature "system of meaning"—that is, a symbol, such as a word or phrase that enables a phenomenon to be perceived in a certain way. Concepts are tools by which one can share meanings. They are unitary and thus do not explain, predict, or state relationships. They are abstractions that are used as building blocks for the development of hypotheses, propositions, and theories. In family analysis, the segments of reality that are identified by concepts are typically qualities, attributes, or properties of social behavior. Examples of concepts within the family area would include the nuclear family, monogamy, roles, norms, values, legitimacy, sex ratio, and so on.

When these concepts take on two or more degrees or values they are referred to as **variables**. "Husband" is a concept; "years married" is

Do concepts make a difference?

> I used to think I was POOR. Then they told me I wasn't poor, I was NEEDY. Then they told me it was self-defeating to think of myself as needy, I was DEPRIVED. Then they told me deprived was a bad image, I was UNDERPRIVILEGED. Then they told me underprivileged was overused, I was DISADVANTAGED. I still don't have a dime, but I have a great vocabulary.

Source: Anonymous.

a variable. The variable may be classified as *independent* (the presumed cause) or *dependent* (the presumed effect). The independent variable is antecedent, or simultaneous, to the dependent variable. Family income (a variable) may be dependent (the presumed effect) upon the number of years of education (the presumed cause).

Concepts and variables are undergoing continuous revision and refinement. Frequently, new concepts must be invented to symbolize some new idea or to identify some social property that had not previously been seen. Thus, *family* may in itself serve as an adequate term for lay people, but the professional differentiates between *families of orientation or procreation, nuclear, conjugal, extended, consanguine, stem,* and *joint.* Because the particular concept used will affect what is seen, it must be constructed in a way that will not distort "reality." An extremely difficult task for the family scholar is to label phenomena in ways that will avoid undesired connotations. Could you imagine a family book bearing titles such as the honky, WASP, palefaced, or uncolored family in American society? Or notice the obviously different connotations of labels or concepts such as nigger, colored, Negro, black, or Afro-American. Halford Fairchild testifies to this argument that the differences are crucial.[11]

Conceptual frameworks

When a set of concepts is interrelated to describe and classify phenomena, in this case phenomena relative to the family, the concepts are generally defined as a **conceptual framework**. In a strict sense of the term, a conceptual framework is not a theory; it is more frequently descriptive rather than explanatory and is generally employed as a classification scheme or taxonomy.

Considerable changes have occurred in the identification of current conceptual frameworks. In 1957, seven basic frameworks or approaches were defined by Hill and others; institutional-historical, interactional-role analysis, structural-functional, situational-psychological habitat, learning theory-maturational, household economics-home management, and the family development or family life cycle approach.[12]

In 1960, in what has become a classic article by Hill and Hansen, the chief conceptual properties and basic underlying assumptions of five

---

11. Halford H. Fairchild, "Black, Negro, or Afro-American? The Differences are Crucial," *Journal of Black Studies* 16 (September 1985): 47–55.

12. Reuben Hill, Alvin M. Katz, and Richard L. Simpson, "An Inventory of Research in Marriage and Family Behavior: A Statement of Objectives and Progress," *Marriage and Family Living* 19 (February 1957): 89–92.

frameworks were provided in taxonomic tables.[13] The frameworks delineated included these approaches: interactional, structural-functional, situational, institutional, and developmental.

These two initial works have stimulated a large number of articles and chapters on conceptual frameworks, frames of reference, and theories that are particularly applicable to the family area but seldom unique to it. These include legal, economic, institutional, evolutionary, biological, psychoanalytic, behavioristic, balance, game, ecological, and general systems frameworks, among others. The five frameworks covered in this chapter tend to appear regularly in the family literature, namely: structural-functional, symbolic interactional, social conflict, social exchange, and developmental. These conceptual classification schemes, models, or frames of reference are not to be substituted for nor are they to replace an interest in the creation of hypotheses, propositions, and theory.

Propositions and hypotheses

Conceptual frameworks can be used to generate or establish propositions, hypotheses, and theories. A **proposition** is a statement about the nature of some phenomenon. It generally involves a statement of the relationship between two or more concepts. For example, "young marriage is related to marital conflict" would be a proposition. If this, or other propositions, are formulated for empirical testing it is then considered a **hypothesis**. Thus a testable hypothesis would be "the younger the age at marriage, the higher the rate of divorce." Hypotheses and propositions are identical, with the exception that hypotheses carry clear implications for testing or measuring the stated relations. Hypotheses serve as the important branch between theory and empirical inquiry. Hypotheses and propositions are formed by combining concepts into statements that set forth some meaningful relationship.

Frequently, a proposition states that if one variable changes in some regular fashion, predictable change will take place in the other. For example, it has been suggested that "as industrialization increases, extended family ties decrease." Thus the two variables (industrialization and extended family) are stated as inversely related: as one increases the other decreases.

An extensive inventory of propositions interrelating family variables was presented by William Goode, Elizabeth Hopkins, and Helen McClure

---

13. Reuben Hill and Donald A. Hansen, "The Identification of Conceptual Frameworks Utilized in Family Study," *Marriage and Family Living* 22 (November 1960): 299–311.

in 1971.[14] They presented an estimated ten thousand propositions that interrelated family variables. Since then, Wesley Burr and thirty-eight other experts in family study have presented the most authoritative and comprehensive work to date on establishing hypotheses and propositions in the area of family.[15] Covering areas such as family networks, change, fertility, work, mate selection, power, recreation, violence, social class, and many others, each author summarized and evaluated previous empirical and theoretical models. This work and others that follow represent yet another step toward systematic theory building in the area of family study.

Theory

When it is possible to interrelate logically and systematically a series of propositions that explain some particular process, the result is a **theory**. A "good" theory should be testable, should be abstract, should have wide application, should be cumulative, and should give grounds for prediction. Thus, a theory is far more than mere speculation or a random collection of concepts and variables. It is a set of logically interrelated propositions that explains some process or set of phenomena in a testable fashion.

Like propositions, theories not only provide explanations of observed reality but also serve as important sources of new hypotheses. Examples of such efforts can be seen in most chapters of the *Contemporary Theory* books by Burr and others. For example, Lewis and Spanier (Chapter 12) identify ninety propositions about factors relating to marital quality and marital stability and show the potential for a social exchange theory in explaining marital relationships.[16]

The use and application of theory, or perhaps more accurately *theoretical frames of reference*, are used extensively throughout this book. While no independent chapters exist on theory per se, you will note subsections that use a particular frame of reference. For example, the **structural-functional** frame of reference is applied extensively in Part II to an analysis of family life-styles. The **social conflict** frame of reference is applied in Chapters 13 and 17 in dealing with the marital system and violence and divorce. The **symbolic interaction** frame of reference is applied throughout the book to an analysis of mate selection, sexual relationships, marital interaction, and child rearing (socialization). The **developmental** framework is applied through Part IV in viewing marriage

---

14. William J. Goode, Elizabeth Hopkins, and Helen M. McClure, *Social Systems and Family Patterns: A Propositional Inventory* (Indianapolis: Bobbs-Merrill, 1971).

15. Wesley R. Burr, Reuben Hill, F. Ivan Nye, and Ira L. Reiss, eds., *Contemporary Theories About the Family*, vols. 1 and 2 (New York: The Free Press, 1979).

16. Burr et al., *Contemporary Theories*, Chapter 12, pp. 268–294.

over the life cycle. **Social exchange theory** is applied to mate selection and the marital system. Other theories—frames of reference—not specifically summarized in detail in this chapter are presented where appropriate to offer a specific explanation of a particular aspect of the family: an orderly replacement theory of change, a complementary-need theory of mate selection, a learning-behaviorist or psychoanalytic theory of socialization, a disengagement theory of old age, and the like. From this list alone, it becomes obvious that many sets of logically interrelated propositions exist that explain some process or set of phenomena. Those more directly pertinent and widely used in a sociology of the family are summarized in the section that follows.

FAMILY THEORIES AND FRAMES OF REFERENCE

A structural-functional frame of reference

The structural-functional frame of reference, sometimes called *functional analysis*, is a major and dominant theoretical orientation in sociology. Within the family area, the scope of the approach is very broad; it provides a framework for dealing with the relationships within the family (husband, wife, sibling, and so on), as well as with the reciprocal influences on the family from other systems within the wider society (such as educational, religious, or occupational influences).

The structural-functional frame of reference has its origin in the functionalist branch of psychology, especially the gestalt position; in social anthropology, and in sociology, especially as seen by social-systems theorists such as Talcott Parsons.[17] The gestalt position focuses on the relation between a whole and its parts. A gestalt is an organized entity or whole in which the parts, although distinguishable, are interdependent. Numerous social anthropologists as well have stressed the impossibility of studying any particular aspect of life detached from its general setting. Functionalism is identified with the study of the interrelationships between the structures of any system.

To talk about social structures is to talk about social organizations, social systems, norms, values, and the like. Cultural structures, social structures, structural interrelations, or any other "structural" terminology refers to the interdependence of parts in a definite pattern of organization. Within this framework, societies (and families) are composed of interdependent parts that are linked together into a boundary-maintaining

---

17. Talcott Parsons, *The Social System* (Giencoe, Ill.: The Free Press, 1951).

Apes provide humans with many models of family structure

> According to the book, *Sociobiology: The New Synthesis*, the great apes, our closest relatives, exhibit a wide variety of family structures. Author Edward Wilson says the social organization varies greatly between species of higher primates, from solitary adults and mother-offspring groups in the orangutans, to monogamous pairs and offspring in the gibbon apes, to large social groups in the baboons, gorillas, and chimpanzees. Baboons, he states, are organized in male-dominated harems that are zealously guarded, while gorillas live in very gentle but male-dominated societies where overt sexual behavior is very rare, and chimpanzees live in large, loosely organized groups characterized by amiable, cooperative activities and sexual promiscuity. Thus nature provides us with many different models for family structure.

Source: Edward O. Wilson, *Sociobiology: The New Synthesis* (Cambridge: Harvard University Press, 1975).

whole and are basically in harmony with each other. Since the parts of a system "need each other," there is a social bond and a high degree of order, cohesion, stability, and persistence. The implication is that groups, systems, or behavior are not purely random, individualistic, or unpredictable. Family groups and systems and the individuals that comprise them, like the other components of a society, are orderly and predictable units that must be viewed in a social context.

The social structure of a family refers to the way in which the social units are arranged, to the interrelationship of the parts, and to the patterns of organization. These patterns differ greatly around the world but, given a particular type of organization, definite recurrent consequences occur. Linda Bryan and others,[18] for example, found that a family structure consisting of stepparents and stepchildren appeared to lend itself to negative stereotypes. They hypothesized that family structure will be a cue by which stereotypes are formed and that stepparents and stepchildren will be seen more negatively than married or widowed parents or their children, but less negatively than divorced or never-married parents or their children. All hypotheses were supported.

To extend this argument of structure producing or resulting in patterned, recurrent consequences suggests that to have one wife or several, for newlyweds to establish a residence separate from parents, for both

---

18. Linda R. Bryan, Marilyn Coleman, Lawrence H. Ganong, and S. Hugh Bryan, "Person Perception: Family Structure as a Cue for Stereotyping," *Journal of Marriage and the Family* 48 (February 1986): 169–174.

husband and wife to share in making the basic decisions, for inheritance to be given to the oldest child, or for there to be premarital sexual freedom is to suggest that recurrent, predictable consequences will occur within that given society and/or family system. *Nuclear, polyandry, partriarchy, avunculocal, bilineal, primogeniture, exogamy, arranged marriage,* or *consanguine* are words that define specific structural arrangements of a given family system. Most of these terms are described and illustrated in the next chapter.

The concepts "structure" and "function" can be discussed separately, although they are interrelated and one implies the other. Speaking in circular terms, social structures are units of society that carry out or result in one or more basic functions. On the other hand, functions can be defined as results or consequences of given social structures. What specifically is meant by function?

Function is generally used in one of two related ways. One is to ask, "What does it do?" That is, in describing functions of the family in the United States or any given society, it is asked what the family does. Why does it exist? What functions does it perform? These functions may be *manifest,* that is, intended and recognized, or *latent,* that is, neither intended nor recognized. These functions may be performed for the individual personality, a particular social system or social institution, or the wider society.

It has been suggested that for individual members, some manifest functions of the family are to provide the basic personality formation, the basic status ascriptions, nurturant socialization, and tension management. For the larger society, some manifest functions are to replace members, to socialize the members to the norms and values of the society, and to act as an agent of social control. Talcott Parsons and Robert Bales suggest that the basic and irreducible family functions are two: (1) the primary socialization of children so that they can truly become members of the society into which they have been born, and (2) the stabilization of the adult personalities of the society.[19]

Families perform latent functions for persons and society as well. These latent functions, while real in the sense that they take place, are neither intended nor recognized. These latent functions may include socializing children to be abusive adults or instilling within them negative definitions of self-worth. For the larger society, some latent functions may be to keep women in inferior positions to men or to perpetuate inequality from one generation to the next. Generally, we do not intend families to fulfill such functions; nevertheless, such latent functions exist.

---

19. Talcott Parsons and Robert F. Bales, *Family Socialization and Interaction Process* (New York: The Free Press, 1955): 16–17.

A second way in which function is used is related to the first usage. It is used in terms of consequences or results of activities that take place. Thus, given a certain type of structural pattern—for example, working mothers—one could ask, "What are some of the consequences (results) of the employment of mothers?" Note that the question is not "What do working mothers do?" but rather "What are some of the results or consequences of this type of behavior pattern?" Are smaller family size, higher levels of mental health, delinquent children, or marital instability consequences of mothers working? Do families in societies that permit mothers to join the labor force have a higher level of living, a "closer" parent-child relationship, or more egalitarian decision-making patterns? Are the consequences similar irrespective of cultural context, time, or location? How does this structure interrelate with other structures? Does it lead to the maintenance or to the breakdown of a particular system? Is it consistent with the value scheme of the particular subculture discussed?

One example of noting manifest and latent consequences can be seen in an analysis of the functions of social conflict among children.[20] Douglas Maynard videotaped reading groups of first-grade children. He found that social conflict among children in these groups had the manifest function of creating their small-group society and its structure. Results of their disputes and arguments produced social organization and created political alignments. Studying these manifest functions served as a prelude to tracing latent functions of the reproduction of authority, friendship, and other social patterns that went beyond any single episode of interaction among children.

To repeat, these terms, *structure* and *function*, are complementary concepts. Although they can be discussed separately, they cannot be understood independently. The structure (parts) to which a social analyst imputes functions (consequences) includes norms, values, roles, rank, power, and sanctions, as well as factors such as emotions, beliefs, and goals.

Today, a major thrust of the structural-functional approach centers around explaining the parts or components (structure) of a society and the manner in which these parts interrelate with one another, both within and outside the particular system under study. Each component of society must be seen in relationship to the whole, since each component acts and reacts upon other components. Thus the task of functional analysis is to explain the parts, the relationship between the parts, the relationship between the parts and the whole, and the functions (both manifest and latent) that are performed by, or result from, the relationship formed by the parts.

---

20. Douglas W. Maynard, "On the Functions of Social Conflict Among Children," *American Sociological Review* 50 (April 1985): 207–223.

Hmm. What theory might explain how this couple carries and provides shade for their infant? (Photo: © Ellis Herwig/The Picture Cube)

On an ideal-type continuum, the level of analysis ranges from macroanalysis to microanalysis. The distinction between these is made purely in terms of the size of the unit chosen for analysis. The macrofunctionalists are concerned with the analysis of relatively large-scale systems and institutions. The microfunctionalists are concerned with the analysis of individual families or of relatively small-scale systems (often designated as *group dynamics*). Both positions conceive of their units of analysis as important to, and interrelated with, the other parts of the larger system.[21]

21. Key concepts in structural-functional theory in sociology are social system, social structure, social function, dysfunctions, manifest and latent functions, functional requisites and prerequisites, equilibrium and order, status and norms.

Some of the leading advocates of this perspective include Talcott Parsons, Robert Merton, Kingsley Davis, Wilbert Moore, Robin Williams, Charles Loomis, Harry Johnson, Emile Durkheim, George Homans, Marion Levy, William Goode, and Robert Winch.

From the perspective of the family, you may wish to examine Robert F. Winch, *The Modern Family*, 3d ed. (New York: Holt, Rinehart and Winston, 1971); Rose Laub Coser, *The Family: Its Structures and Functions*, 2d ed. (New York: St. Martin's Press, 1974); Norman W. Bell and Ezra F. Vogel, *A Modern Introduction to the Family*, rev. ed. (New York: The Free Press, 1968); and William J. Goode, *The Family*, 2d ed. (Englewood Cliffs, N.J.: Prentice-Hall, 1982).

A social conflict frame of reference

Conflict theory may be viewed as a special case of functional theory, as by Lewis Coser,[22] or as an entirely separate theory, as done by Rolf Dahrendorf.[23] Perhaps the most basic assumption of a conflict frame of reference is that conflict is natural and inevitable in all human interaction. Thus, rather than stressing order, equilibrium, consensus, or system maintenance as in functionalism, the focus is on conflict management. Rather than viewing conflict as "bad" and disruptive of social systems and human interaction, conflict is viewed as an assumed and expected part of all systems and interactions, including family systems and marital interactions. If family-employment, husband-wife, or parent-child norms or goals are in frequent conflict (as is to be expected), the issue is not how to avoid it but how to manage, deal with, and/or resolve it. In so doing, the conflict, rather than being disruptive or negative, may strengthen relationships, may force change and as a consequence make them more meaningful and rewarding than they were before.

The classical case for conflict theory stems from Karl Marx who assumed that economic organization, especially the ownership of property, generates revolutionary class conflict.[24] He believed that as the exploited and oppressed proletariats become aware of their oppression and their true "interests," they would revolt and form a revolutionary political organization aimed at overthrowing the dominant, property-holding bourgeoisie. Basic to Marx and influential in the contemporary thinking of conflict theorists are ideas such as: (1) social systems systematically generate conflict, which (2) is an inevitable and pervasive feature of all social systems and (3) is manifest in the bipolar opposition of interests that (4) is brought about by the distribution of scarce resources, most notably power, which (5) results in change in social systems.[25]

Hypotheses stemming from these assumptions suggest that: the more unequal the distribution of scarce resources, the greater the conflict between the dominant and the subordinate; as the subordinate become aware of their collective interests, they increasingly question the legitimacy of existing

22. Lewis A. Coser, *Continuities in the Study of Social Conflict* (New York: The Free Press, 1967).

23. Rolf Dahrendorf, *Essays in the Theory of Society* (Stanford: Stanford University Press, 1968); and Rolf Dahrendorf, "Out of Utopia: Toward a Reorientation of Sociological Analysis," *American Journal of Sociology* 74 (September 1958): 115–127.

24. Karl Marx, *The Communist Manifesto*, trans. Samuel Moore (Baltimore: Penguin, 1967), originally published in 1849 with Friedrich Engels; C. Wright Mills, *The Marxists* (New York: Harcourt, Brace, 1948); and Rolf Dahrendorf, *Class and Class Conflict in Industrial Society* (Stanford: Stanford University Press, 1959).

25. *See* Jonathan H. Turner, *The Structure of Sociological Theory* (Homewood, Ill.: Dorsey, 1974); 79–83.

patterns; the greater the questioning of inequities, the more likely they are to join in overt conflict against the dominant group; and the more overt and/or violent the conflict, the greater the change and the redistribution of these resources.

The family, from this Marxian economic-conflict perspective, serves to support the capitalistic system that exploits working-class workers by paying them lower wages. Similarly, it exploits women, not merely by paying lower wages to those who are employed, but by encouraging them to perform unpaid housework and child care so the husband can devote full time to his capitalist employer.

Feminist conflict theorists, while not denying the economic inequalities argued by the Marxian theorists, do not place the source of all male-female inequalities in economic systems. Some feminists have substituted the word "patriarchal" for "bourgeois" and even for "sex roles." "Sex roles," with its theme of different but equal tasks and power, downplays the structured inequality, that is, male dominance, that is pervasive. This male dominance exists in its own right and cuts across all economic and class lines. In addition, male domination implies female oppression and

TABLE 2—2
Duality of social life: Assumptions of the order and conflict models of society

	Order model	*Conflict model*
Question:	What is the fundamental relationship among the parts of society?	
Answer:	Harmony and cooperation.	Competition, conflict, domination, and subordination.
Why:	The parts have complementary interests. Basic consensus on societal norms and values.	The things people want are always in short supply. Basic dissensus on societal norms and values.
Degree of integration:	Highly integrated.	Loosely integrated. Whatever integration is achieved is the result of force and fraud.
Type of societal change:	Gradual, adjustive, and reforming.	Abrupt and revolutionary.
Degree of stability:	Stable.	Unstable.

Source: D. Stanley Eitzen, *In Conflict and Order: Understanding Society,* 2d ed. (Boston: Allyn and Bacon, 1982): 45.

sexism. The root source of this oppression and sexism is in the home, where for women, employed or not, housework and home are part of the same system. Until women increase their independence from men and gain resources (power, money, education, job opportunities, and the like) that decrease their oppressed status as women, the family will never become an egalitarian institution.

In brief, from either a Marxian or feminist conflict-model or perspective, the family is not the haven posited by an order model such as functionalism (*see* Table 2–2). Functionalists who see the family as the primary socialization agent of youth are seen by conflict theorists as promoting a false consciousness by teaching youth to accept the inequalities between the sexes and classes as "natural." Functionalists who see the family as perpetuating the same "life-chances" from one generation to another (that is, the rich stay rich and the poor stay poor) are seen by conflict theorists as maintaining and promoting inequality based on ascription rather than achievement. Functionalists who see the isolated nuclear family as consistent with the mobility needs of a capitalist society are seen by conflict theorists as disruptive to individual members and their emotional needs. Functionalists who see the modern family as tranquil, passive, and in a state of equilibrium with other units of society are seen by conflict theorists as a system fraught with potential and actual conflict. Conflict, as inevitable in society, in the family, and in interpersonal relationships, leads to change.

Issues related to conflict theory such as power, decision making, marital adjustment, economic factors, and the like are discussed elsewhere, particularly in Chapters 7 and 12.[26]

A symbolic interaction frame of reference

Symbolic interactionism has come into use as a label that indicates a particular and distinctive approach to the study of the group life and personal behavior of human beings. As a social-psychological frame of reference, it addresses itself to two major questions, both of which are

---

26. Key concepts in conflict theory are conflict, competition, negotiation, struggle, resources, scarcity, interests, change, power, and class.

Some of the leading advocates of the perspective include Karl Marx, Georg Simmel, Rolf Dahrendorf, Lewis A. Coser, and Pierre van den Berghe.

From the perspective of the family, you may wish to examine Randall Collins, *Sociology of Marriage and the Family: Gender, Love, and Property,* (Chicago: Nelson-Hall, 1985); Richard F. Curtis, "Household and Family in Theory on Inequality," *American Sociological Review* 51 (April 1986): 168–183; D. H. J. Morgan, *The Family, Politics and Social Theory,* (London: Routledge and Kegan Paul, 1985); Jetse Sprey, "Conflict Theory and the Study of Marriage and the Family," in *Contemporary Theories About the Family,* vol. 2, by Burr et al., pp. 130–159; and Mark Poster, *Critical Theory of the Family* (New York: Seabury, 1978).

of central concern to the family: socialization and personality. The first—socialization—focuses on how the human being obtains and internalizes the behavior patterns and ways of thinking and feeling of the society. The second—personality—focuses on the way in which these attitudes, values, and behaviors are organized.

Within social psychology, symbolic interactionism constitutes both a theoretical perspective and a methodological orientation. Its theoretical uniqueness lies in the extent to which covert activity is a crucial dimension in the understanding of behavior and society. That is, *like* Pavlovian and Skinnerian radical behaviorism,[27] symbolic interactionism includes the observable actions of individuals; *unlike* radical behaviorism, it stresses the importance of "meanings," definitions of situations, symbols, interpretations, and other internalized processes.

Interaction among socialized human beings is mediated by the use of symbols, by interpretation, or by ascertaining meanings for the actions of others. Methodologically, the "world of reality" is known by any means or set of techniques that offers a likely possibility of obtaining what is going on: direct observation, interviews, listening to the conversations of people, securing life history accounts, using letters and diaries, consulting public records, arranging for group discussions, or any allowable procedure that ascertains the subjective meanings. Basically, it involves a phenomenological approach with participant observation, the use of personal documents, and ethnomethodological accounts as the preferred techniques. The use of the quotations from personal interviews is consistent with this particular frame of reference.

The interactionist approach makes the following assumptions:

Marriages and families must be studied at their own level; that is, we cannot infer the behavior of humans, of human interactions, or of social systems from the study of nonhumans or infrahuman forms.

Marriage and family and their components can only be understood in the context of the social setting and society in which they exist. The language spoken, the definitions given to situations, or the appropriateness of any activity only makes sense within a social context.

The human infant at birth is neither social nor antisocial but asocial and learns in interaction with others what is good or bad, accepted or unaccepted behavior.

A social human being is an actor as well as a reactor; that is, he or she can communicate symbolically and share meanings. Thus, individuals do not merely respond to objective stimuli but select and interpret

---

27. Pavlovian and Skinnerian radical behaviorism, parallel to classical and operant conditioning, are described in Chapter 14 under the heading, "A Learning-Behaviorist Frame of Reference."

them. Individuals can interact each with themselves, can take the roles of others, and can respond to symbolic stimuli.

These assumptions, spelled out in more detail in Chapter 14, are basic to an understanding of the significance of this framework as applied to both marital and parental interaction and to human behavior in general.

Concepts from this framework are used extensively throughout the book. For example, the concept "role" is used both within a structural-functional framework and within an interactionist framework. However, its use varies significantly. An institutional or structural concept of role attaches societal expectations to statuses that we occupy. Certain statuses, such as sex, age, and race, are generally ascribed, whereas our marital, occupational, and parental statuses are likely to be achieved. Each of these statuses or status sets carry with them expected, appropriate behaviors. These expectations of what is appropriate for men or women, married or single, homosexual or heterosexual, are termed roles. These are culturally defined expectations, and exist independently of any given person.

Role, as it is used within an interactionist framework, does not deny the institutional usage but, rather than dealing with a package of behavioral expectations wrapped up in a set of rules, it deals with a relationship between what we do and what others do. The expectations (roles) are developed in interaction. The emphasis here is on process. The interactionist concept of role describes the processes of cooperative behavior and of communication. It involves the idea of "role taking," which is not a set of rules associated with a position but involves actions supplied in part by relationships to others whose actions reflect roles that are inferred. Role as a process involves each actor adjusting his or her behavior and reactions to what he or she thinks the other person is going to do. Perhaps a simple example may clarify the difference in the use of these two bodies of thought.

Suppose we have two students, one male and one female. The fact that they occupy student and sexual statuses implies that certain expectations or roles are associated with these statuses. But for the moment let's concentrate on the students as male and female. Some of the rules or expectations traditionally associated with the status "male" in relationship to "female" are that he walk on the outside, open doors, permit her to proceed first, assist her with a chair, and pay the bill. Thus the institutional concept of role emphasizes the society's prescribed expectations for behavior. Whether these rules are actually followed is secondary. The roles (expectations) exist independently of a given individual's fulfillment of them. Failure to conform to the expectations appropriate to status does not eliminate the normative expectations.

In contrast to the institutionalized concept of role, the interactionist concept involves the *process* of determining appropriate behavior in interaction with others. Now, the actor is not the occupant of a position for which there is a standardized set of rules; he or she is a person whose expectations for behavior are supplied in part by his or her relationship to another person or persons. Since the expectations of the other person can only be inferred rather than directly known, there is a continuous process of testing. The clues given by the other person in part determine the expected behaviors (roles) appropriate to that situation. Getting back to our male and female, as they interact the expectations (roles) for appropriate and approved behavior may vary widely from the socially ascribed expectations. The female may quite appropriately pay the bills, open the doors, be the aggressive sexual partner, drive the automobile, and the like. But these too become patterned and recurrent. This is what makes behavior predictable and interaction possible with either strangers or intimate lifelong friends.

These two conceptions of role are not totally independent and separate, for one never escapes the norms or roles provided by a given society. At best, however, the expectations associated with a given status offer only generalized guidelines; they do not determine specific behavior patterns for every situation. Thus, the norm prescribing that a male does not have intercourse with a female on a first date nevertheless may, as the couple interacts, result in coitus. The gestures, the clues, the symbols, the verbal communications, and the clarity of shared meanings may lead to intercourse as a highly appropriate role expectation for the dating partners—within the interactionist concept of role. The behavior of intercourse on a first date, within the institutional concept of role, however, is inconsistent with the culturally prescribed rules for unmarried couples in the United States.

Other concepts that are key to the understanding of this frame of reference include the social self, significant other, reference group, and generalized other. These are clarified and illustrated in various chapters throughout the text, with a more extensive presentation of the symbolic interactionist frame of reference in Chapter 14. At this point, let's be satisfied with recognizing the family as a "unit of interacting personalities"[28] involved in a never-ending, completed, or fixed process.[29]

---

28. Ernest W. Burgess, "The Family as a Unit of Interacting Personalities," *Family* 7 (1926): 3–9.

29. Key concepts in symbolic interaction theory are symbols, interaction, process, status, role, role playing, role taking, role conflict, meaning, reference group, significant other, generalized other, social self, "I," "me," socialization, actor, and identity.

Some of the leading advocates of this perspective include George Herbert Mead, Charles Cooley, William James, Herbert Blumer, Tomatsu Shibutani, Alfred Lindesmith, Anselm L. Strauss, Erving Goffman, and Sheldon Stryker.

From the perspective of the family, you may wish to examine Ralph H. Turner, *Family Interaction* (New York: Wiley, 1970); Sheldon Stryker, "Symbolic Interaction Theory: A Review

A social exchange frame of reference

Seldom does a day pass in which certain exchanges do not take place. Work, gifts, cards, affection, or ideas are given in hopes of getting something in return. Certain exchanges, such as many economic ones, are institutionalized and predetermined—clarified in precise terms prior to the exchange. Thus I know that I can exchange 25 cents for a newspaper or $70 for a membership in the National Council on Family Relations. Other exchanges, including the type found in the social exchange frame of reference, leave unspecified the exact nature of the return, although a return—an expectation of reciprocity—does exist. For example, neighbors who borrow tools or food, friends who invite you to dinner, politicians who promise lower taxes, all expect something in return. That exact something is often unspecified.

Social exchange or social choice theory rests on the belief that human beings attempt to make choices that they expect will maximize their rewards and/or minimize their costs. Social exchange theory seeks to explain why certain behavioral outcomes occur (marriage, sex, employment), given a set of structural conditions (age, race, gender, class) and interactional potentialities. These assumptions are made:

Most gratifications of humans have their source in the actions of other humans (spouse, children, friends, colleagues, fellow workers).
New associations are entered into because they are expected to be rewarding and old associations continue because they are rewarding.
As we receive rewards or benefits from others, we're under obligation to reciprocate by supplying benefits to them in return.
In general, giving is more blessed than receiving, because having social credit is preferable to being socially indebted.

While it may be true that persons (saints) exist who selflessly work for others with no thought of reward, saints are rare, and even they seek social (or spiritual) approval. In brief, social exchange refers to voluntary social actions that are contingent on rewarding reactions from others. These actions cease when the actual or expected reactions are not forthcoming.

Social exchange theory has followed two differing schools of thought

and Some Suggestions for Comparative Family Research," *Journal of Comparative Family Studies* 3 (Spring 1972): 17–32; and Wesley R. Burr, Geoffrey K. Leigh, Randall D. Day, and John Constantine, "Symbolic Interaction and the Family," in *Contemporary Theories About the Family*, vol. 2, by Burr et al., pp. 42–111.

best represented by George Homans[30] and Peter Blau.[31] Homans, the recognized initiator of exchange theory, represents a perspective consistent with that of behavioral psychologists who believe in psychological reductionism and reinforcement theory, where the focus is on actual behavior that is rewarded or punished by the behavior of other persons. Humans, like animals, react to stimuli based on need, reward, and reinforcement. It is expected that in exchange relationships the rewards will be proportional to the cost (a notion of distributive justice).

Blau differs considerably from Homans and represents a perspective consistent with that of the symbolic interactionist.[32] That is, not all exchange is explained in terms of actual behavior of individuals. The exchange is more subjective and interpretative. The exchange, like interaction, is a creative process between actors and not within individuals or in external factors. While humans want rewards, the choices and decisions are limited by social influences such as friends or kin. The human mind responds subjectively to stimuli through conceptualizing, defining, valuing, reflecting, and symbolizing. As a result, the explaining of behavioral outcomes (the goal of social exchange theory) is a function of the actors who interact symbolically, have social selves, and can take roles.

Both Homans and Blau agree that what is important is that each party receives in the exchange something perceived as equivalent to that which is given (to Homans—*distributive justice*, to Blau—*fair exchange*). All social exchange involves a mutually held expectation that reciprocation will occur.[33] If resources or exchange criteria are unequal or imbalanced, one person is at a distinct disadvantage and the other has power over, or controls, the relationship. Specific resources (money, position, physical assets, personality) may be more applicable in one exchange than in another and may have differing values in one exchange than in another. Their worth can only be accurately assessed through participation in actual social markets. Therefore, socialization in exchange and bargaining skills become vital to maximize the use of available resources.

The family literature is filled with many examples of social exchange.

---

30. George C. Homans, *Social Behavior: Its Elementary Forms* (New York: Harcourt, Brace and World, 1961); George C. Homans, "Social Behavior as Exchange," *American Journal of Sociology* 63 (May 1958): 597–606.

31. Peter M. Blau, *Exchange and Power in Social Life* (New York: Wiley, 1964); Peter Blau, "Justice in Social Exchange," *Sociological Inquiry* 34 (Spring 1964): 193–206.

32. *See* Peter Singelmann, "Exchange as Symbolic Interaction: Convergence between Two Theoretical Perspectives," *American Sociological Review* 37 (August 1972): 414–424; Robert B. Schafer, "Exchange and Symbolic Interaction," *Pacific Sociological Review* 17 (October 1974): 417–434; and Richard M. Emerson, "Social Exchange Theory," *Annual Review of Sociology* 2 (1976): 335–362.

33. Alvin W. Gouldner, "The Norm of Reciprocity," *American Sociological Review* 25 (April 1960): 161–178.

As you will note in the chapters on mate selection, Kingsley Davis explains the greater frequency of black male-white female marriage than vice versa by suggesting that black males exchange a higher social status for the "higher" racial status of the white female. Willard Waller suggests in his "principle of least interest" that interest is exchanged for control of the relationship in that the person who is least interested in continuing the dating relationship is in a position to dominate. In arranged marriages, labor, gifts, or a bride price are often exchanged for the right to marry. Robert Winch talks of complementary needs involving an exchange of needs that provide maximum gratification. The higher incidence of premarital sexual behavior of engaged females has been explained by an exchange of sex on the part of the female in return for a commitment on the part of the male. Throughout the text, note the value of different types of resources and the exchange processes at work in understanding authority and power, husband-wife interaction, mate selection, kin relationships, sexual patterns, parent-child conflict, and the like.[34]

A developmental frame of reference

Having its beginning in the 1930s, the family development approach to family study attempts to join together various parts of previously delineated theoretical efforts. Hill and Hansen, discussing the characteristics of the developmental-conceptual framework, have indicated that this approach was not a precisely unique framework but was an attempt to transcend the boundaries of several approaches through incorporation of their compatible sections into one unified theme.[35]

---

34. Key concepts in social exchange theory are exchange, reciprocity, negotiation, transaction, resources, cost, distributive justice, fair exchange, and power.

Some of the leading advocates of this perspective include George C. Homans, Peter M. Blau, Kingsley Davis, Alvin W. Gouldner, John W. Thibaut, Harold H. Kelley, John N. Edwards, and John Scanzoni.

From the perspective of the family, you may wish to examine John N. Edwards, "Familial Behavior as Social Exchange," *Journal of Marriage and the Family* 31 (August 1969): 518–526; Marie Withers Osmond, "Reciprocity: A Dynamic Model and a Method to Study Family Power," *Journal of Marriage and the Family* 40 (February 1978): 49–61; Gerald W. McDonald, "Structural Exchange and Marital Interaction," *Journal of Marriage and the Family* 43 (November 1981): 825–839; F. Ivan Nye, "Choice, Exchange, and the Family," in *Contemporary Theories About the Family*, vol. 2, by Burr et al., pp. 1–41; F. Ivan Nye, ed., *Family Relationships: Rewards and Costs* (Beverly Hills: Sage Publications, 1982); and John Scanzoni, *Sexual Bargaining: Power Politics in the American Marriage*, 2d ed. (Chicago: Univ. of Chicago Press, 1982).

35. Hill and Hansen, "The Identification of Conceptual Frameworks Utilized in Family Study," pp. 299–311.

Sans teeth, sans eyes, sans taste, sans everything

All the world's stage,
And all the men and women merely players,
They have their exits and their entrances,
And one man in his time plays many parts,
His acts being seven ages. At first the infant,
Mewling and puking in the nurse's arms.
Then the whining school-boy, with his satchel
And shining morning face, creeping like snail
Unwillingly to school. And then the lover,
Sighing like furnace, with a woeful ballad
Made to his mistress' eyebrow. Then a soldier,
Full of strange oaths, and bearded like the pard,
Jealous in honour, sudden, and quick in quarrel,
Seeking the bubble reputation
Even in the cannon's mouth. And then the justice,
In fair round belly with good capon lin'd,
With eyes severe and beard of formal cut,
Full of wise saws and modern instances;
And so he plays his part. The sixth age shifts
Into the lean and slipper'd pantaloon,
With spectacles on nose and pouch on side,
His youthful hose, well sav'd, a world too wide
For his shrunk shank; and his big manly voice
Turning again toward childish treble, pipes
And whistles in his sound. Last scene of all,
That ends this strange eventful history,
Is second childishness and mere oblivion,
Sans teeth, sans eyes, sans taste, sans everything.

Source: William Shakespeare, *As You Like It*. Act II, Scene vii.

From rural sociologists it borrowed the concept of stages of the family life cycle. From child psychologists and human development specialists came the concepts of developmental needs and tasks. From the sociologists engaged in work in the professions it incorporated the concept of the family as a convergence of intercontingent careers. From the structure-function and interactional approaches were borrowed the concepts of age and sex roles, plurality patterns, functional prerequisites, and the many concepts associated with the family as a system of interacting actors.[36]

---

36. Ibid., p. 307.

The developmental approach covers a very broad area tending to be both macro- and microanalytic in nature. The peculiar character of this approach lies in its attempt to account for change in the family system over time as well as account for changes in patterns of interaction over time. The major conceptual tool for this time analysis has been termed the *family life cycle*.[37]

The most systematic, widespread, and long-term use of the family life cycle idea is provided by Evelyn Duvall, who has attempted to provide a link between life cycle stages with the developmental-task concept.[38] A *developmental task* is one that arises at or about a certain period in the life of an individual. Successful achievement of the task leads to happiness and success with later tasks, while failure leads to unhappiness in the individual, disapproval by society, and difficulty with later tasks. These tasks have two primary origins: (1) physical maturation, and (2) cultural pressures and privileges.[39] The number of developmental tasks an individual faces are innumerable. Many of them are delineated in human development textbooks.

This theory contends that, like the individual, families have tasks that arise at a given stage in the family life cycle. A family's developmental task is "a growth responsibility that arises at a certain stage in the life of a family, the successful achievement of which leads to present satisfaction, approval and success with later tasks whereas failure leads to unhappiness in the family, disapproval by society, and difficulty with later family developmental tasks."[40] For families to continue to grow as a unit, they need to satisfy at a given stage: (1) biological requirements, (2) cultural imperatives, and (3) personal aspirations and values.

Duvall recognizes and depicts the family life cycle as consisting of eight stages:

Stage 1.   Married couples (without children)
Stage 2.   Childbearing families (oldest child birth–30 months)

---

37. For a discussion and empirical evaluation of this concept, see Steven L. Nock, "The Family Life Cycle: Empirical or Conceptual Tool?" *Journal of Marriage and the Family* 41 (February, 1979): 15–26; Graham B. Spanier, William Sauer, and Robert Larzelere, "An Empirical Evaluation of the Family Life Cycle," *Journal of Marriage and the Family* 41 (February, 1979): 27–38; Graham B. Spanier and Paul C. Glick, "The Life Cycle of American Families: An Expanded Analysis," *Journal of Family History* 5 (Spring 1980): 97–111; and Elizabeth Menaghan, "Marital Stress and Family Transitions: A Panel Analysis," *Journal of Marriage and the Family* 45 (May 1983): 371–386.

38. Evelyn M. Duvall and Brent C. Miller, *Marriage and Family Development*, 6th ed. (New York: Harper and Row, 1985): Chapter 3.

39. Ibid., p. 47.

40. Ibid., p. 61.

Stage 3. Families with preschool children (oldest child $2\frac{1}{2}$–6 years)
Stage 4. Families with school children (oldest child 6–13)
Stage 5. Families with teenagers (oldest child 13–20 years)
Stage 6. Families as launching centers (first child gone to last
child's leaving home)
Stage 7. Middle-aged parents (empty nest to retirement)
Stage 8. Aging family members (retirement to death of
both spouses)[41]

These stages are determined by the age and school placement of the oldest child up to the launching stage, after which the situation facing those remaining in the original family is used. This type of scheme explicitly fails to recognize multiple-child families, overlapping stages, death of a spouse, and many other variations in families. But this scheme, as any, serves as a division for study and analysis, though in reality the family life cycle and each stage within it has no beginning and no end.

Roy H. Rodgers, elaborating on the eight-stage cycle of Duvall, provides the most complex breakdown of the family life cycle.[42] He uses a twenty-four-stage cycle that follows not only the predictable development of a family as the oldest child grows, but keeps the youngest child in focus. His delineation therefore calls for two preschool, three school-age, four teenage, five young-adult, and five launching stages.

Whereas Duvall used the oldest child as the basic determinant of stage divisions, Rodgers believes that this usage does not account adequately for group initiates, thus giving a false impression of a smooth progression from one life-cycle stage to the next. He also rejected using the oldest child on the grounds that there was no way to account for families in which the death of a spouse or child occurred prior to the launching of all children, nor was there a way to handle families in which divorce, disability, or other events might interrupt the smooth progress from one stage to the next.

Rodgers also prefers to use the term *category* in preference to *stage* on the grounds that categories are analytical devices constructed by the researcher, rather than any "real" condition of families. It is Rodgers's belief that "a conceptual framework for family development investigations should lead to a better understanding of the phenomenon being described in the various life-cycle category schemes and, ultimately, should lead to

---

41. Ibid., p. 26.
42. Roy H. Rodgers, *Improvements in the Construction and Analysis of Family Life Cycle Categories* (Kalamazoo, Mich.: Western Michigan University, 1962); Roy H. Rodgers, "Toward a Theory of Family Development," *Journal of Marriage and the Family* 26 (August 1964): 262–270; and Hill and Rodgers, "The Developmental Approach," pp. 181–185.

some theory of family development."[43] One example of an empirical study using family life-cycle categories can be seen in Chapter 12, which includes a section on marital satisfaction over the family life cycle. Chapters 12 through 15 in general follow a family life-cycle model.[44]

SUMMARY

1. This chapter noted the range of disciplines, approaches, and selected frames of reference widely used in the study of the family. The marriage and family area is highly interdisciplinary with no single discipline either asking all the questions or knowing all the answers. This book uses a social science orientation with a major concentration focused on a sociology of the family.

2. Only in the last one hundred years has there been any systematic study of the family. In the mid-1800s, family interests focused on grand evolutionary schemes of change and philosophical speculation. By the turn of the century, social problems relating to the family led to a concern for social reform and with it to some systematic data gathering. This was followed by refinements in research methodology and a concern over social theory. It has only been since the middle of this century that the findings of earlier studies were summarized, conceptual frameworks were systematically presented, and theory building was of central concern.

3. As the foundation upon which the entire book is based, this chapter summarizes the nature of conceptual frameworks, frames of reference, and theory in general and provides an overview of five basic approaches: structural-functional, social conflict, symbolic interaction, social exchange, and developmental.

---

43. Rodgers, "Toward a Theory," p. 263. His attempt to produce and apply this theory can be seen in Roy H. Rodgers, *Family Interaction and Transaction: The Developmental Approach* (Englewood Cliffs, N. J.: Prentice-Hall, 1973).

44. Key concepts in the developmental approach are life cycle, developmental tasks, norms, roles, role sequence, role cluster, role complex, position, positional career, and sanction.

Some of the leading advocates of this perspective include Reuben Hill, Roy H. Rodgers, Joan Aldous, Evelyn Duvall, and Robert J. Havighurst.

From the perspective of the family, you may wish to examine Joan Aldous, *Family Careers: Developmental Change in Families* (New York: Wiley, 1978); Evelyn M. Duvall and Brent C. Miller, *Marriage and Family Development*, 6th ed. (New York: Harper and Row, 1985); Roy H. Rodgers, *Family Interaction and Transaction: The Developmental Approach* (Englewood Cliffs, N. J.: Prentice-Hall, 1973); and Arthur J. Norton, "Family Life Cycle: 1980," *Journal of Marriage and the Family* 45 (May 1983): 267–275.

4. In this chapter and several that follow, considerable attention is given to concepts and their definitions. Although definitions of concepts are seldom the most interesting reading, they are miniature "systems of meaning" that permit the viewing of a phenomenon in a certain way and the sharing of that view with others. In addition, concepts are basic to the development of hypotheses, propositions, and theories. When concepts are interrelated to describe and classify phenomena, the result is a conceptual framework. Conceptual frameworks, generally descriptive classification schemes, provide a basis for the establishment of hypotheses and propositions—statements interrelating concepts. When propositions are logically and systematically interrelated to explain some particular process, the result is theory.

5. One of the most dominant "theories" or frames of reference in sociology today is the structural-functional. This frame of reference has the social system as the basic autonomous unit of which the family is a subsystem. All systems have interdependent parts (structures) that do certain things for the individual or society and have various social consequences (functions). The basic task of functional analysis is to explain the parts, the relationship between the parts and the whole, and the functions that are performed by or result from the relationship formed by the parts. Chapters 3 through 9, as well as major portions of this text, clearly fall within the structural-functional framework.

6. A second frame of reference receiving increasing attention is that of social conflict. Two basic factors of significance in this perspective are the view of conflict (1) as natural and inevitable, and (2) as a major factor that can lead to social change. Marxian conflict-theorists focus on economic inequalities, while feminist conflict-theorists focus on gender inequalities and male dominance. Conflict theory is particularly applicable to a further understanding of the marital relationship, power, the division of labor, and conflict at both a macro (societal) and micro (interpersonal) level.

7. The symbolic interaction frame of reference addresses itself to two major questions, both of central concern to the family: socialization and personality. The basic premises of this approach are that human beings act toward things on the basis of the meanings things have for them; these meanings are derived from interaction with others; and these meanings are modified through an interpretive process. The human being is unique unto himself or herself, understood only in his or her social context, is neither inherently good nor bad, and responds to self-stimulating or symbolically interpreted stimuli.

8. The social exchange framework helps us to understand why certain behavioral outcomes occur given a set of structural conditions and interactional potentialities. Two different approaches to exchange

were examined. One was consistent with a behavioral frame of reference and the other more consistent with an interactionist frame of reference. At various points throughout the book, you will note the use of this framework in dealing with mate selection, marriage, power, and other topics.

9. The developmental frame of reference attempts to join together various parts of other delineated theoretical efforts but has the peculiar characteristic of attempting to simultaneously account for change in the family system and change in patterns of interaction over time. Thus, the central concepts include many used in the other frameworks with the additional basic concept of the family life cycle. An outgrowth of this concept has been numerous attempts to establish, describe, and analyze stages of development.

10. In this text, the general outline from Chapters 10 through 15 follows broad stages of the life cycle, moving from premarital processes to marital, parental, middle years, and aging. Our attention next turns to the family as a social institution, establishing the boundaries of marital, family, and kin groups and systems and examining selected structural features of this basic institution.

KEY TERMS AND TOPICS

Disciplines involved in family study	40	Conceptual frameworks	50
		Propositions and hypotheses	51
Interdisciplinary approaches and concerns	40	Theory	52
		Structural-functional	52
Social science and the family	44	Social conflict	52
Sociology, social psychology, and psychology	44	Symbolic interaction	52
		Developmental	52
Family study (historically)	46	Social exchange theory	53
Concepts and variables	49		

DISCUSSION QUESTIONS

1. Examine the family and marriage books suggested for reading. What disciplines are represented? How do they differ in their content and approach to the family?

2. Since no one discipline has "all the answers" to any family problem, why isn't all research of an interdisciplinary nature? What problems exist in interdisciplinary research?

3. Of what value is a social science approach to the family? How does it differ from any other approach?

4. Are there any disciplines that are completely removed from family study and to which research findings about families are irrelevant?

5. Differentiate between a psychology, a social psychology, a social anthropology, and a sociology of the family.

6. Discuss a "pure" versus an "applied" orientation to the family.

7. Identify folklore that relates to mate selection, weddings, sexual behavior, childbirth, "successful" marriages, and so on. Which tales are likely to be changed by "science"?

8. The period of 1890–1920 was characterized as an era of social reform. It was followed by empirical studies (1920–1950) and, more recently, theory building. Is it likely that these patterns are cyclical? That is, are we likely to get away from theory and return to reform, which will later be followed by a stress on science, followed by theory, etc.? Why or why not?

9. Differentiate between concepts and variables, hypotheses and propositions, and conceptual frameworks and theories.

10. Make a listing of as many family "structures" as you can. Can you think of any form of family organization that exists only as an idea and not as a concrete reality?

11. Discuss what you perceive to be the major functions of the family in the United States. How are these different from the functions of families thirty years ago? What functions do you expect the family to perform thirty years hence?

12. Do you believe that conflict is natural and inevitable in all marriages and families? Is conflict essential for change?

13. What types of assumptions, questions, and concerns are basic to a symbolic interaction frame of reference? How is it similar to or different from other psychological or social-psychological theories? What difference does it make to assume that humans must be studied on their own level, the human infant is asocial, and the like? Relate these ideas to marriage or the family.

14. Write a paragraph on "Who am I." How often did you identify yourself by listing statuses you occupy? Lengthen this list of statuses and write one or two social expectations appropriate to each status. Which role expectations do you personally find displeasing? Are there conflicts between different expectations or between your personal preference and the social expectation? How do you handle them?

15. What exchanges can you identify in explaining male-female sexual behavior, husband-wife spending patterns, or parent-child disciplinary behavior? What is given by each and received in return? Can you think of examples where no reciprocity is expected or given in return for a favor or gift?

16. Identify the stage of the family life cycle for yourself and for your parents. Identify the central problems, concerns, and tasks of families at these particular stages.

17. Develop a family life-cycle model. How many stages does it have? What criteria were used to separate stages? What types of families are omitted from your particular model?

FURTHER READINGS

Adams, Bert N. *The Family: A Sociological Interpretation*. New York: Harcourt Brace Jovanovich, 1986. A sociological, cross-cultural, interpretative look at the family.

Aldous, Joan. *Family Careers: Developmental Change in Families*. New York: Wiley, 1978. A developmental analysis of families covering the framework, the important concepts, and their application from the time families are formed until they are dissolved.

Burr, Wesley R.; Hill, Reuben; Nye, F. Ivan; and Reiss, Ira L. *Contemporary Theories About the Family*. Vol. 1. New York: The Free Press, 1979. This volume on recent family theories and research is the combined work of many scholars attempting to systematically develop interrelated propositions on a wide variety of family topics.

Burr, Wesley R.; Hill, Reuben; Nye, F. Ivan; and Reiss, Ira L. *Contemporary Theories About the Family*. Vol. 2. New York: The Free Press, 1979. This second volume has five chapters dealing with exchange, symbolic interaction, general systems, conflict, and phenomenological approaches to the family.

Collins, Randall. *Sociology of Marriage and the Family: Gender, Love, and Property*. Chicago: Nelson-Hall, 1985. A sociology text that incorporates conflict and feminist perspectives into family issues and studies.

Dail, Paula W. and Jewson, Ruth H. *In Praise of Fifty Years: The Groves Conference and the Conservation of Marriage and the Family*. Lake Mills, Iowa: Graphic Publishing Co., 1986. An overview of issues of concern to family studies that were identified at the fiftieth anniversary of the Groves Conference on marriage and the family in 1984.

Duvall, Evelyn M. and Miller, Brent C. *Marriage and Family Development*. 6th ed. New York: Harper and Row, 1985. A new and revised edition of the Duvall text using a family development and life cycle approach.

Goode, William J. *The Family*. 2d ed. Englewood Cliffs, N. J.: Prentice-Hall, 1982. A brief but intense look at the complex relationships between family systems and the larger social structure.

Gordon, Michael, ed. *The American Family in Social-Historical Perspective*. 2d ed. New York: St. Martin's Press, 1978. A collection of readings reflecting on family subjects in an historical context.

LaRossa, Ralph, ed. *Family Case Studies*. New York: The Free Press, 1984. A presentation and analysis of fourteen case studies that attempts to get students involved in the discovery of how families work.

Lee, Gary R. *Family Structure and Interaction: A Comparative Analysis*. Philadelphia: J. B. Lippincott, 1977. An attempt to document the contributions made by comparative social research to an understanding of family structure and behavior.

Miller, Brent C. *Family Research Methods*. Newbury Park, Calif.: Sage Publications, 1986. A concise synthesis of the methodological techniques used in studying families.

Morgan, D. H. J. *The Family, Politics and Social Theory*. London: Routledge and Kegan Paul, 1985. A British family theorist takes a critical look at how the family is conceptualized and linked with other systems, with a focus on conflict perspectives.

Nye, F. Ivan, ed. *Family Relationships: Rewards and Costs.* Beverly Hills, Cal.: Sage Publications, 1982. An application of choice theory—that is, exchange theory—to various aspects of family relationships.

Scanzoni, John. *Sexual Bargaining: Power Politics in the American Marriage.* 2d ed. Chicago: The University of Chicago Press, 1982. A brief paperback organized around the theme that reward-seeking between males and females generates social exchanges between them that in turn generate conflicts and changes.

Thorne, Barrie, with Marilyn Yalom. *Rethinking the Family: Some Feminist Questions.* New York: Longman, 1982. Twelve essays from a variety of disciplines addressing questions that challenge a monolithic family ideology, that analyze underlying family structures of sex and gender, that question family boundaries, and that examine the ambivalence beween the values of individualism and equality.

Photo: © Alan Carey/The Image Works

3

Marital, Family, and Kinship Organization

Chapter 2 noted a variety of interdisciplinary, social science, and theoretical approaches to family study. Basic to any approach are selected concepts and distinctions that provide "systems of meaning" to an aspect of the world in which we live. You have already noted various ways in which "function" is used by family scholars, dual perceptions of "role"—depending upon its use in a structural or interactional frame of reference—and the different schools of thought evident in the social exchange framework. Likewise, families take on new and varied perspectives when viewed in institutional terms, when seen as a social group or social system, or when differentiated from marriages and kin, orientation and procreation, nuclear and extended, and the like. This chapter makes note of these and other conceptual distinctions in study and understanding of the family.

THE FAMILY AS A SOCIAL INSTITUTION

Frequent reference is made to the family as the most basic of all institutions. It is most closely linked to the supporting institution of marriage. What is meant by this? The concept "institution" refers to certain specific areas of human social life that have become broadly organized into discernible patterns. It refers to the organized means whereby the essential tasks of a society are organized, directed, and carried out. In short, it denotes the system of norms that organize human behavior into stable patterns of activity.

Institution is a noun, *institutionalize* is a verb. The noun *institution* refers to "a system of norms, values, statuses, and roles that develop around a basic social goal."[1] All societies must deal with sexual activity, the care of dependent children, the social relations established by sexual unions, and the birth of children. The institutional norms concerned with these matters constitute the familial or kinship institutions.

The verb *institutionalize* means the establishment of expected, patterned, regular, and predictable behavior; thus, noninstitutionalized behavior is spontaneous and irregular. Typically, a husband-wife fight is noninsti-

---

1. J. Ross Eshleman, Barbara G. Cashion and Laurence Basirico, *Sociology: An Introduction*, 3rd ed. (Boston: Little, Brown and Co., 1988).

tutionalized behavior; a professional boxing match is institutionalized. When something such as dating, premarital sexual behavior, or child rearing becomes institutionalized, this means that it becomes accepted by the society as a necessary, proper, and predictable activity. At this time, although extramarital intercourse is a very common activity in American society, it has not been institutionalized; that is, it has not become a part of our standardized, approved, and culturally safeguarded expected behavior.

Several basic social institutions can be identified in all societies: the familial and kinship, educational, economic, political, and religious institutions appear to have existed in some form in all societies throughout every period of history. Each of these five institutions performs certain functions that are basic for the existence of a given society. However, these are not the only areas that have become institutionalized. In American society, marriage, war, business, communications, medicine, law, science, and recreation have become institutionalized, standardized, and basic to our way of life.

Few institutions have received more recognition, criticism, and critiques than the family system. It has been claimed to be the solution of most problems, on the one hand, and to be the basic cause of problems, on the other. It has been looked upon with hope and dismay. Scientists, clergy, newspaper columnists, parents, and even stockbrokers speak out with authority on this institution. This book is intended to examine the nature of, to describe and interpret, and, hopefully, to get you, the student, to examine and redefine your understanding of this particular social institution: the family.

FAMILIES AS GROUPS OR SYSTEMS

Family and marital **groups and systems** are basic to a sociology of the family and to the family as a social institution. Family *systems* are used in sociology much as physicists and biologists speak of solar or biological systems. In each instance, a reference is made to a configuration of parts that are related interdependently. All systems, whether living or nonliving, have a characteristic organization and pattern of functioning. All major systems have subsystems that are part of the larger system.

To treat the family as a social system is to note the forms of social organization and its modes of functioning. The family system is one example of interrelated statuses that fulfill certain basic functions. It is a subsystem of the larger society that is related to and interdependent with other subsystems in the society. It fulfills selected tasks for the society that are highly patterned, recurrent, and organized. Within the family system are subsystems (marital systems, mate-selection systems, sexual systems, child-rearing systems) which are also highly patterned, recurrent, and organized in order to fulfill selected tasks. Although persons are a part of the system, it is the statuses, roles, norms, ways of ranking, means of social controls, and the values of those persons (the abstractions) that are of significance in dealing with social systems.

The basic units, therefore, of a marital or family system are not persons but the interrelated statuses (positions) and the accompanying expectations (roles) that accompany the interrelated statuses. These interrelated statuses in the family system would include, among others, parent-child, husband-wife, uncle-aunt, grandparent-grandchild, father-mother, or brother-sister. The norms (folkways and mores) and roles, the expectations and values, that accompany these positions are of primary concern to the sociologist. Thus, married males occupy the status of husband. They interact with married females who occupy the status of wife. These interrelated statuses (husband and wife) comprise the marital system. This system too, like the family system or any other system, has sets of norms and expectations that prescribe appropriate and inappropriate behaviors for the specific persons involved. Thus systems are abstractions, forms of social organization comprised of interrelated statuses.

Family and marital *groups*, in contrast to systems, are comprised of people. These people are concrete realities, rather than abstractions, who are physically present and who interact with one another in terms of their ascribed or achieved statuses. If married, we would belong to a two-person marital group. Our family group would consist of the married partners, the children, plus any other relatives included in the extended family context. Marital or family groups can have a specific address, a specific number of members, a specific income, and specific shared rituals. Marital and family groups are temporary, disbanding when their members depart. The system of which they are a part may continue for centuries—long after the departure or death of any specific member or specific family group.

It is the task of a sociology of the family to examine the nature of marital and family groups within societies and to understand the patterns of organization—the marital and family systems that provide order within and between the groups involved.

Marriages and families as primary groups

Sociologists view groups as the core of their attention. They speak of in- and out-groups, primary and secondary groups, formal and informal groups, large and small groups, minority and majority groups, open and closed groups, organized and unorganized groups, independent and dependent groups, voluntary and involuntary groups, and others. Some of these ideal-type constructs are more useful to our understanding of family groups than others. One that appears to be particularly important is that of primary group relationships.

A **primary group** consists of a small number of people who interact in personal, direct, and intimate ways. Primary group relationships are facilitated by: (1) face-to-face contact, (2) smallness of size, and (3) frequent and intense contact. Most families in the Western world operate under these conditions. Unlike most primary groups, the family is of a special nature in that it is so essential both to individuals and to society that its formation is usually legitimized by the community through religious and legal rituals. Whereas most other primary groups can disband voluntarily if the members wish it, the dissolution of the family can only be accomplished through institutionalized means.

Much of the importance of marital, family, and kin groups centers around their function as a primary group. First, for most individuals it is this primary group that serves as the basic socializing agent for the acquisition or internalization of beliefs and attitudes. Second, the family as a primary group constitutes the chief focus for the realization of personal satisfaction. Perhaps more than any other source it is the family that provides each of us with a general sense of well-being, companionship,

The Amish family and community organization

The Amish have a family organization that is monogamous and patriarchal. From the time of marriage until death of one spouse, marriages remain intact. Divorce is extremely rare, desertion is nonexistent, and legal separations are not a matter of awareness—much less of occurrence—among the Amish. These people are highly endogamous in their selection of mates. The birth rate is extremely high when compared with that of the non-Amish American family. Illegitimacy is unknown, due to the fact that a premarital pregnancy necessitates marriage. In short, it would appear that the Amish have one of the most stable and cohesive family systems in the United States.

The Amish family cannot be understood apart from the recognition that it is entirely rural-oriented. Strong religious convictions and the use of a distinctive language and dress have helped to preserve the Amish way of life. Their subculture would be referred to by sociologists as a *Gemeinschaft*. The Gemeinschaft, like the "folk" society, is conceptualized as a small, isolated, traditional, simple, homogeneous society. The folkways and mores are internalized from birth, and face-to-face oral communication retains a strong sense of togetherness. Customs, goals, and styles of life are not questioned as custom becomes sacred. The smallness, the homogeneous character, the self-sufficiency in economic life, and the distinctiveness of the Amish people and community are the key features of this rural subculture in an urbanized American society.

ego worth, security, and affection. Most of us, when away from home for the first time, experience "homesickness" or a nostalgia for the primary group from which our immediate ties have been severed. Third, the family as a primary group also serves as a basic instrument of social control. The family has an extraordinary capacity to punish deviation and reward conformity, since most of us are dependent upon other group members for meeting psychological needs and for realizing meaningful social experiences.

The polar extreme to the primary group is the **secondary group**. Many, if not most, of our involvements in school, work, or the community are not characterized by the intimate, informal, and personal nature of primary groups but rather are characterized by impersonal, segmental, and utilitarian contacts. Secondary groups are basically goal-oriented rather than person-oriented. The personal life of the bus driver, classmate in a lecture, or cigarette salesman is not of major significance in the fulfillment of the goals established for those situations.

In a society dominated by secondary group relationships, the family, time and again, provides the primary relationships that are vital to our health and happiness. It has been argued that the loss or absence of familial networks of social support has been linked to coronary disease, pregnancy disorders, accidents, suicides, mental hospital commitment, school truancy, ulcers, and recovery from certain types of cancer.[2] Without primary group relationships and/or the presence of intimate family bonds, it is doubtful that even survival itself is possible. This idea has been fairly well substantiated with infants and adults who have "no" family or close friends. One possible conclusion to all of this is that rather than being in a state of decay, losing its significant function, and being "on its way out," the U.S. family may be fulfilling a primary group function that has seldom been more crucial and important to the stability of the person or the society.

CHARACTERISTICS OF MARRIAGE, FAMILY, AND KINSHIP GROUPS

Marriage, family, and kin groups are institutionalized social arrangements in all known societies. However, the nature of the arrangements differs greatly across societies, over time, and even within a given society at a specific time. Frequently, the legal and social norms themselves lack clarity as to what does or does not constitute a marriage, family, or kin

---

2. Marc Pilisuk and Charles Froland, "Kinship, Social Networks, Social Support and Health," *Social Science and Medicine* 12 (October 1978): 273–280.

The Amish subculture is one example of a family structure with traditional gender roles, large family size, and intact lifelong marriage. (Photo: © David Strickler/The Picture Cube)

group. For example, is it a marriage if two males live together and recognize each other as spouse, if a male and female live together but have no marriage contract or ever experience a wedding ceremony, or if a man and woman go through a marriage ceremony and then almost immediately separate permanently? Can *any* group of persons be considered a marriage, a family, or a kin group? Let's examine the boundaries of each.

The boundaries of marriage

Throughout the world, marriage is an institutional arrangement between males and females who recognize self and other as husband and wife. Marriage is a social institution that is strictly human and assumes some permanence and conformity to societal norms.

William Stephens, the anthropologist, says that marriage is (1) a socially legitimate sexual union, begun with (2) a public announcement,

Suicide and the family

In 1983, according to information supplied by the U.S. Bureau of the Census, approximately 28,300 persons in the United States committed suicide. This number was equal to 12.3 suicides per 100,000 persons, up from 11.6 in 1970 and 10.6 in 1960. Since 1970, the increase in suicide rates was most dramatic among persons under age 35.

Is it possible that the increase in the number and rate of suicide, particularly in the 15–35 year age group, is a result of less familial support, that is, a decrease in the family as a primary group? If we follow the lead of Emile Durkheim and his classic study of suicide first published in 1897, we would be aware that explanations focusing on the psychology of the individual are inadequate. Second, we would be aware that suicide, most likely the most individual act that anyone is capable of, can only be fully understood in a social and societal context. Third, we would be aware of his notion that the rate of suicide varies inversely with the degree of social integration that a society (or a family?) provides.

Steven Stack attempted to determine the effects of marital dissolution on suicide (*Journal of Marriage and the Family* February 1980). His argument was that a society marked by a high incidence of divorce is low in social integration with respect to the institution of the family. Given a higher incidence of divorce, one indicator of a broken marital and family tie, one would expect more suicidal behavior among those (divorced) persons. His results indicate that the incidence of divorce is closely associated with the rate of suicide even after controlling for the influence of the effects of age composition, percentage black, the rate of interstate migration, and income. While he suggests caution in accepting these results, they do lend some indirect support to the linkage between a lack of social integration in the family and the incidence of suicide and the importance of the family as a primary group.

undertaken with (3) some idea of performance, and assumed with a more or less explicit (4) marriage contract, whch spells out reciprocal obligations between spouses and between spouses and their children.[3]

Ira Reiss, who is interested in providing a universal definition of marriage, says that marriage is "a socially accepted union of individuals in husband and wife roles, with the key function of legitimation of parenthood."[4]

---

3. William N. Stephens, *The Family in Cross Cultural Perspective* (New York: Holt, Rinehart and Winston, 1963): 7.

4. Ira L. Reiss, *Family Systems in America*, 3d ed. (New York: Holt, Rinehart and Winston, 1980): 50.

Can two women or two men divorce?

On May 14, 1984, the Pennsylvania state Superior Court ruled that people of the same sex could not contract a common law marriage, and thus were not eligible to divorce.

Judge Edmund Spaeth, Jr., writing for a unanimous three-judge appeals court, refused to expand common law marriage to include either two men or two women. It was his opinion that the issue had never been legally addressed anywhere in the United States but other jurisdictions had considered whether statutory or ceremonial marriage could be entered into by same-sex couples. These have uniformly held that same-sex persons could not marry.

The judges ruled that marriage as a heterosexual activity dated to the nation's beginnings when statutes spoke, as they do now, of husband and wife and bride and groom which is interpreted to mean male and female. This ruling dismissed an appeal by John DeSanto who had sought for three years to file a divorce action against William Barnsley. Mr. DeSanto claimed that they were married in a common law ceremony on June 14, 1970, before friends and witnesses and now were seeking a divorce.

Any definition of marriage or family is, in a certain sense, arbitrary. Most definitions of marriage exclude persons in same-sex relationships, persons such as children, or persons who do not meet the social or cultural norms that specify what marriage is and who the legitimate partners are. In fact, many phenomenological, conflict, and feminist theorists call into question the very use of labels such as marriage, family, or kin. The suggestion is that the very use of a label reifies, that is, makes real or concrete, a certain reality that ignores the historical origins and the range of meanings that persons in their day-to-day lives give to marriage or family.

Recognizing the danger of reifying the concept, marriage does appear to involve several criteria that are common both historically and cross-culturally. The criteria include:

A heterosexual union, including at least one male and one female
The legitimizing or granting of approval to the sexual relationship and the bearing of children without any loss of standing in the community or society
A public affair rather than a private, personal matter
A highly institutionalized and patterned mating arrangement
An assuming of mutual and reciprocal rights and obligations between the spouses
A binding relationship that assumes some permanence

MARRIAGE AND NUMBER OF SPOUSES

Marital status (single, married, separated, widowed, divorced) and number of spouses (none, one, more than one) are two major components of the boundaries of marriage. With a change in marital status and the number of spouses comes variations in marital interaction patterns; living and sleeping arrangements, exclusive or nonexclusive sexual interactions; the likelihood of and number of children; patterns of support, decision making, and authority; and male-female roles, to mention a few. Obviously, never to have had a spouse is to have a nonmarital status. The never-married single can be expected to share certain characteristics of other single statuses yet in many ways differs from that of the widowed or divorced single. The latter two single statuses are discussed in Chapters 15 and 16 respectively.

Singlehood

In 1985, there were more than 26.1 million males and 21.6 million females in the United States age 15 and over who were never-married singles.[5] These numbers comprise 30 percent of all males and 22.7 percent of all females. White males and white females (28.2 and 20.7 percent respectively) were less likely to be single than black males (43.4 percent), males of Spanish origin (36.6 percent), black females (36.9 percent), and females of Spanish origin (26.0 percent). As expected, the number and percent never-married drops sharply with increasing age. About 98 percent of the men and 92 percent of the women age nineteen and under are single. By age forty-five, only 6.3 percent of the men and 4.6 percent of the women are not and have never been married.

Since 1970, the percentage of those remaining single has risen sharply for persons under thirty years of age. The increase in percentage that are single is particularly apparent in the age groups where most men and women have traditionally married. At ages twenty to twenty-four years, for example, there has been a 63.4 percent increase in the number of single women (from 35.8 in 1970 to 58.5 in 1985) and a 28.2 percent increase in the number of single men (from 54.7 in 1970 to 75.6 in 1985).[6] The increase in the twenty-five to twenty-nine age group is even more dramatic—151 percent for women and 103 percent for men.

Whether the tendency among the younger groups to refrain from

---

5. U.S. Bureau of the Census, *Current Population Reports*, Series P-20, no. 410, "Marital Status and Living Arrangements, March 1985" (Washington, D.C.: U.S. Government Printing Office, 1986), Table 1, p. 17.

6. Ibid., Table 1, p. 17.

Consumer habits of singles are different

> Staying single longer is reshaping the way persons in the United States live and spend their money. For instance, unmarried persons typically spend 50 percent of their food dollars dining out, compared with 37 percent for two-person households. In addition, specialized industries are emerging, such as singles travel agencies and dating services, for people of age-specific categories (such as under thirty). In Michigan, one grocery chain has a singles shopping night where the search extends beyond finding the dairy goods section.
>
> It appears that the buying habits and social attitudes of still-single adults are increasingly mimicking those of married couples. Many singles are fashioning a satisfying independent way of life with the purchases of condominiums, china place settings, and items for the home that once were more likely the province of married couples.

marrying represents merely a postponement of first marriage or a development of a trend toward lifelong singleness is not known. However, Paul Glick states that just as cohorts of young women who have postponed childbearing for an unusually long time seldom make up for the child deficit as they grow older, so also young people who are delaying marriage may never make up for the marriage deficit later on.[7] They may try alternatives and like them.

The legitimacy of singleness as a life-style is increasingly recognized by young people. The 1980 Study of American Families at the Institute for Social Research at the University of Michigan included data from 916 families composed of a mother and her eighteen-year-old child. Most of these respondents no longer regarded getting married as necessarily better than remaining single. This was in spite of the finding that more than 90 percent of the eighteen-year-olds expected to marry. To evaluate the strength of their commitment to marry, they were asked how much it would bother them if they did not marry. Only one-fourth indicated it would bother them a great deal, half said it would bother them a little or some, and the remaining quarter indicated it would not bother them at all if they did not marry.[8]

Apparently a new style of singlehood is emerging that represents one of choice and a status that has potentially positive outcomes, such as pursuing one's career and increasing mobility. Traditionally, the social norm implied that single people were single, not because they wanted to

---

7. Paul C. Glick, "A Demographer Looks at American Families," *Journal of Marriage and the Family* 37 (February 1975): 18.

8. Arland Thornton and Deborah Freedman, "Changing Attitudes Toward Marriage and Single Life," *Family Planning Perspectives* 14 (November/December 1982): 297–303.

be or because it was a life-style that successfully fulfilled human needs, but because they, particularly females, had no one to marry. Bachelors and spinsters or old maids were men and women respectively who were past the common age of marriage and who seemed unlikely to marry. Bachelorhood, while viewed less negatively than spinsterhood, often implied selfishness, immaturity, maladjustment, or, in some instances, not liking women. This image is in sharp contrast to the male who was "smart enough not to get trapped" and the freedom to live a carefree, blissful life of wine and women without the "burden of marriage." Seldom did the "old maid" or "spinster" concept carry similar positive images. To be an old maid was to be frustrated, unattractive, and undesirable as a person.

The life of the single female appears, in general, to be superior to the life of the single male. Several decades ago, Gerald Gurin and others reported that single women experience less discomfort than do single men, express greater happiness, show far less expected frequency of symptoms of psychological distress, and suffer fewer neurotic and antisocial tendencies.[9] Jessie Bernard, as well, argues for the superior status of the single female when compared to the single male.[10] The single female is less likely to have a nervous breakdown, insomnia, nightmares, or dizziness, is more likely to have a higher education and higher median income, and a greater percentage occupy a professional or managerial occupation.

For singles of both sexes, friends are important to their happiness and life satisfaction but with some interesting gender differences. A study in Tennessee showed that single men's life satisfaction was related to self-esteem and the availability of a network of individuals with whom interests and values were shared. For women, life satisfaction was based on the presence of affectional close relationships that provided a sense of security and peace.[11] High levels of self-disclosure and emotional involvement with a few intimate friends were important.

The relationship for females between a single status and a higher educational level, higher median income, higher occupational status, and in general a higher level of achievement is a significant one.[12] As you will

---

9. Gerald Gurin, Joseph Veroff, and Sheila Feld, *Americans View Their Mental Health* (New York: Basic Books, 1960): 42, 72, 190, 110, 234–35.

10. Jessie Bernard, *The Future of Marriage* (New Haven: Yale University Press, 1982 edition), Chapter 3 and Tables 19 and 20, pp. 26–53 and 315.

11. Janet Cockrum and Priscilla White, "Inferences on the Life Satisfaction of Never-Married Men and Women" *Family Relations* 34 (October 1985): 551–556.

12. Charles W. Mueller and Blair G. Campbell, "Female Occupational Achievement and Marital Status: A Research Note," *Journal of Marriage and the Family* 39 (August 1977): 587–593; and Stephen Mergford and Dorothy B. Darroch, "Marital Status and Female Achievement in Australia: A Research Note," *Journal of Marriage and the Family* 42 (August 1980): 653–656.

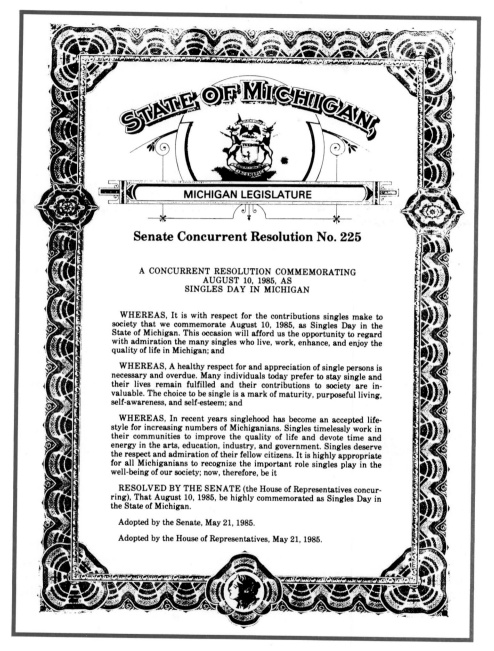

STATE OF MICHIGAN

MICHIGAN LEGISLATURE

Senate Concurrent Resolution No. 225

A CONCURRENT RESOLUTION COMMEMORATING
AUGUST 10, 1985, AS
SINGLES DAY IN MICHIGAN

WHEREAS, It is with respect for the contributions singles make to society that we commemorate August 10, 1985, as Singles Day in the State of Michigan. This occasion will afford us the opportunity to regard with admiration the many singles who live, work, enhance, and enjoy the quality of life in Michigan; and

WHEREAS, A healthy respect for and appreciation of single persons is necessary and overdue. Many individuals today prefer to stay single and their lives remain fulfilled and their contributions to society are invaluable. The choice to be single is a mark of maturity, purposeful living, self-awareness, and self-esteem; and

WHEREAS, In recent years singlehood has become an accepted lifestyle for increasing numbers of Michiganians. Singles timelessly work in their communities to improve the quality of life and devote time and energy in the arts, education, industry, and government. Singles deserve the respect and admiration of their fellow citizens. It is highly appropriate for all Michiganians to recognize the important role singles play in the well-being of our society; now, therefore, be it

RESOLVED BY THE SENATE (the House of Representatives concurring), That August 10, 1985, be highly commemorated as Singles Day in the State of Michigan.

Adopted by the Senate, May 21, 1985.

Adopted by the House of Representatives, May 21, 1985.

FIGURE 3–1
Resolution commemorating Singles Day in Michigan.

The name of the bride

> When a women in the United States marries, the chances are very high that she will take the surname of the husband. Is this a matter of law or social tradition? Apparently social custom and tradition prevail.
>
> According to a comment in *Parade*, in forty-nine of our states, the bride has a right to use any name she wishes and to maintain her own identity. Only in Hawaii does a law exist that requires the wife to assume the husband's name.

note in the discussion of the dual-career marriage in Chapter 4, marriage seems to impede career advancement for females. What is unclear is the extent to which the single status results from educational and economic success or the extent to which success results from the single status.

What is clear is that as the median age at marriage increases so does a longer period of singlehood. With later marriage comes the potential for an increased period of independent living away from the parental home. Some consequences of this pattern, particularly for women, were that they were more likely to plan for employment, lowered their expected family size, became more accepting of the employment of mothers, and were more nontraditional on sex roles than those who lived with parents.[13] Nonfamily living was suggested to lessen parental control and free young adults from parental curfews and supervision over friends and sexual behaviors. Nonfamily living was suggested as well to equip young people with new social and domestic skills and increase their self-confidence in getting along without their families. The longer periods of singlehood with accompanying increases in nonfamily living may lead to further shifts in family life than those presently observed or anticipated.

Monogamy

To most U.S. citizens, the most traditional as well as the "most proper" form of marriage is **monogamy**; one man to one woman (at a time). Throughout the world, this form of marriage is the only one universally recognized and is the predominant form even within societies where other forms exist. Where other forms do exist, most men are too poor to have more than one wife. However, it should be noted that on a societal basis,

---

13. Linda J. Waite, Frances Kobrin Goldscheider, and Christina Witsberger, "Nonfamily Living and the Erosion of Traditional Family Orientation Among Young Adults," *American Sociological Review* 51 (August 1986): 541–554.

only about 20 percent of the societies are designated as *strictly* monogamous, that is, monogamy is the required form.[14]

In the United States, although designated as strictly monogamous, it is possible to have more than one husband or one wife. Since monogamy has never achieved perfect stability, certain married persons end their relationship and most of these remarry. Thus, the second spouse, although not existing simultaneously with the first, is sometimes referred to as fitting into a pattern of *sequential monogamy, serial monogamy,* or *re-marriage* (*see* Chapter 17). Thus, in U.S. society it is both legally and socially approved to have more than one wife or more than one husband as long as they occur sequentially and not simultaneously. To a sizable proportion of our population, replacing marriage partners in a sequentially monogamous fashion is a variation on the lifelong, same-spouse, monogamous pattern. In addition, most nontraditional marital life-styles occur within the context of monogamy. Childless marriage, sexual equality, dual careers, androgynous role patterns, and the like are more likely to occur in a one-male—one-female marriage than in any other type. These marital life-styles are discussed elsewhere throughout this book, usually as found within a monogamous situation.

Polygamy

Distinguished from monogamy is **polygamy**. The suffix *-gamy* refers to marriage or a union for propagation and reproduction. Thus *monogamy* (single), *bigamy* (two), *polygamy* (several or many), *allogamy* (closely related), *endogamy* (within) or *exogamy* (outside or external) describe the nature of marriage. Polygamy refers to the marriage of several or many. Theoretically, there could exist several or many wives (*polygyny*), several or many husbands (*polyandry*), or several or many husbands and wives (*group marriage*), all of which are polygamous marriages, as distinguished from monogamous (one) or bigamous (two) marriages.

The frequency with which the marriage of a plural number of spouses occurs normatively (i.e., as an expected or desired type of marriage) was investigated by George Murdock. In a world sample of 554 societies, polygyny was culturally favored in 415 (77 percent), whereas polyandry was culturally favored in only 4 (less than 1 percent): Toda, Marquesas, Nayar, and Tibet.[15] There is no known society in which group marriage is clearly the dominant, or most frequent, marriage form.[16]

---

14. George P. Murdock, "World Ethnographic Sample," *American Anthropologist* 59 (August 1957): 686.

15. Ibid.

16. William N. Stephens, *The Family in Cross-Cultural Perspective* (New York: Holt, Rinehart and Winston, 1963): 33.

Polygamy at issue in a Utah lawsuit

SALT LAKE CITY, Sept. 11 (AP)—Royston Potter, discharged by a suburban Salt Lake City police force because he is a polygamist, says he took three wives as a matter of religious conviction.

Mr. Potter calls his decision "living the principle," and he has filed a lawsuit reviving a century-old dispute in this mostly Mormon state by challenging antipolygamy laws demanded by Congress before Utah entered the Union.

"It's not so much that you decide that you want one," he said, referring to another wife. "It's necessary as far as a theology goes."

Mr. Potter's lawsuit seeks legal sanction for a practice still embraced by thousands of Utah residents. Polygamists once dodged police raids and served jail terms, but today they are seldom prosecuted.

Mr. Potter, now a janitor, has five children and two more "on the way." He maintains three separate households, which he said he visited "on a rotation-type thing, normally one night at each place." His wives are Denise, 30 years old; Joann, 30, and Mary, 23.

A Third-Degree Felony

Owen Allred, the head of the Apostolic United Brethren, a group that favors polygamy, estimates that 20,000 Utah residents are members of multiple-parent households, even though polygamy is a third-degree felony.

Mr. Potter was discharged in late 1982 when officials in suburban Murray learned of his second wife. He married a third time this year.

His lawyer, Dennis Haslam, said the dismissal was an invasion of privacy, adding, "We felt that he had a religious guarantee to practice plural marriage."

Mr. Haslam said his client was denied due process of law when he was dismissed for practicing polygamy without criminal charges being brought against him.

"It does not matter to Murray City whether he was charged," said the Murray City Attorney, H. Craig Hall, because Mr. Potter freely admitted he was practicing polygamy and would not obey the ban on the practice specified in the 87-year-old State Constitution.

Several words of caution need to be suggested concerning polygamy. First, it is necessary to maintain a clear distinction between ideology and actual occurrence. Occasionally in the United States, a group advocates the right to have as many or as few spouses as desired. Also, when multiple-spouse marriages or communes are located and/or studied, the results are exploited by the mass media and given considerable attention. Perhaps it is uniqueness or rarity that attracts the attention rather than commonality in numerical terms. Second, multiple spouses (except for

Mr. Potter's stand thus not only violated the law but also his oath as a police officer to uphold the State Constitution, Mr. Hall asserted.

In pretrial documents, lawyers for the City of Murray argue that while polygamy is accepted in some cultures, so are blood feuds, tribal warfare, the stoning of adulterers "and many other practices repugnant to our culture and moral values."

No date has been set for trial of the lawsuit, which names the City of Murray, its Civil Service Commission, individual city officials and the state and Federal governments.

Mormon pioneers brought polygamy to Utah in the 1840s after the church's founder, Joseph Smith, said it was a divinely inspired plan.

But it prompted sometimes bloody opposition from non-Mormons, and Congress passed laws preventing polygamists from voting or holding office in Federal territories like Utah. Many were forced into hiding or imprisoned: the church was disincorporated and much of its property seized.

Practice Banned in 1890

In 1890, the church's president, Wilford Woodruff, announced the ban on polygamy among Mormons, saying God had told him to do so in order to prevent further confiscation of property and imprisonment.

In February, Mr. Potter was excommunicated from the Church of Jesus Christ of Latter-Day Saints. But he still considers himself a true Mormon and believes the church was wrong to abandon polygamy.

A spokesman for the church, Don LeFevre, said, "the church doesn't make any excuses for having practiced polygamy in righteousness during the 19th century."

Mr. Potter and other polygamists, many of them former Mormons, believe Mr. Woodruff's decision did not come from God but was a result of pressure from Congress to abandon polygamy in exchange for statehood.

The enabling act for Utah statehood in 1896 insisted the State Constitution forever prohibit polygamy, and attorneys for the state were thus able to argue successfully that the Federal Government should be included as a defendant in Mr. Potter's suit.

Source: *The New York Times*, September 12, 1983, p. 13. Copyright 1983/1984 by The New York Times Company. Reprinted by permission.

group marriage) are only possible on a large scale where an unbalanced **sex ratio** (the number of males per 100 females) exists. Only if the sex ratio is either high or low will polygamy be possible without increasing the number of single persons of one sex. Third, polygamy where it exists, like all forms of marriage, is highly regulated and normatively controlled. Rarely does it involve a strictly personal or psychological motive. Rather, it is likely to be supported by the attitudes and values of both sexes and linked closely to the sex ratio, economic conditions, and belief systems. Polygamy involves a normative system that includes a wide range of obligations among the spouses, children, and wider society. Fourth, polygamy itself has many forms and variations of normative structure that determine who the spouse should be. Examples would be where all the multiple husbands are brothers (*fraternal polyandry*), where all the multiple wives are sisters (*sororal polygyny*), or a levirate and sororate arrangement as existed in the ancient Hebrew family. The *levirate* was a situation (technically, sequential monogamy) in which the wife married the brother of her deceased husband, whereas the *sororate* was a situation in which the preferred mate for a husband was the sister of his deceased wife. From the perspective of families in North America, each of the above represents a nontraditional family form. Polygyny and polyandry will be examined in greater detail.

Polygyny   **Polygyny** is the most frequent form of polygamy. Although not a rare phenomenon throughout the world, researchers and writers often ignore contemporary polygyny. Charles Welch and Paul Glick suggest that this is due in part to the fact that systematic study is hampered by the persistent absence of adequate amounts of readily accessible and reliable data. They, however, selected fifteen African countries to illustrate its incidence (polygynists per hundred married men), intensity (number of wives per polygynist), and general index (number of wives per married man).[17] The incidence of polygyny per hundred men was typically between twenty and thirty-five, that is, from about one in five to one in three married men having more than one wife. The intensity ranged from 2.0 to 2.5. This indicates that most polygynists had two wives rather than three or more. And for the country as a whole, the general index (number of wives per married man) ranged from 1.1 to 1.6. This indicates most men, even in highly polygynous countries had one wife only.

Polygyny appears to be the privilege of the wealthy. Often, having several wives is a mark of prestige, distinction, and high status. Chiefs, the wealthy, the best hunters, and the leaders get the second or third wife. Even in Israel, throughout the Old Testament biblical period, polygyny was practiced but often restricted to men who were rich, occupied leading positions, or had some other claim to distinction. Even today in the Middle East, the "common man" has only one wife.

Why more than one wife? Many circumstances and motives contribute to polygyny. The prestige and status dimension has been mentioned. Sometimes there is a need or a desire to facilitate procreation, particularly that of male children; however, evidence also exists to show that polygyny

17. Charles E. Welch, III and Paul C. Glick, "The Incidence of Polygamy in Contemporary Africa: A Research Note," *Journal of Marriage and the Family* 43 (February 1981): 191–193.

tends to reduce fertility for groups as a whole.[18] This may be a consequence of senior wives insisting on sexual abstinence later in life or of husbands being considerably older at the time second and third wives are added. His death results in widows with significantly lower levels of completed fertility than among monogamous wives.[19]

Other reasons given for polygyny include wife capture (where the men from one village literally take, or capture, wives from another village), the economic value of wifely services, and in some instances religious revelation. The frequently cited example of Mormon polygyny originated in a religious revelation to Joseph Smith, the founder of the Mormon religion. Interestingly, some of the very factors that led to the occurrence of polygyny in this religion were the same factors that led to its being outlawed. It was begun and maintained by a devout conviction of carrying out God's will. It was ended by a revelation from God to the president of the church forbidding the continuation of polygyny.

One way in which Christianity stamped Western society was in this very manner—by outlawing polygyny. Polygyny was frequent among the pre-Christian tribes of Europe as well as in Old Testament Hebrew accounts:

> Gideon, the Israelite judge, had many wives who bore him seventy sons (Judges 8:30). King David had several wives (Samuel 25:39, 43: II Samuel 3:2 ff.: 5:13), and King Solomon, of course, had a huge number of them (I Kings 9:16; Song of Solomon 6:8). Also of King Rehoboam, Solomon's son, it is stated that he had eighteen wives and sixty concubines (II Chron. 11:21). Each of Rehoboam's twenty-eight sons also had many wives (II Chron. 11:23). The frequency of marriage with two women necessitated legislation with reference to the rights of their children (Deut. 21:15).[20]

William Stephens notes that often polygynous women are jealous; however, this is not a universal characteristic.[21] In fact, data from Ibadan, Nigeria, where polygyny is a very common fact of life indicate that among all wives, when asked how they would feel if their husbands took another wife, some 60 percent said they would be pleased: to share the housework, husband care, and child minding and to have someone to gossip and "play" with.[22] Jealousy among plural wives, however, does seem to be considerably more frequent than jealousy among co-husbands. Several

18. *See* Alfred O. Ukaegbu, "Fertility of Women in Polygynous Unions in Rural Eastern Nigeria," *Journal of Marriage and the Family* 39 (May 1977): 397–404; and James E. Smith and Phillip R. Kunz, "Polygyny and Fertility in Nineteenth Century America," *Population Studies* 30 (November 1976): 465–479.

19. L. L. Bean and G. P. Mineau, "The Polygyny-Fertility Hypothesis: A Re-evaluation." *Population Studies* 40 (1986): 67–81.

20. Stephens, *The Family in Cross-Cultural Perspective*, pp. 51–52.

21. Ibid., p. 57.

22. Helen Ware, "Polygyny: Women's Views in a Traditional Society, Nigeria 1975," *Journal of Marriage and the Family* (Feburary 1979): 188.

reasons may exist for this. The greater likelihood of jealousy among co-wives may stem from the fact that they are more frequently chosen, whereas men are more likely to do the choosing in determining whether to be a co-spouse. Having less choice in the matter of being married may contribute to a much greater potential for jealousy. In addition, it has been suggested that multiple husbands are more likely to be brothers than are co-wives. If this is the case, it is possible that jealousy would be less among siblings than among nonsiblings. However, this factor needs additional clarification.

Viewing polygyny cross-culturally, polygynous families evidence specific organizational features:

1. In certain matters, sex particularly, co-wives have clearly defined equal rights;
2. each wife is set up in a separate establishment; and
3. the senior wife is given special powers and privileges.[23]

It has always been suggested that if co-wives are sisters, they usually live in the same house; if co-wives are not sisters, they usually live in separate houses. The deduction follows: for some reason, siblings can better tolerate, suppress, and live with a situation of sexual rivalry than can nonsiblings.

What about polygyny in the United States today? The most frequently cited sources of polygyny are those of certain Mormon fundamentalists living in underground polygynous family units in Utah and neighboring states. The number of these marriages is unknown.

Polyandry This appears to be very unusual and quite rare. Stephens makes several generalizations about polyandry.[24] First, he notes that polyandry and group marriage tend to go together; where you find one you are likely to find the other.

Second, co-husbanding is fraternal. In the few cases in which the husbands are not brothers, they are clan-brothers, that is, they belong to the same clan and are of the same generation. As stated, this factor of being brothers may reduce the likelihood of jealousy. Among the Todas, a non-Hindu tribe in India, it is understood that when a woman marries a man she becomes the wife of his brothers at the same time. In that tribe, jealousy does not seem to present difficulty and disputes among the brothers rarely arise.

---

23. Ibid., p. 63. Note also Joyce Sween and Remi Clignet, "Type of Marriage and Residential Choices in an African City," *Journal of Marriage and the Family* 36 (November 1974): 780–793; and Remi Clignet and Joyce A. Sween, "For A Revisionist Theory of Human Polygyny," *Signs: Journal of Women in Culture and Society* 6 (1981): 445–468.
24. Stephens, *The Family in Cross-Cultural Perspective*, pp. 39–49.

Third, an economic inducement is often mentioned. A man tries to recruit co-husbands so they will work for him. In other instances, co-husbandry is practiced for economic security or as an answer to the land shortage. When several men marry one woman, the fragmentation of holdings, especially in land, is avoided. Thus polyandry, although rare, is one device for conserving limited economic assets.

Stephens suggests that polyandrous societies resort to infanticide to "correct" the ratio of husbands to wives; apparently polygynous societies do so rarely if at all. Where polyandry is frequent, female infanticide is frequently practiced. It is a curious anomaly that male infanticide is rarely, if ever, mentioned in the literature. Female infanticide eliminates the wife surplus among polyandrous families; however, male infanticide does not seem to be used to eliminate the husband surplus in polygynous societies.

Two studies of polyandry among a tribal group in Brazil tended to support some of the ideas just presented.[25] Polyandry was more prevalent in the tribe in earlier years when the sex ratio was very unbalanced (149 males per 100 females), female infanticide had been known to exist, and fraternal polyandry appeared to minimize family conflict. Unlike other reports, the Brazilian tribe had no marriage ceremonies for primary or secondary husbands, and property and inheritance rights were not considerations for marriage. In revisiting the Brazilian tribe in 1980, there was no polyandry but female infanticide was still practiced. There was no apparent cultural consciousness of the linkage between this practice and the shortage of female spouses of marital age. Males were wanted because they served as a protection against enemy raids. While polyandry is rarely found throughout the world, it is another variation of the traditional monogamous marital life-style.

Group marriage   This exists when several males and several females are married simultaneously to each other. Except on an experimental basis it is an extremely rare occurrence and may never have existed as a viable form of marriage for any society in the world. The Oneida community of New York State has been frequently cited as an example of a group marriage experiment (*see* "Oneida Today" insert). It involved economic and sexual sharing based on spiritual and religious principles. The Oneida group was an experimental religious community and not representative of the society. In addition, like most group marriages on record, its time span was limited. Rarely do they endure beyond one or two generations.

Where group marriage does exist, the strong negative reactions of persons who are aware of it force anonymity and secrecy. Thus, it seems

---

25. John F. Peters and Chester L. Hunt, "Polyandry Among the Yanomama Shirishana," *Journal of Comparative Family Studies* 6 (Autumn 1975): 197–207; and John F. Peters, "Polyandry Among the Yanomama Shirishana Revisited," *Journal of Comparative Family Studies* 13 (Spring 1982): 89–95.

Oneida today: Group marriage out—profits in

The Oneida Community began in New York in 1848 with approximately twenty-five members. The leader, John Humphrey Noyes, gave up law to enter the ministry. He preached that human beings were capable of living sinless lives based on a spiritual equality of all persons: materially, socially, and sexually. Monogamy was a sign of selfish possessiveness.

Under the charismatic leadership of this man, the group grew and prospered. The emphasis was on "we" rather than on "I." Economically, there was self-sufficiency and equal ownership of property. They made traps, marketed crops in cane and glass jars, did silk spinning and manufactured silverware. To eliminate feelings of discrimination and sexual inequality, jobs were rotated.

The group differed from most other communal groups in their "group marriage" or pantogamous (marriage for all) relationships. It was felt that romantic love made spiritual love impossible to attain and gave rise to jealousy, hate, and the like; therefore, everyone should literally "love" everyone else. Requests for sexual relationships were made to a central committee. A go-between, usually an older woman, would get the consent of the requested female (women rarely made requests), and, if agreed upon, the couple would go to the woman's bedroom.

Any discord or problems among the members were handled daily in a practice known as "mutual criticism" where the followers would subject themselves to criticism by the rest of the group. The criticized member would sit quietly while the others listed good and bad points. The result was said to be a catharsis, a spiritual cleansing, with remarkably successful outcomes.

When Noyes left the group for Canada in 1879, for whatever reason (outside pressures, age, health, intra-commune strife), the group marriage practice came to an end but the economically successful venture continued.

On November 20, 1880, the group incorporated as Oneida Community, Ltd., to succeed Oneida Community. The present title, *Oneida Ltd.*, was adopted in 1935. Today, you can find Oneida Ltd. listed on the New York Stock Exchange. The past chairman (currently a member of the board) is Peter T. Noyes, a grandson of John Humphrey Noyes, the founder of the Oneida Community. The company makes flatware, silverplated and pewter holloware, jewelry, and gift items. The company also markets tableware products and makes cookware and industrial wire products. This international corporation, with plants in Arkansas, New York (three), Massachusetts, Kansas, England (three), Canada, and Northern Ireland, had net sales in 1986 of approximately 250 million dollars. In May 1987, the stock was selling at 18 and had first quarter earnings of .54 per share. Yes, Mr. Noyes, your children and grandchildren have prospered well. While group marriage is out, profits are in.

reasonable to assume that group marriage will never become very popular. It has various difficulties and shortcomings that include, among others:

1. The difficulty in finding groups of three or more adults of both sexes who can truly live harmoniously with each other
2. The difficulty in establishing a workable division of labor in occupational, recreational, and household tasks
3. The difficulty in finding other individuals with whom one would like to have a group-marriage arrangement and with whom each of the other members can accept and tolerate as spouse
4. The difficulty of avoiding problems, relating to sex, love, and jealousy
5. The difficulty, at the present time, of finding females who are interested in group marriage[26]

The boundaries of the family

The family signifies a set of statuses and roles acquired through marriage and through procreation, adoption, or both. Stephens defines a family as a social arrangement based on marriage and the marriage contract, including recognition of the rights and duties of parenthood; common residence for husband, wife, and children; and reciprocal economic obligations between husband and wife.[27]

Reiss defines the family institution as "a small, kinship-structured group with the key function of nurturant socialization of the newborn."[28] Again, recognizing the dangers of reifying the concept, the family also appears to include and share various criteria or elements:

It arises as a result of marriage.
It includes persons who are united by marriage, blood, or adoption.
Its members share a common residence.
Its members assume reciprocal rights and obligations to one another.
It provides the key function of socialization, particularly of the infant.

It could be said that all marriages are families but not all families are marriages. And certain functions expected in the marital relationship are taboo among certain family members (such as sexual relationships

---

26. Albert Ellis, "Group Marriage: A Possible Alternative?" in *The Family in Search of a Future* edited by Herbert A. Otto (New York: Meredith, 1970): 92–94 *see also* Reese D. Kilgo, "Can Group Marriage Work?" *Sexual Behavior* 2 (March 1972): 8–14.

27. Stephens, *The Family in Cross Cultural Perspective*, p. 8.

28. Reiss, *Family Systems in America*, p. 29.

between brother and sister). As marriages differ structurally in the number of spouses, so do families differ structurally in their size and composition.

A TYPOLOGY OF FAMILY STRUCTURES

One controversy in the family literature has focused on the extent to which families, particularly in the United States, are small, isolated, independent units as opposed to large, interdependent networks. The polar extremes are usually represented by a nuclear-versus-extended dichotomy with modified-extended and modified-nuclear as intermediate positions. The major characteristics of these types are outlined in Table 3–1.

The nuclear and conjugal family

Nuclear and conjugal families refer to the family unit in its smallest form. Generally it includes the husband, wife, and their immediate children. The terms *nuclear* and *conjugal* are at times used interchangeably; however, the conjugal family must include a husband and wife. A nuclear family may or may not include the marriage partners but consists of any two or more persons related to one another by blood, marriage, or adoption, assuming they are of the same or adjoining generations. Thus a brother and sister or a single parent and child are nuclear families but would not, technically speaking, be conjugal families.

Since most persons marry, it is likely that during their lifetime they will be members of two different but overlapping nuclear families. The nuclear family in which they are born and reared (consisting of self, brothers and sisters, and parents) is termed the **family of orientation**. This is the family where the first and most basic socialization processes occur. When an individual marries, he or she forms a new nuclear (and conjugal) family: a **family of procreation**. This family is composed of self, spouse, and children.

The controversy over whether the family in the United States and Canada is nuclear centers on questions related to geographical isolation, economic independence, and social autonomy. Are there families living separately from kin? Do other relatives outside the nuclear unit provide financial assistance or aid in times of need? Are kin ties significant in relation to emotional support, visiting patterns, or social activities? And if the nuclear family is isolated, independent, and autonomous, would this not lead to high divorce, the need for more public assistance programs for the aged, single parents, or poverty, and an increase in personal instability (alcoholism, suicide, mental illness, and the like)? Whatever the actual state of the family, questions such as these seem to be highly relevant to the health of individuals as well as to the functioning of societies.

TABLE 3–1
A typology of family structures

Nuclear	Modified nuclear	Modified extended	Extended
Completely self-sufficient; economically no help	Largely self-sufficient economically; recreation and friendship ties; occasional help in emergencies	Independent economic resources in nuclear family units, but daily exchange of goods and services	Complete economic interdependence of kin network—common ownership of economic resources, occupational cooperation, daily exchange of goods and services
Nuclear family, friends, experts, distant models exclusive agents of socialization, emotional support, and protection	Weak kin network role in socialization, emotional support, and protection	Strong kin network psychological interdependence, but more reliance on non-kin for socialization, emotional support, and protection	Psychological interdependence—socialization, emotional support, protection—almost completely confined to kin network
Complete nuclear family autonomy; kin network influence absent	Nuclear family autonomy, weak kin network influence	Nuclear family autonomy, but strong kin network influence in decision making and resolving conflicts	Arbitrary, linear, intergenerational authority
Minimal contact; geographic isolation; visits on holidays or for family rituals; contact primarily by letter or telephone in literate societies	Regular but not daily contact; kin network within easy visiting distance	Daily contact, geographic proximity	Daily contact, geographic proximity

Source: Betty Yorburg, "The Nuclear and the Extended Family: An Area of Conceptual Confusion," *Journal of Comparative Family Studies* 6 (Spring 1975): 6.

The modified-nuclear and modified-extended family

A number of writers have suggested that the isolated nuclear family is largely fiction, that families of procreation are actually functioning within a network of other nuclear families, offering services and gifts, and maintaining close contact with them.[29] Research by Eugene Litwak led him to suggest that both the idea of an isolated family and the idea of a network of families have some merit. Thus he wrote of a **modified-extended family structure** where nuclear families retain considerable autonomy and yet maintain a coalition with other nuclear families where they exchange goods and services.[30] The modified-extended family differs from the modified-nuclear family in Table 3–1 only in its degree of kin network exchange and support. It differs from extended families in that geographical propinquity, occupational nepotism, or family integration is not required.

The extended family

Extended family refers to family structures that extend beyond the nuclear family. As stated, within the extended family may be a multiple number of nuclear family groupings. Sometimes the terms *consanguine families* and *joint families* are used interchangeably with *extended families*. The consanguine family refers to the joining of nuclear families on the basis of blood relationships or on the basis of descent from the same ancestors so that several generations of offspring are included within one family unit as in an extended family. The difference is that blood ties are emphasized—those between parents and children or between brothers and sisters—over marital ties.

The **joint family** is not used as frequently today as in times past. The term has most often been associated with large families in India where at least two brothers with their own wives and children lived together in the same household. The joint family was consanguine in that the brothers were related by blood and extended in that the wives of the brothers (sisters-in-law) and their children (nephews, nieces, and cousins) lived together. The family was joint in that there existed a common treasury, common kitchen and dining room, and common deities. This Indian form of joint family was usually patrilineal and patrilocal and emphasized filial and fraternal solidarity.

The smallest variety of extended family type is the **stem family**. Normally the stem family consists of two families in adjacent generations,

---

29. Marvin B. Sussman, "The Isolated Nuclear Family: Fact or Fiction," *Social Problems* 6 (Spring 1959): 333–340; James Morgan, "The Redistribution of Income by Families and Institutions and Emergency Help Patterns," in Martha S. Hill et al., eds., *Five Thousand American Families*, vol. 10 (Ann Arbor, Michigan: Institute for Social Research, 1982); and M. S. Grieco, "Family Structure and Industrial Employment: The Role of Information and Migration," *Journal of Marriage and the Family* 44 (August 1982): 701–707.

30. Eugene Litwak, "Occupational Mobility and Extended Family Cohesion," *American Sociological Review* 25 (February 1960): 9–21; and Eugene Litwak, "Geographic Mobility and Extended Family Cohesion," *American Sociological Review* 25 (June 1960): 385–394.

Mexican- or Spanish-Americans and compadrazgo

The Mexican- or Spanish-American family extends beyond the immediate family unit (la casa) to include two other similar but distinguishable systems—the extended family (la familia) and godparents (los compadres). The extended family is generally viewed as the primary and most important institution in the community and the key source of identity and support. The importance of this unit is refected in familism, the idea that the family holds priority over the individual. In other words, individual values and wishes are secondary to the needs and interests of the family unit.

Ties between extended families are promoted by a social system involving godparenthood (compadrazgo). Its most common form is co-parenthood, linking two familes through the baptismal ritual. The godparents are chosen with care from outside the immediate kinship network. It is preferred that the male *compadre* (the more important godparent) be a man of influence, status, and respect in the community. Compadres are expected to develop close relationships and in times of trouble have the right to call on one another for assistance. Compadrazgo is most common among rural families.

based on economic blood ties. An example of this type of family would be the rural Irish where the family consists, for example, of a father and mother living in the same household with a married son, his wife, and children. This type of family is a common device for maintaining intact the family estate. In contrast to the joint family, the plural number of male members of the original family would not pool their resources. Rather, the estate would belong only to the son to whom it is given by the father. The father would continue to live in the place to contribute his labor and derive his living from it. The other sons are given a cash settlement in lieu of their share of the land, and they then leave the family place.

Irrespective of the specific structure of the extended family, Hyman Kempler argues that extended kin have both instrumental and psychological value.[31] Close emotional relationships, especially between grandparents and grandchildren, can be quite important. Close kin serve to relieve parents from being the sole sources of affection and care and can often diffuse overly intense relationships between parents and children. Kin can become important objects of identification and social learning. Older kin can provide experiences of historical continuity and awareness of important aspects of the life cycle. Extended kin are also important for stable trans-

---

31. Hyman L. Kempler, "Extended Kinship Ties and Some Modern Alternatives," *The Family Coordinator* 25 (April 1976): 143–149.

mission of an ideology and value system. Given the importance of these extended relationships, it may seem logical that as or if ties with extended kin weaken or decrease, people would increasingly suggest and experiment with new family forms that incorporate these extended kin features. These forms may include *communes* with a common ownership of goods and sharing of tasks, *family networks* where three or four nuclear families join together to share problems and exchange services, or *affiliated families* where a nuclear family accepts (socially adopts) one or more nonrelated older person who is recognized as part of the kin network. Let us look more closely at the boundaries of the kinship network and the major importance it holds for most of us today.

The boundaries of kinship

The kinship system, like marital and family systems and groups, involves special ties, bonds, and linkages among its members. However, family groups and systems are units upon which the kinship system is built. A kinship system refers to a pattern of social norms regulating those relationships that are directly based on the facts of birth and the birth cycle. It is also a *set* of interpersonal social relationships involving strong interests and emotions, urgent problems of authority and order, and many reciprocal bonds of dependence and support.[32] These relationships, whether created biologically or socially, exist among people who are descended from one another (parents-children) or who have common descent (brother-sister).

Birth is the primary biological point of reference for kinship. But kin relationships are also determined and defined by sex (male or female), birth order (older or younger children), time together (living together or casual visits), and seniority within the kin grouping. These characteristics combine to give each individual a different social position. As Robin Williams states:

> Children are not merely children; they are male or female, older or younger, with siblings or without. The sister of one's father is not in the same biological category as one's mother's sister, but both in our society are "aunt."[33]

As defined, these relationships based on the birth cycle (kinship system) are regulated by patterns of social norms. These norms vary widely from one society to another. Thus, it is impossible to categorize all of them. On the other hand, certain norms exist universally among kin relationships. The most widely used example is that of a taboo on incest. All societies forbid sexual relations between persons in certain

---

32. Robin M. Williams, Jr., "Kinship and the Family in the United States," in *American Society*, 3rd ed. (New York: Alfred A. Knopf, 1970): 47 and 60.
33. Ibid., p. 49.

A family from India prepares to enjoy food natural to their culture. (Photo: ©
Carson Baldwin, Jr./Freelance Photographer's Guild)

kinship positions. Violations of these norms arouse strong feelings among
the kin group as well as in the larger society. All societies also forbid
intermarriage between certain kin group members. The circle of prohibited
relatives for marriage does, however, vary widely in different societies.
One extreme, in ancient Egypt, permitted brother-sister and father-daughter
marriages.[34] The other extreme may be represented by the traditional clan
system of China or certain extended familes in India where the prohibition
extended to a very wide group of relatives including cousins to the sixth
degree.[35]

_____

34. Russell Middleton, "Brother-Sister and Father-Daughter Marriage in Ancient Egypt,"
American Sociological Review 27 (October 1962): 603–611.
35. David F. Mandlebaum, "The Family in India," in *The Family: Its Function and
Destiny*, ed. by Ruth N. Anshen (New York: Harper, 1949): 167–187.

The pattern of social norms tends to treat members of the kin group differently. In most societies, women are accorded lower status than men. The eldest male or the eldest son may be acorded greater prestige, power, and responsibility than younger men. In general, status positions in the kinship network are differentiated by rights, privileges, and obligations; by inheritance; and by general social expectations.

In some societies, kinship is such an integral part of all aspects of the society that it is difficult to differentiate it from other (non-kin) kinds of social institutions and relationships. Particularly in primitive and peasant societies, the political, educational, religious, economic, and property units are so interlinked and meshed with the kinship system or group that it becomes impossible to separate kin networks from non-kin networks. That is, other institutions are part of the kinship system itself. In contrast are the kinship systems known in most Western societies where kinship is separate and clearly distinguished from other institutions and relationships. The economic system, while not totally independent of kin networks or influences, exists separate from and is distinguishable from the kin network. This same differentiation is true for other institutionalized patterns of norms and activity.

Bert Adams suggests that kin groups have tended to fulfill certain functions even when the kinship network is indistinguishable from other institutions.[36] These include: (1) property holding and inheritance; (2) housing and the maintenance of residential proximity; (3) obligation, or helping in time of need; and (4) affection, emotional ties, or primary relationships. It is difficult to do justice to these four basic characteristics of kin groups in this chapter, but their importance merits some attention.[37]

Property holding and inheritance   The holding, ownership, and control of property and the transmission of this property from one owner to another is an issue of central concern to family sociologists and anthropologists in general and to conflict theorists and feminists more particularly. Property tends to indicate wealth and power. Inheritance tends to indicate how this wealth and power is transmitted. Within family systems, this transference is directly linked to inheritance and the rules of descent.

At birth, each of us inherits two separate bloodlines, thus a key issue in most societies (less so in the United States) is whose bloodline, the mother's or the father's, is more important. If the descent pattern is unilineal, as is true in most societies within Asia, India, and Africa, the

---

36. Bert N. Adams, "Kinship Systems and Adaptation to Modernization," *Studies in Comparative International Development* 4 (1968–1969): 55.

37. Those interested in an extensive treatment of kinship should examine Bernard Farber, *Conceptions of Kinship* (New York: Elsevier-North Holland, 1981); and William J. Goode, *The Family*, 2d ed. (Englewood Cliffs, N. J.: Prentice-Hall, 1982), Chapter 7.

The main structural features of the U.S. kinship system

The U.S. kinship system is marked by the following characteristics:

First, the incest taboo everywhere forbids a person to marry father, mother, child, grandparent, uncle, aunt, niece, or nephew. In twenty-nine states intermarriage of first cousins is forbidden; intermarriage of blood relatives is seldom otherwise limited.

Second, marriage is monogamous, and there is no prescriptive pattern for kinship marriages.

Third, no discrimination is made between paternal and maternal relatives for marriage purposes.

Fourth, although the family name descends through the male line, there is little other emphasis upon the male line of descent. The descent system tends to be bilineal or, more strictly, multilineal.

Fifth, there is an emphasis on the immediate conjugal family. In a highly developed consanguine kinship system, by contrast, the tightest unit is the descent group of siblings, a group of brothers and sisters whose spouses enter as strangers and remain always somewhat so. In the United States, the solidarity of spouses is stressed, to the exclusion of in-laws.

Sixth, the immediate family of father, mother, and children tends to be the effective residence, consumption, and social unit. No extended kin groupings are of more than secondary importance in these respects, except among a few relatively small population elements.

Seventh, in urban communities, which are increasingly representative of the country as a whole, the family group is typically a consuming rather than a producing unit. Kinship units as work groups and productive organizations have largely disappeared except in farming and certain types of small retail business.

Eighth, because the nuclear family is the unit and the kinship system is multilineal, U.S. society places relatively little emphasis on family tradition and family continuity.

Ninth, there is comparatively free choice of mates. In fact, U.S. mate selection is to a considerable extent an application of free competition in the institution of marriage. The choice of spouses is purely personal; the kin of the prospective mates have no right to interfere. Parents are usually asked to sanction the marriage choice, but this convention is residual. The individualistic system of mate choice is favored by the autonomous conjugal unit, the discontinuity of generations, the deemphasis of kinship, and the extensive geographic and social mobility found in U.S. society.

Tenth, linked to the father-mother-children unit and free marriage-choice is the tendency for adult children to disperse from the parental household.

Source: Selected sentences taken from Robin M. Williams, *American Society*, 3d ed. (New York: Alfred A. Knopf, 1970): 56–59.

name, property, authority, and marriage controls are traced through one line, usually that of the father and his bloodline—**patrilineal**. Much less frequently do anthropologists note a **matrilineal** pattern, a unilineal system that traces the lineage through the female line. The system of descent most prevalent in the United States is the **bilateral** system where power and property is transferred through both the mother's and father's line to both males and females. One key exception to this pattern is in name, where both sexes tend to assume the name of their father and females take their husband's family name upon marriage.

Patterns of descent take on a special significance to many feminists and conflict theorists because most family systems throughout the world tend to (1) perpetuate power and wealth through successive generations— that is, the rich stay rich and the poor stay poor; and (2) differentiate this power and wealth between the sexes with the males given preferential treatment. The result is that class and sexual inequality is built into most family systems in such a way that the inequalities come to be viewed as "natural" and "legitimate." In other words, some families have the "right" to be wealthier than others, males are expected to be dominant, and females are ordained to be housewives and mothers and submissive to their male counterparts.

Housing and residential proximity   All family systems have rules of residence that establish who lives where and with whom. Since husbands and wives come from different families and since most husbands and wives share the same residence,[38] one or both of them must move. The most common pattern is a **patrilocal** one, in which the bride changes residence and lives with the parents of the groom. In the **matrilocal** pattern, much less frequently found than the former, the newlywed couple lives with the parents of the bride. In the United States, far more frequently found than either of the above is the **bilocal** system, in which the couple lives near the parents of either spouse, or the **neolocal** system, in which the couple lives in a home of their own that may be located apart from both sets of parents. The pattern of residence takes on a special significance as one looks at the third and fourth aspects of kinship, namely the obligation or helping aspect and the affection and emotional ties among kin. Helping patterns and showing affection to grandparents, parents, or siblings take on a different character if you share the same building, live in the same neighborhood or community, or reside hundreds of miles apart.

It appears that residence patterns in the United States show a surprising

---

38. Mitterauer reported on an historic family form in what is now Austria, where married persons did not live with their spouses. *See* Michael Mitterauer, "Marriage Without Co-Residence: A Special Type of Family Form in Rural Corinthia," *Journal of Family History* 6 (Summer 1981): 177–181.

When adult children come home to live

A common, but underresearched event in the lives of many families in the United States is the return of adult children to the parental home. Factors such as a delay in the age at marriage, economic recessions, or divorce tend to increase the likelihood that launching of children from the home may be delayed or that children who left home for reasons such as college, marriage, or a job may return to live. This reuniting of parent-child networks, often including a son- or daughter-in-law, creates a modification in the typical pattern of residential and financial independence and an arena for increased potential conflict.

A report in the *New York Times* included interviews with a number of these families. A major reason for returning to the parental home focused on financial needs. Some couples and individuals couldn't afford the available housing while others felt it was the only way to save money for a home of their own.

Parents and children alike expressed great ambivalence about the housing arrangement. Some of the concerns focused on meal preparation, knowing what to expect and how to behave, adequate space, the loss of privacy which was most acutely felt by younger couples, and still being answerable to parental authority. On the other hand some of the benefits included an opportunity to better enjoy the grandchildren, a sense of continued familial closeness at a time of widespread personal alienation, and a feeling of being needed. Many couples insisted that the added strain on their marriage was more than offset by relief from other domestic tensons such as living "house poor" or being alone a great deal of the time.

degree of local concentration. In the study of Middletown, for example, taking any resident of the city at random, the odds were one in five that a brother or sister lived in the city; one in three that one or both of his or her parents lived there; and two in five that a more distant relative such as a grandparent, aunt, uncle, or cousin lived there.[39] The respondents' immediate families were especially concentrated, with 54 percent of the grown children, 43 percent of the parents, and 31 percent of the brothers and sisters living right in Middletown.[40] These percentages increased considerably when a fifty mile radius was used to establish residence. Thus while newlywed couples establish a residence separate from their parents, this residence tends to be in geographical proximity to parents and siblings. Other studies tend to indicate a similar finding.

39. Theodore Caplow et al., *Middletown Families* (New York: Bantam Books, 1982): 206.

40. Ibid., p. 203.

Obligation, or helping in time of need A range of kinship obligation patterns can be identified. One kin obligation is to *keep in touch*, particularly with parents, to a lesser extent with siblings, followed by other relatives such as aunts, uncles, or cousins. One study found that many extended families had a person who could be considered a "kinkeeper," usually a female, who works at keeping family members in touch with one another.[41] Another kin obligation is to *share services* or *gifts* as gestures of good will and kindness. A third obligation is to *help or assist* when in need. It is likely that all three obligation patterns are observed by most families throughout the world. What is likely to differ is the amount and type of contact, sharing, or helping pattern and the range of kin or relatives that are included.

In Middletown,[42] almost everyone agreed that people ought to keep in touch with relatives and seemed to regard this as more a pleasure than a duty. Obligations to parents were more widely held than obligations to siblings. The authors summarize the norms that govern relations with kin in contemporary Middletown as follows:

1.   People should enjoy contacts with their relations.
2.   Children and parents and brothers and sisters are mutually obligated to remain in permanent contact.
3.   Parents and their grown children are mutually obligated to provide needed help, if at all possible. There is much less obligation of this kind between siblings and practically none between cousins.[43]

The main determinants of the amount of interaction between relatives in Middletown were the distance between their homes and the closeness of their relationship. With increasing distance, visiting is replaced by telephone calls which is replaced by letter writing. Almost no one corresponded regularly with cousins, although they may exchange Christmas cards. Consistently, women do more joint activities with parents and other kin than do men. Again, while Middletown was cited, it appears that these patterns are highly representative of kin obligations elsewhere in the United States.[44]

---

41. Carolyn J. Rosenthal, "Kinkeeping in the Familial Division of Labor" *Journal of Marriage and the Family* 47 (November 1985): 965–974.

42. Ibid., p. 205, and Theodore Caplow, "Christmas Gifts and Kin Networks," *American Sociological Review* 47 (June 1982): 383–392.

43. Ibid., p. 206.

44. *See* Goeffrey K. Leigh, "Kinship Interaction over the Family Life Span," *Journal of Marriage and the Family* 44 (February 1982): 197–208; Susan M. Essock-Vitale and Michael T. McGuire, "Women's Lives Viewed from an Evolutionary Perspective. II. Patterns of Helping," *Ethology and Sociobiology* 6 (1985): 155–173.

Affection and primary relationships   Affection and primary relationships are the emotional and feeling dimension of visits, calls, and letters. Affection can be viewed as being emotionally close to kin. Women seem to be the "specialists" in affective kin relationships. In Middletown, as elsewhere, women expressed more affection than men did for every category of relative. The distribution of affection was highest for mothers, next highest for fathers and near siblings, and lowest for best-known cousins.

The affection dimension between children and parents seems to increase with age but seems to weaken with kin such as cousins. In Middletown, the increased closeness to parents was attributed to children's own maturity, their own parental experience, the belated recognition of the emotional debt they owe, the relaxation of parental authority, the increased needs of parents, and the expectation of bereavement. It can be said that in Middletown, as well as elsewhere, most people feel good about their parents, love them, and make sacrifices for them when necessary.[45] And surprising to many, there is little evidence of any weakening of kinship ties during the past fifty years.

This chapter first focused on the family as a social institution and as a group or system. It then explored the boundaries of marriage, family, and kin; the reader who desires to segment and isolate these three interrelated components for given family members is likely to face many difficulties, for the boundaries of each are seldom precise and distinct. This is true both conceptually and in real life experiences. Pauline Boss and Jan Greenberg, for example, write about family ambiguity as a new variable in understanding family stress.[46] They define boundary ambiguity as not knowing who is in and who is out of the family system. Remarriages, stepparents and stepchildren, in-laws, more distant relatives, and others may or may not be fully recognized as part of a particular family network. While families will differ from one cultural context to another in how they perceive their boundaries, the central notion suggests that a high degree of family boundary ambiguity over time will lead to a high level of stress in the family system. Who is in and who is out become major components in determining task performance, inheritance patterns, visiting, writing, or helping responsibilities, and the like.

Our attention turns in the next chapter to how the marital, family, and kin system are interrelated with other major systems, particularly the economic, employment, work related system. Note how the employment of none, one, or both spouses becomes a ingredient in a better understanding of the functioning of marital, family, and kin networks.

---

45. Caplow et al., *Middletown Families*, p. 220.
46. Pauline Boss and Jan Greenberg, "Family Boundary Ambiguity: A New Variable in Family Stress Theory," *Family Process* 23 (1984): 535–546.

SUMMARY

1. The family as a social institution refers to an organized, formal, and regular way of carrying out certain essential tasks in a society. It refers to the wide system of norms that organizes family units into stable and ongoing social systems. This chapter presented numerous ways in which marital, family, and kin groups and systems are organized to fulfill certain tasks.

2. The family system is an abstraction consisting of interrelated statuses and the social expectations that accompany them. The family group consists of a concrete reality of persons who are physically present and who interact with one another. The family as a primary group, with face-to-face contact, smallness of size, and frequent and intense contact, is distinguished from the secondary group of more formal, impersonal contacts that characterize much of an individual's life.

3. The boundaries of marriage are not always precise and clearly defined. Generally marriage includes a heterosexual union that includes at least one male and one female. It grants legitimacy to children and approval to sexual relationships. It is usually a public affair with reciprocal rights and obligations between the spouses. Finally, it is usually a binding relationship that assumes some permanence.

4. The variations in marriage and number of spouses cover singlehood, monogamy, polygyny, polyandry, and group marriage. The number of people choosing to remain single has risen dramatically since 1970. Available data indicate some extreme differences for the male and female who choose or who involuntarily occupy this particular nonmarital life-syle.

5. Polygyny and polyandry, two forms of polygamy, occur in a wide range of contexts and take numerous forms. The plural spouses may be brothers or sisters, may marry simultaneously or sequentially, and may perform various functions. While polygyny is very common, polyandry is quite rare. Group marriage, as well, occurs extremely infrequently and may never have existed as a viable form of marriage for any society in the world.

6. Like marriage, the boundaries of the family vary considerably. Usually a family arises as a result of marriage and includes people united by marriage, blood, and adoption. The members, some of whom share a common residence, have reciprocal rights and obligations to one another. This institutionalized pattern fulfills certain basic functions for society, particularly as related to infants, socialization, and primary relationships.

7. One typology of family structures differentiates the nuclear/conjugal unit from a variety of types of extended units. Some of these include

families of orientation and procreation, modified-nuclear or modified-extended families, and consanguine, joint, and stem families.

8. The boundaries of kinship serve as an extension of the marital and nuclear family unit. This system too involves special ties, bonds, and linkage among its members. It tends to have key functions and characteristics that include property holding and inheritance, housing and the maintenance of residential proximity, obligation or helping in time of need, and affection and emotional ties.

KEY TERMS AND TOPICS

DISCUSSION QUESTIONS

1. What is meant by the family as a social institution? What does it mean for factors like homosexuality, illegitimacy, or child support to be institutionalized?

2. Differentiate family groups from family systems. Since systems are abstractional, of what relevance are they to an understanding of the family?

3. Describe what would be likely to happen to a person who is removed from all primary-group relationships. Why are they so crucial?

4. In your own words, define marriage and family in a way that would be comprehensive enough to include most societies in the world. How are the two similar or different? Is one necessary for the other? How do they differ from any other group or relationship?

5. What is the likelihood of an increasing percentage of people choosing to remain single? Why or why not? Will this be equally true for males and females?

6.   Why is monogamy so strongly stressed in the United States as the appropriate form of marriage? What advantages or disadvantages do you see in polygyny, polyandry, or group marriage for adults in the United States?

7.   Around the world, when polygamy is culturally approved, polygyny appears to be far more common than polyandry. How is this explained? What factors explain the exceptions?

8.   Thinking of your own kin group, how many persons do you know (uncles, cousins, and so on)? With how many do you interact on a regular basis? What differentiations do you make between kin on your mother's side and kin on your father's side?

9.   What arguments are feminists and conflict theorists likely to make in opposition to traditional unilineal descent and inheritance systems?

10.   Make a list of all your relatives that you personally know and can identify. Which ones do you visit, maintain contact with, and feel obligated toward? How is geographical proximity related to your visits, contacts, or feelings? How many commitments extend beyond parents and siblings?

FURTHER READINGS

Adams, Bert N. *The Family: A Sociological Interpretation*. 4th ed. Orlando, Florida: Harcourt Brace Jovanovich, 1986. An introductory sociology text that emphasizes current analytic frameworks and theoretical conceptions for organizing the wide body of information available on the U.S. family.

Cargan, Leonard, and Melko, Matthew. *Singles: Myths and Realities*. Beverly Hills: Sage Publications, 1982. A look at various dimensions of the single lifestyle such as the never-married, divorced, and widowed, with attempts to dispel traditional stereotypes surrounding them.

Farber, Bernard. *Conceptions of Kinship*. New York: Elsevier North Holland, Inc., 1981. An empirical study of kinship from the central perspective of collaterality, with considerable evidence of kinship as a significant element in maintaining social continuity.

Goode, William J. *World Revolution and Family Patterns*. Glencoe, Ill.: The Free Press, 1963. A description and interpretation of the main changes in family patterns that have occurred over the past half-century in the West, Arabic Islam, sub-Saharan Africa, India, China, and Japan.

Hareven, Tamara. *Family Time and Industrial Time*. New York: Cambridge University Press, 1982. A pioneering study of the largest textile factory in the world at the turn of the century focusing on the behavioral dynamics of families and larger kinship networks when they were subjected to the pressures of the industrial work place.

Kephart, William M. *Extraordinary Groups: An Examination of Unconventional Life-Styles*. New York: St. Martin's Press, 3rd ed., 1986. A look at seven different cultural groups and life-styles that exist in the United States: the old order Amish, the Oneida Community, the Father Devine Movement, the gypsies, the Shakers, the Mormons, and the modern communes.

Lantz, Herman, Schultz, Martin, and O'Hara, Mary. "The Changing American Family from the Preindustrial to the Industrial Period: A Final Report." *American Sociological Review* 42 (June 1977): 406–421. A report of a content analysis of magazines examining the American family in essentially a preindustrial, pre-urban period, 1741–1865.

Lee, Gary, R. "Effects of Social Networks on the Family." *Contemporary Theories About the Family*, vol. 1. Edited by Wesley R. Burr et al. New York: The Free Press, 1979, pp. 27–56. An attempt to establish a series of propositions and review the literature on the exchanges between the family and its social networks (environment).

Lee, Gary, R. "Kinship in the Seventies: A Decade Review of Research and Theory." *Journal of Marriage and the Family* 42 (November 1980): 923–934. The review article on kinship that appears in the special issue of family decade reviews covering the 1970s.

Macklin, Eleanor D., and Rubin, Roger H. *Contemporary Families and Alternative Life-styles*. Beverly Hills: Sage Publications, 1983. A volume resulting from the 1981 Groves Conference on marriage and the family. It covers an extensive range of life-style alternatives including singlehood, childlessness, divorce, stepfamilies, commuter marriages, gay and lesbian relationships, and others.

Simenauer, Jacqueline, and Carroll, David. *Singles: The New Americans*. New York: Simon and Schuster, 1982. A journalistic reporting of three thousand American men and women singles: how they meet others, their problems and pleasures, single parents, and other aspects of their private lives.

Stein, Peter J. *Single Life: Unmarried Adults in Social Context*. New York: St. Martin's Press, 1981. A collection of articles concerning major life issues of the never-married, divorced, and widowed: friendship, intimacy, emotional and physical health, living arrangements, work, raising children, and aging.

Photo: © Camerique Stock Photos/E.P. Jones, Co.

4

Marriage, Family, and Work

The last chapter provided an examination of how marriage, family, and kin groups and systems are organized, showing variation in the number of spouses, presenting a typology of family structures, and noting some of the basic functions of kinship networks. As noted in that chapter, in many societies family-kin networks are such an integral part of all aspects of the society it is difficult to separate and differentiate the family system from other major institutions. One example of these institutionalized linkages in the United States may be represented by the Amish subculture where the boundaries between family roles and responsibilities often are inseparable from their farming occupation, Anabaptist religious teachings, home-oriented educational training for appropriate adult male-female responsibilities, or their community-oriented political system where neighbors and friends provide protection, insurance, welfare, and justice functions. In the wider society—and in most of the nonwestern world—it is much easier to separate the family system from the work, school, church, politics, health, communication, military, recreation, and other systems.

While this chapter will focus primarily on linking marriages and families to the world of employment, work, and the economic system, first it will briefly note how religion, politics, and education affect and are affected by the family. Many of these institutionalized linkages are re-emphasized throughout the text, such as discussions of economic and social-class matters (Chapter 7), interfaith marriage (Chapter 8), the significance of a formal education (Chapters 6, 7, 13, and 17), and governmental policies (Chapter 18).

LINKAGES BETWEEN THE FAMILY AND RELIGION, POLITICS, EDUCATION, AND THE ECONOMY

That **linkages** exist **between** family **systems** and other systems appears obvious, yet at a more macro-level of analysis, it is frequently ignored in family studies. A structural-functional frame of reference reminds us of the interdependence of the parts of a system. As the economy changes so do employment rates and family spending patterns. As wars influence international relations, so do they affect divorce rates. As political decisions determine policies related to health and welfare, so do they affect attitudes toward one-parent families and child support responsibilities. And as education, employment, and the advancement of fertility control methods modify the opportunities and options available to women and men, so do these changes affect male-female, husband-wife, and parent-child interactions and expectations.

Religion and the family Cross-culturally as well as historically, the relationship between the religious system and the family system has been reciprocal.[1] Many family celebrations in most societies are religious ones. Religious norms influence speech patterns, nonmarital as well as marital sexuality, male and female roles, husband-wife and parent-child relations, and so forth. The marriage contract, the baptism of infants and children, and the death rituals frequently involve the clergy and religious organizations.

The pathbreaking study on the relationship between family and religion in the United States was carved out by Gerhard Lenski in the 1950s.[2] In comparing religious groups, he found, for example, that Protestants had higher divorce rates than Catholics, Catholics had more children than Protestants or Jews, Jews and Protestants were more likely than Catholics to see personal autonomy as the key value in preparing children for life, Catholics were less mobile than Protestants and Jews, and so forth. More recently, an increasing body of evidence suggests a general converging of values and behaviors among major religioethnic groups in the United States. Duane Alwin documents substantial changes in the social experiences of groups such as U.S. Catholics to the point that few, if any, differences exist among religioethnic groups in their orientation to the extended family. In dealing specifically with child rearing, he lends support to earlier predictions suggesting a decline in differences in values and orientations between these groups, possibly to the point of nonexistence.[3]

What has not changed is the linkage between the religious system and the family system, between religiosity and familism, and between religious beliefs and practices and family beliefs and practices. What has changed is the convergence of denominational differences. That is, differences between churchgoers and non-churchgoers are more pronounced than differences between particular religious groups such as Protestants

---

1. See, for example, Arland Thornton, "Reciprocal Influences of Family and Religion in a Changing World," *Journal of Marriage and the Family* 47 (May 1985): 381–394, and the entire special section on religion and the family in this issue of the journal, pp. 369–465.

2. Gerhard Lenski, *The Religious Factor* (Garden City, N.Y.: Doubleday, 1961).

3. Duane F. Alwin, "Religion and Parental Child-Rearing Orientations: Evidence of a Catholic-Protestant Convergence," *American Journal of Sociology* 92 (September 1986): 412–440.

or Catholics. Churchgoers, for example, are more likely to be married; have more children; be more conservative on issues relating to sexuality, such as abortion, homosexuality, or premarital sexual relationships; stress more traditional gender roles; and so forth.

In spite of widely held assumptions about the weakening and decline of both religion and the family, evidence from "Middletown" (mentioned in the previous chapter) suggests that family ties in the late 1970s were at least as strong as in the 1920s, and citizens seemed to be at least as religious. Judging from statements today about what people believe, how much money they donate to churches, and how often they attend church meetings, they take their religion at least as seriously as did their grandfathers fifty years previously.[4] The message is clear. "Families that pray together, stay together" irrespective of religioethnic orientation. Differences are linked more closely to intensity of religious participation than to denominational differences.

Many contemporary examples of the linkage between the religious and family systems are provided throughout the text. Examples of recent interest include various social movements started and sustained by religious groups against abortion and the Equal Rights Amendment (ERA). The profamily movement included under its umbrella reestablishing prayer in the schools, outlawing busing for racial balance, and the requirement of parental notification about dispensing contraceptives and contraceptive information to minors. All these issues had the backing of certain fundamentalist and right-wing religious groups and were aimed at the general good of protecting, solidifying, and reestablishing the traditional family. While the degree of success of any of these movements is unclear, the reciprocal linkage between the religious and the family institutions is not.

Politics and the family   As can be witnessed from the preceding paragraph, the divisions between religion, politics, and the family are often hazy. In the 1980s certain religious groups have worked closely with political figures to influence family policy. The Reagan administration took an official stance in favor of a single family type: the perceived traditional family structure.[5] This resulted from a right-wing reaction to changes in family patterns, changes that were defined as "evil" or harmful to the social fabric: abortion, homosexuality, sexual freedom, illegitimacy, broken homes, and the like. Thus the "profamily" movement became a political force.

---

4. Howard M. Bahr and Bruce A. Chadwick, "Religion and Family in Middletown, USA," *Journal of Marriage and the Family* 47 (May 1985): 407–414.

5. See the 1980 Republican National Convention Platform; G. Steiner, *The Futility of Family Policy* (Washington, D.C.: Brookings Institution, 1981); Jerry G. Pankhurst and Sharon K. Houseknecht, "The Family, Politics, and Religion in the 1980s," *Journal of Family Issues* 4 (March 1983): 5–34; and Paul William Kingston and Steven E. Finkel, "Is There a Marriage Gap in Politics?" *Journal of Marriage and the Family* 49 (February 1987): 57–64.

This specific type of profamily action differs from most traditional linkages of the political and family systems. Other linkages between the two systems appear to be more indirect in that social policy and legislation are aimed less at families per se than at improving the living conditions of the population: welfare programs, school lunches, tax deductions, aid to dependent children, Medicare, unemployment compensation, nondiscrimination laws, and so forth. While they had a significant impact on family life, the family, or more specifically a particular type of family, was not the focus of attention of these policies.

The political system represents power, determining who gets what in society. It determines and enforces laws and punishes those who disobey them. It establishes age requirements for marriage, places certain controls on child neglect or abuse, and mandates various types of family support. Some laws and policies are very general, granting families a wide range of freedoms; others are very specific and precise. Does the family have no recourse or power in return?

Many would argue that in most of the world, including the United States, the power of an individual or family is extremely limited. This may generally be the case. On the other hand, collective activity, kin networks, and the solidarity of family ties form vital forces in political activities and voting patterns. The stability of family systems takes on a symbolic importance to political figures. They too attempt to present themselves and their families as moral citizens and supportive of a strong family life. Thus, often in subtle and even deceptive ways, families take on an importance in the political arena. The polity issue is addressed more explicitly in the final chapter.

Education and the family   The family and educational systems tend to supplement one another in teaching selected cultural values, norms, and skills. One intended function of education is to supplement family socialization. The schools use experts (teachers) to teach children knowledge, values, and selected skills that parents frequently are incapable of teaching and that are necessary to have in order to function in a changing world outside the family. The close relation between these two systems appears in many studies that show educational training in the home to be directly linked to the success of training in the school. Why then the school?

Participation in the educational system from early childhood is expected to increase the level of knowledge and mental and interpersonal skills. Ideally, these skills are expected to have positive consequences in marital and parental performance in addition to employment performance. Sometimes the training provided adolescents in the educational system is at variance with that of parents or at a level that exceeds the training that parents have had. Thus the authority of the family may be undermined or the parental skills may be less than that of the child. In such instances parental authoritarianism may give way to more egalitarian parent-child relations or may set the stage for emancipation from the household. Again the linkages between the educational and family systems become evident.

Economy and the family   Perhaps as much as any other institution, the economy influences family organization and interaction. The economy is the component of society concerned with the creation, distribution, and consumption of goods and services. The family contributes labor and skills and in turn receives wages or other forms of compensation (prestige, insurance, services, and the like). The impact of the economic-family linkage is most evident when issues such as unemployment, families in poverty, one-parent families, wife-mother and dual-career employment, or the inequality of wealth and resources are examined.

At a macro-level of analysis, it is difficult to indicate fully the extent to which the economy and economic conditions affect families and their life-styles. Michael Young and Peter Willmott[6] link work and family roles in describing three major changes the family has undergone in the past two hundred years. They argue that in Stage One, prior to the industrial revolution of the eighteenth century, the home was the center of activities, and work and home life were not clearly separated. In Stage Two, with the creation of new production techniques and the development of the factory system, work and home became sharply differentiated, with women responsible for the domestic labor and some paid labor outside the home and men taking over the paid labor activity with few domestic tasks. Stage Three, brought on by technological change and the rise of feminism, resulted in the "symmetrical family." This type of family has as its most important feature the desegregation of roles based on sex. The unity of the family is restored as the consumer rather than as the production unit of Stage One.

Again at a macro-level of analysis, conflict theorists view the economic system as the key to understanding all inequality within or outside of the family system. More than one hundred years ago, Karl Marx's co-writer, Friedrich Engels,[7] argued that marriage represents a class antagonism in which the well-being and development of one group are attained by the misery and repression of the other. In marriage, as in the economy, the dominance of the husbands and the suppression of the wives is evident, and the linkage between the two is unmistakable.

This dominance-suppression issue is at the heart of gender role discussions. Conflict theorists, be they Marxian, feminist, or other, link the male-female division of labor to economic specialization and domination.

---

6. Michael Young and Peter Willmott, *The Symmetrical Family* (New York: Pantheon Books, 1973).

7. Friedrich Engels, *The Origin of the Family, Private Property, and the State* (New York: International Publishing, 1942). (Originally published in 1884.)

Traditional norms state that men are expected to "bring home the bacon," meaning "support the family," thus constituting the basic employed paid-labor force. Women's place is in the home, and domestic chores such as cooking, cleaning, and child care are women's work. This household labor, according to one branch of conflict theory, is intricately linked to a capitalistic type of economic system in that the "free and unpaid" labor of women makes it possible for men to leave the home to work, earn wages, and support the family. His wages, in turn, contribute to his dominant position and make the wife-mother-female dependent on the male.

In light of this discussion, one can understand why "working wives" are those who are employed outside the home. Housework is not "real work," and—as will be shown later in the chapter—remains the task of women whether they are full-time housewives or paid employees outside the home. Let us examine more closely the housewife and employed wife and mother.

Go on—ask me if I work

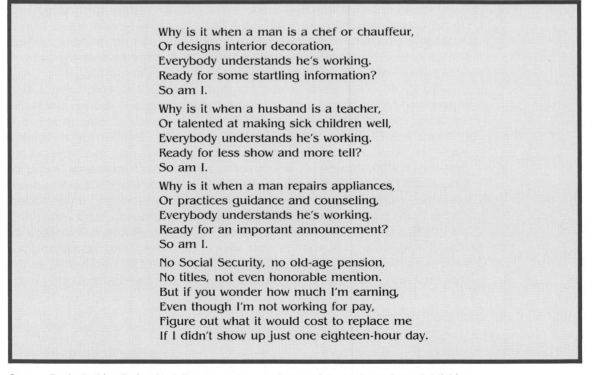

Why is it when a man is a chef or chauffeur,
Or designs interior decoration,
Everybody understands he's working.
Ready for some startling information?
So am I.

Why is it when a husband is a teacher,
Or talented at making sick children well,
Everybody understands he's working.
Ready for less show and more tell?
So am I.

Why is it when a man repairs appliances,
Or practices guidance and counseling,
Everybody understands he's working.
Ready for an important announcement?
So am I.

No Social Security, no old-age pension,
No titles, not even honorable mention.
But if you wonder how much I'm earning,
Even though I'm not working for pay,
Figure out what it would cost to replace me
If I didn't show up just one eighteen-hour day.

Source: Rochelle Distelheim, *McCall's*, December 1976. Copyright © The McCall's Publishing Company.

THE HOUSEWIFE

Traditionally, few roles of women held a higher priority than to be a wife and homemaker. The housewife has been relatively neglected by social scientists as a central problem for research, with the attention granted women in paid employment overshadowing the attention given to women who are not in the paid-labor force (in 1986, 45.3 percent of the female population age sixteen and over and 45.4 percent of married women with a husband present).[8]

The qualifications for the status of housewife are only two: marriage and female. Age, education, specific skills, time off, overtime, level of productivity, and other characteristics are basically ignored in job performance. The role of housewife is generally categorized as a low status position with both low prestige and a low economic value. "I'm only a housewife" is a phrase well familiar to most readers. This exists in spite of the performance of tasks that are economically valuable to society and costly for a family to purchase: cook, baker, waitress, teacher, sexual partner, seamstress, housekeeper, bookkeeper, secretary, chauffeur, nurse, therapist, tutor, counselor, hostess, and recreation director.

Joann Vanek states that there are several important misconceptions about housework.[9] People often think that housewives work fewer hours, at a slower pace, and less strenuously than other workers. Many believe that housework has little productive value. And some believe the present assignment of tasks between husband and wife is equitable.

First, do housewives work less than others? One could argue that household technology, such as canned and processed foods, automatic washers, electric refrigerators, and other "labor-saving" equipment, has reduced the burdens of housework significantly. Data from a national survey of two-parent families with at least one child under twelve reported that the median number of hours per week spent in housework and child care was 41.8 for all white wives and 34.2 for black wives.[10] Among those wives not employed, whites spent 35 hours in housework and an additional 15 hours in child care compared to 28 hours in housework and an additional 10 in child care among blacks. The specific median time allotments for blacks and whites, husbands and wives, employed and non-employed wives can be seen in Table 4–1. Note that while the number of hours that husbands spend in housework and child care increases slightly if the

---

8. U.S. Bureau of the Census, *Statistical Abstract of the United States: 1987*, 107th ed. (Washington, D.C.: U.S. Government Printing Office, 1987), Table 653, p. 382.

9. Joann Vanek, "Housewives as Workers," in *Women Working* by Ann H. Stromberg and Shirley Harkess (Palo Alto, Cal.: Mayfield Publishing, 1978): 392–414.

10. Joyce O. Beckett and Audrey D. Smith, "Work and Family Roles: Egalitarian Marriage in Black and White Families," *Social Service Review* 55 (June 1981): 314–326.

TABLE 4–1
Median values of selected variables, by race and wife's employment status.

	Blacks			Whites		
	Total	Wife employed	Wife not employed	Total	Wife employed	Wife not employed
Wife's hours housework	24.4	21.3	28.1	30.2	25.0	35.1
Husband's hours housework	5.0	5.9	3.9	3.3	4.5	2.4
Wife's hours child care	9.8	9.8	9.9	11.6	9.8	14.7
Husband's hours child care	5.5	6.8	4.9	4.7	5.3	4.1

Source: Joyce O. Beckett and Audrey D. Smith, "Work and Family Roles: Egalitarian Marriage in Black and White Families," *Social Service Review* 55 (June 1981), Table 3, p. 321. Reprinted by permission of The University of Chicago Press, publisher.

wife is employed, husband-wife equity in these tasks is nonexistent. Women, whether housewives or in paid employment, perform most of the domestic work.

Using a national sample to analyze change in men's housework and child care over a ten-year period, Shelley Coverman and Joseph F. Sheley conclude that there were no significant changes in men's mean housework and child-care time through the mid-1970s.[11] Some changes did occur among certain categories of men, such as an increase in the amount of time men with younger children devoted to child care. But they conclude that men's involvement in the traditional "women's sphere" if occurring at all, is lagging considerably behind women's entry into the traditional "men's sphere." Clearly, their findings cast doubt on any significant convergence of sex roles.

In another article, Coverman attempts to explain husbands' participation in domestic labor (housework and child care).[12] Using data from about 700 white, currently married men, three hypotheses were tested on relative resources, sex-role ideology, and demand-response capability. One, the *relative resources* hypothesis, stated that the more resources (e.g., education, income, professional occupation) a husband has relative to his wife, the less domestic labor he does. Clearly, the results did not

11. Shelley Coverman and Joseph F. Sheley, "Change in Men's Housework and Child-Care Time, 1965–1975," *Journal of Marriage and the Family* 48 (May 1986): 413–422.

12. Shelley Coverman, "Explaining Husbands' Participation in Domestic Labor," *The Sociological Quarterly* 26 (1985): 81–97. Note also: Rosalind C. Barnett and Grace K. Baruch, "Determinants of Fathers' Participation in Family Work," *Journal of Marriage and the Family* 49 (February 1987): 29–40.

support this hypothesis. But neither did strong support exist for the idea that men who were better educated, had higher earnings, or were in higher occupational positions than their wives were more likely to participate in housework and child care. Two, the *sex-role ideology* hypothesis stated that the more traditional the husband's sex-role attitudes, the less domestic labor he performs. As with the resource hypothesis, the sex-role ideology hypothesis was not supported either. Three, the *demand-response capability* hypothesis stated that the more domestic-task demands on the husband and the greater his capacity to respond to them, the greater his participation in domestic labor. This hypothesis was overwhelmingly supported. Men who were younger, had a number of children, employed wives, and jobs that did not require long work hours were most likely to be involved in household activities. What her analysis suggests is that neither attitude change nor socioeconomic status will alter the domestic division of labor. It will be altered, however, by the demands placed on a husband to do them—such as having children and an employed wife, combined with fewer hours to spend on paid work.

Second, does housework have little productive value? Again, specific data are difficult to obtain since payroll checks and dollar expenditures seldom accompany this task. But, the work a woman does contributes to the family economy and to the society's total economic output. Without the services referred to earlier (cook, baker, waitress, etc.), the family's standard of living would be lowered drastically and to purchase them would be extremely costly.

Third, is the present holding of power and the assignment of tasks between husband and wife equitable? Vanek argues that it is not.[13] Neither a wage nor a visible product results from her work. She is deprived of economic benefits such as insurance and medical care for her own efforts.

From a Marxist-feminist perspective, housework serves as a prime example of an unequal division of labor between men and women that generates tension, conflict, and change. Being a housewife augments the power of men. As stated earlier, that housewives are excluded from paid employment and an opportunity to support themselves reinforces their dependence on their husbands. Heidi Hartmann pinpoints time spent on housework to support the proposition that the family remains a primary arena where men exercise their patriarchal power over women's labor. She says that

> men's control of women's labor power is the lever that allows them to benefit from women's provision of personal and household services, including relief from child rearing and many unpleasant tasks both within and beyond house-holds, and the arrangement of the nuclear family, based on monogamous

---

13. Vanek, "Housewives as Workers," pp. 405–406.

and heterosexual marriage, is one institutional form that seems to enhance this control.[14]

Another inequality in marriage occurs in the way in which the household tasks are divided. What husbands and wives do is not only different but may not have changed much over several decades. In *Middletown Families,* the way men and women, whether cohabiting or married, divided up household tasks is along traditional lines with the women bearing the brunt of the labor. In 90 percent of the families the wife does all or most of the housekeeping, and in 85 percent of the families with young children, the wife does all or most of the caring for them. About 84 percent of Middletown husbands earn all or most of the family income.[15] These figures parallel a Utah study that showed the wife doing the housekeeping among more than 90 percent of the families and caring for preschool children in about 80 percent of the families (77 percent for Catholics, 80 percent for Protestants, and 85 percent for Mormans). The husband earned all or most of the family income in about 88 percent of the families.[16]

The literature in general suggests that when wives are compared with husbands, "his" marriage is considerably better than "her" marriage. Jessie Bernard[17] stated this most explicitly by reporting that more wives than husbands: report marital frustration and dissatisfaction, negative feelings, and marital problems, consider their marriages unhappy; have regretted their marriage; seek marital counseling; initiate divorce proceedings; have felt they were going to have a nervous breakdown; had more feelings of inadequacy in their marriage; and blamed themselves for their own lack of general adjustment. She described housework as menial labor, isolating, and a dead-end job with no chance of promotion. Finally, she said, in truth, being a housewife makes women sick.

If being a housewive makes women sick, apparently employment outside the home is not the medication needed to make them any better. Evidence from six large national surveys consistently failed to support the hypothesis that women with jobs outside the home are generally happier and more satisfied with their lives than full-time housewives.[18] Both work

---

14. Heidi I. Hartmann, "The Family as Locus of Gender, Class, and Political Struggle: The Example of Housework," *Signs: Journal of Women in Culture and Society* 6 (Spring 1981): 372.

15. Theodore Caplow et al., *Middletown Families: Fifty Years of Continuity and Change* (New York: Bantam Books, 1982): 69.

16. Howard M. Bahr, "Religious Contrasts in Family Role Definitions and Performance: Utah Mormons, Catholics, Protestants and Others," *Journal for the Scientific Study of Religion* 21 (September 1982): 209.

17. Jessie Bernard, *The Future of Marriage* (New Haven: Yale University Press, 1982): 26–53.

18. James D. Wright, "Are Working Women Really More Satisfied? Evidence from Several National Surveys," *Journal of Marriage and the Family* 40 (May 1978): 301–313.

outside the home and full-time housework were found to have benefits and costs attached to them: the net result is that there were found to be no consistent or significant differences in patterns of life satisfaction between the two groups. Constance Shehan, as well, in comparing employed wives and housewives, found no significant difference between the two groups in depression, health anxiety, or life satisfaction. The majority of respondents of both groups were "well-off" psychologically.[19]

While this discussion tended to present the housewife status as negative in terms of low prestige, no salary or fringe benefits, overwork, and the like, it should not be overlooked that many women find satisfaction in the performance of the role. The job is not competitive. The work schedule is highly flexible. The position may be one of choice. Some women prefer housekeeping to any other type of work. Some women define their highest contribution as service to their husband and children. And as reported by Shehan in her study cited above, the home and family are not the only source of gratification that housewives have. Pursuing hobbies, participating in voluntary organizations, and visiting with friends and relatives are important sources of social interaction and interesting activity.

A report from national surveys conducted by the Survey Research Center at the University of Michigan indicated that 50 percent of housewives had a positive opinion of housework and 44 percent had a neutral or ambivalent opinion.[20] Only 6 percent perceived housework as negative. Positive views were inversely related to level of education, that is, housewives with more formal education were less likely to respond positively to housework. They were also most likely to want a career. The least likely to favor housework were college-educated, younger wives. These findings parallel other results that show that women who had wanted a career outside the home were more dissatisfied with their own lives than homemakers who had never wanted a career. It was the career-oriented homemakers who showed the dissatisfaction previous research has suggested characterizes homemakers as opposed to employed women. The home-oriented homemakers, on the other hand, were slightly more satisfied with their lives than employed women.[21]

See also Myra Marx Ferree, "Class, Housework, and Happiness: Women's Work and Life Satisfaction," *Sex Roles* 11 (1984): 1057–1074.

19. Constance L. Shehan, "Wives' Work and Psychological Well-Being: An Extension of Gove's Social Role Theory of Depression," *Sex Roles* 11 (1984): 881–899.

20. Alfreda P. Iglehart, "Wives, Work, and Social Change: What About the Housewives?" *Social Service Review* 54 (September 1980): 317–330.

21. Aloen Townsend and Patricia Gurin, "Re-Examining the Frustrated Homemaker Hypothesis," *Sociology of Work and Occupations* 8 (November 1981): 464–488.

In observing household work, two sociologists found three overall, prevailing views.[22] Some women spoke with disdain about household work. These women could not deny household work as a full-time activity but addressed in detail their "worthless" activities. A second view was rather positive. Household work was justified through such values as "making a good home," "keeping the family happy," or exploring the creative dimensions of child care, cooking, and home decoration. The third view was one of ambivalence. On the one hand, "it was about time" someone noticed the complexity of household work, the amount of labor involved, and who, in fact, bore the brunt of "making a home," especially when they genuinely loved the people for whom household work was being undertaken. One obvious point that did emerge was that few women in their entire sample felt that household work was an entirely worthwhile, dignified activity.

THE EMPLOYED WIFE AND MOTHER

In 1986, 54.7 percent of all females age sixteen and over (a total of 51.7 million) were employed in the labor force. This was up from 46.8 percent (or 38 million) just ten years earlier in 1976 and up from 42.6 percent since 1970 (*see* Table 4–2). Of these 51.7 million females, 25.4 percent were single; 58.5 percent were married; and 16.1 percent were widowed or divorced. While the total number of women in the labor force and the proportion of females in the labor force relative to the female populations have both increased dramatically over the past several decades, the marital distribution, particularly since 1955, has changed very little. Over the past thirty years, at any one time, about one-fourth of the female labor force has been single, three-fifths has been married, and about one in six or seven has been widowed or divorced.

What are some other characteristics of the female work force? Of the married women with a husband present in 1986, 53.8 percent had at least one child under six years of age (*see* Figure 4–1.) This was also true for 73.8 percent of the divorced women.[23] These figures gain added relevance when viewed in the light of certain theoretical orientations that stress the importance of a "mother at-home" for young children (*see* Chapter 14) and the widespread public concern over the working mother.

---

22. Sarah Fenstermaker Berk and Catherine White Berheide, "Going Backstage: Gaining Access to Observe Household Work," *Sociology of Work and Occupations* 4 (February 1977): 41–42.

23. U.S. Bureau of the Census, *Statistical Abstract of the United States: 1986,* 106th ed. (Washington, D.C.: U.S. Government Printing Office, 1986), no. 654, p. 383.

TABLE 4–2
Marital status of women in the civilian labor force, 1950–1986. (Persons 14 years old and over through 1965; 16 years old and over thereafter.)

	1950	1960	1970	1980	1986
Female labor force					
Total (thousands)	17,795	22,516	31,233	44,934	51,732
Single	5,621	5,401	6,965	11,242	13,127
Married	9,273	13,485	19,799	26,828	30,274
Widowed or divorced	2,901	3,629	4,469	6,864	8,332
Percent distribution of female labor force					
Single	31.6%	24.0%	22.3%	25.0%	25.4%
Married	52.1	59.9	63.4	59.7	58.5
Widowed or divorced	16.3	16.1	14.3	15.3	16.1
Female labor force as percent of female population					
Total	31.4%	34.8%	42.6%	51.1%	54.7%
Single	50.5	44.1	53.0	61.5	65.3
Married	24.8	31.7	41.4	50.7	55.0
Widowed or divorced	36.0	37.1	36.2	41.0	43.1

Source: U.S. Bureau of the Census, *Statistical Abstract of the United States: 1987,* 107th ed. (Washington, D.C.: U.S. Government Printing Office, 1987), no. 653, p. 382.

The extent of the legitimacy of these concerns in terms of consequences for the children is examined in the pages that follow.

The largest percentage of employed women in 1985 were in what the U.S. Census categorizes as technical, sales, and administrative support (about 45 percent). This includes occupations such as technicians, retail sales workers, secretaries, and typists. An additional 23 percent were in managerial and professional occupations such as teachers, writers, nurses, and managers; 19 percent were in service occupations such as child-care workers, waitresses, health aides, or hairdressers; 9 percent were operators and laborers, such as machine operators, inspectors, and non-construction laborers; and the remaining percent were in occupations such as mechanics, construction trades, and agricultural occupations.[24] Many occupations are held predominantly by females: registered nurses, 96 percent; secretaries and typists, 98 percent; telephone operators, 93 percent; child-care workers, 97 percent; welfare service aides, 94 percent; and elementary teachers,

24. Ibid., no. 657, pp. 385–386.

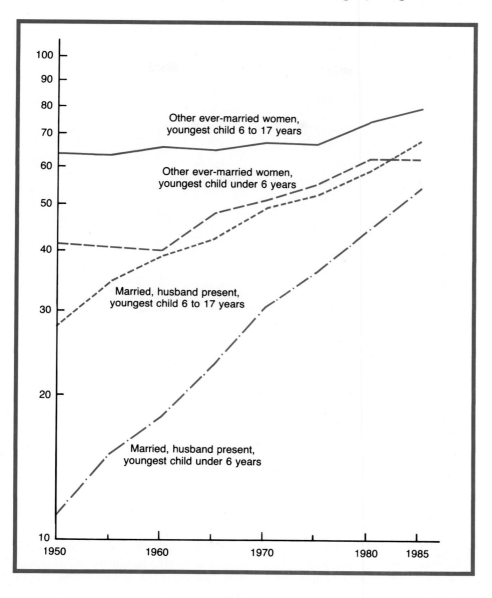

FIGURE 4–1

Labor force participation rates of mothers with children under eighteen years old: March 1950–1982. (*Source:* U.S. Bureau of the Census, *Current Population Reports*, Series P-23, no. 117, "Trends in Child Care Arrangements of Working Mothers" [Washington, D.C.: U.S. Government Printing Office, 1982], figure 1, p. 4; and U.S. Bureau of the Census, *Statistical Abstract of the United States: 1987*, 107th ed. [Washington, D.C.: U.S. Government Printing Office, 1986], no. 654, p. 383.)

Male roles have changed considerably over the past few decades with an increasing number of men learning skills and assuming tasks traditionally associated with the female, wife, and mother. (Photo: © Camerique Stock Photos/E. P. Jones, Co.)

85 percent. In contrast, occupations with few females include engineers and dentists with about 6 percent, the construction trades with less than 2 percent, and fire fighters and mobile equipment mechanics with less than 1 percent. This concentration or absence of women in particular occupations may help us understand differences by gender in income, benefits, power, and authority.

Of those women with incomes, the median income in 1983 was $6,868 (compared to $15,600 for men).[25] The sharpest income discrepancy between men and women appears in the $15,000 and over categories. Fifty-two percent of all employed men fell within this category, as opposed to 22.0 percent of all employed women. Some of the income gap can be explained by the differences just shown in type of work and extent of employment. About two-thirds of employed women were in clerical, service, and blue-collar occupations. In addition, approximately one out of every four employed women was listed as *part time.* If the median income of only the women employed full time in 1984 is used, the median income

---

25. Ibid., no. 742, p. 441.

of women becomes $15,422, a figure still well below the $24,004 of full-time male workers.[26] A simple mathematical computation of these figures indicates that, among full-time workers only, women earned $0.64 to every $1.00 earned by men.

This male-female difference in income is explained by Patricia Roos[27] as the result of women being adversely affected by the sex-segregated character of the labor market. Because of their concentration in selected occupations and industries, women operate in a very different employment context than men. Roos analyzes five measures of positional inequality, or characteristics of jobs, that improve our understanding of why women earn less than men. First, the few occupations in which women work are *low-paying.* Second, the occupations in which women work are *heavily female*—that is, rather than men and women on average doing similar work, women are highly concentrated in a few jobs. Third, working women relative to men are characteristically less likely to *control the means of production.* Women-owned businesses represent only about 5 percent of the U.S. firms. Fourth, women are less likely than men to *exercise authority* over others. Even when they hold authority positions, they are likely to be less important than those held by men. Finally, women are *segregated by industry.* These industries, such as service and retail trade rather than mining, manufacturing, or wholesale trade, both pay less and generate less return to investment.

Reasons for wife-mother employment

Why do wives and mothers work? They work for the same mysterious reasons that husbands and fathers work, although men are much less likely to be asked. Women are asked because of the strong institutionalized bias that has traditionally existed against married women and mothers working for any reason other than economic remuneration. Since the place of a wife—particularly one who is also the mother of preschool-aged children—is widely believed to be in the home, the traditional bias will lead again to the question, "Why do wives and mothers work?"

Many individualistic reasons could be given, but all personal and seemingly idiosyncratic factors share much in common. The most frequently articulated reason for working is money or financial need. One study has

---

26. Ibid., no. 743, p. 441.

27. Patricia A. Roos, "Sex Stratification in the Workplace: Male-Female Differences in Economic Returns to Occupation," *Social Science Research* 10 (September 1981): 195–224. For variations in women's wages *see* Cynthia Rexcoat and Constance Shehan, "Differential Effects of Industrial and Worker Resources in Women's Wages," *Social Science Research* 15 (1986): 1–27.

suggested that in the early years of marriage, wives work primarily in response to perceived family financial needs rather than to achieve individual success goals. Even in working, the wives appeared to be reacting more to traditional (that is, family supporting) wife-mother role expectations than in terms of the self-fulfillment career model idealized by the feminist movement.[28]

Lee Rainwater says that in Western countries with the possible exception of the United States, there is a large unmet demand for jobs on the part of women and concludes that this demand is not motivated primarily by a demand for increased family income but rather by a desire for the nonmonetary gains which women can find in work.[29] Clearly, many factors other than money influence the decision to seek paid employment. Results from Ireland have shown that three factors predict a significant amount of the variance in the married woman's employment status: (1) her perceived approval from four of her important others (husband, mother, father, and closest friend); (2) her own attitude toward maternal employment; and (3) her expected family size.[30] Results from Sweden have shown that marriage itself increases the likelihood of labor-force participation and vice versa.[31] Interestingly, while the opportunities for increased female labor-force participation in Sweden improved the feasibility of marriage, it also increased the feasibility and desirability of divorce.

Interrelated with money, status, approval of significant others, and boredom is a long list of factors that influence the employment likelihood for wives and mothers. Some of these factors include: the availability of jobs; the number and age of her children; her level of education, work experience, and work skills; the income level of her husband; status maintenance and status enhancement; and a range of attitudinal variables, including those of her husband.[32] It is easier to work, as in the middle years, when one does not have children. Generally, it is easier to find a

---

28. Phyllis A. Ewer, Eileen Crimmins, and Richard Oliver, "An Analysis of the Relationship Between Husband's Income, Family Size and Wife's Employment in the Early Stages of Marriage," *Journal of Marriage and the Family* 41 (November 1979): 737.

29. Lee Rainwater, "Mothers' Contribution to the Family Money Economy in Europe and the United States," *Journal of Family History* 41 (Summer 1979): 198–211.

30. Margret Fine-Davis, "Social-Psychological Predictors of Employment Status of Married Women in Ireland," *Journal of Marriage and the Family* 41 (February 1979): 145–158.

31. Robert Schoen and William Urton, "A Theoretical Perspective on Cohort Marriage and Divorce in Twentieth Century Sweden," *Journal of Marriage and the Family* 41 (May 1979): 409–415.

32. See, for example, Marianne A. Ferber, "Labor Market Participation of Young Married Women: Causes and Effects," *Journal of Marriage and the Family* 44 (May 1982): 457–468; Valerie Kincade Oppenheimer, "The Sociology of Women's Economic Role in the Family," *American Sociological Review* 42 (June 1977): 387–406; and Carol S. Aneshensel and Bernard C. Rosen, "Domestic Roles and Sex Differences in Occupational Expectations," *Journal of Marriage and the Family* 42 (February 1980): 121–131.

job if one has training, skills, and experience. The absence of a husband, a part-time employed husband, or a husband with low income forces women into the work force. Generally, an *inverse* relationship exists between the husband's level of income and the percentage of wives employed.

Since opportunities to work are available, Kingsley Davis raises the question of not only why so many wives work, but also why so many of them do not.[33] The answer, he claims, is not that they have calculated the dollar costs and benefits and found that employment does not pay. Rather, it is that they have calculated the psychosocial costs and benefits, and found employment deficient.

Interestingly, a direct relationship exists between economic attainment and an unmarried status. Singleness may be less a "marriage reject" for many employed single women than one of "rejecting marriage."[34] In brief, the lower the husband's income, the higher the percentage of wives employed; the higher the women's income, the more likely she is to be or remain single.

Employed women and children

Few sociocultural differentials have equaled the strength of the inverse relationship between female labor-force participation and fertility. Simply, working women have fewer children. Marital female employment before childbearing has been found to be associated with lower fertility levels later, longer first-birth intervals, and earlier use of birth control.[35] On the other hand, there has been a dramatic increase in labor-force participation among women with school- and preschool-aged children (*see* Figure 4–1). The presence of young children remains a deterrent to women's labor-force participation but only minimally so in contrast to thirty years ago (again note Figure 4–1).

A pregnancy and first birth clearly has a major impact on female employment. A national longitudinal survey of over 19,000 seniors beginning in 1972 with four follow-up surveys reported that the majority of ever-married women have jobs prior to pregnancy: most leave these jobs as the pregnancy progresses, so that only one woman in five remains

---

33. Kingsley Davis, "Wives and Work: The Sex Role Revolution and Its Consequences," *Population and Development Review* 10 (September 1984): 413.

34. Elizabeth M. Havens, "Women, Work and Wedlock: A Note on Female Marital Patterns in the United States," *American Journal of Sociology* 78 (January 1973): 980.

35. H. Theodore Groat, Randy L. Workman, and Arthur G. Neal, "Labor Force Participation and Family Formation: A Study of Working Mothers," *Demography* 13 (February 1976): 115–125.

employed in the month that the child is born.[36] Following the birth, some women return to work but employment rates only rise to about 60 percent of their previous levels. Had these women not become parents, the proportion employed would have steadily increased. Thus, parenthood does lead to an employment deficit. Even women who retained their jobs were found to show some decline in hours at work.

It is often assumed that maternal employment has many effects on a child—all bad. However, research in the last several decades has seriously challenged this view. More than thirty years ago, Ivan Nye reported that adolescent children of part-time working mothers had better relationships with their parents than children of either full-time working mothers or mothers who did not work at all.[37] Since then, few studies seem to exist that report meaningful differences between the children of working mothers in general and the children of nonworking mothers. When differences do exist, it is often explained less by the mother working than by chance factors: social class, part- or full-time employment, age of the children, mother's attitude toward employment, or other social and psychological factors. For example, the occupational status of the position the mother held was found to be of greater consequence to the children than whether she worked or not.[38] Low-status mothers produced the most traditional children; mothers holding high-status positions produced the most non-conventional or liberal offspring; and housewives as well as women in medium-status positions produced children intermediate in their attitudes to the high- and low-status offspring.

Lois Hoffman reviewed research organized around five general hypotheses related to maternal employment and its effect on children.[39] Hypothesis 1 suggested that maternal employment affects the child, particularly the daughter, because the role models provided by working and nonworking mothers differ. Considerable support was provided for this hypothesis. In general, daughters of working mothers had less traditional sex-role concepts, a higher level of female competence, and compared favorably with daughters of nonworking mothers with respect to independence and achievement-related variables.[40] Another source found the

36. Linda J. Waite, Gus W. Haggstrom, and David E. Kanouse, "Changes in the Employment Activities of New Parents," *American Sociological Review* 50 (April 1985): 263–272.

37. F. Ivan Nye, "Adolescent-Parent Adjustment: Age, Sex, Sibling Number, Broken Homes, and Employed Mothers as Variables," *Marriage and Family Living* 14 (November 1952): 327–332.

38. Alan C. Acock, Deborah Barker, and Vern L. Bengtson, "Mother's Employment and Parent–Youth Similarity," *Journal of Marriage and the Family* 44 (May 1982): 441–455.

39. Lois Wladis Hoffman, "Effects on Child," in *Working Mothers* by Lois Wladis Hoffman and F. Ivan Nye (San Francisco: Jossey-Bass, 1974): 126–166.

40. Ibid., p. 136.

status of mother's occupation to be an important influence on son's and daughter's educational and occupational status with the somewhat surprising finding that mother's occupational status had a more powerful effect than father's on son's attainments.[41]

Hypothesis 2 suggested that a child would be affected by the mother's emotional state: morale or satisfactions from employment status, emotional stress because of dual-role demands, and guilt about the child. The data about the mother's emotional state suggest that the working mother who obtains satisfaction from her work, who has adequate arrangements so that her dual role does not involve undue strain, and who does not feel so guilty that she overcompensates is likely to do quite well and, under certain conditions, better than the nonworking mother.[42] This is quite consistent with data on child abuse that show working mothers are not more likely to be abusive. Richard Gelles and Eileen Hargreaves reported that women who worked full time had the lowest rate of overall violence toward their children, while mothers with part-time jobs and mothers who were not working reported higher rates.[43] The tendency for mothers at home and mothers employed part time to hit their children was increased if these mothers had preschool children. Rates of violence were very high where husbands were unemployed.

Hypothesis 3 suggested that maternal employment affects the child through its influence on child-rearing practices. In some studies, maternal employment increased the father's participation in child rearing (*see* Table 4–1 for example), while in others the active participation of the father had a positive effect on the child. It is uncertain, however, that these are directly linked; that is, that the father's activities that result from maternal employment are those that have a positive effect. Children of working mothers were found to have more household responsibilities and experience a milder form of discipline.[44]

Hypothesis 4 suggested that the working mother provides less adequate supervision, resulting in more delinquency. Data suggest that particularly in the lower classes, children of working mothers may receive less adequate supervision, and this less adequate supervision is linked to delinquency. In the middle class, there appears to be some evidence for a higher delinquency rate among children of working mothers although not for reasons of adequate supervision.[45]

---

41. Mary Holland Baker, "Mother's Occupation and Children's Attainments," *Pacific Sociological Review* 24 (April 1981): 237–254.

42. Hoffman, "Effects on Child," p. 142.

43. Richard G. Gelles and Eileen F. Hargreaves, "Maternal Employment and Violence Toward Children," *Journal of Family Issues* 2 (December 1981): 509–530.

44. Hoffman, "Effects on Child," pp. 142–147.

45. Ibid., pp. 151–152.

Hypothesis 5 suggested that the working mother's child is a victim of maternal deprivation. No solid evidence supports this hypothesis.[46]

In brief, maternal employment per se appears to be too broad a concept to produce major distinctions in effects on children. The numbers and percentages of women and working mothers do, however, focus attention on other areas such as an increasing interest in, and need for, day-care services. It also focuses attention on the husband-wife relationship and the balance of power between them, which will be discussed next.

Employed women and marriage

The effect of female employment on a marriage and the marital relationship could be expected to vary considerably depending on whether the employment is full time or part time, on whether there are preschool children, on the age of the couple, on their stage in the life cycle, and on many other factors. For example, one important predictor of happiness in marriage was found to be a woman's freedom to choose among alternative life-styles. Both partners experienced less marital happiness if the wife participated in the labor market out of economic necessity rather than by choice.[47]

A female employment factor that affects the marriage negatively is that of holding a job not traditionally occupied by women. Women holding these positions were about twice as likely to divorce as those with jobs traditionally held by women.[48] Another factor having a significant impact on marital dissolution is the amount of hours the wife works or spends away from the household.[49] The greater the number of hours worked, the greater the probability of marital instability, divorce, or both. In contrast, a female employment factor that affects the marriage positively is the extent to which the family experiences accommodate the wife's employment. Major factors seem to be having a supportive husband and freedom from childbearing responsibilities.[50] The most important conclusion from a

---

46. Ibid., p. 157.

47. Susan R. Orden and Norman M. Bradburn, "Working Wives and Marriage Happiness," *American Journal of Sociology* 74 (January 1969): 392–407.

48. William W. Philliber and Dana V. Hiller, "Relative Occupational Attainments of Spouses and Later Changes in Marriage and Wife's Work Experience," *Journal of Marriage and the Family* 45 (February 1983): 161–170.

49. Glenna Spitze and Scott J. South, "Women's Employment, Time Expenditure, and Divorce," *Journal of Family Issues* 6 (September 1985): 307–329; and Alan Booth, David R. Johnson, Lynn White, and John N. Edwards, "Women, Outside Employment, and Marital Instability," *American Journal of Sociology* 90 (November 1984): 567–583.

50. Sharon K. Houseknecht and Anne S. Macke, "Combining Marriage and Career: The Marital Adjustment of Professional Women," *Journal of Marriage and the Family* 43 (August 1981): 651–661.

review of twenty-seven studies spanning over thirty years and exploring the relationship between employment status and marital adjustment was that the wife's employment status alone appears to have little or no effect on marital adjustment.[51] This finding challenges the common belief that employment of wives per se places marital interaction and harmony in jeopardy.

Employment of the wife is certain to bring changes in the husband-wife relationship. Changes in the roles of companion, housewife, entertainer, lover, and the like are certain to require readjustments on the part of both spouses. The wife's job may reduce the amount of personal care the husband receives, increase his responsibilities for child care and household tasks, and require a modification in his career plans. While these and other changes may at times create stress and conflict, it appears that husbands of employed women evidence no more signs of marital discord and stress than the spouses of housewives.[52] They may, however, experience other consequences of female or dual employment.

Considerable shifts in power in the husband-wife relationship seem to occur when the wife is employed. In general, the wife's power tends to increase. In a later chapter, a resource theory is used to explain shifts in power. Thus, as the wife becomes employed, she gains income, independence, and new contacts (resources) that increase her contribution to the marriage. This increase in power among employed wives appears not only in the United States but cross-culturally as well.

In reviewing the research in this area, Steven Bahr suggested that the increase in power among employed wives tends to be primarily in "external" decisions (for example, finances or the provider role) with less power in "internal" household areas. The effect of employment on power within the child care, socialization, housekeeper, and recreation roles appears to be relatively small.[53] The effects of employment may be more pronounced in the lower class, in small families, and in families without preschool children. Among these groups, employed women have more power.

Employment of mothers affects far more than their children and their marriage. It affects them as well. Employed mothers were likely to enjoy their activities and relationships with children, reveal positive feelings

51. Drake S. Smith, "Wife Employment and Marital Adjustment: A Cumulation of Results," *Family Relations* 34 (October 1985): 483–490.

52. Alan Booth, "Does Wives' Employment Cause Stress for Husbands?" *The Family Coordinator* 28 (October 1979): 445–449; and Alan Booth, "Wife's Employment and Husband's Stress: A Replication and Refutation," *Journal of Marriage and the Family* 39 (November 1977): 645–650.

53. Steven J. Bahr, "Effects on Power and Division of Labor in the Family," in *Working Mothers* by Lois Wladis Hoffman and F. Ivan Nye, pp. 180–181.

about themselves, project an image of ability and confidence, and evaluate their communities as a satisfactory place to live.[54]

In the middle years, with the children gone from the home, the interests of the employed mother are no longer divided between her children and her job. Some women turn from part-time to full-time employment. Some begin work for the first time or at least the first time since the marriage or birth of children. Employment may take on a new meaning, presenting a perspective on the world and her own values considerably different from that known previously.

The employed husband and father

In 1985, 76.3 percent of all males aged sixteen and over (a total of 64.4 million) were employed in the labor force. This was down slightly from the 77.9 percent (56.3 million) ten years earlier in 1975 and down from 80.0 percent (51.2 million) in 1970.[55] As can be seen, while the number of males in the employed labor force increased, the proportion of employed men relative to the total male population decreased. This is unlike the data presented for females which showed both a number and percentage increase. As to the marital status of employed men, about three-fourths are married, about one in five are single, and one in twenty are widowed or divorced.

Apart from number differences in the employment status of males and females, the significant differences center around social norms and expectations. Take note of some of the questions raised about women in the section on the employed wife and mother. Do we seriously raise questions as to why men work, the effect of paternal employment (versus nonemployment) on family size, the "negative" effect of employment on children—especially preschool-aged children—or the career-oriented males as "marriage rejects"? If we ask a boy what he wants to be when he grows up, a "correct" answer is not "married," or "a father," but rather some employment status, particularly one of a prestigious nature: doctor, lawyer, banker, or president. For men, work defines their worth, their success or failure, and their major source of identity.

If that last sentence is true and employment is so important to men,

---

54. F. Ivan Nye, "Effects on Mother," in *Working Mothers* by Lois Wladis Hoffman and F. Ivan Nye, pp. 222–225. *See also* Ronald C. Kessler and James A. McRae, Jr., "The Effect of Wives' Employment on the Mental Health of Married Men and Women," *American Sociological Review* 47 (April 1982): 216–227.

55. U.S. Bureau of the Census, *Statistical Abstract of the United States: 1987*, no. 639, p. 376.

Husband roles among the Amish

Amish family organization and expected gender roles are centered around the father. This patriarchal structure can be seen by the extent to which his wife and children are subject to him. However, the line of authority is not rigid; the wife is consulted, particularly about child rearing, family problems, and decisions relating to home purchases. The children may also be consulted in planning farming matters. However, the husband's word is regarded as final.

The husband's way of life, as with most Amish behavior, stems from the scriptures. As stated in I Corinthians 11:3, "The head of the woman is the man." Thus, both husband and wife are well aware that the husband is the head of the house, although age too is a significant status factor. The oldest male, or grandfather, is respected as the patriarch and his social status increases at least until he reaches the age where he simply moves into the *Gross Dawdy* (grandfather) house and the younger generation takes over.

The husband's major activities center around farming. He will purchase the equipment and livestock without seeking the advice of his wife. He will perform the majority of the farming activities with the assistance of his wife and children. Only on occasion would the husband assist his wife in household tasks.

Personal relationships between husband and wife are quiet and sober, with no apparent demonstration of affection. Irritation between mates, expressed in a variety of ways, is conditioned by informally approved means of expression: the tone of voice, a gesture, or a direct statement. The husband may express disapproval by complete silence at the dinner table and the wife is left to guess what is wrong.

it could be assumed that unemployment is a crucial dimension in their lives. The evidence from depression studies shared the finding that the husband's unemployment had a negative effect on his self-esteem, personal functioning, and marital and family relationships. Similar results appear in more recent studies. Earlier in this chapter, it was stated that rates of violence were very high among unemployed husbands. In a look at blue-collar families, while finding unemployment of men not to have a negative effect on their self-esteem, Jeffry Larson did report that it corresponded to significantly lower marital adjustment, poorer marital communication, and lower satisfaction and harmony in family relations.[56] The unemployed spent less on entertainment, food, gasoline, and home energy consumption, all of which might be expected to effect marital-family relationships.

---

56. Jeffry H. Larson, "The Effect of Husband's Unemployment on Marital and Family Relations in Blue-Collar Families," *Family Relations* 33 (October 1984): 503–511.

Whether unemployed or employed, men's sense of worth and work satisfaction does not exist independently of the family. One paper[57] identified some ways that specific aspects of work-family structures relate to men's satisfaction at work. It was found that men in traditional one-career marriages felt more successful at work than did men in two-career marriages. This traditional family structure added to the man's feelings that he achieved success according to the traditional standards of the culture. Here he enters a career, starts a family in early adulthood, is upwardly mobile, and successfully provides for his family. The work satisfaction for men in two-career marriages was greatly influenced by the presence of children. This two-paycheck marriage appeared to allow the man greater flexibility in his attitudes toward his career and his identification with the "provider" role. Childless men in two-career marriages felt less successful and less self-actualized at work than did fathers in the same type of marriage.

Men, like women, work for financial reasons. But the emphases on getting a job, getting ahead, and gaining prestige or achieving power are stressed in the sex-role socialization process to a far greater extent for men than for women. For men, their work often becomes their home away from home. Bosses or the corporate hierarchy tend to serve as a surrogate parent in holding authority, defining duties, and dispensing rewards and/or punishments. Workmates serve as siblings with their competition, rivalry, friendships, and relatively equal status. In brief, while women are likely to be married to their husbands and gain status and identity through the marriage, men are often married to their work and gain their status and identity accordingly.

THE HOUSEHUSBAND

Work, to men and husbands, is generally defined and described in terms of labor-force employment, not in terms of housework and child care. In an article on men's family work, Joseph Pleck described three different perspectives concerning this work: the traditional, the exploitation, and the changing-roles perspectives.[58]

The *traditional perspective* holds that husbands are not responsible for any substantial amount of housework and child care in the family. The responsibility of the husband to the family is to provide economic support through paid employment. In terms of "role differentiation," the male holds primary responsibility for relationships and needs external to

---

57. Samuel Osherson and Diana Dill, "Varying Work and Family Choices: Their Impact on Men's Work Satisfaction," *Journal of Marriage and the Family* 45 (May 1983): 339–346.

58. Joseph H. Pleck, "Men's Family Work: Three Perspectives and Some New Data," *The Family Coordinator* 28 (October 1979): 481–488.

the family; the female holds responsibility for relationships and needs internal to the family. In terms of "exchange," the husband exchanges his work and economic services for the wife's companionship and household services. In terms of "resources" (*see* Chapter 12) relative to housework and child care, women have *time* for these activities which the full-time employed husband does not have.

The *exploitation perspective,* brought into clear focus by the women's movement, identifies the unequal burden of housework and child care carried by women as an important aspect of their inferior status in society. As suggested previously, one argument suggests that male avoidance of housework and child care is a deliberate strategy to maintain power over women. Studies have revealed that (1) the husband's performance of housework is small in tasks or time relative to the wife's and, more significantly, that (2) husbands of employed wives do *not* spend more time in housework than husbands of nonemployed wives. That is, employed wives do less than nonemployed wives, but husbands work the same amount of time irrespective of the employment status of the wife. What these two findings reveal is a substantial work "overload" on the wives in a combined housewife-employed wife role compared to their husbands. The data in Table 4–1 presented earlier differ somewhat from the data just provided in that the husband's hours in housework and in child care for both blacks and whites did increase if the wife was employed. But the increase was not sufficient to refute the claim of a housework "overload" for the employed wife.

There appears to be a significant disjunction between the perceptions of husband and wife concerning the amount of husband's help with household tasks.[59] Husbands believe that they help more than wives think husbands help. If men hold greater family power and perceive themselves as offering a significant degree of assistance with household labor, it appears unlikely that they will volunteer more or accept the next perspective, that of changing roles.

The *changing-roles perspective,* while acknowledging the traditional and exploitation perspectives, interprets men's work responsibility in a different light. Basically the argument is that in the evolution of work and family roles, as women add a second and new role of paid employment to their traditional role of housewife, men too need to add a second and new role of work in the home and with children to their traditional role of paid employment. The problem today is one of a psychosocial lag between the slower rate of change for men toward housework and the more rapid rate of change for women toward paid employment.

---

59. John G. Condran and Jerry G. Bode, "Rashomon, Working Wives, and Family Division of Labor: Middletown, 1980," *Journal of Marriage and the Family* 44 (May 1982): 421–426.

The first perspective (traditional) sees no reason for change. The second perspective (exploitation) sees little hope for change. The third perspective (changing roles) sees change as possible, likely, and emerging. Evidence for the third perspective is seen in subgroups such as single-parent fathers, fathers deliberately holding part-time jobs, single adoptive fathers, and househusbands; in these situations, men are assuming major household and child care duties. What is not known is the extent to which contemporary househusbands relinquish traditional male roles. A small study of Hispanic househusbands, for example, revealed that their househusband role was brought about by external economic circumstances and was viewed as a temporary status.[60] They did, however, report a greater involvement in family life, increased insight into their spouses' experiences, and as a result, closer relations with their spouses and children.

While there is no question that wives continue to hold the primary responsibility for housework and child care, and while the pace of change may seem both slow and minimal, it seems important to recognize that men's behavior appears to be changing. Men's slow response was found to be not so much reluctance to change, personal weaknesses, or lack of commitment to family life. Rather, the difficulties men face in meeting the newer household demands stem from inconsistencies between family expectations and the expectations of the wider society. Little moral support or logistical help is given men in performing tasks around the house. Because men perceive paid employment as their primary contribution to the family, they are reluctant to acknowledge either that they need help in performing this function or have a responsibility to participate in the homemaking function.[61] While we are not witnessing a major trend toward full-time househusbands, an increased participation of men in household and child care tasks does seem to be taking place in dual-employment and dual-career marriages.

DUAL-CAREER MARRIAGES

While dual-employed marriages and the employment of women have been common, particularly increasing since the Second World War, the common occurrence of dual-*career* marriage is a newer life-style. *Career* is used in place of *work* or *paid employment* to designate a level of commitment and continuous developmental sequence that is intrinsically rewarding,

---

60. Sharon Kantorowski Davis and Virginia Chavez, "Hispanic Househusbands," *Hispanic Journal of Behavioral Sciences* 7 (1985): 317–332.

61. Laura Lein, "Male Participation in Home Life: Impact of Social Supports and Breadwinner Responsibility on the Allocation of Tasks," *The Family Coordinator* 28 (October 1979): 489–495.

conditions less likely to be found in a job taken primarily for additional income purposes. The dual-career argument rests upon assumptions of increasing female access to high-level professions and managerial positions, of norms of gender equality, and of employment motivations centering on personal self-development and interpersonal relationships rather than economics.

Harold Benenson argues that these assumptions about dual careers, while widely believed, are fundamentally flawed and run counter to certain basic realities.[62] For example, in spite of recent gains, married women practicing the elite professions of law, medicine, and college teaching remain a numerically insignificant group among married women as a whole. In spite of high-education levels, most wives of high-income husbands maintain and enhance their families' class position by providing vital assistance to their husbands and children's career advancement. In spite of the dual-career image, women in professions and management positions are far more likely than comparable men to be single, married with no children, or divorced as a consequence of their career involvement. And married women who are in professional and managerial categories are still basically in the traditional female, low-paid professions of school teaching and nursing. Thus, the dual-career pattern tends not to represent equality, access to high-level professions, or work motivations separate from income for the majority of married couples.

Irrespective of these assumptions, dual-career marriages do exist with a range of common problems. Rhona and Robert Rapoport isolated five dilemmas of the dual-career marriage which by their nature set up strains.[63] These were common to all the couples they studied. They are: (1) overload, (2) environmental sanction, (3) personal identity and self-esteem, (4) social network dilemmas, and (5) dilemmas of multiple-role cycling.

The *overload factor* refers to the redistribution or carrying out of tasks that are traditionally done by the wife at home: domestic supervision, child care, social arrangements, and the like. How this overload factor was handled depended on the individuals and their situations but usually involved a considerable strain in their heavy schedule, cutting heavily into free time. Domestic help intruded into family privacy and their work was not always satisfactory. Sometimes standards were deliberately lowered

---

62. Harold Benenson, "Women's Occupational and Family Achievement in the U.S. Class System: A Critique of the Dual-Career Family Analysis," *The British Journal of Sociology* 35 (March 1984): 19–41.

63. Rhona Rapoport and Robert N. Rapoport, *Dual-Career Families* (Harmondsworth, Middlesex, England: Penguin, 1971), pp. 286–296. *See also* A. C. Bebbington, "The Function of Stress in the Establishment of the Dual-Career Family," *Journal of Marriage and the Family* 35 (August 1973): 530–537; and Denise S. Skinner, "Dual-Career Family Stress and Coping: A Literature Review," *Family Relations* 29 (October 1980): 473–481.

for the maintenance of the household. Sometimes the children were pressed into helping roles. The latter tended to be seen as a constructive socialization policy as well as an expedient in the overload situation.

This overload situation is what Karen Fox and Sharon Nickols refer to as the "time crunch."[64] Time is limited to precisely twenty-four hours per day but, dual careers or not, there are multiple roles and tasks to be performed. The way many couples alleviated the time crunch was for the employed wife to spend less time in housework. There is a consistency of data that shows husbands do not provide a corresponding increase in time allocation to housework to offset the wife's decrease.

Environmental sanctions refer to societal pressures which women must endure: sex-role stereotyping, competing with men, child-rearing expectations, and so on. While the mass media and the general sentiment toward married women working are changing in the direction of disparaging the idea of highly qualified women being exclusively housewives, the other factors mentioned are other matters. Unless women at work are outstanding, their deficiencies are likely to be reacted to stereotypically and attributed to "shortcomings" of their sex. If couples have no children, they face the possible hazard of feeling unfulfillment as human beings or as being viewed as odd or unfortunate by others. If they have children, they are expected to provide conventional care, i.e., with the mother staying at home.

Personal identity and *self-esteem* are dilemmas experienced more or less autonomously of environmental sanctions. The individuals studied were socialized in terms of the norms and values of thirty years ago or more. Boys were and are considered to be interested in machines, money, fame, power, and authority. Girls "normally" are interested in beauty, the arts, human relations, and care functions. Variance from these stereotyped interests and activities often produced guilt, ambivalence, sensitivity to criticism, self-doubt, and depression. Some husbands showed irritation or resentment at having to modify their own identities to incorporate a successful wife into their pattern. However, if should be noted that dual-career marriages appear to be as good or better at working through problems that confront them than other families. These families may engage in more purposeful decision making and more open communication, often by a very sharp segregation between home and work roles. What this often means is that at home, the wife becomes "cook" and "my husband's wife."

Social network dilemmas involve relationships with schools, medical facilities, work organizations, friends, or kin. In general, the dual-career families tended to make their network of relationships on a couple basis

---

64. Karen D. Fox and Sharon Y. Nickols, "The Time Crunch: Wife's Employment and Family Work," *Journal of Family Issues* 4 (March 1983): 61–82.

rather than on an individual basis, their relationships with kin tended to diminish except where there were clear responsibilities and/or compatibilities, and they tended to increase the number of people in their networks who were in service relationships with them.

The *dilemmas of multiple-role cycling* involve the need to dovetail the demands of marriage, husband's work, wife's work, children, and so forth as each changes with different stages of the life cycle. For example, in dual-career marriages, occupational establishment often preceded childbearing. With the arrival of children, new demands of time, money, and family tasks posed new dilemmas that needed solutions. This type of role shift, while not unique to the dual-career marriage, was another source of strain.

After reading about the dilemmas and the resultant strains produced by dual careers, one could ask, "Why dual careers?" Clearly, there are gains in this type of life-style. The financial gains are more important than are often acknowledged. The Rapoport study, however, found money to be less crucial than what they subsumed under the general category of "self-expression."[65] These are satisfactions derived from creating something, achieving recognition, expanding energies beyond the home and children, or marital enrichment. One study comparing one- and two-career families found the women in the two-career family to report fewer life pressures and worries, more communication with husbands, more happiness with their marriages, and better physical and mental health. In contrast, the men in the two-career families were in poorer health and were less content with marriage, work, and life in general.[66] More recent results suggest that men are responding less positively to the dual-earner arrangement than women.[67] There may be subtle forms of resistance among men (avoidance of housework, inadequate parenting, domestic violence, high divorce rates) who could potentially benefit most if they had a traditional, conventional wife. It would appear that the husband of the employed wife loses part of his active support system when the wife fails to function as a servant, homemaker, and mother. Employed wives, on the other hand, expand into roles that have more positive value for them.

While the professional employment of women is gaining increasing respectability and acceptance, a state of sexual equality has not and perhaps will not be achieved. This is in spite of a WASP (Wives as Senior Partners)

---

65. Rapoport and Rapoport, *Dual Career Families*, p. 297.

66. Ronald J. Burke and Tamara Weir, "Relationship of Wives' Employment Status to Husband, Wife and Pair Satisfaction and Performance," *Journal of Marriage and the Family* 38 (May 1976): 279–287.

67. Sandra C. Stanley, Janet G. Hunt, and Larry L. Hunt, "The Relative Deprivation of Husbands in Dual-Earner Households," *Journal of Family Issues* 7 (March 1986): 3–20.

marital pattern that is being chosen by some couples where the wife's occupation is seen as more important than the husband's.[68] Wives are still generally expected to give up their own jobs for the sake of their husbands and to shoulder the primary responsibility for housework and child care. Janet and Larry Hunt argue that dual-career families have not represented a radical departure from conventional sex roles. They suggest that as careers become more legitimate for women, careers and families will become increasingly polarized rather than more effectively integrated.[69] They predict a growing institutional separation of careers and families. For the highly successful of both sexes, families will be less necessary, less helpful, and more of a liability than in the past.

Margaret Paloma and others would agree with the idea just presented. Data suggest that the structure of the U.S. family makes it virtually impossible for married career women to have career lines like those of their male counterparts.[70] The dual pressures of both family responsibilities and career obligations for the married career woman may mean the increased separation of career and family or, when integrated, may occur primarily later in life when child care responsibilities are lessened. In brief, today's aspiring married professionals face difficult choices: lowering career aspirations, consciously rejecting parenthood, divorce, withdrawal of one spouse from the top-professional tier, or for some, commuter marriages.

Commuter marriages

What about the dual career where the husband and wife live separately? The pattern of one spouse leaving home temporarily is nothing new and the amount of separation is known to vary both by occupation or profession as well as by distance. Politicians, professional athletes, and various salespersons are known to routinely spend time apart from their spouse. In addition, military service, imprisonment, and seasonal work in selected occupations separate husbands and wives.

---

68. Maxine P. Atkinson and Jacqueline Boles, "WASP (Wives as Senior Partners," *Journal of Marriage and the Family* 46 (November 1984): 861–870.

69. Janet G. Hunt and Larry L. Hunt, "The Dualities of Careers and Families: New Integrations or New Polarization?" *Social Problems* 29 (June 1982): 499–510; and Janet G. Hunt and Larry L. Hunt, "Dual-Career Families: Vanguard of the Future or Residue of the Past?" in Joan Aldous, ed., *Two Paychecks: Life in Dual-Earner Families* (Beverly Hills: Sage Publications, 1982): 41–59.

70. Margaret M. Paloma, Brian F. Pendleton, and T. Neal Garland, "Reconsidering the Dual-Career Marriage: A Longitudinal Approach," in Joan Aldous, ed., *Two Paychecks: Life in Dual-Earner Families* (Beverly Hills: Sage Publications, 1982): 173–192; and Mary C. Regan and Helen E. Roland, "Rearranging Family and Career Priorities: Professional Women and Men of the Eighties," *Journal of Marriage and the Family* 47 (November 1985): 985–992.

Today, the decision for family members to live apart and establish dual residences is increasingly a result of women's participation in the professions and an unwillingness to either divorce or relocate in the community of employment of the spouse. This pattern stands in sharp contrast to the traditional pattern of the married couple and their children living and moving where the husband has employment. Now, however, the wife's career may require her to spend the week days in New York or Chicago while the husband's career may require him to be in Detroit or Boston.

The traditional option would be for one spouse, usually the wife, to give up his or her job to live with the spouse. Newer options include marital separation and/or divorce, with each person pursuing career patterns independently, or remaining married but establishing separate residences with commuting between the residences possible. Both these options have few social or cultural supports. Marriage as defined by most people includes sharing a common residence. Friends or relatives are prone to question the satisfaction with or commitment to a marriage where the husband and wife reside in separate locations. Friends of the couple may exclude invitations to social events of the "single" spouse. And the couple themselves, as well as others, may tend to define aspects of their life-style more like that of single unmarrieds than of married people. The complexity of these living patterns increases for couples with dependent children.

Harriet Gross studied forty-three spouses representing twenty-eight dual-career marriages. Spouses were legally married and lived apart for at least four days at a time for at least several months.[71] For the most part, these couples were not newlyweds, were relatively affluent, and were executives or professionals. About half the husbands and wives saw each other weekly, about 10 percent from once a week to once a month, and about 40 percent less than once a month. Their decision to live apart rested upon advantages such as the freedom it granted to each spouse's work, and also the ability to work long and uninterrupted hours without building meals, sleep, or recreation around the other.

Wives tended to miss the emotional protection they expected from their husbands and sensed that this was a cost of their gain in independence. They also recognized that responsibilities for household and car repairs were theirs to manage singlehandedly. Husbands expressed loneliness and some guilt for being unable to provide the emotional protection they sensed their wives needed. What became evident to the couple was the difficulty of the transition from the older, traditional role definitions to the newly emerging definitions of marital roles that accompanied two-resident living. A summary of Gross's findings suggested that older couples, those married longer, those among whom at least one spouse had an

71. Harriet Engel Gross, "Dual Career Couples Who Live Apart: Two Types," *Journal of Marriage and the Family* 42 (August 1980): 567–576.

established career, and those who were freed from childrearing responsibilities found their life style less stressful.

For many commuter couples, the telephone becomes a means of regular contact. Time together becomes well-planned and not spent in meaningless socializing with uninterested others. The ease of the separation appears to be related to a high career commitment on the part of both parties, financial resources to meet the added expenses of maintaining two places of residence, phone calls, travel to see one another, shorter distances so they can get together more often, and long established patterns of interaction.

SUMMARY

1. This chapter began by briefly looking at selected linkages between the family and other institutions. Cross-culturally as well as historically, major interchanges and connections have existed at a macro-level between basic systems within all societies. Families are linked to religion, not only at weddings and funerals, but in terms of sex roles, sexual behaviors, and family size. Families are linked to politics in terms of social policy and legislation that ranges from taxation deductions for dependents to providing income for the elderly through social security. Families are linked to educations in terms of learning social norms, skills, and mobility patterns.

2. The key focus of the chapter centers on economics, work, and the world of employment. Conflict theorists in particular view the economic system as the key to understanding inequality within or outside the family. Even household labor is intricately linked to a capitalist type of system that enables men to hold a dominant position over women.

3. A primary role for most married women is that of housewife. Often accorded low status, it appears that it involves long hours, is of high productive value, and produces an inequitable assignment of marital tasks. Yet it is a source of satisfaction and gratification for many women, particularly those adhering to more traditional marital-role expectations.

4. The number and proportion of wives and mothers in the paid labor force is increasing yearly. A majority are employed in the traditional female clerical and service occupations. They work for many of the same reasons men work, namely income, but derive many other rewards from their employment as well: status, prestige, recognition, and feelings of success and achievement. Very few negative effects on children are directly attributable to the employment of the mother.

Similar results exist for marriage. While employment of wives affects husband-wife relationships, there are no more signs of marital discord and stress on such relationships than on those where the wife does not work.

5.   The number of employed husbands and fathers is increasing, but the proportion of men working relative to the total male population is decreasing. There is wide-spread agreement on the expectation that men should be employed. Work appears to be the key source of identity, success or failure, and worth for men.

6.   Househusbandry, unlike housewifery, is rarely a full-time job. Three perspectives on the role of husbands in relation to housework and child care were presented: the traditional, the exploitation, and the changing-roles perspectives. Each exists today, but there is evidence that some changes are occurring, although slowly, in the amount of time and frequency men are investing in these household tasks.

7.   The increasing employment of women combined with the constant high employment of men is resulting in a large number of dual-employed and dual-career marriages. Numerous assumptions about these marriages run counter to certain basic realities. They involve various strains for both sexes and force difficult choices between family and career. For some, commuter marriage is the compromise between giving up the marriage or the career.

KEY TERMS AND TOPICS

DISCUSSION QUESTIONS

1.   Show how the family engages in interchanges or is linked to other systems such as religion, politics, or education. What does each contribute to and receive from the other?

2.   Discuss the statement that differences between churchgoers and non-

churchgoers are more pronounced than differences between denominations or particular religious groups.

3. Why is the assumption made that housework is not work when wives and mothers are asked, "Do you work?" What arguments can be made in linking housework to male-female roles, to the dominance-submission issue, or to a capitalistic type of society?

4. One writer stated that "being a housewife makes women sick." What was meant by this? What does research suggest in this regard?

5. What arguments, if any, exist against the employed wife and/or mother? What social factors are most influential in determining who will work? Explain reasons for the increase in female paid employment.

6. Discuss the consequences of employment for the wife and mother on her marriage, on her children, and on herself. Are there circumstances in which the negative consequences overweigh the positive?

7. Discuss the consequences of the employed husband and father on marriage, on children, and on the husband himself. Are there circumstances in which the negative consequences overweigh the positive?

8. Examine the various perspectives on male roles in relation to housework and child care. Do you feel significant changes are occurring on the part of men in the United States or around the world in this regard?

9. What strains may occur in dual-career marriages that are less likely to occur in one-career marriages? What rewards exist in each type?

10. Discuss the pros and cons of commuter marriages. What type of conditions add to or decrease the strain on the couple relationship?

FURTHER READINGS

Aldous, Joan. *Two Paychecks: Life in Dual-Career Families.* Beverly Hills: Sage Publications, 1982. A compilation of twelve articles on the dual-career family, covering such topics as work schedules, marital and family adjustment, conjugal roles, and housework by husbands.

Bahr, Stephen J., ed. "The Economics of Family Life." *Journal of Family Issues* 3 (June 1982). Entire issue. A special issue that deals with a number of questions affecting families: negative income tax, moonlighting husbands, household expenditure patterns, women's nonmarket labor, and others.

Beer, William R. *Househusbands: Men and Housework in American Families.* New York: Praeger, 1982. A study of fifty-six full- and part-time househusbands, providing an overview of the subject including family background, how househusbands feel about the work, and how it has changed them.

Berk, Sarah Fenstermaker. *The Gender Factory: The Apportionment of Work in American Households.* New York: Plenum Publishing Corp., 1985. This book includes a vast amount of research information and looks at who is doing what, what gets produced, and why.

Borman, Kathryn, Quarm, Daisy, and Gidonse, Sarah, eds. *Women in the Workplace: Effects on Families.* Norwood, N.J.: Ablex Pub. Corp., 1984. Nine writings that examine issues such as the role of government in responding to women's economic roles and the care of children, the inequalities of housework, and a look at the future.

Geerken, Michael, and Gove, Walter. *At Home and at Work: The Family's Allocation of Labor.* Beverly Hills: Sage Publications, 1983. A study of women, work, and family that examines the household and marketplace as a single work continuum that both affects and is affected by the nuclear family.

Hayes, Cheryl D., and Kamerman, Sheila B., eds. *Children of Working Parents: Experiences and Outcomes.* Washington, D.C.: National Academy Press, 1983. A follow-up to the *Families That Work* book by a panel of experts on work, family, and community, and on what is known about the outcomes for children of changes in parental employment.

Hood, Jane C. *Becoming a Two-Job Family.* New York: Praeger, 1983. A role-bargaining study of how sixteen working- and middle-class couples renegotiated the market-work/house-work bargain after the wives returned to the job market.

Kamerman, Sheila B., and Hayes, Cheryl D., eds. *Families That Work: Children in a Changing World.* Washington, D.C.: National Academic Press, 1982. The initial book by a panel on work, family, and community reporting on changes in family work patterns and relationships and the consequences these have for children.

Lewis, Robert A., and Sussman, Marvin B., eds. *Men's Changing Roles in the Family.* New York: The Haworth Press, 1986. A look at men's roles as persons, husbands, and fathers in the context of work, friendship, and caring relationships. Excellent bibliography and filmography listing.

Pleck, Joseph H. *Working Wives, Working Husbands.* Beverly Hills: Sage Publications, 1985. Data from two national studies are used to examine the time working wives and husbands allocate to housework with a major focus on work overload and its consequences.

Reskin, Barbara F., and Hartmann, Heidi I., eds. *Women's Work, Men's Work: Sex Segregation on the Job.* Washington, D.C.: National Academic Paress, 1986. A report by the Committee on Women's Employment and Related Social Issues that reviews evidence showing that employment segregation by sex has grave consequences for women (particularly women), men, families, and society.

Sekaran, Uma. *Dual-Career Families: Contemporary Organizational and Counseling Issues.* San Francisco: Jossey-Bass, 1986. Drawing from numerous research studies, this book presents a portrait of the dual-career family, looks at organizations and their policies, and provides a framework for counseling spouses involved.

Voydanoff, Patricia. *Work and Family Life.* Beverly Hills: Sage Publications, 1987. An examination and review of the current knowledge on the relationship between work and family.

Winfield, Fairlee E. *Commuter Marriage: Living Together, Apart.* New York: Columbia University Press, 1985. A brief, readable description of married couples who maintain separate residences.

II

FAMILY LIFE-STYLES: CULTURAL AND SUBCULTURAL VARIATIONS

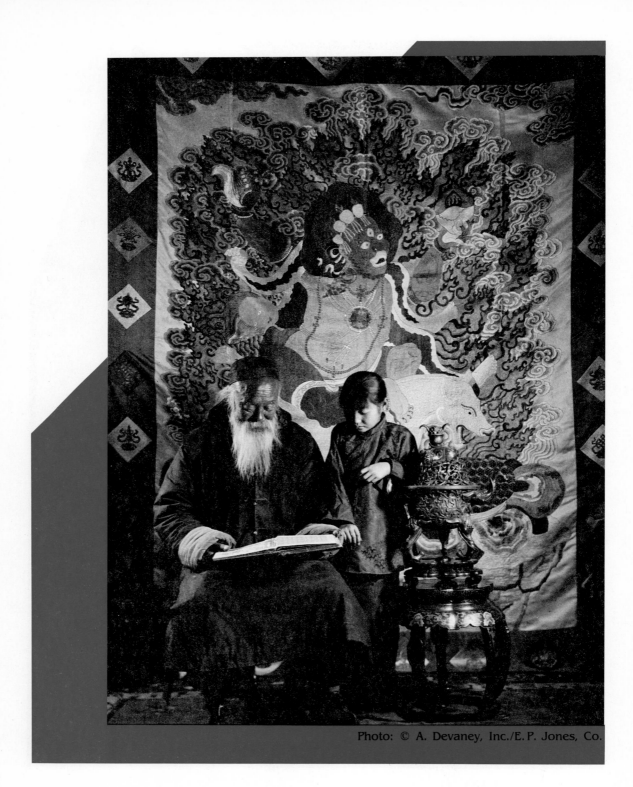

5

Life-Styles among Chinese Families

This chapter examines at least three family systems of the Chinese of mainland China: the traditional system, the system brought about by the Marriage Law of 1950, and the contemporary Chinese family system. Each of these patterns of family organization and life-styles differs considerably from the others when viewed in either an historical or contemporary perspective. While major changes have occurred in the traditional Chinese family, none of the new forms is viewed as simply experimental or as a trial. Each includes ways of life that its members have learned to regard or were instructed to regard as good and important.

Much is to be gained by examining the Chinese family or any family system other than our own. While a fascination may exist in examining the bizarre or sensational, perhaps more fruitful outcomes may be in gaining a perspective on the possible variety and wide range of family patterns and practices. Equally important may be to discover the threads of commonality among family systems: the prevalence of monogamy, the strong ties between mother and child particularly during the child's early years, the lack of unregulated promiscuity, the status affiliation afforded by the family, the significance of the kin networks as a system of support, and the like. An examination of families other than our own may decrease our own ethnocentrisms and provincial orientations; may enable us to consider alternatives to traditional practices; may help us to understand the close linkages between families and the larger social and cultural context within which those families operate; may alert us to question the obvious and destroy false stereotypes; may, in addition to *describing* life-styles and social patterns, help us in *explaining* human behavior and social organization; and may lead to a discovery of more general propositions and principles. The person who "knows it all" may be one who has had no exposure to life-styles other than his or her own. Thus, let's examine selected family systems beyond the North American boundaries with a particular focus on families in mainland China.

THE CHINESE OF MAINLAND CHINA

Mainland China has a land area about equal to that of the United States but a population more than four times as large. It opened its borders and allowed observers to enter the country in the early 1970s. It provides a remarkable case of a massive country with more than one billion inhabitants, accounting for about 22 percent of the world's population, making a transition from a patriarchal family system using ancient techniques of agricultural labor to a more egalitarian system under a developing and modernizing economy.

Until the early part of this century, the Chinese family is said to have withstood extensive change for nearly two thousand years. With the end of the Ch'ing Dynasty in 1911, the culmination of the Chinese Revolution in 1949 and the Marriage Law of 1950, dramatic changes were brought about in the lives of Chinese families of all classes and in the lives of women in particular.

While this brief presentation tends to describe the traditional and emerging Chinese family as a relatively uniform entity, there are many exceptions to the generalized patterns presented. In addition to class and gender differences described in some detail, differences also existed in the traditional family between clans, villages, and regions of the country. For example, women were not expected to work in the fields in the north but the practice was acceptable in the south. Women are described as severely oppressed, yet some women were highly educated and became known for their music, art, or poetry. Suicide is described as a socially acceptable solution to a variety of problems, yet its practice was not considered widespread. Recognizing such limitations, our attention is first directed to the traditional Chinese family.

THE TRADITIONAL CHINESE FAMILY

In a broad sense, the **traditional Chinese family** refers to the type of general system that existed up to approximately 1900 or even 1950. Two important status distinctions that need to be understood in this traditional system centered around class differentiations as witnessed particularly within the clan and the sex differentiation as witnessed in the father-son relationship and the oppression of women.

The clan in traditional China

The clan system of traditional China was extremely important to the maintenance of ancestral linkages and group solidarity. A **clan,** sometimes referred to as the **tsu,** included all persons with a common surname who traced descent from a common ancestor. The *tsu,* operated through a council of elders, often involved several thousand persons, sometimes included entire villages, and was comprised of everyone from the gentry to peasants. The **gentry** were intellectuals who did no manual labor but who received income as landlords or from holding government offices or academic positions. The **peasants** comprised the bulk of the population. They cultivated the land, were generally very poor, and often aspired for the attainment of gentry status. In a country greatly "overpopulated" in the sense that the cultivated land was not sufficient to give the average peasant an adequate livelihood, infant and general mortality rates were high. Widespread conditions of poverty contributed to undernourishment and lack of medical care. Indirect consequences of poverty, particularly for females, included infanticide, abandonment, selling and out-adoption (giving up of children for adoption), nonmarriage, and late marriage.

The significance of this large clan group to the family can be seen in the functions it performed: lending money to its members; helping individual families to pay for extravagant weddings and funerals; establishing schools; exercising judicial authority within the clan; acting as a government agent in collecting taxes; and maintaining ancestral graves and *tsu* property.[1] This "family" network performed most of the functions we generally associate with government: taxes, law enforcement, schools, welfare, etc. As you might guess, the *tsu* came under serious attack when the revolutionary government came into power.

The clan network was maintained in a variety of ways. One widely described practice included **ancestor worship.** An individual existed by virtue of his (not her) ancestors, and they in turn continued to exist through their descendants. In life, parents cared for children and the children, in turn, took on care and shelter of their parents in old age. After death, while the form of care changed, the duty did not. In life, parents were served and respected. In death they were served and worshipped. If in life parents needed food, clothing, shelter, and money, then when dead, the children supplied them with these essentials. The transfer of goods from this world to the next was achieved primarily by burning. Food, however, could be offered directly. In return, the ancestors gave blessings and assistance through their supernatural powers. They, like Greek gods, could bless warfare, hunting, or agriculture or punish with famine, defeat, sickness, or death. Thus, there was a continuing reciprocal relationship between the living and the dead clan members.[2]

---

1. Paul Chao, *Women Under Communism: Family in Russia and China* (Bayside, N. Y.: General Hall, 1977): 123.

2. An excellent treatment of ancestor worship as well as Chinese kinship can be found in Hugh D. R. Baker, *Chinese Family and Kinship* (New York: Columbia University Press, 1979).

Closely related to ancestor worship was the principle of **filial piety,** the duty and subordination of a son to his father. Giving proper deference to parents and other ancestors tended to perpetuate and maintain property within the family, grant universal authority to the male elders, serve as a major source of both formal and informal social control, and perhaps above all, maintain stability and continuity, that is, prevent drastic change.

Gender roles in traditional China

As the principle of filial piety alone would suggest, an extremely favorable position of males relative to females existed in the traditional Chinese system. In traditional Chinese cosmology, the world was composed of two complementary elements: the **yin,** the female, stood for all things dark, weak, and passive; the **yang,** the male, stood for all things bright, strong, and active.[3] Paul Chao says that a wife had to obey three persons: her father before marriage, her husband after marriage, and her son after her husband died.[4]

At all stages of life, recognition of women never approached that of men. Female infanticide was common, especially among the poorer peasants, for girls were both an expense to raise and later would need a dowry to marry. Marriages were not based on love and "free choice" but were arranged by parents through matchmakers. Since persons with the same surname or from the same clan could not marry, marriage usually meant the female would be completely removed from her family, friends, and community. In addition, many women only met their husbands for the first time on their wedding day and then entered a husband-wife relationship that was considered subordinate and supplementary to the parent-son, particularly father-son, relationship.

The wife's chief responsibilities were to bear male children and to aid in the work. Failure of a wife to bear male children could lead to repudiation and the obligation of a husband, among the gentry at least, to take a concubine or additional wives. A woman could have only one husband and if he died, she was not allowed to remarry. A wife or mother had few legal or property rights but could wield some power over other women, particularly her daughters-in-law. The latter peacefully endured harsh treatment until they, in turn, became mothers-in-law.

Not all women tolerated the harsh treatment. Margaret Wolf[5] says that for peasant women, suicide was a socially acceptable solution to a variety of problems that offered no other solution. A young widow, par-

---

3. Katie Curtin, *Women in China* (New York: Pathfinder Press, 1975): 10.
4. Chao, *Women Under Communism,* p. 124.
5. Margaret Wolf, "Women and Suicide in China," in Margaret Wolf and Roxanne Witke, *Women in Chinese Society* (Stanford: Stanford University Press, 1975): 111–141.

ticularly a childless one, could expect little from the future. Even among the gentry women, suicide was considered a proper response for those "whose honor" had been tampered with or who in any way brought dishonor or disgrace to her husband's family.

Another indication of the oppression of women is seen in the traditional practice of binding women's feet. The feet, bound from early childhood, were reduced to three inches in length from toe to heel with the result of permanent crippling. **Footbinding,** extending back to the tenth century, was prevalent among the upper classes not so much as a sign of beauty but to restrain women's movement. Peasant women, heavily involved in agriculture and production, were exempted from this practice. Footbinding, as well as other oppressive practices, came under heavy attack in the Chinese Revolution.

CHANGES IN THE CHINESE FAMILY

It is difficult to distinguish any major single influence behind the dramatic changes that occurred in the Chinese family. Events in Russia, in the Western world, and within China itself combined to force new patterns of existence in all social areas, including the family.

Major changes in the Chinese family were greatly influenced by the Russian Revolution and the Bolshevik party. Between 1917 and 1927, the Soviet government passed laws aimed at revamping marriage and divorce laws, granting free abortions on demand, and giving women legal equality with men. The ideas of Friedrich Engels[6] clearly provided a basis for the formulation of official family policy in both the Soviet Union and mainland China. Of prime significance was his principle that as private property emerges, man's status prevails over that of women. Some of his claims included: family property elevates man's position; monogamy was instituted for women only; the married woman sells her body once and for all into slavery; a woman becomes the slave of a man's lust and a mere instrument for the production of children.[7]

While the Bolshevik Revolution and the teachings of Karl Marx, Engels, and Vladimir Lenin influenced events in China, Judith Stacey notes that the course of the family revolution in China digressed in noteworthy ways from the Russian case.[8] First, the Chinese Communist party's (CCP) attack on traditional family life was never as radical as that of the Bolsheviks.

---

6. Friedrich Engels, *The Origin of the Family, Private Property and the State* (New York: International Publishers, 1942). Originally published by Charles H. Kerr, Chicago, 1902.

7. Ibid., pp. 49–51, 56, 65.

8. Judith Stacey, "Toward a Theory of Family and Revolution: Reflections on the Chinese Case," *Social Problems* 26 (June 1979): 500.

Changes in the marriage laws of 1950 and 1980 have enacted a marriage system in China that focuses on monogamy, freer choice of partners, and more equal rights for men and women. (Photo: © Audry Toppins/Rapho-Photo Researchers)

The CCP was involved in significant efforts to conform the Confucian family, but it never advocated or promoted the "withering away" of the family. On the contrary, the Maoists in China saw family reform as the means to more successful and harmonious marriage and family life. Second, because reform goals were comparatively temperate, they were also implemented with greater effort and effectiveness. Third, the consequences of these different approaches to family transformation were significantly different. For example, in rural China, the Communist Revolution appears to have strengthened a reformed version of traditional peasant family structure, eradicating the worst abuses of Confucian patriarchy yet making it possible to realize traditional values of extended three-generational households and more geographic stability.

Since the system of family property and the concept of traditional family solidarity were incompatible with communist ideals, it became mandatory to make a major effort to change the traditional system. A Chinese Communist party conference in 1922 called for voting rights for all regardless of sex and the abolishment of all legislation restricting women. The low status of women and the traditional maltreatment of wives, daughters-in-law, and domestic maids were branded as vestiges of the evils of the traditional family system. As Chao states, the attempt of the communist government to bring about a fundamental, drastic revolution in the family system was implemented by means of the Marriage Law of 1950, whose effect was to implant in the minds of people, especially youths, new ideas regarding marriage and the family and to dismiss the Confucian virtue and ethics of the family.[9]

The following quotations from Chairman Mao Tse-tung provide a clear picture of his goal, which was the elimination of sexual differences in work and family life.

> Protect interests of the youth, women and children, provide assistance to young student refugees, help the youth and women to organize in order to participate on an equal footing in all work useful to the war effort and to social progress, ensure freedom of marriage and equality as between men and women, and give young people and children a useful education. . . .
> Enable every woman who can work to take her place on the labor front, under the principle of equal pay for equal work.[10]

The Marriage Law of 1950

Ideals such as those of Mao just cited were the basis for the new Marriage Law officially promulgated by the Chinese Communist Central Government at Peking on May 1, 1950. The two major principles of this law are:[11]

1. The abolishment of the feudal marriage system which was based on arbitrary and compulsory arrangements and the supremacy of man over women and which was in disregard of the interests of children. Enacted instead was a new, democratic marriage system based on

---

9. Chao, *Women Under Communism,* p. 126.
10. Ibid., p. 127.
11. These principles are derived from Chao, ibid., Appendix II, pp. 221–226.

free choice of partners, monogamy, equal rights for both sexes, and the protection of the lawful interests of women and children.

2. The prohibition of bigamy, concubinage, child betrothal, interference in the remarriage of widows, and the extraction of money or gifts in connection with marriage.

The law, in defining the rights and duties of husband and wife, gives them equal status in the home. The marital pair are in duty bound to love, respect, assist, and look after each other, live in harmony, and engage in productive work. Both have the right to a free choice of occupation and free participation in social activities. They have equal rights to possess or manage property. Each has the right to use his or her own family name.

The law, in defining the relations between parents and children, prohibits infanticide and provides a duty of parents to rear and educate their children and a duty of children to support and assist their parents. Children born out of wedlock enjoy the same rights as children born in lawful wedlock. With the consent of the mother, the natural father may have custody of the child.

Divorce is granted when husband and wife both desire it. When only one party insists on divorce, the district People's Government may try to effect a reconciliation. If this fails, the county or People's Court makes a decision without delay after assurance that appropriate measures have been taken for the care of children and property. Interestingly, the law prohibits a husband from applying for a divorce when his wife is pregnant, and he may only apply one year after the birth of a child.

No matter which parent gets custody of the children, they remain the children of both parties. Both parents have the duty to support and educate their children. If a divorced woman remarries and her husband is willing to pay the cost of maintaining and educating the children, the father is entitled to have his cost reduced or eliminated.

After divorce, the wife keeps property that belonged to her prior to her marriage. The disposal of other family property is subject to agreement between the husband and wife or, if agreement cannot be reached, it is based on a decision by the People's Court. Debts incurred jointly are paid out of property jointly, but debts incurred separately are paid off by the person responsible.

Changes resulting from the Marriage Law

It may be difficult to imagine a greater contrast in family systems than between the traditional Chinese family system and that prescribed by the Marriage Law of 1950. The traditional system arranged marriage by parents. The communist government took the view that arranged marriage is a bourgeois form that makes the woman a slave to her husband and his family. The traditional system emphasized the subjugation of woman and the lack of freedom in love or marital choice. The communist government encouraged marriage for love and free choice of spouse. To those whose marriages were typed as "feudalistic," old-fashioned, compulsory, arranged, business matches, polygamous marriages, loveless marriages, or marriages in which the in-laws or the husband held supreme authority, the government was ready to give "easy" divorces.

Drastic changes such as these, in China or elsewhere, are likely to be threatening to the stability and authority patterns of families and households. Elisabeth Croll, drawing on case studies from the early 1960s, found that parents felt their controls to be threatened. They frequently perceived the operation of free-choice marriages to be a direct attack on their authority. The initiative of young people in the marriage negotiations was commonly interpreted as a direct expression of disobedience or rebellion against parental authority. She quotes a poem taken from a July 1962 Peking publication:

> With freedom of marriage,
> Gone is the father's prestige;
> Now comes the Marriage Law,
> Mothers are no longer held in awe. [12]

Lucy Jen Huang, writing in this same time period, remarked on the new freedom of mate selection suggesting that, due to the increasing number of women participating in the labor force, most young people now met through working together under various circumstances: in offices, in factories, or on farm cooperatives. [13] Other changes in mate selection patterns included: (1) a shorter dating and courtship period, (2) the exploitation of males by females capitalizing on their new freedom to negotiate, (3) a simple wedding ceremony in contrast to the traditional elaborate and expensive weddings, and (4) early marriage, meaning as soon as the legal age of eighteen for women and twenty for men was reached.

Certain practices of the traditional Chinese family came under sharp attack as incompatible with the newer communist ideology. Thus, the confiscation of lineage property, the subsequent collectivization of family landholdings, the mobilization of women for regular agricultural work, and the expansion of education and other nonfamilial activities for youth in particular clearly had an important impact. [14] Filial piety, footbinding,

---

12. Elisabeth Croll, *The Politics of Marriage in Contemporary China* (Cambridge: Cambridge University Press, 1981): 33.

13. Lucy Jen Huang, "Some Changing Patterns in the Communist Chinese Family," *Marriage and Family Living* 23 (May 1961): 137–139.

14. You may be interested in Part III, pp. 131–297 of William J. Parish and Martin King Whyte, *Village and Family in Contemporary China* (Chicago: The University of Chicago Press, 1978).

and the oppression of women common in the traditional family were defined as serving neither the revolution nor the economic goals of the state. The existence of the *tsu* or clan was supplanted by urban and rural people's communes.

In spite of changes such as those described, a strong stable family system has emerged. Paul Chao says:

> There is no doubt that China has succeeded remarkably in removing the traditional family system to help industrialization and make women participate in production in rural and urban areas. Weakening a good deal the traditional family, the Chinese Communists have not destroyed the family as an economic unit as well as a social unit, but established nurseries and kindergartens where old women are called for taking care of babies while their mothers are free to work outside the home. All Chinese families have joined communes in productive units, they have had a stable base of agriculture and small-scale industry that is self-reliant. The family continues to be an economic unit, though the state has brought home to people the greater importance of the state. [15]

THE CONTEMPORARY CHINESE FAMILY

Whether viewing the family in traditional China, China under the revolution, or contemporary China, mention must again be made to use caution in perceiving the family as a uniform entity, either by region, clan, or class. Drastic changes have taken place in family systems throughout the nation. But the changes have been neither uniform nor complete.

In noting family patterns in rural versus urban areas, Martin King Whyte[16] says that trends since 1949 have not reduced the gap between rural and urban family patterns, but have widened it still further. In Chinese cities, clan organizations were never as important as in villages. The patterns of family to be found in contemporary cities also seem somewhat more varied than is the case in the countryside. Patrilocal residence (in the man's father's house) after marriage is less the general rule in cities than it is in the villages. Urban youths marry later than rural youths. Urban parents play a less central role in choice of mate. Marriage finance is negotiated less between the two families in urban areas. In husband-wife relations, it appears that while women do more of the domestic chores than do men this factor is more pronounced in rural areas. Urban divorce is said to be more evenhanded or even-biased in favor of women.

The continuation of and changes in rural-urban differences are documented in terms of the average number of children ever born per family.

---

15. Chao, *Women Under Communism*, p. 155.
16. Martin King Whyte, "Family Change in China," *Issues and Studies* 16 (July 1979): 48–62.

As recently as 1955, the average number of children was 6.39 in rural areas compared to 5.67 in urban areas. Twenty years later, by 1975, these figures were 3.95 (rural) and 1.78 (urban). In 1981, the comparable figures were 2.91 (rural) and 1.39 (urban).[17] These figures reveal both the long-standing discrepancy in number of children between the cities and country, as well as the powerful impact of the one-child policy (discussed later).

Like rural-urban differences, age, sex, and educational differences exist as well. But, recent information clearly illustrates, that irrespective of age, sex, or education, the traditional family no longer holds attraction to Chinese rulers. This is particularly evident in the new national **Marriage Law of 1980** that went into effect in January 1981. The People's Republic of China promulgated a marriage law that replaced the marriage law of 1950 described earlier. This new law reflects the massive changes that have taken place in the intervening thirty-year period since the end of the Chinese Revolution and the earlier marriage law. As described, the 1950 law was aimed at correcting many of the practices of the previous feudal society: arrangement of marriages by parents, the inequality of husbands and wives, bigamy and concubinage, the extraction of gifts in connection with marriage, and the like. The new law provided a model for the responsibilities of family members to each other and a guide for their relationships.

In presenting China's marriage law of 1980, Rachel Hare-Mustin[18] indicates the concern for the lawful rights and interests of women, children, and the aged, a change in the minimum age for marriage, the encouragement of family planning, and the emphasis on personal independence and equality among family members. Under the new law, a man may choose to become a member of the woman's family and the children may adopt the mother's name. Provisions are made for adoption and the rights of stepchildren. Although still not common, divorce is easier to obtain and granted when mutual affection no longer exists and mediation has failed.

While a new law has been passed, many traditional family patterns continue. For example, a patrilineal and patrilocal pattern still exists in taking the father's surname and in the bride moving to her husband's village. Both sons and daughters are eligible to inherit under the law but married-out daughters are not likely to inherit from either her blood family or her family by marriage.

---

17. Xiangming Chen, "The One-Child Population Policy, Modernization, and the Extended Chinese Family," *Journal of Marriage and the Family* 47 (February 1985): 193–202. *See also* William R. Lavely, "Age Patterns of Chinese Marital Fertility, 1950–1981," *Demography* 23 (August 1986): 419–434.

18. Rachel T. Hare-Mustin, "China's Marriage Law: A Model for Family Responsibilities and Relationships," *Family Process* 21 (December 1982): 477–481. *See also* John W. Engel, "Marriage in the People's Republic of China: Analysis of a New Law," *Journal of Marriage and the Family* 46 (November 1984): 955–961.

Ceremonies for the dead, like those for the living, are much curtailed today. In cities, cremation appears to have become the norm. But in the countryside burial remains common, although the place of burial is often viewed as a waste of land. And since the land no longer belongs to the family, increased difficulty exists in maintaining kin loyalty, totally irrespective of any religious significance. Religious beliefs in general have been labeled as superstitious, and religious practices have been discouraged.

It would appear that while the family in mainland China today is different from the traditional one, many parallels exist. Filial piety is seen in the relationships between parents and children and to the extent to which sons and daughters-in-law care for their parents. John Dixon reports that the problems of urban youth, especially juvenile delinquency, have always been and continue to be a source of concern for the Chinese Communist party. He claims that this problem has been compounded by a weakening of family discipline, by the inevitable delays in job assignments for young people, by a youth policy dominated by the permanent deportation of young people to distant places, and by a continuing confusion as to youth's proper role in Chinese society.[19]

While women in China have made significant progress toward emancipation, aspects of traditional sex-role differentiation still persist.[20] In work outside the home, women still experience discrimination in pay and important jobs. In the political area, only a small proportion of the persons elected to the Central Committee of the Chinese Communist party are women. In household tasks, most responsibilities have remained the woman's. In mate selection, accounts exist of women who retain bourgeois ideas in selecting a husband who will support them. After years of communist rule, sons are valued over daughters, the traditional protective attitude toward girls seems to survive, and most of the important jobs in politics, the educational system, agriculture, factories, and hospitals are held by men.

Marriage in urban areas is no longer an arrangement between families based upon economic and social alliances that take little account of the personal preferences of the young people. Yet, more than three decades after the Marriage Law made free choice legal, the role of the matchmaker

19. John Dixon, "The Welfare of Urban Youth in China 1949–79," *Journal of Adolescence* 4 (March 1981): 1–12. *See also* Thomas B. Gold, "China's Youth: Problems and Programs," *Issues and Studies: A Journal of China Studies and International Affairs* 18 (August 1982): 39–62; and Wei Zhangling, "Chinese Family Problems: Research and Trends," *Journal of Marriage and the Family* 45 (November 1983): 943–948.

20. Rachel T. Hare-Mustin and Sharon E. Hare, "Family Change and the Concept of Motherhood in China," *Journal of Family Issues* 7 (March 1986): 67–82. For an excellent review of the women's movement in China and the role of women in the family and economy *see* Joan M. McCrea, "The Socio-Economic Role of Women in the People's Republic of China," *Women's Studies International Forum* 6 (1983): 57–72.

Only children, better children?

During the third birth planning campaign (1971–79), Chinese authorities intensified efforts to improve maternal and child health care. Officials believed that parents would be more willing to have fewer children if they expected those children to survive and grow up in good health. Antenatal and obstetrical care was upgraded. For example, health workers identified high-risk women during pregnancy so that they could deliver in well-equipped hospitals. Proper techniques for handling the umbilical cords of newborns were introduced, thus eliminating neonatal tetanus. Premature babies were followed up intensively. Child health stations began providing preventive care, such as vaccinations against tetanus, measles, polio, tuberculosis, diphtheria, pertussis, and the like. As a result of these and earlier efforts, infant mortality declined from over 200 deaths per 1,000 births in 1949 to about 50 by the mid-1970s. In some areas health workers now check on infants in the home and on young children at nurseries and kindergartens. They also give mothers advice on hygiene and nutrition.

As average family size becomes smaller, children become more precious and parents become increasingly concerned that their children be "perfect." In keeping with the one-child campaign, begun in 1979, the slogan of the third birth planning campaign has been expanded to *wan xi shao you,* "later, longer, fewer, and better." Even more emphasis has been placed on maternal and child health. For example, in Shifang county, Sichuan province, children from one-child families receive routine monthly health check-ups, take first priority in clinics, and can use special registration desks and pharmacy windows in the health centers. In addition, interest in education, psychological problems, and childhood diseases is increasing.

Recently Chinese officials have also expressed interest in genetic matters such as the frequency of abnormal births and genetic counseling to avoid such births. Marriages are forbidden between close blood relations. Individuals whose children could develop hereditary diseases are persuaded not have any. Reportedly amniocentesis is widely used. In a 1981 speech Vice-Premier Chen Muhua said:

> Eugenics is also an important aspect of planned parenthood. Do not give birth to physically unhealthy or mentally retarded children, for that will

is still crucial. To some extent, the continuing activity of matchmakers bespeaks a society in which members of the opposite sex still find it extremely difficult to meet or interact casually. Powerful cultural restraints, such as the fear of gossip at one's school or workplace, constrain male-female interaction. As stated by Hershatter:

> The restraint required of schoolgirls is particularly pronounced. They are expected to deny any interest in affairs of the heart, and to react with appropriate embarrassment or even disgust when the subject is broached. Some groups of young people, like university students, are discouraged by

put more burdens on the family and society and make the state and nation lose time.

Pamphlets on sex education and contraception that are routinely distributed to newlyweds now contain information on genetics; questions about the physical status of prospective mothers have appeared in surveys of birth planning practices. Genetic research institutes are being set up, and counselors are being trained.

Current birth planning rhetoric often refers to the need to improve "the quality of the population." This phrase is directed at educational opportunities as well as at eugenics and health care. According to a speech by Xu Dixin, President of the Chinese Population Association, at the opening of the Third National Conference of Population Science in 1981, only 0.5 percent of the population is college-educated and only 22 percent reached the middle-school level. There are shortages of teachers, educational materials, and school buildings. Under these circumstances, and in a country where traditionally learning has been highly valued, Chinese families prize the educational rewards of the one-child certificate. According to a Chinese newspaper article, many would rather have a single well-educated child than two or three poorly educated children.

Chinese officials express a growing interest in the psychosocial implications of the one-child family. They are concerned that only children might be spoiled and pampered by their relatives and have behavioral problems in school. The 1979 survey of one-child families in Hefei city, Anhui province, warned that

> most of the single children are well-developed, but, due to favorable economic conditions as well as love and overindulgence on the part of parents and grandparents, some of them tend to be willful, selfish, and even eccentric.

Parents of only children are urged to cooperate with the schools to solve this problem. Also, Chinese officials have recommended that government departments publish pamphlets and hold child psychology classes to teach parents how best to raise their only children.

Source: Pi Chao Chen and Adrienne Kols, "Population and Birth Planning in the People's Republic of China," *Population Reports,* Series J, 25 (January/February 1982): J-602. Information Program, Johns Hopkins University, Baltimore, Maryland 21295.

the school authorities from courting and are forbidden to marry while they are in school.[21]

This context provides a role for friends, relatives, or one of the

---

21. Gail Hershatter, "Making a Friend: Changing Patterns of Courtship in Urban China," *Pacific Affairs* 57 (Summer 1984): 239.

surviving marriage arrangers, usually women, who receive a fee. This, of course, occurs at some risk since their activity is denounced as feudal (traditional) as well as capitalist (money-making). Some individuals work directly through parents in finding a good match and in proposing it to both parties.

One-child family policy

One area of significant changes in the 1970s has been the decrease in the birthrate and an increase in one-child families. As a result of an intensive Chinese family planning program (called *birth planning* by the Chinese), the birthrate was reduced from 34 per 1000 in 1970 to 18 per 1000 in 1979. By 1980, an estimated 51 percent of all births in China were first births and by 1981, 57 percent of couples with only one child had pledged not to have another and had received **one-child certificates.**[22] This certificate entitles a couple to increased income, lower-cost health care, better nursing, larger pensions, and eventually preferential treatment in schooling and employment for their only child. In some areas, a slightly larger monetary bonus is allowed if the couple's first child is a girl than if it is a boy. In rural areas of many provinces, couples today can have two children if their first child is a girl, giving recognition to the preference for a son and providing a practical way of dealing with its implications.[23] Otherwise, couples who have more than two children have penalties imposed on them.

To overcome the traditional desires for a son to provide support in old age, the government has designed additional incentives for the one-daughter family. Today, property can be distributed to daughters as well as sons, daughters are legally responsible for the parents' welfare in the same way as sons, and a daughter as well as a son may take over the father's job when he retires. These practices may not, however, eliminate fear, especially in rural areas, about security in old age. In rural areas the welfare of the aged is closely tied to the economic well-being of the communes and, increasingly, also to the ability of individual households to realize higher incomes. It has been suggested that as the rural population as a whole ages, the changing balance between labor force participants

---

22. Pi Chao Chen and Adrienne Kols, "Population and Birth Planning in the People's Republic of China," *Population Reports*, Series J, 25 (January/February 1982): J-577. *See also* Dudley C. Poston and Mei-Yu Yu, "The One-Child Family: International Patterns and their Implications for the People's Republic of China," *Journal of Biosocial Science* 18 (1986): 305–310; and Dudley L. Poston, Jr., "Patterns of Contraceptive Use in China," *Studies in Family Planning* 17 (September/October 1986): 217–227.

23. Fred Arnold and Liu Zhaoxiang, "Sex Preference, Fertility, and Family Planning in China," *Population and Development Review* 12 (June 1986): 221–246.

The Chinese government, through billboards and other means, emphasizes the multiple benefits derived from effective birth planning and a one-child family. (Photo: © George Gerster/Photo Researchers

in their prime productive ages and the aged may have a serious negative impact on productivity and, by extension, on the well-being of the aged.[24]

It will be of interest to see the extent to which the Marriage Law of 1980 permitting men and women to marry at ages twenty and twenty-two, respectively, will lead to an increase in the birth rate. Younger ages at marriage tend to be associated with early childbirth. The twenty- and twenty-two-year marriage age contrasts sharply with the marriage requirement of the 1970s, which stipulated twenty-three and twenty-five years, respectively, for women and men in the rural areas and twenty-five and twenty-eight years for their urban counterparts. Yuan Tien[25] suggests that the new legal minimum ages at marriage has already resulted in an instant

---

24. Alice Goldstein and Sidney Goldstein, "The Challenge of an Aging Population," *Research on Aging* 8 (June 1986): 179–199.

25. H. Yuan Tien, "Age at Marriage in the People's Republic of China," *The China Quarterly* 93 (March 1983): 90–107.

The United States and China's family planning

In November 1986, James Scheuer (Democrat, N.Y.), a member of the House Science and Technology Committee, led a congressional delegation to China. Their intent was to study China's family planning program and to discuss charges that the government was using coercion and forced abortion to reduce the population growth. Charges of this type, made by conservatives in the Reagan administration, prompted Washington to withdraw financial support from the United Nations Fund for Population Activities.

Representative Scheuer indicated the importance of recognizing that if China had not instituted a comprehensive family planning effort in the 1960s, including the one-child per family policy, unchecked population growth would have pushed the population by the year 2025 to an estimated 5.2 billion. This is a sum far exceeding today's total world population.

As reported in the *New York Times* (January 24, 1987), the delegation during their ten days in China found that the much publicized one-child policy was not what it seemed. The national average is actually 2.2 children per family, with the strongest adherence to the one-child policy occurring in urban areas where housing is in short supply. The policy is far less rigid in the rural areas where 80 percent of the Chinese reside.

Last year nearly 50 percent of the births in China were in families that already had one child. Flexibility is given to the local officials who run the family planning program in the field. "Practical difficulties" such as when a first child is mentally or physically handicapped, is female, has a father who is a disabled serviceman, or when both parents are single children, provide justification for sanctioning second children. Indications are that the policy may be relaxed even further by 1990 or 2000. If the current birth rate of 2.2 children per family can be maintained, China can meet its goal of not exceeding 1.2 billion people by the year 2000.

The United Nations Fund for Population Activities spends $10 million a year in China. This is an amount equal to less than 1 percent of China's own $1 billion annual commitment to birth planning. Their program involves expert assistance in training and introduction of the full array of contraceptive technology. Even so, anti-abortion zealots in the U.S. Government have successfully blocked U.S. contributions to the fund and have irritated relations with China by misapplication of a federal law that prohibits contributions to any agency involved in the management of a coercive abortion or involuntary sterilization program. The fund's role in China's birth-planning program is not a "management" role and as Scheuer suggests, "The administration should set aside its ideological interpretation of the law, administer the law objectively, and follow Congress's legislative intent in an intelligent manner."

upsurge in the numbers of young people getting married with estimates of at least 14 million in 1981, more than twice the number of 1980. And Tien indicates as well that by the time of their first wedding anniversary more than 85 percent of the women had conceived.

One evaluation of future problems resulting from the one-child family policy includes, among other things, (1) experiencing an aged population which (2) will place increasing pressure on social welfare and (3) present a labor shortage in the twenty-first century. An unexpected result of this one-child-per-couple policy is (4) the revival of female infanticide across mainland China. This seems to be particularly true in rural areas which in 1980, 1981, and 1982 had a consistently higher sex ratio than the urban areas.[26]

The one-child family policy has both direct and latent effects in the physical formation of the extended family, the manner in which family members relate to one another, and the content and features of inter-generational ties. Xiangming Chen states that first, the thrust of the one-child policy's impact has begun to weaken the extended family network by greatly trimming the average family size. The absence of siblings; the subsequent loss of in-laws, uncles, and aunts; and the thinning out of extended consanguineous relationships remove a large number of branches from the previously complex family tree.[27]

Second, Chen goes on to state that the immediate and long-term effect of reduced family size is reflected in expected changes in the power relationships among the generations. Taking care of one child usually requires less time and effort than two or more and this further lessens married women's traditional role of child rearing and related household chores. It reinforces the fact that the great majority of married Chinese women work and, thus, may facilitate the formulation of an equal marital relationship between the husband and the wife by giving the latter more leisure time and bargaining power.

Divorce

Have family size and gender role changes led to an upsurge in divorce? Apparently not. Divorce does not appear to be widespread. While permitted, it requires mutual consent and assurance that appropriate measures have been taken for care of any children and property. One study in Kwangtung

---

26. Tin-yu Ting and Hsin-mu Chen, "Involuntary Family Size: An Evaluation of Mainland China's One-Child Family Policy," *Issues and Studies: A Journal of China Studies and International Affairs* 22 (February 1986): 45–63.

27. Xiangming Chen, "The One-Child Population Policy, Modernization, and the Extended Chinese Family," *Journal of Marriage and the Family* 47 (February 1985): 193–202.

Province suggested *no* cases of divorce in that locality in recent years.[28] Most marriages were stable, most individuals expected to stay married for life, and both the local kinship structure and government policy favored such stability.

It appears that the statements of Marx and Engels regarding family property, monogamy, marital love, married women selling their bodies into slavery, and the like are not reaching fruition in mainland China. The communist government is making major efforts to renovate housing, maintain stability in monogamous marital relationships, and provide for the care and protection of children by responsible parents. For all intents and purposes, important roles are assigned to the family system, and it is not heading toward decay or abolishment. There seems to be a melting of the traditional and the revolutionary in many aspects of Chinese family life. As Mao himself said, "Let the past serve the present."

SUMMARY

1. This chapter on family life-style in mainland China examines, in one sense, at least three family systems. The traditional Chinese family that existed for several thousand years stands in sharp contrast to the family proposed in the Marriage Law of 1950 which, in turn, seems to contrast with the contemporary Chinese family.

2. The traditional Chinese family withstood extensive change for a period covering two thousand years. It was characterized by sharp class and gender distinctions. The gentry, who were well-educated and owned the land, stood in contrast to the peasants who cultivated it. Similarly, the male, highly valued from birth onward, stood in contrast to the female whose purpose was to serve, honor, and bear male children for the men.

3. The Marriage Law of 1950 was the official promulgation by the Chinese Communist party (CCP) to abolish the supremacy of men over women, the arrangement of marriages, female infanticide, footbinding, and the like. In turn, it created a family system that gave men and women equality in jobs or in the home, permitted widows to remarry, allowed women to own and hold property, legitimized illegitimacy, and sanctioned divorce. The general goal of Mao was to protect the interests of women, youths, and children, who under the traditional system had had few legal rights or privileges.

---

28. Parish and Whyte, *Village and Family in Contemporary China*, p. 192.

4. The Chinese family system today appears to be a blend of the traditional and that proposed by the law. The clan has been replaced by the rural and urban commune; the oppression of women, youths, and children has been vastly decreased; the worship of ancestors has declined; women have entered the labor force in great numbers; daughters-in-law are no longer estranged newcomers to the family unit; and suicide and divorce are infrequent.

5. Some recent changes in policy and practice are noted in the new Marriage Law of 1980 that went into effect in 1981. The old Marriage Law of 1950 was aimed at correcting many of the practices of the previous feudal society. The new marriage law provides a model for the responsibilities of family members to each other and a guide for their relationships.

6. A specific area of dramatic change in the contemporary Chinese family is evident in the one-child family program. Nearly half of all births in China are first births and the majority of these couples received a one-child certificate indicating a pledge to have no more. Incentives are given to the one-child family, with some additional incentives if that child is a female.

7. Certain family and class distinctions continue to exist. Sex-role differentiation remains in the home as well as in economic, political, or educational spheres; parents and matchmakers still play a major if not direct role in the arrangement of marriages; and sexual norms remain restrictive. The contemporary Chinese family is alive and well, vastly different from the traditional family in structure and function, yet not in a state of decay or withering.

8. The next chapter brings us to the United States, where black families are examined. This family system stands in sharp contrast to any of the Chinese families examined.

KEY TERMS AND TOPICS

DISCUSSION QUESTIONS

1. What value exists in studying family life-styles other than one's own?

2. How is it possible that the traditional Chinese family system withstood extensive change for several thousand years? Is it possible for any family system to resist change in the twentieth century? How?

3. Describe the significance of the clan or the *tsu* to the individual member of a Chinese family. How did it influence marriage, children, employment, and the like?

4. Why were women so oppressed in the traditional Chinese family? Include in your response some justification for practices such as female infanticide, footbinding, arranged marriage, and the prohibition against widows remarrying.

5. Contrast the efforts to transform the family by the Bolsheviks in Russia and the Maoists in China.

6. Attempt to evaluate the degree of success of the Marriage Law of 1950 based on what we know about the contemporary Chinese family.

7. Discuss some of the implications of a one-child policy in terms of population control, family interaction, preference for a male child, and effect on the only child.

8. How is the decrease in age at marriage likely to affect Chinese families, population control, or gender and work roles?

9. What similarities exist between the contemporary Chinese family and that of other systems such as the contemporary kibbutz family? Include a discussion of communes, sex roles, child rearing, divorce, and religion in your response.

10. Based on urban-industrial changes, population growth, trends in mainland China, or general family trends in a world-wide perspective, what thirty-year projections can you make in regard to kinship or clan networks, sex or gender roles, frequency of marriage and/or divorce, and family size in mainland China?

FURTHER READINGS

Baker, Hugh D. R. *Chinese Family and Kinship.* New York: Columbia University Press, 1979. An extensive analysis of kinship, primarily in traditional China, but with a final chapter on kinship in the twentieth century.

Chen, Pi Chao, and Kols, Adrienne. ``Population and Birth Planning in the People's Republic of China.'' *Population Reports* Series J, 25 (January/February 1982): J-578-618. A comprehensive overview of population in China: its distribution, changes, methods of birth planning, current policies, program results, and demographic projections.

Coale, Ansley J. *Rapid Population Change in China, 1952–1982.* Washington, D.C.: National Academy Press, 1984. A report on China over a thirty-year period by the Committee on Population and Demography, with Chapter 3 on marriage and Chapter 4 on childbearing in China since 1950.

Croll, Elisabeth. *The Politics of Marriage in Contemporary China.* Cambridge: Cambridge University Press, 1981. An anthropological approach to the study of change in marriage resulting from the Marriage Law of 1950. Most emphasis is placed on the early 1960s rather than on recent years.

Goode, William J. *World Revolution and Family Patterns.* New York: The Free Press, 1963. This book deals with world changes in family patterns and has chapters on the West, Arabic Islam, sub-Saharan Africa, India, China, and Japan.

Hanley, Susan B., and Wolf, Arthur P. Eds. *Family and Population in East Asian History.* Stanford: Stanford University Press, 1985. A collection of thirteen papers on various aspects of family and fertility in East Asia, including five from China.

Lewis, Myrna. "Aging in the People's Republic of China," *International Journal of Aging and Human Development* 15 (1982): 79–105. This article provides a profile of the Chinese elderly, an historical perspective, retirement, daily life, health care, and death, with scattered comments on family involvement in these events.

Osmond, Marie Withers. "Cross-Societal Family Research: A Macrosociological Overview of the Seventies," *Journal of Marriage and the Family* 42 (November 1980): 995–1016. A decade review article that examines methodological and substantive issues in cross-societal family research.

Parish, William L., and Whyte, Martin King. *Village and Family in Contemporary China.* Chicago: University of Chicago Press, 1978. A study describing the economic and political structures of contemporary rural Kwangtung as they effect change in village and family life.

Salaff, Janet W. *Working Daughters of Hong Kong: Filial Piety or Power in the Family.* Cambridge: Cambridge University Press, 1981. An intense look at ten working daughters to see what happens to families when traditional rural families are confronted with the dense population and industrialization of Hong Kong.

Song, Jian, Tuan, Chi-Hsien, and Yu, Jing-Yuan. *Population Control in China: Theory and Application.* New York: Praeger Publishers, 1985. Written primarily for demographers, the authors focus on population growth trends and apply population control theories to China's planned birth program.

Photo: © Jeffry W. Myers/Freelance Photographer's Guild

6

Life-Styles among Black Families

Anyone who has any interest in the area of race relations or, more specifically, in the black-white issue in U.S. society, cannot afford to overlook the role of the family in this total, complex situation. In our society it is the family, and more specifically the conjugal family, that serves as the focal point for the accumulation of material resources by individuals; for the purchase, distribution, and consumption of those resources; for the development and formulation of personality; and for the formation of identity.

Black families are basically more similar than dissimilar to the dominant family forms that exist in the larger society. For blacks or whites, social status is positively related to marital stability, children receive their basic identity and status subscription within the family context, and parents ascribe to the basic achievement and mobility values that exist within the larger society. On the other hand, there are, of course, clear variations by social class, ethnicity, and religion. In addition, unique historical experiences, such as slavery, legal and social segregation, and economic discrimination, have resulted in differences in life-styles and value patterns for blacks. These factors will be discussed in the sections that follow.

MAJOR TRANSITIONS OF THE BLACK FAMILY

There are various ways in which black families are unique and different from white families in U.S. society. Many of these differences can be traced to selected historical factors unique to black families and then various changes that have taken or are taking place can be noted. These changes are identified as major social transitions[1] that include:

1. from Africa to the United States,
2. from slavery to emancipation,

---

1. These transitions are updated and modified from Andrew Billingsley and Amy Tate Billingsley, "Illegitimacy and Patterns of Negro Family Life," in Robert N. Roberts, *The Unwed Mother* (New York: Harper, 1966): 133–149.

3.   from rural and southern areas to urban and northern ones,
4.   from negative to positive social status,
5.   from negative to positive self-image.

From Africa to the United States

Three factors in the transition from Africa to the United States have profound relevance. First is color. It is this factor that is the most influential characteristic of black people in society, and it is color that defines them as such. Blacks who can "pass" as whites are confronted with a different set of interaction patterns than are blacks who cannot "pass."

Second is cultural discontinuity. The system of behavior that was socially learned and shared by members of the African society was not applicable to the social conditions to be faced in the United States. It is perhaps difficult, if not impossible, to find any other group who came or was brought to the United States who faced such a disruption of cultural patterns. Yet many African cultural patterns were maintained.

Third is slavery. Again, unlike almost any others in the United States, the African did not choose to come. With few exceptions, Africans came here only as slaves. The impact of slavery on family patterns and norms at the time of slavery, as well as its significance for understanding black families today, has become an issue of controversy. For decades, most sociologists accepted almost uncritically the interpretations of black family history given by E. Franklin Frazier, Stanley M. Elkins, and W. E. B. DuBois. They emphasized the instability of marriages and family ties, the disruption of husband-wife and kin networks, the extent of matrifocality, and the lack of authority of fathers.[2]

A number of studies have raised serious questions about the conclusions of these earlier writers. Herbert Gutman vigorously attacks the "misdirected emphasis" on marital and family disruption by showing that most households (70 to 90 percent) have had a husband or father present and have had two or more members of a nuclear family unit.[3] The matrifocal family has been infrequent; unmarried black women under thirty have lived with their parents, middle-aged black women have lived with their husbands and children, elderly black women have lived with their husbands

2. E. Franklin Frazier, *The Negro Family in the United States*, rev. ed. (New York: Macmillan, 1957); Stanley M. Elkins, *Slavery: A Problem in American Institutional and Intellectual Life* (Chicago: University of Chicago Press, 1959); and W. E. B. DuBois, *The Philadelphia Negro* (Philadelphia: University of Pennsylvania Press, 1899).

3. Herbert G. Gutman, *The Black Family in Slavery and Freedom, 1750–1925* (New York: Pantheon, 1976), Chapters 1 and 10 in particular.

Slave descendant fights race listing

NEW ORLEANS, Sept. 14 (AP)—A Louisiana woman who is a descendant of an 18th-century black slave has asked a court to declare her white. The woman's birth certificate says she is black.

Susie Guillory Phipps, 48 years old, of Sulphur also wants the courts to declare unconstitutional a 1970 state law that labels anyone with one thirty-second "Negro blood" as black.

"I am white," Mrs. Phipps told Commissioner Anthony Vesich of Orleans Parish Civil District Court on Monday. "I am all white. I was raised as a white child. I went to white school. I married white twice."

Mrs. Phipps, the great-great-great-great-granddaughter of a black slave and a white planter, said Louisiana should no longer classify her as a Negro on the basis of her 18th century ancestry.

Mrs. Phipps is one of six members of a family in the Lake Charles area who are suing to have the State Bureau of Vital Records change the racial classification on their birth certificates from black to white.

Mrs. Phipps, a light-skinned woman with Caucasian features and straight black hair, described herself as the darkest member of her family.

She said other relatives were reluctant to testify for fear that the state would change the birth certificates of their blond, blue-eyed children from white to black.

She said she was unaware of the black ancestry registered on her birth certificate until five years ago, when she applied for a copy of it to obtain a passport and a clerk told her that "on the book, I was a colored girl."

or their married children, and subfamilies headed by single, widowed, or abandoned mothers have been incorporated into large households. Frank Furstenberg and others caution as well against presenting a monolithic interpretation of slavery as having only a destructive impact on the black family.[4] They argue that the slave family was considerably stronger than has been believed. It was not patterned by instability, chaos, and disorder but rather by two-parent households. While a somewhat higher proportion of black families have been headed by a female than has been true for other ethnic groups, reasons other than slavery conditions explain it.

4. Frank F. Furstenberg, Jr., Theodore Hershberg, and John Modell, "The Origins of the Female-headed Black Family: The Impact of the Urban Experience," *Journal of Interdisciplinary History* 6 (Autumn 1975): 211–233; Herman R. Lantz, "Family and Kin as Revealed in the Narratives of Ex-slaves," *Social Science Quarterly* 60 (March 1980): 667–675; and Mike Meacham, "The Myth of the Black Family Matriarchy Under Slavery," *Mid-American Review of Sociology* 8 (1983): 23–41.

Her attorney, Brian Begue, argued that the practice of assigning racial designation on birth certificates was unconstitutional, and that the standard of one thirty-second was an inaccurate test of racial makeup. By state calculations, Mrs. Phipps and her siblings have three thirty-seconds black ancestry, he said.

Testifying for the family was Dr. Munro Edmonson, a professor of anthropology at Tulane University, who cited research indicating that the average American white person had 5 percent traceable Negro genes and the average American black had 25 percent traceable white genes.

The attorney for the state, Jack Westholz, said the birth certificate had been filled out by the woman's parents, who apparently listed their children's race as black because that was what the parents' own birth certificates read.

Stanley G. Brown, state registrar for vital records, testified that hospitals had instructions to record a child's race based on a statement of its parents, unless there was a "glaring inconsistency."

Mr. Westholz attacked Mrs. Phipps's assertion today with depositions from two relatives who said they considered themselves black and had raised their children as such. Quoting from a deposition given last year by Victor Guillory, an uncle of Mrs. Phipps, Mr. Westholz said, "We were all raised that way. I knew nothing else."

Mr. Westholz also quoted from a deposition by one of Mrs. Phipps's aunts by marriage, who said she had told her children to think of themselves as black, despite their light skin.

Source: The New York Times, September 15, 1982, p. 10. Copyright © 1982/1983 by The New York Times Company. Reprinted by permission.

In the first place, the great majority of black families were couple-headed. Second, ex-slaves were more likely to reside in couple-headed households. Third, when property holding among the different ethnic groups was held constant, variations in family composition largely disappeared. Finally, we were able to show that economic status had a powerful effect on the structure of the black family because blacks suffered extremely high mortality and females with children faced difficulties in remarrying.[5]

Perhaps there is some accuracy to both the traditional view that emphasized instability and family disruption and the more contemporary view that emphasizes high degrees of stability and couple-headed households. Data on family residential patterns for blacks in a southern farming

5. Furstenberg et al., "The Origins of the Female-headed Black Family," p. 232.

county in 1870 and 1885 reveal some interesting differences.[6] The 1870 data, drawn from the first census after the Civil War, show high percentages of black families in nonfamily or nonnuclear family households. This lends support to traditional beliefs. In 1885, following fifteen years of accommodation to the reconstruction period, data indicate that the two-parent family was the norm. The major changes in the two-parent black family structure over this time may have been brought about by an ability to carry out what had long been an ideal norm as well as a need for an economic partnership and a community defense against hostility.

Supporters on both sides of this controversy are likely to agree that slavery in the United States had a major impact. In the United States, slavery assumed inferiority. The slave had no legal rights, marriages were not licensed, many female slaves were sexually used and abused, and miscegenation,[7] which violated the social norms of the times, was frequent.

From slavery to emancipation

In 1863, a proclamation issued by Abraham Lincoln freed the slaves in all territories still at war with the Union. At last the slave was free from servitude, bondage, and restraint—at least in theory. For thousands of Afro-Americans, however, emancipation brought with it a freedom to die of starvation and illness. In many ways this transition presented a crisis for many black families.

Billingsley and Billingsley state that three patterns of family life emerged from this crisis.[8] First, the majority of blacks remained on the plantations as tenants of their former owners with little or no wages for their labor. Second, families that had been allowed to establish common residence worked common plots of ground for extra food for the family. Families where the man was an artisan, preacher, or house servant made the transition with the least difficulty. Third, and perhaps most disruptive of family life, in situations where only loose and informal ties held a man and woman together, those ties were severed during the crisis of emancipation. This occurred despite the presence of children. In search of work, many men joined large bands of other homeless men who wandered around the countryside. This factor entrenched some females as the major productive and dependable family element.

---

6. Barbara Finlay Agresti, "The First Decades of Freedom: Black Families in a Southern County, 1870 and 1885," *Journal of Marriage and the Family* 40 (November 1978): 697–706.

7. *Miscegenation* refers to marriage and interbreeding between members of different races, especially in the United States between whites and blacks.

8. Andrew Billingsley and Amy Tate Billingsley, "Illegitimacy and Patterns of Negro Family Life," p. 139.

Emancipation did offer some advantages for the black family. As stated by Andrew Billingsley:

> Although family members could be whipped, run out of town, or murdered, they could not be sold away from their families. Marriages were legalized and recorded. The hard work of farming, even sharecropping, required all possible hands—husband, wife, and children. . . . Some "screens of opportunity" did enable large numbers of families to survive, some to achieve amazingly stable and viable forms of family life, and a few to achieve a high degree of social distinction.[9]

From rural and southern areas to urban and northern ones

In 1984 there were 28.5 million blacks in the United States comprising 12.1 percent of the 236.7 million total population. Geographically, they were overrepresented in the South (where they comprised 18.6 percent of the total population) and underrepresented in the other three regions (9.9 percent in the Northeast; 9.1 percent in the North Central; and 5.2 percent in the West). The movement of blacks from rural areas and from the South has in general followed that of the rest of the population; however, very few blacks have migrated to western states, with the exception of California. In 1930 about four-fifths of all blacks lived in the South compared to slightly more than half (53 percent) in 1980. Likewise a change has occurred in the transition to metropolitan areas. In 1960, 64.8 percent of all blacks lived in SMSA's (standard metropolitan statistical areas). By 1970 this figure increased dramatically to 79.1 percent and by 1980 had increased slightly more to 81.1 percent. Fifty-eight percent of blacks were in central cities, a drop from the 60.0 percent of blacks who lived in central cities in 1970.[10]

The significance of these migration patterns largely evolves around their selectivity: not all ages or complete families were caught up in the movement to urban areas or to the north, since the industrial pool preferred young men. This had a tremendous impact both on the community left behind and on the community into which blacks migrated. It affected family life by disrupting the nuclear family and by geographically separating extended-family ties; it affected the educational-occupational structure of both communities; and it had an effect on other factors such as housing,

---

9. Andrew Billingsley, *Black Families in White America* (Englewood Cliffs, N.J.: Prentice-Hall, 1968): 71.

10. U.S. Bureau of the Census, *Current Population Reports,* Series P-20, no. 37, and Series P-20, no. 374, "Social and Economic Characteristics of the Population in Metropolitan and Nonmetropolitan Areas" and "Population Profile of the United States: 1981" (Washington, D.C.: U.S. Government Printing Office, 1971 and 1982), Table 2, p. 20, and Table 3–6, p. 23.

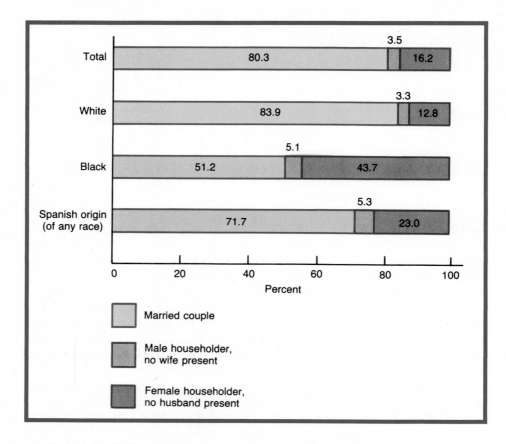

FIGURE 6–1
Family type as a percent of all family households by race and Spanish origin:
1985. (*Source*: U.S. Bureau of the Census, *Current Population Reports*, Series
P-20, No. 411, "Household and Family Characteristics: March 1984"
[Washington D.C.: U.S. Government Printing Office, 1986]. Figure from Table
D, p. 5.)

ghetto life, and patterns of discriminatory behavior. Black males, in particular, brought with them aspirations for economic improvement that
they expected to have fulfilled but which, for many, were not. Unlike the
middle-class mobility patterns due to a job offer involving relocation, the
lower-class male was more likely to migrate because of current unemployment or an irregular work schedule.

On the other hand, the consequences of the shift from rural to urban
and northern areas that has occurred and is taking place today are not
all negative. Many stabilizing factors and positive aspects have resulted.
Although the city is often portrayed as a center of evil in our society, in

a very real sense it has been the center of hope. As stated by E. E. LeMasters and John DeFrain:

> With all of its problems for parents, the urban community actually offers many advantages: better school systems, with special classes for the handicapped child; better social welfare services, both private and public; better medical and public health facilities; more tolerance for racial and religious minorities; and greater chance for vertical social mobility.[11]

Occupational and earnings gains as well appear to result from residence in the North. While men who migrate to the North as adults have lower returns than northern natives, the occupational and earnings achievements of black men who migrated to the North as children closely resemble those of men who are natives of the North.[12]

The geographical transitions have been occurring for the last sixty years or more. In some ways these transitions produce a generation gap among blacks. On the one hand we have a sizable number of transplanted parents who were reared in rural Mississippi or Alabama in a highly segregated society, and who would be considered blue-collar class or else are living below the poverty level. On the other hand we find an increasing number of children of these parents living in large urban centers; they are integrated into the school system, have aspirations and hopes for a college education, and have occupational and earnings achievements considerably higher than exist in southern states and equivalent to persons born in the North.

From negative to positive social status

Some would argue that the single most important variable to understanding the black family today is social class. Many family forms are more likely to be the consequence of class rather than either skin color or race. Major differences seem to exist within the black family if a distinction is made between those living below the poverty level and the "middle class" of the subculture. It is the black middle class that is seldom publicized. This is a stratum in which most of the marriages are stable, two-parent units where husbands have a high school education or better and occupy positions in business, government, or our educational systems. These families are basically more similar than dissimilar to the dominant white-family form that exists in our society.

---

11. E. E. LeMasters and John DeFrain, *Parents in Contemporary America: A Sympathetic View* (Homewood, Ill.: The Dorsey Press, 4th ed., 1983): 224.

12. Dennis P. Hogan and Michele Pazul, "The Occupational and Earnings Returns to Education Among Black Men in the North," *American Journal of Sociology* 87 (January 1982): 905–920.

This shift from a negative to a positive social status includes a shift in the approach to and the interpretation of black families. The traditional and old model of the black family projected a negative stereotype, viewing the family as being one monolithic lower-class entity—as a social problem in itself, as a pathology of illegitimacy and broken homes, as centering around the female as a dominating matriarch, and as including males with low self-esteem.[13] The emerging or new model challenges these negative views, stressing the black family as a variety of types at different social-class levels, rejecting the social problem and pathology orientation as an expression of middle-class ethnocentrism, viewing the family as having strengths such as egalitarianism, self-reliant males, strong family ties, and high achievement orientations, and, finally, being worthy of study as forms of social organization in its own right.

The old model of the black family was vividly portrayed twenty years ago by Daniel Patrick Moynihan in his now classic **Moynihan Report.**[14] It was his contention that there had been a serious weakening in the black social structure and that there was a trend away from family stability in lower socioeconomic levels. He concluded in his report that the structure of family life in the black community constitutes a "tangle of pathology" and that at the heart of the deterioration of the fabric of black society is the deterioration of the family. The major block to equality centers around the matrifocal family. The implication is that young blacks grow and are reared in a mother-centered family without the helpful influence of both parents. This, in turn, Moynihan argued, was a major reason why blacks were making only limited gains during the prosperous 1960s.

Billingsley, Frazier, and others disagreed directly and strongly with Moynihan's central tenet.[15] They contended that the black family is not a cause of the "tangle of pathology" but rather that it is an absorbing, adaptive, and amazingly resilient mechanism for the socialization of its children and the civilization of its society.[16]

More recent data indicate that in terms of delinquency, aspirations, educational expectations, perceptions of the education desired by the parents, self-conceptions, and notions of appropriate gender-role behavior of adults, the empirical evidence does not provide adequate support for

---

13. *See* Leonard Lieberman, "The Emerging Model of the Black Family," *International Journal of Sociology of the Family* 3 (March 1973): 10–22; also note Warren D. Ten Houten, "The Black Family: Myth and Reality," *Psychiatry* 33 (May 1970): 145–173.

14. Daniel P. Moynihan, *The Negro Family: The Case for National Action* (Washington, D.C.: U.S. Government Printing Office, U.S. Department of Labor, 1965).

15. Billingsley, *Black Families in White America;* Frazier, *The Negro Family in the United States;* and Sally Bould, "Black and White Families: Factors Affecting the Wife's Contribution to the Family Income Where the Husband's Income Is Low to Moderate," *The Sociological Quarterly* 18 (Autumn 1977): 536–547.

16. Billingsley, *Black Families in White America,* p. 33.

A glimpse at West Point cadets reminds us of how an increasing number of black males and females are entering positions of leadership in the military, business, the professions, and government. (Photo: © T.C. Fitzgerald/The Picture Cube)

the conclusions of the Moynihan Report.[17] In fact, Alan Berger and William Simon suggest that even in the lower-class broken family, there is no indication that the black family is dramatically different from the white family in the way it treats its children and the results it produces. Billingsley further supports this opinion in a point made later in this chapter: the majority of blacks live in two-parent nuclear families with the man gainfully employed and working every day but who is often unable to earn enough to pull his family out of poverty.

Let's examine if specific shifts have occurred from a negative to a positive social status as portrayed primarily by census data in regard to employment, income, and education. Note particularly (1) the tremendous gains made in recent years in the United States for both black males and

17. Alan S. Berger and William Simon, "Black Families and the Moynihan Report: A Research Evaluation," *Social Problems* 22 (December 1974): 145–161; and Roberta H. Jackson, "Some Aspirations of Lower Class Black Mothers," *Journal of Comparative Family Studies* 6 (Autumn 1975): 171–181.

TABLE 6–1
Unemployment rates by sex and age, 1960, 1970, and 1985 (annual averages)

	Black			White		
	1960	1970	1985	1960	1970	1985
Adult males	9.6	5.6	15.3	4.2	3.2	6.1
Adult females	8.3	6.9	14.9	4.6	4.4	6.4
Teenagers*	24.4	29.1	40.1	13.4	13.5	15.7

* Teenagers include persons sixteen to nineteen years old.
Source: U.S. Bureau of the Census, *Current Population Reports,* Series P-23, no. 42, "The Social and Economic Status of the Black Population in the United States" (Washington, D.C.: U.S. Government Printing Office, 1972), Table 37, p. 53; and U.S. Bureau of the Census, *Statistical Abstract of the United States, 1987,* 107th ed. (Washington, D.C.: U.S. Government Printing Office, 1987), no. 642, p. 378.

females and (2) the major disparities that still exist between blacks and whites.

Employment   An increasing number of blacks are entering positions of leadership in the professions, in business, and in government. This is overshadowed, however, by the number and rate of blacks who are not employed. For many years the unemployment rate among blacks was double the rate of the nation as a whole. That is, if the national unemployment rate was 5 percent, one could assume a 10 percent rate for blacks. In 1985, the annual average unemployment rate was 6.1 for white males and 15.3 for black males. The unemployment rate for black females was slightly lower than that for black males (*see* Table 6–1) but they joined black males in having unemployment rates more than twice that of white males or females. Evidence does not support the widespread belief that a double negative status (i.e., being both black and female) provides an occupational advantage, although black middle-class wives may have higher employment rates than white middle-class wives because of economic need.[18] Most black females who are employed are overrepresented in service, clerical, and blue-collar jobs that generally are low status and earn a low income. The 1985 unemployment rate for black teenagers was most dramatic: 40.1 percent. Employment opportunities for less-educated, unskilled, young blacks are not sufficient to meet the employment and income needs of this segment of our population during

18. Bart Landry and Margaret Platt Jendrek, "The Employment of Wives in Middle-class Black Families," *Journal of Marriage and the Family* 40 (November 1978): 787–797.

TABLE 6–2

Median income in current dollars of white and black families, 1950–1985

Year	White ($)	Black ($)	Difference ($)	Ratio: black to white
1985	29,152	16,786	12,366	58
1984	27,686	15,432	12,254	56
1983	25,837	14,561	11,276	56
1982	24,603	13,598	11,005	55
1981	23,517	13,266	10,251	56
1980	21,904	12,674	9,230	58
1975	14,268	8,779	5,489	62
1970	10,236	6,279	3,957	61
1965	7,251	3,993	3,258	55
1960	5,835	3,230	2,605	55

Source: Adapted from U.S. Bureau of the Census, *Statistical Abstract of the United States: 1987,* 107th ed. (Washington, D.C.: U.S. Government Printing Office, 1987), no. 732, p. 436.

times of economic prosperity, and this group also suffers disproportionately during times of economic recession.

Income   There is no doubt that the black population made substantial social status gains over the past thirty years. These gains seem to exist whether one looks at occupation, education, or income. Yet, irrespective of absolute gains, the paradox is that blacks remain significantly deprived when compared to whites at the same status level. The economic gap that separates the whites and blacks in the United States is growing, despite all the efforts of recent years.

According to census data (*see* Table 6–2), the dollar gap between blacks and whites actually grew in the last quarter century. In 1960, the median white family income was $5,835; the median black family income was $3,230—a dollar gap of $2,605. By 1975, after widely heralded social reforms, white income soared to $14,268 and black income rose to $8,779, with a constantly increasing dollar difference reaching $5,489. As of 1985, the median income for white families was $29,152 and for black families $16,786, with a dollar difference of over $12,000.

The ratio of black to white income was fifty-eight in 1985. However, ratios mean very little when dollar amounts are insufficient to maintain families. In 1985, the poverty threshold for a nonfarm family of four was $10,989.[19] This figure is only about fifty-eight hundred dollars less than

19. U.S. Bureau of the Census, *Statistical Abstract of the United States, 1987,* 107th ed. (Washington, D.C.: U.S. Government Printing Office, 1987), p. 416.

the median family income for blacks in 1985 and includes 31.3 percent of the total black population. The seriousness of the implications to family life is illuminated by at least one study, which found the husband's income to be the most important predictor of marital disruption in black families.[20] In general, an established sociological finding positively relates socio-economic status to marital stability.

Education Transition from a negative to a more positive social status can also be seen by examining the percentages of the black population age twenty-five years and over who have completed at least a high school education. In 1985, 58.4 percent of black males and 60.8 percent of black females had completed four years of high school or more. This is in contrast to the comparable 1970 percentages of 30.2 and 32.6 for black males and females respectively.[21]

These changes appear quite dramatic for the time span involved. The figures may be equally dramatic in understanding mate selection and marriage for black men and women. If more black females than males are completing high school, note the implications this has for black women finding a mate with an education or income equal to or better than their own. Note the potential for increased strain and conflict for marriages that exist in a society that stresses a male provider role. Addressing these issues directly, Paul Secord and Kenneth Ghee suggest that strains in black marriages would be somewhat relieved if black men had better employment prospects, more occupational mobility, and higher educational attainment relative to black women.[22] The educated black woman who still expects her husband to be the primary provider is likely to be dissatisfied with his performance. The educated black woman who is more likely than the less educated to expect her husband to be more sensitive, emotionally nurturant, and companionable may have difficulty in finding the black husband who can fulfill her expectations. Factors such as these help us understand the high incidence of divorce and separation among black couples.

Apparently, dissatisfaction with spouse is not only a female-wife issue. One study of blacks in the United States, in testing the relationship between marital status and life satisfaction, found that for men, the married were significantly less satisfied with life than were the divorced, separated, or

---

20. Robert L. Hampton, "Husband's Characteristics and Marital Disruption in Black Families," *The Sociological Quarterly* 20 (Spring 1979): 255–266.

21. U.S. Bureau of the Census, *Statistical Abstract of the United States: 1987*, no. 198, p. 121. The comparable figures for white males and white females were 76.0 and 75.1 respectively in 1985 and 54.0 and 55.0 in 1970.

22. Paul F. Secord and Kenneth Ghee, "Implications of the Black Marriage Market for Marital Conflict," *Journal of Family Issues* 7 (March 1986): 21–30.

widowed. For women, widows showed the highest mean level of satisfaction, followed by the divorced and married. The separated and single had the lowest level of satisfaction. The author suggests that the difficulties many black men have in providing adequately for their families often lead to difficulties in spousal relationships and satisfaction with their own lives. They also attribute their findings to points made earlier: the disparities in education—with women marrying less-educated men—and the sex-ratio issue—where black women have a more restricted field of eligible partners than do white women.[23]

Frazier, writing in 1957, seemed convinced that conformity to more traditional family norms and stable marriage patterns would result as the educational and economic position of blacks improved.[24] It was his conviction that a black middle class would arise made up of salaried professionals and white-collar workers, and family stability would evolve in relation to economic improvement. Generally, as economic conditions improve, the incidence of family disorganization decreases, family life becomes increasingly stable, there are higher aspirations for children, and there is a greater conformity to the sexual mores of society. For black families, however, there is the added dimension of male-female disparities in education and in eligible marital partners.

From negative to positive self-image

A basic tenet of social psychology states that we develop our selves, our identities, and our perceptions of our worth in interaction with others. As the black is the last to be hired and the first to be fired, as he or she interacts in a white world, and as the black child interacts in a society that encourages feelings of inferiority and degrades self-worth, it might be expected that a self-fulfilling prophecy would be operative: the growing black child believing and acting out the societal messages bestowed upon her or him. The prevailing view of blacks over the years has been that they suffer from negative self-esteem manifested in feelings of self-hate and a lack of self-actualizing behavior.

Numerous studies call into question that prevailing view. Although it cannot be denied that racism and discrimination abound and take their toll on blacks, empirical evidence from at least fifteen studies does not support the view of negative self-evaluation.[25] From studies he reviewed

---

23. Richard E. Ball and Lynn Robbins, "Marital Status and Life Satisfaction Among Black Americans," *Journal of Marriage and the Family* 48 (May 1986): 389–394.

24. Frazier, *The Negro Family in the United States*, p. 333.

25. *See* for example Janet G. Hunt and Larry L. Hunt, "Racial Inequality and Self-image: Identity Maintenance as Identity Confusion," *Sociology and Social Research* 61 (July

Children, irrespective of color or ethnicity, enjoy imitating adult behaviors.
(Photo: © Jeffry W. Myers/Freelance Photographer's Guild)

comparing blacks and whites on measures of self-esteem, Guterman[26] concluded that the level of self-esteem among blacks does not differ significantly from that of whites or else is actually higher than that of whites. A Detroit study[27] on the quality of life reported higher levels of self-evaluation among blacks than among whites. Specifically, 75 percent of blacks, compared to 61 percent of the whites, were completely or highly satisfied with themselves.

A follow-up on that study was done to see whether levels of self-evaluation vary among blacks based on demographic characteristics or

---

1977): 539–559; Anthony R. Harris and Randall Stokes, "Race, Self-evaluation and the Protestant Ethic," *Social Problems* 26 (October 1978): 71–85; and Castellano B. Turner and Barbara F. Turner, "Gender, Race, Social Class, and Self-Evaluations Among College Students," *The Sociological Quarterly* 23 (Autumn 1982): 491–507.

26. Stanley S. Guterman, ed., *Black Psyche: Modal Personality Patterns of Black Americans* (Berkeley, Calif.: Glendessary Press, 1972): 87.

27. *A Study of the Quality of Life: Metropolitan Detroit* (Ann Arbor: Institute for Social Research, University of Michigan, 1975).

Does slavery live today?

In the *Journal of Black Studies* (December 1986) Joe Feagin's article titled "Slavery Unwilling to Die: The Background of Black Oppression in the 1980s" appeared. In this article, Feagin argues that the semislave system remains firmly in place in regard to employment, housing, and educational segregation as well as in terms of violence, ideological racism, color coding, and resistance to intermarriage. And, he proclaims, the likelihood of future change without militant black action is close to zero.

Why is this so? Basically, it resides in the ideological position of white U.S. citizens who vigorously oppose any significant government program, whether it be affirmative action in jobs or prosecution of homeowners and realtors who discriminate. Whites tolerate a few black employees at work, a few black students at school, and a few black families in the larger residential neighborhood but most whites do not accept more substantial desegregation. Survey after survey shows whites do not favor federal government intervention to see that blacks get fair treatment in jobs or housing or in getting rid of segregation in schools.

In brief, most white U.S. citizens believe that the tremendous imbalance of power, reflected in a system of semislavery, should not be eradicated by race-conscious action. And Feagin (p. 199) concludes that "this does not bode well for the future of blacks in the United States."

Source: Joe Feagin, "Slavery Unwilling to Die: The Background of Black Oppression in the 1980s," *Journal of Black Studies* (December 1986): 199.

satisfaction with internal and external factors in their lives.[28] It was found that older blacks tended to appraise themselves more positively than did younger blacks. Blacks with less education generally had a higher self-evaluation than those with more education. Those with higher evaluations of themselves felt they had more control over life plans, were more satisfied with their job, income, and life as a whole. High self-evaluation was strongly associated with satisfaction with family life, particularly for women. This finding further strengthened the notion that the family plays an important role in shaping blacks' attitudes about themselves. The family for blacks has been one of the primary sources of support and a major reference group for boosting self-pride.

How is it possible that blacks have positive concepts of themselves in spite of oppressive social and economic conditions? Foster and Perry[29] provide several explanations. One is that over the past few decades, black organizations and social interactions have served to bolster self-pride,

---

28. Madison Foster and Lorraine R. Perry, "Self-valuation Among Blacks," *Social Work* 27 (January 1982): 60–66.

29. Ibid., p. 65.

What does it feel like to be white?

I wonder what it feels like to be white. I have no idea, but I am, on occasion, curious.

I've never, on the other hand, found myself wondering what it feels like to be male, although I have wanted in times of stress to have bulging biceps so I could knock an adversary flat on his back.

But white is something else again. I wonder if the collective white experience, if indeed there is such a thing, can be probed, explored, and subjected to the same kinds of generalizations that routinely are applied to the collective black experience?

I doubt it. Still, I can't resist the temptation to ask, in a general way, some questions that come from my experience.

I wonder if little white girls played with little black dolls whose hair had to be oiled and straightened into submission? Of course, that's an unfair question. Little black girls didn't play with those dolls either. We played with pink or brown cloth-bodied babies whose hair could be brushed and teased into big fat curls.

Kinky hair, mahogany skin, thick lips, and a wide nose were not things you paid money for. No. You paid money to straighten your hair, to lighten your skin, to buy a lip liner to make your lips look smaller. I started thinking about all of this after I was given a new face by an extremely nice makeup artist who brushed dark powder down the sides of my nose to narrow it and then outlined my lips in brown to give them less substance and more form.

Somehow I never thought my lips would become a metaphor for life.

The usual questions

In any event, I wonder what it would feel like to walk into the Free Press one day and be a member of the majority population?

I wonder what it would feel like to walk into a General Motors management meeting or to go into a restaurant in Traverse City and see your skin tone repeated over and over again throughout the room?

I wonder what it feels like to walk into an office or store filled with white shoppers and not feel out of step, if only for a second?

identification with blackness, and appreciation of black culture and life. Second, historical black writing and poetry "damn as a falsehood" the concept of inferiority. Third, the family, church, fraternal groups, friendships, and general social relationships provide positive support systems that influence blacks' self-evaluation. Hoelter[30] supports these views by suggesting that blacks get more than whites out of interpersonal rewards

---

30. John W. Hoelter, "Race Differences in Selective Credulity and Self-Esteem," *The Sociological Quarterly* 23 (Autumn 1982): 527–537.

I wonder what it feels like never to have been told: "I never think of you as black."

I wonder what it feels like to go through an entire week at work without being asked:

My opinion on a black political or social situation.
The name of a black expert on a particular subject.
If a story is racially significant.

I wonder what it feels like to go on vacation, get a deep tan, walk up to a black person and put your tanned arm next to that black arm and say: "See how dark I am? We're almost the same color."

I wonder what it feels like to have someone ask what nationality your parents are?

Are there answers?

I wonder what it feels like to be able to go to almost any movie at any time and see people who look like you up on the screen—to see loving, laughing, fighting, heroic, or cowardly people, each one reflecting an aspect of humanity. I've often thought that the controversy over "The Color Purple" really stemmed from the fact that blacks are woefully underrepresented in movies. Thus, every "black" movie becomes a statement about black life and is given greater significance than it deserves.

I wonder what it feels like to set up a lunch date with a stranger at a fancy restaurant in some upscale suburb and have to give a detailed description about what you'll be wearing and the color of your hair?

Perhaps there are no answers to these questions. Perhaps the inherent generalizations make them meaningless.

Still, I do wonder . . . about the questions and about the responses I'll get from those folks, black and white, who think they know the answers.

Source: Susan Watson, *Detroit Free Press,* June 18, 1986, p. 3A.

because those significant others perceived to give the most positive evaluations have a greater impact on the self-esteem of blacks compared to the impact of similar evaluations on whites. His study concludes that the black community, or at least the segment that "counts," serves to enhance rather than destroy its members' self-images.

All of these factors suggest that the black community and family teach their children to act, feel, and think positively and to be proud. These are factors that may explain the finding, surprising to many, that suicide rates in the United States are considerably lower for blacks than for whites. For example, in 1983, the suicide rate per 100,000 population was 10.5 for black males and 19.3 for white males. The rate was 2.1 for black females and 5.6 for white females.[31] Clearly, not all blacks have high self-concepts and self-esteem, but significant progress has taken place in the transition from a negative to a positive self-image among blacks.

PATTERNS OF BLACK FAMILY LIFE

At least three distinct patterns of black family life have emerged from the social transitions described. These can be referred to as the **matricentric female-headed pattern,** the **middle-class two-parent pattern,** and the **patriarchal affluent pattern.** Although these refer primarily to the nuclear family unit, they do not exclude other relatives. Not uncommon among black nuclear families is the presence of nephews, aunts, grandparents, cousins, and other adult relatives. These extended kin, plus unrelated kin living in as roomers, boarders, or guests, exert a major influence on the life-style of black families. At this point, you, the reader, need to recognize (1) the wide range of family structures beyond the matriarchal, egalitarian, and patriarchal family patterns and (2) the extreme resiliency of the black family institution. Neither the mother-centered nor any other type of family is necessarily "falling apart" but is capable of major adaptations to the historical and contemporary social conditions confronting it.

The matricentric female-headed family pattern

The matricentric female-headed family pattern, the least stable of the three patterns, is one in which the female is the dominant member. The female may be a mother or grandmother who resides with children, usually without the continuous presence of a husband or father. These one-parent family units raise one-half of all black children. Early motherhood, lack of education, and insufficient income lead to the characterization of this family pattern as "multiproblemed." Here is where we are most likely to find families below the level of poverty.

There were 8.9 million blacks and 22.9 million whites below the poverty level in 1985.[32] Low-income blacks comprise 31 percent of the

---

31. U.S. Bureau of the Census, *Statistical Abstract of the United States, 1987,* 107th ed. (Washington, D.C.: U.S. Government Printing Office, 1987), no. 115, p. 76.

32. Families are classified as being above or below the poverty level by using a poverty index based on a sliding scale of money income that is adjusted for such factors as family size, composition, and farm-nonfarm residence. The poverty threshold for a family of four was $10,989 in 1985 (see Chapter 7 and Table 7–2).

black population, nearly three times the comparable proportion of low-income whites (11.4 percent) and higher than the 29 percent of those of Spanish origin. Families with female households without a husband comprise a sizable proportion of low-income families. In 1985, 50.5 percent of all black families, 53.1 percent of Spanish-origin families, and 27.4 percent of all white families below the census-defined poverty level were female households with no husbands present.[33] It is a debated issue whether the family structure of the female householder with no husband present explains the family's poverty or whether the poverty explains the family's structure. It is likely that each contributes to the other and that governmental policies contribute to both.

The matricentric pattern may take several forms. One is the family in which there is no father. In this situation, the child is given the surname of the mother who lives in her own house or the house of her parents with her own children. Second is the family that has a temporary father or a series of temporary fathers. The father may appear when he has a job and live with his wife and then leave when the income ceases. A third subtype of the matricentric pattern is one in which the father may be present but the mother is the dominant authority figure. These families include those having fathers who cannot support a family and who cannot exercise the authority of parenthood.

Robert Staples indicates that the proliferative growth of female-headed households is probably the most significant change in the black family in the last thirty years.[34] One of the most visible reasons for the dramatic increase in households headed by women has been a corresponding increase in out-of-wedlock births. While the non-marital sexual activity rate of black and white women is converging, the black female initiates intercourse at earlier ages, is more likely to be engaged in unprotected intercourse, and is less likely to marry or have an abortion if she becomes pregnant.

The likelihood of becoming pregnant is greatest among black teenagers who are from high-risk environments. A study conducted by the research division of the Chicago Urban League showed that considered in combination, teenagers who are from high-risk environments (lower class, resident in a ghetto neighborhood, non-intact family, five or more siblings, a sister who became a teenage mother, and lax parental control of dating) have rates of pregnancy 8.3 times higher than girls from low-risk environments (upper class, resident in a good neighborhood, intact family,

33. U.S. Bureau of the Census, *Current Population Reports*, Series P-60, no. 154, "Money Income and Poverty Status of Families and Persons in the United States: 1985" (Washington, D.C.: U.S. Government Printing Office, 1986), Table 15, p. 21.

34. Robert Staples, "Changes in Black Family Structure: The Conflict Between Family Ideology and Structure Conditions," *Journal of Marriage and the Family* 47 (November 1985): 1005–1013.

four or fewer siblings, no sister who became a teenage mother, and strict parental control of dating).[35]

A less visible reason than out-of-wedlock births for the increase in female-headed households is related to the shortage of men relative to the number of women during the marriageable years. The decline in the supply of black males, rather than factors such as an economic motivation brought on by welfare dependency,[36] appears to be the driving force behind the increase in black female-headed families.

According to the U.S. Bureau of the Census, in 1984 there were 1.6 million more black women than black men over the age of fourteen. Since there is an excess number of black males at birth, the shortage of males over age fourteen is attributed both to their higher infant mortality rate and a considerably greater mortality rate of young black males through homicide, accidents, suicide, drug overdose, and war casualty. To these numbers can be added black males who are divorced or separated due to military service, unemployment, or institutional confinement—such as prison or mental hospitals—and those with serious alcohol or drug problems. Factors such as these magnify the serious disadvantages of black women in choosing from the eligible and desirable males in the marriage pool or in staying married.

Female-headed households are not the predominant family pattern among black families in the United States nor are they exclusive to black families. In 1985, of the 6.8 million black families in the United States, 2.96 million or 43.7 percent were female-headed households with no husband present (see Table 6–3). This compares to 12.8 percent of white families and 23.0 percent of Spanish-origin families. Of those women heading households among black families with children under the age of eighteen, about one-fourth were married with the husband absent, only 7 percent were widowed, one-fourth were divorced, and 44 percent were single.

An examination of Table 6–3 will show how these figures compare with white and Spanish-origin families for the same year. In 1985, women heading white female-headed households that included children under the age of eighteen were considerably more likely to be widowed or divorced and much less likely to be single. Women heading Spanish-origin families were most likely to be married but separated from their husbands. Note from the same table that the average number of children under the age

---

35. Dennis P. Hogan and Evelyn N. Kitagawa, "The Impact of Social Status, Family Structure, and Neighborhood on the Fertility of Black Adolescence," *American Journal of Sociology* 90 (January 1985): 825–855.

36. William A. Darity, Jr. and Samuel L. Myers, Jr., "Does Welfare Dependency Cause Female Headship? The Case of the Black Family," *Journal of Marriage and the Family* 46 (November 1984): 765–779.

TABLE 6–3
Selected characteristics of white, black, and Spanish-origin family households, 1985

Characteristic	White	Black	Spanish-origin
Total number of family house- holds in the United States	54,400,000	6,778,000	3,939,000
Female householder, no husband present	6,941,000	2,964,000	905,000
Percentage of Total	12.8%	43.7%	23.0%
Average number of children un- der eighteen per family			
Total	0.93	1.37	1.56
Female householder	1.07	1.63	1.70
Male householder	0.71	1.03	0.82
Marital status of female householder families with children under eighteen, by percent			
Married, husband absent	23.2%	24.2%	39.5%
Separated	(20.5)	(22.1)	(36.2)
Other	(2.7)	(2.1)	(3.3)
Widowed	9.4	6.9	7.9
Divorced	55.6	25.1	29.3
Single (never married)	11.8	43.8	23.3
Total	100.0%	100.0%	100.0%

Source: U.S. Bureau of the Census, Current Population Reports, Series P-20, no. 411, "House-hold and Family Characteristics: March 1985" (Washington, D.C.: U.S. Government Printing Office, 1986), Tables D, 2 and 11, pp. 5, 17–20, and 67–70.

of eighteen per family is greater for female-headed household families with no husband present than for all other families irrespective of race. Male-headed householders, however, have fewer children per household than either female-headed householders or all other households irrespective of race.

In our society it has been assumed that adults cannot maintain family stability unless they are married and living with their spouse. Perhaps stability indicates factors other than the presence of two parents. An increase in income, a greater availability of housing, and the maintaining of kin ties with persons other than a spouse may permit more families to maintain a degree of stability equal to that of families with both parents present.

The middle-class two-parent family pattern

Family stability, life satisfaction, and personal happiness are not dependent on a two-parent family pattern, but marriage itself appears to contribute to the life satisfaction of black adults. Generally, married black persons tend to be happier than unmarried black persons. National survey data from more than 2200 black persons found this relationship to hold regardless of gender, age, education, or structure of the respondents' family of orientation (reared by both parents, one, or neither).[37]

The two-parent family is the type of family structure most commonly found among blacks in our society. This is one in which the husband and wife are living together in their first marriage. Here we have two parents in distinctive but complementary and flexible roles. The husband is more likely to have stable employment and at least an operational level of education. Families of this type are more likely to be middle-class or higher-income working-class families[38] but are not limited to these classes. For example, one study of black families in a predominantly lower-class urban area focused on intact—that is, husband-wife—families and found little, if any, evidence that husband-fathers renounced their positions in the family or of reversed husband-wife roles where the female assumed the traditional male responsibilities. The results overwhelmingly indicated that in these intact lower-class families, the husbands were the main providers for their families, were positive role models for their children, participated actively in child rearing, and were active participants with their spouses in the decision-making process.[39]

As of March 1985, 68.7 percent of all ever-married black men (age 15 and over) were living with their wives. The other 31.3 percent included 12.8 percent who were married without a wife present, 6.2 percent who were widowed, and 12.3 percent who were divorced. Of all ever-married black women (age 15 and over), 49.5 percent were living with their husbands. The other 50.5 percent included 21 percent who were widowed, 13.4 percent who were married with the husband absent, and 16.1 percent who were divorced. Comparable data on the marital status of ever-married white persons and those of Spanish origin can be see in Table 6–4.

---

37. Ann Creighton Zollar and J. Sherwood Williams, "The Contribution of Marriage to the Life Satisfaction of Black Adults," *Journal of Marriage and the Family* 49 (February 1987): 87–92.

38. *See* Noel A. Cazenave, "Middle-Income Black Fathers: An Analysis of the Provider Role," *The Family Coordinator* 28 (October 1979): 583–593.

39. Bernice McNair Barnett, Ira E. Robinson, Wilfred C. Bailey, and John M. Smith, Jr., "The Status of Husband/Father as Perceived by the Wife/Mother in the Intact Lower Class Urban Black Family," *Sociological Spectrum* 4 (1984): 421–441; and Ira E. Robinson, Wilfred C. Bailey, and John M. Smith, Jr., "Self-Perception of the Husband/Father in the Intact Lower Class Black Family," *Phylon* 46 (1985): 136–147.

TABLE 6–4
Marital status of ever-married persons fifteen years old and over by race and sex, March 1985

Marital status	White		Black		Spanish-origin	
	Male	Female	Male	Female	Male	Female
Married, spouse present	85.3%	71.4%	68.7%	49.5%	79.8%	70.1%
Married, spouse absent	3.1	3.6	12.8	13.4	9.1	10.1
Separated	(2.0)	(2.8)	(10.8)	(12.0)	(4.2)	(8.4)
Other	(1.1)	(0.8)	(2.0)	(1.4)	(4.9)	(1.7)
Widowed	3.2	14.9	6.2	21.0	3.4	9.7
Divorced	8.4	10.1	12.3	16.1	7.7	10.1
Total	100.0%	100.0%	100.0%	100.0%	100.0%	100.0%

Source: Percentages figured from data presented in U.S. Bureau of the Census, *Current Population Reports,* Series P-20, no. 410, "Marital Status and Living Arrangements: March 1985" (Washington, D.C.: U.S. Government Printing Office, 1986), Table 1, pp. 18–19.

This majority pattern destroys the myth that the majority of black men are separated or divorced from their wives. That nearly one-fifth of ever-married black women are widowed adds significantly to the percentage of black women with no husband present. Clearly the majority of adults are currently married and live in husband-wife families with their spouses.[40]

Despite being a dominant pattern, the two-parent intact family has been relatively neglected by most social scientists. In contrast, several excellent studies have been done on black families characterized by the divorced or absent husband.[41] Perhaps the two-parent family pattern has been ignored because these families are relatively stable, conforming, achieving, and cause few problems to anyone.

One study of stable black families in Indianapolis was done by Scanzoni. These families included husbands and wives who had lived together for five years or more.[42] Using black interviewers, data were gathered

---

40. In 1985, while most black adults were married, a very high percentage of both black males (43.4 percent) and females (36.4 percent) age fifteen and over were never-married singles. The comparable figure for white males was 28.2 percent, for white females 20.7 percent, for Spanish-origin males 36.6 percent, and Spanish-origin females 26.0 percent. U.S. Bureau of the Census, *Current Population Reports* Series P-20, no. 410, "Marital Status and Living Arrangements, March 1985 (Washington, D.C.: U.S. Government Printing Office, 1986), Table 1: 18–19.

41. For instance, *see* Elliot Liebow, *Tally's Corner* (Boston: Little, Brown, 1967); and Lee Rainwater, "Crucible of Identity, The Negro Lower-Class Family," *Daedalus* 95 (1966): 172–216.

42. John H. Scanzoni, *The Black Family in Modern Society* (Boston: Allyn and Bacon, 1971).

from four hundred households in an attempt to describe and analyze the urban black family system above the under class or lower class. A central hypothesis of Scanzoni's study was that an inextricable link exists between economic resources and black family structure.

The inescapable conclusion of Scanzoni is that:

> The black family in America, as much as the white family, is shaped by its relationship to the economic-opportunity structure. This relationship is mediated primarily via the occupation of the male head-of-household. Where he is not present, as is often the case in the lower class, this has certain negative consequences for the family. And where he is present, the degree of his integration with the opportunity system influences most, if not all, aspects of husband-wife and parent-child interaction.
>
> That there is a "black community" and a "white community" reflects in part differential access to the economic rewards of the total society. That there are certain "black family patterns" which may differ somewhat from "white family patterns" reflects this same differential economic access.[43]

More recent support for the influence of economic resources on both family structure and satisfaction with family life comes from a study of southern black husbands. Husbands in families with greater per capita financial resources tended to be more satisfied with life in their families.[44] The authors suggest that reciprocity is involved, with higher incomes leading to greater satisfaction, but also greater satisfaction lending itself to cohesion and stability, and thence, higher incomes.

It appears that families in which both husband and wife are present are those from which black leaders emerge. A three generation analysis of the social origin of contemporary blacks from the United States revealed that most of these eminent blacks were reared in stable families, with 67.8 percent living with both parents (15.3 percent lived with mother, 4.1 percent with father, 5.6 percent with a relative, and 4.9 percent with someone else).[45] Interestingly, these eminent blacks were also predominantly the descendants of families characterized by antebellum (before the Civil War) freedom, lighter skin, urban residence, and higher educational and occupational attainment. It is in the two-parent family pattern that the father plays a more dominant role and the children develop a greater identification with him. The role of the father as playmate, teacher, and disciplinarian to his children is less likely to take place in the matricentric form of family organization when he is present and impossible when he is not.

---

43. Ibid., pp. 309–310.

44. Richard E. Ball and Lynn Robbins, "Black Husbands' Satisfaction with Their Family Life," *Journal of Marriage and the Family* 48 (November 1986): 849–855.

45. Elizabeth I. Mullins and Paul Sites, "The Origins of Contemporary Eminent Black Americans: A Three-Generation Analysis of Social Origin," *American Sociological Review* 49 (October 1984): 672–685.

Once again we return to the point made at the beginning of this chapter. Families are not isolated groups existing independently from the society of which they are a part. The success or failure of a two-parent pattern or a matricentric pattern relates very closely to the opportunity structure which is provided to them.

The patriarchal affluent family pattern

The patriarchal affluent family pattern can perhaps more accurately be illustrated by using Willie's concept of "affluent conformists." [46] These are two-parent families heavily represented among professional and higher income blacks. Both spouses are likely to have college or graduate degrees and the husband-father is likely to take the primary responsibility for most of the major decisions. Among these families, the problems so often associated with blue-collar or poverty-level families are almost nonexistent. Endogenous marriages are highly encouraged. Much of a given generation's wealth is inherited from a previous generation. These wealthier blacks in large part tend to isolate themselves from the majority of black families and many college graduates from this background do not engage actively in black organizations.

A patriarchal family pattern exists among many middle- and lower-class families as well. In interviews with both the husbands and wives of forty-three black working-class families in Ohio, it was found that both sexes perceived the power structure of the family to reside with the husband.[47] Specifically, only 2 percent saw the wife as dominant, 25 percent saw equality, and 73 percent saw the husband as dominant. These results differ profoundly from the popular stereotype of the matriarchal black family. Another study of black married couples from an urban North Carolina area demonstrated that the husband-led power pattern was associated, in general, with the highest level of marital quality.[48] Egalitarian and wife-led couples reported similar, lower levels of marital quality. In this research report of black couples, the husband-dominant family was suggested as the goal to be obtained rather than egalitarianism. Husband-wife equality in power, it was suggested, could be construed to be the effect of the financial and social discrimination that prevented black husbands from clearly surpassing their wives in income and education and thus assuming undisputed leadership of their families.

---

46. Charles V. Willie, *A New Look at Black Families*, 2nd ed. (Bayside, New York: General Hall, 1981): 58.

47. Jerry M. Lewis and Paul Sites, "Decision Making in Black Working Class Families," unpublished paper sent to the author.

48. Bernadette Gray-Little, "Marital Quality and Power Processes Among Black Couples," *Journal of Marriage and the Family* 44 (August 1982): 633–646.

For our purposes, perhaps the most noteworthy features of this particular pattern of family life are its stability and strict patterns of socialization and social control defined according to the values shared by the dominant group in our society. As suggested previously, if economic factors are held constant, black families, particularly at the higher socioeconomic levels, differ little from white families. One difficulty with this economically based perspective, however, is that it ignores the influence of social-cultural forces and transitions, such as those described earlier in the chapter, in the lives of U.S. blacks. And black families in the United States cannot be understood without acknowledging the importance of race and culture.

SUMMARY

1. The black family in U.S. society, like any family system, is not a uniform entity, nor is it isolated and separate from other social systems within the community and society. The basic structural patterns, the interpersonal processes, and the personal value positions can only be understood within the context in which they exist.

2. In U.S. society, black families have been and still are affected by numerous major social transitions. The transition from Africa to the United States is relevant to understanding factors such as the influences of skin, color, slavery, and cultural discontinuity. The transition from slavery to emancipation had a major influence on the emergence of multiple family forms, occupational patterns, kin relationships, and the forms of families. The transition from rural and southern to urban and northern areas, while presenting the opportunities for better wages, schools, and health services, also tended to disrupt kin ties and community linkages.

3. The transition from negative to positive social status is in the process of occurring; although major gains have taken place in income and education, the lag behind the white community is major and significant.

4. The transition to a positive self-concept and self-valuation appears to be one area where blacks in the United States excel. Several recent studies suggest a higher level of self-esteem and self-valuation among blacks than among whites. The family and other primary and secondary groups provide positive support systems that influence blacks' evaluation.

5. From these major social transitions, distinct patterns of black family life have emerged. The *matricentric* female-household family, while not the most prevalent, is the family type where multi-problems are most frequently found. In these families a father may not exist, may

be present only temporarily, or may be present but unable to exercise authority. Those families with a female householder and no husband present are most likely to be low-income, have a greater number of children than white families or other black families, and appear to face the greatest difficulties in meeting the daily demands of existence.

6. The *middle-class* two-parent family, the most prevalent type, is one in which both husband and wife are living together and the spouses have distinctive and complementary roles. These families, often ignored in the social science literature, are relatively stable, conforming, and achieving. They desire to participate in the economic and social benefits of the larger society and tend to share the general values and goals of the larger society.

7. The *patriarchal* affluent family pattern, although less common than the other forms, is heavily represented among blacks in the higher socioeconomic levels of society. Here the father is present, makes most of the major decisions, and is dominant in most respects. Noteworthy features of this pattern are its stability and strict patterns of socialization and social control.

8. This chapter and the one preceding it focused on the family patterns and life-styles of two major groups: the Chinese of mainland China and the blacks of the United States. Significant differences in structure and interaction patterns seem apparent in historical and contemporary settings. A further continuity of thought exists as we turn our attention to the next chapter to variations in family life-styles among families that are identified with particular social classes.

KEY TERMS AND TOPICS

DISCUSSION QUESTIONS

1. Is there a unique Afro-American family today?
2. What black family characteristics of today can be traced directly to an African

heritage? How does an understanding of slavery contribute to an understanding of patterns of black family life today?

3. Compare black and white families on dimensions such as family size, educational level, rural-urban residence, and marriage rates. How can differences be explained? What differences exist if one controls for social class?

4. From the use of state census data, contrast the demographic characteristics by race of your county or state with national data. Explain similarities or differences that may exist.

5. Examine the "Moynihan Report." What data are presented that are subject to interpretations other than those given? Why did this report become an object of alarm and controversy?

6. What significance for families is attached to movements from south to north or from rural to urban residences? Are these factors any different for blacks than for whites?

7. How do you explain the level of self-evaluation among blacks? What place does the family hold in your explanation?

8. What dangers lie in dealing with the black family as a homogeneous grouping? Describe variations in life-styles and marital patterns within the black family.

9. It has been claimed by several scholars that life for black families in the inner city appears to be getting worse. Explain.

10. Discuss the unique role and status of the woman in the black family. How is it explained? Why or why isn't it likely to change?

FURTHER READINGS

Billingsley, Andrew. *Black Families in White America.* Englewood Cliffs, N.J.: Prentice-Hall, 1968. A look at the black family as a complex institution within the black community, which is in turn highly interdependent with other institutions in the wider white society.

Engram, Eleanor. *Science, Myth, Reality: The Black Family in One-Half of Research.* Westport, Conn.: Greenwood Press, 1982. An investigation of the interaction between social science, institutionalized beliefs that unfold as truth, and that which is true as applied to black families in the United States. The latter one-fourth of the book includes a comprehensive bibliography.

Frazier, E. Franklin. *The Negro Family in the United States.* Chicago: University of Chicago Press, 1966. First published as a research monograph in 1939. This book gives an historical look at the black family. It has been revised on several occasions to bring it up to date.

Gutman, Herbert G. *The Black Family in Slavery and Freedom, 1750–1925.* New York: Pantheon Books, 1976. An historical look at the black family that dispels the popular notions of mother-centered, one-parent, disorganized, and pathological family conditions under slavery.

Hill, Robert B. *The Strengths of Black Families.* New York: Emerson Hall, 1971.

The director of the research department of the National Urban League strips away many myths and stereotypes surrounding the black family.

Liebow, Elliot. *Tally's Corner.* Boston: Little, Brown, 1967. A sensitive analysis of the life-styles of black men who hang out on a particular street corner in Washington, D.C.

McAdoo, Harriette Pipes, ed. *Black Families.* Beverly Hills, Cal.: Sage Publications, 1981. A collection of twenty articles addressing a variety of issues and differences in black families.

McAdoo, Harriette P., and McAdoo, John L., eds. *Black Children: Social, Educational, and Parental Environments.* Beverly Hills, Cal.: Sage Publications, 1985. A collection of empirical research focusing on the experiences of black children and their parents as they develop skills to be functional in both black and non-black cultures.

Moynihan, Daniel Patrick. *The Negro Family: The Case for National Action.* Washington, D.C.: U.S. Government Printing Office, 1965. This, the "Moynihan Report," created a major controversy by arguing that the structure of family life in the black community was increasingly unstable and was the fundamental source of weakness in the community.

Peters, Marie F., and McAdoo, Harriette P. "The Present and Future of Alternative Life-styles in Ethnic American Cultures." In Eleanor D. Macklin and Roger H. Rubin, eds., *Contemporary Families and Alternative Lifestyles.* Beverly Hills: Sage Publications, 1983, Chapter 14, pp. 288–307. The vast diversity of black family life-styles is examined in this chapter: singlehood, cohabitation, single-parents, extended and augmented, dual-income, and polygamous formation, and the effects of the sex ratio and of social class.

Stack, Carol B. *All Our Kin: Strategies for Survival in a Black Community.* New York: Harper, 1974. An anthropologist who lived in the Flats, the poorest section of a black community in a midwestern city, reports on men, women, kin, and domestic networks.

Staples, Robert. *Black Masculinity: The Black Male's Role in American Society.* San Francisco: The Black Scholar Press, 1982. An examination of the black male in the United States, including sections on crime and violence, sex and sexuality, and male-female relationships.

Staples, Robert. *The World of Black Singles: Changing Patterns of Male/Female Relations.* Westport, Conn.: Greenwood Press, 1981. A comprehensive examination of college-educated single black Americans: their dating patterns, sexuality, interracial relationships, and friendship patterns.

Willie, Charles V. *A New Look at Black Families.* 2d ed. Bayside, N.Y.: General Hall, 1981. A detailed analysis of eighteen case studies of contemporary black families from different income levels: six affluent, six working class, and six poor.

Willie, Charles V. *Black and White Families: A Study in Complementarity.* Bayside, N.Y.: General Hall, 1985. A presentation of forty-eight case studies including twenty-four white and twenty-four black, middle-class, working-class, and poor families.

Photo: © Alan Carey/The Image Works

7

Social Class Variations in Family Life-Styles

The discussions in the two previous chapters on Chinese and black families included aspects of social class. In the traditional Chinese family, the life-styles of the gentry were radically different from those of the peasants. In contemporary Chinese families, while class extremes have been diminished, class and power distinctions were shown clearly to still exist. Among black families, specific attention was given to the life-styles of families from different social classes. In this chapter the class dimension is examined: what it means, how it is determined, and how families who comprise a general class category experience and express differing life-styles. The chapter ends with a discussion of family mobility—changing life-styles by moving from one class category to another.

THE MEANING OF SOCIAL CLASS

The concept of "social class" refers to an aggregate of individuals who occupy broadly similar positions on scales of wealth, prestige, and power. As even the most untrained observer can note, some kinds of work, some styles of life, and some types of homes, automobiles, or dress are viewed as more prestigious than others. All persons, families, and societies differentiate some roles and positions as more important, more powerful, more privileged, more prestigious, and more highly rewarded than others. This differential in power, prestige, money, and the like results in inequality between persons and families. The grouping or ranking of persons in a hierarchy of unequal positions is referred to in sociology as **social stratification.** This term, borrowed from geology, refers to a differential ranking of people into horizontal layers (strata) of equality and inequality.

Two of the theories described in Chapter 2, the **functionalist** and the **conflict theories,** are particularly relevant to our understanding of social class and the stratification system. A functionalist perspective views stratification as both an inevitable and necessary feature of society. The assumption is that all societies have a wide range of tasks that need to be performed in a society. These tasks are essential for the stability and maintenance of that society but they carry with them differential levels of prestige and rewards. Someone must collect the garbage, repair faulty plumbing, and perform the labor to assemble automobiles, while others must teach students, plan defense strategies, research the activity of molecules and atoms, and engage in heart surgery. Some tasks require greater levels of skill and training and these are likely to be more highly rewarded. This unequal distribution of social rewards is functional for society because it enables all roles and tasks to be completed, with those that demand the most scarce talents being performed by the most able and skilled persons.

For many years, this functionalist perspective was the predominant one among sociologists and for many, remains so today. However a number of people began to question why some families are highly rewarded with family fortunes for generations when they perform little of value to society; why people such as film stars or boxers earn millions overnight for doing tasks that are viewed as less important than those of social workers, scientists, or even the president, who may not earn as much in a lifetime; and why poor people need to stay poor from one generation to the next. Sociologists also began to raise value questions about the justice of unequal rewards and the fairness of assignment by birth of certain groups to positions of low prestige, wealth, and power. An awareness of these and other inequities among persons and families led conflict theorists to reject a functionalist view of a stratified society.

Conflict theorists saw a stratified society, not as leading toward stability and order, but one leading to dissatisfaction, alienation, and exploitation. The differentiation of economic rewards led one of the classical theorists of nineteenth-century sociology, Karl Marx, to believe that conflict in capitalist countries would result between those who have and those who have not; between those who control the means of production and those whose labor is the instrument of production; between management and labor; between the bourgeoisie who use capital, natural resources, and labor for profit, and the proletariat who sell their labor to buy the products produced by their labor. Translated into family terms, this means conflict between the families that own and control the wealth and means of production and the families who are forced to work for wages and produce the products or provide the services. Translated into gender terms, this means conflict between the males (husbands) who are employed and receive higher wages and the females (wives) who are less likely to be employed and receive lower wages.

Rayna Rapp[1] uses this Marxian dichotomy in analyzing family and

---

1. Rayna Rapp, "Family and Class in Contemporary America: Notes Toward an Understanding of Ideology," *Science and Society* 42 (Fall 1978): 278–300; also in Barrie Thorne with Marilyn Yalom, *Rethinking the Family: Some Feminist Questions* (New York: Longman, 1982): 168–187.

class in the contemporary United States. While granting recognition to class variations in households and families, she argues that social class is a shorthand for a process, not a thing. That process is one by which different social relations to the means of production are inherited and reproduced. Categories of people get swept up at different times and places and deposited into different relations to the means of production and to one another. People then get labeled "blue collar" or "white collar." While people carry these class category labels, Rapp stresses that it is important to recognize class not as a static place that individuals inhabit but as a process determined by the relationships set up in capital accumulation.

Erik Wright and others[2] make similar arguments in their explicitly Marxian relational perspective of the U.S. class structure. They define classes not in terms of categories of occupations, but in terms of social relations of control over investments, decision-making, other people's work, and one's own work. National survey data using these dimensions of social relations of production yielded four general results the authors see as particularly important: (1) the working class is by far the largest class in the U.S. class structure; (2) close to half of all locations within the class structure have a "contradictory character," meaning that their class content is determined by more than one basic class and implying that no simple scheme of class polarization represents the U.S. class structure; (3) lower status white-collar occupations are as polarized as manual occupations, and thus it makes little sense to consider these white-collar occupations as part of the middle class; and (4) women and blacks are considerably more polarized than white males, with the result that a sizeable majority of the United States working class is composed of women and minorities.

THE DETERMINATION OF SOCIAL CLASS

The discussion presented thus far would suggest that class is determined by examining who owns, manages, oppresses, and controls. This group is distinguished from those who are managed, oppressed, and controlled. However, only relatively recently has class been analyzed in terms of ownership and authority relations. Traditionally, class determination and categorization was based on an examination of the husband's or head-of-household's occupation. These occupations were ranked on a scale of

---

2. Erik Olin Wright, David Hachen, Cynthia Costello, and Joey Sprague, "The American Class Structure," *American Sociological Review* 47 (December 1982): 709–726.

Dress styles, the display of jewelry, or the type of beverage consumed all serve as clues to one's class position. (Photo: © Antonio Mendoza/The Picture Cube)

prestige, and all other family members were granted the same ranking. More recently, while occupational prestige has remained the key determinant of social class, the employment and occupational prestige of the wife and other family members has been considered as well.[3] Other determinants of inequality have included dimensions such as income, wealth, education, and self-rankings.

In determining social class, almost any criterion or prestige indicator (income, occupation, education, etc.) can be placed on a continuum and divided into any number of categories or strata. The studies of "Middletown" (Muncie, Indiana), among the most famous community studies in sociology,

---

3. Marc L. Berk and Paul W. Kingston, "Working Couples and Class Identification," *Sociological Spectrum* 2 (January/March 1982): 31–39; Judith Treas, "U. S. Income Stratification: Bringing Families Back In," *Sociology and Social Research* 66 (April 1982): 231–251.

used two classes: the business class and the working class.[4] Most students may think in terms of three classes: upper, middle, and lower. The classical work by August Hollingshead, entitled *Elmtown's Youth,* subdivided the community into five classes: upper, upper-middle, lower-middle, upper-lower, and lower-lower.[5]

If social class or a stratification system represent systems of inequality, who is to determine that objectively there are two, five, or seventeen classes of strata? Perhaps few distinct and separate strata exist at all, but rather they represent a continuum of inequalities of wealth, income, prestige, power, age, sex, or race. What is clear is that differences do exist among families in their income and spending power, in their owning or serving production processes, in their recognition of wealth and power differentials, and in the consequences these differences have for families and their members.

CONSEQUENCES OF SOCIAL CLASS TO FAMILY MEMBERS

The real significance of the class structure stems from some of its consequences. In addition to influencing our chances to live (which determine the likelihood of being born in the first place), of living through the first year, or of reaching retirement, social class influences our early socialization, the organization of society, the role expectations and role projections that we hold, the values that we stress, the types of behavior defined as deviant, and the likelihood of mental illness. In addition, class affects the likelihood of an education, its type, the motivation to get it, and the ends for which education is meant. It affects dropout rates, scores on intelligence tests, grades, occupational-vocational aspirations, and almost any other factor related to education.

Most significantly, social class both determines and results in important differences in influence, power, and opportunities. The ascribed status of birth into a certain social stratum has important consequences for the ability to make decisions and wield power. The links of differing classes to political organizations, financial institutions, and corporate boards affect the available opportunities and rewards. To be bourgeoisie or proletariat, management or labor, represents a determinant of one's class position

4. Robert S. Lynd and Helen Merrell Lynd, *Middletown* (New York: Harcourt, Brace and World, 1939); Robert S. Lynd and Helen Merrell Lynd, *Middletown in Transition* (New York: Harcourt, Brace and World, 1937); and Theodore Caplow et al., *Middletown Families* (New York: Bantam Books, 1982).

5. August B. Hollingshead, *Elmtown's Youth* (New York: Wiley, 1949).

as well as being an influential factor in determining the consequences that result from the position.

Similar consequences of class hold true for marriages and families. Social class affects the age at which one is likely to marry, the success of that marriage, the meanings attached to sexual behavior, the size of family, the recreation engaged in, the type of food eaten, the discipline and care given to children, sleeping arrangements, and contraceptive usage. On this last point for example, a survey of sexually active black adolescents from Chicago showed that 41 percent of the young women from the highest social class used contraceptives at first intercourse, but only 17 percent of those from the lowest class did so. For males, 32 percent of adolescents from the highest class compared to 11 percent from the lowest practiced contraception at first intercourse.[6] Irrespective of race, ethnicity, or gender, differences in behaviors are evident at varying class levels.

Although it is true that there are no sharply defined boundaries from one class to another, a great many of the normal life experiences of certain people are highly similar to other people who share a similar class sub-culture. For example, where polygyny is practiced, it is the men of higher social or economic position who are most likely to have a number of wives. Divorce rates go up as class level goes down. Birth rates increase as social class levels drop. Upper-social-strata young persons are granted less freedom of choice of a mate than are lower-social-strata persons. In the Western world particularly, the age of men at marriage rises with class position. If class lines are crossed in marriage, the woman is more likely to be upwardly mobile (hypergamy). The upper social stratum has more extended kinship networks than does the lower stratum. Higher-social-strata couples are more likely to use contraceptives than are lower-social-strata couples. One could continue indefinitely with a list of family variables that are highly related to class position. This list is not meant to be complete nor has each relationship been established to hold true cross-culturally. A key point is, however, that within a culture as well as between cultures, significant regularities occur between a family's attitude and behavior patterns and the class position that that family occupies.[7]

---

6. Dennis P. Hogan, Nan Marie Astone, and Evelyn M. Kitagawa, "Social and Environmental Factors Influencing Contraceptive Use Among Black Adolescents," *Family Planning Perspective* 17 (July/August 1985): 165–169.

7. Note for example, Russell W. Rumberger, "The Influence of Family Background on Education, Earnings and Wealth," *Social Forces* 61 (March 1983): 755–773; and Anne Locksley, "Social Class and Marital Attitudes and Behavior," *Journal of Marriage and the Family* 44 (May 1982): 427–440.

WEALTHY FAMILIES

Wealthy families have been identified as the "very rich," the "upper class," and the "ruling class." Compared to other categories of families, relatively little recent data are available on them. Rayna Rapp observed that one sociologist (either quite naive or quite sardonic) commented, "We know so little about the wealthy because they don't answer our questionnaires."[8] Indeed! They fund them rather than answer them.

This grouping of families, while small in number relative to other groupings, is large in power and influence. They possess enormous resources of wealth and social standing. They have a network of affiliations on important boards in banking, insurance, and manufacturing. These are the elite who own and control the means of production and make the rules for the workers to follow.

When we turn to the family structure of the very rich, some interesting bits and pieces emerge. Families are described by researchers as extremely lineal and concerned with who they are, rather than what they do. They are quite ancestor-oriented and conscious of the boundaries that separate the "best" families from the others. Families are obviously the units within which wealth is accumulated and transmitted.

Women in this class are said to serve as gatekeepers of many of the institutions of the very rich. They launch children, serve as board members at the private schools, run social and service clubs, and facilitate the marriage pools through events like debuts and charity functions. Susan Ostrander conducted interviews with thirty-six upper-class women and indicated that they held a clear preference for being with people like themselves (such as through private and exclusive clubs by invitation only), felt a sense of being better than other people (materially, morally, and in terms of volunteer work and contributions to the community), and conveyed an awareness that people define and judge them by who they are rather than by what they do.[9] As wives, like traditional wives in other social classes, they held a subordinate position to their husbands, had an unequal voice in family decisions, and maintained sole responsibility for home and family. But at this class level, women did not perform the nitty-gritty tasks of housework and child care. Women of other races and classes did such work for them. At this class level, women did not need—economically, personally, or socially—to seek paid work outside the home. At this class level, their accommodative and supportive function to their husbands enabled the men to manage the economic and political affairs

---

8. Rapp, "Family and Class in Contemporary America," p. 297.

9. Susan A. Ostrander, *Women of the Upper Class* (Philadelphia: Temple University Press, 1984).

of the society and to perpetuate the dominance of the upper class. Without doubt, the upper class is very gender segregated. Interestingly, this gender segregation is an accepted fact, virtually unchallenged by upper-class women. Why? Ostrander suggests that perhaps the gains of *gender* equality are not enough to balance the losses of *class* equality.

By any measure, this category of persons is the smallest numerically of all social classes but has the highest prestige and influence. Since they are at the very top of the class hierarchy, the members maintain their positions by preserving symbols of status such as genealogies, autobiographies of ancestors, heirlooms, and records of ancestral achievement. They also maintain their position by carefully controlling the marriage choices of their children.

It seems reasonable to assume that many changes are taking place among families of wealth parallel to changes in the society in general. For example, since mid-century the continuing push of egalitarian and democratic forces, the push for racial and class integration of private and "Ivy-League" schools, the assumption by the middle classes of status symbols once associated only with the rich, and so on would lead one to assume the death of "high society." Yet, in an interesting study of upper-class marriages, Paul Blumberg and P. W. Paul found a major theme of continuity in these marriages over the last thirty years.[10] They stated:

> Although tremendous forces have shaken American society in the past generation, the upper class has maintained itself remarkably intact, and having done so, is perhaps the most untouched group in American life. . . . It is the upper-class territory of school, neighborhood, club, and bluebook which remains the most racially segregated turf in America.[11]

MIDDLE-CLASS FAMILIES

Ask most Americans to what class they belong and you will likely be told "middle." Relatively few people could honestly respond "wealthy" and few people take pride in responding "poor" even if it's true. Furthermore, a response of middle class generally carries positive connotations, implying that while some people occupy a higher occupational status and prestige position, others obviously occupy a lower position. The middle-class families form the linkage between the powerful wealthy families and the working class and powerless, financially poor families. Residing in a middle position,

---

10. Paul M. Blumberg and P. W. Paul, "Continuities and Discontinuities in Upper-Class Marriages," *Journal of Marriage and the Family* 37 (February 1975): 63–77.
11. Ibid., p. 75.

the possibility exists of moving upward as well as the threat of moving downward. One consequence of this appears to be that the middle classes are very conscious of social values, involved in the major issues brought on by social change, and relatively rigid in moral standards. Some middle-class families closely resemble the wealthy families in their economic status and degree of influence. Other middle-class families vary little from the blue-collar workers in terms of their family patterns. This suggests that a precise analysis of the middle class as a distinct family type or life style is highly ambiguous in its results and extremely difficult.

From a Marxian perspective, the middle class is comprised of the **bourgeoisie:** those people who own small amounts of productive resources and have control over their working conditions in ways not found among the **proletariat:** those working-class people who work for wages. In the United States, particularly since the middle of this century, the number of small-scale entrepreneurs and professionals who stand outside the wage-labor–capital relation has decreased significantly. Today, middle class is more likely to refer to people employed as professionals or corporate and government bureaucrats. In Middletown[12] this group was categorized as the business class: those who made their living by selling or promoting ideas and by arranging the goods and services produced by the working class. They wore suits to their jobs in offices, banks, and businesses.

Middle-class families are likely to receive salaries rather than the hourly wage prevalent among blue-collar or working-class families. This more stable income resource base appears to be one key factor in differentiating this class grouping from those below it. The higher levels of income and greater "job security" allow for some discretionary spending and leisure activities. With this stable resource base is likely to come a range of amenities that lessen the shock of unanticipated crisis events: medical coverage, pension and retirement plans, bank credit, investment income, and the like. Rayna Rapp suggests that middle-class households probably are able to rely on commodity forms rather than kinship processes to ease both economic and geographic transitions.[13]

In the same article, Rayna Rapp goes on to suggest two hunches she has about middle-class kinship patterns. One is that kinship probably shifts from the lateral to the lineal. By this she means that material and economic resources are invested lineally among parents, children, and grandchildren rather than being dispersed into larger kin networks, as is more likely to be found in blue-collar and poor families. Some evidence of this is seen in the emphasis given to children's education, wedding gifts, music and art lessons, and so forth. Her second hunch is that

---

12. Caplow et al., *Middletown Families,* p. 86.
13. Rapp, "Family and Class in Contemporary America," p. 181.

friendship rather than kinship is the nexus within which the middle class invests its psychic and familial energies. Friendship allows for a great deal of affective support and exchange but usually does not include major resource pooling.

These hunches appear to be consistent with findings from a study in England of middle-class couples, suggesting that the experience of higher education and a professional career promoted value systems emphasizing personal autonomy and the ability to develop and carry out rational plans.[14] The women commenced their married lives with high expectations of being able to realize their family building plans by preventing unwanted conceptions, by conceiving when they chose to do so, and by controlling events rather than being subject to forces over which they have little influence. Wives who exercised initiative and responsibility at work were likewise effective in their other social roles. This ability to control and logically plan one's own life seems to be highly characteristic of this class and may partially explain the belief of many menbers that people of all classes should be able to do likewise.

The nuclear family of the middle class tends toward the ideal of equality of status between husband and wife. For example, in Middletown,[15] the overwhelming majority regarded family roles as joint activities. More specifically, business-class women were more than twice as likely as working-class women to say that housekeeping should be equally shared between spouses (31 percent versus 14 percent), while working-class women were more likely to say that housekeeping is mainly a wife's responsibility (85 percent versus 69 percent). The tendency toward the *ideal* of equality is evident in the extent of role enactment: the actual behavior of Middletown families shows more division of roles by sex than their opinions called for. In about 84 percent of Middletown families, the husband earns all or most of the family income. In 85 percent of the families with young children, the wife does all or most of the caring for them. Role flexibility was supported in principle at the same time that families faithfully practiced quite traditional roles.

Another widely studied area showing differences between the middle-class grouping and those below them is in parent-child relations and in childbearing practices. More than twenty years ago Melvin Kohn[16] suggested that, in terms of discipline, middle-class parents were more likely to use

---

14. Diana Woodward, Ann Heath, and Lynne Chisholm, "Patterns of Family Building and Contraceptive Use of Middle-Class Couples," *Journal of Biosocial Science* 10 (January 1978): 39–58.

15. Caplow et al., *Middletown Families*, pp. 67–70.

16. Melvin Kohn, "Social Class and Parent-Child Relationships: An Interpretation," *American Journal of Sociology* 68 (January 1963): 471–480; and Melvin Kohn, *Class and Conformity* (Homewood, Ill.: Dorsey, 1969).

reason, verbal threats, or withdrawal of rewards to punish a child or solicit the child's compliance. In contrast, blue-collar parents were more likely to rely on physical punishment. Kohn's reasoning was that by virtue of experiencing different conditions of life, members of different social classes come to see the world differently and develop different conceptions of social reality, different aspirations, and different conceptions of desirable personality characteristics. The middle class (white-collar occupations), in contrast with the lower class (blue-collar occupations), requires the individual to: (1) deal more with the manipulation of ideas, symbols, and interpersonal relations, (2) be involved in work that is more complex and requires great flexibility, thought, and judgment, and (3) be less closely supervised. From these occupational differences come different values that are reflected in patterns of discipline. Middle-class values are likely to deal with self-direction, freedom, individualism, initiative, creativity, and self-actualization. Thus parents encourage in their children *internal* standards such as consideration, curiosity, and self-control. Discipline is based on the parents' interpretation of a child's motives for a particular act.[17]

Kohn's ideas in regard to parent-child interaction by social class have received widespread attention and attempts at extension and replication. For example James and Sonia Wright[18] used national survey data to examine some of the main theses discussed on previous pages. They found that since Kohn's original survey there have been clear trends in self-direction values among middle-class parents and that social class is the primary source of differentiation in childrearing values. Even studies outside the United States tend to confirm the effect of social class on childhood socialization with the middle-class tendency to use psychological rather than physical approaches to discipline.[19] This class effect appears to be largely due to the higher level of educational attainment of middle-class parents.

---

17. In contrast, lower-class or blue-collar workers deal more with the manipulation of physical objects, require less interpersonal skill, have more standardization of work, and are more closely supervised. This leads to values of conformity to *external* standards such as orderliness, neatness, and obedience. Discipline is based on the consequences of the child's behavior rather than on the interpretation of motive for the behavior. *See,* for example, Gary W. Peterson and David F. Peters, "The Socialization Values of Low-Income Appalachian White and Rural Black Mothers: A Comparative Study," *Journal of Comparative Studies* 16 (Spring 1985): 75–91.

18. James D. Wright and Sonia R. Wright, "Social Class and Parental Values for Children: A Partial Replication and Extension of the Kohn Thesis," *American Sociological Review* 41 (June 1976): 527–537.

19. Robert C. Williamson, "A Partial Replication of the Kohn-Gecas-Nye Thesis in a German Sample," *Journal of Marriage and the Family* 46 (November 1984): 971–979.

BLUE-COLLAR FAMILIES

Blue-collar or "working-class" families are made up of workers classified by the U.S. Bureau of the Census as employed in (1) precision production, craft, and repair, (2) machine operating, assembling and inspecting, (3) transportation and material moving, and (4) handling, equipment cleaning, helping, and laboring. Service works are generally also classified as blue collar occupations. In 1985 such workers constituted 48 percent of all working householders in families (*see* Table 7–1).

The job of a blue-collar worker generally requires some sort of manual skill.[20] The "elite" of the blue-collar workers—electricians, plumbers, and highly skilled operators—frequently earn more than members of the middle classes. For example, public school teachers, generally assigned to a middle-class position, are likely to average $3,000 to $6,000 a year less than do certain blue-collar workers. However, formal education beyond a trade or high school is not generally required for the manual skills necessary for the members of this class. Physical health is quite crucial to blue-collar workers, since many jobs are dependent upon an ability to perform physical labor. These groups are generally represented by trade unions. A great amount of faith is placed in the unions to protect persons from those above them in the work hierarchy, to provide help with family medical expenses, and to prevent a dismissal from work.

Since members of this class are almost completely dependent on the swings of the business cycle in our wage-price-profits system, the economic stability described among middle-class families is less prevalent. Most income is received from wages earned by the hour, the piece, the day, or the week. To supplement the income of the husband, a considerable proportion of wives are employed outside the home. Unlike a sizable proportion of female workers from the middle class, the blue-collar wife is more likely to take a job out of economic necessity than the desire for a career. She is also likely to be the target of frequent and severe sexual harassment. James Gruber and Lars Bjorn, in an article titled "Blue-Collar Blues," predicted that women with lower status—namely black, young or "unattached" (single or divorced) women, as well as those who have low seniority or job status—will experience sexual harassment. Over a third of the blue-collar women autoworkers reported harassment in the form of sexual propositioning, abusive language, physical attacks, and other behavior such as body language, whistling, and stares.[21]

---

20. For a perceptive view of the meaning of work in the working class, *see* Lillian Breslow Rubin, *Worlds of Pain: Life in the Working-Class Family* (New York: Basic Books, 1976), Chapter 9, pp. 155–184.

21. James E. Gruber and Lars Bjorn, "Blue-Collar Blues: The Sexual Harassment of

TABLE 7–1
Occupation and median income of families with working householders, 1985

Occupation group	Number (in thousands)	Percent	Median income
White-collar workers			
Executive, administrative, and managerial	6,807	14.1	$46,448
Professional specialty	5,910	12.2	44,207
Technical and related support	1,305	2.7	36,659
Sales	5,367	11.1	34,793
Administrative support, including clerical	4,282	8.9	28,695
Blue-collar workers			
Precision production, craft, and repair	9,270	19.2	31,077
Machine operators, assemblers, and inspectors	3,901	8.1	27,009
Transportation and material moving	3,020	6.2	28,499
Handlers, equipment cleaners, helpers, and laborers	1,880	3.9	22,716
Service workers			
Private household	185	0.4	9,418
Service, except private households	4,472	9.3	21,723
Farming, forestry, and fishing	1,900	3.9	17,749
Total	48,335	100	31,966

Source: U.S. Bureau of the Census, *Current Population Records,* Series P-60, no. 154, "Money Income and Poverty Status of Families and Persons in the United States: 1985" (Washington, D.C.: U.S. Government Printing Office, 1986), Table 1, p. 6.

The strains associated with the uncertainties of many facets of life to members of this class present a high degree of family instability. Divorce occurs with greater frequency among this grouping than among any of the higher income, education, or occupational groupings.

It is the blue-collar family, more than any other, whose members conform to the traditional image of husband and wife roles.[22] The husband's role is to be a good provider, and the wife's role, although she is often

Women Autoworkers," *Work and Occupations* 9 (August 1982): 271–298. Note also: James E. Gruber and Lars Bjorn, "Women's Responses to Sexual Harassment: An Analysis of Sociocultural, Organizational, and Personal Resource Models," *Social Science Quarterly* 67 (December 1986): 814–826.

22. Note in particular Rubin, *Worlds of Pain,* Chapters 5–7, pp. 69–133.

employed, is to do housework and care for the children. As the primary wage earner, the husband is the final authority and disciplinarian.

The wife and mother rears the children. If the family is broken by divorce or separation, it is with her that the children will remain. It is expected that she will remain faithful to her husband as long as he remains faithful to her. If these obligations are broken, the offended party is likely to seek separation or divorce.

The role of children is definitely one of subordination to the parents. Unlike middle-class parents who stress that children stay in school and who make major sacrifices to keep them there, the working-class blue-collar families are more likely to expect that children will leave school after fulfilling the minimum legal requirements or at most after completion of high school. Boys and girls are taught to be self-sufficient, to be tough-minded, and to be able to compete for personal rights and privileges. Working-class boys begin their heterosexual intercourse experiences earlier and have them more frequently than do boys from middle- and white-collar families. Working-class girls marry early, with a high proportion of pregnancies conceived premaritally. Many teen-aged girls interviewed by Rubin reported that when they grow up they will marry for love and that it will be better than their parents' marriage. While love may be desirable, what they get is babies. Forty to 60 percent of teen-aged pregnancies are conceived premaritally and approximately 50 percent of working-class women married in their teen years.[23]

Although it is now more than twenty-five years old, a vivid glimpse into the lives of these families can be found in Mirra Komarovsky's book *Blue Collar Marriage*.[24] Using a case-study approach, fifty-eight "stable" families with children were interviewed. The respondents were chosen from a community the author termed Glenton that had a total population of about 50,000.

Husbands and wives in Glenton knew what was expected of them and generally agreed about marital ideals. However, the role consensus or the clarity of role definition was not necessarily suited to the conditions of life under which Glenton's families had to live. A transition to new roles was often hindered by certain circumstances such as the poverty of some young couples, the poor occupational adjustment of the young unskilled workers, and the need to reside in the parental home after marriage. The following illustration of a thirty-two-year-old husband, taken from Komarovsky's book, illustrates how unfavorable these circumstances can be. This quote might well have come from a blue-collar worker who experienced the recession of the early 1980s.

---

23. Ibid., Chapter 4.
24. Mirra Komarovsky, *Blue Collar Marriage* (New York: Random House, 1962).

You keep thinking you can do almost anything and get away with anything when you're still young. There had been a couple of big layoffs when we got married, but work was still pretty good and I thought I could do anything and that I was going places and I was going to be somebody. Nothing was good enough for my wife, and we didn't think nothing of charge accounts and buying things. We hadn't been married long and I got my first layoff. They said I was young. They laid off others and they said they was old. We couldn't keep up our payments on the furniture, and we lost every stick of it, and she was pregnant. And I mean to tell you. We went and stayed at her ma's for a few days, and then up to my ma's for a while. There wasn't no room for us at her ma's and my ma had a spare room, and we must have stayed there about a month while I was looking for work and then I got it, and then we moved out again. And then this time, we got one thing by paying the whole money on it that we borrowed the money for. We borrowed it from people, and not the bank. And we bought a bed. We figured we could sit on that, and we had our cooking pots and could eat out of them. But we didn't want to think of sleeping on the floor anymore. It would have been all right if it was summer and she wasn't pregnant.[25]

The majority of men and women interviewed saw the principal marital ties as sexual union, complementary tasks, and mutual devotion. Within this class, if one of the functions of modern marriage is to be friends, to share one's hurts, worries, and dreams with another person, a large number of couples fail to find such fulfillment.

FAMILIES AND THE FEMINIZATION OF POVERTY

According to data supplied by the U. S. Bureau of the Census, in 1985 more than 33 million persons in the United States were below the poverty level.[26] This included 7.2 million families (*see* Figure 7–1). This figure equals 11.4 percent of all families or about one out of every eight families in the United States classified as having an income below the poverty level. For white families the poverty rate was 9.1 percent compared to 25.5 percent for Spanish-origin families, and 28.7 percent for black families. Among families with a female householder with no husband present the percentages increase to 27.4 for white families, 50.5 for black families, and 53.1 for Spanish-origin families. The single-parent family is discussed

25. Ibid., p. 47. Reprinted by permission.

26. U.S. Bureau of the Census. *Current Population Reports*, Series P-60, no. 154. "Money Income and Poverty Status of Families and Persons in the United States: 1985" (Washington, D.C.: U.S. Government Printing Office, 1986), Table B, p. 3.

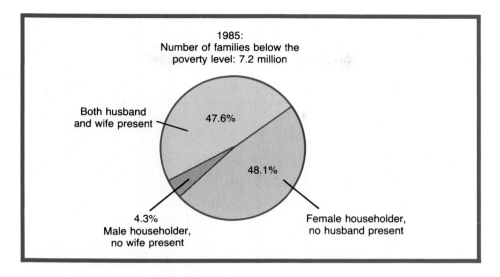

FIGURE 7–1
Families below the poverty level, by type of family, 1985. (*Source:* U.S. Bureau
of the Census, *Current Population Reports,* Series P-60, no. 154, "Money
Income and Poverty Status of Families and Persons in the United States: 1985"
[Washington, D.C.: U.S. Government Printing Office, 1986], Table B, p. 3.)

in the section that follows. The female-headed single-parent family is one
important aspect of the feminization of poverty.

A variety of interwoven demographic and socioeconomic trends are
evident in the feminization of poverty. First is the one just mentioned:
the female-headed family where women are living independently with
custody and primary responsibility for their dependent children. Second
is the rise in teen and young parenting where economic self-sufficiency
is difficult. Third is the income inequality where women earn much less
than their male counterparts in the labor market. Fourth is the inadequate
level of personal and child support from absent husbands, social assistance,
and other programs.

For example, one study showed that child support varies greatly by
race and marital status, with non-blacks twice as likely as blacks and ever-
married six times as likely as never-married to receive child support.[27]
Seldom is the amount received adjusted for inflation, further contributing
to the increasing feminization of poverty. In combination, factors such
as these place a disproportionate number of women below the level of

27. Andrea H. Beller and John W. Graham, "Child Support Awards: Differentials and
Trends by Race and Marital Status," *Demography* 23 (May 1986): 231–245.

Families in poverty tend to be overly-represented with single parents (mothers), unplanned pregnancies, high rates of unemployment, and a dependence on governmental assistance. (Photo: © Polly Brown/The Picture Cube)

poverty. This is true not only in the United States, but in Canada and most other industrialized countries as well.[28]

A logical question is, How are figures on poverty derived? How is it determined that a family be considered at the poverty level or not? Cannot a three-person family live on much less than a seven-person family? Obviously, the small family can live on less than the large one and family

---

28. Deborah A. Abowitz, "Data Indicate the Feminization of Poverty in Canada, Too," *Sociology and Social Research* 70 (April 1986): 209–213; and Sheila B. Kamerman, "Women, Children and Poverty: Public Policies and Female-Headed Families in Industrialized Countries," *Signs: Journal of Women in Culture and Society* 10 (1984): 249–271.

TABLE 7–2

Weighted average poverty thresholds in 1985

Size of family unit	Threshold
1 person (unrelated individual)	$ 5,469
15 to 64 years	5,593
65 years and over	5,156
2 persons	6,998
Householder 15 to 64 years	7,231
Householder 65 years and over	6,503
3 persons	8,573
4 persons	10,989
5 persons	13,007
6 persons	14,696
7 persons	16,656
8 persons	18,512
9 persons or more	22,083

Source: U.S. Bureau of the Census, *Current Population Reports,* Series P-60, no. 154, "Money Income and Poverty Status of Families and Persons in the United States: 1985" (Washington, D.C.: U.S. Government Printing Office, 1986), Table A-1, p. 33.

size is a key factor in determining the poverty threshold. The poverty index is based solely on money income and does not reflect noncash assistance or governmental benefits such as food stamps, medicaid, or public housing. The poverty index is based on the Department of Agriculture's 1961 Economy Food Plan and reflects the different consumption requirements based on family size and composition. Operating on the assumption that families of three or more persons spend approximately one-third of their income on food, the poverty level is set at three times the cost of the Economy Food Plan. Poverty thresholds are updated every year to reflect changes in the Consumer Price Index. Thus, as can be seen in Table 7–2, the average poverty threshold for a family of four in 1985 was $10,989. For one person it was $5,469, and for a family of eight it was $18,512.

The poverty rate in 1985 dropped slightly from the level in 1983, the highest level since 1966. Among the factors contributing to the increase in poverty in the early 1980s was a recession, an associated rise in unemployment, and tightening of eligibility standards for certain government aid programs. Hit the hardest and receiving the largest increase in rates of poverty were metropolitan areas, in particular the central cities; persons under age forty-five, and more specifically young people; and blacks and persons of Spanish origin. These data are consistent with a study that indicated the factors most highly associated with poverty to be: female-headed families, large family size, minority group status, age (children, youths, the aged), unemployment and underemployment, and lack of income from sources other than wages.[29]

The greatest amount of public assistance goes to households below the poverty level. In 1985, this was true of nearly three-fourths of all households receiving food stamps, half of those receiving free or reduced-price school lunches, 55 percent of those in publicly owned or other subsidized housing, and 59 percent of those with one or more members covered by medicare.[30] Clearly, cuts in governmental food, housing, and health benefits hit those living at a poverty level the hardest.

Given the nature of welfare legislation, the state of the job market, and segregated slum housing, households and family life are unstable. In human terms, not only do the poor pay more but they share more as well. Stack's monograph dealing with strategies of survival in a black community provides vivid descriptions of the way "what goes round comes round."[31] That is, clothing, furniture, food, appliances, money, and kids make the rounds among individuals and households. People give what they can and take what they need. These exchange patterns result in a **fictive kinship** by which friends are turned into family. The swapping of goods and services results not merely in the norms of reciprocity that seem prevalent in most social exchanges, but also in stable friendships that pattern those of kin. As Stack says:

> Non-kin who live up to one another's expectations express elaborate vows of friendship and conduct their social relations within the idiom of kinship. Exchange behavior between those friends "going for kin" is identical to exchange behavior between close kin.[32]

Poverty is directly linked to unemployment or underemployment and since employment is irregular, income is irregular. Because income is irregular, a considerable amount of insecurity exists in regard to food, clothing, shelter, transportation, and other essential items. Children may be forced or encouraged to contribute to the financial needs of the family, and few remain in school beyond the minimum legal age. These conditions contribute to and are highly related to other concerns. For example, families

---

29. Catherine S. Chilman, "Families in Poverty in the Early 1970s: Rates, Associated Factors, Some Implications," *Journal of Marriage and the Family* 37 (February 1975): 49–60.

30. U.S. Bureau of the Census, *Current Population Reports,* Series P-60, no. 155, "Receipt of Selected Noncash Benefits: 1985" (U.S. Government Printing Office, Washington, D.C., 1987), Table A, p. 2.

31. Carol B. Stack, *All Our Kin: Strategies for Survival in a Black Community* (New York: Harper & Row, 1974), Chapter 3, pp. 32–44.

32. Ibid., p. 40.

Who is to blame for rising poverty?

Poverty is on the rise. Despite the supposed economic recovery, there are more poor Americans today than there have been for almost 20 years. Last year the poverty rate rose to 15 percent; since 1978, the numbers of the poor increased by 10 million people, or by 40 percent. The black poverty rate rose to 36 percent, triple the white rate. Half of all black children are poor; a fifth of all children are poor.

The rise in poverty has touched off a search for the causes. One popular target is the Reagan administration, whose policies have been based on the "trickle-down" theory, which assumes that if you give tax breaks and other incentives to the rich, they'll invest and spend more, and the prosperity will filter down to the have-nots. That hasn't happened. In fact, the gap between affluence and poverty has widened. Worse, cuts in programs aiding the poor and jobless have meant not only more poverty, but more extreme poverty.

Sensitive to the political implications of rising poverty and hunger in America, the administration has been taking defensive steps. The president named a task force to find out what's behind the mounting reports of hunger. A good place for the task force to start would be to examine the impact of federal cuts in nutrition programs, cuts that save the government small change while inflicting suffering on millions.

One disturbing aspect of the search for the causes of rising poverty is the old game of blaming the victim. In its latest form, that means blaming the increase in female-headed households for the rise in poverty, especially among blacks.

Female-headed families are far more likely than others to be poor, but they are poor because females—especially black women—face massive discriminatory barriers to employment. Not enough people go beyond conventional thought to question why society refuses to provide day care facilities that would enable more mothers to work, and why it refuses to provide training and job opportunities that would help them out of poverty.

Nor does it explain the different poverty rates between white and black female-headed households. White families headed by women suffer a poverty rate of 28 percent, but among similar black families, the rate is 35 percent. That indicates that racial discrimination and lack of economic opportunity are at the root of rising poverty.

Along with discrimination, a long stagnant economy painfully undergoing restructuring is behind the rise in poverty. For the past dozen years, we've had one recession after another, each deeper than the last. Jobs have been wiped out, especially among people whose skills are limited and not transferable to other industries.

If we are serious about wanting to know why we are poor, we'll stop blaming the victims of poverty and adopt policies that end poverty instead of spreading it.

Source: John E. Jacob, *Detroit Free Press,* September 23, 1983, p. 11. Reprinted with the permission of the Detroit Free Press.

in poverty have the highest rates of divorce, psychoses, and physical disabilities; the least amount of dental and health care; the largest proportion of people on public welfare; the greatest rejection rate from the armed services; the highest crime rate; the largest number of children; the highest rate of venereal disease; the most unemployment; and, as perceived by many middle-class persons, "the most of the worst."

The majority of persons and families below the level of poverty typically live below this level for intermittent periods of time. But within the poverty population is a U.S. **underclass** characterized by persistent poverty and a variety of associated problems, such as welfare dependency, crime, and substance addiction. The underclass is geographically concentrated in ghettos of cities and its members have high participation in the underground economies that flourish in the neighborhood. Kelly argues that underclass crime and welfare dependency, while overdetermined by objective economic circumstances, is also influenced by stress mediated at the social, psychological, and social network levels. The primary locus of this mediation exists in family, kinship, and informal social networks.[33] A key point is that extended and fictive kin networks are critical intervening variables in the analysis of economic and stress-related behaviors among the underclass.

It is difficult for most students and teachers to describe the life-styles of families in poverty without imposing middle-class evaluations upon them. To even use terms such as "poor," "poverty," "lower class," or "underclass" may be imposing negative connotations and interpretations on persons and families who occupy this grouping. To describe families in terms of unemployment, welfare, illegitimacy, venereal disease, crime, and disabilities is to repeatedly apply negative labels and convey an impression of fault and blame.

Rayna Rapp notes that it is particularly ironic that the ideology of family, so important to poor people, is used by ruling-class ideologies to blame the poor for their own condition. She notes that the very poor have used their families to cement and patch tenuous relations to survival; out of their belief in "family" they have invented networks capable of making next-to-nothing go a long way.[34] A middle- or ruling-class response is that their notion of family is inadequate, deviant, or even pathological. Perhaps the family is less inadequate or pathological than the relationship between the family or household and the productive resources available to them. Few people rationally and consciously choose or desire the styles of life that accompany poverty. The single-parent situation is no exception.

---

33. Robert F. Kelly, "The Family and the Urban Underclass," *Journal of Family Issues* 6 (June 1985):159–184.

34. Rayna Rapp, "Family and Class in Contemporary America," pp. 179–180.

THE SINGLE PARENT AND POVERTY

Because the section on the single parent follows the section on poverty should not lead readers to assume all one-parent families are poor. They are not. But Norton and Glick, in presenting a social and economic profile of one-parent families, state that by most objective measures, the vast majority of these families hold a disadvantageous position in society relative to other family groups.[35] They are characterized by a high rate of poverty, a high percentage of minority representation, relatively low education, and high rate of mobility. In short, they generally have little equity or stature in U.S. society and constitute a group with pressing social and economic needs.

These pressing social and economic needs become most acute among black and Spanish-origin female-headed families, over half of whom fall below the poverty level. Census data indicate that in 1984 the median income of families with a female householder with the husband absent was $9,466. This is about one-half the $18,346 median income of the male householder with the wife absent and less than one-third the $31,216 median income of married male householders with the wife present (married two-parent family).[36] That same year, using the poverty index developed by the Social Security Administration described in the previous section of this chapter, more than one-third (37.6 percent) of all families with a female householder and no husband present were below the poverty level.[37] As indicated previously, this included 27.4 percent of white, 50.5 percent of black, and 53.1 percent of Spanish-origin female households without a husband present. The social concern about female-householder families increases when it is noted that, in addition to the proportion at a poverty level, a large proportion of these families are on welfare, and women with unstable sources of income feel less able to plan for their lives (fate control).[38]

Who are these single parents? How many children in the United States reside in this type of family structure? Drawing from 1985 census data, more than 16 million children under the age of 18 or about one in four was not living with both parents. As can be seen in Table 7–3, this included

---

35. Arthur J. Norton and Paul C. Glick, "One Parent Families: A Social and Economic Profile," *Family Relations* 35 (January 1986): 9–17.

36. U.S. Bureau of the Census, *Current Population Reports*, Series P-60, no. 154, "Money Income and Poverty Status of Families and Persons in the United States: 1985" (Washington, D.C.: U.S. Government Printing Office, 1986), Table 14, p. 20.

37. Ibid., Table 14, p. 20.

38. Sally Bould, "Female-headed Families: Personal Fate Control and the Provider Role," *Journal of Marriage and the Family* 39 (May 1977): 339–349.

20 percent of the white, 60 percent of the black, and 32 percent of Spanish-origin children. Most of these were living with mother only (15 percent white, 51 percent black, and 27 percent Spanish-origin) but about 2 percent were living with the father only, and the remaining 2.5 percent were not living with either parent.

The number of children in a single-parent context is quite dramatic when children's actual living arrangements are considered over a period of time rather than considered for a given year or at a single point in time. Sandra Hofferth, drawing data from the Panel Study of Income Dynamics (interviews with a national probability sample of about 5,000 families that have been followed longitudinally since 1968), projects that 70 percent of white·children born in 1980 will spend at least some time

TABLE 7–3

Living arrangements of children under 18 years: 1985 (Excludes persons under 18 years old who were maintaining households or family groups)

Living arrangements of children and marital status of parent	1985			
	All Races	White	Black	Spanish Origin*
All children under age 18	62,475	50,836	9,479	6,057
Living with both parents	46,149	40,690	3,741	4,110
Living with one parent	14,635	9,139	5,114	1,746
Living with neither parent (Numbers in Thousands)	1,691	1,007	624	201
Living with two parents	73.9%	80.0%	39.5%	67.9%
Mother only	20.9	15.6	51.0	26.6
Father only	2.5	2.4	2.9	2.2
Other; relatives only	2.1	1.4	5.7	2.5
None; relatives only	0.6	0.6	0.9	0.8
Percent	100.0%	100.0%	100.0%	100.0%
Marital status of Single Parents				
Never married	25.7%	13.4%	48.1%	23.9%
Married, spouse absent	25.6	26.3	24.2	40.7
Widowed	7.5	8.4	5.1	7.4
Divorced	41.2	51.9	22.6	28.0
Percent	100.0%	100.0%	100.0%	100.0%

* Person of Spanish Origin may be any race.

Source: U.S. Bureau of Census, *Current Population Reports,* Series P-20, No. 410, "Marital Status and Living Arrangements March: 1985," (Washington, D.C.: U.S. Government Printing Office, 1986), Table A-8 and A-9, pp. 71 and 72.

with only one parent before they reach age eighteen.[39] For black children born in 1980 the projection is 94 percent. These figures stand in sharp contrast to the 19 percent of white children and 48 percent of black children born between 1950 and 1954 who have lived with one parent.

Why the dramatic increase? How is it possible that 70 percent of white and 94 percent of black children will probably experience a single-parent living arrangement before they reach age eighteen? An overly simplified but partial answer to this question can be obtained by examining the marital status (never married, married but spouse absent, widowed, or divorced) of single parents by race and ethnicity (black, white, Spanish-origin) as presented in the lower third of Table 7–3. Of all white single parents, more than one-half are divorced (52.0 percent) and another one-fourth are married but with a spouse absent (26.0 percent). Thus, most of these children under age eighteen came from a two-parent household but as a result of divorce or an absent parent now find themselves in a one-parent context. Black children, in contrast, are highly likely to have been born into a single-parent situation because the mother never married (48.0 percent). Less than one-fourth of black children entered a one-parent situation because of divorce. Thus, while white one-parent families typically result from divorce and black one-parent families typically result from a never-married parent, Spanish-origin one-parent families balance between divorce (28.0 percent), a married but absent parent (40.0 percent), and a never-married parent (24.0 percent). Relatively few one-parent situations of any of the three groups result from widowhood, as might be expected since most widowhoood occurs at older ages when the children are no longer teenagers or younger. But given the increase in births to unmarried women, the frequency of divorce, and the number of married couples with a spouse absent, it can be projected that the vast majority of children born in the 1980s will experience a one-parent living arrangement.

Over the past several decades, the major increase in single-parent families has occurred among children living with mother only. Similar increases have not taken place in the percentage of persons living with the father only; however it is of interest that these father-child families have only recently come to the attention of researchers at all. The mother was always the focus of attention, since she gave birth to the child, was primarily responsible for the nurturant socialization responsibilities, was more likely to be a widow than was the husband likely to be widower, and was generally given legal custody of the children by the courts in cases of divorce and separation. Thus, as could be expected, most literature

---

39. Sandra L. Hofferth, "Updating Children's Life Course," *Journal of Marriage and the Family* 47 (February 1985):93–115.

on this topic deals with the mother-child unit. Even this literature, rather than dealing with the mother who is present, deals with the father who is absent: the fatherless family.

Let's turn our attention briefly to these two single-parent situations: the mother-child family (the father-absent family) and the father-child family (the mother-absent family).[40]

Mothers as single parents (the father-absent family)

In 1985 more than thirteen million children under the age of eighteen were in homes with a mother-only—father-absent situation and the number increases yearly. Concurrent with this factor is the widely held view that every child needs a father or his social equivalent.

The trend toward an increasing percentage of children in homes without a father present represents an issue of national concern. Heather Ross and Isabel Sawhill[41] state that these concerns focus on: (1) the precarious financial status of female-headed families, almost half of whom are poor, spend some time on welfare, and run a high risk of living under conditions of poverty; (2) the possible effect on children of not having an adult male influence in the home; and (3) the lack of clarity about how public policy has contributed to these changes and the role it could play with respect to this type of family structure.

Using national data of five thousand American families, taken from the Panel Study of Income Dynamics conducted by the Survey Research Center at the University of Michigan, Sara McLanahan compared the levels of stress of two-parent (male-headed) and one-parent (female-headed) families.[42] She looked at three types of stressors: the presence of chronic life strains, the occurrence of major life events, and the absence of social and psychological supports. The *chronic life strains* included income, education, number of children under eighteen years in household, age, and race. Two-parent and female-headed families differed only slightly with respect to age of head and number of children, but had notable differences in levels of education, race, and family income. Female-headed

40. Readers interested in this topic should consult the special issue of *Family Relations* on "The Single Parent Family" 35 (January 1986) as well as the annotated bibliography compiled by Benjamin Schlesinger in that issue, pp. 199–204.

41. Heather L. Ross and Isabel V. Sawhill, *Time of Transition: The Growth of Families Headed by Women* (Washington, D.C.: Urban Institute, 1975), pp. 3–4.

42. Sara S. McLanahan, "Family Structure and Stress: A Longitudinal Comparison of Two-Parent and Female-headed Families," *Journal of Marriage and the Family* 45 (May 1983): 347–357.

families were more likely to experience the strains commonly associated with being poor, black, and less educated.

Major life events included observed changes during the past year in a variety of areas such as financial status, employment status, household composition, place of residence, and health. Life events scores, as with life strains, indicated that female-headed families were most likely to experience disruption, particularly in areas of income change, household composition change, and resident change. Female heads were less likely to be in the labor force, and those that were employed were more likely to experience employment-related events than were working male heads.

Social and psychological supports included variables such as known neighbors, living within walking distance of relatives, participation in clubs and organizations, free household help received, self-esteem, and hopefulness. There was no difference between the two-parent and female-headed families in terms of living near relatives. Female-headed families were more likely to receive free household help but knew fewer of their neighbors, participated in fewer clubs and organizations, reported much lower self-esteem, and were much less optimistic about the future. McLanahan's conclusion was that single female heads with children experience more stress than their married two-parent counterparts in all three areas, and suggests that the higher incidence of major life events experienced by female heads is primarily a function of the marital disruption process rather than a characteristic of the state of single parenthood.

What happens to children in female-headed families? Barbara Cashion reviewed the social psychological research pertaining to female-headed families published between 1970 and 1980, and concludes that children in these families are likely to have good emotional adjustment, good self-esteem except when they are stigmatized, intellectual development comparable to others in the same socioeconomic status, and rates of juvenile delinquency comparable to others in the same socioeconomic status.[43] Major problems in these families stem from *poverty* and *stigma.* Poverty as a general social problem is associated with problems in school, juvenile delinquency, the mother's poor attitudes about her own situation and, as noted earlier, in her sense of not being in control. The negative stigma is associated with a lowered self-esteem in children and in the labeling or defining of father-absent children as problematic even in situations where problems are minimal or nonexistent. Cashion's general conclusion is that the majority of female-headed families, when not plagued by poverty, have children as successful as those from two-parent families.

While most research reported was carried out in the United States,

---

43. Barbara G. Cashion, "Female-Headed Families: Effects on Children and Clinical Implications," *Journal of Marital and Family Therapy* (April 1982): 77–85.

similar findings come from cross-cultural studies on female-headed families and households. Bilgé and Kaufman contend that such families are found to be neither pathological nor inferior. To condemn female-headed or one-parent families as abnormal or "pathological," they claim, is "a coverup for the economic inequalities of our society."[44] Around the world, one-parent, female-headed families function to bring up children and provide emotional support. When combined with an extended network of concerned kin, it can often tender more emotional support and offer more options to family members than an isolated nuclear family. This suggests that no single family form produces an optimal milieu for a growing child and that mother-child forms, like others, can provide the support systems and methods of socialization that are positive to a child's emotional, intellectual, and social development.

Fathers as single parents (the mother-absent family)

The father-child family, like the mother-child family, is a result of widowhood, divorce, separation, nonmarriage, and, more recently, single-parent adoption. While only about 2 percent of all children under age eighteen are living with their fathers only, Thompson and Gongla[45] suggest that the number of single-parent families maintained by fathers may very well begin to increase as a by-product of the following:

1. men's changing life-styles,
2. normative shifts favoring single fatherhood,
3. noncustodial fathers' desire to continue their parenting role,
4. single fathers' greater access to economic resources and better economic well-being than single mothers,
5. research findings that suggest single fathers and single mothers can effectively function as custodial parents, and
6. research that suggests that the positive and negative experiences of being a single parent are similar for both fathers and mothers.

Research on fathers as single parents has been relatively infrequent and generally limited to small nonprobability samples. Yet they may prove to be more insightful than mother-child studies in light of the extreme

---

44. Barbara Bilgé and Gladis Kaufman, "Children of Divorce and One-Parent Families: Cross-cultural Perspectives," *Family Relations* 32 (January 1983): 59–71.

45. Edward H. Thompson, Jr. and Patricia A. Gongla, "Single-Parent Families: In the Mainstream of American Society," in Eleanor D. Macklin and Roger H. Rubin, *Contemporary Families and Alternative Lifestyles* (Beverly Hills: Sage Publications, 1983): 97–124.

importance placed upon mothers as key agent of socialization. Can men "mother"?

This is a question posed by Barbara Risman who surveyed fathers about their experiences as homemakers, the nature of the father-child relationship, and overall role satisfaction.[46] Her major finding was that most men felt comfortable and competent as single parents, regardless of the reason for custody or their financial status. This was true even though four out of five single fathers had no outside housekeeping help, either paid or volunteer. These men felt very close to and very affectionate toward their children, were glad to be fathers, and had little trouble fulfilling either the instrumental or expressive functions of single parenthood. Clearly successful mothering is not an exclusively female skill. Men *can* "mother."

In a number of ways, fathers who maintain a family alone are better situated than their female counterparts. Fathers as single parents are known to have higher levels of education, are more likely to be in the labor force, and as shown earlier, are much better situated economically. One study suggested that the greatest strain single-parent fathers experienced in their transition to single parenthood was in becoming single rather than in becoming single parents. Many fathers experienced loneliness and missed a wife's companionship. The presence of children helped them adjust to being single.[47]

Can any conclusions be drawn from the data available? It does seem clear that, just as a two-parent family does not guarantee happiness, adjustment, and well-behaved children, neither does a one-parent family signify the opposite. Nor are the findings meant to imply that the absence of a father or mother has no effect whatsoever. There are definite limitations on time and energy for the fulfillment of various tasks. Children in single-parent families are assumed to have more responsibility than children in two-parent families. Gender-role patterns tend to remain traditional, with children doing sex-stereotyped chores and engaging in sex-stereotyped activities. But Marie Richmond-Abbott contends that since single parents exhibit behavior typically stereotyped as both masculine and feminine, this context may serve as a model and be the vanguard of more nontraditional and flexible sex-role values and behavior by the children.[48]

Many other effects of single parenthood can be cited. In regard to the power structure, with one parent it is impossible for the child to play

---

46. Barbara J. Risman, "Can Men 'Mother'? Life as a Single Father," *Family Relations* 35 (January 1986): 95–102.

47. Richard M. Smith and Craig W. Smith, "Child Rearing and Single-Parent Fathers," *Family Relations* 30 (July 1981): 411–417.

48. Marie Richmond-Abbott, "Sex-Role Attitudes of Mothers and Children in Divorced, Single-Parent Families," *Journal of Divorce* 8 (Fall 1984): 61–81.

one adult against the other. This situation may also create certain problems in adjusting to the parent of the opposite sex. In terms of affectional support, the danger of the one-parent family is that the demands of one to fulfill the needs ordinarily met in marriage by two may prove intolerable to the solitary parent, with the result being physical and emotional exhaustion.

What about the parent-absent family, those 6.6 percent of black children, 3.3 percent of Spanish-origin children, and 2.0 percent of white children who in 1985 were living with neither parent (Table 7–3)? Apparently most of these children, while not living with a parent, are living with relatives, especially grandparents. As they get older they become more likely to live in families with brothers or sisters, or with other relatives. White children are more likely than black children to be placed in public agencies and institutions.[49] The conditions that result in children living separately from their parents, the effect of parent absence on the children, and the existing support services for these children are questions in need of research.

FAMILY MOBILITY: CHANGING CLASS LIFE-STYLES

One fundamental characteristic of families and class is the extent to which there is opportunity to move from one class to another. Although mobility is often thought to mean improvement, it can be upward, downward, or lateral. The first two types are referred to as *vertical social mobility* (upward or downward) and the latter is referred to as *horizontal social mobility*.

The likelihood of social mobility

The likelihood of vertical social mobility may be regarded as a function of three separate phenomena. First is the *opportunity structure* to which the individual has access. This is the organizational structure of a society that defines the ultimate achievement possibilities for the individual as well as the channels available to realize the achievements. Different opportunity structures apply to different individuals, groups, or subcultures within the same society. However, the structure of the society, including the presence or absence of jobs, the availability of educational and training

---

49. Raymond Montemayor and Goeffrey K. Leigh, "Parent-Absent Children: A Demographic Analysis of Children and Adolescents Living Apart from Their Parents," *Family Relations* 31 (October 1982): 567–573.

programs, and other social characteristics, will in large part determine the extent to which mobility occurs.

The second component of the likelihood of vertical social mobility may be said to be the *individual* him- or herself. In this regard, personality characteristics determine the individual's capacity for exploiting the opportunity structure and will influence the likelihood of mobility. These characteristics may include factors such as intelligence, motivation, motor skills, and value systems.

The third component may be termed the *frictional factor.* That is, two identically equipped individuals confronting the same opportunity structure may nevertheless attain disparate levels of mobility. These factors, inherent neither in the individual nor in the opportunity structure, may be referred to as chance, luck, or fortune.[50]

Bradley Schiller postulates that the family's economic circumstance is the key accessibility condition for the various opportunity strata available to sons.[51] Thus each economic class confronts a separate and distinctive set of achievement opportunities. In comparing the pattern of socioeconomic achievement of children from welfare families with that of the general population, sharp differences are found. Schiller suggests that the lack of achievements of poor children is largely due to the inequality of opportunity that exists along class lines. That is, a substantial portion of the underachievement of sons who grew up in families receiving Aid to Families with Dependent Children (AFDC) cannot be explained by differential abilities or by the sons' motivations or aspirations. The argument that the poor remain poor because they lack the motivation to rise above their origin receives little empirical support.

The extent of social mobility

The American dream suggests that in this land of opportunity anyone can go from "rags to riches." The widespread belief is that with hard work and endurance, any motivation to get ahead will enable anyone who so desires to move upward on the social-class ladder. Data do seem to suggest that social mobility in our society probably is increasing. However, social mobility and equality of opportunity probably never have been as widespread as U.S. citizens believe.

It has been estimated that one of every four or five persons moves upward at least one social-class level during his or her lifetime. It is among blue-collar workers that the greatest amount of upward mobility occurs.

---

50. Bradley R. Schiller, "Stratified Opportunities: The Essence of the 'Vicious Circle,' " *American Journal of Sociology* 76 (November 1970): 427.

51. Ibid., pp. 426–439.

Empirical studies of social mobility suggest several general conclusions. One is that more children will find themselves at the same level as their parents than at any other level. Secondly, a substantial proportion of sons and daughters have experienced some mobility. Third, upward mobility is more prevalent than downward mobility. Fourth, when mobility does occur, it is likely to mean a shift to class levels adjacent to those of the individual's parents, that is, short-distance mobility is more frequent than long-distance mobility.

Consequences of social mobility

It is unlikely that many of us would reject the opportunity for upward social mobility. With this opportunity we envision a better job, higher income, a more luxurious home, a more prestigious neighborhood, opportunities to travel, better clothes, a new car, freedom from debt, and generally a more luxurious as well as refined life-style. And many, if not most, who are reading this believe that education is one means to obtain these rewards. Within our society, with its fairly open class system and its increasing requirements for specialized and highly trained technicians and experts, brain power frequently means higher status. But a closer investigation of the open class system shows that not all consequences of mobility are positive. In various ways, the costs of upward social mobility may be great and its penalties quite severe.

Many students will discover, or may have already discovered, some disruptive effects of their increased education (a potential contribution to upward social mobility). The most obvious is likely to be an increasingly estranged relationship with parents. Particularly if parents are working-class people of limited formal education, many students will find that they are modifying their beliefs and value systems in ways that may conflict greatly with those of their parents. The paradox of this situation is that these are frequently parents who make major sacrifices to provide a college education for their children, with the painful consequence of having their children become socially distant from them.

There are instances in which marriage itself may be threatened by upward social mobility. The wife who works to assist her husband in completing his education may find that his value system and life-style changes while hers remains more static. Success in business may encourage certain husbands to seek the friendship of more "sophisticated" females. Career-oriented wives may discover the existence of many men whose values and behavior patterns are more to their liking than those of their husbands. Two existing spouses may not be equally interested in mobility or may differ in their ability to readjust to the new requirements of a higher social status. These and many other examples of social mobility illustrate how this supposedly desirable phenomenon may disrupt husband-wife relationships.

Mobility can be a disruptive process leaving persons isolated, detached, lonely, and emotionally distressed. In a review of empirical studies dealing with the emotional climate in the family, Kenneth Kessin reports that generally the data suggest stressful emotional relationships, tension, and parent-child estrangement associated with actual or anticipated mobility.[52] Upwardly mobile wives were found to identify less with their extended family and express less neighborhood integration than did nonmobile wives. One general conclusion for married women was that mobility tended to produce social isolation and was detrimental to extended family relations.

Obviously, not all social mobility has negative consequences. In a relatively open class system, a high rate of social mobility may tend to stabilize the social order by providing outlets to persons with particular skills or talents who are dissatisfied with their present social status. The possibility for upward social mobility may prevent the rebellious and revolutionary tactics that result from persons who are frustrated in their social position and have little opportunity for advancement. Families may receive new recognition and social prestige by their social climbing. Thus the question is not so much whether social mobility is good or bad, but rather what types of consequences to individuals and families result within societies that have closed or open class systems?

SUMMARY

1. *Social classes* refers to aggregates of individuals who occupy differential portions on scales of wealth, prestige, and power. This differential ranking results in inequalities between persons and families.

2. Two theories particularly relevant to an understanding of social class are those of functionalism and conflict. The former sees a stratified system as inevitable and necessary for the fulfillment of tasks needed to maintain a society. The latter sees a stratified system as leading to dissatisfaction and conflict between the laborers who are the instrument of production and the owners and managers who control the means of production.

3. The determination of social-class position varies widely from examining who owns, manages, and controls production to noting differential rankings of occupational prestige, income, or education. This chapter makes no effort to establish a set number of strata or classes but

---

52. Kenneth Kessin, "Social and Psychological Consequences of Intergenerational Occupational Mobility," *American Journal of Sociology* 77 (July 1971): 5.

notes some of the consequences of differential ranking of persons and families, and then provides a description of four general social categories of families: the wealthy, the middle class, blue-collar families, and families in poverty.

4. Wealthy families are identified as the very rich, the upper class, and the ruling class. This group of elite owns and controls the means of production. Families are concerned with who they are and serve to protect their names and wealth.

5. Middle-class families serve as the linkage between the small group of wealthy families and the group of working-class, blue-collar families. They are the bourgeoisie who own small amounts of productive resources. They are the professionals and corporate white-collar bureaucrats. Family resources are directed lineally to the children and grandchildren. Married couples tend toward the ideal of equality between the spouses but in reality perform highly segregated roles. In child rearing they were found to use reason, verbal threats, or withdrawal of rewards to punish their children.

6. Blue-collar or working-class families comprise nearly half of all U.S. workers. They do not have the economic stability found in middle-class families since they are more highly dependent on the swings of the business cycle in our wage-price-profits system. Marriages are more unstable than among the higher social groupings, husband-wife roles are highly traditional, and children are subordinate to the parents. Early marriage and parenthood are frequent.

7. Families in poverty include about one in nine U.S. families altogether, but include more than one-fourth of Spanish-origin families and one-third of black families. Evident in the feminization of poverty is the growth in female-headed families and the rise in teen and young parenting, income inequality, and inadequate personal and child support. The greatest amount of public assistance goes to these households but many rely on the swapping of goods and services. This results in a *fictive kinship* where friends become like family. Most serious poverty is characterized by an underclass of persistent poverty and a variety of associated families.

8. A disproportionate number of single-parent families are families in poverty. This is particularly true of female-headed households where no husband or father is present. Increasing rates of unmarried motherhood and high rates of divorce and spouse-absent families make it probable that the majority of children born in the 1980s will experience a one-parent living arrangement before they are eighteen. Clear differences exist between mothers as single parents and fathers as single parents, with the fathers faring much better. Studies suggest children from this type of family structure compared well with those from a two-parent structure when socioeconomic status is controlled.

9. What are the chances for and consequences of family social mobility? Social mobility does seem to be increasing, but was probably never as widespread as has been widely believed. While seen as desirable by most persons, upward mobility can result in new recognition and social prestige or may bring rejection and social isolation. Clearly, extended-family cohesion is likely to decrease and lower levels of family participation are likely to result.

10. This chapter concludes Part II, which examined structural and sub-cultural variations in family life-styles. Part III examines premarital structures and processes and deals primarily with mate selection. In a general sense, the next eight chapters follow the marital and family life cycle, from the point of selecting a mate and premarital factors through marriage, parenthood, middle years, and, finally, the later years. As you will note a variety of frames of reference or theoretical approaches (structural-functional, exchange, conflict, psychoanalytic, behaviorist, symbolic-interactional) are used in the examination of these organizational and processual patterns at various stages of the life cycle.

KEY TERMS AND TOPICS

DISCUSSION QUESTIONS

1. What is meant by social class? How many classes exist? How is that determined?

2. Compare and contrast a functionalist perspective of class with that of the conflict perspective.

3. Discuss "all men (women, families) are created equal."

4. How valid are the ideas of Marx on class conflict between the bourgeoisie and the proletariat? Where does the middle class fit into his scheme?

5. Make a stratification study of the families in your home community. Where

do they live, work, and worship? Where does or will their children attend college (if at all)? What kind of cars do they drive? What hobbies do they pursue? What are their family sizes, attitudes toward child rearing, and the like? Outline their style of living.

6. Describe the family and work life of the very rich. Summarize the life-styles of the husband, wife, sons, and daughters.

7. Discuss: "When a college student from a middle-class family takes a job in a factory, he or she becomes a member of the working class." Or: "When the same student becomes unemployed, he or she enters into the poverty level."

8. What is meant by "fictive kin" and the "feminization of poverty"? Explain reasons for their existence.

9. What kind of programs or policy may be effective in getting families above a level of poverty? Should food stamps, subsidized housing, welfare programs, etc. be cut or eliminated? Why or why not?

10. How do you explain the increases in one-parent families? Why is this increase of concern to policy makers or to the general public? What differences exist in one- or two-parent situations? Does it make a difference if the single parent is a father or a mother? Why?

11. What types of factors foster upward mobility? Downward mobility?

12. Why are many consequences of upward social mobility disruptive to kin and community ties?

FURTHER READINGS

Blumberg, Paul M., and Paul, P. W. "Continuities and Discontinuities in Upper-Class Marriages." *Journal of Marriage and the Family* 37 (February 1975): 63–77. A study of the social characteristics and changes in upper-class marriages.

Dalphin, John. *The Persistence of Social Inequality in America.* Cambridge, Mass.: Schenkman, 1981. A brief paperback that examines why inequality exists in the United States, how it is perceived, and why income, wealth, and power are concentrated in the hands of the upper class.

Gecas, Viktor. "The Influence of Social Class on Socialization." *Contemporary Theories About the Family.* Vol. 1. Edited by Wesley R. Burr et al. New York: The Free Press, 1979: 365–404. An inventory of findings on social class and socialization to determine how and why social class affects parental behavior.

Greif, Goeffrey L *Single Fathers.* Lexington, Mass.: Lexington Books, 1985. Questionnaire returns from over 1100 single fathers who had custody of their children were used to describe how they handle various aspects of parenting, including housework, child care, going to work, the legal system, and interpersonal relationships.

Komarovsky, Mirra. *Blue Collar Marriage.* New York: Random House, 1962. A case study of fifty-eight working-class families that provides a wealth of material on most aspects of blue-collar married life.

Levine, Edward M. "Middle-class Family Decline," and Novak, Michael, "In Praise of Bourgeois." *Society* 18 (January/February 1981): 72–78 and 60–67. Two articles on the middle-class family in U.S. society: the former examining its decline and the latter praising its virtues.

Ostrander, Susan A. *Women of the Upper Class.* Philadelphia: Temple University Press, 1984. Interviews with thirty-six upper-class women and a look at their lives as wives, mothers, club members, and volunteers.

Rapp, Rayna. "Family and Class in Contemporary America: Notes Toward an Understanding of Ideology." *Science and Society* 42 (Fall 1978): 278–300; also in Barrie Thorne with Marilyn Yalom, *Rethinking the Family: Some Feminist Questions.* New York: Longman, 1982: 168–187. An examination of class differences from a conflict perspective between those who own and control the means of production versus those who provide the labor and work for wages.

Rubin, Lillian Breslow. *World of Pain: Life in the Working-Class Family.* New York: Basic Books, 1976. A subjective analysis of fifty working-class families and a comparison group of twenty-five professional middle-class families.

Treas, Judith. "Trickle Down or Transfers? Postwar Determinants of Family Income Inequality." *American Sociological Review* 48 (August 1983): 546–559. An empirical assessment of two competing theories of income redistribution: the expansion of social welfare and macroeconomic expansion.

Vanfossen, Beth Ensminger. *The Structure of Social Inequality.* Boston: Little, Brown, 1979. A book that draws heavily upon empirical research and sociological theory in analyzing the determinants, correlates, and consequences of inequality.

Williams, Terry M., and Kornblum, William. *Growing up Poor.* Lexington, Mass.: D. C. Heath and Co., 1985. An investigation of U.S. teenagers who are growing up under extremely difficult economic and social conditions.

Yorburg, Betty. *Families and Societies: Survival or Extinction.* New York: Columbia University Press, 1983. A brief portrait of changes in family life. Chapter 6 examines class differences in U.S. families.

III

THE CREATION
OF THE MARITAL STATUS:
PREMARITAL
STRUCTURES
AND PROCESSES

Photo: © Alan Carey/The Image Works

8

Homogamy and Endogamy in the Selection of Mates

With this chapter we shift our discussion from family institutions and variations in family life-styles to premarital structures and processes in the creation of the marital status. This chapter examines five normative structures surrounding mate selection in the United States: age, residence, class, religion, and race. The terms generally employed to describe mate selection among those who share similar characteristics are **homogamy** and **endogamy:** homogamy denotes something about the likeness or similarity of married couples; endogamy refers to in-group marriages of almost any kind. That people marry those like themselves more often than could be due to chance is known as *assortive mating.* [1] The "assorted" mates are matched on specific structural dimensions.

Homogamy and endogamy are critical factors in the continuity of the U.S. family system (as well as of other social institutions). Homogamy functions to maintain the status quo and conserve traditional values and beliefs. These functions can be dysfunctional in that they reduce or eliminate contact with other people and cultures and restrict the free choice of a mate. But as long as marriage is perceived to be an important and significant institution in the United States or in any society, it is not very difficult to understand why the same characteristics that are viewed as important in a society (age, race, religion, class) are also important in the selection of a mate.

It is common for students to operate on the idea that they are free to marry anyone they please. In reality, there is probably no society in which people actually choose their marriage partners on a completely individual basis. Only when persons consciously consider the socialization processes that lead them to prefer certain types of persons for marriage, consider the social pressures to marry certain types of persons, and investigate the extent of homogamy and endogamy within a given society, do they become aware of the limited freedom of choice that does exist.

Studies throughout the world report high rates of racial, religious, class, educational, and age homogamy. No society in the world leaves

---

1. Paula Dressel presents a theoretical model of twelve propositions relevant to the prediction of degrees of endogamy and homogamy in mate selection. *See* Paula L. Dressel, "Assortive Mating in Later Life," *Journal of Family Issues* 1 (September 1980): 379–396.

the selection of a marriage partner unregulated and indiscriminate. Whether the choice is by the persons getting married, by parents, relatives, delegated persons or groups, or by specific social agencies, it is always subject to regulation by social and cultural controls.

One should not be led into believing that endogamy and homogamy are the preferred or required norms in all respects. The most universal of all norms regarding marriage—the incest taboo—is an exogamous norm. Exogamy rules that members of a society marry outside their kin group. Thus, all marriages are exogamous in that they are forbidden between members of the same nuclear-family unit. Generally, the same could be said for sex. **Exogamy** and **heterogamy** are often used interchangeably. However, technically speaking, exogamy *requires* differences whereas heterogamy *denotes* differences. If both heterogamy and exogamy are used to indicate marriage between persons of a different group, then no "purely" endogamous marriage exists.

Our discussion of homogamy, exogamy, or both in the selection of mates will be confined to specific characteristics or groups that are culturally conceived as relevant to the choice of a spouse, particularly as exists within the United States. A marriage could conceivably be considered endogamous in regard to race, exogamous in regard to kin, heterogamous in regard to religion, and homogamous in regard to values and personality traits.

FACTORS INFLUENCING RATES OF INTERMARRIAGE

Prior to discussing specific dimensions of mate selection such as age or race, several general questions need to be addressed. For example: Who is included or excluded in determining whether a marriage is, in actuality, mixed? How are rates influenced by the reporting of them, particularly in using figures of marriages as opposed to individuals? What social and cultural factors are likely to foster or affect the likelihood of intermarriage? These three questions appear to be applicable to any intermarriage whether based on age, class, race, religion, height, weight, or eye color.

Who is included in a mixed marriage?

How much age difference must exist before a marriage becomes age-exogamous? Is a marriage between a Methodist and a Lutheran (both Protestant) an interfaith marriage? At what point does any difference or characteristic determine homogamy or heterogamy, endogamy or exogamy? Obviously, in any study or in any reporting of rates some definition must be used to determine whom to include or whom to exclude. In research, *operational definitions* are used; in other words, variables are defined according to the way they are measured. As a result, an age difference of more than four years may be arbitrarily defined as age exogamous. Or an interracial marriage may be defined as any marriage in which the couple defines themselves accordingly irrespective of color or lineage. This problem of what is or is not an intermarriage is a serious one in determining rates or in comparing studies. Greater attention is devoted to this issue in dealing with specific social dimensions.

Can intermarriage rates be influenced?

Specifically, can intermarriage rates be influenced by the reporting of marriages as opposed to individuals? Most published rates of mixed marriage (or intermarriage) are based on the total number of a group's *marriages.* But sometimes they are interpreted as if they were based on the number of *individuals* who marry. A **marriage rate** refers to the percentage of marriages that are mixed of all marriages involving individuals in a specific category. A **marriage rate for individuals** refers to the percentage of married individuals in a specific category who enter a mixed marriage.

Suppose we have ten marriages, four that are black-white, or interracial, and six that are white-white, or intraracial. Is the mixed (interracial) marriage rate 40 percent or 25 percent? Four of the ten marriages (40 percent) are interracial, but four of the sixteen white persons (25 percent) married interracially.

Unless none of the marriages or all of the marriages are mixed, the mixed-marriage rate for marriages is always greater than the mixed-marriage rate for individuals. Thus, if your objective is to prove that mixed marriages are occurring in greater frequency, you could use the mixed-marriage rate for marriages. If you wish to prove that the incidence of mixed marriage is not as great, you could use the mixed-marriage rate for individuals. Statistically, both figures would be accurate. Thus, one way to lie with statistics "honestly" is to use the rate that best fits your purpose or interest.

In addition to distinguishing rates between marriages and individuals, it is also possible to distinguish a group's **actual rate** of intermarriage from its **expected rate.** The ratio between the two is important in determining if intermarriage is greater than could be expected to occur by chance or if marriage partners had been chosen randomly. The *expected intermarriage rate* is the percentage of people who would have selected a mate outside their own group if they had chosen their marriage partners randomly, knowing the frequency distribution of the particular groups in the population. The *actual rate* refers to those marriages that do take place. Glenn, for example, illustrates that based on the relative size of religious categories, 68 percent of Protestants, 26 percent of Catholics, and only 2.3 percent of Jews could be expected to be endogamous with random mating. In actuality, as will be shown later, an overwhelming majority of Protestant, Catholic, and Jewish members marry endogamously.[2] Clearly, assortive mating processes are operative for religious as well as most social groupings: people marry endogamously in frequencies far greater than could be expected simply by chance or at random.

What factors foster intermarriage?

Actual rates of intermarriage are influenced by various factors, many of which center around the normative eligibility rules for mate selection, such as role compatibility, value consensus, and similarity in age, class, religion, or race. However, apart from the normative rules there are non-normative factors that favor endogamous marriages. Consider, for example, factors such as group size, sex ratio, controls over marriage, the development of cultural similarities, the romantic love complex, and the influence of certain psychological factors.

Size of a group   The size of a group relative to the larger population is likely to influence the extent to which the actual intermarriage rate is larger or smaller than would be expected by chance. Generally the larger the group, the lower its intermarriage rate. Or the smaller the group relative to the total population, the faster its rate goes up with each intermarriage. For example, in Utah, the heart of the Mormon population in the United States, marriages are highly endogamous. But in Florida, where Mormons constitute less than 1 percent of the population, it was ascertained that about two-thirds of the Mormons living there had married a non-Mormon.[3] That such a difference exists in the proportion of Utah and Florida Mormons who marry interfaith stems far less from the difference in degree of religious intensity of members in Florida than from the probability that Florida Mormons will meet and interact with persons from a non-Mormon background.

Similarly, a study of intermarriages in Hawaii over more than a thirty-year period supported the effect of group size on intermarriage. The larger the group, the smaller the rate of intermarriage in Hawaii, whether the groups were age cohorts, ethnic groups, residential communities, occupational groups, or people with the same marital status.[4]

---

2. Norval D. Glenn, "A Note on Estimating the Strength of Influences for Religious Endogamy," *Journal of Marriage and the Family* 46 (August 1984): 725–727.

3. Brent A. Barlow, "Notes on Mormon Interfaith Marriages," *The Family Coordinator* 26 (April 1977): 148.

4. Teresa Labov and Jerry A. Jacobs, "Intermarriages in Hawaii, 1950–1983," *Journal of Marriage and the Family* 48 (February 1986): 79–88.

Heterogeneity   Blau and others propose that in addition to size, the degree of heterogeneity in the community will influence the rate of intermarriage.[5] This too found support in the Hawaii study.[6] The more heterogeneous the opposite sex, the more outmarriage was observed.

Sex ratio and group controls   The sex ratio (number of males per 100 females) is likely to influence the rate of intermarriage. In a community or setting where one sex outnumbers the other, traditional barriers are crossed with increased frequency as the sex with greater numbers selects from the smaller pool of available partners. Intermarriage rates are likely to be influenced as well by the extent of social or *group controls* over the individuals involved. The Amish and Jews, both religious minorities in the United States, maintain group sanctions through teachings and religious practices that discourage marriage with "outsiders."

Cultural similarities   Another factor that influences intermarriage rates is the development of cultural similarities and the elimination of differences. As ethnic minorities attend public schools, work in diverse social environments, and identify with the new or larger society, the differences in language, dress, or traditional practices decrease and the likelihood of intermarriage increases.

Romantic love complex   An increase also occurs as a result of what might be called the *romantic love complex,* the idea that love is more important than group controls, cultural differences, or homogamous characteristics. Related to this complex is a personal choice ideal that suggests each person has the right to choose whom to marry with minimal interference from others.

Psychological factors   Finally, intermarriage rates are likely to be influenced by certain psychological factors: rebellion against one's own group, feelings of alienation, emotional immaturity, or other psychological characteristics. As is the case with all factors mentioned, no given individual influenced by any of these factors will necessarily intermarry. But probabilities of intermarriage increase under conditions or circumstances such as those described.

The discussion that follows examines the role of selected social-structural dimensions as they affect interpersonal relations in the selection

5. Peter M. Blau, Terry C. Blum, and Joseph E. Schwartz, "Heterogeneity and Intermarriage," *American Sociological Review* (February 1982): 45–62.

6. Ibid., p. 85.

of a marriage partner. These include age, residence, social class, religion, and race. Obviously, this list is not, nor is it intended to be, inclusive of all social structures relating to the selection of a mate. However, it should give a clear indication of the extent to which endogamous marriages are predominant in the United States.

AGE AT MARRIAGE

Age homogamy

Most couples in the United States are relatively homogamous in terms of the age at which they marry. Although a person is "free" to marry someone considerably older or younger (within legal limits), most single persons select a member of the opposite sex from a closely related age group. In 1985, the median age at first marriage was 25.8 for males and 23.3 for females, an age difference of 2.5 years (*see* Table 8–1).

An examination of Table 8–1 shows that the median age at first marriage as well as the age difference between males and females has changed considerably since the turn of the century. From 1890 until the mid-1950s, the trend in the United States was toward an earlier age at marriage and a narrowing of the age difference between bride and groom

TABLE 8–1
Median age at first marriage, by sex, for the United States: 1890–1985

Year	Male	Female	Difference	Year	Male	Female	Difference
1985	25.5	23.3	2.2	1973	23.3	21.0	2.2
1984	25.4	23.0	2.4	1972	23.3	20.9	2.4
1983	25.4	22.8	2.6	1971	23.1	20.9	2.2
1982	25.2	22.5	2.7	1970	23.2	20.8	2.4
1981	24.8	22.3	2.5	1960	22.8	20.3	2.5
1980	24.7	22.0	2.7	1950	22.8	20.3	2.5
1979	24.4	22.1	2.3	1940	24.3	21.5	2.8
1978	24.2	21.8	2.4	1930	24.3	21.3	3.0
1977	24.0	21.6	2.4	1920	24.6	21.2	3.4
1976	23.8	21.3	2.5	1910	25.1	21.6	3.5
1975	23.5	21.1	2.4	1900	25.9	21.9	4.0
1974	23.1	21.1	2.0	1890	26.1	22.0	4.1

Source: Adapted from U.S. Bureau of the Census, Current Population Reports, Series P-20, no. 410, "Marital Status and Living Arrangements: March 1985" (Washington, D.C.: U.S. Government Printing Office, 1986), Table A-1, p. 67.

at first marriage. Data for 1890 show the median ages at first marriage to be 26.1 years for males and 22 for females, an age difference of 4.1 years. In 1956, the median age at first marriage reached an all-time low (22.5 for men and 20.1 for women). Since that time there has been a gradual, though not continuous, increase in the median age at first marriage for both men and women. In the last ten years there has been about a two-year increase in the median age at first marriage for both males and females.

How would you explain this incredible two-year increase in just a ten-year period? Are people delaying marriage because they are spending more time in school? Is it due to increased job opportunities or lack of them? Does an absence of a satisfactory level of income lead people to delay marriage? Can it be attributed to an increase in cohabitation that delays or replaces marriage? Or might the "marriage squeeze," relating to a shortage of marital partners, be a contributing factor? The marriage squeeze is described in the next section.

Age homogamy is in itself a function of the age at marriage. Without exception, the median age at marriage for grooms is always higher than that for brides. It is estimated that in six out of seven marriages in the United States, the male is as old or older than his bride. And an empirical study of marital-age heterogamy showed that in 1980, 27 percent of these males were five or more years older. In contrast, only 3.1 percent of the males were five or more years younger.[7] In both types of age heterogamy (husband older as well as husband younger), when compared with homogamous-age marriages (operationally defined as plus or minus four years), a tendency existed for the heterogamous marriages to be characterized by lower-educational level, multiple marriages, lower-family income, and lower-occupational status of the husband.

Why the overwhelming likelihood that males will be older than females? Several explanations include the husband's slower physiological maturity than that of his wife, the traditional responsibility of the husband to be the major breadwinner (which requires more preparation time), the slight excess of males through the early twenties, the mating gradient (described later in this chapter), or the continued subjugation of women. This last gender argument is consistent with the proposition that suggests female-male age differences decrease or narrow as societies become more egalitarian.

Age differences in marriage are the smallest at the younger ages and increase as age goes up. Although it is the usual pattern for men to choose women younger than themselves, the difference in their ages increases as the age at first marriage for the male increases. This indicates

---

7. Maxine P. Atkinson and Becky L. Glass, "Marital Age Heterogamy and Homogamy, 1900–1980," *Journal of Marriage and the Family* 47 (August 1985): 685–691.

Not only is the median age of all marriages increasing, the frequency of divorce and widowhood tends to remarriage among many older couples. (Photo: © Harold M. Lambert Studio/E. P. Jones, Co.)

that as men get older they increasingly marry younger women. A different pattern exists for women. As women get older they marry men who are more nearly their own age.

The reason for these seemingly contradictory data is that in the first case the median age of the bride is based on the actual age of the groom. In the latter case the median age of the groom is based on the actual age of the bride. That is, men of actual age (such as fifty-five, sixty-three, or sixty-eight) tend to marry brides who, taken together, constitute a computed median age that is considerably younger. For women, their actual age (such as fifty-five, sixty-three, or sixty-eight) is very close to the computed median age of the men they marry. There are considerable differences in average ages at marriage between previously married persons such as widows and divorcees, but the generalizations of differences in age at marriage seem to hold true regardless of age, sex, or previous marital status.

A final question dealing with age homogamy is whether age differences make a difference in the quality of marriage. Are May-December marriages, as referred to in the popular literature, more problem-ridden and less stable? Evidence tends to suggest they are not. An analysis of two public use data sets yielded no significant differences in marital quality among couples from various age-dissimilar categories.[8] This finding, a dramatic contradiction to conventional wisdom, might suggest that age is becoming a less compelling determinant of adult attitudes and behavior in U.S. society.

The marriage squeeze

The "marriage squeeze" is used to describe the effects of an imbalance between the number of males and females in the prime marriage ages. Consider the hypothetical population where males age twenty-five typically marry females age twenty-two. If the annual number of births is decreasing each year, the twenty-five-year-old males will be looking for brides among the smaller cohort (an age-specific group) of females born three years later. The males would be caught in a marriage squeeze because they are encountering a shortage of females. Conversely, if a population experiences a substantial increase in the annual number of births, the same process would operate but it would be the females who would be caught in the marriage squeeze. That is, the male population born three years earlier would be smaller in number than the larger number of females born three years later.

The marriage squeeze phenomenon is a significant factor in marriage behavior. In the 1950s it was men who faced a shortage of women. The situation reversed in the 1980s to women facing a shortage of men and will reverse again in the 1990s and the turn of the century to a shortage of women. How are these imbalances and shifts explained? Basically, the 1950s marriage squeeze was the result of a decline in the absolute number of births each year during the late 1920s and early 1930s, combined with the fact that men tended to marry women two or three years younger than themselves. Because there were more men born in 1930 than women born in 1932 or 1933, the pool of women two or three years younger

---

8. Hernan Vera, Donna H. Berardo, and Felix M. Berardo, "Age Heterogamy in Marriage," *Journal of Marriage and the Family* 49 (August 1985): 553–566.

For females: does waiting to marry mean not marrying?

Yale sociologists Neil B. Bennett and Patricia H. Craig and Harvard economist David E. Bloom provided the traumatic news. White, college-educated women born in the mid-50s who are still single at age 30 have only a 20 percent chance of marrying. By age 35 the odds drop to 5 percent. Forty-year-olds have a 2.6 percent probability of tying the knot. Within days this news set off a profound crisis of confidence among the growing ranks of single women in the United States.

Their study was titled, innocently enough, "Marriage Patterns in the United States." But the dire statistics confirmed what everybody suspected all along: that many women who seem to have it all—good looks, good jobs, advanced degrees, high salaries—will not have mates.

It should be noted, the study does not say that women should get married or even speculate about how many would like to do so. The study does not say that women need to suffer a stigma of singleness, being unmarried indicates a low lovability quotient, or not marrying consigns a woman to emotional impoverishment. What it does say is that for those who wait, "not now" may mean an increased probability of "never," particularly to the huge cohort of baby-boom women.

from whom to choose was smaller. Thus a male marriage squeeze. A reverse female marriage squeeze resulted in the 1970s and early 1980s due to the increased number of births during the post-World War II "baby boom" of the 1950s. And finally, given the sharp decline in the birth rate in the 1960s and 1970s, we can predict a return to the male marriage squeeze in the 1990s. Assuming a two- or three-year difference in marriage age, the smaller female population born several years later than the larger male population born earlier will have a larger pool from which to select.

Spanier and Glick[9] demonstrate how the marriage squeeze affected black females far more than white females in the mid-1970s. While the ratio of white males to females remained fairly close to 100 in the marriage age group, the ratio for black males to females was lower. In the 20–24-year age group there were 11 percent more black females than black males. This increased to 16 percent in the 25–29-year age group and to more than 19 percent among those 30–34. This marriage squeeze resulted in a restricted field of eligibles for black women, causing an unusually large proportion of black women to remain unmarried or to marry men who tend to be older, who have lower educational attainment, and who have previously been married.

9. Graham B. Spanier and Paul C. Glick, "Mate Selection Differentials Between Whites and Blacks in the United States," *Social Forces* 58 (March 1980): 707–725.

Heer and Grossbard-Shechtman[10] argued that the marriage squeeze against females in the 1970s was instrumental in reducing both the proportion of females who could marry and the compensation which men were obliged to give women for traditional wifely and maternal duties. Combined with a contraceptive revolution, it became increasingly possible for women to have sexual relationships without procreative or marital intent. These factors in turn served to increase divorce and illegitimacy and fostered the women's liberation movement. Schoen and Baj, however, caution us against giving the marriage squeeze a mystique that credits it with an importance beyond its due.[11] Testing its impact in five western countries, they conclude that its influence on recent marriage behavior seems less than that of other forces: the changing structure of industrial labor markets, increased female labor-force participation, low fertility, and changing sex roles. In contemporary third world countries, however, they suggest that its importance is probably much greater than has been appreciated to date.

The law and the age at marriage

The legal control of age, marriage, and divorce in the United States lies with the states rather than with the federal government. Most state laws have two provisions regarding age at marriage: one is the age at which young people may marry *without* the consent of their parents; the other is the age at which young people may marry *with* parental consent. To be married *without* parental consent, all states require that the groom be eighteen (except Mississippi, which requires both men and women to be twenty-one). To be married *with* parental consent, the minimum age is typically sixteen for both sexes. As of 1985, a number of states (Delaware and Ohio) required males to be eighteen with or without parental consent; several states (Arizona, California, Georgia, Indiana, Iowa, Kansas, Kentucky, and Massachusetts) had no minimum age with parental consent; and a few states (Alabama, New Hampshire, Rhode Island, Texas, and Utah) permitted marriage for males at age fourteen with parental consent. No state has a legal age at marriage for females that is older than that for males; however, at least eleven states permit females to marry younger

---

10. David M. Heer and Amyra Grossbard-Shechtman, "The Impact of the Female Marriage Squeeze and the Contraceptive Revolution on Sex Roles and the Women's Liberation Movement in the United States, 1960 to 1975," *Journal of Marriage and the Family* 43 (February 1981): 49–65; *see also* Robert Schoen, "Measuring the Tightness of a Marriage Squeeze," *Demography* 20 (February 1983): 61–78.

11. Robert Schoen and John Baj, "The Impact of the Marriage Squeeze in Five Western Countries," *Sociology and Social Research* 70 (October 1985): 8–19.

than males with parental consent.[12] Over the past decade, a majority of states lowered the legal minimum age for marriage. Interestingly, this came at a time when the median age at marriage was increasing sharply, lessening the need for concern over young marriages.

The concern over young marriages

Data presented about the median age at marriage show that half of all males and females marry for the first time below the ages of twenty-five and twenty-three respectively. Some of these marriages occur among adolescents or teenagers, an age category that most people view as too young for marriage. The consequences of these teenage marriages are fairly well known, and most are defined as both serious and unfortunate. The consequences include a high incidence of dropping out of school,[13] high unemployment rates among teenagers (refer back to Table 6–1), higher than average fertility rates[14] (the consequences of young parenthood are discussed in Chapter 13), lower than average lifetime earnings, and a high divorce rate[15] (estimated for teenage marriages to be from two to four times that for marriages begun by persons after age twenty).

Some support was found for the idea that people who marry young are unprepared for the mate selection process and marital role performance, experience relatively low marital satisfaction as a result, and therefore appear disproportionately in divorce statistics.[16]

Apart from these young marriages, by itself, age at marriage does not appear to be a major point of difficulty in family life. Considering the upturn in the divorce rate in the latter half of the 1960s and in the 1970s and considering the stabilization or increase in ages at marriage, it is not

---

12. These figures came from *The World Almanac and Book of Facts: 1986* (New York: Newspaper Enterprise Association, 1986): 85.

13. Alan C. Kerckhoff and Alan A. Parrow, "The Effect of Early Marriage on the Educational Attainment of Young Men," *Journal of Marriage and the Family* 41 (February 1979): 97–107; and Gus W. Haggstrom, David E. Kanouse, and Peter A. Morrison, "Accounting for the Educational Shortfalls of Mothers," *Journal of Marriage and the Family* 48 (February 1986): 175–186.

14. Margaret Mooney Marini, "Effects of the Timing of Marriage and First Birth on Fertility," *Journal of Marriage and the Family* 43 (February 1981): 27–46.

15. Kristin A. Moore and Linda J. Waite, "Marital Dissolution, Early Motherhood and Early Marriage," *Social Forces* 60 (September 1981): 20–40; and Stephen J. Bahr and Richard J. Galligan, "Teenage Marriage and Marital Stability," *Youth and Society* 15 (June 1984): 387–400.

16. Gary R. Lee, "Age at Marriage and Marital Satisfaction: A Multivariate Analysis with Implications for Marital Stability," *Journal of Marriage and the Family* 39 (August 1977): 493–503; and Alan Booth and John N. Edwards, "Age at Marriage and Marital Stability," *Journal of Marriage and the Family* 47 (February 1985): 67–75.

likely that any rise in the divorce rate can be accounted for by age at marriage.

RESIDENTIAL PROPINQUITY

Well established in the sociology-of-the-family literature is the idea that mate selection involves a "propinquity factor." A lengthy list of studies over the last thirty years seems to have established the general conclusion that in the United States, urban persons tend to marry someone who lives within a fairly limited distance of his or her home. Evidence to support this idea usually takes the form of a frequency distribution or cumulative percentage of marriages in some community, classified by the distance separating the bride's residence from the groom's residence just prior to marriage.

Studies of propinquity

Most studies take the lead of James Bossard who, in the early 1930s, checked five thousand consecutive marriage licenses in which one or both applicants were residents of Philadelphia.[17] A tabulation was made of the distance between the residences of the couple. Of the total number of applicants, one in eight gave the same address, one in six lived less than a block from one another, one in four lived within two blocks or less, one in three lived within five blocks or less, and one in two lived within twenty blocks or less. The obvious point is that the percentage of marriages decreased steadily and markedly as the distance between residences of the contracting parties increased.

Since the work of Bossard, at least a dozen studies have been conducted that support an inverse relationship between mate selection and distance between contracting parties. Most have been concerned exclusively with proximity of addresses just before marriage, and their findings have been based on the records of marriage license applications.

Since most propinquity studies were completed two or three decades ago, it is difficult to determine whether place of residence is as significant a factor in mate selection today. One might also expect considerable variations among different groups such as rural residence, marriage among college students, or age. However, it is expected that people would tend to marry those who live near them.

---

17. James H. S. Bossard, "Residential Propinquity as a Factor in Marriage Selection," *The American Journal of Sociology* 38 (September 1932): 219–224.

Explanations of propinquity

How can one account for the propinquity factor in mate selection? One obvious explanation is that we meet and interact with people who live near us and attend the same schools, churches, and social events. While the pool of potential mates increases dramatically with increasing distance, proximity facilitates contact. We are less likely to meet and get to know intimately those who don't live near us. We are not likely to "fall in love with" or marry those we don't meet.

Another explanation has been called the **norm-segregation theory.** This theory suggests that we marry people who adhere to similar cultural norms and that these people reside in segregated clusters. People of similar normative categories related to race, class, religion, ethnic affiliation, or educational level tend to cluster together residentially. Neighborhoods and communities often tend to be characterized by norm-homogamous groupings. Thus the combinations of norm-similarity and geographical proximity provide an additional explanation of residential propinquity in mate selection.

In a highly mobile society one might expect nearness of residence to become a less relevant factor in mate selection. For certain groups and persons this will likely be true. Higher-status groups may be less propinquitous than lower-status groups because factors such as cost and time may be more readily accessible. Higher-status groups may be willing to travel farther and at greater cost than lower-status groups. Propinquity differences of class and occupational groups could then be ascribed to differential perception of the time-cost function.

One final point is that propinquity does not mean nonmobility. As individuals move about for college, jobs, military service, or whatever, they become increasingly more likely, as time passes, to marry someone currently close by than someone formerly propinquitous. Again the time and cost factors become operative. The individual who spent her childhood and adolescent years in Pennsylvania but goes to school and takes a job in Los Angeles may well marry someone from the southern California area. Most people do not become intimately acquainted with many eligible persons of the opposite sex but those they do are likely to be residentially propinquitous.

SOCIAL STATUS

Class endogamy, in our own society and around the world, is a desirable social norm, particularly for higher-status parents in regard to their children. Whether mates are selected by the individuals themselves, parents, or by someone else, conditions supporting class endogamy are essential to

Looking for a mate? Go west women and go east men

The nation has a supply of never-married men and women. As of 1980, there were 25 million single males aged 15 and over compared to 21 million single females of the same ages. But where does one go to meet them? The husband-hunter should go to Alaska, Hawaii, Wyoming, Nevada, or the Pacific Coast states. The wife-hunter has his best chances in Massachusetts, Minnesota, New York, Pennsylvania, New Jersey, or any of the New England States.

In addition, females should avoid cities and search out rural areas: the opposite is true for males. Urban areas have about 115 single males per 100 females compared to about 139 in rural areas. The nation's capital, Washington, D.C., may be the best place of all for males, as the number of never-married single women actually exceeds the number of never-married single men.

All states have more unmarried males than females but the numbers and ratios vary widely. California has an excess of nearly 700,000 never-married single men over single women. In contrast, Maine, Rhode Island, and Vermont have an excess of fewer than 10,000 single males. Alaska, while small in numbers, has the best ratio of single men to single women: for every never-married single female there exist 1.7 never-married single males. Hawaii, Washington, Oregon, California, Montana, Idaho, Wyoming, and Nevada have ratios exceeding 1.3 single males to each single female.

Source: Ratios were figured state by state from census material provided in the *United States Summary of General Population Characteristics* (Washington, D.C.: U.S. Government Printing Office, 1983), Vol. 1, Table 65, p. 146.

preserve family lineage and status. On the other hand, persons from lower statuses have much to gain by marriage to persons of a higher standing. Irrespective of the desired or preferred circumstances, most marriages are class endogamous.

Class endogamy

Numerous studies in the past fifty years have found that both men and women marry persons from within their own class with a greater consistency than could be expected simply by chance. As early as 1918, an analysis of marriages in Philadelphia showed that intermarriage between men and women in the same industry was distinctly more common than chance expectancy, revealing something of an endogamous trend.[18]

18. D. M. Marvin, "Occupational Propinquity as a Factor in Mate Selection," *Publications of the American Statistical Association* 16 (1918–19): 131–150.

In a study at Western Michigan University, endogamous norms were found to exist among married college students.[19] In extensive personal interviews with the married students living in university housing, it was found that men from high-status homes, where the father was a professional or a marginal professional, were most likely to marry women who had fathers in the same occupational strata. The same was true of the middle grouping of business, secretarial, and minor government occupations, as well as for the lowest grouping of skilled, unskilled, or farming occupations. The same pattern existed for married women.

Like occupational endogamy, educationally endogamous or homogamous marriages occur at levels higher than expected by chance. Richard Rockwell, in examining marriage cohorts from census data, found that for virtually every marriage cohort, at least half of all marriages that *could* have been homogamous *were* homogamous.[20] However, he did find that educational homogamy is lower now than at the beginning of the century. Nevertheless, both education and occupation remain major factors in mate selection.

This intraclass pattern is often viewed by exchange theorists as a process in which individuals attempt to achieve the best possible bargain for themselves and their children by weighing marital resources and alternatives.[21] If this is true, it would be highly surprising if the endogamy pattern were not the most prevalent. It is at similar class levels where the marital resources would most likely be similar. If this is the case, what does a person of lower social class have to trade with persons of a higher social status? Let us examine some of these patterns of marriage across class lines.

Mésalliance

Marriage with a person of an inferior position has been termed **mésalliance.** Special cases of mésalliance are **hypergamy,** denoting the pattern wherein the female marries upward into a high social stratum, and **hypogamy,** where the female marries downward into a lower social stratum.

With particular reference to the United States, a number of writers have concluded that hypergamy is more prevalent than hypogamy—women

19. J. Ross Eshleman and Chester L. Hunt, *Social Class Factors in the College Adjustment of Married Students.* (Kalamazoo: Western Michigan University, 1965): 32.

20. Richard C. Rockwell, "Historical Trends and Variations in Educational Homogamy," *Journal of Marriage and the Family* 38 (February 1976): 83–95.

21. Exchange theorists view mate selection and other reciprocal interactions as a bargaining process. What is received is dependent upon what is available to give in return and vice versa (*see* discussion in Chapter 2).

marry men of higher status more frequently than men marry women of higher rank. On the basis of an exchange-theory argument, the social advantages of hypergamy seem to exist primarily for the low-status woman. For equity to occur, this type of exchange would require that the woman be exceptional in those qualities the culture defines as desirable. Depending on the society, qualities in women that determine status might include factors such as shade of skin color, facial and morphological features, and relative age. Glen Elder suggests that throughout history some women have been able to exchange their physical beauty for a young man's lineage, accomplishments, or mobility potential.[22] Typically, a woman is expected to use her attractiveness to gain certain legitimate ends such as recognition, status, and a husband.

Men in the United States rank physical attractiveness at or near the top among the qualities they desire in women, and this seems to be especially true of the upwardly mobile or strongly ambitious. Thus it would be expected that a male who achieves status through his occupation exchanges his social rank for the beauty and personal qualities of the female. The idea that physical attractiveness is of great exchange value, particularly among women of working-class origin, was one factor that Elder attempted to determine.[23]

Elder's research confirmed his basic hypothesis. Women who became upwardly mobile through marriage were characterized by physical attractiveness, a desire to impress and control others, high aspirations for the future, and an avoidance of steady dating. Among women from the working class, physical attractiveness was more predictive of marriage to a high-status man than was educational attainment, while the relative effects of these factors were reversed among women of middle-class origins.

Certain ideas related to mésalliance seem to be confirmed. One is that males, when they marry outside of their class, will more frequently marry down than up. And the higher the occupational stratum of the male, the more commonly he is found to have married down. Conversely, when females marry outside of their class they will more frequently marry up than down. In brief, hypergamy is more prevalent than hypogamy. This notion extends to dating as well and is referred to as the mating gradient.

The mating gradient

If, as stated, when persons marry outside their social class men tend to marry down and women tend to marry up, then we can assume the same

---

22. Glen H. Elder, Jr., "Appearance and Education in Marriage Mobility," *American Sociological Review* 34 (August 1969): 520.

23. Ibid., pp. 519–533.

processes occur prior to marriage. When men and women date or engage in intimate types of personal interaction, it can be expected that women will seek out similar or higher status men and men will seek out similar or lower status women. This tendency has been called the **mating gradient.** It results from the suggestion that men at the top have a wider range of mate choice than do men at the bottom, with the reverse true for women: those at the top having a more narrow range than those at the bottom.

As stated by Gerald Leslie and Sheila Korman:

> An interesting implication of the . . . mating gradient is that it works to keep some of the highest-status women and the lowest-status men from marrying. Women at the highest levels have a smaller pool of potential mates to begin with because it is not generally acceptable for them to marry downward. In addition, these high-status women must compete both against one another and against women from other status levels for high-status men. To the extent that high-status men marry downward, they leave high-status women without partners. Among men, the reverse obtains. The lowest-status men generally are not eligible to marry higher-status women; yet higher-status men may select lower-status spouses. Thus, unmarried women may be, disproportionately, high-status women, and unmarried men may be, disproportionately, low-status men.[24]

The mating gradient also seems to operate in dating on college campuses. It is the freshman male and the senior female that have the smallest choice of probable dating partners. The freshman girl is the choice of college males at any class ranking, whereas the freshman male must, to a greater extent, limit his choices to the freshman females. At the other extreme, the situation is reversed. By the time the male and female are seniors, the male can select from any of the class rankings of females, whereas the female is more limited to senior or junior men.

Class heterogamy and marital conflict

What about the consequences of social-class heterogamy (hypergamy or hypogamy) in terms of marital conflict or divorce? One literature search of social-class heterogamy and marital success revealed highly inconsistent findings regarding the hypothesis that marrying someone of a higher or lower social class background leads to marital incompatibility and divorce.[25] Leonard Pearlin attempted to explain the inconsistency of findings relating

---

24. Gerald R. Leslie and Sheila K. Korman, *The Family in Social Context*, 6th ed. (New York: Oxford University Press, 1985): 376.

25. Norval D. Glenn, Sue Keir Hoppe, and David Weiner, "Social Class·Heterogamy and Marital Success: A Study of the Empirical Adequacy of a Textbook Generalization," *Social Problems* 21 (April 1974): 539–550.

class intermarriage to marital success by suggesting that only those to whom status advancement is important and who have married mates of lower status are apt to have a sense of loss.[26] This feeling leads, in turn, to a disruption of reciprocity, expressiveness, affection, and value sharing in marital exchange. In brief, the suggestion is that status heterogamy by itself is a trivial element of marriage. Status inequalities became an important force in marital relations only when combined with certain status values: marrying down while striving to move up. This brings disruption because it involves the sacrifice of something valued, namely status. From an exchange perspective, when status consciousness invades marriage, exchange equivalence is difficult to maintain.

In an attempt to test the Pearlin hypothesis, Stephen Jorgensen found the conflict to be true for wives but not for husbands.[27] That is, a positive relationship existed between social-class hypogamy (wife marrying down) and the wife's perception of marital conflict frequency given that she values status advancement at the same time. The explanation for this finding was that although a high percentage of wives are entering the labor force, the social status of married women still depends to a large extent on the career aspirations and accomplishments of their husbands. On a normative basis, males are not as dependent on their wives for social placement as the role of primary breadwinner remains his major responsibility.

RELIGION

All studies have found that the number of people who marry within their own religion is far greater than chance occurrence can explain. Carter and Glick, using census data, inferred in 1976 that if all persons had completely disregarded religion as a factor in mate selection, 56 percent of married couples would have spouses of like religion and 44 percent would have spouses of a different religion.[28] This inference is based on the assumption that 70.4 percent of the Protestants in the United States would have married Protestants, that 26 percent of Catholics would have married Catholics, and that 3.6 percent of Jews would have married Jews. The sum of the squares of these three values equals 56.49 percent: the *expected* percentage

---

26. Leonard I. Pearlin, "Status Inequality and Stress in Marriage," *American Sociological Review* 40 (June 1975): 334–357.

27. Stephen R. Jorgensen, "Social Class Heterogamy, Status Striving, and Perceptions of Marital Conflict: A Partial Replication and Revision of Pearlin's Contingency Hypothesis," *Journal of Marriage and the Family* 39 (November 1977): 653–661.

28. Hugh Carter and Paul C. Glick, *Marriage and Divorce: A Social and Economic Study,* rev. ed. (Cambridge, Mass.: Harvard University Press, 1976): 358.

While religious endogamy is the norm, an increasing number of interfaith and interethnic marriages take place each year. (Photo: © Carolyn Hine/The Picture Cube)

of endogamous marriages. The *actual* percentage of all married couples with a spouse of the same religion was 91.4 for Protestants, 78.5 for Catholics, and 92.8 for Jewish. These figures substantiate the major influences that religion, or at least religious affiliation, plays in the selection of a marital partner.

Determining if a marriage is interfaith

Determining what is within one's religion can be an extremely complex research problem. To even define, much less measure, a mixed religious or interfaith marriage involves problems that few persons have satisfactorily resolved. For example, if you were engaged in a research study to determine the frequency of interfaith marriage at your school or in your community, would you, as suggested at the beginning of this chapter, place a Methodist–Lutheran marriage in the intra- or interfaith category? Would a devout Catholic married to a person reared in the Catholic tradition but presently indifferent to religion make a mixed marriage? If an atheist marries an agnostic would they be marrying endogamously or exogamously? If a Protestant marries a Catholic and then the Protestant converts to Catholicism, is this an inter- or intrafaith marriage?

Most studies of interreligious marriage are limited to three broad categories—Catholic, Protestant, and Jewish—with only an occasional breakthrough to account for finer classifications. Rarely are any divisions made in Catholicism. In Judaism, even though definite differences regarding interfaith and intra-Jewish marriages have been found to exist within the three major branches—Orthodox, Conservative, and Reform—it is relatively infrequently that studies distinguish among them. The same is true among some of the major denominations of Protestantism: Methodist, Presbyterian, Lutheran, Baptist, and the like. This lack of differentiation is very unfortunate, for even the most untrained persons in religious thought recognize differences in beliefs and practices *among* Protestant denominations to say nothing of those *within* denominations.

To deal with interfaith marriage solely on the basis of Catholic–Protestant, Catholic–Jewish, or Protestant–Jewish sets up an artificial distinction. However, it does provide general data that make possible the testing of hypotheses concerning the significance of religious endogamy within the major religious categories in the United States.

The frequency of interfaith marriage

The frequency of interfaith marriage is determined in most research studies by checking religious affiliation on public records or by asking people directly. From these studies, indications seldom exist as to the frequency of conversion or anticipated conversion of a spouse or interdenominational mixtures with religious groups. They do indicate that among Protestants, Catholics, and Jews in the United States, intermarriages are most common among Catholics and least common among Protestants and Jews.[29] In addition, interfaith marriages are most frequent among those persons who are religiously less devout than among the religiously more devout.

Irrespective of religious affiliation, most marriages are endogamous. Using combined data from six United States national surveys conducted from 1973 to 1978, Glenn reported a rate of 92.6 of Protestants married to Protestants, 88.2 of Jews married to Jews, and 82.0 of Catholics married to Catholics. Overall, 89.7 percent of all Protestants, Catholics, and Jews were married to persons of the same religion.[30]

While these figures may appear to be quite high, Glenn reported a substantial decrease in religious homogamy since 1957. He concludes that in the recent past in the United States, norms of religious endogamy have not been as strong as most writers addressing the topic have thought them to be. The apparent fact that many persons are now willing to marry a person of a different religion and to change their own religion to that of the spouse led Glenn to state that "marriage in the United States has become very largely a secular institution, with religious institutions exerting only weak influences on marital choice."[31]

It is interesting to note that endogamy is not merely the predominant pattern when the broad Protestant–Catholic–Jewish classification is used but is also the predominant pattern among Protestant denominations as well. Not only are Protestants married to other Protestants, as previous studies have shown, but they are married to Protestants who share the same denominational affiliation. The ratio of mixed marriages does not vary much across denominational lines.

Some consequences of interfaith marriages

The general opposition to interfaith marriages stems from the widespread belief that they are highly unstable and create a multitude of problems that intrafaith marriages do not experience. Some empirical evidence supports this belief. Heaton suggests that interreligious marriages are

---

29. Norval D. Glenn, "Interreligious Marriage in the United States: Patterns and Recent Trends," *Journal of Marriage and the Family* 44 (August 1982): 555–566.

30. Ibid., Table 1, p. 557. These percentages differ slightly from the Carter and Glick figures reported earlier due to different time periods as well as different data bases.

31. Ibid., p. 564.

Louisiana repeals black blood law

NEW ORLEANS, July 5—Gov. David C. Treen signed today into law legislation repealing a Louisiana statute that established a mathematical formula to determine if a person was black.

The law establishing the formula, passed by state legislators in 1970, said that anyone having one thirty-second or less of "Negro blood" should not be designated as black by Louisiana state officials.

The legislator who wrote the law repealing the formula, Lee Frazier, a 34-year-old Democrat representing a racially mixed district in New Orleans, said recently that he had done so because of national attention focused on the law by a highly publicized court case here.

The case involves the vigorous but thus far unsuccessful efforts of Susie Guillory Phipps, the wife of a well-to-do white businessman in Sulphur, La., to change the racial description on her birth certificate from "col.," an abbreviation for "colored," to "white."

She has spent thousands

Mrs. Phipps, whose skin is white, has spent thousands of dollars on legal proceedings to prove that she is white in the eyes of the state as well and that a mistake was made on her birth record.

"I really felt badly that this had made not only local but national headlines," said Mr. Frazier. "Louisiana was made the laughingstock of the nation."

He said his research showed that the designation of race on official documents in this area from the late 1700's and its purpose was "to keep control over land ownership, to keep the landowner from having to share his land with his illegitimate children who were family members."

According to H. M. Westholz Jr., a State Health Department lawyer who represented Louisiana in Mrs. Phipps's case, the repeal of the blood law will probably have no effect on the Phipps case because, he says, "the formula was not a central issue in the case."

Earlier this year, a state civil district judge upheld the state's position that there was insufficient evidence to show that the birth certificate was inaccurate. The case is being appealed to the Louisiana State Court of Appeals.

It superseded "long line" of laws

Mr. Westholz said the 1970 blood law had superseded "a long line" of state court opinions that use the term "any traceable amount" of black ancestry as "the proper way to define a Negro." He said that as a practical matter the law was "useless" and "impossible" to apply because of the difficulty in precisely determining a person's racial background. An Assistant Attorney General said there was no reason to expect that the earlier criteria would return to use with the law's repeal.

Mr. Westholz said Mrs. Phipps had lost her case against the state because most of the older records attesting her racial background and other evidence indicating race had corroborated the information on her birth certificate, placed there by a midwife.

He said publicity generated by the case had brought "a surge" of requests from applicants wishing to change the description of their race on old birth records. In 1980 he said, the state stopped mentioning race on birth records except in the state's confidential files, kept for statistical purposes.

Mrs. Phipp's lawyer, Brian Begue, says that the law was "a bad law" but that its repeal was worse. He lobbied vigorously against the repeal.

From "laughable" to "obscene"

"You're not doing any good to repeal this law without having something to take its place," Mr. Begue said in an interview. "You're exchanging the one thirty-second rule, which is laughable, to 'traceable amount,' which is obscene."

Mr. Begue said that "in the absence of a legislative expression of a standard" for determining race, repeal "creates a vacuum into which 'traceable amount' is drawn." He described the legislators' action as "a vain and useless gesture for an election year."

The bill's author, Mr. Frazier, says the key to the success of the law's repeal is other legislation passed last week that allows a person to change birth records by presenting "a preponderance of evidence" to prove that the record was wrong. The old state law was much more stringent, he said, requiring evidence that left "no room for doubt."

Mr. Frazier said that in the future it would be possible for a person to change birth records by sworn statements from family members, doctors and others.

Mr. Begue rejoins: " 'Preponderance of evidence' looks good but there's no way out if you look white and all your records say you're colored. If your records say you're colored, then your blue eyes, blond hair, white skin and sister's color don't matter, because we don't know what makes a person colored."

Mr. Westholz describes the new legislation requiring "preponderance of evidence" rather than "no room for doubt" as "a dramatic improvement."

A third viewpoint is offered by Ronald Davis, State Assistant Attorney General. Mr. Davis says he is pleased because the repeal of the law means that "the state is not in the business of officially determining race."

He said the new legislation "will make it easier for people to change their racial designation" and that "it is meaningful from a symbolic point of view because Louisiana had appeared to be in the Dark Ages."

Mr. Davis said Mr. Begue's fears that repeal was a step backward were groundless. "There is no reason for 'traceable amount' to creep back into the criteria," he said.

less satisfying than religiously homogamous marriages.[32] Other evidence includes higher aggregate levels of marital happiness reported by persons in religiously homogamous marriages and slightly higher divorce rates for certain types of religiously heterogamous marriages.

Caution must be given in the interpretation of findings from these cross-sectional, homogamous-heterogamous comparisons even if their reports are accurate. Marriages that were unhappy and have already ended in divorce do not contribute to unhappiness in the currently married population. Nevertheless, even taking this factor into account, it is likely that lower levels of happiness and slightly higher rates of divorce occur among the interreligious marriages than among the intrareligious homogamous marriages.

What about the children of interfaith marriages? It has been argued that these children, compared to children of homogamous marriages, are subjected to less intense and less consistent religious socialization with the consequence of being weakly religious themselves. In other words, the assertion is that interfaith marriages have a secularizing effect on the children. For the most part, this assertion was not found to be true. Larry Peterson, in studying over 1,000 adult Catholics, claimed that contrary to the secularization hypothesis, interfaith marriages have relatively inconsequential effects on religious commitment.[33] Offspring from interfaith marriages did not consistently score lower on the general religiosity measures than offspring of homogamous marriages. Catholics who are the offspring of interfaith marriages and Catholics who form them were as firmly committed to Christianity in general and Catholicism in particular as Catholics in homogamous families. In sum, the negative consequences often assumed of interfaith marriages on the success of the marriage or the secularization of the children do not appear to find much empirical support.

Race

Of all the norms involving intermarriage, few are more widely held or rigorously enforced than in the area of race. Despite scientific findings and the removal of legal barriers, the restrictions concerning interracial marriage still remain the most inflexible of all the mate-selection boundaries.

Among most people of the world, interracial marriage is accepted both legally and socially. With the possible exception of the Republic of

---

32. Tim B. Heaton, "Religious Homogamy and Marital Satisfaction Reconsidered," *Journal of Marriage and the Family* 46 (August 1984): 729–733.

33. Larry R. Peterson, "Interfaith Marriage and Religious Commitment among Catholics," *Journal of Marriage and the Family* 48 (November 1986): 725–735.

South Africa, few countries are as race conscious as the United States. The intermingling of people of different races is nothing new in world affairs. Based on historical and biological evidence, the idea of a "pure race" is totally inaccurate—race mixture has been going on throughout all of recorded history, and some evidence suggests that even in prehistory racial intermingling occurred. As there is no evidence to support a pure race, neither is there evidence to support the idea that racial mixtures result in biologically inferior offspring. Biologically, there is nothing to prevent marriage of persons of different races.

Removal of the legal prohibition against interracial marriage in the United States came in 1967 when the United States Supreme Court struck down as unconstitutional a 1924 Virginia law forbidding marriage between persons of different races. According to the Court, a law of this type violates rights guaranteed to all persons under the Fourteenth Amendment to the Constitution. Irrespective of the Supreme Court's decision declaring such laws unconstitutional, the social mores and the disfavor placed on interracial marriage by all major racial, religious, and ethnic groups are so strong in most areas that relatively few marriages of this type take place.

The strength of the prohibition against interracial marriage, particularly black-white marriage, in itself increased the difficulty of obtaining the type of research evidence necessary to substantiate factors such as frequency, male-female differences, or the stability of marriages of this type. It must be noted and made clear that a discussion of race in relation to marriage is not independent of, or isolated from, age, residence, social class, religion, educational level, region of the country, whether the marriage is black-white or Oriental-Caucasian, whether it involves a marriage or a remarriage, or any other dimension. To deal with racial endogamy alone is impossible.

The frequency of black-white intermarriage

Determining the frequency of black-white marriage is exceedingly difficult. As with religion, there is the matter of classification. If a black passes for white and marries a white, is this an intermarriage or an endogamous marriage? If, as is on the law books of various states, a person is one-eighth or one-sixteenth black (an empirical impossibility), would it not be an intermarriage irrespective of which race one marries? Even if a categorization could be agreed upon and precisely determined, it could be argued that social sanctions against such marriages are so severe in most parts of the United States that the reported number of such marriages would be less than the actual number.

In 1960, for the first time, the United States census was tabulated to show the number of husbands and wives who had the same or different

TABLE 8–2
Interracial married couples: 1970 and 1985

	1970	1985	Percent increase
Total married couples	44,597,000	51,114,000	14.7
Interracial married couples	310,000	792,000	155.5
Percentage of total	0.70%	1.55%	
Black-white married couples	65,000	164,000	152.3
Percentage of total	0.15%	0.32%	
Husband black, wife white	41,000	117,000	185.4
Wife black, husband white	24,000	47,000	95.8
Other interracial married couples	245,000	628,000	156.3

Source: Adapted from U.S. Bureau of the Census, *Statistical Abstract of the United States: 1987,* 107th ed. (Washington, D.C.: U.S. Government Printing Office, 1986), Table 48, p. 39.

racial backgrounds. This information, like all census information involving race, does not denote any clear-cut scientific definition of biological stock. Rather, it is based on self-identification by respondents. The data represent self-classification by people into one of fifteen groups listed on the census questionnaire.[34]

As can be seen in Table 8–2, of the 51.1 million married couples in the United States, in 1985, 792 thousand, or 1.5 percent of the total, were classified as interracially married. Only 164 thousand, or 0.32 percent of the total number of married couples, were classified as black-white married couples. While caution must be advised on the accuracy of these census-assembled figures because they are based on self-reports and devoid of reliability or validity checks, it does provide one valuable source of information on frequency, the increase over time, and the black husband/white wife or white husband/black wife differential.

Several findings appear of interest in Table 8–2. For example, while the number of married couples increased by 14.7 percent since 1970, the number of interracial married couples increased by 155 percent. Yet, the number of interracial marriages relative to the total number of marriages is small: 1.5 percent of all interracial marriages and only 0.32 or one-third of 1 percent of black-white marriages. In brief, interracial marriages are increasing in the United States but their occurrence is still infrequent.

Interracial marriage rates vary widely from one state to another. For

---

34. These fifteen groups listed in the race item on the census questionnaire included: white, black, American Indian, Eskimo, Aleut, Chinese, Filipino, Japanese, Asian Indian, Korean, Vietnamese, Hawaiian, Samoan, Guamanian, and "other."

example, the percentage of black-white marriage reported for 1967–1970 by Thomas Monahan was 1.94 in the District of Columbia, .73 in Massachusetts, and .45 or higher in Alaska, Hawaii, Maryland, New Hampshire, Rhode Island, Connecticut, and New Jersey. In contrast, North Carolina, Georgia, Tennessee, Alabama, Mississippi, and Louisiana had a percentage of black-white marriage under .09. The rates are much higher when all racially mixed marriages are considered. For example combining white-other or black-other rates with the black-white rates, the percentages vary from 32.54 in Hawaii, 10.79 in Alaska, and 2.11 in Montana to .03 in Alabama and .07 in Mississippi.[35]

Heer suggests that although marriages between blacks and whites are relatively infrequent in number, they are sociologically important because they serve as an indicator of the relationship between the two races. He hypothesizes that a low frequency of black-white marriage serves to reinforce the pattern of inequality between the two races. He advances several reasons for this:

> First of all, on a per-capita basis white persons hold a far higher share of the nation's wealth than do blacks and a low frequency of racial intermarriage makes it unlikely for a black to inherit wealth from a white. Secondly, blacks are by and large excluded from the many unionized manual jobs to which entrance is strongly determined by kin connections because existing jobs of this type are usually held by whites and black persons rarely have white kin. Thirdly, the lack of close relatives among whites affects the socialization of black youth. In particular, they cannot obtain an easy familiarity with the social world of whites and hence are inhibited from applying for jobs demanding such familiarity even when their technical qualifications are completely satisfactory. Finally, over the long run it may be surmised that prejudice against blacks on the part of white persons would be diminished if the proportion of whites with black relatives were substantial rather than negligible, as at present.[36]

Male-female intermarital racial differences

Most articles and books dealing with black-white marriage indicate that black males marry white females more frequently than white males marry black females. This black husband-white wife contention is strongly supported by census data (*see* Table 8–2). Of the 164,000 reported black-white marriages in 1985, 117,000 or 71 percent of them included a black

---

35. Thomas P. Monahan, "An Overview of Statistics on Interracial Marriage in the United States, with Data on Its Extent from 1963–1970," *Journal of Marriage and the Family* 38 (May 1976), Table 5, p. 227.

36. David M. Heer, "The Prevalence of Black-White Marriage in the United States, 1960 and 1970," *Journal of Marriage and the Family* 36 (May 1974): 246.

husband and a white wife. Forty-seven thousand or 29 percent of the total had a black wife and a white husband.

There is a lack of consensus on the reasons for a differential incidence of interracial marriage by sex. The two most frequently cited are differences in socioeconomic status and differences in sexual norms. Let's examine these two reasons briefly.

The first, suggested by Kingsley Davis more than thirty-five years ago, is that if marriages between black men and white women largely involve black males of high social status and white females of low social status, then the groom can trade his class advantage for the racial caste advantage of the bride.[37] That is, an exchange process is in operation where the higher-status black male offers his higher socioeconomic status for the preferred color status of the lower-class white female. The result is racial hypogamy and class hypergamy for the female. She marries down racially and up in social status or class, exchanging one for the other. Several attempts, however, to test the thesis of racial hypogamy–class hypergamy have not brought forth much support. This implies that for the female to marry up, she would generally have a lower level of education or lower status occupation than her husband. Neither Heer[38] nor Lewis Carter[39] found the wives of black males to be of lower educational attainment.

The second frequently cited explanation for a preponderance of black male–white female marriages revolves around sexual norms. The argument is that sexual norms allow white men to take sexual advantage of black women without marrying them.[40] But little research seems to support this argument. It seems very probable that the sexual norms, at least on college campuses, may be actually the reverse of Davis's contention. That is, if the sexual norms are not equal, the black male may actually have greater sexual access to the white female than vice versa.

Since neither of these explanations appears to have much empirical support, I would hypothesize that differential norms operate for white and black males in relation to females. For example, for both races the males are more likely to be the mate selection–marriage initiators. In addition, given the greater societal approval accorded to whites, it may be a more prestigious factor for a black male to initiate interaction with a white female than for a white male to initiate interaction with a black female. Other factors or explanations as well may be operative.

---

37. Kingsley Davis, "Intermarriage in Caste Society," *American Anthropologist* 43 (July/September 1941): 388–395.

38. Heer, "The Prevalence of Black-White Marriage," pp. 253–255.

39. Lewis F. Carter, "Racial-Caste Hypogamy: A Sociological Myth?" *Phylon* 29 (Winter 1968): 347–350.

40. Davis, "Intermarriage in Caste Society," pp. 388–395.

The success of interracial marriages

Do black-white marriages succeed?

A generally accepted view is that those who enter a racially mixed marriage are more likely to get divorced. Analyzing a set of data in the state of Iowa covering almost thirty years, Monahan inferred that blacks, both males and females, have contributed almost twice as many divorces to the picture as one would expect from their proportion of marriages. But when the divorce rate of mixed marriages of blacks with whites was examined, Monahan found that in Iowa the mixed marriages were more enduring (i.e., less likely to divorce) than were black-black marriages. As a whole, in Iowa black-white marriages would appear to have a greater stability than do marriages where both parties are black, and intermarriages of black males with white wives are more enduring than marriages of whites with white.[41]

Monahan found a somewhat similar pattern in Hawaii by examining the rates of divorce.[42] He concluded that, whatever the explanation, interracial marriage does not necessarily lead to a weakening of family ties. Despite the considerable increase in interracial marriage in Hawaii, the divorce rate had stabilized at a level lower than in previous decades, and, as a whole, the mixed-race marriages were only moderately less successful than the same-race marriages.

Recognizing that Iowa and Hawaii may be unique cases, recognizing that interracial marital success depends upon which races are intermarrying and the circumstances surrounding the marriage, and recognizing different methodological and research problems, the findings of Monahan should certainly lead to a serious questioning of the negative aspects of interracial marriage to the couple themselves. The question then follows, What about the children? Are they at risk for developing personality and adjustment problems?

Popular literature, often based on speculation or on unrepresentative case histories, is strongly biased toward the notion that offspring of cross-racial-ethnic marriages are likely to suffer from adjustment problems. Data from Hawaii, at least, suggest that this literature is incorrect.[43] There, children of cross-ethnic-racial marriages are not much different from children of endogamous marriages. And male offspring of exogamous marriages,

---

41. Thomas P. Monahan, "Are Interracial Marriages Really Less Stable?" *Social Forces* 48 (June 1970): 464–469.

42. Monahan, "An Overview of Statistics on Interracial Marriage," pp. 40–47.

43. Ronald C. Johnson and Craig T. Nagoshi, "The Adjustment of Offspring of Within-Group and Interracial/Intercultural Marriages: A Comparison of Personality Factor Scores," *Journal of Marriage and the Family* 48 (May 1986): 279–284.

for example, scored higher in social desirability and lower in interpersonal abrasiveness measures than did offspring of endogamous marriages. Daughters of exogamous marriages were found to be more extroverted with no other differences approaching significance. Results such as these may be due to the low level of community-wide stigma associated with mixed marriages in Hawaii. If that is true, then pressures outside the marriage and the parent-child relationship are the key dimensions in producing negative effects of such marriages on offspring.

Whether dealing with husband-wife, parent-child, or employer-employee relationships, the success of the relationship depends upon the total situation and not merely upon the fact that one partner is black and the other is white. Interpersonal relationships of any sort are affected by external forces as well. Thus parents, kin, neighbors, local politicians, or society in general lend support or opposition with varying degrees of pressure and influence on the marriage, family, or job situation. Success is relative, extending far beyond the boundaries of any two persons—with skin color alike or different.

The trend in intermarriage

As was evident in Table 8–2, the trend in interracial marriages is upward. Between 1970 and 1985, the number of interracially married couples in the United States more than doubled. Yet the total incidence (792 thousand) is still so low that these marriages relative to all marriages (51.1 million) are not likely to have any major effect in the achievement of assimilation, racial integration, decreasing social distance, or even in affecting black-white relationships in general.[44]

It is hard to imagine a set of conditions under which black-white marriage rates would increase so rapidly as to achieve any large inter-mingling within the foreseeable future. It is likely that interacting forces are at work. For example, if schools become integrated, if educational opportunities become available to blacks, if job opportunities increase, then it is likely that the incidence of interracial marriage will increase. And if black-white marriages continue to increase, this may play some role, albeit small, in bringing blacks near to equality with white.

---

44. Gurak and Fitzpatrick describe the intermarriage patterns of five Hispanic groups in New York City arguing that intermarriage provides an excellent indicator of assimilation and of the social distance separating ethnic groups. *See* Douglas T. Gurak and Joseph P. Fitzpatrick, "Intermarriage Among Hispanic Ethnic Groups in New York City," *American Journal of Sociology* 87 (January 1982): 921–934.

SUMMARY

1. *Homogamy* and *endogamy* refer to the extent of intermarriage among people who share similar characteristics or are of like groups. This chapter examined the nature of intermarriage and five normative structures surrounding mate selection in the United States: age, proximity of residence, class, religion, and race. The choice of a mate along these and other structural dimensions has significant consequences for the society, the marriage, or the persons involved.

2. The reporting and interpreting of any type of intermarriage has its difficulties. The boundaries of race, class, or religion are rarely clear-cut and precise. Rates for individuals are often confused with rates for marriages. Actual rates of intermarriage vary according to numerous social factors such as group size, heterogeneity, sex ratio, controls over marriage, the development of cultural similarities, the romantic love complex, and the influence of certain psychological factors.

3. Most couples in the United States are relatively homogamous in the age at which they marry. Since the turn of the century, the tendency has been for the male-female age difference at the time of marriage to narrow. Age at marriage as well decreased for both sexes between 1890 and the mid-1950s. Since then there has been an increase, which has accelerated in the last decade.

4. The marriage squeeze is used to describe the effects of imbalance between the number of males and females in the prime marriage ages. This squeeze resulted in a shortage of women in the 1950s, a shortage of men in the 1980s, and predictably will result in a shortage of women at the turn of the century. The marriage squeeze is particularly acute among black women.

5. The age at marriage is of major concern when it involves teenagers. These concerns relate to higher rates of high school drop-outs, unemployment, fertility, and divorce.

6. Mate selection involves a "propinquity factor." Studies seem to conclude that people choose mates who live within a fairly limited distance of their own homes. Explanations for propinquity center around the opportunity to meet, a norm segregation theory, and a time-cost factor.

7. Mate selection studies conclude that marriages are highly endogamous by social class far greater than could be expected to occur simply by chance. When marriage occurs with someone from a lower position (mésalliance) it may denote hypergamy or hypogamy. The general tendency for men to date and marry downward more frequently than upward has been termed the *mating gradient*. The literature on social

class heterogamy and marital success reveals highly inconsistent findings.

8. Religious endogamy, although less rigid than racial endogamy, remains an important factor in mate selection. Precise data on the frequency of intermarriage are difficult to determine. There seems to be consensus that the religiously devout marry endogamously in greater frequency than the religiously less devout and that endogamous marriages have higher levels of happiness and slightly lower rates of divorce than the interfaith marriages. Those with no religion have lower rates of marital happiness or success.

9. In the United States, racial endogamous norms are more rigorously enforced than any others described in this chapter. Findings suggest that black males marry white females more frequently than white males marry black females. The success of these marriages tends to contradict public opinion. While the trend in interracial marriage is upward, the incidence is low and the number will, in all probability, have little effect on an integration of the races.

10. In general, intermarriage of all types appears to be on the increase, but endogamous marriages continue to occur in frequencies far greater than one could expect to occur by chance alone. The next chapter continues to concentrate on mate selection, but the frame of reference shifts from a structural orientation to more of a processual and interactional orientation. What are the explanations of choosing one mate over another? What are the processes followed in moving from meeting to marriage? These and related issues follow.

KEY TERMS AND TOPICS

DISCUSSION QUESTIONS

1. Differentiate between endogamy and exogamy, homogamy and heterogamy. What is meant by assortive mating? What constitutes intermarriage or a mixed marriage?

2. Discuss factors that are likely to increase the incidences of intermarriage. What factors operate most strongly to discourage or prohibit them?

3. What trends do you predict in regard to age at marriage, place of residence, social class, religion, and race?

4. What are the laws in your state regarding age at marriage? Do differentiations exist for male and female as to the age at marriage? Why is this? What legal changes do you think would be advisable?

5. Describe the marriage squeeze. What factors account for a shift from a shortage of women to a shortage of men and a return to a shortage of women? Why is the marriage squeeze so significant for black women?

6. Explain what is meant by and the reasons for residential propinquity. Can you think of situations, circumstances, or both that would decrease the influence of residence on the choice of a mate? What are various consequences of marriage to the "guy next door" as opposed to someone 2,000 miles away?

7. Discuss hypergamy and hypogamy—their likelihood, their explanation, and some consequences of their occurrence.

8. Does the mating gradient occur in your school? Why or why not? Is the basic pattern likely to change in ten years?

9. Take a brief survey among your friends as to the importance of religious endogamy in dating or marriage. What additional problems, consequences, or both may be more likely in interfaith than intrafaith marriages?

10. To what extent is an exchange theory adequate in explaining interclass or interracial marriages? What are factors offered in exchange? How are exceptions handled?

11. In regard to black-white interracial marriages: Why are they so infrequent? How do you explain the predominance of black husband–white wife marriages rather than the reverse? What objections to interracial marriages are likely to lack empirical support?

12. Discuss this idea: With the integrating of our schools, jobs, and neighborhoods, soon everyone will be marrying anyone.

FURTHER READINGS

Aldridge, Delores P. "Interracial Marriages: Empirical and Theoretical Considerations." *Journal of Black Studies* 8 (March 1978): 355–368. A readable, concise summary of findings relating to interracial marriages.

Carter, Hugh, and Glick, Paul C. *Marriage and Divorce: A Social and Economic Study.* Rev. ed. Cambridge, Mass.: Harvard University Press, 1976. Presents a systematic documentation of important trends and variations in demographic aspects of marital behavior in the United States during recent decades.

Heer, David M., and Grossband-Shechtman, Amyra. "The Impact of the Female Marriage Squeeze and the Contraceptive Revolution on Sex Roles and the

Women's Liberation Movement in the United States, 1960 and 1975." *Journal of Marriage and the Family* 43 (February 1981): 49–65. A fascinating empirical account arguing that the advent of the Women's Liberation Movement was directly linked to a female marriage squeeze and the revolution in contraceptive technology.

Lenski, Gerhard. *The Religious Factor: A Sociological Study of Religion's Impact on Politics, Economics and Family Life.* Garden City, N.Y.: Doubleday, 1961. A study completed in Detroit attempting to discover the impact of religion on secular institutions including the family.

Mayer, Egon. *Love and Tradition: Marriages between Jews and Christians.* New York: Plenum Press, 1985. A look at Jewish–Christian marriages within a historical and cultural context based on survey data and personal interviews over a ten-year period.

Murstein, Bernard. I. "Mate Selection in the 1970s." *Journal of Marriage and the Family* 92 (November 1980): 777–792. One of the decade review articles dealing with major trends in mate selection issues and research.

Otto, Luther B. "Antecedents and Consequences of Marital Timing." *Contemporary Theories About the Family,* vol. 1, edited by Wesley R. Burr et al. New York: The Free Press, 1979, pp. 101–126. A review of the literature and an attempt to establish models relating to the timing of marriage.

Photo: © Bruce Rosenblum/The Picture Cube

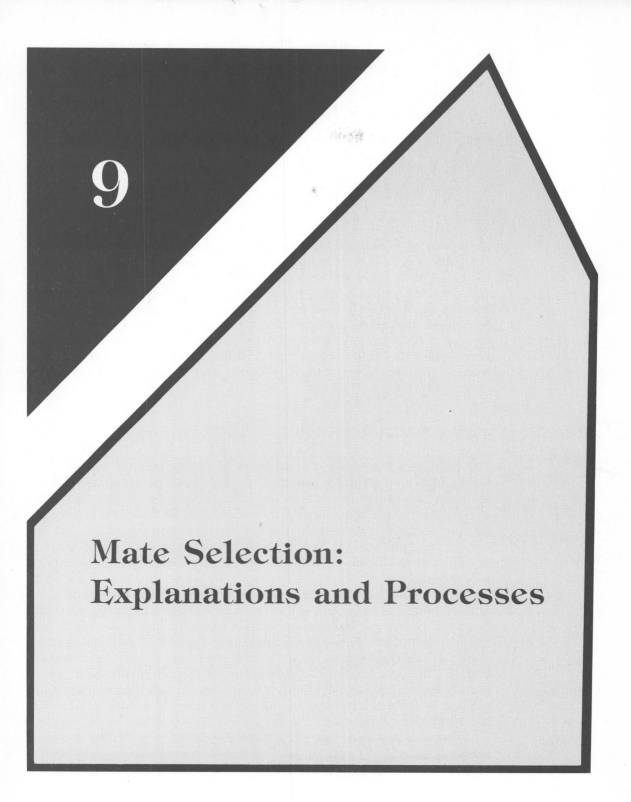

9

Mate Selection:
Explanations and Processes

As should have become very clear from reading the last chapter, mate selection is not simply a matter of preference or free choice. Despite the increases in freedom and opportunities that young people have to select "anyone they please," many factors that are well beyond the control of the individual severely limit the number of eligible persons from whom to choose. The taboo on incest and the restrictions placed on age, sex, marital status, class, religion, race, and others in most societies narrow considerably the "fields of eligibles." A sizable volume of research suggests that all societies have systems of norms and sometimes specific rules about who may marry whom.

ARRANGED MARRIAGE VERSUS FREE CHOICE OF MATE

The processes followed in the selection of specific marital partners vary widely from one society to another. On an ideal-type continuum, these methods may vary from totally arranged marriages at one extreme to total free choice of mate at the other. Where marriages are arranged, the couple have nothing to say about the matter. The selection is usually, but not always, made by parents or kin. The other extreme, total free choice, is so rare that to discuss it would simply be conjecture. The United States is, however, one of the few societies of the world that approaches this end of the continuum. In its extreme form, parents and kin are not consulted and in some instances not even informed of the impending marriage. Between these two extremes are various combinations of arranged–free choice possibilities. Parents may arrange and give their son or daughter a veto power. The son or daughter may make his or her own selection and give the parents the veto power. One of the persons to be married, usually the son, may select the bride with his parents. Regardless of the method of mate selection, every society has a set of norms to prescribe the appropriate procedure.

Where mate selection is arranged, the family is generally the chief and only source of employment; rather than establishing a new family, marriage is a means of providing for the continuity and stability of the existing family. Arranged marriage has the effect (functions) of providing the elders with control over the younger family members and control over who from the outside enters and becomes part of the family unit. In addition, it preserves family property, furthers political linkages, protects economic and status concerns, and keeps the family intact from one generation to another. As a result, almost without exception, the chosen partners must share similar group identities. Racial, religious, and particularly economic statuses must be similar. Arranged marriage, rather than being based on criteria such as romantic love, desire for children, loneliness or sexual desire, will likely include factors such as the size of the bride's price, the reputation of the potential spouse's kin group, levirate and sororate obligations, and traditions of prescribed marriage arrangements.

An example of an arranged marriage between the groom and the bride's parents is provided by John Peters, who spent eight years in the jungles of northern Brazil. He described mate selection among the Shirishana as follows:

> The female has no choice in the selection of her spouse. Any person who is in the *Wanima* kinship relationship to the potential bride and who is acceptable to her family could be her mate. The selection is generally made when the female is three years of age and the male 14 to 20 years of age. (In several instances the male has been an estimated 34 years.) The selection may be initiated by the mother of the male, but more commonly is done by the male himself. On occasion a male has asked the family of a pregnant woman that the unborn child become his wife, should it be a girl.[1]

Arranged marriages result in a commitment among the selected partners that is, in many instances, as binding as the marriage itself. Since the marriage exists primarily to fulfill social and economic needs, concerns such as incompatibility, love, or personal need fulfillment are not at issue. As a result, divorce is practically unknown or occurs only infrequently. Instances where marriages must be terminated frequently bring a great sense of shame and stigma to the entire family and kin group.

Evidence suggests that as traditional cultures are exposed to "Western" models of modernization and as they industrialize and adopt new technology from the outside world, those segments of cultures with the greatest exposure to these influences tend to increasingly depart from an arranged marriage pattern to one of increasing "free" or "love" matched marriages. Gary Lee and Lorene Stone[2] extend this proposition slightly by suggesting

---

1. John Fred Peters, "Mate Selection Among the Shirishana," *Practical Anthropology* 18 (January/February 1971): 20–21.
2. Gary R. Lee and Lorene Hemphill Stone, "Mate Selection Systems and Criteria: Variation According to Family Structure," *Journal of Marriage and the Family* 42 (May 1980): 319–326.

Mail-order brides give men an empty dream come true

Mail-order brides are back in the news. I say back because of the previous boom in the mail-order bride business that took place in this country roughly 150 years ago. News is cyclical. One learns that in the newspaper business.

When the West was being won (or lost, from the perspective of native Americans), lots of hearty men who went alone into the wilderness found they had little to do after their fortunes were found. There were very few discos in which to meet members of the opposite sex. What good is money without someone to share it? Finding a wife in the wilderness, however, was impossible.

The mail-order bride business evolved to fill this need. Through it, women with few marriage prospects at home, impoverished women, adventuresome women, all kinds of women offered themselves to brokers as potential brides. Love might come, but partnership was the bargain. Thus was the story line provided for "Paint Your Wagon" and "Seven Brides for Seven Brothers."

Young, beautiful, and obedient

The phenomenon of contemporary mail-order brides is similar, with one un-wholesome difference. The old-time bridegrooms were attempting to coax a little reality into their unreality. The new-time bridegrooms are trying to replace reality with unreality. They are surrounded by genuine women, but want fantasy creatures.

The modern mail-order brides are primarily young Oriental women, many from the Philippines. They are willing to marry lonely American men in return for the opportunity to live in relative comfort as U.S. citizens. Their opportunities for a comfortable life-style at home are limited. They have that in common with some of our pioneer mothers.

Men who have availed themselves of this contemporary service are happy to explain its appeal. They complain that American women are too outspoken, too demanding, too self-interested. These men say they yearn for an "old-fashioned' wife, one who is docile, domestic, and subservient.

that autonomous mate selection based on romantic attraction is more likely to be institutionalized in societies with nuclear family systems than in those in which families are typically extended. In other words, extended families tend to exert greater control over the mate selection process than do nuclear families.

As suggested, total free choice is practically nonexistent anywhere in the world. This would imply freedom to choose a person for marriage without regard to the wishes of anyone else, and certainly not the wishes of parents or kin groups. Also, it would imply that instrumental consid-erations such as money, power, social rank, occupation, education, age,

One recent mail-order bridegroom explained himself on TV recently: "Look at me. How else is a man my age with my looks going to get a beautiful, talented, 25-year-old women who will love him, live with him and be faithful to him?"

How indeed? This man was grossly overweight and well over 50, with a face to stop a truck. He exhibited little wit, charm, or grace. Maybe he's a great guy, but there was no evidence.

His bride sat expressionless at his side. She had long black hair and almond eyes. She was pleasant appearing, but not beautiful. I know nothing of her talent. I'll accept that she is 25.

Till death parts them

I wonder if this man and others like him understand how ridiculous they are. They reach for a dream. They convince themselves it can be ordered from a catalog and bought for the price of an airline ticket and a marriage license.

The fantasy each cherishes is that he will find a young, beautiful woman who will fall in love with him on sight, or after a brief exchange of letters. That's pretty silly, especially since these men generally admit they've had trouble in past romantic pursuits.

Then this exotic child-woman is supposed gladly to abandon her past life and culture, marry the dreamer, be happy, faithful, and obedient, devoting all her energies to serving her master for the rest of his or her life, whichever comes first.

One wonders if these men also believe in Santa Claus and the Tooth Fairy.

The lonely men in the Wild West weren't so silly. But they weren't looking for ego props. The catalog women pay a high price for their trip to the U.S. Living with a loonie tune and playing to his fantasies can't be any fun at all.

Source: Nickie McWhirter, *Detroit Free Press,* March 7, 1984, p. 1-B. Reprinted with the permission of the Detroit Free Press.

incest, family ties, or even sex would not be major considerations in the choice. Limited free choice takes these factors into consideration and permits a choice of a mate by the spouses themselves within the limits of the permitted social groupings. Given this choice, then, love and prestige ratings become significant as do the processes of getting to know one another and of moving the relationship toward increasing commitment. Personal needs and values also become significant. Thus our attention is turned to the premarital dyad and to various theories and processes that explain mate selection.

Mate selection and marriage in Swaziland

Swaziland, an independent country in Africa, is located between the Republic of South Africa and Mozambique. Mate selection and marriage in Swazi society differs from western marriage in various ways.

First, rather than marriage being a union of two individuals, it is essentially a union of two groups of kinsmen. The opinion of senior members of the lineage is often as important as that of the prospective bride and groom. Second, there is a clearly stated rule that children born to the union belong to the kin group of the father. Third, the residence pattern is patrilocal. Fourth, marriages are legitimized only after the payment of *brideswealth.* This is a form of compensation to the kin of the bride for their loss of the woman and her procreative capacities. The amount of brideswealth ranges from ten to twelve head of cattle for a commoner's daughter to as many as fifty or sixty for an important royal princess.

Fifth, marriage is closely related to the continuance of society, therefore childlessness is viewed as a serious problem. Sixth, the production of as many children as possible is a primary aim of marriage. Thus, polygyny is not only permissible, it is considered the ideal form of marriage. Finally, divorce is kept to a minimum as the termination of a marriage is an extremely complex process.

Source: Gary P. Ferraro, "The Persistence of Brideswealth in Swaziland," *International Journal of Sociology of the Family* 13 (Spring 1983): 1–16.

INDIVIDUALISTIC EXPLANATIONS OF MATE SELECTION

With a decrease in kinship control over mate selection, particularly in Western societies, has come a freedom that has brought about an enormously complex system. It would seem obvious that this process occurs long before the first "date." Since in the United States it is possible to have more than one mate (although legally only one at a time), for many the mate-selection process never ends. Most psychological and other "individualistic" theories explaining this choice are based on a wide range of experience, along with a variety of subconscious drives and needs.

Instinctive, innate, or biological

One of the oldest, and perhaps most radical, explanations of mate selection suggests that what guides a man to a woman is instinct (rarely was it thought to be the other way around). Instinct is established by heredity and deals with unlearned behavior. In my opinion, there is no such thing as a human instinct, but to many biologists and psychologists instincts are basic to human behavior.

The mate selection process in the United States includes a wide range of activities that couples can enjoy in getting to know one another. (Photo: © Camerique Stock Photos/E. P. Jones, Co.)

Related to the instinct theory is the genetic-similarity argument.[3] The idea is that genetically similar others, be they strangers or kin, have a tendency to seek each other out and provide supportive environments. In contrast, genetically dissimilar others have a tendency to form natural antipathies and provide mutually hostile environments. As assortative mating in animals is based on genetic similarity, so too is assortative mating in humans.

As far as is known, no one has ever discovered any instinctive, unconscious, or purely biological determinants for mate selection. Of course,

3. J. Philippe Rushton, Robin J. H. Russell, and Pamela A. Wells "Genetic Similarity Theory: Beyond Kin Selection," *Behavior Genetics*, 14 (1984): 179–193.

the fact that they are unconscious or innate make them difficult, if not impossible, to discover. However, to attribute explanations of selecting a mate to the unconscious adds little more to our understanding of basic processes involved in mate choice than does explaining it by spirits, fairies, or supernatural powers.

Parental image

Closely related to the instinct theory is the psychoanalytic idea of Sigmund Freud and his followers suggesting that a person tends to fall in love with and marry a person similar to his or her opposite-sex parent. This, too, is generally unconscious and centers around the **Oedipus complex.** To a male child, early in his life his mother becomes his first love object. But the presence of his father prohibits him from fulfilling his incestuous desire, and, as a result, the male infant develops an antagonism toward his father for taking his love object from him. This, in turn, results in an unconscious desire to kill his father and marry his mother. The male infant's desire for his mother and fear of his father is so great that he develops a fear of castration or, as Freud called it, **castration anxiety**— a fear that his father wants to emasculate him by removing the penis and testes. But since the father is also protective, helpful, and respected by the mother, a great amount of ambivalence exists, which is resolved only by a primary type of identification with the father. The Oedipus complex is thus temporarily resolved for the male, but the repressed love for his mother remains. By adolescence, when the male is free to fall in love, he selects a love object that possesses the qualities of his mother.

The opposite, but parallel, result occurs for the female. She at an early age becomes aware of lacking a male sexual organ and develops *penis envy.* Feeling castrated, her feelings are transformed into the desire to possess a penis, especially the father's. These feelings for the forbidden object remain repressed throughout childhood, but her love for her father, known as the **Electra complex,** culminates in marriage when she selects a mate with the qualities of her father. Both the Oedipus complex and the Electra complex are discussed more fully in Chapter 14.

Although it seems vey reasonable to believe that young people, in selecting a mate, would be keenly aware of the qualities of their parents and the nature of their marriage, no clear evidence has been produced to support the hypothesis that the boy seeks someone like his mother and that the girl seeks someone like her father. There are times when very close resemblances seem to exist between a man's wife and his mother and between a woman's husband and her father. Jedlicka[4] argues

---

4. Davor Jedlicka, "Indirect Parental Influence on Mate Choice: A Test of the Psychoanalytic Theory," *Journal of Marriage and the Family* 46 (February 1984): 65–70.

that this occurrence is more frequent than could be expected by chance; however, whether the explanation is rooted in Oedipus or Electra complexes is subject to question.

Complementary needs

The theory of complementary needs in mate selection was developed and enhanced by Robert F. Winch. It was his belief that although mate selection is homogamous with respect to numerous social characteristics such as age, race, religion, ethnic origin, residential propinquity, socioeconomic status, education, or previous marital status, when it comes to the psychic level and individual motivation, mate selection tends to be complementary rather than homogamous. The idea grew out of a modified and simplified version of a need-scheme theory of motivation; but rather than the needs being similar, they will tend to complement one another.

To test his hypothesis of mate selection, Winch subjected to intensive study twenty-five husbands and their wives. In each of three early papers, Winch claimed that the bulk of the evidence from these couples supports the hypothesis that mates tend to select each other on the basis of complementary needs.[5] Conversely, in each of these three papers, he claimed that support is not available for the conflicting hypothesis that spouses tend to be motivationally similar.

Several years later, Winch published his book on mate selection.[6] For mate selection to take place on the basis of love, that is, due to complementary needs, it is understood that both man and woman must have some choice in the matter. The theory would not be operative in settings where marriages are arranged (as by parents, marriage brokers, or others). Thus love will likely only be an important criterion under culture conditions where: (1) the choice of mates is voluntary, (2) the culture encourages premarital interaction between men and women and (3) where the marital friendship is culturally defined as a rich potential source of gratification. Since love is defined in terms of needs, the general hypothesis is that where people marry for love, their needs will be complementary.

Reports by Winch and his colleagues led to a constant flow of articles attempting to retest the complementary needs hypothesis. The results

---

5. Robert F. Winch, Thomas Ktsanes, and Virginia Ktsanes, "The Theory of Complementary Needs in Mate Selection: An Analytic and Descriptive Study," *American Sociological Review* 19 (June 1954): 241–249; Robert F. Winch, "The Theory of Complementary Needs in Mate Selection: A Test of One Kind of Complementariness," *American Sociological Review* 20 (February 1955): 52–56; and Robert F. Winch, "The Theory of Complementary Needs in Mate Selection: Final Results on the Test of the General Hypothesis," *American Sociological Review* 20 (October 1955): 552–555.

6. Robert F. Winch, *Mate Selection* (New York: Harper, 1958).

were basically negative, failing to provide empirical support to the idea that people tend to choose mates whose needs complement their own.

> One reason can be that the theoretical considerations concerning complementarity are incorrect. Another reason may be that the theory of complementarity is correct in principle but that it is much too little specified. A third reason may be that the measurement of needs is not in agreement with the theory.[7]

Any or all of these reasons may be correct. What is clear is that relatively little empirical support exists for the theory of complementary needs as originally formulated. In fact, most research attempting to explain mate selection on the basis of personality traits, whether similar, different, complementary, or some combination thereof, seems to have bogged down into a morass of conflicting results. Most findings suggest the probable futility of further pursuit of personality match.[8] In spite of the research, unsupported theories—whether instinctive, mother-images, complementary needs, or personality traits—die hard and further research on these ideas is sure to follow.

SOCIOCULTURAL EXPLANATIONS OF MATE SELECTION

Age, residential propinquity, class, religion, and race are sociocultural factors that influence mate selection. Any factor in which social norms and endogamous factors play a part in who marries whom falls into this category. Roles and values, although basic to norms of endogamy, can also be viewed as interaction processes that explain the choice of a mate.

Role theory

Role theory, at least to this author, appears to be conceptually more justifiable as an overall explanation of marital choice than any of the previous explanations of theories. All social humans or, more specifically all marriageable persons, have expectations regarding the behavior desired by themselves and by their prospective mates. One perception of role, as described in Chapter 2, refers to a set of social expectations appropriate

---

7. Jan Trost, "Some Data on Mate Selection: Complementarity," *Journal of Marriage and the Family* 29 (November 1967): 738.

8. *See,* for example, J. Richard Udry, "Personality Match and Interpersonal Perception as Predictors of Marriage," *Journal of Marriage and the Family* 29 (November 1967): 722–724.

to a given status: husband, wife, male, female, single, and the like. These expectations, implicit or explicit, have been internalized and serve to direct and influence personal behavior as well as the behavior desired in a prospective marriage partner. Basically, we tend to desire (internalize) the roles defined by our society, subculture, and family.

Roles and personality needs differ in a very important respect. With role, the focus of attention is on behavior and attitudes appropriate to a situation irrespective of the individual, whereas with personality needs, the focus is on behavior and attitudes that are characteristic of the person or individual irrespective of the situation. The difference is crucial. Role focuses on definitions, meanings, and social expectations. In regard to mate selection, individuals select one another on the basis of role consensus, role compatibility, or on the basis of courtship, marital, and family-role agreement.

Role consensus or agreement, widely used as an indicator of marital success or adjustment and found to have a strong, positive association with marital satisfaction,[9] has been applied relatively infrequently to mate selection. However, similar processes could be expected to be as operative prior to marriage in the selection process as after marriage. Where role discrepancies exist, marriage is less likely to occur in the first place. Would Joe, who expects a wife to care for children, cook meals, and clean the house, marry Mary, who despises these activities? Or reciprocally, would Mary want to marry Joe if that is what he expects of her?

Disparity in role agreement can be obtained by listing series of expectations associated with various statuses and comparing the responses of the couple. The expectations of the couple on any given dimension can be used: decision making, recreation, sex, church attendance, care of children, employment, and the like. A given role expectation is less crucial than the agreement of the persons involved. For example, if Joe expects that sleeping on the Sabbath is more important than church attendance, no conflict exists if Joe's spouse holds a similar expectation or attaches little importance to the expectation. The role itself is not as important as the consensus of the partners in regard to the role. Also the role expectation itself may change as the situation changes. Maybe Joe's spouse thinks Joe should attend church on the Sabbath but does not expect him to do so when out of town or on vacation.

In brief, the couple likely to marry is the male and female who share similar role definitions and expectations. This assumes, of course, that forces such as an existing marriage, age, parents, money, schooling, or other sociocultural factors do not hinder or prevent it.

---

9. Stephen J. Bahr, C. Bradford Chappell, and Goeffrey K. Leigh, "Age at Marriage, Role Enactment, Role Consensus, and Marital Satisfaction," *Journal of Marriage and the Family* 45 (November 1983): 795–803.

Heterosexual interaction and the selection of marital partners is not limited to any specific age grouping. (Photo: © Alan Carey/The Image Works)

Value theory

A value theory of mate selection suggests that interpersonal attraction is facilitated when persons share or perceive themselves as sharing similar value orientations. Values define what is good, beautiful, moral, or worthwhile. They are the criteria or conceptions used in evaluating things (including objects, ideas, acts, feelings, and events) as to their goodness, desirability, or merit. Values are not concrete goals of action but are criteria by which goals are chosen.

A value theory of mate selection suggests that when persons share similar values, this in effect validates oneself, thus promoting emotional satisfaction and enhancing the means of communication. When a value is directly attacked or is ignored under circumstances that normally call it to attention, those who hold the value are resentful. Because of this emotional aspect it seems reasonable to expect that persons will seek their informal social relations with those who uncritically accept their basic values and, thus, provide emotional security. Such compatible companions are most likely to be those who feel the same way about "important" things, i.e., those who possess similar values. This accounts for the tendency to marry homogamously and explains why friendships (homophily) and marriages involve people with similar social backgrounds.

In brief, the theory posits that: (1) persons with similar backgrounds learn similar values; (2) the interaction of persons with similar values is rewarding, resulting in effective communication and a minimum of tension; and (3) rewards leave each person with a feeling of satisfaction with his or her partner and thus a desire to continue the relationship.

The theory of value consensus helps explain the findings that exist dealing with homogamy, endogamy, propinquity, parental image, complementary needs, or ideal-mate conception. Sharing values brings people together, both spatially and psychologically. Thus a person may want to marry a member of the same religious denomination, for example, because this might be a very important value in and of itself, or because persons who share similar social backgrounds will likely be socialized under similar conditions and consequently develop similar value systems. The same would hold true for other explanations, such as parental image. Since it is parents who are the major socializing agents for most children, it could be expected that a relationship would exist between personal values and values of parents as well as between values desired in a mate and values of parents. Thus it is perhaps not parent image that influences marital choice but rather parent-image influence via the internalization of a set of values.

Exchange theory

Exchange theory was described briefly in Chapter 2. Also, as mentioned in several instances in the previous and current chapters, the idea of some type of exchange is basic to the mate selection process. Whether it is an exchange of higher economic status for a preferred color status, an exchange of athletic prowess for beauty, or an exchange of sex for money, the central idea is that some type of transaction and bargaining is involved in the mate selection process. Prior to 1940, a major contribution of Willard Waller's treatise on the family was his analysis of courtship conduct as bargaining and/or exploiting behavior. In his words: "When one marries he makes a number of different bargains. Everyone knows this and this knowledge affects the sentiment of love and the process of falling in love."[10]

---

10. Willard Waller, *The Family: A Dynamic Interpretation* (New York: Cordon, 1938): 239.

Today it is doubtful that "everyone knows this." The criteria Waller used for exchange have since come under attack, but the fact that bargaining takes place in the mate selection process has received further investigation and support.

Numerous articles lend support to mate selection as a process of social exchange.[11] They suggest that few people get something for nothing. And although bargaining may not always take place, some type of social exchange will. The difference between bargaining and exchange is that bargaining implies a certain purposive awareness of the exchange of awards. Bargaining entails the knowledge of what one has to offer and what the other person can get, whereas under a simple exchange this awareness is not always readily apparent.

Exchange theorists argue that the behavior of socialized persons is purposive or goal-oriented and not random. Implicitly this indicates that behavior is rewarded and intended to avoid nonrewarding situations. It also indicates that each party in a transaction will attempt to maximize gains and minimize costs. Over the long run, however, in view of the principle of reciprocity, actual exchanges tend to become equalized. If reciprocity does not exist—that is, nothing is given in return—the relationship will likely terminate. A key factor in exchange theory that may deter or delay a termination of an inequitable exchange is the lack of an alternative to the current relationship. But if an alternative to the current relationship is perceived as superior to the present relationship, one of the partners will terminate the present relationship in favor of the more attractive alternative.

There are perhaps few areas where social exchange appears more evident than in the research dealing with dating and mate selection. Even though much dating behavior is overtly intended for the specific purpose of marriage, transactional processes are in operation. In dating, for example, the male may consider sexual intercourse as a desired goal and highly valued reward. To achieve this reward he may have to offer in exchange flattery (my how beautiful you look tonight), commitment (you are the only one I love), goods (I thought you might enjoy these flowers), and services (let me get you a drink).

The social exchange approach to the explanation of mate selection neither explains how interaction arises nor describes the larger social environment, rather, it seeks to explain why certain behavioral outcomes take place.

---

11. Michael M. McCall, "Courtship as Social Exchange: Some Historical Comparisons," in *Kinship and Family Organization,* ed. by Bernard Farber (New York: Wiley, 1966); and James W. Michaels, Alan C. Acock, and John N. Edwards, "Social Exchange and Equity Determinants of Relationship Commitment," *Journal of Social and Personal Relationships* 3(1986): 161–175.

Sequential theories

Up to this point it should be evident that, although single factors were stressed as significant in the process of mate selection, most explanations take into account factors implied in other explanations. Several writers consciously and intentionally combine or place in sequence selected single factors: role, values, needs, exchanges, and the like. Three of these ideas will be considered briefly: the "filtering" idea of Alan Kerckhoff and Keith Davis, [12] the process or development idea of Charles Bolton[13] and the SVR idea of Bernard Murstein. [14]

Kerckhoff and Davis   Kerckhoff and Davis introduce a longitudinal perspective during the mate selection period. They hypothesize that (1) the degree of value consensus is positively related to progress toward a permanent union, and (2) the degree of need complementarity is positively related to progress toward a permanent union. [15]

To test these hypotheses, the authors conducted a longitudinal study of college students who were engaged, pinned or "seriously attached." The authors considered the degree of consensus in family values, the degree of need complementarity, and the movement of the couple toward a permanent union. They found that value consensus was significantly related to progress in the relationship for only the short-term couples, whereas complementarity was significant for only the long-term couples. They interpreted the finding to indicate a series of "filtering factors" operating in mate selection. Early in the relationship social attributes such as religion, education, and the occupation of the father are in operation. As the relationship continues, a consensus of values becomes significant. Still later in the relationship, complementary needs play an important part. They suggest that the complementary factor is seen later in the relationship due to the unrealistic idealization of the loved ones in the early states of the relationship.

Bolton   Bolton sees mate selection as a development of a relationship. Rather than basing mate selection on the personal or social attributes of the specific individuals involved, mate selection is viewed from the per-

12. Alan Kerckhoff and Keith Davis, "Value Consensus and Need Complementarity in Mate Selection," *American Sociological Review* 27 (June 1962): 295–303.

13. Charles Bolton, "Mate Selection as the Development of a Relationship," *Marriage and Family Living* (August 1961): 234–240.

14. Bernard I. Murstein, "Stimulus-Value-Role: A Theory of Marital Choice," *Journal of Marriage and the Family* 32 (August 1970): 465–481.

15. Kerckhoff and Davis, "Value Consensus and Need Complementarity in Mate Selection," p. 366.

spective of the development process itself. Like many other explanations of mate selection, endogamous or homogamous factors are included, but unlike many other explanations, mate selection is herein viewed as a developmental process wherein the interpersonal transactions have their own course of events and one interaction tends to shape another.

This perspective parallels very closely the symbolic interactionist frame of reference described in Chapter 2. At that point, role was viewed in two ways: (1) as a package of behavioral expectations attached to a status, and (2) as the relationship between what we do and what others do with the role or expectations developed in the interaction process. Mate selection is seen to occur in much the same manner as in the second view. That is, the outcome of the interaction of the individuals involved is not mechanically predetermined, but rather, it is the end product of a sequence of interactions characterized by advances and retreats along the paths of available alternatives. In short, the development of love relations is problematic because the product bears the stamp of what goes on between the couple as well as what they are as individuals.[16]

Murstein   A third sequential explanation of mate selection is provided by Murstein who sees mate selection as a three-stage sequence involving stimulus-value-role (SVR). These three stages refer to the chronological sequence in the development of the relationship. Social exchange theory is used within each to explain the dynamics of interaction and attraction.

SVR theory holds that in a relatively "free choice" situation, as exists in the United States, most couples pass through three stages before deciding to marry. In the stimulus stage, an individual may be drawn to another based on the perception of his or her own qualities that might be attractive to the other person. Because initial movement is due primarily to non-interactional cues not dependent on interpersonal interaction, these are categorized as "stimulus" values.

If mutual "stimulus" attraction has occurred between a man and a woman, they enter the second stage of "value comparison." This stage involves the appraisal of value compatibility through verbal interaction. They may compare their attitudes toward life, politics, religion, sex, and the role of men and women in society and marriage. If, as they discuss

---

16. Ibid., p. 236. In many ways the dyadic formation theory of Lewis follows the process or developmental idea of Bolton. Lewis posited six pairing processes experienced by dating couples: the achievement by pairs of (1) perceiving similarities, (2) rapport, (3) openness, (4) role-taking accuracy, (5) interpersonal role fit, and (6) dyadic crystallization. *See* Robert A. Lewis, "A Developmental Framework for the Analysis of Premarital Dyadic Formation," *Family Process* 11 (1972): 17–48; and Robert A. Lewis, "A Longitudinal Test of a Developmental Framework for Premarital Dyadic Formation," *Journal of Marriage and the Family* 35 (February 1973): 16–25.

> "We met and fell in love at first sight."
> "Then why didn' you get married?"
> "Oh, we met again and the second sight was different."

these and other areas, they find that they have very similar value orientations, their feelings for one another are likely to develop. Bolton suggests that couples may decide to marry on the basis of stimulus attraction and verbalized value similarity. But for most persons it is important to be able to function in compatible roles, an ability that is not as readily observable as verbalized expressions of views on religion, politics, and the like. For this reason Murstein places the role stage last in his three-stage time sequence leading to marital choice.

The role stage requires the fulfillment of many tasks before the couple is ready to move into marriage. They must increasingly confide in each other and become more aware of each other's behavior. They must measure their own personal inadequacies and those of their partner since, for example, moodiness, inability to make decisions, dislike of the self, and neuroticism may be hard to bear in the marriage situation. Finally, they must attain sexual compatibility whether by achieving a good sexual relationship in practice or by agreement as to the degree of sexuality that will be expressed during this "role" stage prior to marriage.

While agreement may exist on the importance of a stimulus attraction, value similarity, and role consensus, do these exist in sequence and is there a progression of stages? One test of Murstein's theory provided little support for a sequence of value and role stages with difficulties encountered in identifying when couples were in a particular stage or when they moved from one to another.[17]

Other sequential ideas exist. For example, Bert N. Adams establishes a series of propositions in summarizing mate selection that include (1) conditions or barriers such as proximity, (2) early attractions such as physical attractiveness, similar interests, disclosure or rapport, (3) deeper attractions such as the development of consensus, personality similarity, lack of unfavorable parental intrusion, empathy, or role compatibility, and (4) a final series of escalators or perpetuators that move the persons toward marriage: defining other as "right" or "the best I can get."[18]

---

17. Geoffrey K. Leigh, Thomas B. Holman, and Wesley R. Burr, "An Empirical Test of Sequence in Murstein's SVR Theory of Mate Selection," *Family Relations* 33 (April 1984): 225–231.

18. Bert N. Adams, "Mate Selection in the United States: A Theoretical Summarization,"

Without exception, each of the sequential theories of mate selection sees the movement toward marriage in terms of a series of changing criteria, stages, or patterned regularities. However, the progression to marriage may not be as orderly as postulated by the proponents of the sequential models. Rodney Cate and co-authors,[19] for example, identify alternative pathways to marriage and suggest that existing models represent an overly simplistic view of the mate-selection or heterosexual-relationship development process. As the course toward marriage was earlier claimed *not* to reside in personality traits or needs, perhaps it does not reside totally on interactional sequential factors either. Factors external to the person or couple (family-kin influence socioeconomic conditions, community heterogeneity, technological changes, etc.) are likely, from a sociological perspective at least, to be important factors or dimensions in an understanding of the process of changing status from single to married.

PROCESSES OF STATUS CHANGE: SINGLE TO MARRIED

The mate selection process is the manner in which an individual changes status from single to married. All human societies have some socially approved and structured procedure to follow in getting married. They vary from one society to another and, particularly in industrialized societies, include a wide range of variance within a society. A mate selection process that involves the individuals themselves only exists where there is some degree of personal choice in marital partners. As described, where marriages are "arranged" the process generally occurs between kin groups. In any case, it is rare for mate selection processes to exist independently of other institutions such as schools, churches, or business.

In the United States, the mate selection process, particularly for first marriages, is highly youth-centered and competitive. It involves a wide range of social relationships prior to marriage that involves an increasing degree of commitment. Writers use different terminology to describe this process but generally it involves a series of stages that may include group activities; casual dating; going steady; being pinned; cohabiting; being engaged; or some other type of classification indicating a more binding relationship or a marriage commitment. The flexibility of the system permits

in *Contemporary Theories About the Family*, vol. 1, ed. by Wesley R. Burr et al. (New York: The Free Press, 1979): 259–267.

19. Rodney M. Cate, Ted L. Huston, and John R. Nesselroade, "Premarital Relationships: Toward the Identification of Alternative Pathways to Marriage," *Journal of Social and Clinical Psychology* 4 (1986): 3–22; and Rodney M. Cate and James E. Koval, "Heterosexual Relationship Development: Is It Really a Sequential Process?" *Adolescence* 18 (Fall 1983): 507–514.

this process to be followed once or many times prior to marriage, covering a time span of days to years, and including or omitting one or several of those stages.

Perhaps the mate selection process in the United States can be compared to a male-female game, which has rules, goals, strategies, and counter-strategies.[20] In one sense, playing the game is voluntary since it is not mandatory that everyone play, but it is probably more difficult to avoid than to achieve. In elementary school (or before) parents inquire about boyfriends or girlfriends. As children mature, the pressure from parents, peers, and, usually by now, an internalized self-concept, all encourage getting involved. The goals of the game may simply involve enjoyment, affection, group approval, learning to play better, or getting a mate. Since a double standard exists, females have a different set of rules, norms, and goals than do males.

The social norm for the male in the United States implies that his basic goal in this game is to move the relationship toward sexual intimacy. Even before the first "date" or meeting, a key question is "Will she or won't she?" The extent to which direct or "rapid" approaches are used to answer the question will depend on a wide range of social and interpersonal factors: previous marriage, age, social class, income, religion, beauty, friends, and so on.

The social norm for the female in the United States implies that her basic goal in this game is to move the relationship toward commitment. Even before the first date, key questions might be "Will he ask me out again?" or "Is he a potential husband?" To get the commitment, the female has the responsibility to regulate the progression of the intimacy goal of the male. To get intimacy (sex is a more accurate term at this point), the male must convince the female that she is not like all other girls but is different, unique, and special.

These two norms work reciprocally. Progress toward one calls for progress toward the other. They work together. As commitment increases, intimacy increases and vice versa. Most communication in this game is likely to be in the form of nonverbal cues, signs, gestures, and other symbolic movements.

Suppose the rules are not followed—the male makes no moves toward intimacy or the female makes no moves to halt the intimacy or to get a commitment. The female, after one date, may say to herself or others, "What a nice guy, he really is a gentleman," or the like. Suppose after

---

20. This idea is an expansion of Waller and Hill's "courtship bargains" and "courtship barter." *See* Willard Waller (revised by Reuben Hill), *The Family: A Dynamic Interpretation* (New York: Holt, Rinehart and Winston, 1951): 160–164.

two, four, or eight dates, he still makes *no* move toward intimacy. Now the female is likely to ask questions such as "What's wrong with him?" or "What's wrong with me?" Suppose the female makes no moves to stop or slow down the intimacy moves of the male, or, she makes the initial moves. The game may continue to be played but now under a new set of rules and conditions.

More extensive analysis of stages for mate selection such as dating, going steady, and getting pinned or engaged can be found in most more "functionally oriented" marriage textbooks. Thus they will be touched upon only briefly at this point.

Dating

One form of behavior experienced by most adolescents in the United States is dating. Of all the stages of the mate selection process, dating is the one that carries the least commitment in continuing the relationship. Dating has been defined as a U.S. invention that emerged after World War I among college students and other young adults. In most of the world where parents have an extensive involvement in the selection of marriage partners, dating is not a relevant factor to be considered. However, as shifts occur away from family control over the selection of a marriage partner, an increasing amount of emphasis is placed on establishing social structures that permit the persons themselves to interact and get to know one another. In the United States, dating is one of these structural patterns, although certainly not the only one established for purposes of male-female interaction.

The traditional "date"—where the male called a female several days or a week ahead and verbally contracted a time and activity, picked her up at her house, wined and dined her at his expense, took in a movie or social activity, and returned her to her residence prior to the time established by her parents—may be a dying or dead event. Today it seems more likely that dating involves students or youth congregating in groups, evolving into pairs while retaining allegiance to the group, sharing food or entertainment expenses, and engaging in less highly structured and predetermined behaviors. Apart from the student scene, one consequence of the later age at marriage has been the emergence of new forms of partner selection for dating. These include computer matchups, videotape selections, singles clubs, newspaper advertisements, singles bars, and other less formal opportunities for meeting.[21]

---

21. Note, for example: Stanley Woll, "So Many to Choose From: Decision Strategies in Videodating," *Journal of Social and Personal Relationships* 3 (1986): 43–52; and Rosemary Bolig, Peter J. Stein, and Patrick C. McKenry, "The Self-Advertisement Approach to Dating: Male-Female Differences," *Family Relations* 33 (October 1984): 587–592.

Bundling as a mate selection process

Bundling is frequently associated with the Amish courtship system. A practice that was started in Northern Europe, brought to America, and practiced in the New England colonial family, bundling has been known to take several forms. The most common was using a bed with a "bundling board." Under this arrangement a boy and a girl would lie on the bed without undressing. Second was the use of "bundling bags." Under this system, the female got into a large sack with a wax seal at the neck. Obviously, this seal was supposed to remain unbroken. Third, there were also instances recorded where the female's ankles were tied together.

To understand bundling, it must be seen in the context in which it occurred. Among New England families and among the Amish, wood and candles were commodities that required much time and labor. To use these commodities throughout the evening hours would be a waste of materials. Also, where winters are cold and distances of travel are sometimes great, bundling provided an opportunity for the male and female to visit alone without disturbing the rest of the family or using the heat and light commodities. One should also recognize that within the household were likely to be parents, six to fourteen children, and often grandparents and other relatives. Thus the sexual connotations that many people associate with it today were perhaps minimal. Add to this the rigid sexual codes that existed and one should get a relatively accurate picture of bundling in its social context. This subject has been widely exploited by the popular press; however, it is not known that bundling exists today among the Amish.

The fact that dating is not what it once was does not mean it doesn't exist or is unimportant. It has, however, changed its structure. Sheila Korman,[22] in looking at nontraditional dating behavior, found that while feminists tended to initiate dates and share dating expenses more than nonfeminists, even the nonfeminists who held traditional beliefs were venturing into these nontraditional forms of heterosexual dating interactions.

Among feminists or nonfeminists, males or females, writers agree that dating fulfills various functions for the individual. Dating may be:

1. *A form of recreation.* It provides entertainment for the individuals and is a source of immediate enjoyment. Since it's something that's fun to do as an end in itself, it carries no future obligations or commitments.

---

22. Sheila K. Korman, "Nontraditional Dating Behavior: Date-Initiation and Date Expense-Sharing Among Feminists and Nonfeminists," *Family Relations* 32 (October 1983): 575–581.

2.   *A form of socialization.* It provides an opportunity for individuals of the opposite sex to get to know each other, learn to adjust to each other, and to develop appropriate techniques of interaction.

3.   *A means of status grading and status achievement.* By dating and being seen with persons who are rated "highly desirable" by one's peer group, an individual may raise his or her status and prestige within his or her group.

4.   *A form of courtship.* It provides an opportunity for unmarried individuals to associate with each other for the purpose of selecting a mate whom they may eventually marry.

The primary reasons for dating and the functions the date fulfills influence the dating role. In other words, it could be expected that persons who date for recreation will behave differently from those who date for socialization, status achievement, or mate selection. For example, emotional involvement, sexual intimacy, exclusivity of the relationship, who pays the bills, or discussions of future plans could be expected to differ depending on if the motive for dating is to have something to do, to be "seen with" a prestigious person, or to find a husband or wife. It could be expected that the person who is more emotionally involved and more committed to the relationship will be hurt most if the relationship ends. It could be expected that the person with the lower status or prestige will have less say (power) in what interactions and activities occur.

This idea parallels that of Waller nearly fifty years ago, in what he termed **the principle of least interest.**[23] He observed that seldom are both persons in a dating relationship equally interested in continuing the relationship. Since both parties are not equally emotionally involved, if the dating were terminated, it would be more traumatic for one than for the other. Thus, essentially, the principle of least interest says that the person who is less interested in continuing the dating relationship is in a position to dominate, and possibly exploit, the other party.

This principle may also suggest a factor involved in the continuation or breakup of a relationship. If an imbalance or unequal interest exists, it would suggest difficulty in continuation and further development of a relationship. Consistent with exchange theory, when a perception of equity does not exist in what one is receiving relative to what one is giving, the relationship is more likely to end or result in a power imbalance where one can dominate the other. This principle, by the way, may not only apply to dating interactions but to friendships or marriages as well.

---

23. Waller, "The Family: A Dynamic Interpretation," p. 275.

Steady dating, going with someone, or being pinned

In the mate selection process, it is highly typical that most adolescents make the move from an uncommitted relationship to a premarital relationship that involves some commitment to one another and an exclusion of others. Irrespective of the term used, whether *going steady, steady dating, going with someone, being pinned,* or any other, societies that permit the individuals themselves to choose their spouses need some device for individuals to lessen the open competition with others and at the same time provide anticipatory socialization for the marital role. Opportunities are needed to focus in on the "field of eligibles," to get to know what is expected of self and others, and to get to know someone better without a major commitment or norm of permanence attached to the relationship. Steady dating or "going with someone" fills the gap between recreational or dalliance dating and engagement or marriage.

Philippine courtship folk beliefs

If on the day of their betrothal either the groom or the bride gets sick, it is a sign that their married life will not last long.

The bride should not fit the wedding dress or her wedding will be cancelled; or one of the party may die and the wedding not be consummated.

And when a maiden weds let the older women instruct her well. And on the day of the wedding she is not to see the groom, not until at the altar. Else, the wedding might not go through or an accident might happen to either the bride or the groom. As soon as the ceremony is over let her rise ahead of the groom and lean on his shoulder. Thus, she will always be able to make him do as she wishes and not have an overbearing husband.

If the wedding dress is torn before the wedding it is a bad omen; if it is wet, somehow, it is also bad.

During the wedding ceremony, the two candles that are lighted in front of the couple mean the length of their lives, and if the candle near the girl is brighter than that of the boy, that means that the girl will live longer than the boy.

For a bride to be sad on her wedding day means bad luck. For a bride to be late at her wedding means bad luck. For a bride to sleep soundly and awake cheerful indicates eternal happiness.

After the wedding, if the girl walks ahead of the man and groom, she will rule the husband.

Source: Francisco Demetrio y Radaza, S. J., ed., *Dictionary of Philippine Folk Beliefs and Customs,* Book III (Cagayan de Oro City, The Philippines: Xavier University, 1970), pp. 633, 635, 637, 639, 642, 644.

The functions filled by this form of interaction are highly similar to those described under dating. They may provide recreation, socializing experiences, status achievement, or selection of a mate. The specific patterns of activity or meanings attached to the relationship may vary considerably from one context to another.

On college campuses, at least in the 1960s, a series of terms (*pinned, pearled, lavaliered,* etc.) and a variation of meanings were available to categorize relationships as perhaps more serious than steady dating but with less commitment than engagement. Perhaps the best known of these arrangements was that of pinning. The custom involved a gift of the male's fraternity or dormitory pin to the female. The pin was considered a temporary gift and was returned to the male in case the pair broke up. Pinning was one means of publicly announcing to the campus community that the couple had a commitment to one another. In many instances, the commitment may have been little more serious than steady dating, whereas others may have defined it as similar to engagement.

Engagement

Engagement in some form has existed in almost every society in the world. Since marriage is seldom taken lightly, most societies have provided some social structure to instill an awareness in the couple and the community that the relationship is a serious one and that marriage will likely occur. In many societies engagement is considered extremely important and much more binding than it is in the Western world today. Since it implies the final transition in the process of changing status from single to married, and since it involves a transfer from dating availability to dating exclusiveness, various rituals, gifts, and interactions occur to implant in the minds of the couple and the public the importance of the relationship.

Engagement serves a variety of functions for both the couple and society. For the couple, it provides a clear indication that marriage is about to occur. Due to the exclusive nature of the relationship, personal and interpersonal testing can continue with less threat from competitive forces. A more thorough awareness of marital-role expectations, value consensus or dissensus, and future aspirations can be examined. It provides the final opportunity prior to the legal union for the couple to understand self in relation to the partner. It is likely that many couples view an engagement as a kind of trial marriage, including total sexual intimacy, the sharing of certain financial obligations, and in some instances living together (note the nonmarital cohabitation section that follows).

Engagement also provides the function of making public the plans of the couple. This can best be seen by the placement of the female's or couple's picture in community newspapers. In colonial days the announcement was accomplished by the posting of *banns.* A number of days or weeks prior to the marriage, a public notice of intent to marry would be published, posted at key locations in the community, and announced in the churches. In the smaller folk- or gemeinschaft-like communities characterized by a sense of solidarity and a common identity, the word traveled quickly and the community served as a key force in the binding of the relationship. Today, in our urbanized societies, it could be questioned how significant the formal newspaper announcement is in making public the plans and applying community pressures upon the couple.

An engagement ring, like a public announcement, serves the purpose of enabling the female to publicly and continuously display her symbol of commitment. The ring, which involves a financial commitment on the part of the male (and sometimes on the part of the female), symbolizes the seriousness of the relationship and the intent of a forthcoming marriage. In a time of calling for equality between sexes, perhaps the time is near when the male will expect an engagement ring as well. At least one article has suggested that the emergence of a groomal shower, a male variation of the traditional female bridal shower, is a reflection of our changing attitudes toward marriage and an indication of some movement toward greater egalitarianism.[24]

NONMARITAL HETEROSEXUAL COHABITATION

Is it possible that mate selection in the 1980s is not marriage-oriented, is not oriented toward a single partner, and does not stress permanence? Is it possible that a decrease in a double sexual standard will totally eliminate the male-female sex game described earlier? Is it possible that dating, pinning, and engagement are premarital structural arrangements only significant as historical phenomena? Or are we simply witnessing major modifications in, and additional alternatives to, traditional mate selection and marriage processes?

An alternative to marriage and an increasingly prevalent nonmarital arrangement is nonmarital cohabitation, living together, or consensual unions. These involve a situation where a man and a woman who are not married to each other, neither by ceremony nor by common law, occupy the same dwelling. The arrangement, among the young or the old, may or may not be marriage-oriented, may be the beginning of a long-range life-style or be for short-term convenience, may or may not involve an intimate, unrestricted sexual union, and may or may not include the knowl-

---

24. Felix M. Berardo and Hernan Vera, "The Groomal Shower: A Variation of the American Bridal Shower," *Family Relations* 30 (July 1981): 395–401.

edge of parents among youths or perhaps the knowledge of the children among older people.

The extent to which, for all practical purposes, nonmarital cohabitors are married couples minus a legal marital document could be questioned. One way to answer this is to note if these relationships, like dating, serve functions such as recreation, socialization, status grading, or selecting a marriage partner or if they serve functions of marriage such as procreation, exclusive sexual intimacy, extension of a kin network, economic partnership, tension management, or socialization of children. Maybe what exists today is a large number of nonmarried marrieds. Let's examine these couples: their prevalence, how they differ from noncohabitants, some consequences of their cohabitation, living together if they are elderly, and legal factors related to their cohabitation.

The prevalence of nonmarital cohabitation

How prevalent is the living together of persons who are not married to one another? U.S. census reports show some interesting data. Since 1970, the United States had witnessed a dramatic increase in the number of unmarried couples who live together. In 1985 there were about 2.0 million unmarried couple households, a 354 percent increase since 1970 when there were an estimated 523,000 households of this type.[25] More than two-thirds (69.6 percent) of the unmarried households in 1985 consisted solely of the two partners, and nearly one-third (30.4 percent) of the couples had one or more children living with them. Nearly one-fourth of all households with two unrelated adults were under age 25, about 40 percent were age 25–34, about 29 percent were 35–64, and about 8 percent were age 65 and over.

Another way to examine the prevalence of nonmarital cohabitation is to look at married couples who had cohabited with each other prior to their marriage. This approach, rather than counting the nonmarried persons who are cohabiting, counts the marriages in which the couple cohabited prior to the marriage. This perspective places cohabitation in the sequence of a couples' relationship from dating to marriage. This was done in Oregon by checking all marriage licenses in one county for 1970 and 1980.[26] Couples were coded as cohabiting if they supplied identical home

25. U.S. Bureau of the Census, *Current Population Reports,* Series P-20, no. 410, "Marital Status and Living Arrangements, March 1985 (Washington, D.C.: U.S. Government Printing Office, 1986), Table A-13.

26. Patricia A. Gwartney-Gibbs, "The Institutionalization of Premarital Cohabitation: Estimates from Marriage License Applications, 1970 and 1980," *Journal of Marriage and the Family* 48 (May 1986): 423–434.

Cohabitors and noncohabitors: characteristics and differences

Eleanor Macklin, in an overview of nonmarital heterosexual cohabitation, found the following variables to differentiate between people who have and have not cohabited nonmaritally:

1. *Age.* As a group, cohabitants tend to be somewhat younger than married people.
2. *Religiosity.* Cohabitors have consistently been found to have lower rates of church attendance and higher rates of no religious affiliation.
3. *Race.* Cohabitation rates among blacks are about three times those among whites. Interracial couples were more frequent among currently cohabiting than among currently married couples.
4. *Geographic area.* Cohabitants are more likely to be living in large metropolitan areas and in the northeast and the west.
5. *Socioeconomic status.* Findings appear inconsistent. On the one hand unmarried cohabitants tend to be characterized by low income levels and high unemployment. On the other hand unmarried cohabiting women are more likely to be employed and have had more education than married women.
6. *Unconventionality.* Unconventional behavior is or was more likely among cohabitants: drug usage, oral sex, attendance at rock concerts, participation in meditation, and the like. They tend as well to espouse more liberal attitudes.
7. *Personality.* Cohabitants tend to see themselves as more androgynous and more liberated from traditional sex role characteristics. Men see themselves as less competitive and more emotionally supporting. Women see themselves as more assertive, independent, and intelligent.
8. *Age of children.* Among divorced persons, cohabitation incidence declines with age of the children involved.

Source: Selected from Eleanor D. Macklin, "Nonmarital Heterosexual Cohabitation: An Overview," in Eleanor D. Macklin and Roger H. Rubin, eds., *Contemporary Families and Alternative Lifestyles* (Beverly Hills: Sage Publications, 1983): 57–59.

addresses on their application. In 1973, 13 percent gave identical home addresses. By 1980, the percentage cohabiting increased to 53 percent. The author, Patricia Gwartney-Gibbs, suggests that when over half of a marrying population cohabits premaritally, as was the case in her study, it signals that a new normative pattern in courtship and marriage rituals may be emerging. Cohabitation prior to marriage may indeed become institutionalized as a new step between dating and marriage for many couples.

As the data indicate, nonmarital cohabitation is not an exclusive domain of youth and college students. In fact, more than one hundred

Josie recommends nonmarital cohabitation

Josie is a 30-year-old undergraduate student at Wayne State University. She was raised in a devout Catholic family, got married at age 20, divorced at age 27, moved back to her parents' home for two years, then, over a year ago moved in with Joe. Was that a good idea for her, and would she recommend it to others? In her words:

"Cohabitation is definitely a good idea before you get married. You get a clearer idea about someone when you see them morning, noon, and night rather than on an occasional evening and weekend. In many ways I'm very traditional. I do all the housework and cooking but I want to work full time when I finish school. Joe accepts that but he'd be just as happy with me in the traditional housewife role.

"I guess I'm very traditional in my commitment to Joe. I wouldn't even consider going out with or sleeping with anyone else, although I did go to bed with several men after my divorce. But now I'm really committed to Joe and would be badly hurt if he went out with someone else. I know he feels the same. I love him and know he loves me.

"We have thought about marriage but I don't believe that would change much. The only reason I can think of for marrying is that it might be a statement on the part of each of us of the trust we really have for each other. Sometimes I feel that my life is secondary to his, less important, since he's earning all the money. But I saved quite a bit from when I worked full time before I went back to school. Since I have a merit scholarship and he pays all the groceries, I don't see anything changing with marriage. I don't ask him for money now and don't think I could any easier if we were married.

"Joe's really a great guy. Unlike my ex-husband, we can talk openly about anything. For example, my ex-husband would never talk about sex—what I liked or how I felt—and he never seemed to hear me or give any expression of hearing. Now it's so different. For me, physical pleasure isn't enough. I must feel strongly about someone and be able to communicate and share openly with them.

"I really believe God led me to Joe. He's all I ever could want in a guy— warm, affectionate, expressive, willing to talk, caring. We might marry someday but he brings it up more than I do. I like living with him and don't see how marriage would improve anything. So for now, I'm happy with things as they are."

thousand persons in the United States over age sixty-five were living in a two-person household with an unrelated adult of the opposite sex. But the large increase as well as the available information on nonmarital cohabitants exists primarily among the young. Apart from census data, most of the estimates of prevalence come from research using college students, with the estimates varying according to the particular definition of cohabitation (who is included) and the population from which the estimate is drawn (private small colleges, state universities, region of country, etc.). ·

Charles Cole reviewed ten cohabitation surveys to assess its prevalence on U.S. college campuses.[27] The percentages ranged from lows of 9 and 12 percent at a small liberal arts college and a large state university both in the Midwest to highs of 31, 33, and 36 percent at two universities in the Northeast and one in the Southwest. The male-female ratio for cohabitation was consistently higher for males.

Unmarried cohabitation is not unique to the United States. Jan Trost reports that in Sweden all those persons married and younger than thirty had cohabited prior to marriage and more than half of all cohabitants age twenty to twenty-four were unmarried.[28] He estimated that in Iceland, two-thirds of all persons marrying had lived together before marriage. In Norway, Finland, Denmark, and the Netherlands from 5 to 10 percent of all cohabiting couples were unmarried.

Most prevalence rates deal with those who *had* cohabited, not those that currently *are* cohabiting. The difference in the two may be major and lead to misperceptions. For example, in a nationwide sample of 2,510 young men, Richard Clayton and Harwin Voss reported that 18 percent of the respondents had lived nonmaritally with a woman for six months or more but at the time of the interviews only 5 percent were cohabiting.[29] For some young men, cohabitation served as a prelude to marriage. For others, especially those who had experienced marital disruption, cohabitation served as a temporary or permanent alternative to matrimony.

Comparing cohabiting and noncohabiting couples

Eleanor Macklin, in an overview of the literature, compared cohabiting couples with married couples and noncohabiting engaged or going steady couples.[30] She found that nonmarried cohabitants indicate significantly

27. Charles Lee Cole, "Cohabitation in Social Context," in *Marriage and Alternative: Exploring Intimate Relationships* ed. by Roger W. Libby and Robert N. Whitehurst (Glenview, Ill.: Scott, Foresman, 1977), Table 2, p. 68.

28. Jan Trost, "Cohabitation in the Nordic Countries: From Deviant Phenomenon to Social Institution," *Alternative Lifestyles* 4 (November 1981): 401–427; and Jan Trost, "Attitudes Toward and Occurrence of Cohabitation Without Marriage," *Journal of Marriage and the Family* 40 (May 1978): 393–400.

29. Richard R. Clayton and Harwin L. Voss, "Shacking Up: Cohabitation in the 1970s," *Journal of Marriage and the Family* 39 (May 1977): 273–283.

30. Eleanor D. Macklin, "Nonmarital Heterosexual Cohabitation: An Overview," in Eleanor D. Macklin and Roger H. Rubin, eds., *Contemporary Families and Alternative Lifestyles* (Beverly Hills: Sage Publications, 1983): 49–74.

less commitment than do married couples. When compared with engaged couples, the unmarried cohabitants tended to be as committed to their partners and to the relationship but less committed to the idea of marrying their partner.

In regard to a division of labor, it was noted that cohabiting couples tended to mirror the society around them and engage in sex-role behavior characteristic of other couples their age. The same was true for exclusivity. While most believed in sexual freedom within the relationship, most voluntarily restricted their sexual activity as evidence of their commitment to the relationship. In regard to communication, satisfaction, and problems experienced, few differences have been noted between married and unmarried cohabiting couples.

In providing a profile of social and economic characteristics of unmarried cohabiting individuals, Spanier notes several items of interest.[31] One, there were approximately equal numbers of never-married and ever-married cohabiting women, whereas the number of men was more heavily represented by those in the ever-married category. This means it was more likely for a previously married man to be living with a never-married woman than vice versa. Two, unmarried couples were more likely than married couples to live in metropolitan areas. Three, cohabitation rates among blacks were three times that of whites. Four, unmarried cohabiting men were less likely to be employed and unmarried cohabiting women were more likely to be employed than married men and women respectively. And, five, low income was found to be especially characteristic of unmarried couples.

Numerous studies compared unmarried cohabitants with legally married couples. One found major differences in territoriality and privacy.[32] The unmarried were far more likely to have an area for being alone. Whereas marriage norms oppose physical separateness and promote togetherness, unmarried couples were likely to maintain rights to another residence as well as to have places within the residence for being alone. Based on this privacy factor, the authors concluded that unmarried cohabitation is not an accurate portent of what a married relationship would be like.

A second, in a matched sample of fifty cohabiting and fifty married couples, revealed that cohabiting couples were less church-oriented, more antiestablishment, more pessimistic, more fearful of close ties, more withdrawn, more likely to experience internal conflicts, more restless, and

---

31. Graham B. Spanier, "Married and Unmarried Cohabitation in the United States: 1980," *Journal of Marriage and the Family* 45 (May 1983): 277–288.

32. Paul C. Rosenblatt and Linda G. Budd, "Territoriality and Privacy in Married and Unmarried Cohabiting Couples," *The Journal of Social Psychology* 97 (October 1975): 67–76.

more impulsive. In general cohabitants tended to be more discouraged and less well adjusted than marrieds.[33]

A third examined interpersonal violence among married and cohabiting couples and found cohabitors to be more violent than marrieds.[34] The authors caution against viewing cohabitation as a unitary phenomenon, however, since cohabitors over age thirty, divorced women, those with high incomes, and those who had been together for over ten years had lower rates of violence than their married counterparts.

Consequences of unmarried cohabitation

Is unmarried cohabitation a cure-all for traditional sex- or gender-role inequality, for creating successful long-term relationships, for lowering divorce or marriage rates, and the like? Apparently not exactly. Rebecca Stafford et al. studied the division of labor in household tasks using matched samples of married and cohabiting college men and women.[35] Both cohabiting groups still divided housework along traditional lines with the women bearing the brunt of the labor. Compared to their parental generation, the young men were sharing the dishes and laundry more and the young women were sharing the lawn mowing and home repairs more. But women in both the married and unmarried groups still took most of the responsibility for and performed most of the household tasks. Apparently unmarried cohabitation is not a cure for gender inequality.

Another study of living together considered two major questions: (1) the degree to which a sample of living-together couples could be considered to contribute to a predicted decline in marriage rates by adopting the arrangement as a life-term life-style; and (2) the degree to which a basis for a successful long-term relationship had been established by the living-together couples.[36]

These questions were examined by comparing living-together, un-

---

33. James W. Crooke, James F. Keller, and Edward Markowski, " A Comparison of Sociocultural Characteristics and Personality Traits of Cohabiting and Legally Married," *International Journal of Sociology of the Family* 6 (Spring 1976): 87–98.

34. Kersti Yllo and Murray A. Straus, "Interpersonal Violence Among Married and Cohabiting Couples," *Family Relations* 30 (July 1981): 339–347.

35. Rebecca Stafford, Elaine Barkman, and Pamela Dibona, "The Division of Labor Among Cohabiting and Married Couples," *Journal of Marriage and the Family* 39 (February 1977): 43–57.

36. Judith L. Lyness, Milton E. Lipetz, and Keith E. Davis, "Living Together: An Alternative to Marriage," *Journal of Marriage and the Family* 34 (May 1972): 305–311. *See also* Carl A. Ridley, Dan J. Peterman, and Arthur W. Avery, "Cohabitation: Does It Make for a Better Marriage?" *The Family Coordinator* 27 (April 1978): 129–136; and Jeffrey M. Jacques and Karen J. Chason, "Cohabitation: Its Impact on Marital Success," *The Family Coordinator* 28 (January 1979): 35–39.

Trauma for unmarried couples who break up

A psychologist in Colorado studied unmarried couples who were living together and found that breaking up can be as traumatic for them as getting a divorce. The researcher, Kitty Mika, said that unmarried couples often say they are living together because they're not ready for marriage but may be kidding themselves about how easily they can withdraw from such a relationship.

Fifty persons were interviewed who had been involved in live-in relationships that didn't work. All the respondents were over twenty-one and had recently broken up with their live-in lovers.

The men and women reacted differently to the end of a live-in relationship. Women seemed to fall apart initially and look better later. Men were still suffering two years later. After the separation, the women showed emotional turmoil, while the men seemed happy until you talked with them.

Ms. Mika suggests that it's a good idea to look at what you're doing before you do it. You can get pretty attached to people, even when you don't expect to.

Source: Based on data supplied in an Associated Press article.

married couples with going-together (conventional, seriously dating) couples. It was found that the going-together couples held traditional orientations toward each other with a commitment to marriage forming a strong part of this orientation. The living-together couples appeared to come to their arrangement with varied expectations. The living-together women seemed to desire security through eventual marriage, whereas the men indicated that the arrangement was more likely to be an alternative to marriage.[37] Had the women come to the situation with motivations similar to those of the men, this living-together group would be expected to have very low marriage rates. If the females' desires to be married are fulfilled, the rates could be unchanged or only slightly depressed. Thus, the answer to the first question dealing with living together as a factor in declining marriage rates appears to be yes for men and no for women.

The second question was to what degree the living-together couples established a basis for a successful long-term relationship. It was found that, to a very striking degree, living-together couples did not reciprocate the kinds of feelings (need, respect, happiness, involvement, or commitment to marriage) that one would expect to be the basis of a good heterosexual relationship.[38] Another study examining the relationship between cohab-

---

37. Ibid., p. 305.
38. Ibid., p. 310.

itation and subsequent marital quality found that having cohabited pre-maritally was associated with signficantly lower perceived quality of communication for wives and significantly lower marital satisfaction for both spouses.[39] Part of this effect was accounted for by differences between cohabitors and noncohabitors on sex-role traditionalism, church attendance, and other sociocultural variables but even after controlling for such differences the cohabitors still exhibited lower marital satisfaction for both husbands and wives. These types of data do not lend support to the contentions that cohabitation serves as an effective training period for marriage or that it results in improved mate selection.

The reader should be reminded that most cohabitation data reported in this section come from United States couples. Consequences of cohabitation are likely to vary considerably in different societies. In many parts of the world it may be defined as deviant and inappropriate heterosexual behavior. In contrast, reports from Sweden suggest that unmarried cohabitation may be viewed more as a variety of marriage than an alternative to it.[40] Differences between those who marry and those who do not appear to be that the former have a marriage license. Those who cohabit without marriage are not victims of ostracism and appear to differ little in social characteristics and behavior from the married.

While unmarried cohabitation may not be a cure-all for heterosexual or marital problems, it would appear that it has definite functional value. Among other factors, for many couples it provides a financially practical condition, a warm, homelike atmosphere, more privacy than a dormitory or co-operative housing arrangement, easy access to a sexual partner, an intimate interpersonal relationship, a nonlegal, nonpermanent, nonbinding union, and a form of trial marriage. At this point it appears to be an institutionalized life-style for a temporary time period. In no way can it be viewed as a threat to the institution of marriage. The literature strongly indicates that the great majority of both cohabitants and noncohabitants desire to marry at some point in the future.

Cohabitation among the elderly

It was earlier stated that more than one hundred thousand persons (1984 figures) over the age of 65 are cohabiting with a person of the opposite sex.

---

39. Alfred DeMaris and Gerald R. Leslie, "Cohabitation with the Future Spouse: Its Influence upon Marital Satisfaction and Communication," *Journal of Marriage and the Family* 46 (February 1984): 77–84.

40. Bo Lewin, "Unmarried Cohabitation: A Marriage Form in a Changing Society," *Journal of Marriage and the Family* 44 (August 1982): 763–773.

Since 1970, the *proportion* of unmarried couples involving persons 65 and over has declined significantly, while the *number* has remained relatively constant. In 1970, they numbered about 115,000 persons representing 22 percent of the total with no children present. By the mid-1980s they numbered about 110,000 but represented only 8 percent of those with no children present. The negligible change in number and significant change in proportion of cohabiting older persons is noteworthy given the significant increase in the elderly population. This may be explained by changes in Social Security regulations which make remarriage more practical for the elderly unmarried, as may the large increase in young unmarried couples who have no children.

The advantages of nonmarital cohabitation for older persons are likely to be similar to those for college-aged and younger persons: companionship, financial savings, sexual gratification, and the like. Two areas in which older persons may differ from younger ones might include: (1) greater disapproval from their age cohort in general and their friends and associates in particular, and (2) interference in their relationships with their children and grandchildren. This may be a fruitful area for research.

Cohabitation and the law

It has been suggested that family law is undergoing a more rapid rate of change in substance and procedure than any other area of the law. Note for example the legal concerns surrounding male alimony, test-tube babies, surrogate motherhood, embryo transplants, abortion, contraceptives for minors, rights of illegitimate children, joint custody, spousal immunity, or divorce kits for the "do-it-yourselfer." Beyond these are the issues related to unmarried cohabitation.[41] The legal controversy becomes acute when one partner dies or the couple separates. At this point problems tend to arise in the areas of real and personal property, insurance, wills, estates, and child custody. The legal rights, particularly for women and children, are unclear. Traditionally, an unmarried woman who intentionally lived with an unmarried man acquired no property rights. If she contributed any service, she was not entitled to recover an interest in resulting property. Similar situations existed for children. They were considered illegitimate and on the death of the father received no financial or property benefits.

Within the past decade there appears to be a trend toward increasingly

---

41. Charles F. Crutchfield, "Nonmarital Relationships and Their Impact on the Institution of Marriage and the Traditional Family Structure," *Journal of Family Law* 19 (1980–81): 247–261; and F. Patrick Hubbard and Mary Johnson Larsen, "Contract Cohabitation: A Jurisprudential Perspective on Common Law Judging," *Journal of Family Law* 19 (1980–81): 655–706.

granting legal protection for the "spouse" and the children of cohabitants.[42] In 1973, a California appellate court held that a meretricious spouse (one who is intentionally living with a person of the opposite sex and is unmarried) had the same property rights as a married person. Three years later, in the much publicized case of Michelle and Lee Marvin who had an alleged oral contract at the beginning of their seven-year nonmarital relationship, the California Supreme Court set a precedent by defining the value of the woman's services for the purpose of property settlement. This decision also recognized the validity of an oral contract between cohabitants by making it legally binding upon both parties. A similar trend seems to be occurring for children born of cohabiting nonmarried parents. In 1972 a Supreme Court decision found the Social Security Act to be discriminatory against illegitimate children in the payment of death benefits. Another court held a father responsible for child support. Decisions such as these have reduced but not eliminated the negative legal consequences of cohabitation for adults or children. Wide variation exists in state laws and most states have not defined the rights of cohabitants or their children.

SUMMARY

1. The processes followed in mate selection vary widely from one society to another, ranging from totally arranged marriages to limited "freedom of choice." The difference is centered in who is making the choice.

2. A range of explanations exists as to who selects whom and why. At one extreme are individualistic explanations with the answers rooted in instincts, genetic similarity, needs, drives, parental images, and complementary needs. In contrast are sociocultural explanations with the answers rooted in norms, roles, values, and social exchanges.

3. Sociocultural explanations operate at a more conscious level, are more readily testable, and have greater research support than individualistic explanations. These, too, are not fully adequate to explain mate selection, but they do appear to be more fruitful. One sociocultural theory involves roles—the internalized, learned, social expectations as to what attitudes and behavior are appropriate or inappropriate in the selection of a mate. In brief, the couple likely to marry is the male and female who share similar role definitions and expectations.

42. Lenore J. Weitzman et al., "Contracts for Intimate Relationships: A Study of Contracts, Within, and in Lieu of Legal Marriage," *Alternate Lifestyles* 1 (August 1978): 303–378; and Lenore J. Weitzman, *The Marriage Contract: Spouses, Lovers, and the Law* (New York: The Free Press, 1981).

4. Closely related to role theory is the idea that interpersonal attraction is facilitated when persons share or perceive themselves as sharing similar value orientations. This sharing of values, in effect, validates one's self and thus promotes emotional satisfaction and enhances the means of commmunication.

5. Exchange theorists view mate selection as a bargaining or social-exchange process. While not explaining how interaction arises, the theory does explain the behavioral outcomes. The mate selection choice is based on the selection of persons who share equivalent resources, each having something to offer that is desired by the other. Relationships may continue in unequal exchanges if no better alternative to that relationship is perceived.

6. Some writers see mate selection as the result of several of these processes operating simultaneously or sequentially. One explanation involves a series of "filtering factors." Another sequential explanation sees mate selection as a developmental process of interactions between individuals, the outcome of which is not mechanically predetermined but is the end product of a sequence of events along the paths of available alternatives. A third sequential explanation involves a three-stage chronological sequence involving stimulus, value, and role (SVR).

7. The mate selection process is the manner in which an individual changes status from single to married. The process involves all sorts of rules and roles applicable to male-female interaction. Generally, it involves a series of types of dating that fulfills a variety of functions and leads to increasing degrees of intimacy and commitment such as steady dating and engagement.

8. Finally, consideration was given in this chapter to unmarried heterosexual cohabitation, living together, or consensual unions. Descriptive data were provided to indicate prevalence; a comparison was made between cohabiting and noncohabiting couples; and some of the consequences of unmarried cohabitation were examined. Brief attention was devoted to cohabitation among the elderly and cohabitation and the law. While certain legal and social difficulties may result, the rapid increase in unmarried heterosexual cohabitation represents an attractive life-style, even if temporary, for couples of all ages.

9. This chapter and the previous one provided an overview of selected structural characteristics, functions of and processes involved in the selection of mates. Examined were selected types of endogamous and exogamous marriages as well as various explanations as to why certain mate choices occur. Although the male-female sexual relationship is generally an important dimension to consider in understanding mate selection, only minimal attention was given to it.

10. Sexual relationships, of significance to marriage and the family throughout the world, are more fully analyzed and described in Part IV. Chapter 10, on nonmarital sexual standards and relationships, further enhances an understanding of this and the previous chapter on mate selection. Attention is now directed to sexual norms and relationships.

KEY TERMS AND TOPICS

Arranged marriage versus free choice of mate	292	Dating	310
Individualistic explanations	296	Bundling	311
Oedipus and Electra complexes	298	Principle of least interest	312
Castration anxiety	298	Engagement	314
Complementary needs	299	Nonmarital heterosexual cohabitation	315
Role, value, and exchange theories of mate selection	300	Consequences of cohabitation	321
Sequential theories of mate selection	305	Cohabitation among the elderly	323

DISCUSSION QUESTIONS

1. Would there be any advantages for young people to have their marriage arranged for them? Would the consequences in marriage be different? How?

2. To what extent was or is your mate likely to be a result of instincts, innate drives, parental image, or complementary needs?

3. In spite of the logical and rational basis of the theory of complementary needs, why is there so little empirical support for it?

4. In what ways is role theory consistent or inconsistent with homogamy and value and sequential theories?

5. List a number of role expectations that you hold for yourself and your spouse. Have a dating partner do the same. Then on a rating scale of one to five indicate whether you agree or disagree with the expectations. Compare and discuss the results. Examples: "I expect the male should do the laundry." "I expect the female to see that the children get religious training." "Both the husband and wife should be employed full-time."

6. What do you value most? Could you marry anyone who did not share these values? Why?

7. To what extent is the portrayal of the male-female game in the mate selection process an accurate one?

8. Recall your own past love affairs or those of your friends. Is the "principle of least interest" applicable? How was it manifested?

9. How important is it to restrict the "field of eligibles" today—whether in the form of going steady, being pinned, or some other concept or arrangement? Is it more important for females than males? Why or why not?

10. How do you explain the frequency of premarital cohabitation? In what ways is or is not cohabitation a trial marriage?

11. What advantages or disadvantages of cohabitation exist for males in contrast to females, for youths in contrast to the elderly, or in verbal contracts in contrast to legal, written ones?

12. Review some of the legal implications of cohabitation. Should it be viewed and treated as a marital relationship?

FURTHER READINGS

Adams, Bert N. "Mate Selection in the United States: A Theoretical Summarization." Vol. 1. *Contemporary Theories About the Family*. Edited by Wesley R. Burr et al. New York: The Free Press, 1979: 259–267. An attempt to develop propositions and a theoretical model on who married whom.

Bell, Robert R. *Marriage and Family Interaction*. 6th ed. Homewood, Ill.: Dorsey Press, 1983. Chapter 3 on dating and mate selection, Chapter 4 on love, Chapter 6 on the never-married, and Chapter 7 on cohabitation present a sociological analysis of these areas.

Eekelar, John M., ad Katz, Sanford N., eds. *Marriage and Cohabitation in Contemporary Societies*. Toronto: Butterworth and Company, 1980. An international and interdisciplinary overview of areas of legal, social, and ethical issues surrounding cohabitation and marriage.

Eshleman, J. Ross, and Clarke, Juanne N. *Intimacy, Commitments and Marriage: Development of Relationships*. Boston: Allyn and Bacon, 1978. A look at the process of becoming a human being, the development of relationships, and variations in commitments throughout the life cycle.

Korman, Sheila K. "Nontraditional Dating Behavior: Date-imitation and Date Expense-sharing Among Feminists and Nonfeminists." *Family Relations* 32 (October 1983): 575–581. A study of women students seeks to determine the extent to which feminists are more likely to engage in nontraditional behaviors in dating in order to equalize the bargaining element.

Lewin, Bo. "Unmarried Cohabitation: A Marriage Form in a Changing Society." *Journal of Marriage and the Family* 44 (August 1982): 763–773. A look at cohabitation in Sweden, testing the hypothesis that unmarried cohabitation is a variety of marriage rather than an alternative to it.

Macklin, Eleanor D. "Nonmarital Heterosexual Cohabitation: An Overview." In Eleanor D. Macklin and Roger H. Rubin, eds., *Contemporary Families and Alternative Lifestyles*. Beverly Hills: Sage Publications, 1983: 49–74. A comprehensive overview of cohabitation among the unmarried covering its prevalence, the nature of relationships, their characteristics, a comparison with noncohabiting couples, and the effects of cohabitation.

Mullan, Bob. *The Mating Trade*. London: Routledge and Kegan Paul, 1984. A cross-national look at topics ranging from choosing partners from arranged marriages in Jewish and Japanese cultures to contemporary mating industries, such as computer and videodating.

Murstein, Bernard I. *Paths to Marriage.* Newbury Park, Cal.: Sage Publications, 1986. A concise theoretical and research-oriented work on marital choice, including historical, sociocultural, developmental and tactical determinants.

Rubin, Lillian B. *Just Friends: The Role of Friendship in Our Lives.* New York: Harper and Row, 1985. While not a book on mate selection, it is a clear expression of friendship relationships between women, men, women and men, couples, families, and kin.

Spanier, Graham B. "Married and Unmarried Cohabitation in the United States: 1980." *Journal of Marriage and the Family* 45 (May 1983): 277–288. Data from the March 1980 Current Population Survey are used to contrast married couples living together with unmarried heterosexual cohabitors. Provides an excellent look at trends as well as a profile of the social and economic characteristics of cohabitors.

Waller, Willard. *The Family: A Dynamic Interpretation.* New York: Holt, Rinehart and Winston, 1951. (Revised by Reuben Hill. Originally published by Cordon in 1938.) One of the classical early textbooks on the family, taking a look at the personal interactive aspects of marriage and the family.

IV

SEXUAL NORMS AND RELATIONSHIPS

Photo: © Pamela Price/The Picture Cube

10

Sexual Relationships in Premarital and Nonmarital Contexts

Few topics occupy as much widespread attention and thought as do matters relating to sex, both as a social and as a personal phenomenon. The significance of sex in modern life is evidenced by the recent controversies centering around abortion, gay liberation, sex education in the public schools, pornographic literature, X-rated movies, the availability of contraceptives to adolescents, and the general concern over sexual identity and male-female roles, to mention a few.

Ira Reiss, in a sociological analysis of human sexuality, defines sexuality as erotic and genital responses produced by the cultural scripts of a society.[1] He suggests that sexuality is universal in that everywhere it is viewed as important and in need of societal regulation of some sort. The basic reason for this importance is that it encompasses the elements of physical pleasure and self-disclosure. These are crucial elements in forming relationships in a society, sexual or otherwise.

All societies have social norms that grant approval to certain sexual behaviors and disapproval to others. Perhaps the most universal taboo on sexual behavior relates to incest; the most universal approval is granted to sexual behavior in marriage (both are discussed in Chapter 11). Clearly, no society grants unrestricted sexual liberties: all societies control sexuality. John DeLamater[2] and Christie Davies[3] both argue that social institutions, primarily family and religion, are the source of both general perspectives and specific norms that govern sexual expression. In the United States, for example, the Judeo-Christian doctrine embodies a procreational orientation toward sex. Acts that have no reproductive value such as masturbation, sodomy (anal, oral, bestiality), or homosexuality are taboo and sinful, as are activities that threaten the family unit such as incest and adultery. The family plays a primary role in the regulation and control of

---

1. Ira L. Reiss, *Journey into Sexuality: An Exploratory Voyage* (Englewood Cliffs, N.J.: Prentice-Hall, 1986), p. 37.

2. John DeLamater, "The Social Control of Sexuality," *Annual Review of Sociology* 7 (1981): 263–290.

3. Christie Davies, "Sexual Taboos and Social Boundaries," *American Journal of Sociology* 87 (March 1982): 1032–1063.

sexual conduct through the socialization process, controlling who marries whom and providing negative sanctions when sexual norms are violated.

Processes of controlling sexuality take many forms. Some societies attempt to enforce norms of chastity by secluding single girls. Some provide escorts or duennas when girls are with the opposite sex in public. Ethnic and subcultural differences regulate sexual matters by a lifelong process of instilling sexual norms into the consciousness of the members within that ethnic group.

The stratification system also serves to regulate sexual expression. Class and caste systems operate both to separate groups geographically as well as to define appropriate or inappropriate sexual partners. Sex is also highly regulated by the statuses we occupy. Males may behave differently from females in many situations, priests behave differently from school teachers, divorcees behave differently from married persons, and grandparents behave differently from grandchildren.

Most societies use the reproductive cycle to regulate sex. Taboos may be placed against sexual intercourse during pregnancy, during the menstrual period, immediately following childbirth, or through the period of lactation. Special events also serve to regulate sex. Intercourse may be required or forbidden during times of certain festivities, religious ceremonies, weddings, harvest time, or the like. Quite clearly, there are no societies which do not use various means to regulate and control the sexual behavior of its members.

Sexual control may be indicated by the forms of sexual outlet granted social approval, availability or both to members of a given society. Certain societies display pornography openly, whereas others prosecute those who sell or display this type of literature. Some societies have burlesque movie houses; others forbid them. Whereas the most approved sexual outlet occurs in marriage, the norms of most societies discourage practices such as rape, child molesting, bestiality, voyeurism, prostitution, homosexuality, group sex, and the like.

In our own society, as well as in virtually all others, the primary and most pervasive sexual interest is with heterosexual behavior and relationships, both marital and nonmarital. These relationships generally refer to far more than simply coitus or sexual intercourse. They may include overt acts such as kissing, petting, and the like but also are likely to include attitudes, social values, and norms appropriate to the acts.

Many distinctions can be made in classifying heterosexual relationships. Most often they involve one male and one female, but multiple partners are at times involved. They may involve persons who are not married but whose relationship is marriage-oriented (premarital). They may involve persons who are not married and to whom marriage is not a factor (nonmarital). They may involve a husband and wife (marital). They may involve a married person with a partner other than his or her spouse (extramarital).

If you can't talk of rock, how can you discuss sex?

This column is about sex. Parental discretion is advised.

The Reagan administration seems to be going ahead with a rule requiring that any organization receiving federal funds for dispensing contraceptives to a minor must notify the parents within 10 days of the request.

The administration's heart is in the right place. But trying to put such a rule into effect presents problems. Many parents can't talk with their teenagers about rock music, much less discuss with them the subject of sex.

Let's assume that the Wallingfords have just received a letter from Planned Parenthood, noting that their daughter Sue Anne has requested a prescription for the Pill.

Both are waiting for her when she comes home from school.

"And what were you doing in school?"

"I don't know. I just went to class, and stuff."

"What kind of stuff?" Wallingford yells.

"You know, just stuff. What are you guys all excited about?"

"Are you sure you didn't sneak off in a clothes closet and do it with some boy?"

"Do what? And with what boy?"

"Any boy. We know everything," she says, waving the letter from Planned Parenthood. "So what do you have to say for yourself?"

"I knew if I asked you for permission to buy the Pill you wouldn't give it to me."

"You're damn right we wouldn't give it to you. What kind of parents do you think we are?" Wallingford says.

They may involve a sexual exchange of married partners (swinging or wife/husband swapping). They may involve divorced or widowed persons who were once married but are currently socially and legally single (post-marital). This chapter will examine selected sexual standards and relationships that exist in premarital and nonmarital contexts.

PREMARITAL SEXUAL STANDARDS

Several decades ago Ira Reiss stated that logically there can be three major types of sexual standards: one stating that premarital sexual intercourse is wrong for both sexes; one stating that premarital intercourse is right for both sexes; and one stating that premarital intercourse is right for one sex but wrong for the other.[4] Today, empirical evidence would

---

4. Ira L. Reiss, *Premarital Sexual Standards in America* (Glencoe: The Free Press, 1960): 82.

"I know what kind of parents you are. That's why I went somewhere else to protect myself."

"To protect yourself from what?"

"Having a baby."

"What do you know about having babies?" Mrs. Wallingford says.

"Well, when the male's sperm fertilizes the woman's ovum . . ."

"That's enough of that kind of dirty talk," Wallingford shouts.

"Relax, Daddy-O. I haven't done it. But if I ever decide to, I want to be protected. They told us at the clinic, it's the woman and not the man who has to take precautions. Men couldn't care less about the consequences."

"You seem to know a lot about sex, young lady," Wallingford says. "You certainly didn't learn any of this at home."

"I know. That's why I went to the clinic. Every time I brought up the subject you said it was none of my business."

"It isn't any of your business," Mrs. Wallingford says. "You're 17 years old and nice girls don't discuss such things with their parents."

"Where are you going?"

"To the basketball game with Jack."

"So that's where you're going to do it," Wallingford cries.

"How am I going to do it at a basketball game?"

"In the parking lot," Wallingford says. "That's where I used to do it."

"I can't take any more of this. Goodby."

After Sue Anne leaves, Mrs. Wallingford wipes the tears from her eyes. "You know, George, I think we both would be happier today if Planned Parenthood had never let us know."

Source: Art Buchwald, *Detroit Free Press*, February 10, 1983, p. 13-B. By permission of the author.

suggest that the United States, although not most countries, has sexual standards that fit all three possibilities: a single standard of abstinence, a single standard of permissiveness, and a double standard. The second standard, that intercourse is right for both sexes, often subdivides people into two groups: (1) those who accept intercourse only when there is a stable relationship with engagement, love, or strong affection present, and (2) those who accept intercourse when there is a mutual physical attraction, regardless of the amount of stability or affection present.

Although many people have tendencies toward more than one standard, most can be classified as adhering predominantly to one or another. In summary they are:

1. *Abstinence.* Premarital intercourse is wrong for both women and men

regardless of circumstances. This single standard may permit norms of kissing, petting, mutual masturbation, or even oral-genital stimulation as long as the vagina has not been penetrated by the penis.

2. *Permissiveness with affection.* Premarital intercourse is right for both women and men under the condition that there is a stable relationship with engagement, love, or strong affection present. This person-centered single standard grants an approval to intercourse when love, a marriage commitment, or both are present.

3. *Permissiveness without affection.* Premarital intercourse is right for both women and men regardless of the degree of affection or commitment. This body-centered single standard places the emphasis on the pleasure surrounding the physical aspects of the act.

4. *Double standard.* Premarital intercourse is acceptable for men but wrong and unacceptable for women. Women and men are judged differently for the same behavior.

The argument for the double standard, which suggests that "that's the way men are," "boys will be boys," or "men 'need' coitus more than females," has little basis in fact. Men and women appear to be very similar in their needs, drives, and responses. Research findings of Masters and Johnson more than twenty years ago indicate that women have as definite an orgasm as do men and that, in general, women have a greater potential for sexual responsiveness than do men, since they tend to respond faster, more intensely, and longer to sexual stimulation. Aside from obvious anatomical variants, men and women are homogeneous in their physiologic responses to sexual stimuli.[5] Kinsey came to the same conclusion almost fifteen years earlier when he reported:

> The anatomic structures which are most essential to sexual response and orgasm are nearly identical in the human male and female. The differences are relatively few. They are associated with the different functions of the sexes in reproductive processes but they are of no great significance in the origins and development of sexual response and orgasm. If females and males differ sexually in any basic way, those differences must originate in some other aspect of the biology or psychology of the two sexes. They do not originate in any of the anatomic structures which have been considered here.[6]

In brief, the justification for a double standard, based on the innate needs or drives of men being basically different from those of women,

5. William H. Masters and Virginia E. Johnson, *Human Sexual Response* (Boston: Little, Brown, 1966), Chapter 17 and p. 285.

6. Alfred C. Kinsey, Wardell B. Pomeroy, Clyde E. Martin, and Paul H. Gebhard, *Sexual Behavior in the Human Female* (Philadelphia: W. B. Saunders, 1953): 593.

Sexual standards in Sweden

Scandinavian countries, particularly Sweden, are often viewed by U.S. citizens as "sexually liberated" and without a double standard. While not true in absolute terms, in comparison with the United States this would appear to be accurate. Swedish norms about premarital intercourse, sex education, availability of abortion and contraception, free clinical treatment of venereal disease, and the open discussion of human sexuality are more permissive and sexually equal than those in the United States.

Swedish policy on sexual matters has been adopted explicitly to reduce sexual inequality. Young Swedes, both men and women, are permitted to responsibly and freely express their sexuality. Most young people live together and have intercourse before marriage. But most relationships, rather than being indiscriminate or promiscuous, are cultivated in a context of intimacy with particular persons. Couples are not as likely to be forced into marriage by pregnancy as occurs among couples in the United States. What this means is that women are not penalized if they become pregnant before marriage. The adverse effects of pregnancy are reduced by government assistance in the forms of child care centers, abortion clinics, sex education classes, and the like. Government policy, while protecting the rights of women, also aims at guaranteeing equal opportunity to every child in Sweden, irrespective of the circumstances of birth.

has little if any empirical support. The differences that exist—and certainly many do—are basically social, learned differences. Since they are learned, any differences that exist can be relearned to equalize the situation and correct the imbalance of accepting male indulgence and condemning female indulgence.

Although the double standard is thought to have been weakened by the feminist movement (with its platform of equality), the development of contraception (with its removal of much of the fear of pregnancy), and the Industrial Revolution (which gave women greater economic opportunities), the double standard is still very much a part of U.S. society, as will be shown later in this chapter. And few would dispute the notion that the double standard is relevant to far more than sexual behavior and standards. It is applicable to business, politics, religion, education, and any other sphere of social life.

SEXUALIZATION AND SEXUAL SCRIPTS

Sexualization, that is, sexual socialization, is the process by which persons learn and internalize their sexual self-concepts, values, attitudes, and

Sexual scripts designate the who, what, where, when, and why questions of sexuality and are in turn modified by new sexual experiences. (Photo: © Frank Siteman/The Picture Cube)

behaviors. It is a process that begins at birth and continues into adulthood and old age. Details of the socialization process, be it in regard to sexuality, gender, violence, or other factors, are described in Chapter 14. Our attention at this point will focus specifically on the learning and development of sexual knowledge, attitudes, and values. These aspects of sexualization appear to be the key to understanding sexual behavior.

Symbolic interaction theory would posit that we become sexual beings through the process of social interaction. As suggested previously, while there is an important biological and hormonal basis to sexual development, simply having genitals associated with the female or male does not guarantee that our gender identity or preferences follow anatomical components. This is evidenced in transvestism (dressing in the clothing of the opposite gender), transsexualism (trapped in the body of the wrong gender), or homosexuality (sexual activity or preference for same gender relationships). It is evidenced as well in the wide range of acceptable or nonacceptable attitudes and behaviors that exists among persons in general: sexual abstinence, cunnilingus, fellatio, masturbation, sadism, sodomy, voyeurism, or sexual positions in heterosexual coitus. Research on hermaphrodites (persons with both male and female sex glands) seems to provide strong evidence that conventional patterns of masculine and feminine behavior can be altered.

Symbolic interaction theory would posit as well that sexual behavior can only be understood in terms of internalized symbolic meanings. This suggests that the definitions of the situation, and the meanings or interpretations given to various behaviors, are basic to understanding that behavior or lack of behavior. If premarital coitus is defined as sinful, if masturbation is believed to cause insanity, and if homosexuality is perceived as perverted, these meanings and definitions will have a major, but not absolute, influence on behavior or the absence of it. That is, definitions, attitudes, meanings, values, and other internalized mental processes predispose behavior.

These ideas, basic to a symbolic interaction frame of reference, parallel the ideas of John Gagnon and William Simon. They conceptualize the outcome or product of what is here termed sexualization in terms of *sexual scripts.*[7] The sexual script designates the who, what, where, when, and why of sexuality. Like a script for a play or movie, it provides an overall blueprint of what sexuality is and how it is practiced.

Scripts are the plans that people have in their heads. The sexual script defines *who* one does sex with. Sex is not allowed with certain categories of people, but others are fantasized about and on the "approved list." The script defines *what* sexual behaviors are right or wrong, appropriate or inappropriate. While kissing or masturbation may be on the approved list, intercourse or oral sex may not. The script includes the *whens* and *wheres* of sex. Is it appropriate only at night in the dark in a bedroom? Is it appropriate at noon in an automobile? And finally, it includes the *why* issue. Is sex for fun, intimacy, reducing tension, procreation, or some other reason? One's sexual script is the internalized notions of these who, what, when, where, and why questions. It is learned in interaction with others and contains notions of the society, subculture, reference groups, and significant others in which we are members and with whom we interact. In interaction with others we build our scripts, those cognitive schemes that we carry in our heads and that affect our actual conduct.

The process by which these sexual scripts are formulated tends to illustrate the importance of adult socialization in contrast to the Freudian emphasis on the early years (*see* Chapter 14). At puberty, a young person may be largely ignorant of adult sexuality. Adolescence is a period when adult sexual scripts become formulated, experienced, and modified. Scripts are devices for organizing, guiding, and understanding our behavior. They

---

7. John H. Gagnon, *Human Sexualities* (Glenview, Ill.: Scott Foresman 1977), pp. 5–9; and William Simon and John H. Gagnon, "Sexual Scripts: Permanence and Change," *Archives of Sexual Behavior* 15 (1986): 97–120.

justify action that is in accord with them and cause us to question those that are not. Simon and Gagnon[8] argue that for behavior to occur, something resembling scripting must occur on three distinct levels: cultural scenarios, interpersonal scripts, and intrapsychic scripts.

Cultural scenarios are the instructional guides that exist at the level of collective life. The enactment of virtually all roles reflects the institutions, groups, and social context in which we were born, raised, and function. *Interpersonal scripts* transform the person trained in cultural scenarios and general social roles to context-specific behavior. What we do is influenced by the response of others. These cultural scenarios and interpersonal scripts result in *intrapsychic scripting,* an internal dialogue, a world of fantasy, or—in interaction terms—a personal self that is in reality a social self. The private world of individual wishes and desires is bound to social life. All sexual behavior involves and includes all three levels of scripting.

Sexual scripting, like the general process of sexual socialization, follows the life cycle. Until recently, infancy, childhood, and old age were periods where the appearance of sex-seeking behavior was viewed as pathological in that these people were either too young or too old to be capable of comprehending or experiencing the full meaning of the behavior. In the context of this and most family texts, sexual life cycles tend to be subsumed under headings of premarital, marital, extramarital, or postmarital experiences. Any of these ideas suggest profound changes in the requirements and meanings attached to sexual scripts. Thus, a traditional premarital sexual script that suggests "nice girls don't" changes to "nice girls do" after they are married. According to Simon and Gagnon, the power of sexual scripts—perhaps the power of the sexual—is tied to the extrasexual significances of confirming identities and making them congruent with appropriate relationships.[9]

This section on sexualization and sexual scripts focuses on the processes by which sexual definitions and meanings become internalized; they are part of the basic process of socialization in general and may become more clearly understood after reading Chapter 14. At this point, let us examine briefly the consistency between the attitudinal and behavioral aspects of sexual scripts.

Sexual attitudes and behavior: how consistent are they?

Sexual scripts include both attitudinal and behavioral components. How consistent are sexual beliefs, values, and attitudes with what is done?

8. Ibid., pp. 98–104.
9. Ibid., p. 117.

One could assume that, for the most part, attitudes and behavior are highly related. In earlier editions of this text, I hypothesized that when they differ, beliefs about what is appropriate or proper sexual behavior tend to be more conservative than actual behaviors. The contention was that socialization practices in Judeo-Christian cultures lead to the internalization of sexual attitudes and beliefs that are highly restrictive (don't masturbate, engage in oral-genital sex, have premarital intercourse, and the like). During adolescence, as young people get involved in the courtship process, as going steady and a commitment type of relationship take place, behaviors will probably go beyond the boundaries of what is believed to be proper. After engaging in the behavior, the belief toward that behavior is likely to change in the direction of greater permissiveness. An interaction process is at work. More permissive behavior modifies the belief.

There are several reasons for greater permissiveness of actual behavior than of belief about proper behavior. It is likely that traditional values continue to be applied even when the behavior is changed. Also, it is possible that premarital sexual behavior is subject to more rapid social change than are attitudes. When behavior exceeds the belief limits, this conflict may produce guilt. While guilt is likely to be a common component of the sexualization process, a tendency exists to continue the behavior until it is accepted. Once accepted, the feelings of guilt are reduced or totally eliminated.

Considerable support appears to exist for the ideas just presented. One example comes from a study of about 3,500 high school students.[10] Selected results indicated that 83 percent of sexually experienced adolescents cited a best age for first intercourse that was older than the age at which they themselves experienced that event, and 43 percent of them reported a best age for first coitus older than their current age. Among the sexually active who agreed with the statement that they would only have sex if using birth control, about one-fourth used no contraceptive at last intercourse. A much higher proportion of virgins believed premarital sex is wrong than did non-virgins, and even among the non-virgins about one-fourth of both sexes said they believe sex before marriage is wrong. In other words, findings such as these tend to suggest that attitudes or beliefs are more restrictive or conservative than behavior, whether the adolescents were sexually active or virgins. And as could be expected, those who engaged in various sexual behaviors had more permissive sexual scripts than those who did not. The authors of this study conclude that the majority of young people have values and attitudes consistent

---

10. Laurie S. Zabin, Marilyn B. Hirsch, Edward A. Smith, and Janet B. Hardy, "Adolescent Sexual Attitudes and Behavior: Are They Consistent?" *Family Planning Perspectives* 16 (July/August 1984): 181–185.

Even in public places such as city streets, couples in the United States can be observed expressing intimate exchanges. (Photo: © Alan Carey/The Image Works)

with responsible sexual conduct, but not all of them are able to translate these attitudes into personal behavior.

ANTECEDENTS OF SEXUAL BEHAVIOR

Antecedents of sexual behavior are factors that preceded or took place prior to a given sexual activity. Many antecedents are related to, or associated with, the presence or absence of nonmarital intercourse. Simple logic would seem to indicate that a major antecedent or preceding factor in explaining or understanding premarital sexual behavior would be parental influence in the sexual socialization process. For example, is it not logical to assume that individuals brought up in sexually conservative homes will have less premarital heterosexual involvement than those from more liberal home environments? In other words, homes in which parents do not openly display affection, have a rigid and concerned attitude toward nudity, never discuss sex openly, and never have books or pamphlets available on sexual subjects would be expected to produce or lead to more conservative behavior or less sexual involvement by their children. This hypothesis was put to a test in a national probability sample of nearly 1,200 college students. Interestingly, the findings showed no significant relationship for males or females between parental sexual conservatism and premarital socio-sexual involvement.[11] This seems to indicate that perceived sexual conservatism leads neither to increased nor decreased sexual activity.

In fact, data from two independent studies that include teenagers and their mothers indicate that neither parental attitudes toward premarital sex nor parent-child communication about sex and contraception appear to affect teenagers' subsequent sexual and contraceptive behavior.[12] Teens who communicated little with their mothers were as likely to use effective birth control as were those who communicated well. Authors of both studies suggest that the findings do not indicate that family communication counts for very much in terms of either sexual behavior or contraceptive usage. One reason may be that parental communication about sex and contraception is generally so vague or so limited as to have no impact.

How about the related issue of parental discipline? Would we not

---

11. Graham B. Spanier, "Perceived Parental Sexual Conservatism, Religiosity, and Premarital Sexual Behavior," *Sociological Focus* 9 (August 1976): 285–298.

12. Susan F. Newcomer and J. Richard Udry, "Parent-Child Communication and Adolescent Sexual Behavior," *Family Planning Perspectives* 17 (July/August 1985): 169–174; and Frank F. Furstenberg, Jr., Roberta Herceg-Baron, Judy Shea, and David Webb, "Family Communication and Teenagers' Contraceptive Use," *Family Planning Perspectives* 16 (July/August 1984): 163–170. *See also* Kristin A. Moore, James L. Peterson, and Frank F. Furstenberg, "Parental Attitudes and the Occurrence of Early Sexual Activity," *Journal of Marriage and the Family* 48 (November 1986): 777–782.

Sex and the single Russian—"your place or mom's?"

MOSCOW—"It's our No. 1 national problem," a young carpenter complained recently. He wasn't referring to the faltering economy, the frequent food shortages, or some foreign policy setback. He was talking about how tough it is for young singles here to find a place for romancing.

"I'm 24, and I live in a two-room flat with my mother, grandmother, and younger sister," he said. "Figure out for yourself how many times in a month the apartment is empty and I can have a girl over. Weeks go by without an opportunity, and I really don't have any other place available."

For Soviet singles, finding a bedmate is a lot easier than finding a bed. Housing here is in such short supply that even young marrieds must move in with their parents, and it's practically unheard of for single people to have their own pads.

The younger generation may be liberal about lovemaking, but most of their parents disapprove of premarital sex and would rather not have it taking place in their apartments.

"My mother knows I have girls over when she's away," said a 26-year-old medical technician from Minsk who is lucky enough to have his own bedroom. "But it's something we never talk about because she definitely doesn't like the idea."

Occasionally, he confessed, he sneaks a lover in late at night after his mother has been asleep for some time. "But if she ever woke up, oy-oy-oy!" he said with a grimace, holding his head in mock horror.

As for little love nests—even makeshift ones—away from home, they're very difficult to find here. In the summer many singles snuggle up in the parks, but in the winter it's too cold for cuddling outdoors, with temperatures frequently falling below zero.

"Forget about going to a hotel," said a Leningrad lass. "In the first place it's almost impossible to get a reservation, and in the second place you have to present your internal passports when you register. Two unmarried people would get chased away or worse, because strictly speaking that sort of thing is against the law."

Singles sometimes overcome these obstacles by making friends—or private arrangements—with a hotel employee. "I know a night clerk," said a student in Stavropol, "and for five rubles he finds me an empty room for a few hours.

expect adolescents from homes with very strict discipline and rules about dating to be more sexually conservative and those from homes with few rules and lenient discipline to be sexually permissive? Survey data from several thousand adolescents (ages 15–18) and their parents were analyzed to determine how parental discipline was related to the sexual permissiveness of their children.[13] As just hypothesized, sexual permissiveness

13. Brent C. Miller, J. Kelly McCoy, Terrance D. Olson, and Christopher M. Wallace,

It's a service he provides for a lot of young people, and the money he makes this way is much more than his salary."

The Saturday night standby of so many young Americans—the back seat of a car—is not accessible to most singles here. An automobile can cost several years' salary, and special permission is needed to purchase one.

A young Yugoslav studying at Moscow State University—where unmarried students can be expelled for making love in their rooms—is constantly besieged by classmates who want to borrow his car. "Sometimes they offer me money and gifts," he said.

What makes the problem easier to put up with is the fact that this is still a puritanical society where mass media stimulation does not take place. Suggestive advertising, sexy songs, girlie magazines are strictly forbidden in the Soviet Union.

"Here, having sex is not a fixed idea," said 23-year-old Sergei, who is studying the management of mass demonstrations at an institute in the Ukraine. "We're not busy thinking about it all the time, which I think is the case with young men and women in the West."

Still, he said, when the opportunity presents itself, young people here feel no compunction to turn it down. "We're interested in having sex, but it's not the main thing on our minds," he said.

Another factor interfering with the sex lives of singles here is the absence of social activities oriented toward the unwed. Singles bars do not exist, and admission to the only discotheque in this city is limited to a few hundred people at a time. Long lines form outside every Saturday night.

A survey by two Leningrad sociologists showed that most Soviets meet their spouses at work, at school, or on vacations. The problem of meeting a potential mate is so serious among older women that lonely hearts clubs have recently been set up in several of the principal cities.

In the age brackets above 30, single women greatly outnumber single men, and the disparity increases with age.

A young Muscovite, an engineer, may have put it all in perspective when he said: Even if you meet someone, "finding a place where you can make love when you want to is even more difficult than finding a comfortable pair of shoes in the shops. And frankly, I haven't been able to find either yet."

Source: Jim Gallagher, The Chicago *Tribune,* February 1, 1979, Section 2, pp. 1–2. Copyrighted © 1979, Chicago *Tribune.* Used with permission. All rights reserved.

was highest among adolescents who viewed their parents as not being strict or not having rules about dating. But interestingly, adolescents who experienced very strict parental discipline and many dating rules were

"Parental Discipline and Control Attempts in Relation to Adolescent Sexual Attitudes and Behavior," *Journal of Marriage and the Family* 48 (August 1986): 503–512.

more permissive than those with moderate parental strictness and rules. In other words, a curvilinear relationship was found in that both strict and lenient disciplinary patterns resulted in higher levels of sexual permissiveness with the lowest permissiveness among adolescents with moderately strict parents.

How might the above findings be explained? First, perhaps children do not interpret the presence or absence of sexual behavior on the part of parents as being particularly relevant to their own sexual needs and experiences. Second, perhaps parental disciplinary behaviors are a consequence of adolescent permissiveness. That is, if parents suspect their teenager is engaging in sexual intercourse they may impose more dating rules. Third, while parents may be extremely influential in general socialization, they may be less influential than significant others outside the home, particularly peers, in sexual socialization.

Support for this latter idea comes from a national probability sample of fifteen- to nineteen-year-old women.[14] A majority of young women had views on socioeconomic status which were like their parents' views. But in regard to premarital sex, very little agreement existed between parents and peers and more young women were influenced by friends than by parents. The same study showed that sexually experienced young women influenced by their peers were more likely to use contraceptives than those influenced by their parents. Sexually experienced women whose views were like their parents' were more likely to "deny" their sexual behavior and either fail to use contraceptives or to use mainly nonmedical methods, such as withdrawal, thereby implying a lack of readiness on their part to engage in sex.

The relevance of formal sex education

Formal sex education, that is, education dealing with the general area of sexuality in a structured context of classes, seminars, workshops, clinics, and the like, is generally supported by the public. Disagreement exists over such issues as appropriate content, who should teach it, the inclusion or exclusion of moral values, and so forth.

The need for formal sources of education stems from many sources, including the difficulty many parents and children face in communicating openly and freely about sexuality and birth control. Even when parents

---

14. Farida Shah and Melvin Zelnik, "Parent and Peer Influence on Sexual Behavior, Contraceptive Use, and Pregnancy Experience of Young Women," *Journal of Marriage and the Family* 43 (May 1981): 339–348. For an extensive overview of literature on this and related topics see W. M. Strahle, "A Model of Premarital Coitus and Contraceptive Behavior Among Female Adolescents," *Archives of Sexual Behavior* 12 (1983): 67–94.

have accurate knowledge and make conscientious efforts to encourage sexual discussion and effective contraceptive behavior, emotional factors in the relationship may make such discussions difficult. Sexually active teenagers, who are likely to perceive their parents as wanting them to be sexually inactive, are not likely to discuss their oral-genital or intercourse experiences with them. Neither are they likely to seek out contraceptive information or devices from them. And numerous efforts to require clinics

Ethical values in sex education in Sweden

All children in Sweden receive sex education. It is compulsory, and as a result Swedish children between the ages of five and fifteen are likely to have a better understanding and knowledge of sexual matters than children anywhere in the world. Sex education, or as it is termed today, "education about living together," is an indispensable component of the school curriculum at all grade levels. Contraception information is given to six- and seven-year-olds. Ideas about sexually transmitted diseases, nocturnal emissions, and homosexuality are taught to ten- and twelve-year-olds. By the junior-high-school level, masturbation, intercourse, abortion, sexual deviations, impotence, love, companionship, and so forth are common and acceptable topics for the classroom. What about values and ethics? Are these topics taught in a vacuum of appropriateness, morality, and responsibility?

The Swedish National Board of Education has issued a teachers' manual that stresses the broad ethical dimensions and foundations of human, and particularly, sexual relationships. As summarized from Carl Gustof Boethius (*Family Planning Perspectives*, November/December 1985, p. 277) these include, among others:

No human being is to be regarded and treated as a means of selfish gratification.
The use of psychological pressure and physical force in any context is a violation of the personal freedom of others.
Sexuality involves more than casual sex (not implying moral disapproval of sexual relationships but stressing the more sustained interpersonal relationships).
Schools should support the conviction that sexual fidelity in a permanent relationship is a duty (a conviction held by nearly all young people).
Frankness about sexual life in words and deeds is a goal but pornography that degrades humans is distinguished from nonpornographic illustrations and texts.
Men and women must be subject to identical standards of sexual morality (the old double standard is viewed as having an undesirable effect on sexual relationships).
Schools should not discourage sexual relationships among the mentally or physically handicapped, prisoners, or the aged.
Schools should try to promote an atmosphere of tolerance.

and agencies to inform parents of their adolescents' inquiries about contraception and abortion may have the unintended consequence of more unwanted pregnancies and sexually transmitted diseases rather than the intended consequence of improving parent-child communication.

The difficulty in communication between parents and children; the inadequate factual information from parents or peers; the widespread discomfort and embarrassment in the area of sexuality and contraception; the need for privacy about sex and birth control; the spread of sexually transmitted diseases; the growth in teenage, unwanted, and out-of-wedlock pregnancies; and so forth are reasons supporting formal sex education programs and clinics. Do these formal programs and clinics, as some infer, lead the sexually inactive to become active, increase knowledge, decrease unwanted pregnancies, or in short, make any difference at all?

The results of formal programs are mixed at best. Few lead to the negative consequences feared or the positive consequences hoped for. In general, it appears that sex knowledge gain through school classes and programs has little, if any, influence on premarital sexual behavior or on the subsequent probability that a teenager will begin to have intercourse. Data provide overwhelming support for the claim that the decision to engage in sexual activity is *not* influenced by whether or not teenagers had sex education in school.[15] In fact, a large proportion of teenagers initiate coitus before they have taken a sex education course.

Sex education does, however, influence knowledge and behavior regarding contraceptives. Sexually active teenagers who have had formal instruction report knowing how to use more methods of contraception and use them more effectively than do adolescents who have had no instruction.[16] Also, sexually active women who had sex education were less likely than those who did not to become pregnant. The availability of contraceptives, like the taking of a sex education course, does not appear, however, to have much influence on premarital sexual behavior.

Further evidence of no direct relationship between the initiation of sexual activity and the availability of contraceptives resulted from a study of adolescent women seeking contraceptives from a family-planning clinic.[17] Ninety-six percent of the adolescents had already had sexual intercourse

---

15. Melvin Zelnik and Young J. Kim, "Sex Education and Its Association with Teenage Sexual Activity, Pregnancy and Contraceptive Use," *Family Planning Perspective* 14 (May/June 1982): 117–126.

16. Deborah Anne Dawson, "The Effects of Sex Education on Adolescent Behavior," *Family Planning Perspectives* 18 (July/August 1986): 162–170; and William Marsiglio and Frank L. Mott, "The Impact of Sex Education on Sexual Activity, Contraceptive Use and Premarital Pregnancy Among American Teenagers," *Family Planning Perspectives* 18 (July/August 1986): 151–162.

17. Ruth Kornfield, "Who's to Blame: Adolescent Sexual Activity," *Journal of Adolescence* 8 (1986): 17–31.

before coming to the clinic for the first time. Over half the adolescent women who had been sexually active before coming to the clinic had never used any kind of contraceptive protection at all, and many of those who had used it in an irregular fashion. Most adolescents came to the clinic after they had made a conscious decision to continue to be sexually active and did not want to become pregnant.

While most research shows that formal education programs fail to achieve their intended purposes, exposure to informal education, peer-group interaction, mass media publications, and the like explains the considerable variation in behavior. Even greater variation is explained by factors such as dating frequency and religiosity. All these factors do not discount the idea that courses and programs have merit beyond the prevention of intercourse or unplanned pregnancies. Many courses provide young people with a greater understanding of human physiology, interpersonal relationships, and social values.

PREMARITAL HETEROSEXUAL INTERCOURSE

Premarital sexual intercourse indicates that at least one of the partners is single and has not been previously married. It is premarital in that the person has never been married, not in the sense that the relationship is confined to the person one will marry.

Cross-culturally, it appears that most societies permit or even encourage premarital relationships, particularly for the males. The taboo that falls primarily on females appears to be more a precaution against childbearing out of wedlock rather than a moral sanction. Using a global perspective, the crucial question, particularly for females, may not be whether premarital intercourse will be permitted, but whether unmarried motherhood will be allowed. It is likely that a commitment to norms of chastity lessens as a separation of premarital intercourse from pregnancy becomes possible. Thus, if contraceptives, sterilization, abortion, or other social arrangements exist to prevent or terminate a pregnancy, premarital sexual permissiveness will increase.

Has premarital permissiveness increased in the United States as it has become increasingly possible to separate intercourse from pregnancy? Using the mid-1960s as a point in time for comparison, let's note the changes that have occurred in the frequency of intercourse prior to marriage.

The frequency of premarital intercourse prior to the mid-1960s

The difference between the *ideal* norm and the *real* norm is significant: the ideal norm portrays what ought to be; the real norm portrays what

Premarital sex as a societal characteristic, not an individual one

Leonard Beeghley and Christine Sellers assert that the rate of premarital sex is a characteristic of a society, not an individual. Their argument suggests that rates of behavior reflect how social organization influences people's range of options. Their article shows that the rising rate of premarital sex during this century can be accounted for by changes in the American social structure which was much different in 1900 than it is today.

In 1900:

1. The time between puberty and marriage was less.
2. There was little public reference to sexuality.
3. Youths were closely supervised by parents and community.
4. Likely results of sex were venereal disease and pregnancy.
5. Traditional roles meant that to secure a suitable mate, women had to withhold sex.
6. Social norms preached sexual abstinence.

These characteristics of society, without exception, existed independently of individuals and directed their behavior in one way rather than another, with the result that the rate of premarital sex was low.

Today, social organization has changed.

1. The gap between puberty and marriage allows more time for premarital sex.
2. Sexual pervasiveness conveys the idea that premarital sex is okay.
3. Social autonomy provides the opportunity for premarital sex.
4. Medical care and contraception reduce the risks of venereal disease and pregnancy.
5. Egalitarian sex role norms encourage more complete relationships rather than exploitive ones.
6. The norm of sexual abstinence has declined, meaning increased social acceptance.

These factors exist independently of individuals and direct their behavior in a different way. The result is a high rate of premarital sex. Individual morality has not declined but society has changed and these changes have led to changes in the rate of premarital sex.

Source: Leonard Beeghley and Christine Sellers, "Adolescents and Sex: A Structural Theory of Premarital Sex in the United States," *Deviant Behavior* 7 (1986): 313–336.

is. More than thirty years ago, one finding of the Kinsey report that was shocking to the U.S. population was that about 50 percent of all the married women studied had had premarital coitus.[18] Few findings so

18. Kinsey et al., "Sexual Behavior in the Human Female," p. 292.

sharply illustrate the disparity between the ideal norm or value of premarital virginity and the real norm of actual behavior. It should be noted that a considerable proportion of the premarital coitus had occurred in the year or two immediately preceding marriage, with a portion of it confined to the period just before marriage.

A second significant difference exists between *incidence* and *prevalence.* Incidence is the occurrence or nonoccurrence of an experience. Generally, one has or has not had intercourse, is or is not a virgin, has or has not experienced orgasm. Prevalence is a different matter. Premarital intercourse may have occurred once or a thousand times. It may occur infrequently or on a regular basis. Thus, the incidence rate (number who have or have not) differs considerably from the prevalence rate (frequency).

In summarizing the incidence of premarital intercourse as indicated from approximately twenty different studies completed prior to 1955, Winston Ehrmann noted that the incidence for males ranged from 32 to 73 percent and for females from 7 to 47 percent.[19] At the time of his writing, there had been considerable unanimity of opinion that the percentage of college women engaging in premarital coitus ranged from 15 to 25 percent. Virtually all analyses up to that time, and up to ten years later, appeared to be in accord with Robert Bell's (1966) conclusion:

> On the basis of the available evidence, it appears that the greatest changes in premarital coitus for the American female occurred in the period around World War I and during the 1920s. There is no evidence that the rates since that period have undergone any significant change. Probably the most important change in female premarital sexual behavior in more recent decades has been an increase in premarital petting.[20]

Changes in frequency of premarital intercourse in the 1960s

Since the mid-1960s, many social forces have appeared on the U.S. scene that have led to behavioral changes regarding premarital coitus and have the potential for producing further changes. A high proportion of college students had been deeply involved in the civil rights movement and later in the protest over the Vietnam War. On most university campuses, the birth control pill became available and acceptable for personal use to a large number of unmarried college women. In addition, around the mid-1960s sexual candor became increasingly legitimized in the mass media, even by one of the most conservative of the media—television. The result of these social forces developing in the latter half of the 1960s has led

---

19. Winston Ehrmann, *Premarital Dating Behavior* (New York: Bantam Books, 1959): 41–42.
20. Robert R. Bell, *Premarital Sex in a Changing Society* (Englewood Cliffs, N.J.: Prentice-Hall, 1966): 57.

to an increase in the rejection of many traditional values and to the development of increasingly important patterns of behavior common to a general youth culture. In 1970, three separate articles appeared in the *Journal of Marriage and the Family* suggesting an increased rate of premarital coitus among college women along with less feelings of guilt about these experiences.

The first, a 1970 article by Robert Bell and J. B. Chaskes, reported on a 1968 replication of a 1958 study of premarital sexual behavior and attitudes.[21] The two groups of female students were alike in social-class background (as measured by the education and occupations of their father), in age, in class standing, in religious background, and in the mean age of their first date. There were some significant changes from 1958 to 1968 in regard to premarital intercourse. The number of women having premarital coitus when in a dating relationship went from 10 percent in 1958 to 23 percent in 1968, and the coitus rates while going steady went from 15 percent in 1958 to 28 percent in 1968. While there was some increase in the rates of premarital coitus during engagement, the change was not as striking as for the dating and going-steady stages. The data suggest that the decision to have intercourse in 1968 was much less dependent upon the commitment of engagement and more a question of individual decision regardless of the level of the relationship.

The second report on change in the sexual behavior of college students came from Gilbert Kaats and Keith Davis. They stated:

> In marked contrast to pre-1962 data on sexual behavior of college women were our findings in the spring of 1967 at the University of Colorado of a reported premarital coital rate of 41 percent—a figure about twice as high as that which has traditionally been reported at other universities. . . . Conversely, the figure for males, 60 percent, was nearly identical with that which has been reported since the turn of the century. If the findings could be replicated they may suggest that this university is much more "liberal" in this area than most or that we are experiencing a marked shift in the behavior of college women.[22]

The authors noted a converging of sexual behavior (sexual egalitarianism) between males and females. Yet, despite this convergence, considerable evidence is found among men and women alike for the existence of a strong double standard. Both male and female respondents considered virginity for the female more important than for the male. Sisters, more than brothers, would be encouraged by their siblings not to engage in premarital intercourse.

21. Robert R. Bell and J.B. Chaskes, "Premarital Sexual Experience Among Co-eds, 1958 and 1968," *Journal of Marriage and the Family* 32 (February 1970): 81–84.

22. Gilbert R. Kaats and Keith E. Davis, "The Dynamics of Sexual Behavior of College Students," *Journal of Marriage and the Family* 32 (August 1970): 390.

Women who rated high on physical attractiveness were found to have higher premarital coital rates. In spite of not differing from the less attractive women in most of the attitudinal measures or on background items (such as age, semester in college, family background, birth order, strength of religion, dating status, sorority membership, reasons for abstaining from or indulging in premarital coitus, and frequency in experiencing sexual urges), women rated high on physical attractiveness were more likely to hold a favorable self-picture, rated themselves as physically attractive, had more friends of the opposite sex, believed that more of their friends had had intercourse, dated more frequently, had been in love more often, had had more petting experiences, and had a higher rate of experience with intercourse.[23]

The third study, appearing in 1970, was written by Harold Christensen, who had devoted several decades to studying sexual behavior cross-culturally.[24] His study involved behavior as well as attitudes, studied males as well as females, compared three separate cultures, and measured identical phenomena in the same manner in the same populations at two different points in time.

In 1958, Christensen administered questionnaires to college samples in three cultures differing on a restrictive-permissive continuum: the highly restrictive Mormon culture in the western intermountain region of the United States; a moderately restrictive midwestern culture in the central United States; and the highly permissive Danish culture. The study was repeated in 1968 using the same questionnaire and was administered in the same three universities. Attitudes concerning premarital coitus were found to have liberalized considerably during the decade for both sexes (especially for females) in both the Danish and the two U.S. cultures studied. Females still had more restrictive attitudes than males, but the difference was less than had been the case earlier.

What these studies and others appear to agree upon is that significant changes took place in the 1960s in the sexual behavior of the never-married. These changes were most pronounced for females and moved in the direction of increased permissiveness. One report explained this greater change among females by differentiating between *developing* and *established,* or existing, sexual scripts.[25] The conditions found prior to the mid-sixties and proposed as causes of change in sexual behavior (freedom of youth from parental control, the development of a strong youth culture, the availability of the birth control pill) could not be expected

23. Ibid., p. 398.

24. Harold T. Christensen and Christina F. Gregg, "Changing Sex Norms in America and Scandinavia," *Journal of Marriage and the Family* 32 (November 1970): 616–627.

25. David Reed and Martin S. Weinberg, "Premarital Coitus: Developing and Established Sexual Scripts," *Social Psychology Quarterly* 47 (1984): 129–138.

to have automatically provided new sexual scripts. Men had an *established* traditional script pattern for premarital coitus that permitted permissiveness. Women, in contrast, had had no sexual script for premarital coitus, and time was needed to develop one in response to the changed conditions. Thus, a *developing* script pattern for women led to greater changes in their behavior than that for men. While the male-female differences decreased, a distinct double standard remained. What about the 1970s and 1980s?

Frequency of premarital intercourse in the 1970s and 1980s

Have the major changes reported for the 1960s come to a halt? Apparently not in the 1970s, although we might predict a leveling off of permissiveness in the late 1980s given the general trend toward increased social conservatism and the heightened concern about AIDS.

Reports of adolescent and premarital-nonmarital sexual behaviors in the 1970s indicate a continuation of the increased levels of permissiveness witnessed in the 1960s. An analysis of premarital sexual behavior and attitudes over an extensive period of time—1965, 1970, 1975, and 1980— reveals some interesting changes.[26] One is a continued but asymptotic increase in reported premarital sexual behavior among both men and women. What this indicates is that the increase in rate of premarital coitus continued between 1975 and 1980 but at a lower rate of increase than occurred earlier. This might lend early support to my prediction of a leveling off of permissiveness in the late 1980s. The reported change in the percentage of college males engaging in premarital sexual activity increased by 12 percent between 1965 and 1980. In 1965 and 1970, 65 percent of the males reported having had premarital intercourse, increasing to 74 percent in 1975 and to 77 percent in 1980. For females the increase was 35 percent between 1965 and 1980 with 29 percent reporting premarital intercourse in 1965, increasing to 37 percent in 1970, 57 percent in 1975 and 64 percent in 1980. Note that in addition to the increase for both sexes, the increase was far greater for females, resulting in a narrowing of the difference between men and women.

Apart from samples of college students, nearly all research reports indicate an increased permissiveness of premarital sexual behaviors in the 1970s. Melvin Zelnik and others showed by national probability samples of females aged 15 to 19 that in 1971, 28 percent were nonvirginal (23 percent of the white teenagers and 54 percent of the black teenagers).

---

26. Ira E. Robinson and Davor Jedlicka, "Change in Sexual Attitudes and Behavior of College Students from 1965 to 1980: A Research Note," *Journal of Marriage and the Family* 44 (February 1982): 237–240.

By 1976, just five years later, 55 percent had had sexual intercourse (incidence) and most of these, 85 percent, had had it more than once (prevalence).[27] The average age at which young women had their first sexual experience was 16.2 compared with 15.7 among the men. A majority of young women interviewed in 1979 first had intercourse in the context of a "commitment relationship" such as being engaged or going steady, but most young men indicated their first sexual partner was in a more casual relationship.[28] For both sexes the initiation of sex appears to have been a spur-of-the-moment decision. Only 17 percent of the men and 25 percent of the women planned their first act of intercourse. While most adolescents did not want to get pregnant or get their partners pregnant, a large proportion of them did not use a contraceptive method.

A recent national study found that 47 percent of women aged 15 to 44 (or their partners) used any contraceptive at first intercourse. The leading method at first intercourse was the condom, followed by the pill and withdrawal. Use of a contraceptive at first intercourse increased sharply in the 1980s because of an increase in the use of the condom. The proportion who used a method at first intercourse varied from 22 percent among Hispanic women to 74 percent among Jewish women: it was higher among white than black women, higher in higher socioeconomic categories. A higher age at first intercourse increased the likelihood that intercourse was planned, that sex and contraception were discussed with the partner, and that the degree of commitment to the relationship was higher.[29]

A review of thirty-five studies conducted over the past eighty years notes two major trends that are apparent.[30] One is a major increase in the proportion of young people reporting coital involvement. The second is a more rapid increase in the proportion of females reporting coital involvement than males, although the initial base for males was greater. Today the proportion of men and women reporting coital involvement is nearly equal. These changes support a major shift in the standards governing sexual behavior that are cited at the beginning of this chapter from the double standard toward the single standard of permissiveness with affection. This shift includes a current standard of intercourse being appropriate in love relationships (without the requirement of progression toward marriage) and permissible in casual relationships without exploitation.

---

27. Melvin Zelnik, Young J. Kim, and John F. Kantner, "Probabilities of Intercourse and Conception Among U.S. Teenage Women, 1971 and 1976," *Family Planning Perspectives* 11 (May/June 1979): 177–183.

28. Melvin Zelnik and Farida K. Shah, "First Intercourse Among Young Americans," *Family Planning Perspectives* 15 (March/April 1983): 64–70.

29. William D. Mosher and Christine A. Bachrach, "First Premarital Contraceptive Use: United States, 1960–1982," *Studies in Family Planning* 18 (March/April 1987): 83–95.

30. Carol A. Darling, David J. Kallan, and Joyce E. VanDusen, "Sex in Transition, 1900–1980," *Journal of Youth and Adolescence* 13 (1984): 385–399.

He needs sex for intimacy; she needs intimacy for sex

This is about a marriage that is falling apart. Only the names and some of the identifying details are changed.

He complains to her, "If we just had better sex, everything would be all right again."

She complains to him, "If everything were just all right again, we would have better sex."

Then they glower at each other. A separation is in the works. That ought to take care of the sex part, and the all right part, too.

Maybe these people don't read magazines or books. Lots of shrinks and quasi-shrinks have written about this kind of standoff.

An old problem

Part of what's been written is that many, if not most, women need to feel intimate with a man before they are comfortable having sex with him. A woman likes to feel she is privileged to share a man's dreams and secrets, because he thinks she's special. She likes to feel chosen, appreciated, cherished, loved . . . add whatever warm and wiggly qualities you like to the string.

Only after she has achieved this intimacy is she eager to engage in sex. Sex is an affirmation and culmination of the closeness the two of them share.

Lots of men, however, do it the other way around. Sex is the path to intimacy. A man is not ready to share his private world or thoughts with a woman until after they have had sex. Before that, he feels alienated and separated, somehow in jeopardy and at risk. The sex act is the green light that tells him he's safe with this particular woman. She won't hurt or damage him. It's OK to get close and closer. She gives him her body. She cares about him.

The honeymoon never lasts

Evidently, marriage doesn't change these basics. The people I know who are splitting have been married nearly 20 years. He's still saying more and better sex would mend the marriage. She's still saying the marriage needs mending before better sex is possible. They're both sick of mouthing these lines, and

Norval Glenn and Charles Weaver, drawing on data from seven national samples, suggest that the so-called "sex revolution" in the United States has been real but has been restricted to premarital heterosexual relations. Attitudes toward extramarital and homosexual relations remain distinctly restrictive.[31]

---

31. Norval D. Glenn and Charles N. Weaver, "Attitudes Toward Premarital, Extramarital, and Homosexual Relations in the U.S. in the 1970s," *The Journal of Sex Research* 15 (May 1979): 108–118.

they've pretty much quit. He's looking for an apartment. She's looking for a lawyer.

I don't know who's right. Maybe nobody's right. Probably they're both right, sort of.

I think it's funny how we court each other, bending and yielding, understanding and responding to each other's needs and whims when we are unmarried or newly married. Then, when it could be much easier to do all those things, because we know each other better and have more time to study each other, we give up on it.

We abandon what was formerly successful behavior and expect that will have no effect on our partner or the union. It always does. A marriage is a living organism, highly sensitive to even slight changes in its environment. When a significant change persists, the organism is sometimes permanently damaged.

That special touch

The woman in the vignette above says she has no interest anymore in attempting a reconciliation. It's been too cold around the house for too long, she says. She has no feeling that her husband thinks she's special. He doesn't share. He doesn't hug. He doesn't tell her she's wonderful. She says it will be better to feel alone and be alone than to feel alone and unloved by a husband demanding his sexual privilege. Maybe.

I don't know what he feels. Frustrated. Confused, probably. Cheated, emasculated, that he's married to a crazy lady who doesn't understand his need to feel secure before he can feel intimate.

Maybe it's all the same thing. If sharing sex is security for a man, confirming to him that a woman thinks he's special, certainly being stroked and sweet-talked represents the same security for a woman. One is an act, one is a voice. Both say the same thing: I love you; you are special.

Why is that so difficult a lesson for us to learn? Vive la difference, of course, but la difference is not so much as we make it.

Source: Nickie McWhirter, *Detroit Free Press,* January 20, 1982, p. 1-D. Reprinted with the permission of the Detroit Free Press.

One factor seems clear: major changes have occurred in sexual attitudes and behaviors over the past two decades. This may be related to a general social and political liberalization, a decline in religious belief, an increase in the number of working women, the greater availability of contraceptives, or a variety of other factors. Factors such as the conservative religious and political orientation of the 1980s and the rise in herpes,

AIDS, and other sexually transmittable diseases may well lead to more restrictive sexual attitudes and behaviors in the future.

SUMMARY

1. Premarital sexual relationships are generally thought to include a wide variety of sexual activities performed by those who have never been married. "Nonmarital" may be a more encompassing concept, referring to any type of sexual activity occurring outside of marriage, but the intent of this chapter was not directed to nonmarital sexual activities involving married or previously married persons. Irrespective of marital status or gender, all sexual activities have controls or restrictions placed upon them. These activities include coitus but in a more general sense encompass a wide variety of touching, kissing, and caressing activities as well.

2. Three major types of heterosexual standards are possible in regard to coitus. One states that premarital intercourse is wrong for both sexes (a single standard of abstinence), a second states that premarital intercourse is right for both sexes (a single standard of permissiveness with or without affection), and the third states that premarital intercourse is right for one sex but wrong for the other (a double standard). The United States has sexual standards that fit each logical possibility, but most are variants of basic types.

3. Sexualization was described as the process by which people acquire their sexual self-concepts, values, attitudes, and behaviors. Attention was given to learning processes in social interaction and the need to consider meanings and definitions of the situation to more fully understand behavior. These meanings and definitions make up our sexual scripts, designating the who, what, when, where, and why of sexuality.

4. Sexual attitudes and behaviors are highly interrelated. When they differed, it was argued that attitudes and beliefs will be more conservative or restrictive than will actual behavior. During adolescence, more permissive behaviors in dating, love, and interpersonal relationships will tend to modify the belief-attitudinal script.

5. Selected antecedents to sexual behavior include parental influence; however, neither parental attitudes nor parent-child communication appear to affect teenagers' subsequent sexual and contraceptive behavior. Parental discipline appears to have a curvilinear effect with both the most restrictive and permissive disciplinary patterns resulting in greater permissiveness.

6. Formal sex education programs seldom result in the type of positive

consequences desired or negative consequences feared. The decision to engage in sexual activity is not influenced by sex education classes but appears to have some effect on contraceptive knowledge and effective use.

7. Premarital heterosexual intercourse has attracted widespread attention, particularly for females. The greater interest in females focuses not merely on premarital sexual norms but on norms linked to unmarried parenthood, an issue traditionally of less concern for males.

8. Studies completed prior to the mid-1960s indicate that rates of premarital coitus had not undergone any significant change since the 1920s, except for an increase in premarital petting among females. The 1960s witnessed major changes in the sexual behavior of the never-married. These changes were most pronounced for females and moved in the direction of increased permissiveness, lessening the male-female difference but not eliminating a double standard.

9. The 1970s appeared to be a decade that continued the trends of the 1960s. Studies on college campuses as well as nationwide surveys showed a continual increase in premarital sexual permissiveness. While there was a narrowing of group differences, clear racial and male-female distinctions remained.

10. The chapter that follows continues an examination of human sexuality, with attention focused on the marital relationship, married persons, or previously married ones. Most of the social and cultural factors of significance prior to marriage continue to influence sexuality within a marital context.

KEY TERMS AND TOPICS

DISCUSSION QUESTIONS

1. It was mentioned that all societies control sexual activities. How is this done? Why?

2. What are the pros and cons of the maintenance of a premarital sexual standard of: (1) abstinence? (2) permissiveness with affection? (3) permissiveness without affection? (4) a double standard?

3. Compare the sexual norms portrayed by the Catholic church, selected Protestant groups, soap operas on TV, *Playboy* magazine, the law, nudists, or topless bar girls. Wihtin the same society, how can such differences be explained?

4. In your opinion, which is more important to understanding sexual behavior: (1) biological needs, drives, hormones, and the like, or (2) norms, values, attitudes, and so on? Explain.

5. Are males and females inherently different in sexual socialization? If so, in what ways does society contribute to the difference?

6. Give some thought to your own sexual scripts. What factors do you define as most influential in your current attitudes relating to inappropriate or acceptable sexual behaviors in regard to physical intimacy—with whom, where, why, under what conditions, and so forth?

7. Examine the relationship between what you believe and what you do or have done. For you, how accurate is the idea that behaviors often exceed the acceptable belief-value script which in turn modifies the belief or value?

8. How would you explain the finding that parental attitudes and parent-child communication seem to have little effect on adolescent sexual behavior and contraceptive usage?

9. Discuss the impact, if any, of sex education on sexual attitudes, sexual behavior, or contraceptive usage. Contrast the impact of formal sex education classes relative to the impact of peers and informal sources.

10. Contrast the degree of sexual permissiveness prior to the 1960s to that of the 1960s, 1970s and 1980s. How do you account for the changes that have occurred?

FURTHER READINGS

Byrne, Donn, and Fisher, William A., eds. *Adolescents, Sex, and Contraception.* Hillsdale, N.J.: Lawrence Erlbaum Assoc., 1983. A book of readings on the noncontraceptive sexual behavior of adolescents, the reasons for that behavior, and possible solutions to the problem.

Chilman, Catherine S. *Adolescent Sexuality in a Changing American Society.* New York: John Wiley and Sons, 1983. A combination of research-based knowledge and theory from the social sciences, oriented to human service professionals who work with adolescents.

Clayton, Richard R., and Bokemeier, Janet L. "Premarital Sex in the Seventies." *Journal of Marriage and the Family* 42 (November 1980): 759–775. One of the decade review articles covering the epidemiology (prevalence and incidence) and the etiology (correlates and causes) of premarital sexual attitudes and behavior.

Feldman, Harold, and Parrot, Andrea, eds. *Human Sexuality: Contemporary Issues.* Beverly Hills, Cal.: Sage Publications, 1984. Representatives of opposing moral, religious, legal, and political positions debate questions of contemporary human sexuality.

Francoeur, Robert T. *Becoming a Sexual Person.* New York: John Wiley and Sons, 1984. A brief edition of a more extensive text that covers sex in cultural, personal, impersonal, and social contexts.

Gagnon, John H. *Human Sexualities.* Glenview, Ill.: Scott, Foresman, 1977. An examination of the range of human sexualities including gender roles, sexual response, masturbation, homosexuality, offenses and offenders, therapies, and other topics.

Hayes, Cheryl D., ed. *Risking the Future: Adolescent Sexuality, Pregnancy and Childbearing.* Washington, D.C.: National Academy Press, 1987. An excellent report on adolescent sexuality and fertility including five chapters on trends, determinants, and consequences, and four chapters on preventive interventions and policies.

Kinsey, Alfred C.; Pomeroy, Wardell; and Martin, Clyde. *Sexual Behavior in the Human Male.* Philadelphia: W. B. Saunders, 1948. With the following book, these are the classic Kinsey studies presenting an intensive analysis of male and female sexual behaviors ranging from sexual activities to male-female comparisons of the anatomy, physiology, psychology, and neural mechanisms of sexual response.

Kinsey, Alfred C.; Pomeroy, Wardell; Martin, Clyde; and Gebhard, Paul. *Sexual Behavior in the Human Female.* Philadelphia: W. B. Saunders, 1953. With the preceding book, these are the classic Kinsey studies presenting an intensive analysis of male and female sexual behaviors ranging from sexual activities to male-female comparisons of the anatomy, physiology, psychology, and neural mechanisms of sexual response.

Reiss, Ira L. *Journey into Sexuality: An Exploratory Voyage.* Englewood Cliffs, N.J.: Prentice-Hall, 1986. An attempt to develop an overall explanation of human sexuality that will apply cross-culturally and explain how society organizes and shapes our sexual lives.

Reiss, Ira L. *The Social Context of Premarital Sexual Permissiveness.* New York: Holt Rinehart and Winston, 1967. A systematic sociological study of premarital sexual attitudes with an integration of six basic propositions into one theory of sexual behavior.

Whitehurst, R. N., and Booth, G. V. *The Sexes: Changing Relationships in a Pluralistic Society.* Toronto: Gage Publishing, 1980. A readable, at times provocative, book covering sexuality historically, theoretically, and cross-culturally with particular attention devoted to sexual identities and variations, contemporary and over time.

Photo: © Barbara Alper/Stock, Boston

11

Sexual Relationships
in Marital Contexts

Were it not for the legal and social norms pertaining to sex, there would be very little reason for differentiating marital sex from premarital, non-marital, extramarital, postmarital, or any other type of sexual relationship. This is why, although both married and unmarried men and women were included in the research population of the Masters-Johnson studies, no controls were made for marital status. Early in their investigation, a non-married group provided the opportunity for comparison-controlled studies with established marital groups. However, in their words:

> The unrehearsed physiologic and anatomic response patterns of the unmarried were recorded and contrasted to the mutually conditioned and frequently stylized sexual response patterns of the marital units. This technique for experimental control was abandoned as soon as it was established une-quivocally that there is no basic difference in the anatomy and physiology of human sexual response regardless of the marital status of responding units.[1]

The legal and social norms regarding sex in American society make coitus between husband and wife the one totally approved type of het-erosexual activity. Cross-culturally as well, marital coitus is recognized as the most important of all sexual outlets because of the significant role it plays in the maintenance of the family system.

SEX AND MARRIAGE

Few would deny the importance of sexual intercourse to marriage. It is the one factor that, normatively at least, differentiates the marital relationship from any other social relationship. The relative importance of the sexual aspects of a marriage as compared with nonsexual aspects of a marriage will differ by sex, social class, and other factors. Let's examine, first, some selected results of the Kinsey studies; then we'll turn our attention to recent changes in marital sexual activity and sexual adjustment; finally

---

1. William A. Masters and Virginia E. Johnson, *Human Sexual Response* (Boston: Little, Brown, 1966): 16–17.

we'll turn to other factors that relate to married persons but involve a nonspouse: extramarital coitus, incest, and postmarital coitus.

Selected results of the Kinsey studies

Sexuality was brought into the public arena with the publication of the **Kinsey studies** in 1948 and 1953. This landmark research revealed two major surprises: (1) that what people actually did was far more permissive than the publicly proclaimed legitimate sexual codes, norms, and values, and (2) that most people, married and single, were extremely misinformed or uninformed about sexuality. This research set the stage to make sexuality a legitimate area of research and provided a wealth of information making sexuality a legitimate subject for discussion as well.

While this research may today be viewed as "old," you will quickly note that while the frequencies and statistics may be different, many of Kinsey's findings and interpretations hold true over time. Let's note several examples. Question whether the following findings would be equally valid today.

The frequency of marital coitus, according to Kinsey, decreased with age, dropping from an average of 3.7 times per week during the teens to about 2.7 at the age of thirty, 1.4 at the age of forty, and 0.8 at the age of sixty.[2] Male and female estimates were highly comparable although females tended to estimate the frequencies of their marital coitus higher than males estimated them. Females who desired less coitus than they had were likely to overestimate, whereas males who wished for more than they obtained were likely to underestimate. The incidence and frequency of marital coitus reached their maximum in the first year or two after marriage. From that point, they had steadily dropped into minimum frequencies in the oldest age groups. There was no other activity among females to show such a steady decline with advancing age.[3]

Kinsey stated that one tragic finding for a number of marriages was that many of the husbands reported that early in their marriages they had wanted coitus more often than their wives, and the younger married females reported that they would be satisfied with lower coital rates than their husbands wanted. On the other hand, in the later years of marriage, many of the females expressed the wish that they could have coitus more frequently than their husbands were then desiring it. Over the years, most

---

2. Alfred C. Kinsey, Wardell B. Pomeroy, Clyde E. Martin, and Paul H. Gebhard, *Sexual Behavior in the Human Female* (Philadelphia: W. B. Saunders, 1953): 77.

3. Ibid., p. 348.

Contrasts in legislating sex

Two news items present an interesting picture of contrasts in legislating sex.

The West German Bundesrat (upper house) passed legislation permitting homosexuality and the swapping of marital partners among consenting adults. Taking effect in 1975, the law also permits the sale of pornography to anyone eighteen years of age and over. The West German Minister of Justice explained the legislation was an attempt to progress from the attitudes of the nineteenth century.

Dade County voters in Florida in 1977 repealed a gay rights ordinance that barred discrimination against homosexuals in jobs, housing, and public accommodations. Anita Bryant, who actively campaigned for repeal with the support of her church-based Save Our Children organization, said that if homosexuality were the normal way, God would have made Adam and Bruce.

females became less inhibited and developed an interest in sexual relations that they might then maintain until they were in their fifties or even sixties.[4]

There were surprisingly few differences between the frequencies of marital coitus among females of the several educational levels represented in Kinsey's sample. But the men provided an interesting contrast. In the lower educational groups, about 80 percent of the total outlet in the early years of marriage was provided by marital coitus, and the incidence for this group increased to 90 percent as the marriage continued. For the college-educated men, marital coitus provided 85 percent of the total outlet during the early part of marriage, but by the time he reached the age of 55, only 62 percent of his total sexual outlet was provided by marital coitus. At no time in their lives did college-bred males depend on marital intercourse to the extent that lower-level males did throughout most of their marriages.[5]

Kinsey suggested that only upper-level males become increasingly interested in extramarital relations as they grow older.[6] Why is this so? It may be that increased frequency of extramarital intercourse is due to: (1) a conclusion that the early restraints on their sexual lives were not justified, (2) a conclusion that extramarital experience should be secured before old age has interfered with the capacity to do so, (3) an increasing dissatisfaction with the relations with restrained upper-level wives, or (4)

---

4. Ibid., p. 353.

5. Alfred C. Kinsey, Wardell B. Pomeroy, and Clyde E. Martin, *Sexual Behavior in the Human Male* (Philadelphia: W. B. Saunders, 1948): 567.

6. Ibid., p. 568.

Secrets of a trim, attractive body

Do you want to achieve or maintain a good-looking, sleek body? In a report in *Sexology*, a New York doctor, Abraham I. Friedman, stated that "sex is the ideal substitute for the gratification of emotional overeating."

Dr. Friedman, who has worked exclusively on weight control problems, said that increased sexual activity can help overweight people lose as much as four to five pounds a month in addition to the loss from regular dieting. He said the cause of many of his patients' overeating was emotional and that most of them had sexual difficulties. "They were substituting food for sex and love."

Dr. Friedman reported that the center of sexual response is in the same area of the brain that contains the center of appetite control. So, aside from the calories burned up (about 200) in the physical activity of lovemaking, "it is very likely that the increased activity of one center—sex—may have a dampening effect on the other—appetite."

Psychologically, there is a close link between our basic needs for food and sex. "When people are deprived of love and sex," said Dr. Friedman, "they often turn to food and overeat." Conversely, pounds and inches can be lost by sensibly substituting one basic need for another. The doctor said that for every three times you substitute sex for a 700-calorie snack, you'll lose more than one pound."

Moral: Next time you feel the urge to reach for a peanut-butter-and-banana sandwich, now you know what you really should be reaching for.

a preoccupation of the educated male with the professional or business affairs of his life leading to a decrease in marital intercourse—and perhaps to increased nonmarital opportunities.

The precoital techniques used in marriage were quite the same as those found in premarital petting that may or may not have led to coitus. In Kinsey's sample:

> Simple lip kissing between the spouses had almost always (99.4 percent) been an accompaniment to the marital coitus. In order of descending incidences, the other techniques which were used at least on occasion had included the manual stimulation of the female breast by the male (in 98 percent); the manual stimulation of the female genitalia by the male (in 95 percent); the oral stimulation of the female breast (in 93 percent); the manual stimulation of the male genitalia by the female (in 91 percent); extended oral techniques in deep kissing (in 87 percent); and finally the oral stimulation of the female genitalia by the male (in 54 percent) and of the male genitalia by the female (in 49 percent).[7]

7. Kinsey, *Sexual Behavior in the Human Female*, p. 361.

How do Kinsey's data compare with more recent research? Note selected similarities and differences in marital sexual activity reported by Kinsey at the middle of the century with reported activity today.

Changes in marital sexual activity and related factors

Some of the changes in frequency of sexual activity mentioned in the last chapter on premarital sexual behavior appear to be paralleled in marriage. Charles Westoff, reporting on data from national probability samples of married women of reproductive age in 1965 and 1970, showed an increase in this five-year time period in the overall coital frequency.[8] The increase was slightly higher among women in their twenties than among older women, but the increase appeared among women at all ages studied. This rise in reported coital frequency was found to exist almost regardless of method of birth control used and even where no method was used. Thus, it is not accurate to attribute the increase in coital frequency entirely to the increase in the proportion of women using the pill. On the other hand, Westoff noted that it seems reasonable to infer that the greater use of more reliable methods decreased anxiety about unintentional pregnancy and, therefore, relaxed some of the constraints on sexual expression (or perhaps on the willingness to talk about it).

Since there remains an increase in coital frequency over and above that accounted for by types of exposure to risk, how can this increase be explained? In addition to the influence of modern contraceptive technology, the availability of legal abortion could be said to further reduce anxiety about unwanted pregnancy. Other factors likely include the increase in openness about sex since the mid-1960s, the exploitation of sexual themes by the mass media, the developing emphasis on women's right to personal fulfillment, a shift from the traditional passive sexual role to more assertive behavior among women, and the viewing of sex itself as a more natural, less taboo topic.

Figure 11–1 supports what Kinsey and other studies suggest about the relationship between coital frequency and age, the length of time together, or years married. In each category the frequency of coitus decreases.

Philip Blumstein and Pepper Schwartz, in an intensive examination of couples in the United States (married, cohabitors, gay men, and lesbians), found that for all couples, the frequency of sex declined with the length of time together.[9] Their data for married couples can be seen in Figure

---

8. Charles F. Westoff, "Coital Frequency and Contraception," *Family Planning Perspectives* 6 (Summer 1974): 136–141.

9. Philip Blumstein and Pepper Schwartz, *American Couples* (New York: Pocket Books, 1983): 195–201.

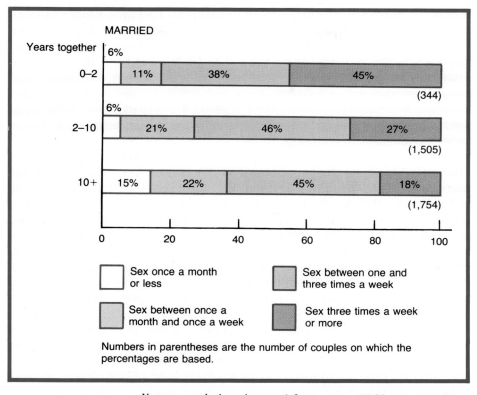

FIGURE 11–1

Years married and sexual frequency. (Philip Blumstein and Pepper Schwartz, *American Couples.* [New York: Pocket Books, 1983], p. 196.)

11–1. For those married up to two years, 45 percent reported sex three times a week or more. This drops to 27 percent for those married two to ten years and to 18 percent for those married ten or more years. The opposite situation is equally true. Whereas only 17 percent of those married two years or less had sex less than once a week, this increased to 27 percent for those married two to ten years, and to 37 percent for those married ten years or more. This last figure, assessed in reverse, would tell us that 63 percent of the married couples, even after ten years of marriage, have sex at least once a week. People who jest that marriage "ruins" sex by making it non-existent or even humdrum, find little support in these findings.

The first year of marriage is clearly the time of most frequent marital coitus. However, a striking finding of a study of persons married five years or less was the wide range of responses. Men reported monthly frequencies from 1 to 43, while the women's reports ranged from 2 to 45.[10] Male and

10. Cathy Stein Greenblat, "The Salience of Sexuality in the Early Years of Marriage," *Journal of Marriage and the Family* 45 (May 1983): 289–299.

female responses were fairly similar in that both had wide ranges, similar average frequencies (14.43 for men and 13.81 for women), and similar medians (12.0 for men and 12.5 for women). The best predictor of frequencies in the next few years proved to be frequency in the first year. After the first year, everything that happens to a couple—children, jobs, commuting, housework, financial worries, fatigue, familiarity—combines to reduce intercourse frequency while nothing leads to increasing it. Despite the lower frequencies, sex was considered by the respondents as important or very important in marriage.

The discussion of declining coital frequency with age should not be interpreted to mean that sex becomes unimportant in marriage after age twenty-five, forty, or sixty. But it may call for a redefining of aging sexual behavior and the development of values that maximize the sexual relationship of aging couples. This may include the elimination of a stereotype that only links sex with youth and the early years of marriage. This may include viewing sexual activity as being more than "performance" oriented, more than genitally or intercourse oriented, and more than orgasm oriented. Other forms include nongenital sexual pleasuring and oral and digital manipulations that may or may not result in actual physiological orgasm and/or ejaculation.[11]

Many factors other than contraceptive usage and age have been found to be highly related to marital sexual activity. For example, intercourse is less frequent during menstruation. This was true even among a highly educated sample of married couples where one might anticipate less adherence to tradition.[12] Intercourse appears as well to be related to stress within the marriage. John Edwards and Alan Booth indicate that the more severe the marital strain, the lower the frequency of marital coitus.[13] They suggest that the sexual behavior of both males and females is largely contextual, determined to a greater extent by present circumstances (like marital strain) than past background.

Westoff reported that coital frequency increases with the amount of education of the wife, is higher among women who work in paid employment than those who do not work (highest among career-motivated women), and is positively associated with the effectiveness of contraception.[14] The

---

11. Martha Cleveland, "Sex in Marriage: At 40 and Beyond," *The Family Coordinator* 25 (July 1976): 233–240; Ruth B. Weg, *Sexuality in the Later Years: Roles and Behavior* (New York: Academic Press, 1983); and Catherine G. Adams and Barbara F. Turner, "Reported Change in Sexuality From Young Adulthood to Old Age," *The Journal of Sex Research* 21 (May 1985): 126–141.

12. Naomi M. Morris and J. Richard Udry, "Menstruation and Marital Sex," *Journal of Biosocial Science* 15 (1983): 173–181.

13. John N. Edwards and Alan Booth, "Sexual Behavior In and Out of Marriage: An Assessment of Correlates," *Journal of Marriage and the Family* 38 (February 1976): 73–81.

14. Westoff, "Coital Frequency and Contraception," pp. 139–140.

Length of time together is definitely linked with a decline of interest in sexual activity. Familiarity might just breed boredom or indifference rather than contempt. (Photo: © Frank Siteman/Stock, Boston)

highest frequencies are reported by women who are using the pill or the IUD or whose husbands have had vasectomies. The lowest frequencies are associated with the use of the rhythm method and the douche.

It is of interest to note that national survey data of married women under age forty-five show that, except for sterilization, Catholic and non-Catholic contraceptive practices are quite similar.[15] As of 1975, between 75 and 80 percent of both groups were using contraception. Very small percentage differences exist in the use of the pill (34 percent for both non-Catholic and Catholic), IUD (9.0 vs. 7.6), diaphragm (4.1 vs. 3.5), condom (9.6 vs. 14.9), or foam (3.9 vs. 2.6). Sterilization was more common for both non-Catholic wives (17.5 percent vs. 12.9) and husbands (15.6 vs. 13.1).

While certain female-male or Catholic–non-Catholic differences appear to be decreasing, marital sexual activities still vary considerably in numerous

15. Charles F. Westoff and Elise F. Jones, "The Secularization of U.S. Catholic Birth Control Practices," *Family Planning Perspectives* 9 (September/October 1977): 203–206.

respects, such as by social class. Contrary to the notion that the lower classes are less sexually inhibited, the middle and upper classes are more likely to have intercourse in total nudity, use a variety of positions in intercourse, and engage in oral-genital contacts. While the stratification literature suggests that working-class people are increasingly adopting middle-class values and behaviors, Weinberg and Williams suggest that social class is still an important determinant of sexual behavior.[16] Compared to the lower and working class, middle-class men and women started their sexual activities at a later age, were more likely to enjoy their first sexual experiences, and were more likely to react positively to masturbation.

One key reason for these differences may be related to gender roles. Generally, the lower the class, the greater the division between traditional male and female roles. Where there exists a high degree of role segregation between husbands and wives, the couple will tend not to develop as close or as gratifying an interpersonal sexual relationship. Where husbands and wives are likely to segregate work, recreational, or domestic activities into male or female roles, so too are they likely to clearly differentiate sexual roles. The result? Different sexual expectations and behaviors by social class.

Autoeroticism in marriage

Masturbation, or autoeroticism, is widely recognized as a common sexual outlet. One would assume and expect that if masturbation is considered a substitute for intercourse, the frequency of masturbation would be low among the married who have daily access to a sexual partner. This hypothesis was not borne out by researchers. J. S. Greenberg and F. X. Archambault did not find significant differences between frequencies of masturbation and intercourse.[17] Hans Hessellund found that while there was a significant difference in intercourse frequency among married and unmarried subjects, there were no significant differences in frequency of masturbation between married and unmarried subjects.[18]

In or out of marriage, more men than women masturbate and do so more frequently. Hessellund tentatively concluded that for men masturbation functions more as a supplement to sexual life, while for women it is to a greater extent a substitute for intercourse.[19] Gagnon and Simon

---

16. Martin S. Weinberg and Colin J. Williams, "Sexual Embourgeoisment? Social Class and Sexual Activity: 1938–1970," *American Sociological Review* 45 (February 1980): 33–48.

17. J. S. Greenberg and F. X. Archambault, "Masturbation, Self-Esteem and Other Variables," *Journal of Sex Research* 9 (February 1973): 41–51.

18. Hans Hessellund, "Masturbation and Sexual Fantasies in Married Couples," *Archives of Sexual Behavior* 5 (1976): 133–147.

19. Ibid., p. 139.

A substitute for overeating and drinking

Dr. Sol Gordon, professor emeritus at Syracuse University and the author of many books on sexuality, suggests in *Psychology Today* (October 1986) that if you must have a compulsion, please choose masturbation rather than overeating or overdrinking. Nobody has ever died from overmasturbating.

While written somewhat in jest, he argues that the issue is more important than it appears. Masturbation is one of the biggest concerns of young people, and they need to know that masturbation is a normal expression of sexuality. While few take seriously the myths that masturbation causes acne, tired blood, mental illness, or blindness (Gordon questions if that's why he wears glasses), most parents don't give outright approval to their children to masturbate. Some people suggest it may be all right if done in private and if not done too much. But Gordon questions how much is too much? After every meal, twice a week, once a year?

Since teenagers and adults have strong sexual urges, Gordon questions why we create dumb solutions, such as taking cold showers. He questions the value of how we deal with anxieties—by eating when not hungry or drinking when not thirsty. Why not encourage people to masturbate, which is a much more effective solution to coping with high levels of anxiety, tension, or sexual needs. In his thirty years of clinical work, he has yet to hear about a rapist, child molester, or chronically sexually dysfunctional person who grew up feeling comfortable about masturbation. In response to researchers who suggest that masturbation itself provides a powerful stimulus for sexual abuse, Gordon says this is found to be true only if the molester despises masturbation, feels guilty about it, or both.

Source: Sol Gordon, "What Kids Need to Know," *Psychology Today* 20 (October 1986): 22–26.

attribute the continued masturbation of men after marriage—and not only when their wives are absent—to continuation of the acting out of sexual fantasies that first developed in early adolescence.[20]

For women, it could be predicted that as gender role training includes the development of sexual imagery, an increase in masturbatory activity, for both married and single women, would follow. Masturbation permits independent and autonomous control of pleasure, producing an orgasm that females particularly find to be more intense physiologically than occurs from intercourse. This may result from the fact that the masturbator does not have to regulate his or her own sexual pleasure to the sequence or routines of another person and thus inhibit the power of self-gratification.[21]

---

20. John H. Gagnon and William Simon, *Sexual Conduct* (Chicago: Aldine, 1973): 65.
21. Ibid., p. 65.

Rape in marriage

Until recently, marital rape has been ignored in the marital-family literature. It has been brought to light more recently as a feminist issue involving an act of physical violation against women. It is only in the past few decades that victims of rape, in or out of marriage, were recognized as people who needed assistance.

Rape, simply defined, is forced sex without consent. Legal definitions generally involve three separate factors: sexual intercourse involving vaginal, anal, or oral penetration; force or threat of force; and nonconsent of the victim. As recently as 1977, laws in twenty-nine states specifically stated that a man cannot be prosecuted for raping his wife.[22] Yet Russell reports that one out of every seven women interviewed who had ever been married reported at least one, and sometimes many, experiences of rape by her husband.[23]

Bowker, in reviewing studies of marital rape, makes several points.[24] First, marital rape may be more common than all other kinds of rape combined. Second, marital rape is commonly found among battered wives. Third, motivating factors for marital rape include anger, the need to dominate, and occasionally sexual obsession. Fourth, marital rape may be as psychologically disturbing as nonmarital rape and have long-term severe effects. Fifth, marital rape within violent marriages seems to affect women's self-esteem negatively as well as their attitudes toward men and heterosexual behavior. And sixth, husbands who rape their wives are likely to have problems with alcohol, to have had serious dysfunctions in their families of orientation, and to dominate totally their marriages.

Frieze reported similar findings from interviews with women in attempting to investigate the determinants and consequences of marital rape.[25] Sexual pressuring or being forced to have sex was the most commonly reported form of marital rape. Most of the women felt the cause to lay in their husbands' belief that such an action served to prove his manhood. They all saw the rape as the responsibility of the husband and brought on by factors in his personality rather than by the wife's provocation. Her study confirms that marital rape is a serious matter, that many women undergo severe emotional and behavioral reactions, that it is often associated with battering, and that the women need sources of help. What

22. "The Marital Rape Exemption," *New York University Law Review* 52 (May 1977): 306–323.

23. Diana E. H. Russell, *Rape in Marriage* (New York: Macmillan, 1982).

24. Lee H. Bowker, "Marital Rape: A Distinct Syndrome?" *Social Casework* (June 1983): 347–348.

25. Irene Hanson Frieze, "Investigating the Causes and Consequences of Marital Rape," *Signs: Journal of Women in Culture and Society* 8 (1983): 533.

seemed clear was that the quality of the couple's sexual relationship was closely linked with the health of the marriage.

SEXUAL ADJUSTMENT

Sexual adjustment has been highlighted by certain writers as the keystone to marital adjustment. However, it is highly unlikely that adjustment of any sort is a dichotomous either/or phenomenon. Within any marriage, there are certain times and situations in which sex is "better or worse" than other times or situations. Also, to assume that frequency of intercourse, attainment of female orgasm, or an uninhibited sex life is equal to sexual adjustment is both misleading and false. It is very difficult to separate sex from the total complex of interaction that constitutes married life. Sexual adjustment may be one indicator of general marital adjustment, but it is doubtful that sexual adjustment alone will maintain an otherwise poor relationship. Dissatisfaction in a marriage is likely to be reflected in the frequency and performance of marital coitus, and conflict in sexual coitus may be symptomatic of other tensions within the marital relationship.

The Blumstein and Schwartz study of couples in the United States cited earlier supports this linkage between sexual adjustment and the quality of the relationship.[26] Their findings led to the overwhelming conclusion that a good sex life is central to a good overall relationship. Their married couples felt so strongly about having sex often that those who said they have it with the partner infrequently tended to be less satisfied with the entire relationship. What is not known definitively is whether an unsatisfactory relationship leads to less frequent sexual activity or whether the problems begin in the bedroom and eventually corrode the entire relationship. This author tends to lean more heavily toward the notion that when nonsexual parts of a marital relationship are going poorly, the quality and frequency of the sexual relationship will decline as well.

The last statement is not meant to deny the effect that sexual inadequacies have on the quality of a relationship. Masters and Johnson estimate that 50 percent of all marriages in the United States have some form of sexual inadequacy, such as primary or secondary impotence, vaginismus, premature ejaculation, orgasmic dysfunction, unequal level of response, or others.[27] This may be a partial explanation for the popularity of sex manuals.

---

26. Blumstein and Schwartz, *American Couples*, pp. 201–206.
27. William H. Masters and Virginia E. Johnson, *Human Sexual Inadequacy* (Boston: Little, Brown, 1970): 351–369.

Marriage/sex manuals

An indirect indication of the desire for sexual adjustment in marriage may stem from the sale of marriage manuals. This assumes, perhaps falsely, that the purchases are made (1) primarily by married persons and (2) for purposes of improving sexual relations within marriage. One national bestseller, *The Joy of Sex*, claims to be a "gourmet guide to love making" and was followed one year later by *More Joy of Sex*, stated to be a love-making companion to the former book.[28] Whether books such as these are read, the advice is followed, or the relationship is affected is another issue. Sales alone, however, indicate widespread interest and present great potential for influencing public opinion.

What kind of messages do sex manuals portray? One publication reporting on models of female sexuality in forty-nine United States sex manuals from 1950 to 1980 indicated that they generally reflect one of three distinct models.[29] The first model of female sexuality, and the one predominant in the 1950s and 1960s, portrays males and females as *different and unequal*. Female sexuality was naturally emotional and male sexuality was more animalistic or physical. This model assumed that female sexual response lies dormant until it is awakened by an experienced and skillful male partner, teacher, and leader. The second model most prevalent in the early 1970s was one of *humanistic sexuality*. These manuals portray sex as a basic human quality and remove it from the context of marriage. That is, partners are no longer referred to as husband and wife but as male, female, partner, or couple. Traditional sex roles in the bedroom are denounced and sex is portrayed as an experience to be explored, experimented with, and fun without rules or roles. The third model, *sexual autonomy*, prevalent since 1975, portrays women as independent agents, self-sufficient and in control of their own sexuality. Whereas the first two models view the sexual experience dyadically as primarily an interactive phenomenon, this model focuses on the private sexual experience of women, who are told to take responsibilty for their own satisfaction. Orgasm, a product of learning, is viewed as every woman's right with or without a man, thus emphasizing both coital and noncoital techniques.

Brissett and Lewis, who described sex manuals in the 1960s as stressing work themes requiring a good deal of study, practice, and preparation, examined more recently published manuals to see if the old work ethic

---

28. Alex Comfort, ed., *The Joy of Sex* (New York: Simon and Schuster, 1972); Alex Comfort, ed., *More Joy of Sex* (New York: Simon and Schuster, 1973).

29. Martin S. Weinberg, Rochelle Ganz Swensson, and Sue Kiefer Hammersmith, "Sexual Autonomy and the Status of Women: Models of Female Sexuality in U.S. Sex Manuals from 1950 to 1980," *Social Problems* 30 (February 1980): 312–324.

Intimacy and sexual behaviors take many forms and exist in many contexts. Most sex manuals tend to encourage variations in patterns of sexual expression. (Photo: © Susan Rosenberg/Photo Researchers)

still prevails.[30] They found that basically it does. What a person can choose, however, is, to a certain degree, the style of work, and to a much greater degree, the life-style surrounding the work. Unlike the previous manuals analyzed, the recent manuals do not define good sexual relations as merely a product of proper techniques, diligent applications, and marital orgasm. The newer manuals seem obsessed with making sexual relations interesting through the stylization of its time, place, equipment, and maneuvers. Instead of feeling guilty for having too much sexual pleasure, sexual partners now may very well experience anxiety for not having enough. Since almost everything is now permitted in the realm of sexuality, Brissett and Lewis suggest that it is just possible that "nothing any longer is good enough."[31]

Unfortunately, many popular manuals, magazines, and journals, in fulfilling a basic function of educating and informing men and women about sex, have also contributed to a fear of sexual performance. To be

---

30. Dennis Brissett and Lionel S. Lewis, "The Big Toe, Armpits, and Natural Perfume: Notes on the Production of Sexual Ecstasy," *Society* 16 (January/February 1979): 63–73.
31. Ibid., p. 73.

FIGURE 11—2

informed about the average number of coital experiences per week among married couples, multiple orgasms, or coital positions may be very interesting but may also lead to serious questioning and doubts about one's own performance. The male and female whose sexual practices do not conform to the social norms may seriously question their own adequacy or "normality." If other couples are having intercourse three or four times a week and we are engaging in coitus once a month, is something wrong? If other women during orgasm turn blue, feel the earth move, hear bells chime, or pant and scream ecstatically, am I less of a woman if I quietly experience a pleasant sensation? Masters and Johnson state that these grave self-doubts and usually groundless suspicions are translated into fears of performance.

It should be restated that fear of inadequacy is the greatest known deterrent to effective sexual functioning, simply because it so completely distracts the fearful individual from his or her natural responsivity by blocking reception of sexual stimuli either created by or reflected from the sexual partner.[32]

Dealing with sexual inadequacies

Probably no therapy program for dealing with sexual inadequacies has ever been undertaken with as solid a research base as that of the Reproductive Research Foundation under the directorship of Masters and Johnson. The purpose of their treatment program is aimed at restoring sex to its natural context so it functions like breathing—that is, without conscious effort and with spontaneity. The types of dysfunctions they attempt to correct include primary (total) and secondary (partial) impotence, premature ejaculation, and ejaculatory incompetence on the part of the male; orgasmic dysfunction and vaginismus on the part of the female; and dyspareunia (painful intercourse); and the aging process on the part of both sexes.[33]

Two concepts that appear particularly significant to the behavioral scientists are what Masters and Johnson term the **spectator role** and the **sexual value system**. The spectator role involves learning to eliminate the negative effect of self-consciously trying to produce certain sexual results. It attempts to eliminate the deliberate placing of the mind on what is desired rather than on a "natural response." In reference to the spectator role of the impotent husband, the authors note:

> As sex play is introduced and mutual attempts made by marital partners to force an erective response, the impotent husband finds himself a spectator to his own sexual exchange. He mentally is observing his and his partner's response (or lack of it) to sexual stimulation. Will there be an erection? If and when the penis begins to engorge, how full will the erection become? When erection is obtained, how long will it last? The involuntary spectator in the room demands immediate answers for these questions from the anxious man in the bed, so intensely concerned with his fears of sexual performance. Rather than allowing himself to relax, enjoy sensual stimulation, and permit his natural sexual responsivity to create and maintain the erective process, he as a spectator demands instant perfomance.[34]

---

32. Masters and Johnson, *Human Sexual Inadequacy*, pp. 12–13.

33. Here, *dysfunction* refers to a sexual malfunction, usually social and psychological in origin. *Primary impotence* refers to the inability to ever achieve or maintain an erection sufficient for intercourse. *Secondary impotence* refers to failure at some times, success at others. *Premature ejaculation* refers to ejaculation before, immediately upon, or shortly after penetration. *Orgasmic dysfunction* refers to the inability and failure of the female to reach orgasm. *Vaginismus* refers to the psychosomatic illness that affects a woman's ability to respond sexually by virtually closing the vaginal opening to male entry. *Dyspareunia* refers to painful intercourse.

34. Ibid., p. 65.

The problem is compounded because the wife too is operating in the spectator role. In her attempt to provide her husband with an erection, she too may be questioning what she is doing wrong in assisting him to perform adequately.

The sexual value system, termed *SVS* by Masters and Johnson, refers to those sensory experiences an individual has had under circumstances that he or she finds pleasurable on the one hand and, on the other, is not offensive to the values he or she has learned from society (e.g., family, church, school, peer group, or other). Physiologically, male and female sexual responses are very similar, but where the female differs radically is in her sexual value system—her psychosocial aspect of sexuality.

In many ways society prohibits the female in U.S. society from developing a positive sexual value system. Whereas the male may often be praised or honored in his sexual performance, the reality of the female's sexual function still carries many implications of shame and misbehavior—neither of which contributes to high levels of marital sexual harmony. Many women are reared in our society to believe that "nice girls don't involve themselves," "sex is for reproductive purposes," or "sex is a man's privilege."

Treatment of sexual dysfunction, according to Gagnon and others, is viewed in the broad context of sexual scripts.[35] Rather than explaining and treating narrowly conceived terms such as vaginismus or premature ejaculation, one needs to look at the total script. Solutions to problems means focusing on both the performance and the cognitive script and modifying what one does and/or what one thinks. If, as Masters and Johnson claim, the greatest overall cause of malfunction is fear, this too is part of our sexual script. And problem-solving thus revolves around modification of the behaviors and ideas that make up our performance and cognitive sexual scripts.

EXTRAMARITAL COITUS

A chapter on sexual relationships in marital contexts may well be incomplete without a look at sexual relationships among married persons with persons (married or single) other than their spouse.

The terms *extramarital coitus* or *adultery* refer to nonmarital sexual intercourse between a man and a woman, at least one of whom is married at the time to someone else. Almost without exception in the United States, adultery is legally punishable. And although actual prosecution is rare,

---

35. John H. Gagnon, Raymond C. Rosen, and Sandra R. Leiblem, "Cognitive and Social Aspects of Sexual Dysfunction: Sexual Scripts in Sex Therapy," *Journal of Sex and Marital Therapy* 8 (1982): 44–56.

the moral condemnation that accompanies extramarital coitus is, in general, much stronger than that directed at premarital or postmarital coitus. It is widely held that adultery is condemned in practically all Western cultures because of the threat it poses to the family unit. Secondly, it is assumed (and sometimes falsely so) that marriage provides a socially approved legitimate sexual partner, and thus sexual deprivation is minimized.

Lynn Atwater argues that several myths contribute to an unrealistic faith in sexual exclusivity in the United States.[36] One is that one person can and will supply all of another's emotional, social, and sexual needs. A second is that people grow to love each other more as years go by. A third is that sexual exclusivity comes easily and naturally. These myths lead us to blindly believe that if only our partners are faithful, all of our emotional needs will be satisfied. Yet the extent of extramarital relations suggests otherwise.

Sexual relationships in general have traditionally held very different standards for men and women. While a double standard continues to exist, the previous chapter illustrated a trend toward a convergence of attitudes and behavior in the area of premarital sex. There does not seem to be evidence for such a trend regarding extramarital sex. Today, much greater concern centers around the extramarital behavior of the wife than that of the husband. Kinsey noted that most societies permit or condone extramarital coitus for the male if he is reasonably circumspect about it and if he does not carry it to extremes that would break up his home, lead to the neglect of his family, outrage his in-laws, stir up public scandal, or start difficulties with the husband or other relatives of the women with whom he has his relationships.[37] On the other hand, such extramarital activity is much less frequently permitted or condoned for the female. And when it is permitted, it usually occurs on special occasions or with particular persons (such as at certain orgiastic ceremonies, for the new bride as part of the marriage ceremony, or in a few instances, as a means of entertaining the husband's guests).

Even though a double standard exists in the United States, it is far less pronounced than in many countries that provide and permit considerable freedom for the male with harsh restrictions and taboos placed on the female. For example, Japan prior to World War II could be considered a "man's world." Shin'ichi Asayama, reporting on Japan, noted that all Japanese husbands enjoyed some form of sexual contact outside of marriage.[38] In contrast, infidelity by a wife was condemned as a crime from

---

36. Lynn Atwater, *The Extramarital Connection* (New York: Irvington Publishers, 1982): 18.

37. Kinsey, *Sexual Behavior in the Human Female,* p. 414.

38. Shin'ichi Asayama, "Adolescent Sex Development and Adult Sex Behavior in Japan," *The Journal of Sex Research* 11 (May 1975): 107.

Can you afford both a querida and a wife?

> Polygyny is not permissible for the Christian Filipino male, but those who can afford it have a querida. In the Philippines, the querida system involves a married man, usually of higher status, seeing, supporting, and possibly having children by a woman other than his wife. While a "mistress relationship" is frowned upon, the civil code provides for the maintenance of his illegitimate children. The double standard is seen in that equal privileges do not exist for the wife. He can separate from her for adultery on her part, but she cannot do likewise. Nor can the wife bring an action for legal separation against the husband unless he maintains his mistress in the same dwelling as his legitimate wife. The wife can, of course, simply leave him or refuse to cohabit, which would be a separation de facto. But the former would simply create additional problems of support and custody of the children.
>
> The frequency of this keeping of a "mistress," "second wife" (not legally), or querida, is unknown. But an informal survey of priests from twenty-two dioceses suggests that the percentage of men with queridas is about one or two, although in certain urban social strata it is probably much higher.
>
> The querida often represents a serious threat to a wife and children in diminishing their man's affection and support. Thus while wives may know about their husband's querida, they may pretend they do not. As long as the man adopts some measure of self-control and fidelity, his morality is secure and his role adequately discharged. The wife, in turn, avidly participates in religious life and, in effect, prays for two, her piety making up for both her own and her husband's failings.

both a legal and moral point of view. Since World War II, the social and economic conditions for women have improved, changing the situation radically. However, sexual freedom for women does not approach the same level as for men. Even today, it is felt that Japanese men openly enjoy more sexual freedom than do U.S. and probably European men. Women in the United States enjoy more freedom than Japanese women, but U.S. women seem to be less tolerant than Japanese women about their husbands' extramarital sexual relations.[39]

A unique feature of extramarital sex involving Japanese women is their emotional involvement with their partner. While Japanese women may not approve of extramarital sex, once exposed to the opportunity they are inclined to be emotionally involved. Women in the United States, in contrast, are less likely to be pushed into an extramarital relationship by an unhappy marriage but rather are pulled or drift into the relationship.[40]

---

39. Minako K. Maykovich, "Attitudes Versus Behavior in Extramarital Sexual Relations," *Journal of Marriage and the Family* 38 (November 1976): 693.

40. Ibid., pp. 696–698.

In the absence of restrictive cultural norms regarding sexual activity, U.S. women who engage in extramarital sex approve of it, but their commitment to it is weak. This is consistent with Ralph Johnson's findings that 60 percent of adulterous wives had high marital adjustment (compared to 30 percent of the husbands), showing a low association between extramarital sex and marital dissatisfaction for U.S. wives.[41]

Like any other sexual outlet, it is impossible to know with any high degree of accuracy how frequently adultery takes place. Kinsey's figures indicate that by age forty, 26 percent of the females and 50 percent of the males had experienced extramarital coitus.[42] Minako Maykovich found that 32 percent of middle-class U.S. women aged thirty-five to forty had experienced extramarital sex at least once.[43] Ralph Johnson noted that 69 percent of the husbands and 56 percent of the wives in his study indicated a positive inclination to interact with a person of the opposite sex when their spouse was out of town. This does not mean coitus would result from such interaction but it does indicate the potential, given the opportunity.[44]

What factors account for or are highly related to extramarital coital experience? Of all the factors that Kinsey examined, religious devoutness, more than any other, affected the active incidences of extramarital coitus, particularly for the females. The lowest incidences of extramarital coitus had occurred among those who were most devoutly religious, and the highest incidences had occurred among those who were least closely connected with any church activity. This was true of all the Protestant, Jewish, and Catholic groups in the sample.[45]

David Weeks and Joan Jurich employed five national surveys to investigate the relationship between attitudes toward extramarital sexual relations and a measure of size of community of present residence.[46] Size of community was strongly and directly related to extramarital attitudes. As persons from small communites are more likely to be politically conservative, to be less supportive of the Equal Rights Amendment, to express greater opposition to sex education, communism, or welfare, so are they more likely to disapprove of premarital and extramarital sexuality. Greatest approval of extramarital sexual relationships was found to exist among persons who reside in or near large metropolitan centers, as well as

41. Ralph E. Johnson, "Some Correlates of Extramarital Coitus," *Journal of Marriage and the Family* 32 (August 1970): 454.

42. Kinsey, *Sexual Behavior in the Human Female,* p. 437.

43. Maykovich, "Attitudes Versus Behavior," p. 695.

44. Ralph Johnson, "Some Correlates of Extramarital Coitus," p. 452.

45. Kinsey, *Sexual Behavior in the Human Female,* p. 424.

46. David L. Weis and Joan Jurich, "Size of Community of Residence as a Predictor of Attitudes Toward Extramarital Sexual Relations," *Journal of Marriage and the Family* 47 (February 1985): 173–178.

Please reply in confidence

Chicago West Suburbs—Happily marrieds, 26 and 33, white, would like to hear from social minded married for fun evenings and good times. Phone and photo please.

Pontiac Area Marrieds — Attractive, would like to hear from other similar-minded adults for dining, nights out, and games. Not necessarily in that order.

Texas Marrieds — Late 30s, attractive, Latin, would like to hear from other Latin or Anglo marrieds for adult fun and friendship. Answer all. Phone and photo please.

Florida Marrieds — Liberal minded, affectionate, attractive, late 20s, would like to hear from other similar qualified marrieds. We can travel. Phone, photo, and address if possible.

Jersey Marrieds — White, 29 and 30, happily married, discreet and liberal-minded. Would like to hear from other liberal-minded marrieds who enjoy photography and correspondence. Age and race no barrier. Photo please with phone will bring prompt reply.

Northern Calif. Marrieds — Attractive, white, liberal-minded. Would like to hear from other marrieds for adult fun. Discretion assured. Will answer all who include phone and photo.

Southern N. Y. Area — Attractive and happily marrieds, 28 and 25, white, would like to hear from other liberal-minded marrieds. Phone and photo and must be discreet.

among those who hold permissive premarital sexual attitudes, who are either unmarried or unhappily married, and who have high levels of education.

In developing a model of permissive attitudes toward extramarital sexuality, Saunders and Edwards suggested that permissive attitudes are significantly affected by factors such as the diffuseness of one's intimacy conception, the comparison level of alternatives available, the autonomy of interaction with the opposite sex, and the degree of perceived satisfaction with one's marriage.[47] They stress, in any research having to do with extramarital sexual permissiveness, the importance of differentiating between males and females and distinguishing between attitudes and behavior. Their model explained more variance for females than males and was directed toward permissive attitudes rather than actual behaviors.

Atwater, in studying fifty feminist-oriented women, suggests that ex-

---

47. Janice Miller Saunders and John N. Edwards, "Extramarital Sexuality: A Predictive Model of Permissive Attitudes," *Journal of Marriage and the Family* 46 (November 1984): 825–835.

tramarital coitus for these women is a direct response to the women's movement. They are breaking out of a traditional scene that demanded faithfulness for them but not for their husbands. And extramarital behavior for women is an arena where they are free to establish the kinds of sexual patterns they prefer with no social pressure to maintain less than satisfactory relationships, no deep investment of love and romance, and no long-term institutional pattern that defines sex as having purposes other than personal pleasure. For these women, participation in extramarital sex signals continued liberation from traditional sexuality and, in Atwater's words, is "the final assault on the double standard."[48]

Another partial assault on the double standard is a specific type of extramarital coitus referred to as "swinging," "consensual adultery," "mate swapping," "wife swapping," "co-marital sexual behavior," or "group sexual activities." Swinging is having sexual relations (as a couple) with at least one other individual. It also involves a willingness to swap sexual partners with a couple with whom the spouses are not acquainted and/or to go to a swinging party and be willing for both spouses to have sexual intercourse with strangers. The term wife swapping at times refers to the same activity, although this term may be objectionable to groups sensitive to sexual inequality. One rarely hears of husband swapping although that occurs with equal, if not greater, frequency.

Swinging, group sex, mate swapping, key clubs, and such are a reorganized nontraditional pattern of sexual expression for some married couples. While it involves a single standard of sexual permissiveness, it is doubtful it will find widespread acceptance or approach the frequency of nonconsensual extramarital sexual relationships. It differs from adultery, however, in its nonsecrecy, openness, and greater degree of honesty between the marital partners.

INCEST

Incest refers to sexual intercourse between certain family members, particularly those within and closest to the nuclear family: father-daughter, mother-son, brother-sister, stepfather-stepdaughter, and the like. A taboo on incest is believed to be universal in human culture although sexual relations between family members do occur.

George Murdock, in drawing data from 250 societies, set forth a number of empirical conclusions concerning incest taboos. Among others, these included: a universal application to all persons of the opposite sex within the nuclear family; a universal application to at least some relatives

---

48. Atwater, *The Extramarital Connection*, pp. 190–191.

outside the nuclear family but variations as to which specific relatives are included or excluded (such as aunts or uncles, half-siblings, nieces or nephews, cousins); a universal principle of no instances where relatives outside the nuclear family are more stringently tabooed than ones within it; a lack of coincidence of the taboo with nearness of actual biological relationship outside the nuclear unit; a tendency of incest taboos to be associated with those relatives who are given terms such as *mother*, *sister*, or *daughter*; a failure of taboos against adultery or fornication to exceed in strength the taboo against incest; and an apparent universal violation of the incest taboo in spite of the strength of this sexual prohibition.[49]

Particularly within the United States, a constant finding in all existing surveys is the overwhelming predominance of father-daughter incest.[50] If incest is defined in a broad·sense to include sexual stimulation and arousal, it could be argued that brother-sister incest is extremely prevalent and mother-child incest is universal. However, for our purposes, the more specific definition of intercourse will be used.

Because of the secrecy which surrounds the violation of this most basic sexual taboo, no accurate statistics exist on its prevalence. In the United States, most data come from police or court records, and it is highly probable that most cases of incest are not reported. It does, however, seem reasonable that more incest than is reported occurs in intact families and escapes the attention of social agencies and survey researchers. One report indicated that approximately 10 percent of all women report a childhood sexual experience (not necessarily intercourse) with a relative, and 1 percent are victims of father-daughter incest.[51] Family sexual abuse occurs in all social classes and in urban as well as rural environments. The most frequent victim is a daughter, and the most frequent perpetrator is a biological father but often is a step- or foster father or even a boyfriend or lover of the mother.

In interviews with a random sample of more than 900 adult women in San Francisco, Diana Russell found that while the most frequent incest perpetrators were biological fathers (since most women lived with and were accessible to biological fathers), the next largest group were step-fathers.[52] The likelihood of incestuous abuse was far greater if a stepfather was the principal figure in the woman's childhood years (17 percent or one out of approximately every six women) than if a father was the principal

49. George P. Murdock, *Social Structure* (New York: Macmillan, 1949): 284–289.

50. Judith Herman and Lisa Hirschman, "Father-Daughter Incest," *Signs: Journal of Women in Culture and Society* 2 (Summer 1977): 735–756.

51. Judith Herman, "Father-Daughter Incest," *Professional Psychology* 12 (February 1984): 76–80.

52. Diana E. H. Russell. "The Prevalence and Seriousness of Incestuous Abuse: Step-fathers vs. Biological Fathers," *Child Abuse and Neglect* 8 (1984):15–22.

figure (2 percent or one out of approximately forty women). And perhaps more significantly, when stepfathers sexually abused their daughters, they were much more likely than any other relatives to abuse them at the most serious level (forced penile-vaginal penetration, oral–vaginal-penis sex, or anal intercourse) in contrast to experiences such as digital penetration of the vagina, touching of breasts, buttocks, thigh, leg, forced kissing, and so forth. She explains these differences by suggesting that stepfathers, not being biologically related to their daughters, may feel less bound by the normative taboo on incest. Another explanation was that the bonding that commonly occurs between biological fathers and daughters may often be absent between stepfathers and daughters. A third explanation suggested that the daughter, often feeling betrayed by the mother who remarried, may compete with the mother for the attention of the stepfather. Whatever the explanation, the far greater prevalence and seriousness of stepfather-daughter incest over biological father-daughter incest suggests that daughters in remarriage face substantial risks of incestuous abuse.

Explanation for the taboo against incest

How can the taboo against incest be explained? One theory attributes it to the recognition by primitive people of the dangers of close inbreeding.[53] However, it is doubtful that early societies were aware of the genetic effects or the principles of heredity. Even if they were, it seems logical that it would have been used to produce a higher quality human such as has since been widely adopted with animals. Furthermore, these variable taboos do not coincide with biological nearness, thus discounting the idea that incest rules have their basis in biological or genetic factors.

A second explanation attributes incest prohibition to instinct. But if it were instinctive, avoidance of incest would be automatic. How would one explain the diversity of the taboos and their lack of correlation with actual consanguinity?[54] It is a fallacy to attempt to explain social phenomena that vary widely from one society to another on the basis of a relatively stable biological factor, and thus instinctive interpretations of social phenomena are rarely seen in the social sciences.

Some writers regard the prohibition of incest as habits formed during childhood. Habits of avoidance result from the dulling of the sexual appetite through prolonged associations. This idea suggests that to grow up in the same household with a person of the opposite sex eliminates that person as a sexual or marital partner. However, as Murdock suggests,

---

53. Melvin Ember, "On the Origin and the Extension of the Incest Taboo," *Behavior Science Research* 10 (June 1975): 249–281.

54. Ibid., p. 290.

Brother and sister wed

A brother and sister—separated 20 years by adoption—have been charged with incest after officials learned they married May 25 [1979] even though they were aware of their relationship.

Free on personal recognizance were David J. Goddu, 22, and Victoria M. Pittorino, 23, of Lawrence, Massachusetts.

The marriage was performed in nearby Andover by Justice of the Peace Elven Salter, who apparently was unaware they were related.

It was not clear how they met, but it may have been through adoption records, their natural mother said in an interview published yesterday in the Lawrence *Eagle Tribune*. She asked that her name be withheld.

"They know they are brother and sister. But I guess they think they're in love and I know they don't think this is wrong," she said. "They told me they won't have any children. But it's still a nightmare."

Incestuous marriages are automatically void under Massachusetts law. Incest, engaging in sex with a relative, is punishable by imprisonment of up to 20 years.

"We were happy for David," said David's father, James Goddu of Holyoke. "Now we wish it never did happen."

The sibling newlyweds face a district court hearing July 25 in Lawrence, where they were arrested last week, police said.

Lawrence police officer Tom Duggan stopped David for speeding last Wednesday. At that time, Duggan said, David reported he and his bride were wanted on a warrant for incest.

The warrant was sworn by a policeman in nearby Methuen, according to the *Eagle Tribune*, but the officer said he did not know who made the original complaint.

Victoria was arrested on Thursday, Duggan said.

"I had no idea that this was happening," said Goddu, who said he had not spoken to his son. "I don't know why they did it. I think they were ignorant of the law."

Their natural mother, who is moving from Methuen to an undisclosed location, said she permitted her children to be placed in foster homes when the boy was 18 months old and the girl 3 years and later agreed to adoption after her marriage broke up.

The woman told the newspaper her children stayed with her for a week last month. "Vicki called me and said, 'We got married,'" said the mother. "She sounded so happy. I was horrified."

"It never would have happened if they'd been brought up together," she said. "They weren't, and they found each other and they found me. I wish they had never found me."

Said Goddu: "I wish the laws were more strict about disclosure information to adopted children."

Source: Honolulu *Star Bulletin*, June 18, 1979, p. C-18.

this theory does not harmonize with cases where marriage with a housemate is actually favored, is inconsistent with the widespread reference for levirate and sororate unions, is contradicted by the enduring attachments between husband and wife that occur in most societies and, above all, overlooks, and even inverts, the vast body of clinical evidence showing that incestuous desires are regularly engendered within the nuclear family and are kept in restraint only though persistent social pressure and individual repression.[55]

Sigmund Freud's explanation of the incest taboo relates to the Oedipus and Electra complexes. His idea, like many others, does not account for the variation and extension of such taboos beyond the immediate nuclear family. Nor does it suggest why they are so regularly a part of culture, receiving the approval of society and incorporated everywhere in sanctioned cultural norms.

Murdock suggests that no unitary theory of incest taboos appears capable of accounting for all their aspects. For his explanation, he draws upon psychoanalysis, sociology, cultural anthropology, and behavioristic psychology. According to Murdock:

> It thus appears that a complete scientific explanation of incest taboos and exogamous roles emerges from a synthesis of the theories of four separate disciplines that deal with human behavior. *Psychoanalytic theory* accounts for the peculiar emotional quality of such taboos; for the occurrence of violations, which neither an instinct hypothesis nor Westermarck's theory of acquired aversion explains; for the diminished intensity of taboos outside of the nuclear family; and for the universal occurrence of incest avoidance tendencies which serve as a basis for cultural elaboration. *Sociological theory* demonstrates the social utility of both intra-family and extended incest taboos and thus accounts for the universality. *Psychological behavior theory* reveals a mechanism by which extension occurs and that by which social utility becomes translated into custom, thus supplying an essential part of the reasons for both the universality and the variety of extended taboos. *Cultural anthropology*, finally, contributes to our explanation of the varied conditions of social structure and usage which channelize generalization or produce discrimination, and thus accounts for the differential incidence of exogamous rules and extended incest taboos, for their correlation with conventional groupings of kinsmen, and for their lack of correspondence with actual biological relationship.[56]

It would be difficult to imagine the nature of the full system of rules within the family and between families if there were no prohibitions against sexual relations and marriage between members of the same nuclear family. Take simply the confusion of statuses that would result should

---

55. Murdock, *Social Structure*, p. 291.
56. Ibid., p. 300.

inbreeding occur. "The incestuous male child of a father-daughter union . . . would be a brother of his own mother, that is, the son of his own sister; a step-son of his own grandmother; possibly a brother of his own uncle; and certainly a grandson of his own father."[57]

Some writers argue that the incest taboo is not universal and in certain instances is highly dysfunctional. The cases most frequently mentioned are those of brother-sister marriages among the Incas, the Hawaiians, and the ancient Egyptians. However, for our basic purposes, isolated instances such as these rarely pertain to a society as a whole but only to limited groups of high prestige where maintenance of status takes precedence over other factors. Exceptions to the taboo on incest are sanctioned primarily among royalty and rarely for commoners.

POSTMARITAL COITUS

Compared to the subjects of premarital, nonmarital, marital, or extramarital coitus, relatively little attention has been given to the subject of coitus after the dissolution of marriage through death, separation, or divorce. An intense interest exists in the sexual activities of the young prior to marriage and the importance of coitus in marriage. But after marriage, the importance of coitus enters into a state of limbo between an activity that is vital and necessary to psychological and emotional health and an activity that contradicts the conventional morality of confining coitus to marriage. Paul Gebhard states that the escape from this dilemma is to ignore and minimize the problem as much as possible, but if forced to take a position to condemn publicly and condone privately.[58] This dilemma between the public and private norms as they relate to postmarital coitus indicates a social permissiveness insofar as publicity is kept minimal. It may also contribute to the low level of available information as well as to the high level of curiosity about the sexual activity of formerly married persons.

The incidence of postmarital coitus

It is generally assumed that most if not all previously married men and women engage in coitus. Based on questionnaires, interviews, and direct

---

57. Kingsley Davis, "Legitimacy and the Incest Taboo," in *A Modern Introduction to the Family* ed. by Norman W. Bell and Ezra F. Vogel (Glencoe, Ill.: The Free Press, 1960): 401.

58. Paul Gebhard, "Postmarital Coitus Among Widows and Divorcees," in *Divorce and After* ed. by Paul Bohannan (Garden City, N. Y.: Doubleday, 1970): 81–96.

observations, plus consultations with psychologists and social scientists who have studied the matter, Hunt wrote:

> Of all the people one might meet in the World of the Formerly Married at any given moment, almost none of the men and only about one-fifth of the women have had no sexual intercourse at all since their marriages broke up. Obviously, time plays a part in this: the longer a person remains an FM, the greater the likelihood that he or she will have begun having postmarital sexual activity. But most people start very soon; five out of six FMs begin having sexual intercourse within the first year, most of them with more than one partner.[59]

The data given refer to incidence, not frequency. That is, almost all of the male and about 80 percent of the female formerly marrieds had had coitus at least once.

Reporting on the incidence of postmarital coitus based upon interviews with 632 white females, the Institute for Sex Research, with which Kinsey was associated, found major differences between the postmarital sexual behavior of the widowed and the divorced. Eighty-two percent of the divorced had had such coitus compared to 43 percent of the widowed.[60] At all ages, substantially more divorced women had had coitus than had widowed women. The age-specific incidence of postmarital coitus indicated that during their twenties and thirties, roughly two-thirds to three-quarters of the divorced had coitus in contrast to one-third to one-half of the widowed. In their forties, the divorced widened their lead: about three-fifths to two-thirds of them experienced coitus, as opposed to roughly one-quarter to one-third of the widowed. After age fifty, the differences lessened as age exerted its leveling influence, but they were still very marked.

Gebhard found enormous differences between the widowed and the divorced deriving from several interrelated factors.[61] One of these was religion, with the critical matter proving to be the degree of devoutness rather than the denomination. From 30 to 40 percent of the widowed were labeled devout on the basis of church attendance, as opposed to 15 to 29 percent of the divorced. There was a moderate tendency for both groups to become more devout with increasing age. A second factor was prior experience in coitus outside of marriage. If an individual had had premarital or extramarital coitus, he or she was more likely to engage in postmarital coitus. No great differences existed in premarital coitus (28 percent widowed, 37 percent divorced), but greater differences existed in

---

59. Morton M. Hunt, *The World of the Formerly Married* (Greenwich, Conn.: Fawcett, 1966): 119.

60. Gebhard, "Postmarital Coitus Among Widows and Divorcees," p. 84.

61. Ibid., p. 86.

Do the words "mistress," "other woman" and "paramour" conjure up visions of a potential home wrecker, a "kept woman" who sits around in a black lace teddy keeping martinis on ice for her lover?

Scratch that image, says author and Ohio State University sociology professor Laurel Richardson.

"The contemporary Other Woman is likely to be our neighbor, our sister, our daughter, our mother, ourselves: regular, normal, everyday single women," writes Richardson, author of "The New Other Woman" (Free Press).

Most often, they are career women, some of whom earn more than their lovers. They come from all social strata. Many are divorced and raising children alone. Often, she says, the last thing they want is for their lovers to become their husbands.

Changes have occurred, Richardson said during a recent Detroit visit, because there are many more single women today. "Women are delaying marriage, divorcing more often, and they are in daily contact with married men at work," she says.

"Between 40 and 50 percent of husbands report having at least one affair during their marriages, and almost 70 percent of married men under age 40 imagine they will have one," Richardson says. "Fifteen percent of married men are chronic womanizers and will have repeat affairs."

Single women don't set out to become the "other woman," but fall into these relationships because there are so few single men for them to date, she says. Today there are 33 million single women in America, Richardson says, and one in five does not have a potential mate.

Given the imbalance, "it is likely that the single woman over 25 who has never had a relationship with a married man will be in the minority," she says.

These women have to "learn to feel good about themselves and the lives they choose," Richardson says.

Problems arise, she says, when a woman's married lover—who started out as the object of a carefree fling—suddenly becomes the most important thing in the woman's life.

Although she thinks she's going into an affair with her eyes open, romantic mist may soon cloud her vision, Richardson says. The secret nature of the affair itself creates a situation in which it's easy for a woman to fall in love, changing the nature of her supposedly light-hearted dalliance.

"Mystical explanations for her falling in love are unnecessary," writes Richardson. "The conditions—secrecy, privacy and time constraints—under which her relationship with a married man is built are aphrodisiacal enough to afford ample explanation."

Soon, the woman is spending too much of her leisure time waiting for her married lover to call, waiting for him to get away from home, leaving her calendar free for spur-of-the-moment opportunities. And when the affair ends, many go through the same traumas a divorcing woman does, without the support system.

"I wrote the book because I saw how one of my best friends suffered when her relationship ended," says Richardson, who was in the midst of a divorce herself at the same time the friend was ending an affair. Friends and family rallied around Richardson, but her friend, who had kept her affair secret, had no one with whom to share her pain.

Richardson does not condone or condemn such relationships, but points out the pitfalls. "I want the book to help these women handle their guilt and other feelings they never expected to have," she says.

Richardson says she tried to start an "other woman anonymous" group at Ohio State to help gather material for her book, but could find no one interested in revealing herself. Over eight years, she interviewed women at conferences and eventually conducted in-depth interviews with 55 women aged 24 to 65.

Their case histories are unique, but touch on common themes. Most of the couples met through work. Once they succumbed to a mutual sexual attraction and established relationships, the women faced similar problems, involving sex, emotional entanglements, guilt and fighting the logistics of the affair.

She says "other women" should keep these points in mind:

Do not withdraw from your regular life. Continue to see friends and family, and keep busy rather than saving all your free time for your lover.

Include someone in your life who knows about your relationship. This person, a sister, a best friend, is a source of realistic feedback: "They can say to you, 'Don't kid yourself.'"

Don't give away your independence. If your lover tries to control your activities and you comply because you're afraid to upset him or end the affair, you may be in for further emotional trouble.

It may be better to be involved with more than one married man, to cut down the strength of attachment to a single man. Also, Richardson says, it's not uncommon for a woman to discover she isn't the only "other woman" in a man's life.

Plan for the ending at the beginning. The women Richardson interviewed seldom married their lovers. One of the most successful endings, she says, involved a psychiatrist and his patient who remained friends after their affair ended and she married someone else.

What is her advice to the wife?

If she loves him and wants to maintain the marriage, Richardson says, "She should ignore (the affair) as long as possible." With luck, the affair might end before it becomes public knowledge and the wife feels pressured to take action.

Richardson suggests the wife talk to a counselor and not automatically feel she is at fault, or take rash action.

"Having the love of a man is the strongest cultural imperative women have been conditioned to seek to value themselves," says Richardson. When their husbands find love elsewhere, or if a single woman has no man in her life, they often feel a personal devaluation. Meanwhile a man's feeling of self-worth comes from his success in work, Richardson says, and does not depend as much on a woman's love.

Source: Marj Jackson Levin, *Detroit Free Press*, November 22, 1985, pp. 1B and 4B. Reprinted with the permission of the Detroit Free Press.

extramarital coitus (8 percent widowed, 33 percent divorced). The divorced had a "head start" on the widows in that 31 percent were having extramarital coitus in their final year of marriage. A third factor centered around the type of relationship desired. Widows appear to be more interested in an emotional rather than a purely sexual relationship. Emotional relationships take longer to develop than do sexual ones. A fourth factor was the trauma of being widowed. Even after the initial phase of acute grief has ameliorated, the widow may find it difficult to find a mate who measures up to the image of her deceased husband, an image which tends to benefit from selective memory. A fifth factor related to remarriage. Divorcees were more likely to engage in coitus. That is, many women who would have ordinarily avoided coitus for moral (or other) reasons had it when marriage seemed impending.

It is perhaps surprising to note that when the coital-orgasm rate in the postmarital period is compared to that of the previous marriage, both the widowed and divorced have a greater orgasmic response in postmarital life. Of those having coitus, 57 percent of the divorced and 48 percent of the widowed had a higher percentage of orgasm during their postmarital life than in their former marriage.[62] This may be attributable to the greater proportion of postmarital women who decide whether or not coitus will occur. It may also be attributable to the newness and the happier emotional relationships of the postmarital situation. Particularly for the divorced, one can generally assume unhappiness in the terminal years of the marriage. And it has been demonstrated that marital unhappiness is associated with a lower orgasm rate for wives.[63] A third factor accounting for the higher postmarital orgasm rate may relate to the relaxation of inhibition that accompanies age, experience, and maturity. It could be assumed that different partners and new experiences would result in learning-educational benefits.

SUMMARY

1. Marriage legitimizes the sexual relationship. The social norms that surround sex and marriage are the key factors in differentiating marital sex from premarital, extramarital, or any other circumstance outside the marital relationship. Coitus within marriage comprises a larger proportion of the total sexual outlet than any other type of heterosexual

---

62. Ibid., p. 92.
63. Paul Gebhard, "Factors in Marital Orgasm," *The Journal of Social Issues* 22 (April 1966): 90.

activity and is recognized cross-culturally as important in the maintenance of the family system.

2. Studies indicate that the incidence and frequence of marital coitus reach their maximum in the first year or two after marriage, with a steady decline from that time on. As in premarital coitus, marital coital rates showed an increase during the latter part of the 1960s. A variety of explanations account for this shift including a decrease in exposure to the risk of pregnancy and an increased societal openness about sexual matters.

3. Two issues within marriage typically ignored are autoeroticism and rape. While frequency of intercourse varies considerably in or out of marriage, the frequency of masturbation appears less likely to do so. Rape, on the other hand, may be more common in marriage than in any other context. It is often associated with physical brutality.

4. Sexual adjustment is one factor in marital adjustment, but it is doubtful that this factor alone would maintain an otherwise "poor" marital relationship. The interest in this topic can be seen in the widespread sale of sexual manuals and books. These reflect a variety of models concerning relations between the sexes and the nature and meaning of sexuality. It is possible that some of these manuals provide a major disservice to sexual adjustment by providing advice that operates negatively against adjustment by failing to see sex in a total social context of values and norms, by focusing on techniques, and by engendering feelings of inadequacy in not being able to meet the expectations given.

5. One of the most extensive, research-based programs for dealing with sexual inadequacies is the Reproductive Biology Research Foundation under the directorship of Masters and Johnson. Two concepts of significance to the social scientist include the spectator role and the sexual value system. Treatment of sexual dysfunctions was viewed in the broad context of sexual scripts.

6. As indicated, not all heterosexual coitus of married persons occurs with the spouse. Extramarital coitus, incest, and postmarital coitus appear to be widespread with major differences between males and females and across cultures. Extramarital coitus appears to be highly related to premarital permissiveness, to marital strain, to alienation and powerlessness, to community size, to higher levels of education, to autonomy of interaction, and other factors. Swinging, or co-marital sexual behavior is a form of extramarital coitus involving both husband and wife.

7. Incest, while exhibiting a universal taboo, appears to be an occurrence that is neither unknown nor rare. Growing up with stepfathers, in contrast to biological fathers, greatly increases the likelihood of incestuous abuse as well as the seriousness of it. The chapter includes

an examination of various explanations for this widespread taboo on sexual relationships between selected family members.

8. The chapter concludes with an examination of postmarital coitus. Among the formerly married, nearly all the men and the large majority of the women engage in coitus at some time. Major differences in the incidence of coitus exist between divorced and widowed women.

9. This chapter could fit within the framework of Part V, as well as serve as the concluding chapter to this section on sexual norms and relationships. It examined sexual relationships in marital contexts by reviewing key findings, discussing sexual adjustment and inadequacies in marriage, and concluding with extramarital, incest, and postmarital coitus. All are significant to marital interaction. Continuing within a premarital and marital life-cycle sequence, attention is directed in the following chapter to marital structures and processes.

KEY TERMS AND TOPICS

DISCUSSION QUESTIONS

1. Examine the two volumes of the Kinsey studies. What do you perceive to be their most significant findings? To what extent are their findings influenced by their samples, their methods of gathering data, and their interpretation of the data? How applicable are these findings today?

2. In what ways is marital coitus likely to be influenced by employment of husband and/or wife, income, religion, number and/or presence of children, age, and other factors? How do you explain changes that have taken place?

3. Discuss the implications and seriousness of marital rape. What types of control, punishments, laws, programs, and the like might be effective in dealing with this issue?

4. What, in your estimation, constitutes "good" sexual adjustment in marriage? Is it possible to have "good" sexual adjustment and "poor" marital adjustment? Is the opposite possible?

5. Describe husband-wife and male-female differences in sexual response through the life cycle. How are these differences explained?

6. Review five leading sex manuals. To what extent are social norms and values discussed? In what ways might they be helpful, harmful, or both to marital sexual relationships?

7. Make a list of sexual difficulties in marriage. Are some of them unsolvable? What factors are most likely to lead to these difficulties? What factors are significant in resolving them?

8. Examine the significance of concepts such as the spectator role or sexual value system.

9. What are the arguments for and against extramarital sex, swinging, or mate swapping? How can they be disruptive to or improve marriage?

10. Which explanations for the universality of the incest taboo can you accept? Are there possible explanations other than those given in the chapter? What are they?

11. In what ways is postmarital coitus different from marital or premarital coitus? In what ways would you expect similarities or differences between the sexual behavior and activity of the divorced versus the widowed?

12. Read the insert on "The New Other Woman." Why do these "other woman" select married men? What are the pros and cons of such relationships?

FURTHER READINGS

Atwater, Lynn. *The Extramarital Connection*. New York: Irvington Publishers. 1982. A sociological perspective of extramarital involvements based on intensive interviews with fifty women.

Cuber, John F., and Harroff, Peggy B. *The Significant Americans: A Study of Sexual Behavior Among the Affluent*. New York: Appleton-Century, 1965. A research study by the authors through interviews with 437 American men and women who were designated as elites, top influentials, or upper-middle-class.

Libby, Roger, W., and Whitehurst, Robert N. *Marriage and Alternatives: Exploring Intimate Relationships*. Glenview, Ill.: Scott, Foresman, 1977. Like their earlier book, *Renovating Marriage*, this book breaks from tradition in looking at alternatives to marriage for sexual and intimate relationships.

Mahoney, E. R. *Human Sexuality*. New York: McGraw-Hill, 1983. A multidisciplinary research-based textbook written by a professor of sociology.

Masters, William H.; Johnson, Virginia E.; and Kolodny, Robert C. *Human Sexuality*. Boston: Little, Brown, 1982. The founders and directors of the Masters and Johnson Institute in St. Louis and the authors of *Human Sexual Inadequacy* and *Human Sexual Response* provide an introductory textbook integrating the biological, psychosocial, and cultural elements of human sexuality.

Murdock, George P. *Social Structure*. New York: The Free Press, 1965. Although recommended reading for a general and excellent cross-cultural perspective on family structure, the book also extensively analyzes sexual patterns and incest.

Offir, Carole Wade. *Human Sexuality*. New York: Harcourt Brace Jovanovich, 1982. A textbook on human sexuality, covering a wide range of topics including the psychobiology of sex, sexual behavior and relationships, sexuality across the life span, and sex as a social and medical issue.

Richardson, Laurel. *The New Other Woman: Contemporary Single Women in Affairs with Married Men*. New York: The Free Press, 1985. The author dispels old stereotypes of the "other woman" based on interviews with single women who were involved in relationships with married men.

Russell, Diana E. H. *Rape in Marriage*. New York: Macmillan, 1982. A study involving more than 900 interviews of wives in San Francisco to discover the incidence and circumstances surrounding rape by husbands.

Schulz, David A. *Human Sexuality*. Englewood Cliffs, N.J.: Prentice-Hall, 2nd ed., 1984. A textbook covering sexuality issues from many perspectives: cross-culturally, gender roles, love, commitment, fantasy, anatomy, problems, disease, the law and others.

Shepher, Joseph. *Incest: A Biosocial View*. New York: Academic Press, 1983. Combining biological theory and ethnographic data, the author presents a genetic and mathematical model of a sociobiological theory of incest.

Weg, Ruth B., ed. *Sexuality in the Later Years: Roles and Behavior*. New York: Academic Press, 1983. A multidimensional exploration of human sexuality and sensuality among the elderly and the widespread destructive stereotypes associated with this age group.

V

MARITAL AND FAMILY RELATIONSHIPS: PATTERNS OF INTERACTION THROUGHOUT THE LIFE CYCLE

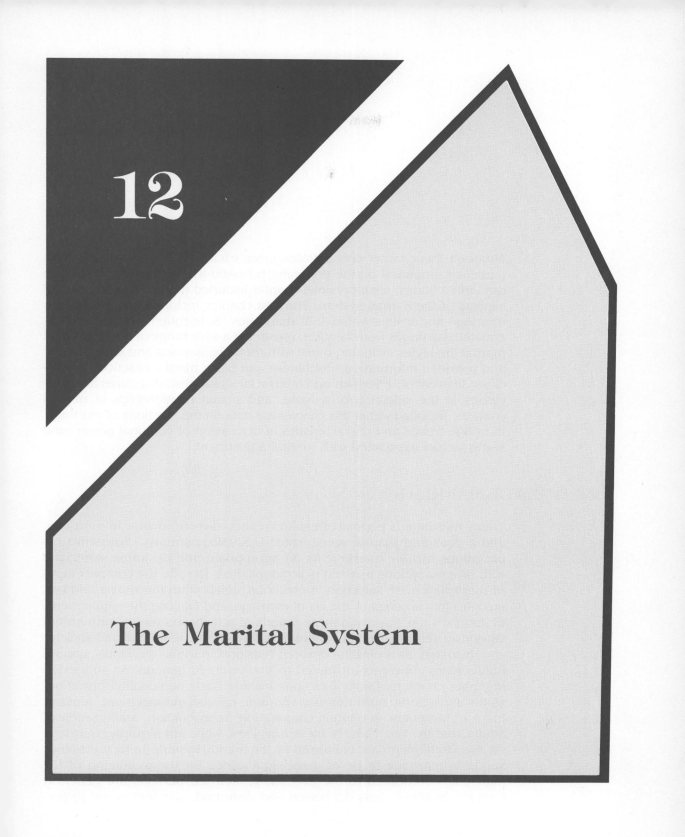

12

The Marital System

Although this chapter concentrates more exclusively on marriages, with particular emphasis on the dominant husband-wife patterns and roles in the United States, each previous chapter included discussions of selected aspects of the marital system. The first chapter included census data on marriage and issues within U.S. marriages. Subsequent chapters differentiated marriages from families; presented a wide range of nontraditional marital life-styles including those with multiple spouses and dual careers; and provided information on Chinese and black marital practices, social-class differences, interfaith and interracial situations, structures and processes in the selection of a mate, and sexual relationships in marital contexts. Included within this chapter are data on the functions of marriage, marriage trends and characteristics, a discussion of conjugal power, and some factors associated with marital adjustment.

FUNCTIONS OF MARRIAGE

Today marriage is popular. Despite conflict, divorce, delays in marrying, and a changing marital scene, most U.S. citizens marry. Normative expectations include marriage as an appropriate and desirable state, and with rare exceptions this end is accomplished. Despite the complex tasks of mastering mate selection interactions, celebrating the rituals and ceremonies that accompany the act of marriage, and fulfilling the requirements of domestic life, few avoid these rounds of activity and remain unmarried. Obviously, marriage fulfills various functions for the individual and society.

Marriage, as an institutionalized relationship within the family system, fulfills many functions attributed to the family in general. As suggested in earlier chapters, family functions include basic personality formation, status ascriptions, nurturant socialization, tension management, replacement of members, economic cooperation, reproduction, stabilization of adults, and the like. Many of these functions, while not requiring marriage for their fulfillment, are enhanced by the marital system. In fact, evidence suggests marriage to be of great significance for the well-being of the individual. Compared to the unmarried, married persons are generally happier, healthier, less depressed and disturbed, and less prone to pre-

Marriage vows: before and after

He married her because among other things, her hair looked so beautiful.

He divorced her because she spent so much time fixing her hair.

She married him because his muscles rippled so much when he swam.

She divorced him because he spent more time in the bedroom doing sitting-up exercises than anything else.

He married her because she was such an adept conversationalist, never at a loss for a word.

He divorced her because she never got off the telephone.

She married him because he loved to take her dancing.

She divorced him because he was "tired" most of the time.

He married her because she was so "vivacious."

He divorced her because she was too restless.

She married him because he could support her in lavish style.

She divorced him because he had too firm a hold on the purse-strings.

He married her because their families shared a common background.

He divorced her because her family kept interfering in their affairs.

She married him because he had a robust masculine appetite and appreciated her cooking.

She divorced him because he never wanted to take her out to eat.

He married her because she was quick, neat, and intelligent.

He divorced her because she had absolutely no patience with the children, who were sometimes slow, slovenly, and stupid.

She married him because he was a "real sport."

She divorced him because he refused to give up the sporting life.

He married her because they shared the same intellectual and political beliefs.

He divorced her because she wasn't interested in anything but the house and the kids.

She married him because he was so courteous and attentive in all the little things that matter so to a woman.

She divorced him because he was so punctilious about little things, and so oblivious to important things.

He married her because all the other men were so impressed with her magnificent figure.

He divorced her, after the third child, because she had "let herself go."

Source: Sidney Harris, copyright Publishers-Hall Syndicate.

mature death, with some evidence suggesting the differences in well-being between unmarried and married persons are becoming greater rather than smaller.[1] Weingarten as well, in a national study comparing

1. Ruut Veenhoven, "The Growing Impact of Marriage," *Social Indicators Research* 12 (January 1983): 49–63; Ronald C. Kessler and Marilyn Essex, "Marital Status and Depression:

first married, currently divorced, and remarried adults found the currently divorced less exuberant about life than either of the married groups.[2] Recognizing that neither marriage nor remarriages are panaceas that wipe away all traces of distress or chronic pain, "couplehood" seems to provide some benefits that make adjustment to today's world substantially easier.

The functions of marriage differ as the structure of marriage differs. For example, where marriage is specifically an extension of the kin and extended-family system, then procreation, passing on the family name, and continuation of property become a basic function. Thus, to not have a child or, more specifically, to not have a male child, is sufficient reason to replace the present wife or add a new wife. In the United States, while most children are born of a married couple and while most married couples want children, to not have children is rarely a sufficient reason to remarry. Nor is the undesirability or impossibility of having a child, as with a career-oriented woman, sterile persons, or older women, a sufficient reason for not marrying. Thus why marriage?

The chapter on mate selection processes mentioned that, for arranged marriages, important factors include the bride's price, the reputation of the potential spouse's kin group, levirate and sororate arrangements, and traditions of prescribed marriage arrangements. Where marriage is based on "free choice," individualistic forces are accorded greater significance. Thus in the United States, marriage has many functions and involves many positive as well as negative personal factors: establishment of a family of one's own, children, companionship, happiness, love, ego support, economic security, an approved sexual outlet, affection, escape, elimination of loneliness, pregnancy, ad infinitum. The greater the extent to which the perceived needs of marriage are met, and the fewer the alternatives in the replacement of the unmet needs, the greater the likelihood of marriage and the continuation of that marriage. Why marriage? At a personal level, any perceived reason may explain marriage; but at a social level, all societies sanction certain reasons and renounce others. Thus personal factors operate within the confines of social boundaries; the functions that marriage performs are determined and qualified by the social and cultural context.

The social and cultural context of the United States is currently witnessing a variety of marital forms other than the traditional monogamous, sexually exclusive marriage pattern for the fulfillment of individuals' per-

---

The Importance of Coping Resources," *Social Forces* 61 (December 1982): 484–507; and Norval D. Glenn and Charles N. Weaver, "The Contribution of Marital Happiness to Global Happiness," *Journal of Marriage and the Family* 43 (February 1981): 161–168.

2. Helen R. Weingarten, "Marital Status and Well-Being: A National Study Comparing First-Married, Currently Married, Currently Divorced, and Remarried Adults," *Journal of Marriage and the Family* 47 (August 1985): 653–662.

ceived needs. A familiar pattern is sequential or *serial monogamy*: the marriage, divorce, remarriage, divorce pattern. Another familiar pattern is *adultery*, the maintenance of the marriage with a secret satisfaction of sexual and emotional needs outside the conjugal relationship. *Nonmarital cohabitation*, a relatively common practice today, involves a male and a female sharing a common residence. These and other nontraditional patterns have been examined previously. In the United States, as around the world, marriage or some alternative exists to fulfill basic functions generally attributed to the husband-wife relationship.

MARRIAGE TRENDS AND CHARACTERISTICS

In 1985, of the 182.3 million persons age 15 and over in the United States, 108 million or 59.3 percent of them were married. As can be seen in Figure 12–1, the percentages married differed considerably by sex, race, and Spanish origin. Nearly 64 percent of white males, but less than 40 percent of black females age 15 and over, were married. One study found marital status to be perceived more favorably and rated as more secure than the unmarried.[3] Married persons were seen as happier than either divorced or widowed and more reliable than the never-married.

That marriage is viewed favorably may help us understand why 2.4 million marriages occurred in 1985, a marriage rate (number of marriages per 1,000 population) of 10.2.[4] This rate has varied widely over the past fifty years (*see* Figure 12–2). It has fluctuated under the influence of wars, changing economic conditions, sex ratio of the marriageable population, and the number of potential brides and grooms present in the general population. Characteristically, the marriage rate has risen at the outset of a major war, declined during the course of the conflict, and increased sharply in the immediate postwar years. This was the experience for World Wars I and II and was probably true during the Civil War. Economic recessions and depressions generally have had an inhibiting effect on marriages, as have shifts in the age distribution of the population resulting in a smaller proportion of the population at the young adult ages.

In 1932, at the depth of the Depression, the rate plunged to a low of 7.9, probably unprecedented in this country except perhaps during the Civil War. The influence of World War II is unparalleled in the history of marriage rates in the United States. Just before and immediately after the United States' entry into the war, the rate rose sharply as young men

3. Claire Etaugh and Joann Malstrom, "The Effect of Marital Status on Person Perception," *Journal of Marriage and the Family* 43 (November 1981): 801–805.

4. U.S. Bureau of the Census, *Statistical Abstract of the United States, 1987*, 107th ed. (Washington, D.C.: U.S. Government Printing Office, 1987), no. 80, p. 58.

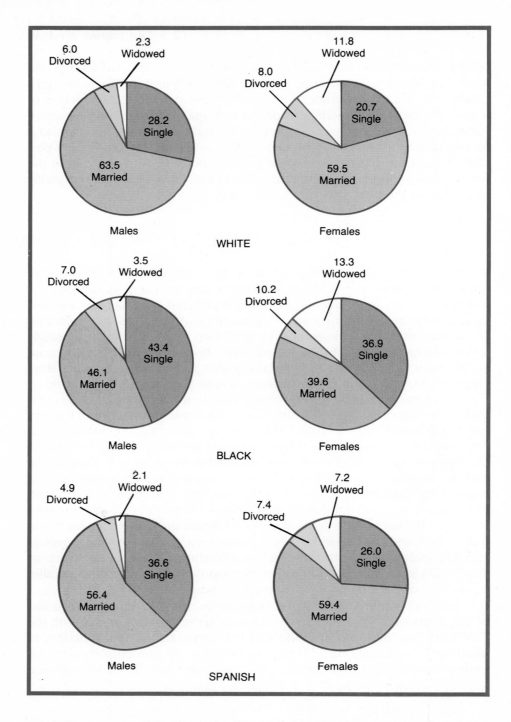

FIGURE 12–1
Marital status of persons fifteen years old and over by sex, race, and Spanish origin, 1985. All figures represent percentages (*Source:* U.S. Bureau of the Census, *Current Population Reports,* Series P-20, no. 410, "Marital Status and Living Arrangements: March 1985" [Washington, D.C.: U.S. Government Printing Office, 1986], Table 1, pp. 18–19).

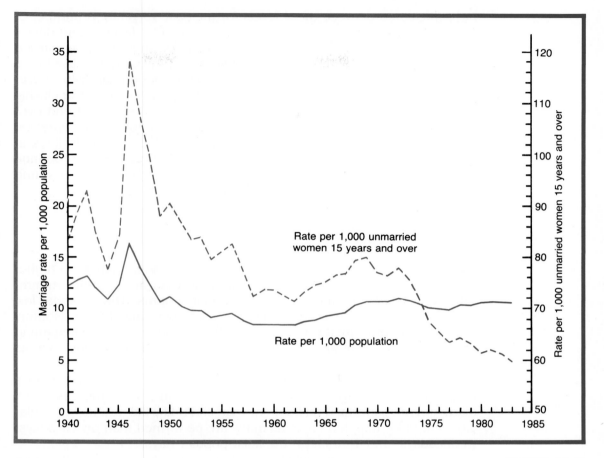

FIGURE 12–2

Marriage rates: United States, 1940–1983. (*Source:* National Center for Health Statistics, "Advance Report of Final Marriage Statistics, 1983," *Monthly Vital Statistics Reports,* vol. 35, no. 1 [Public Health Service, Hyattsville, MD., May 2, 1986], Figure 1, p. 2.)

sought to avail themselves of the deferred status granted to married men or simply wanted to marry before going overseas. The end of the war and the return of millions of men to civilian life precipitated an upsurge in marriages. In 1946 the marriage rate reached 16.4, an unprecedented and to date unsurpassed peak. By 1949 the rate had returned to the pre–World War II level, dropping as rapidly as it had climbed. This marked the end of twenty years of the most frequent and pronounced fluctuations in the history of United States marriage rates.

Dropping back to rates below 9.0 in the late 1950s, the marriage rates increased through the 1960s to a level of between 10 and 11 and have fluctuated between these levels for the past 15 years. A number of recent changes in family life have been attributed to declines and delays in marriage. These include increases in sexuality among the unmarried and an accompanied increase in out-of-wedlock births, an increase in the independence of young people, nonmarital cohabitation, labor-force participation of women, a reduction in fertility, a temporary shortage of eligible males in the marriage market (a marriage squeeze), and the trend over the past few decades of increase in divorce.[5] Although these represent dramatic changes from the past that could suggest further declines in marriage, strong evidence exists that people in the United States continue to value marriage. Marriage is viewed as important among both young and old and remains a popular choice for most U.S. citizens.

Variations in marriage rates

In the United States, marriages have a distinct *seasonal* pattern: a higher number of marriages typically occur in June than in any other month, with August and July the next most popular months. The seasonal low for marriage tends to occur in January, February, and March. Monthly variations are also greatly affected by holidays, the ending and beginning of school years, climatic conditions, and religious holy periods such as Lent.

Marriages also vary widely by *day* of the week. Over half of all marriages take place on Saturday (55 percent). More than three times as many marriages are performed on Saturday than on Friday, the next most popular day, and more than ten times as many are performed than on Tuesdays, Wednesdays, and Thursdays, the least popular days.

Marriage rates in the United States consistently show distinct differences by *geographic regions*. The western states have the highest rate, followed closely by the South. The northeastern region has the lowest rates. Within regions, however, there is wide variation among states, particularly in the West. In 1984, rates for the western states ranged from 117.9 in Nevada to less than 8 per 1,000 in Pennsylvania and West Virginia. Other states with a rate of marriage at 8.4 per 1,000 population or lower included Rhode Island, Connecticut, New Jersey, Nebraska, and Oregon.[6]

Marriages are reported by, and subject to laws of, the state where the ceremony is performed. Lenient marriage laws attract couples from

5. Willard L. Rodgers and Arland Thornton, "Changing Patterns of First Marriage in the United States," *Demography* 22 (May 1985): 265–279; Thomas J. Espenshade, "Marriage Trends in America: Estimates, Implications, and Underlying Causes," *Population and Development Review* 11 (June 1985): 193–245.

6. *Statistical Abstract of the United States: 1987*, no. 124, p. 81.

Marital adjustment, an abstract concept, includes dimensions of happiness, affectional expression, enjoying common activities, and sharing similar expectations. (Photo: © Alan Carey/The Image Works)

out of state, particularly if the adjoining states have more restrictive laws. A high marriage rate for a state is generally associated with a high proportion of marriages in which both bride and groom live outside the state. The major attractions are laws that do not require a waiting period between the date of application for a license and issuance of the license or between license issuance and the ceremony, or laws that do not require a medical examination. These factors have a two-pronged effect—they lower the rates of the states from which the couples are drawn and raise the rates of the states to which they are attracted.

POWER IN CONJUGAL RELATIONSHIPS

One important aspect of the marital system is the power positions of husband and wife—as individuals and in relation to each other. There appears to be considerable agreement that power refers to the ability to influence others and affect their behavior. Conjugal power would refer to the ability of the husband and wife to influence each other. It is often measured by determining who makes certain decisions or who performs certain tasks.

Power involves the crucial dimensions of authority and influence. Social norms determine who has *authority*, in that the culture designates the positions that have the "legitimate" and prescribed power (authority). In some societies, authority is invested in the husband; in others, it rests with the oldest male in extended-family situations, and in some it goes to the mother-in-law. Other family members can *influence*, that is exert pressure upon, the person with authority. The president of the United States has the prescribed authority to make a wide range of decisions, but he can be influenced by the press, the public, or his own family, none of whom are given the authority to make political decisions. The husband may have authority over his wife and children, but he is greatly influenced by them.

Characteristics of conjugal power

Mary Rogers makes several key points about power.[7] First, she argues that power is a capacity or an ability to influence others, *not* the exercise of that ability. Ability does not denote social action. The perceived or real ability to influence can affect outcomes even when the exercise of that ability is not undertaken. Second, an individual's power must be viewed relative to specific social systems and the positions (statuses) a person occupies within a given social system. Note that power is not inherent within a person. Power must be viewed in dynamic terms; one must note that the power of individuals to influence others is linked to the social statuses and social roles they occupy and perform within special social systems. Third, if power is an ability to influence others, resources are the primary determinants of that ability. A *resource* is "any attribute, circumstance, or possession that increases the ability of its holder to influence a person or group."[8] Attributes might include age, sex, race, health, and level of energy; circumstances might include location, friendships or acquaintances, flexibility, or access to information; possessions might include money, land,[9] property, goods, and so on. The contention is that persons with greater resources have an advantage over those without those resources. In a social-exchange perspective, they can bargain with others from a position of strength.

Rebecca Warner and others make a strong case for broadening the conceptualization of resources to include selected features of family and

7. Mary F. Rogers, "Instrumental and Infra-Resources: The Base of Power," *American Journal of Sociology* 79 (May 1974): 1418–1433.

8. Ibid., p. 1425.

9. Support for control over land as a source of women's power can be seen in Sonya Salamon and Ann Mackey Keim, "Land Ownership and Women's Power in a Midwestern Farming Community," *Journal of Marriage and the Family* 41 (February 1979): 109–119.

kinship structures (family organization).[10] It was argued, for example, that wives will have more power in marriages in societies with nuclear rather than extended family structures and in societies with matrilateral rather than patrilateral customs of residence and descent. Ethnographic data on over one hundred nonindustrial societies provided support for these propositions, highlighting the fact that organizational resources may be as important as material and personal resources in understanding conjugal power.

Processes of conjugal power

The processes in the use of power within marriage are dimensions often overlooked. Since marriage involves two or more people, and since social power involves the ability of one person to influence others, it becomes necessary to ask questions that involve persons in relation to each other. For someone to influence, someone else must be influenced. And in being influenced, how does this affect the use of power by the influencer? Jetse Sprey indicates that in any reciprocal power relationship, compliance itself must be considered a potential source of influence.[11] If there is total compliance by one spouse to the demands of the other, such an event must be seen as part of a reciprocal exchange of power from which it is not logically possible to determine who is the more powerful. For example:

> A wife may threaten her husband with divorce unless he stops his heavy drinking. If we assume that she has the ability to carry out her threat, the fact remains that it is up to her spouse to accept or reject her demand. By refusing to comply, he will force her to either carry out the threat or to retreat. In both instances her conduct would be influenced by his. If he decides to stop his drinking she indeed did influence his conduct, but his decision to comply in turn determines her course of action. There is an additional aspect to this case: in a marriage, a threat to divorce affects *both* its sender and its receiver, since each must face the consequences if it is carried out. Both spouses presumably are aware of this and can be expected to perceive a threat of this nature within this shared context. To interpret, therefore, the outcome of the above confrontation as a mere "win" for the wife, and to code it as an indication of her "power," seems rather unrealistic, to put it mildly.[12]

---

10. Rebecca L. Warner, Gary R. Lee, and Janet Lee, "Social Organization, Spousal Resources, and Marital Power: A Cross-Cultural Study," *Journal of Marriage and the Family* 48 (February 1986): 121–128.

11. Jetse Sprey, "Family Power and Process: Toward a Conceptual Integration," in *Power in Families*, ed. by Ronald E. Cromwell and David H. Olson (New York: Wiley, 1975).

12. Ibid., p. 68.

This illustration and others that could be given clearly demonstrate the complexity of understanding power processes. The use of power is often indirect; the outcome may have no "winner" or finality; and the nature of the interaction will vary from one group and system to another and from one social context to another.

Conjugal power and decision making

One of the ways in which conjugal power has traditionally been measured is to determine which spouse makes the major decisions and how the husband and wife decision-making patterns vary by area of concern. One of the most widely cited studies and one that served as a major stimulant to many studies that followed was done by Robert Blood and Donald Wolfe.[13] In an attempt to measure the balance of power between husbands and wives, they interviewed 731 city wives in metropolitan Detroit.

They selected eight situations that they felt would include both masculine as well as feminine decisions about the family as a whole. These included: (1) what job the husband should take, (2) what kind of car to get, (3) whether or not to buy life insurance, (4) where to go on a vacation, (5) what house or apartment to take, (6) whether or not the wife should go to work or quit work, (7) what doctor to have when someone is sick, (8) and how much money the family can afford to spend per week on food.

The wives' answers to the eight situations revealed that two decisions were primarily the husband's province (his job and car), two were primarily the wife's province (her work and food), while all the others were joint decisions in the sense of having more "same" responses than anything else. Even the wife's working turned out to be quite a middling decision from the standpoint of the mean score, leaving only the food expenditures predominantly to the wife.

Even though published more than twenty-five years ago, perhaps the responses of the wives to these eight decision-making questions are not surprising even today. Both legally and socially in the United States, it is expected that the male is responsible for the economic support of his wife and children. His job and his work are his primary exertions in both time and energy. Factors related to automobiles might also be expected to be primarily the concern of the husband; although most wives in our society have operators' licenses, when the husband and wife travel together it is likely to be the husband who does the driving. Traditionally, it has also been the husband who cares for repairs and upkeep of the automobile.

---

13. Robert O. Blood, Jr. and Donald M. Wolfe, *Husbands and Wives: The Dynamics of Married Living* (Glencoe, Ill.: The Free Press, 1960): 20.

Whether or not to buy life insurance, where to go on a vacation, and what house or apartment to take are decisions that are more likely to be shared equally by husband and wife than by either spouse separately. It could be assumed that both have equal competencies in these choices. Furthermore, these areas affect both partners more equally than do the other decision-making areas.

Blood and Wolfe's theoretical explanation of why husbands make certain decisions, wives make others, and there is joint involvement in still others is based on resource availability. That is, the source of authority and power lies in the comparative resources each spouse has available. The balance of power is weighted toward the partner who has the greater resources as perceived by the spouse.

Joint decision-making, sharing of marital power, perceptions of both self and spouse as doing a fair share of family work, and a feeling of equity appear to be positively related to marital satisfaction and negatively related to depression.[14] Findings such as these lend support to social exchange theories and equity models that suggest personal happiness and the highest levels of satisfaction with a marriage occur in the context of each partner defining their spouse as contributing a fair share to housework and child care and perceiving equity in the exchange. Evidence shows less depression among spouses who share marital power. For many married persons, particularly wives, an inequitable balance of marital power is a serious problem.

Differences in wife-husband responses

Considerable criticism has been made of studies of decision making and task performance that elicit responses from wives only (such as the Blood and Wolfe study). Evidence suggests that when husbands respond, they report less power for themselves than their wives claim for them, that wives tend to overestimate the power of their husbands, and that discrepancies exist in the reports of husbands and wives about their respective roles. Interviews with nearly 500 married couples in the midwest, for example, revealed that spouses accurately perceive their partner's expectations about half the time. Also, spouses think they carry more responsibility for household duties than their partners think they do.[15] In spite of twenty

14. Sara Yogev and Jeanne Brett, "Perceptions of the Division of Housework and Child Care and Marital Satisfaction," *Journal of Marriage and the Family* 47 (August 1985): 609–618; John Mirowsky, "Depression and Marital Power: An Equity Model," *American Sociological Review* 91 (November 1985): 557–589; and Bernard Davidson, "A Test of Equity Theory for Marital Adjustment," *Social Psychology Quarterly* 47 (1984): 36–42.

15. Dana V. Hiller and William W. Philliber, "The Division of Labor in Contemporary Marriages: Expectations, Perceptions, and Performance," *Social Problems* 33 (February 1986): 191–201.

years of repeated warnings about husband-wife discrepancies and "wife only" research, recent data report a continued reliance on these methods.[16]

Susan Douglas and Yoram Wind explain incongruency in husband-wife responses in two ways.[17] First, they suggest that an important source of discrepancy is the measurement instrument. Incongruence frequently appears to be associated with questions that may be open to differing interpretations. Some of the measures used suffer from too great a reliance on recall concerning decisions or acts which took place sometime in the past or which involved multiple decisions and acts. Second, they suggest that most families do not have clearcut, consistent patterns of authority across different areas, and that investigation of authority patterns should first be conducted relative to specific areas of family life, rather than developing overall authority measures aggregating across areas.

In addition to methodological concerns such as a one-spouse response, a number of writers have questioned the theoretical accuracy of explaining power based on resources. The theory of resources (in reality a proposition rather than a theory) contends that the more a partner controls resources of value to him- or herself and the mate, the greater his or her relative power. Here data show some mixed and inconsistent results. To understand why we will examine the theory of resources issue more intensely.

The theory of resources issue

Sprey makes several interesting points in regard to the "resource" argument.[18] One, he questions how individuals without authority or other resources manage to influence the family process. Housewives in patriarchal families and children in most households fit into this category. Second, he suggests that while the availability of a given resource will be a necessary condition for its use, the *absence* of a resource among other members may serve to limit, or even neutralize, its usefulness for those who have access to it. A child, for example, may use ignorance or lack of knowledge to counteract a parent's expertise in a given dispute. Third, he suggests that the distribution of resources is relative: defined and guided by the

---

16. Janet Bokemeier and Pamela Monroe, "Continued Reliance on One Respondent in Family Decision-Making Studies: A Content Analysis," *Journal of Marriage and the Family* 45 (August 1983): 645–652. Also, Szinovacz illustrates how couple data can be used as a methodological tool. *See* Maximiliane E. Szinovacz, "Using Couple Data as a Methodological Tool: The Case of Marital Violence," *Journal of Marriage and the Family* 45 (August 1983): 633–644.

17. Susan P. Douglas and Yoram Wind, "Examining Family Role and Authority Patterns: Two Methodological Issues," *Journal of Marriage and the Family* 40 (February 1978): 35–47.

18. Sprey, "Family Power and Process," pp. 76–78.

rules and role prescriptions of the system in question. Yet, while systems provide boundaries and rules, they do not determine outcomes. Outcomes, influenced by resources as related to the system involved, are a result of reciprocal influencing.

This "theory of resources," which I've been discussing, provides the conceptual core around which many of the later studies have been built. Several authors have stressed that power is not merely based on an individual's resources but on the comparative contributions (resources) and exchange processes of the husband and wife relative to each other. Hyman Rodman, for example, developed a "theory of resources in a cultural context" that takes into account the "theory of resources," the "theory of exchange," the comparative contributions of both husband and wife, and the cultural context in which the interaction occurs.[19] His argument is that one must not only be aware of resources in attempting to explain conjugal power, but must consider as well the cultural context in which decision making takes place. Thus, in certain societies it is the upper and middle status groups, the highest income, educational, and occupational groups, that first accept norms of marital egalitarianism. This in effect diminshes the impact of resources upon power in marital settings.

This idea not only had support in Greek and Yugoslavian families tested by Rodman, but among husbands in United States families as well. Mark Rank[20] found that increments in wives' resources correlated positively with wives' influence, supporting the theory of resources argument. But increments in husbands' resources correlated negatively with husbands' influence, thus not supporting the greater resources leading to greater influence and power argument. The explanation is that as husbands gain higher levels of income, education, or occupational prestige, they come in contact with sets of egalitarian norms regarding spousal relations. In brief, as both husbands and wives gain resources, women become less economically dependent upon their spouses while men become socialized into an egalitarian ethic. Wesley Burr et al., as well, found similar results among Mormons in Utah.[21] One clear finding was that normative structure was much more important than resources in accounting for the variance in power.

The power dimension of marriage is too complex and vast to cover

---

19. Hyman Rodman, "Marital Power in France, Greece, Yugoslavia, and the United States: A Cross-National Discussion," *Journal of Marriage and the Family* 29 (May 1967): 320–324; Hyman Rodman, "Marital Power and the Theory of Resources in Cultural Context," *Journal of Comparative Family Studies* 3 (Spring 1972): 50–69.

20. Mark R. Rank, "Determinants of Conjugal Influence in Wives' Employment Decision Making," *Journal of Marriage and the Family* 44 (August 1982): 591–604.

21. Wesley R. Burr, Louise Ahern, and Elmer M. Knowles, "An Empirical Test of Rodman's Theory of Resources in Cultural Context," *Journal of Marriage and the Family* 39 (August 1977): 505–514.

Meaningful conversation and marriage don't mix

At a party the other evening, people were discussing marriage. Marilyn turned and looked at her husband lovingly (as if she had just popped a Geritol tablet) and said, "Dan and I have a good marriage because we have meaningful conversations with one another."

I couldn't get it off my mind. On the way home I asked my husband, "Have we ever had a meaningful conversation?"

"I don't think so," he said.

"That's hard to believe," I persisted. "In 26 years we've never had one?"

"Not that I can remember."

We drove along in silence for about 20 minutes. Finally I said, "What is a meaningful conversation?"

"You're kidding! You actually don't know?"

"No. What is it?"

"Well," he said, "it's a conversation with meaning."

"Like the oil embargo and Paul Harvey?"

"Exactly."

"What about them?" I asked.

"What about who?"

"The oil embargo and Paul Harvey."

"It doesn't have to be a conversation about the oil embargo and Paul Harvey," he said. "It could be a discussion on anything in your daily schedule that is pertinent."

"I shaved my legs yesterday."

"That is not pertinent to anyone but you."

"Not really. I was using your razor."

"If you read the paper more," he said, "your conversations would be more stimulating."

"Okay, here's something meaningful I read just yesterday. In Naples— that's in Italy—police were searching for a woman who tried to cut off a man's nose with a pair of scissors while he was sleeping. What do you think of that?"

"That's not meaningful," he said.

A few minutes later I offered, "Suppose it was the American Embassy and the woman was a spy, and the nose belonged to Henry Kissinger which held secret documents about an oil embargo between Saudi Arabia and Paul Harvey?"

He drove in silence. "How long have Dan and Marilyn been married?"

"Twelve years," I said.

"They must pace their meaningful conversations."

Source: From *At Wit's End* by Erma Bombeck. Reproduced through the courtesy of Field Newspaper Syndicate.

adequately in a portion of one chapter. Interested persons may want to examine a review article on power provided by Gerald McDonald[22] and an overview of social processes and power in families by John Scanzoni.[23]

ADJUSTMENT IN MARRIAGE

Marital adjustment, happiness, satisfaction, or a number of variables that attest to the quality of a marriage may be the most frequently studied dimension in the marriage and family field.[24] Many attempts have been made to assess the quality of marital relationships, using such concepts as "marital adjustment," "success," "satisfaction," "stability," "happiness," "consensus," "cohesion," "adaptation," "integration," "role strain," and the like. Sometimes these terms are used interchangeably; other times each denotes something different. Sometimes the terms are used in a psychological sense, referring to the state of one of the marital partners; sometimes they are used in a social-psychological sense, referring to the state of the relationship; and sometimes they are used in a sociological sense, referring to the state of the group or system. In addition, there are times the terms are used to refer to the achievement of a goal and other times they are used to refer to a dynamic process of making changes. All the concepts emphasize a dimension that contrasts with maladjustment, dissatisfaction, instability, unhappiness, and so forth.

As indicated, irrespective of the label and the diversity of operational definitions, research on this issue attempts to assess marital quality. Johnson and others, while agreeing that marital quality is a useful umbrella term for summarizing the literature, question its utility as a research tool since it is so multidimensional.[25] It may include marital happiness, interaction, problems, disagreements, or instability, for example, all of which appear to be empirically distinct concepts. They cannot fruitfully be combined into a single measure, and as such, the concept of marital quality is not well-suited for research purposes. For our purposes, and perhaps due to the lack of any single concept that incorporates the multiple dimensions of quality, the general concept of adjustment will be used.

---

22. Gerald W. McDonald, "Family Power: The Assessment of a Decade of Theory and Research, 1970–1979," *Journal of Marriage and the Family* 42 (November 1980): 841–854.

23. John Scanzoni, "Social Processes and Power in Families," in *Contemporary Theories About the Family*, vol. 1, ed. by Wesley R. Burr et al. (New York: The Free Press, 1979), pp. 295–316.

24. Graham B. Spanier and Robert A. Lewis, "Marital Quality: A Review of the Seventies," *Journal of Marriage and the Family* 42 (November 1980): 825–839.

25. David R. Johnson, Lynn K. White, John N. Edwards, and Alan Booth, "Dimensions of Marital Quality: Toward Methodological and Conceptual Refinement," *Journal of Family Issues* 7 (March 1986): 31–49.

Marriages of high quality tend to include periods of privacy, separate from children or daily tasks, where couples can share thoughts or simply enjoy quiet times together. (Photo: © Harold M. Lambert Studio/E. P. Jones, Co.)

The adjustment of married mates is unlike any other human relationship. It may share many conditions of friendship groups, peer groups, work groups, or religious groups, but the husband-and-wife relationship differs. Marriage, involving two sexes in physical propinquity, is public and binding in nature. Being publicly sanctioned, marriage becomes more difficult to break. Being binding, the members must act as a unit and cooperation becomes essential. Every decision must take into account the desires and wishes of the spouse. These forces determine the level of adjustment, the nature of the interaction, and the degree of conflict.

A social conflict frame of reference, as described in the second chapter, includes the basic assumption that conflict is natural and inevitable in all human interaction. This is true of marital interaction as well. As couples interact, as they define and redefine their relationship to one another, and as they perform daily activities and fulfill role expectations, conflict is inevitable: conflict over one's work, over children, over criticism, over in-laws, over expenditures, over sex, and, as stressed in popular literature prior to the days of the pump, even matters such as how one squeezes the toothpaste. The "adjustment" of a marriage is not therefore based on whether conflict exists but on how conflict is managed in a way mutually satisfactory to the marital partners. Let us examine more fully the dimensions of marital adjustment and how it is measured.

Dimensions of marital adjustment

From the introductory statement it should be clear that **marital adjustment** is a varied concept that lacks a general consensus of definition. A general concept is likely to include a relative agreement by husband and wife on issues perceived to be important, sharing similar tasks and activities, and showing affection for one another. *Marital success*, as distinguished from marital adjustment, generally refers to the achievement of one or more goals: permanence, companionship, fulfilling the expectation of the community, and so forth. *Marital happiness*, distinguished from either adjustment or success, is an emotional response of an individual. Whereas happiness is an individual phenomenon, marital success and adjustment are dyadic achievements or states of the marriage.

Jessie Bernard states that the major dimensions of any human adjustment problem are: (1) the degree or extent or nature of the *differences* between or among the parties involved, (2) the degree or extent or nature of the *communication* between or among the parties, and (3) the *quality of the relationship* between or among them—that is, its positive or negative affectivity, friendliness, or hostility.[26]

Differences may be a matter of degree or they may be categorical: no flexibility, no leeway. Often matters of principle are categorical and thus the most difficult to resolve. Thus "we will never miss Mass" or "premarital sex is wrong," if taken categorically, do not permit flexibility in dealing with a mate or spouse who feels differently. On the other hand, differences of degree permit give-and-take, bargaining, and negotiation.

One specific example of how differences as well as the nature of those differences affect the quality of marriage involves sex-role attitudes.

---

26. Jessie Bernard, "The Adjustment of Married Mates," in *Handbook of Marriage and the Family*, ed. by Harold T. Christensen (Chicago: Rand McNally, 1964): 690.

What keeps a marriage going?

Jeanette Lauer and Robert Lauer reported in *Psychology Today* (June 1985) the responses of 351 couples who had been married for 15 years or more as to why their marriages had lasted. Men and women showed remarkable agreement on the keys to an enduring relationship. The top seven reasons that both men and women gave, in order of frequency were:

My spouse is my best friend.
I like my spouse as a person.
Marriage is a long-term commitment.
Marriage is sacred.
We agree on aims and goals.
My spouse has grown more interesting.
I want the relationship to succeed.

Other reasons, in differing order of importance for men and women, included things like laughing together; agreeing on a philosophy of life, on how and how often to show affection, and on their sex life; being proud of the spouse's achievements; discussing things calmly; and having a stimulating exchange of ideas.

These couples were not blind to each others' faults but believed their strengths more important than their deficiencies and the difficulties. Some said they would stay together no matter what, thus, divorce was not an option. The authors suggest that for most of these couples, "till death do us part" is not a binding clause but a gratifying reality.

Source: Jeanette Lauer and Robert Lauer, "Marriages Made to Last," *Psychology Today*, 19 (June 1985): 22–26.

A study done of military couples on sixteen bases in Europe and the United States examined sex role congruency and assessed how these attitudes were related to the marital relationships.[27] The marriages they found to have the lowest level of marital quality were those with a traditional husband and a modern wife. Interestingly, however, the modern husbands and traditional wives had a quality of marriage similar to marriages where both spouses were modern or both were traditional. Apparently nontraditional men who honor the rights of the wife to pursue independent interests and who jointly share household tasks find it acceptable to have wives who behave traditionally. The point is that differences as well as the nature and extent of those differences affects dyadic or interpersonal adjustment.

---

27. Gary Lee Bowen and Dennis K. Orthner, "Sex-Role Congruency and Marital Quality," *Journal of Marriage and the Family* 45 (February 1983): 223–230.

The second dimension, communication, of necessity involves inter-action. Few people would doubt or question the importance of communication to successful relationships of any kind. Yet communication is an extremely complex factor in marital relationships: it may be verbal or nonverbal, explicit or tacit, may clarify or mislead, draw relationships closer together or tear them apart. To not talk at all, to talk constantly, to order, to nag, to scold, to praise, may each be used to convey a certain message. One study found that communication styles that were relaxed, friendly, open, dramatic, and attentive were used by happily married couples.[28] Another study found the perceptions of marital communication on the part of both husband and wife to affect the kind (male or female) of sterilization procedure chosen.[29] Clearly, the style and nature of communication cannot be dismissed as insignificant to marital interaction, decision making, and adjustment.

The quality of the relationship is a third major dimension of adjustment. A friendly and loving spouse does not automatically mean adjustment, but it makes accommodation easier. Making sacrifices or changes in plans becomes easier when spouses have a love and genuine concern for one another. If the quality of the relationship is affection, results are far different than if it is hatred or hostility. These three dimensions—differences, communication, and quality of the relationship—are each important for understanding the process of adjustment.

Evaluating marital adjustment

The measurement of marital adjustment began in a serious way in the late 1920s.[30] Ten years later, comprehensive studies were conducted to determine personality factors associated with marital adjustment[31] and to predict marital success.[32] The latter study was the beginning of a much larger longitudinal study published more than a decade later.[33] Both studies

28. James M. Honeycutt, Charmaine Wilson, and Christine Parker, "Effects of Sex and Degrees of Happiness on Perceived Styles of Communicating In and Out of the Marital Relationship," *Journal of Marriage and the Family* 44 (May 1982): 395–406. *See also* James M. Honeycutt, "A Model of Marital Functioning Based on an Attraction Paradigm and Social Penetration Dimensions," *Journal of Marriage and the Family* 48 (August 1986): 651–667.

29. Frank D. Bean, Margaret Pruitt Clark, Gray Swicegood and Dorie Williams, "Husband-Wife Communication, Wife's Employment and the Decision for Male or Female Sterilization," *Journal of Marriage and the Family* 45 (May 1983): 395–403.

30. Gilbert V. Hamilton, *A Research in Marriage* (N.Y.: Albert and Charles Boni, 1929).

31. Lewis M. Terman, *Psychological Factors in Marital Happiness* (New York: McGraw-Hill, 1938).

32. Ernest W. Burgess and L. S. Cottrell, Jr., *Predicting Success or Failure in Marriage* (New York: Prentice-Hall, 1939).

33. Ernest W. Burgess and Paul Wallin, *Engagement and Marriage* (Philadelphia: J. B. Lippincott, 1953).

by Ernest Burgess on marriage and engagement measured adjustment by concentrating primarily on five areas: agreements and disagreements, common interests and activities, demonstration of affection and sharing of confidences, dissatisfaction with the marriage or engagement, and feelings of personal isolation and unhappiness.

The most widely used measurement of marital or interpersonal adjustment in the past decade is the Dyadic Adjustment Scale developed by Graham Spanier.[34] The scale consists of thirty-two items centering around four basic components: dyadic satisfaction, dyadic cohesion, dyadic consensus, and affectional expression. *Satisfaction* is measured by asking questions such as "Do you confide in your mate?" "Regret that you married?" and inquiring into the degree of happiness in the relationship. *Cohesion* focuses on whether the couple does things together and exchanges ideas.[35] *Consensus* measures the extent of agreement on issues such as finances, friends, religious matters, or household tasks. *Affectional expression* refers to the extent of agreement regarding demonstrations of affection, sex relations, and showing love.

Two researchers from Australia, in testing Spanier's Dyadic Adjustment Scale, suggest Spanier's thirty-two items are unnecessary and that, for quick screening purposes, one global self-rating item is sufficient.[36] This item presents seven degrees of happiness in the marital relationship, ranging from extremely unhappy to perfect; each partner is to indicate the one best describing their relationship. While many criteria have been used to evaluate the quality of relationships, perhaps Bernard's statement summarizes the issue. She claims:

> It is universally preferred that husbands and wives be fond of one another, that they live without quarreling and bickering, and that they find satisfaction in their relationship; but if a choice has to be made between this desideratum and stability, stability is given precedence in some societies, marital happiness and satisfaction in others.[37]

Bernard goes on to make a significant point for evaluating a marital

---

34. Graham B. Spanier, "Measuring Dyadic Adjustment: New Scales for Assessing the Quality of Marriage and Similar Dyads," *Journal of Marriage and the Family* 38 (February 1976): 15–28; and Graham B. Spanier and Linda Thompson, "A Confirmatory Analysis of the Dyadic Adjustment Scale," *Journal of Marriage and the Family* 44 (August 1982): 731–738.

35. A model of marital cohesion that is more inclusive than the one used here can be seen in Joe F. Pittman, Jr., Sharon Price-Bonham, and Patrick C. McKenny, "Marital Cohesion: A Path Model," *Journal of Marriage and the Family* 45 (August 1983): 521–531.

36. C. F. Sharpley and D. G. Cross, "A Psychometric Evaluation of the Spanier Dyadic Adjustment Scale," *Journal of Marriage and the Family* 44 (August 1982): 739–741.

37. Bernard, "The Adjustment of Marital Mates," p. 730.

relationship. She says a criterion should be set up in terms not of the best imaginable relationship but of the best possible one.[38] Thus a marriage may be said to be successful to the extent that it provides the highest satisfaction possible, not the highest imaginable. However unsatisfactory it may be in terms of happiness, it may still be judged better than the alternatives.

From this relativistic and exchange point of view, a marital relationship is successful (1) if the satisfaction is positive, that is, if the rewards to both partners are greater than the cost, and (2) if it is preferable to any other alternative. Two examples follow:

1. A and B do not like one another; they get on one another's nerves; the costs of remaining married are great in frustration and loneliness. But the rewards are great also; together they can afford a lovely home; they have high status in the community; the children are protected from scandal; the church approves of them; etc. This relationship is "successful" or "good," not because it is the best imaginable, but only because it is the best possible in the sense that the satisfactions are greater than the costs.

2. An example in which a marital relationship is sucessful only because it is better than any alternative would be the marriage of a dependent woman to, let us say, an alcoholic, in which the costs in misery were much greater than the rewards in security or status; but the spread between costs and satisfactions would be much greater if she left him. She would then be alone; she would not have the protection of the status of marriage; she would not even have the occasional sober companionship of a husband, etc. Bad as it is, therefore, her marriage seems better to her than any alternative she has.[39]

Udry suggests that the dimension of marital alternatives appears to be a better predictor of marital disruption than are measures of satisfaction.[40] Using longitudinal data of married couples from sixteen United States urban areas, he measured the respondents' perceptions of how much better or worse they would be without their present spouse and how easily that spouse could be replaced with one of comparable quality. Marital alternatives were found to correlate positively with resources of the self and negatively with the spouse's resource. In the ensuing year or two after these resources were measured, couples in which spouses were high in marital alternatives had several times the disruption rate of couples low in alternatives.

---

38. Ibid., p. 732.

39. Ibid., pp. 732–733.

40. J. Richard Udry, "Marital Alternatives and Marital Disruption," *Journal of Marriage and the Family* 43 (November 1981): 889–897.

Factors related to marital adjustment

Many statistical studies have been geared to find factors associated with marital adjustment that couldn't be explained by chance alone.[41] But often the findings quoted in texts and popular literature are those that support the opinions of the writer, and contradictory evidence is frequently discounted or ignored completely. Many writers are prone to a Pollyanna-like view of marriage characterized by a tendency to view consistently nonargumentative discussions, agreements, similarity, and the like as good or positive and conflict, anger, disagreements, or differences as negative. Conflict is generally viewed in the context of divorce and not as inevitable to a marriage. The literature traditionally has tended to lack research data on conflict and conflict management as crucial aspects of marriage (note conflict theory in Chapter 2).

In a chapter entitled "Marital Conflict as a Positive Force," Scanzoni argues that, in understanding the dynamics of husband-wife interaction, the first step is to divest ourselves of the notion that equilibrium or stability for all is a necessary ideal; the second step is to rid ourselves of the idea that conflict is ipso facto bad or unhealthy within marriage.[42] Conflict brings into the open the issues that one or the other partner considers unjust or inequitable. If disagreement is brought into the open, bargained over, and resolved in a way that is satisfactory to both partners, the outcome may be a new, more positive level of marital adjustment or solidarity. In contrast, failure to engage in conflict when injustice is perceived may result in a less beneficial, less rewarding situation for both marital partners and actually increase the chances for dissolution of the marriage.

Conflict, when viewed from this perspective of injustice, should not be confused with difficulties and discord brought about by factors such as economic hardship or facing unexpected income constraints. These too produce conflict and change in marital relations. Longitudinal data of couples who suffered income loss during the major depression (1929–1933) showed marked decline in marital quality and an increase in marital discord.[43] Men who lacked adaptive resources became more difficult to live with, more tense, irritable, and explosive. This behavior in itself produced conflict but appeared to be related less to interpersonal inequities than

41. For eighty-seven propositions dealing with marital quality and a list of more than one hundred fifty references on this subject, *see* Robert A. Lewis and Graham B. Spanier, "Theorizing About the Quality and Stability of Marriage" in *Contemporary Theories About the Family*, vol. 1, ed. by Wesley R. Burr et al. (New York: The Free Press, 1979): 268–294.

42. John Scanzoni, *Sexual Bargaining: Power Politics in the American Marriage*, 2d ed. (Chicago: The University of Chicago Press, 1982): 61–102.

43. Jeffrey K. Liker and Glen H. Elder, Jr., "Economic Hardship and Marital Relations in the 1930s," *American Sociological Review* 48 (June 1983): 343–359.

to disrupted patterns of social interaction and adverse psychological changes brought about by economic loss.

In general, by 1970 the following had all been delineated as variables correlating positively with marital happiness: higher occupational statuses, incomes, and educational levels for husbands; husband-wife similarities in socioeconomic status, age, and religion; affectional rewards, such as esteem for spouse, sexual enjoyment, companionship; and age at marriage.[44] However, later data raise serious questions about the "accuracy" of many of these "well-established" positive correlations with marital happiness.

Norval Glenn and Charles Weaver analyzed data from three national surveys to estimate the direct effects of each of ten independent variables on the reported marital happiness of white males and females aged 18 through 59.[45] Contrary to predictions based on theory and previous evidence, all of the estimated direct effects were weak or nil. For example, socioeconomic status, years of schooling, duration of marriage, age at marriage, church attendance, the presence of children, or wife's employment outside of the home all indicated little or no positive relationships to marital happiness. Many of these findings are inconsistent with textbook generalizations and earlier evidence. These differences may be due to differences in measurement, sampling, and methods of analysis but, as suggested by Glenn and Weaver, they may also reflect changes associated with the steep increase in marital instability since the early 1960s. In their words:

> If, as we suspect, the persons most likely to enter into unsuccessful marriages are generally the same people who are most likely to terminate unsatisfactory marriages, then even the strongest predictors of the success of marriages may bear little or no relationship to the happiness of individuals in intact marriages. In other words, to the extent that marital "mistakes" are quickly rectified by divorce, they may contribute little in the long run to marital unhappiness.[46]

What the previous paragraphs are suggesting is that the high divorce rates of the 1970s may have been the results or "solutions" to unhappiness in many marriages that would have remained intact in earlier decades. Getting divorced means these unsatisfactory marriages are no longer available to substantiate findings that were supported earlier. These statements do not mean that all unsatisfactory marriages terminate in divorce or that all satisfactory marriages remain intact. But marital quality, hap-

44. Mary W. Hicks and Marilyn Platt, "Marital Happiness and Stability: A Review of the Research in the Sixties," *Journal of Marriage and the Family* 32 (November 1970): 555.

45. Norval D. Glenn and Charles N. Weaver, "A Multivariate, Multisurvey Study of Marital Happiness," *Journal of Marriage and the Family* 40 (May 1978): 269–282.

46. Ibid., p. 280.

piness, satisfaction, and the like do seem to be highly interrelated. Let's see what happens when we examine marital satisfaction over the life cycle.

Marital satisfaction over the life cycle

The developmental concept as applied to adjustment in marriage has stimulated interest in changes over the life cycle. This approach, which deals with changes over time, has been used to test the issue of spouses' value similarity (which appeared to have a significant impact upon adjustment in the later years of marriage),[47] equity in marital roles (which appeared to increase for both husbands and wives over the life cycle),[48] variations in the life course of U.S. women (with blacks having greater variation than whites in factors such as having more children and having them sooner),[49] and perceived marital quality (which supported a curvilinear, U-shaped trend).[50]

What happens to marital satisfaction over the life cycle? Using an eight-stage family life cycle, Boyd Rollins and Harold Feldman traced the pattern of general and specific aspects of marital satisfaction.[51] Separate questionnaires were obtained from husbands and wives in 799 middle-class families. The results suggest that husbands and wives are influenced in different ways by stage or family life-cycle experiences. In general, family life-cycle experiences were associated with marital satisfaction more for wives than husbands. Especially in this subjective area of feelings about marital interaction, the dependent-children stages of the family life cycle were associated with negative evaluations of the marriage by the wife.

One pattern of marital satisfaction, as indicated by the percentage of individuals who reported their marriage was going well "all the time," can be seen in Figure 12–3. The pattern of satisfaction for wives steadily

47. James M. Medling and Michael McCarrey, "Marital Adjustment over Segments of the Family Life Cycle: The Issue of Spouses' Value Similarity," *Journal of Marriage and the Family* 43 (February 1981): 195–203.

48. Robert B. Schafer and Patricia M. Keith, "Equity in Marital Roles Across the Family Life Cycle," *Journal of Marriage and the Family* 43 (May 1981): 359–367.

49. Graham B. Spanier, "Marital Trajectories of American Women: Variations in the Life Course," *Journal of Marriage and the Family* 47 (November 1985): 993–1003.

50. Stephen A. Anderson, Candyce S. Russell, and Walter R. Schumm, "Perceived Marital Quality and Family Life-Cycle Categories: A Further Analysis," *Journal of Marriage and the Family* 45 (February 1983): 127–139; Walter R. Schumm and Margaret A. Bugaighis, "Marital Quality over the Marital Career: Alternative Explanations," *Journal of Marriage and the Family* 48 (February 1986): 165–168.

51. Boyd C. Rollins and Harold Feldman, "Marital Satisfaction Over the Family Life Cycle," *Journal of Marriage and the Family* 32 (February 1970): 20–28.

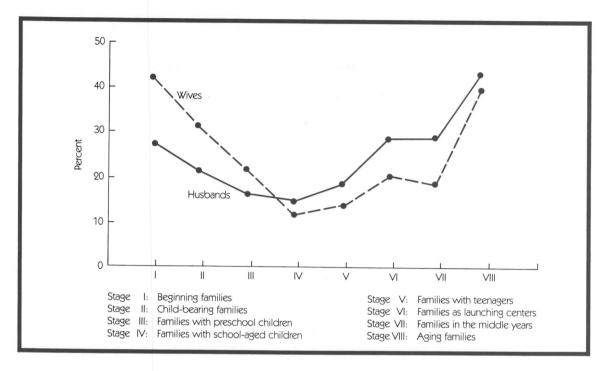

FIGURE 12–3
The percentage of individuals in Rollins and Feldman's study who reported that their marriage was going well "all the time." (*Source:* Boyd C. Rollins and Harold Feldman, "Marital Satisfaction Over the Family Life Cycle," *Journal of Marriage and the Family* 32 [February 1970]: 25.)

declined from the beginning (Stage I) to the school-age stage (Stage IV), then increased slightly, with a rapid increase from the empty-nest stage (Stage VII) to the retired stage (Stage VIII) of the family life cycle. For the husbands, there was considerably less satisfaction from the beginning, which declined slightly to the school-age stage (Stage IV), a slight increase to the empty-nest stage (Stage VI), a leveling off in the middle years (Stage VII), and then a rapid increase to the retired stage (Stage VIII). The amount of change for husbands, although statistically significant, was found by the authors to be less than that for the wives.

A major study of 1,140 families by Olson and McCubbin and their colleagues[52] attempted to discover how families managed their lives and what explains their relative success and failure. Central to their analysis was a seven-stage family life-cycle model (Stages II and III, the childbearing and preschool-children stages used in eight-stage cycles, were combined

---

52. David H. Olson, Hamilton I. McCubbin, and Associates, *Families: What Makes Them Work* (Beverly Hills: Sage Publications, 1983).

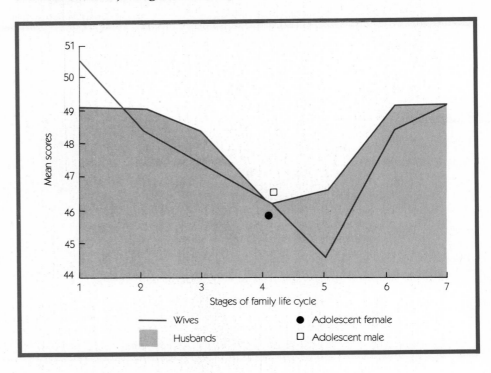

FIGURE 12—4
Family satisfaction. (*Source:* David H. Olson, Hamilton I. McCubbin, and
Associates, *Families: What Makes Them Work* [Beverly Hills: Sage Publications,
1983], Figure 10.5, p. 181 Copyright © 1983 by Sage Publications, Inc.
Reprinted by permission of Sage Publications, Inc.)

into a single stage). Their results confirm the findings of numerous other
studies, including the Rollins-Feldman one just described, indicating that
adults' satisfaction with marriage and family tends to have the shape of
a U-curve (*see* Figure 12—4).[53] There was a decline in satisfaction following
the birth of the first child through adolescence and a subsequent rise as
the children were launched from the nest. One explanation for the dramatic
increase in satisfaction found following the launching state is interpreted
as a result of the relaxation of sex roles between the parents. Women see
themselves as freer to look for work and organizational roles outside the
home, and men find themselves with decreased financial responsibility
and more ability to be passive and dependent.

Results of studies showing the effects of children on the marital
happiness of parents appear to be highly consistent. Overwhelming evidence

---

53. Canadian data as well show a curvilinear relationship. *See* Eugene Lupri and
James Frideres, "The Quality of Marriage and the Passage of Time: Marital Satisfaction Over
the Family Life Cycle," *Canadian Journal of Sociology* 6 (1981): 283–305.

suggests that in American society the presence of children in the family lowers marital happiness or satisfaction for the parents. This is true as well for subpopulations delineated on the basis of sex, race, level of education, religious preference, employment status, and other groupings. Glenn and McLanahan, in their own national surveys and reviewing many others, find no evidence for distinctly positive effects, and strong evidence for negative effects, of children on marital quality.[54] Given this highly consistent evidence, they suggest it is ironic that most U.S. citizens want to have and do have children and may serve as an example of the social function of ignorance. That is, people are motivated to perform the essential functions of reproduction and child care by the false belief that the psychological rewards of having children outweigh the costs or penalties. Perhaps there are perceptions of rewards, but the research evidence does not find them in terms of the effect of marital satisfaction.

The Olson-McCubbin study *Families*, as well as other research, provides some precautionary notes to the life-cycle data presented. First, while consistent variation from stage to stage is found, the amount of change may be neither as great nor as significant as is often implied in textbooks such as this. For example, adding data from those marriages that had dissolved would reduce the increase in satisfaction reported by most studies. Second, while male-female husband-wife differences are found in most studies, these differences tend to be overplayed. Often the sex differences were even less pronounced than were differences across the life cycle. Third, Spanier and Lewis, in reviewing studies in the 1970s of marital quality over the career of the marriage, argue that reliance on cross-sectional data for the study of trends can be very misleading.[55] That is, comparing groups who are at different stages in the life cycle (cross-sectional comparisons) rather than by following the same group over time through stages (longitudinal) does not adequately account for cohort effects, age-correlated effects, social desirability, or the tendency found in longitudinal studies to report as happy those marriages which survive over time.

A fourth precautionary note alluded to in the third point just described raises a question common to all marital adjustment research, that of marital conventionalization. Marital conventionalization is seen as the extent to which marriages are appraised in terms of social desirability, idealization

54. Norval D. Glenn and Sara McLanahan, "Children and Marital Happiness: A Further Specification of the Relationship," *Journal of Marriage and the Family* 44 (February 1982): 63–72. *See also* Jay Belsky, Mary E. Lang, and Michael Rovine, "Stability and Change in Marriage Across the Transition to Parenthood: A Second Study," *Journal of Marriage and the Family* 47 (November 1985): 855–865.

55. Graham B. Spanier and Robert A. Lewis, "Marital Quality: A Review of the Seventies," *Journal of Marriage and the Family* 42 (November 1980): 829.

of the spouse, and conservatism. Indicators of conservative orientations often include measures of traditional family morality, religious activity, premarital sexual abstinence, and general conservative ideology. Gary Hansen made an attempt to test the relationship between marital adjustment and conventionalization and concluded that conventionalization and adjustment measures each contaminate the measure of the other but not to the extent that they invalidate their use.[56] That is, marital adjustment measures are not so hopelessly contaminated by social desirability and conventionality that they must be cast aside.

Similar findings are suggested by Anderson et al., who tested whether the relationship between perceived marital quality and family life-cycle categories was an artifact of marital conventionalization.[57] They found it was not. Clearly, the curvilinear trend of the family life cycle over time could not be attributed to an artifact of marital conventionalization. Conventionalization was no more influential during later life-cycle stages than for any other stage.

Having examined selected aspects of the marital system, including trends, characteristics, power, and adjustment over the total life cycle, let us return to earlier stages and investigate the parental system. The next two chapters take a look at the transition to parenthood, including unwed parenthood and factors such as family size and birth order followed by parent-child interaction and socialization up to the launching stage.

SUMMARY

1. The marital system fulfills many functions that differ as the structure of marriage differs. Where marriage is an extension of the kin-group or the extended-family system, individualistic factors become relatively unimportant. In contrast, where marriage exists primarily for the individual and the conjugal relationship, the functions that marriage fulfills for the kin group decrease in importance. In either case, the functions that marriage performs will, to a large extent, be predictable on the basis of the social and cultural context that surrounds marriage.

2. In the United States, marriage rates have increased significantly since the end of the Civil War. These rates fluctuate under the influences of war, changing economic conditions, sex ratio of the marriageable population, and the number of potential brides and grooms present

---

56. Gary L. Hansen, ``Marital Adjustment and Conventionalization: A Reexamination,'' *Journal of Marriage and the Family* 43 (November 1981): 855–863.

57. Anderson, Russell, and Schumm, ``Perceived Marital Quality and Family Life-Cycle Categories,'' p. 134.

in the general population. The rate of marriage varies by season, day of the week, and region of the country.

3. An important and widely researched area of marriage deals with the power positions of husband and wife as individuals and in relation to each other. Power refers to the ability to influence others and to affect their behavior. Power, often measured by determining who makes certain decisions, includes the crucial dimensions of authority (legitimized power) and influence. The processes of family power focus on the interaction and dynamic aspects of decision making or conflict management. The outcomes of family power deal with the product, decision, or results of the process.

4. Studies of decision-making outcomes indicate that certain decisions are made primarily by the husband, others primarily by the wife, and others jointly. Who makes which decision has been widely explained by a theory of resources—the one with the information, education, income, and so forth makes the decision. This theory has been the topic of considerable debate and criticism but has led to a further development of resource exchange, resources in a cultural context, or a theory of comparative resources.

5. As with power, many attempts have been made to measure adjustment in marriage. Although lacking a general consensus of definition, adjustment generally includes relationships that are high in husband-wife agreement and high in the sharing of activities, tasks, and affection. Only infrequently has conflict been viewed as a basic aspect of marriage, the management of which is crucial in adjustment.

6. A number of writers suggest that marital alternatives may be a better predictor of marital disruption than are measures of adjustment or satisfaction.

7. When marital adjustment and satisfaction are examined throughout the life cycle, satisfaction appears to be highest at the beginning of marriage, with low points coming when families have school-aged children and teenagers. Studies indicate a curvilinear relationship throughout the life cycle—the beginning and the end of marriage are points of highest satisfaction.

8. Several notes of precaution are extended in dealing with the satisfaction—life-cycle data. First, differences, while existing, are often not as dramatic as often presented. Second, while sex differences exist as well, these too should not be overplayed. Third, reliance on cross-sectional data can produce misleading conclusions. Fourth, the issue of conventionalization must be recognized although studies suggest the issue is not serious enough to invalidate marital adjustment criteria.

9. Generally, it is the marital system that precedes and is basic to the parental system to which we direct our attention in the chapter that follows.

KEY TERMS AND TOPICS

DISCUSSION QUESTIONS

1. Why do people marry? What functions for the individual or society does marriage perform? Are any of these universal?

2. Check marriage rates in your state or community. How do they compare with other states and with national data? What variations occur by month and day of week?

3. Differentiate power, authority, and influence. How can each be determined and measured?

4. Make a list of ten decision-making areas. Take a brief survey among friends to determine whether their father, mother, or both jointly made these decisions. Are certain decisions consistently made by one or the other sex?

5. What is your theory of conjugal power? Can you think of instances where the person with the greatest resources does not have the most power? Are there instances where persons with very few resources still have a high degree of power?

6. Women's movements are striving for more power. What types of power issues relate to the role of wives, mothers, and marriage? What are some recommended changes and means of attaining these changes?

7. What is the significance of conflict in a marriage? Can it be beneficial?

8. Describe the nature of marital success, i.e., What is it? How can it be measured? Is success the same as adjustment, happiness, and compatibility?

9. Select two or three of the most "ideal" marriages of which you are aware. What factors tend to make those marriages "ideal"? Do the same features exist in each marriage?

10. What factors indicate conventionality and conformity? Is the conventional marriage the "adjusted" or "successful" marriage?

11. How would you explain the curvilinear relationship between marital adjustment and the family life cycle?

FURTHER READINGS

Aldous, Joan. "Family Interaction Patterns." *Annual Review of Sociology* 3 (1977): 105–135. An examination of family interaction patterns including power as exchange, conflict-management processes, the conceptualization of love, and family communication.

Bernard, Jessie. "The Adjustments of Married Mates." *Handbook of Marriage and the Family*. Edited by Harold T. Christensen. Chicago: Rand McNally, 1964, pp. 657–739. One of the most comprehensive discussions of the dimensions and models of marital adjustment available.

Blumstein, Philip, and Pepper Schwartz. *American Couples.* New York: Pocket Books, 1983. An intensive look at money, work, sex, and the lives of couples in the United States: married, cohabitors, gays, and lesbians.

Galvin, Kathleen M., and Brommel, Bernard J. *Family Communication: Cohesion and Change.* Glenview, Ill.: Scott, Foresman, 1982. A family textbook using a communication perspective in dealing with the development of relationships, intimacy, roles, power, decision making, and conflict.

Hendrick, Clyde, and Hendrick, Susan. *Liking, Loving, and Relating.* Monterey, Cal.: Brooks/Cole, 1983. A paperback that examines a range of issues dealing with relationships: attraction, affiliation, loving, marriage, and selected issues in contemporary relationships.

Hunt, Richard A., and Rydman, Edward J. *Creative Marriage.* 2d ed. Boston: Allyn and Bacon, 1979. A look at the marital dyad in terms of their communicating, personal roots, opportunities, and difficulties.

Kammeyer, Kenneth C. W., ed. *Confronting the Issues: Sex Roles, Marriage, and the Family.* 2d ed. Boston: Allyn and Bacon, 1981. A collection of readings built around controversies within marriage and the family. Section I deals with attacks, defenses, and alternatives to marriage as an institution.

Lewis, Robert A., and Spanier, Graham, B. "Theorizing About the Quality and Stability of Marriage." *Contemporary Theories About the Family.* Vol. 1. Edited by Wesley R. Burr et al. New York: The Free Press, 1979, pp. 268–294. An attempt to explain why some marriages fail and others do not, with the ultimate goal to build a partial theory of marital stability.

Olson, David H., and McCubbin, Hamilton, I. *Families: What Makes Them Work.* Beverly Hills: Sage Publications, 1983. More than 1,100 couples and nearly 2,700 individuals in intact marriages and families from 31 states were studied at seven stages of the family life cycle on five dimensions: family types, family resources, family stress and changes, family coping, and family satisfaction.

Scanzoni, John. *Sexual Bargaining: Power Politics in the American Marriage.* 2d ed. Chicago: University of Chicago Press, 1982. As referred to earlier, sexual bargaining deals with motivations to marry, marital conflict as a positive force, and marital change in the past and future.

Scanzoni, John. "Social Processes and Power in Families." *Contemporary Theories About the Family.* Vol. 1. Edited by Wesley R. Burr et al. New York: The Free Press, 1979, pp. 295–316. A review of the conjugal power literature and an attempt to analyze power between spouses in terms of general social theory.

Wells, J. Gipson. *Current Issues in Marriage and the Family*. 3d ed. New York: Macmillan, 1983. A collection of readings dealing with the following issues: to marry or not; marriage versus cohabitation; men's and women's roles; to have children or not; abortion; divorce; marital fidelity; and the future.

Photo: © Harold M. Lambert Studio/E. P. Jones, Co.

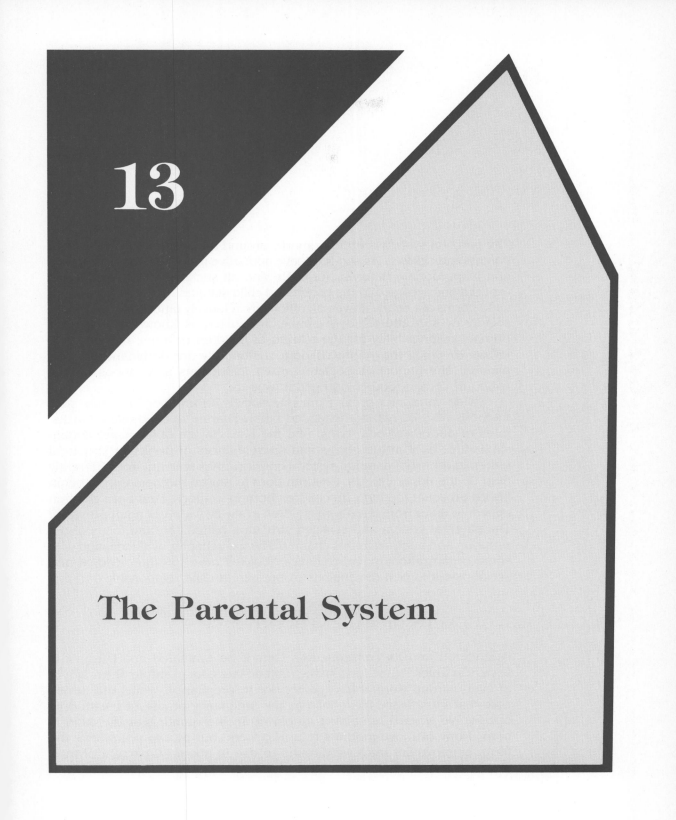

13

The Parental System

The parental system centers primarily around the interrelated statuses of parents and children. All societies have normative restrictions on appropriate and inappropriate behavior for both, and all societies have sets of role expectations accorded to the parent and child statuses. Some of the parent-child norms are nearly universal; others are relatively unique to a particular society or subculture. For example, no society is known to place the primary responsibility for the rearing of children on men; no society is known in which the young children customarily are dominant over the parents; and almost all societies place restrictions and taboos on the eating of certain foods by pregnant women.

Wide variations occur from one society to another in family size, methods of child rearing, extended family sharing in child-related tasks, rates of out-of-wedlock births, and the like. On the other hand, certain similarities exist in the norms and consequences of particular structural patterns within the parental system. Lower classes rear children differently than do the upper classes. Children born to unwed mothers do not begin life on an equal footing with children born in wedlock. First-born children appear to differ from later-born children in a wide variety of adult activities. The parental system and selected structural pattens are the focus of description and analysis in this chapter. The next chapter, while dealing with some organizational characteristics, focuses more on interactional and social-psychological dimensions of the parent-child relationship.

SOCIAL CONSEQUENCES OF PARENTHOOD

Parenthood and its consequences cannot be evaluated apart from the society in which it functions. In the United States, for example, the majority of ever-married women have jobs prior to pregnancy. Waite and others note that most leave these jobs as the pregnancy progresses, with only one in five women remaining employed in the month that the child is born. Many of these mothers return to work, but by two years after the birth, employment rates were found to rise to about 60 percent of their previous levels. Thus, one major social consequence of parenthood in the United States is the withdrawal of women from employment. In contrast, fathers showed higher levels of work activity than would be expected of them at the time of the first birth.[1]

Another consequence of parenthood, at least in the short run, relates to marital stability. In spite of the data presented in the previous chapter on how marital satisfaction drops with the presence of children and data presented later in this chapter showing how childless marriages have higher levels of marital adjustment than couples with children, a national longitudinal study shows strong, positive effects of the first birth on the marital stability of young adults. It was estimated that by the time the first child reaches age two, more than 20 percent of the parents would have been divorced or separated if the child had not been born compared to actual disruption rates of 5 to 8 percent.[2]

Lynn White and Alan Booth refer to this factor as the "braking hypothesis." They suggest that although children do not prevent divorce, they may cause couples to approach the divorce decision more slowly.[3] In spite of a persistent negative correlation between the presence of children and marital happiness, they too found that new parents were significantly less likely to divorce over a three-year period than those who remained childless. Their explanation for these seemingly inconsistent findings was not that persons in more stable marriages have children (a selectivity argument) and was only partially based on the argument that a new baby causes major negative changes in marital structure. Rather, their argument focused on a differential propensity to divorce. Childless couples, they suggest, give greater selectivity to marital happiness than parents. The result is a greater willingness of childless couples to divorce when unhappy. Whatever the reason, fewer divorces seem to occur when very young children are present. Studies reported in Chapter 17 indicate how older children do not provide the same deterrent to divorce.

The social realities of parenting in the United States and much of the world stress the wife and mother as the primary caretaker and responsible person. Parenting tends to be viewed as primarily a maternal duty, de-emphasizing the role of the father in this task—and at times suggesting that fathers are not important in the parenting process or, if

---

1. Linda J. Waite, Gus W. Haggstrom, and David E. Kanouse, "Changes in the Employment Activities of New Parents," *American Sociological Review* 50 (April 1985): 263–272. *See also* Ellen Hock, M. Therese Gnezda, and Susan L. McBride, "Mothers of Infants: Attitudes Toward Employment and Motherhood Following Birth of the First Child," *Journal of Marriage and the Family* 46 (May 1984): 425–431.

2. Linda J. Waite, Gus Haggstrom, and David E. Kanouse, "The Consequences of Parenthood for the Marital Stability of Young Adults," *American Sociological Review* 50 (December 1985): 850–857.

3. Lynn K. White and Alan Booth, "The Transition to Parenthood and Marital Quality," *Journal of Family Issues* 6 (December 1985): 435–449.

important, they tend to be indifferent, incompetent, inadequate, or derelict in their parental role.

This neglect and indifference of fathers does not seem to be empirically supported. In a study covering five countries (United States, Ireland, Spain, Japan, and Mexico), it was found that U.S. men do not associate or interact with children much differently from men in other countries.[4] Men were found to associate with children less than women, but in the United States when societal norms allowed them access to children, the men associated with children in large numbers and responded to their children rather actively. The authors concluded that on balance, there is no compelling reason to assume paternal deprivation by U.S. men toward their children. Changes in society are offering men new contexts for fathering activities. This is particularly evident in nontraditional contexts such as dual-earner families, househusband fathers, stepfathers, fathers in the military, adolescent fathers, single custodial and noncustodial fathers, widowers as single fathers, and gay fathers.[5] For fathers and mothers, becoming a parent means assuming new roles and responsibilities.

THE TRANSITION TO PARENTHOOD

What is involved in the transition to parenthood? What must be learned and what readjustments of roles must take place in order to move smoothly from a childless married state to parenthood? What is the effect of parenthood on the adult? In what ways do parents, and in particular mothers, change as a result of their parental experiences? These closely related questions were of central concern to Alice Rossi in her analysis of the parental role.[6]

Rossi's discussion on the impact of parenthood followed a comparative approach by asking in what basic structural ways the parental role differs from other primary adult roles such as the marital role and occupational role. She concentrated on four unique and salient features of the parental role.[7] First, for women, there is cultural pressure to assume the role. Whereas men have freedom of choice where work is concerned, the cultural pressure for a young woman is to consider maternity necessary for her

---

4. Wade C. Mackey and Randal D. Day, "Some Indicators of Fathering Behaviors in the United States: A Crosscultural Examination of Adult Male-Child Interaction," *Journal of Marriage and the Family* 41 (May 1979): 287–299.

5. Shirley M. H. Hanson, "Fatherhood: Contextual Variations," *American Behavioral Scientist* 29 (September/October 1985): 55–77.

6. Alice S. Rossi, "Transition to Parenthood," *Journal of Marriage and the Family* 30 (February 1968): 26–39; and Alice S. Rossi, "A Biosocial Perspective on Parenting," *Daedalus* 106 (Spring 1977): 1–31.

7. Rossi, "Transition to Parenthood," p. 30.

Parenthood requires the learning of many new skills including the differentiation of play from conflicts among siblings or peers. (Photo: © Camerique Stock Photos/E. P. Jones, Co.)

fulfillment as an individual and to secure her status as an adult. Perhaps today, this cultural pressure has decreased with the declining birth rate, the movement of increasing numbers of women into the paid labor force, and the emphasis on two-child or childless families.

Second, the parental role is not always a voluntary decision. Pregnancy may be the unintended consequence of a sexual act that was recreative in intent rather than procreative. Also, the termination of a pregnancy is not always socially sanctioned.

Third, the parental role is irrevocable. To give birth to a child is always to have a child. It is possible to have ex-spouses and ex-jobs, but it is not possible to have ex-children. Once the birth occurs, there is little possibility of undoing a commitment to parenthood except, of course, in instances of abandonment or placing the child for adoption.

Fourth, the parental role is unique in the preparation U.S. couples bring to it. Rossi says there is: (1) paucity of preparation, (2) limited learning during pregnancy, (3) abruptness of transition, and (4) lack of guidelines to successful parenthood.[8] The paucity of preparation is witnessed

---

8. Ibid., p. 35.

Surrogate mothers

In the past few years surrogate motherhood has provided a controversial alternative for an increasing number of marriages in which the woman is infertile. A surrogate mother is a woman who, for a fee, contracts to be impregnated through artificial insemination, to carry the child, and after delivery, to relinquish the child, as well as all parental rights, to the biological father. Usually the biological father is married to an infertile woman who hopes to adopt the child. The increased demand for newborn white babies and the decrease in their supply has led a number of infertile couples to seek alternative ways to obtain a baby. One of these ways is to locate and hire a surrogate mother.

Who are these surrogate women? Dr. Philip Parker, a psychiatrist at the School of Medicine at Wayne State University, interviewed more than 200 white women applying for surrogate motherhood. These women were referred to him by a well-known attorney in Dearborn, Michigan who has negotiated numerous contracts between surrogate mothers and couples. Dr. Parker found that the mean age of interested surrogate mothers was twenty-five. More than half were married, about one in five were divorced and about one-fourth had never been married. About 40 percent were Catholic and nearly 60 percent were Protestant. About 40 percent were unemployed at the time of the interviews or were receiving some form of financial aid or both. Among the 60 percent of those working or with a working spouse the total family income ranged from $6,000 to $50,000. More than half had at least a high school education. More than 90 percent had at least one previous pregnancy; 80 percent had at least one birth. About 90 percent of these women said they required a fee for their participation and most wanted at least $5,000.

Not all surrogate mothers were applying strictly for the money, however.

by our educational system's teaching of subjects in science and mathematics but not in areas relevant to family life: sex, home maintenance, child care, interpersonal competence, empathy, and the like. The limited learning during pregnancy makes adjustment to parenthood potentially more stressful than marital adjustment, whereas during the engagement period preceding marriage, couples have opportunities to share social experiences, engage in sexual experimentation, and the like in preparation for their marriage. There is a lack of any realistic training for parenthood during the anticipatory stage of pregnancy. The abruptness of transition occurs when a new mother starts out immediately on twenty-four-hour duty. The birth of a child is not followed by any gradual taking on of responsibility, as in the case of a professional work role. Finally, the lack of guidelines to successful parenthood stems from an inability to be able to say just what parental role prescriptions have what effect on the adult characteristics of the child.

Other factors included the perceived degree of enjoyment and desire to be pregnant, the desire to "give" a baby, and to resolve feelings they had regarding a previous voluntary loss of fetus or baby through abortion or relinquishment.

Of the more than 200 surrogate mother applicants interviewed by Dr. Parker, followup interviews were conducted with 25 who since had given birth or become pregnant. Of these, 22 did receive or are receiving a $10,000 fee. Twelve of them had already delivered, received the fee, and did not seem to have any adverse psychological consequences relating to this fee. One surrogate mother who had delivered changed her mind during the pregnancy and refused the $10,000 fee once she established a relationship with the parental couple. Dr. Parker reported that, in general, the fee became less important as the pregnancy developed and as the surrogate established a relationship with the parents-to-be.

Most surrogates felt very contented with the special attention given them, described the pregnancy as doing and producing something (a baby) that only a woman could do, and experienced a sense of accomplishment in giving the gift of a baby to a needy couple. This giving, Dr. Parker suggests, appeared to help many surrogates deal with prior unresolved voluntary losses of a fetus or child. He states that no evidence has been found to support the notion that surrogate motherhood, with or without a fee, leads to serious adverse psychological consequences. Therefore, in spite of descriptions by opponents to surrogate motherhood as baby-buying, slavery, or black marketeering, Dr. Parker feels that all parties involved can benefit if properly selected. Surrogate motherhood should not be prohibited.

Parenthood as a crisis or a transition

"Everybody" loves a newborn infant. Some love them more when they belong to someone else. But what effect does that "lovable" newborn and later the young child have upon parents? Several decades ago, E. E. LeMasters began what was to result in a series of studies by hypothesizing that the birth of a couple's first child is a critical event.[9] He claimed that parents in our society have a romantic notion about child rearing and that they tend to suffer from a process of disenchantment after they become parents. In his study of forty-six middle-class couples, he reported evidence that supported his hypothesis of disenchantment: 83 percent of

9. E. E. LeMasters, "Parenthood as Crisis," *Marriage and Family Living* 19 (November 1957): 352–355.

the couples reported an "extensive" or "severe" crisis in adjusting to the birth of their first child.

Unconvinced that LeMasters and several other writers were correct, a series of studies was done that questioned the advisability of labeling the arrival of the first child as a *crisis*. Writers noted that a crisis perspective places the emphasis on negative outcomes and overlooks the positive and gratifying aspects of parenthood. Over several decades the emphasis shifted from crisis to difficulties to transition. Reports suggested only slight amounts of difficulty in adjusting to the first child, with mothers reporting greater amounts of difficulty than fathers, and black parents reporting greater difficulties than white parents. Few findings existed to warrant the label of crisis, and it became more appropriate to refer to beginning parenthood as a *transition* rather than a *crisis*.

Whether it should be termed *crisis* or not, there is little doubt that when a dyad (husband and wife) becomes a triad (parents and child), a major reorganization of statuses, roles, and relationships takes place. The effect of the birth of a child and the preschool years of the children on the adjustment of the parents seems fairly well established. As noted in the previous chapter, general marital satisfaction of couples tends to decrease after the birth of their children through the preschool and school years until the children are getting ready to leave home. LaRossa suggests that when you ask parents how their lives have changed after their babies were born—rather than asking whether they were bothered or gratified—the one consistent response deals with time.[10] Both parents report that sleep time, television time, communication time, sex time, and even bathroom time are in short supply as the result of a child. The "crisis" earlier writers made reference to may realistically be a need to adjust to the additional time it takes to do all the additional tasks that accompany the presence of children.

The value of parenthood

Apparently not all children are problematic, produce a crisis situation, or are viewed negatively. In spite of unplanned pregnancies, a decreasing birth rate, a decrease in the average family size, and an increase in childless marriages (all discussed later in this chapter), women continue to want and voluntarily have children. In fact, nearly half of all currently married women over the age of thirty who had never borne a child and who were

---

10. Ralph LaRossa, "The Transition to Parenthood and the Social Reality of Time," *Journal of Marriage and the Family* 45 (August 1983): 579–589. Similar time problems are reported in Julie A. Kach and Paul E. McGhee, "Adjustment of Early Parenthood," *Journal of Family Issues* 3 (September 1982): 375–388.

According to a report in *Family Planning Perspectives* (January/February 1987), slightly more than two percent of ever-married women aged 15–44 adopt a child. Those most likely to adopt are older women, sterile women, and women who have never had their own children. Both the proportion of U.S. women who adopt a child and the proportion of U.S. women who place their babies for adoption appear to have remained relatively stable since the mid-1970's. This apparently ended the sharp downtrend in adoptions prior to 1975 that reflected the wider availability of abortion as a means of resolving an unwanted pregnancy.

Who places their child for adoption? Eighty-eight percent of the mothers have never been married. White women are much more likely to place their babies for adoption (12 percent) than black women (less than one percent). Unmarried women who place their babies for adoption are less likely to be receiving some form of public assistance, less likely to be poor, and more likely to have completed high school than unmarried women who keep their babies.

What are the material consequences for adopted children? They have overwhelmingly greater economic advantages than do children who remain with their never-married mothers. Only two percent of adopted children were living below the poverty level compared with 62 percent of children who remained with their never-married mothers.

sterile for noncontraceptive reasons were found to have adopted at least one child.[11] In addition, given the fights over child custody and the estimated 500,000 to 750,000 incidents of child snatching (the abduction of a child by one parent from another) each year,[12] it must be assumed that children are of value, satisfy certain needs for individuals and couples, and fulfill basic functions for society.[13]

Lois Hoffman listed basic values that incorporate the many satisfactions children provide in various cultures.[14] The first is the idea that having children satisfies a need for attaining adult status and a social identity.

---

11. Christine A. Bachrach, "Adoption as a Means of Family Formation: Data from the National Survey of Family Growth," *Journal of Marriage and the Family* 45 (November 1983): 859–865.

12. Richard J. Gelles, "Parental Child Snatching: A Preliminary Estimate of the National Incidence," *Journal of Marriage and the Family* 46 (August 1984): 735–739.

13. For a review of research on satisfaction with parenthood and parenting, *see* Ann Goetting, "Parental Satisfaction: A Review of Research," *Journal of Family Issues* 7 (March 1986): 83–109.

14. Lois Wladis Hoffman, "The Value of Children to Parents and the Decrease in Family Size," *Proceedings of the American Philosophical Society* 119 (December 1975): 430–438; and Lois Wladis Hoffman and Jean Denby Manis, "The Value of Children in the United States:

Particularly for females, parenthood establishes a person as a truly mature, stable, and acceptable member of the community. For many women, it is defined as their major role in life and the fulfillment of womanhood.

A second value of children relates to an expansion of the self, a tie to a larger entity, and an attaining of a kind of immortality. The "carrying on of the family name" and the establishment of a continuity between the past and the future are basic to this value.

A third value is to help to expand the parents' self-conception by evoking new, previously untapped dimensions of personality. Motherhood may be seen as synonymous with virtue. A good father may bring self-respect.

A fourth value relates to primary group ties and affection. Hoffman found that two-thirds of the respondents in a nationwide sample of married women under forty with at least one child indicated that children satisfied their desire for love and the feeling of being in a family.

Ranked close to this was a fifth value of stimulation and fun, stated by 60 percent of the respondents. This included statements such as "they keep you young," "they bring a liveliness to your life," or "they're fun."

Other values include a feeling of achievement and competence, power, social comparison, and economic utility. Some of these values are more prevalent in cultures outside the United States. Power, for example, is a significant value in certain villages in India where the new bride moves into the household of her husband's family where she lives in a subservient role to her mother-in-law. By having sons, she gains some control over her own life and over her childless sisters-in-law. Eventually, when her sons bring home brides, she becomes the powerful and dominating mother-in-law.[15] In the United States, power can be seen in the control and influence parents hold over other human beings—their children. A value like economic utility tends to have greater significance in rural areas or in certain countries. Children provide inexpensive labor and, in addition, are often viewed as important to care for parents in their old age.

The concern over young parenthood

Chapter 8 had a brief subsection entitled, "The Concern over Young Marriages." The concern over young parenthood—primarily teenage parent-

A New Approach to the Study of Fertility," *Journal of Marriage and the Family* 41 (August 1979): 583–596.

15. T. Poffenberger and S. B. Poffenberger, "The Social Psychology of Fertility Behavior in a Village in India," in *Psychological Perspectives on Population*, ed. by J. T. Fawcett (New York: Basic Books, 1973): 135–162.

Vatican condemns birth from frozen embryo

On April 17, 1984, the Associated Press in Rome reported that the Vatican newspaper condemned the process used to conceive a child from a frozen embryo. The report was in response to an announcement one week earlier by scientists that a healthy girl named Zoe had been delivered by doctors at Monash University in Melbourne. Zoe was the first birth announced in Australia resulting from that method.

In an editorial appearing in *L'Osservatore Romano*, Gino Concetti, a theologian, said that one understands the desire of sterile couples to have children, but one must realize that not everything one desires can be right. He said the new technique is unacceptable because it requires the act of masturbation to obtain sperm and, according to the Roman Catholic Church, masturbation is "a deviation and a grave sin." Thus the condemnation of artifical insemination and the use of a frozen embryo.

hood—is directly linked to the concern over young marriage, with premarital births related to greater levels of marital instability. Similarly, a young age at first marriage is related to an increased risk of marital dissolution for both blacks and whites. Combining a premarital birth with a young age at first marriage yields a strong likelihood of subsequent marital dissolution.[16]

Young parenthood magnifies the general issues surrounding parenthood in general that have been discussed thus far. When parenthood, and more specifically motherhood, occurs at an early age, it is likely to have a negative effect on occupational attainment, marital stability, asset accumulation, and the woman's health. When compared to women in the twenty- to thirty-five-year age group, teenage mothers are most likely to postpone prenatal care, have a child of low birthweight, and experience a higher rate of infant mortality.[17] The evidence strongly suggests that the bulk of the adverse consequences of teenage childbearing may be of social and economic origin, rather than attributable to the effects of young age per se. At the macro-level, trends in the age at first birth have important effects on the pace of social change, period fertility trends, and the state of the economy.[18] It affects as well the milieu in which children are raised,

16. Jay D. Teachman, "Early Marriage, Premarital Fertility, and Marital Dissolution," *Journal of Family Issues* 4 (March 1983): 105–126; and John O. G. Billy, Nancy S. Landale, and Steven D. McLaughlin, "The Effect of Marital Status at First Birth on Marital Dissolution Among Adolescent Mothers," *Demography* 3 (August 1986): 329–349.

17. Michael K. Miller and C. Shannon Stokes, "Teenage Fertility, Socioeconomic Status and Infant Mortality," *Journal of Biosocial Science* 17 (1985): 147–155.

18. Ronald R. Rindfuss and Craig St. John, "Social Determinants of Age at First Birth," *Journal of Marriage and the Family* 45 (August 1983): 553–565.

the kinds of opportunities available to them, and their intellectual development.

In a study of 400 young adolescent mothers, their partners, progeny, and parents, Frank Furstenberg explored when, how, and why childbearing before the age of eighteen jeopardizes the life prospects of the young mother and her child.[19] Four out of five of the adolescent mothers became pregnant within two years following the onset of intercourse, which typically occurred at age fifteen. Fewer than one in four of the teenagers' mothers admitted that they had known that their daughters were having sexual relations prior to the pregnancy. While most of the adolescents had some limited knowledge of birth control, they tended to be most aware of those forms to which they had the least access, and their control was confined largely to "getting the boy to use something." Contraception was much more likely to be practiced by couples who had a stable romantic relationship.

As might be expected, the pregnancies were greeted by both adolescents and parents with astonishment. Three-quarters of the expectant mothers wished they had not become pregnant and half could not tell their parents for several months. Those women who married were more likely than those who did not to indicate positive feelings toward the pregnancy.

Furstenberg's results, consistent with other studies, found that premarital pregnancy greatly increased the probability of eventual marital dissolution. A comparison group of classmates who married but had not conceived premaritally had one-half the probability of the marriage breaking up after two years than that for the adolescent mothers. Although unplanned pregnancy may not *cause* the breakup of the marriage, it is an important link to a weak economic position of the male who fathers a child out of wedlock. Most of the men—young, inexperienced, and unskilled—had a low earning potential before they wed. Again, like other studies, economic resources are strongly linked to marital stability.

The problems of young parenthood are further compounded by additional unwanted pregnancies. Estimates vary, but Furstenberg indicates that most published studies show that at least half of the teenage mothers studied experience a second pregnancy within thirty-six months of delivery. In his sample, one-fourth of the women became pregnant within twelve months of the birth of the first child, and by three years, half of the women with two children had become pregnant a third time.

Pregnancy, marriage, or both was a principal reason for leaving high school. One-fourth of the adolescents never returned, and half never

---

19. Frank F. Furstenberg, Jr., "The Social Consequences of Teen-age Parenthood," *Family Planning Perspectives* 8 (August 1976): 148–164. The data presented in this section came from this report.

graduated, this in contrast to 18 percent of the comparison group who did not graduate.

One-quarter of the respondents had obtained most, if not all, of their income from working. Welfare barely edged out income from spouse as the second most common source of support. Welfare was not, however, a contributing factor in the encouragement of childbearing out of wedlock. The welfare mother was not significantly more likely to become pregnant after she went on relief than the young mother who was not receiving support. In any case, nearly half of all adolescent mothers were living below the poverty level.

The presence of one or more children made holding a full-time job very difficult. Most of the women who worked had another individual to share the responsibilities of caring for the child. Few of the mothers could be classified by any standard as rejecting parents.

Furstenberg argues for social programs that are preventive rather than reactive. These would include educational, vocational, medical, or contraceptive programs that continue to provide services for as long as the need for service exists and that are geared to the client rather than the professional. The principal reason so many young mothers encounter problems is that they lack the resources to adequately cope with a poorly timed birth.

One major resource available to the young parent comes from their nuclear families: parents and siblings. This is often in the form of free room and board and partly or wholly subsidized child care. This assistance can significantly alter the life chances of the young mother, enhancing her prospects of educational achievement and economic advancement. Were it not for the increased poverty and dependency, the social isolation, less schooling, and the increased levels of childbearing (much of which is unwanted and out of wedlock), there would be far less concern over young parenthood.[20]

The concern over unwed parenthood

Closely related to and often simultaneous with the concern over young parenthood is the issue of unwed parenthood with the attached label of

---

20. You may want to note Catherine S. Chilman, "Social and Psychological Research Concerning Adolescent Childbearing: 1970–1980," *Journal of Marriage and the Family* 42 (November 1980): 793–805; K. Denise Dillard and Louis G. Pol, "The Individual Economic Costs of Teenage Childbearing," *Family Relations* 31 (April 1982): 249–259; Frank L. Mott, "The Pace of Repeated Childbearing Among Young Mothers," *Family Planning Perspectives* 18 (January/February 1986): 5–12; and Frank L. Mott and William Marsiglio, "Early Childbearing and Completion of High School," *Family Planning Perspectives* 17 (September/October 1985): 234–237.

illegitimacy placed upon the child. Illegitimacy or legitimacy is only characteristic of the human family since no other animal grouping has regulations that define who has the right to procreate and rear a fully accepted member of society. It is the family and marital system that universally fulfills the function of giving legal status and social approval to the birth of a child. To be born outside the family is to be illegitimate, a label generally defined as a social problem and an economic burden. Legal changes granting equal rights to children born in or out of parental wedlock are in process, but the unwed parent is still viewed disapprovingly, with the approval and congratulations reserved for the married parent and the child born into a conjugal family unit.

A family unit requires someone to assume the roles of sociological father and sociological mother. Even though some degree of premarital sexual license exists in about 70 percent of the societies for which information is available, childbirth outside marriage is not approved in those societies. The suggestion is that marriage bestows legitimacy on parenthood more than on sex. That is, most societies are more concerned with illegitimacy than with sexual intercourse outside marriage.

This greater concern for unwed parenthood than for unwed intercourse may be the key to understanding the emphasis and attention given to the mother and the relative lack of attention given to the father. Despite his obvious involvement in the pregnancy, the male is studied far less frequently and assigned a less deviant label. One study described these men as "non-deviant rule breakers."[21] The unwed fathers shared a view that the consequences of their actions were both morally and socially unacceptable, were prepared to receive some form of social sanction or moral condemnation, but for the most part, the sanctions either did not develop or were minor in severity. The double standard described in the chapter on premarital sexual behavior is not merely operative on sexual behavior, it is even more in evidence with regard to the pregnancy consequences that result from sexual behavior.

Some antecedents of out-of-wedlock adolescent pregnancy come from over 2,000 young adults first surveyed as seventh-grade students and followed up ten years later. Among the males, having a girlfriend become pregnant was associated with school difficulties, low parental socioeconomic status, and high popularity. Among females, pregnancy risk was related to race, low socioeconomic status, father absence, number of siblings, school difficulties, family stress, and popularity.[22] Sexual differences in

---

21. Erdwin H. Pfuhl, Jr., "The Unwed Father: A 'Non-Deviant' Rule Breaker," *The Sociological Quarterly* 19 (Winter 1978): 113–128.

22. Cynthia Robbins, Howard B. Kaplan, and Steven S. Martin, "Antecedents of Pregnancy Among Unmarried Adolescents," *Journal of Marriage and the Family* 47 (August 1985): 567–583.

Do welfare benefits encourage early childbearing?

When unmarried teenagers become pregnant, as a starting proportion now do, they can choose abortion, adoption, marriage, or welfare. Some people say it is that last option, the government dole, that is encouraging the tremendous upsurge in children having children.

Two Harvard researchers, David Ellwood and Mary Jo Bane, examined the impact of welfare, and, in particular, the Aid to Families with Dependent Children (AFDC) program, on family structure and living arrangements. As reported in *Family Planning Perspectives* (September/October 1985) they did their study because of widespread concern that the availability of AFDC—which supports mainly single women and their children—encourages out-of-wedlock childbearing and is destructive of family relationships.

What they found was that the level of welfare benefits in a state seems to have *little* impact on the decisions of unmarried women to have children. It does, however, appear to have a substantial effect on the living arrangements of young single mothers. In states where benefit levels are high, unmarried mothers are considerably more likely to move out of their parents' home and set up their own households. Also, young married mothers are somewhat more likely to become divorced or separated.

The authors conclude that a dramatic cut in welfare would change the lives of poor women. It would reduce the income of single mothers and influence where many young single mothers live. But welfare (AFDC alone or AFDC plus food stamps) would do little to slow the growth of single-parent families and early childbearing.

experiencing pregnancy were attributed to the possibility that some males were unaware they had impregnated girls, the greater ease males have in the denial of causing a pregnancy, and the tendency of adolescent girls to date older males.

As of 1979, one-third of unmarried white teenagers and 43 percent of unmarried black teenagers had conceived within 24 months of becoming sexually active.[23] Thus, still relevant is a question Kingsley Davis posed more than forty-five years ago. "Why doesn't society solve the problem of illegitimacy by requiring the use of contraceptive methods and, when these fail, abortion?"[24] His answer was that to break the normative relations

23. Michael A. Koenig and Melvin Zelnik, "The Risk of Premarital First Pregnancy Among Metropolitan-Area Teenagers: 1976 and 1979," *Family Planning Perspectives* 14 (September/October 1982): 239. On black teenage pregnancy see: Joyce A. Ladner, "Black Teenage Pregnancy: A Challenge for Educators," *Journal of Negro Education* 56 (1987): 53–63.

24. Kingsley Davis, "Illegitimacy and the Social Structure," *American Journal of Sociology* 45 (September 1939): 221–222.

between sexuality and the family, so that adults would as a matter of course decide rationally whether they would enjoy sex within or outside the family, would also reduce the strength of the motive to marry and found a family. The radical changes necessary to eliminate illegitimacy would very likely come close to eliminating the family system too. If this is true, the concern over childbirth in or out of wedlock is well understood.

One central element in understanding unwed parenthood is the class status of the child. It could be expected that unwed parenthood among the lower classes would be of less concern to a society than would unwed parenthood among the higher classes. With less property to protect or to inherit and with lineage and family honor less a focus of attention in the lower classes, families have less to lose if a birth out of wedlock occurs. The expected result of this would be more frequent unwed births among the lower classes.

Among the higher classes, since property and family name is at stake to a greater degree, some expected results are likely to include pressure on the couple to marry, turning over the child to an adoption agency, or

TABLE 13–1
Births to unmarried women, by race and age of mother, 1950–1984

Race and Age	1950	1960	1970	1980	1984
Total live births (in thousands)	141.6	224.3	398.7	665.7	770.4
White	53.5	82.5	175.1	320.0	392.0
Black and other	88.1	141.8	223.6	345.7	378.4
Percent of all births	4.0%	5.3%	10.7%	18.4%	21.0%
Total rate (# per 1,000)	14.1	21.6	26.4	29.4	31.0
White	6.1	9.2	13.8	17.6	20.1
Black and other	71.2	98.3	89.9	77.2	71.4
Number (in thousands) by age of mother					
Under 15 years	3.2	4.6	9.5	9.0	9.1
15–19 years	56.0	87.1	190.4	262.8	261.1
20–24 years	43.1	68.0	126.7	237.3	279.2
25–29 years	20.9	32.1	40.6	99.6	137.0
30–34 years	10.8	18.9	19.1	41.0	59.3
35 years and over	7.7	13.6	12.4	16.1	24.8
Percent 19 years and under	41.8	40.9	50.2	40.9	35.1

Source: U.S. Bureau of the Census, *Statistical Abstract of the United States: 1987*, 107th ed. (Washington, D.C.: U.S. Government Printing Office, 1986), no. 86, p. 61.

leaving home to bear the child. Births can be avoided altogether via abortion, which is more accessible to the educated and financially able.

Rates of birth outside of marriage   At the very time that birth rates are steadily declining or leveling off (to be discussed later in this chapter), the **rates of birth outside of marriage** are showing a dramatic increase. The number of births to unmarried women exceeded 770,000 in 1984 (*see* Table 13–1). This represents more than a 500 percent increase in the number of such births since 1950. Equally dramatic is the change in the *percentage* of all births to unmarried women. In 1950, the percentage was 4.0. By 1984, the same figure was 21.0, an increase of 525 percent.

The rate varies widely by race, with much of the difference explained by social class. The differences in stigma attached to unwed births, the likelihood of reporting, and the access to, and use of, contraceptives and abortion account for a major proportion of the white–non-white difference.

The incidence of live births by age of mother shows a profound change. Unwed mothers are getting older. In 1970, 50.2 percent of births were to teenage mothers compared to 35.1 percent in 1984. The number of mothers under age 15 actually dropped in the same time interval. While teenage unwed mothers ages 15–19 increased by 70,700 or 37 percent between 1970 and 1984, the increase in those ages 20–24 was 152,500 or 120.4 percent. Even greater increases occurred among the 25–29 and 30–34 age categories (up 237 and 210 percent respectively).

Unwed parenthood is no longer most prevalent among teenagers when compared to other age categories. Most unwed births in 1984 were to mothers in the 20–24 age category and older. These age changes might suggest fewer problems related to emotional immaturity, dropping out of school, and skills to care for the child, but whether it means fewer income and employment problems is unclear. Let's examine if having a child out of wedlock matters.

Does birth out of wedlock make a difference?

Again we return to the question relating to the concern over unwed parenthood. Does it really make a difference that more than 770,000 births each year are outside of wedlock? Do these children experience more social, economic, and health handicaps than children born in wedlock? Is the presence of both a male and a female parent essential to the growth and development of a child? Does the unmarried mother face increased emotional and economic difficulties that seriously affect both the mother and the child? Some of these specific questions are discussed elsewhere (note the section on the single parent in Chapter 7 on social class, Chapter

6 on the black family, and Chapter 14 on parent-child socialization in particular); however, several research studies are worthy of consideration here.

Empirical research indicates that birth outside of wedlock does have an impact on the child, the parent, and society, both in the United States and elsewhere. In Great Britain, the National Child Development Study showed that by age seven, children born out of wedlock fared considerably worse than children born in wedlock on a number of social, economic, and health measures.[25] Differences persisted even after social class was taken into account.

Similar findings exist in the United States as evidenced in studies completed in California.[26] Information from a sample of two-year-old legitimate and illegitimate children indicated that despite significant social changes, illegitimate children continue to face poorer life chances than legitimate children. They were found to have a higher infant mortality rate, and the unadopted illegitimate children fared quite poorly on a number of measures including school performance. Unmarried mothers were less likely to marry within three years after the birth than the general population of unmarried women and were more likely to separate from their husbands if they did later marry. It is of interest to note that adopted children born to unwed mothers did as well or better than legitimate children.[27] It would appear from the data in the Berkov and Sklar study that, despite a decrease in the degree of stigma attached to birth out of wedlock and the proliferation of services and programs for these children and their mothers, these children do not begin life on an equal footing with legitimate children, and their handicaps persist beyond the hazards of infancy.[28]

Other data clearly support negative and long-lasting repercussions of teenage and/or unwed childbearing. Young parents acquire less education than their contemporaries; they are often limited to less prestigious jobs and, in the case of the women, to more dead-end ones. From the moment of pregnancy awareness, both young parents and unwed mothers have

---

25. This research is discussed in E. Crellin, M. L. Kellmer Pringle, and P. West, *Born Illegitimate: Social and Educational Implications* (London: National Foundation for Educational Research in England and Wales, 1971).

26. Beth Berkov and June Sklar, "Does Illegitimacy Make a Difference? A Study of the Life Chances of Illegitimate Children in California," *Population and Development Review* 2 (June 1976): 201–217.

27. Similar findings are reported in Christine A. Bachrach, "Children in Families: Characteristics of Biological, Step-, and Adopted Children," *Journal of Marriage and the Family* 45 (February 1983): 171–179.

28. Berkov and Sklar, "Does Illegitimacy Make a Difference?" p. 215. *Also see* Wendy Baldwin and Virginia S. Cain, "The Children of Teenage Parents," *Family Planning Perspectives* 12 (January/February 1980): 34–43.

difficult decisions and adjustments to make. Little toleration is extended to the young unwed mother who wishes to keep her child as her own, although greater toleration does exist in the lower-class strata where the commitment to the norm of legal marriage is less and where the punishments for deviation and the rewards for conformity are lower.

In 1935, the United States Congress established a national policy of providing financial aid to a mother and her children when they did not have financial support. This Aid to Families with Dependent Children (AFDC) program enabled a mother to keep her children with her. Programs such as these receive constant protests from taxpayers who argue (falsely) that mothers want more children to increase their aid (*see* insert, Do Welfare Benefits Encourage Early Childbearing?). Increased aid is seldom a central motivational factor in the birth of additional children.

FAMILY SIZE AND RELATED FACTORS

Birth rates and birth expectations

Most married couples want, have, or expect to have children. In 1984, there were 3.67 million births in the United States, a rate of 15.5 births per 1,000 population.[29] The same year, 20.3 percent of all ever-married women aged 15 to 44, either by choice or circumstances, were childless.[30]

The birth rate is one of the best documented series of descriptive social data available today. Census data show quite clearly the increase and decrease in number and rate of births in the United States. In 1910 the birth rate was 30.1 per 1,000 population, decreasing to 18.7 during the Depression years of the mid-thirties, increasing to 25 in 1955, steadily decreasing between 1957 and 1975, and increasing from 14.6 in 1975 to 15.7 in 1985. The decline in the fertility rate for U.S. women was especially sharp between 1971 and 1973 but was a continuation of the drop in the level of fertility since the peak year of the baby boom in 1957.

What do demographers and journalists mean when they talk about a "baby boom"? Simply stated, the baby boom was a post—World War II "disturbance" that upset what had been a century-long decline in the U.S. fertility rate. It was an unanticipated, pronounced, and consequential rise in the United States birth rate during the late 1940s and 1950s (*see* Figure 13–1). Theories as to its cause include increases in normative pressure on women to have children, the disruption and dislocation brought about

---

29. U.S. Bureau of the Census, *Statistical Abstract of the United States: 1987*, 107th ed. (Washington, D.C.: U.S. Government Printing Office, 1987), no. 82, p. 59.

30. Ibid., Table 93, p. 64. (Comparable figures for 1940 were 26.5, 1950, 22.8, 1960, 15.0, 1970, 16.4; and 1980, 18.8 percent).

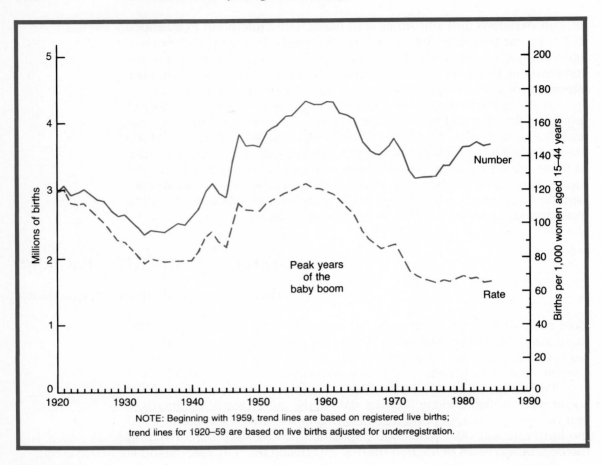

FIGURE 13–1
Live births and fertility rates: United States, 1920–1984. (*Source:* National
Center for Health Statistics, "Advance Report of Natality Statistics, 1984,"
Monthly Vital Statistics Reports, vol. 35, no. 4 [Public Health Service,
Hyattsville, Md., July 18, 1986], Figure 1, p. 2.)

by war, the postwar economic prosperity, and the longterm psychological
effects of growing up during the Depression. Bean suggests that social
and cultural conditions during the era supported having families, while
at the same time increasing the cost of having large families.[31] This
postwar spurt in annual births did not represent a return of the large
family of the nineteenth century. What happened was a movement away
from singlehood, childless marriage, and one-child families, and a bunching

31. Frank D. Bean, "The Baby Boom and Its Explanations," *The Sociological Quarterly*
24 (Summer 1983): 353–365.

That's snow business

> In May 1979, doctors at Michael Reese Hospital in Chicago reported a 20 percent increase in pregnancies over the normal for that time of year. They claimed that the consequences of the "Great Blizzard of January 1979" in that area should become apparent by mid-September.

together of births. Only a minor part of the baby boom could be attributed to increases in the proportions having three or more births.[32]

In 1985, the average number of lifetime births *expected* by currently married women ages 18–34 was 2.19, a decline from a 2.34 average exactly ten years earlier in 1975 and a 3.05 average reported in 1967.[33] A comparison of the average number of lifetime births expected by currently married women versus the never-married women indicated that single women expect a lower average number of births than do wives (1.82 versus 2.19 in the 18–34 age group). The difference in lifetime birth expectations between married and single women decreases with age, indicating both a reduction in the remaining number of reproductive years and a decrease in marriage prospects at later ages for single women. If women now in their late teens and twenties live up to their expectations for the future, the number of persons who come from "large" families will be a much smaller proportion of the population than at the present time.

There seems to be some disagreement as to whether the number of children and family size will continue its downward trend or perhaps level off at no more than two children. Due to factors such as improved methods of birth control, liberalized abortion laws, and increased acceptance of birth planning by Catholics, we might anticipate a decrease in the number of unplanned and unwanted births. We do know that since the early 1960s there has been a trend to delay first births. Women who delay childbearing have fewer children and are significantly better off economically than either average-age childbearers or the childless. And by retirement age the delayed childbearer with only one or two children appears better off than all other women.[34]

32. Leon F. Bouvier, "America's Baby Boom Generation: The Fateful Bulge," *Population Bulletin* 35 (1980): 4. Published by The Population Reference Bureau, Inc., Washington, D.C.

33. U.S. Bureau of the Census, *Current Population Reports*, Series P-20, no. 406, "Fertility of American Women: June 1985" (Washington, D.C.: U.S. Government Printing Office, 1986), Table 5, p. 26.

34. Sandra L. Hofferth, "Long-Term Economic Consequences for Women of Delayed

Baby boomers having children

As of 1985, the birthrate in the United States is up from 10 years earlier but has leveled off since 1979. The Census Bureau recorded 3.75 million births or 15.7 births per 1,000 people in 1985. That's up from 14.6 in 1975. But it's below 1970's 18.4 births per 1,000 and 1960's 23.7. Since 1979 the number of births per 1,000 population ranged between 15.5 and 15.9.

The increase in births since the 1970s is an echo of the past. More children are being born because there are so many women of childbearing age—women born during the post-war baby boom. But births per 1,000 population vary widely by region and state.

The Northeast and Midwest are regions with a birth rate below the national average, while the South and West are above. Figures for 1985 show the West with 17.7 births per 1,000, whereas the Northeast had 13.9 births per 1,000.

Alaska at 24.1 and Utah at 23.4 top the nation in births per 1,000 population, well ahead of third place New Mexico, which had 19.9 births per 1,000. The high rate in Utah reflects the Mormon high fertility rate. Non-Mormons in Utah have a rate close to the nation as a whole (*Journal of Marriage and the Family*, May 1985: 459). At the low end of the scale, Connecticut had the lowest birthrate in the nation at 11.6 per 1,000 people. The bottom quartile were all in the Northeast and Middle Atlantic areas of the United States.

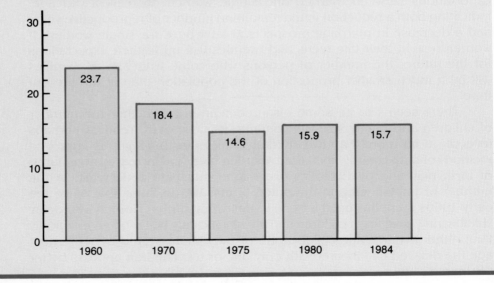

Thus, with delayed childbearing, we not only get fewer children who are better off economically, but a lengthened time until the new generation

Childbearing and Reduced Family Size," *Demography* 21 (May 1984): 141–155; and Jane Riblett Wilkie, "The Trend Toward Delayed Parenthood," *Journal of Marriage and the Family* 43 (August 1981): 583–591.

Breakdown of live births per 1,000 residents by state, 1985			
1. Alaska	24.1	26. Missouri	15.3
2. Utah	23.4	27. Wisconsin	15.3
3. New Mexico	19.9	28. Oregon	15.1
4. Texas	19.2	29. Ohio	15.0
5. North Dakota	18.6	30. Arkansas	14.9
6. Arizona	18.5	31. Tennessee	14.8
7. Louisiana	18.1	32. Michigan	14.8
8. California	17.9	33. Vermont	14.8
9. Wyoming	17.4	34. South Carolina	14.7
10. Idaho	17.4	35. Indiana	14.7
11. Hawaii	17.3	36. Alabama	14.6
12. South Dakota	17.3	37. Iowa	14.6
13. Washington	17.3	38. Virginia	14.6
14. Colorado	17.1	39. New York	14.4
15. Georgia	16.7	40. North Carolina	14.4
16. Nevada	16.4	41. Florida	14.4
17. Mississippi	16.2	42. Massachusetts	14.2
18. Montana	16.0	43. Rhode Island	14.0
19. Nebraska	16.0	44. Maine	13.9
20. Kansas	15.9	45. Kentucky	13.9
21. Minnesota	15.8	46. Maryland	13.7
22. Delaware	15.8	47. Pennsylvania	13.7
23. New Hampshire	15.8	48. New Jersey	13.7
24. Oklahoma	15.7	49. West Virginia	13.2
25. Illinois	15.4	50. Connecticut	11.6

Source: U.S. Bureau of the Census, *Statistical Abstract of the United States*: 1987, 107th ed. (Washington, D.C.: U.S. Government Printing Office, 1986), no. 84, p. 60.

reaches childbearing age. The consequence is a decrease in population growth over the longer term but an upturn in growth in the short run. This appears to be happening. Increases in first-order birth rates have been substantial in the baby-boom cohorts of women now aged 25–39 who have delayed births. This is combined with the older women who had the high fertility and earlier timing patterns of the 1950s and 1960s who already had all the children they wanted when they were younger.

It seems probable that people are not having as many children as previously because whatever needs are involved in wanting children are satisfied in other ways. For example, jobs and careers for women appear to be an alternative to children or to influence the decision to have fewer children. Many other variables have been found to be related to marital fertility: socioeconomic status, religion, race, education, urbanization, female income, child-care arrangements, gender roles, age at marriage, age at first birth, interval since last birth, age of women, and others.[35] Even the size of the family of origin (number of brothers and sisters) appears to influence marital fertility. And, of course, many couples make a conscious choice to have no children or for some reason, fail to have them. Let us examine briefly these childless marriages.

Childless marriage

For many years the myth existed that because of a maternal instinct, all women wanted children. This "instinct" even went one step further and assumed that once a child was born, the mother would "instinctively" want, love, and care for him or her. These assumptions were given major blows as statistics, research reports, newspaper accounts, and gossip networks revealed the widespread termination of pregnancies through legal and/or illegal abortions, the commonality of mothers abusing and even killing their children, and the discovery that women who never had children—in or out of marriage—did not suffer physical or emotional damage. These and other factors tended to dispel the notion of the biological linkage between being female and a natural desire for and love of children.

There is little doubt that children place enormous demands on parents in terms of emotional and financial costs. Yet, most married couples, either voluntarily or involuntarily, have children. It is possible that many of these couples have children because they were never socialized to believe that not having them is a viable alternative to marriage and family life. Since marriage legitimizes the sexual union and the birth of children, voluntary childless marriage may not have been viewed as a realistic choice.

Most cultures and societies impose social pressures upon couples to be "fruitful," meaning "to bear children." The marriage is not complete or socially mature until children are born of the union. One study asked respondents to describe their perceptions of fictitious individuals assigned one of six family size statuses. Voluntary childless couples and parents of one child were found to be viewed most negatively.[36]

---

35. For example, *see* Sandra L. Hofferth, "Childbearing Decision Making and Family Well-Being: A Dynamic Sequential Model," *American Sociological Review* 48 (August 1983): 533–545; Mary G. Powers and Joseph J. Salvo, "Fertility and Child Care Arrangements as Mechanisms of Status Articulation," *Journal of Marriage and the Family* 44 (February 1982): 21–34; Jay D. Teachman, "Historical and Subgroup Variations in the Association Between Marriage and First Childbirth: A Life-Course Perspective," *Journal of Family History* 10 (Winter 1985): 379–401; and William D. Mosher, David P. Johnson, and Marjorie C. Horn, "Religion and Fertility in the United States: The Importance of Marriage Patterns and Hispanic Origin," *Demography* 23 (August 1986): 367–379.

36. Denise F. Polit, "Stereotypes Relating to Family-Size Status," *Journal of Marriage and the Family* 40 (February 1978): 105–114.

Census material shows that in 1985, 9.9 percent of ever-married women between the ages of thirty-five to forty-four were childless. This figure increases to 23.3 percent among the twenty-five to thirty-four-year-old married women and to 41.9 percent among those eighteen to twenty-four years of age. These younger age groups have not, however, completed their childbearing years and most expect to have children at some time in their lives. Only approximately 10.4 percent of all women and 6.2 percent of currently married women age eighteen to thirty-four do not expect to have any children in their lifetimes.[37]

The impact of education on this childless expectation is striking. The proportion expecting no lifetime births is only 7.6 percent for women who are not high school graduates. This increases to 9.3 percent for high school graduates, 11.8 percent for those with one to three years of college, 14.9 percent for those with four years of college, and 17.0 percent for women with five years or more of college.[38] The discussion on dual-career marriages in Chapter 4 showed that both marriage and children hinder careers for women. And these data just presented indicate that with an increased level of educational training comes an increased proportion of women who never expect to have a child.

While the percentage of childless married couples is small, an increase in expectations for childlessness led Judith Blake to question whether this increase will contribute to extremely low fertility rates in the United States.[39] Her results suggest it will not. There was found to be a high level of consensus that nonparenthood is not an advantaged status. Although offspring were not regarded as economic investments, they were viewed as important social investments among all groups, and particularly among the less advantaged. Men were significantly more likely to regard childlessness as disadvantageous than were women. This suggests that even with a change in women's job opportunities, a significant increase in childlessness will not occur. In Blake's words:

> The fact that men of all strata view nonparenthood as distinctly disadvantageous suggests that they may be willing to help women lower the opportunity costs of childbearing and rearing in order to have a family—a small family, perhaps, but a family nonetheless.[40]

Not only are women more likely than men to view children as a disadvantage, voluntarily childless women, whether married or single, rate the costs of a child higher and the satisfactions lower than other groups

---

37. U.S. Bureau of the Census, *Current Population Reports*, Series P-20, no. 406, "Fertility of American Women, June 1985" (Washington, D.C.: U.S. Government Printing Office, 1986), Table 2, p. 13 and Table 10, p. 41.

38. Ibid., Table 8, p. 32.

39. Judith Blake, "Is Zero Preferred? American Attitudes Toward Childlessness in the 1970s," *Journal of Marriage and the Family* 41 (May 1979): 245–257.

40. Ibid., p. 256.

of women (such as parents or those who desire to become parents).[41] In particular, educated professional women, who have lived with and enjoyed an adult-centered life-style, gave high ratings to the restrictions and disruptions of children and to general life-style costs. They gave low ratings to the emotional satisfactions and personal fulfillment a child might give them, but felt their current life-style choices—especially careers—did meet such needs.

If parenthood seems to interfere with personal happiness and one's freedoms, it seems to interfere with marriage and family life as well. As is noted in several chapters, children impose a strain on marriage. Does this also mean or suggest that couples without children have higher levels of health and marital adjustment and satisfaction than do couples with children? Apparently it does. When voluntarily childless wives, undecided wives, and postponing wives were compared with mothers, the results from one study indicated that all three groups of childless wives have higher mean levels of marital satisfaction than do mothers.[42] Karen S. Renne found that childless marriages were more likely to be happy ones that tended to improve with time while parental marriages tended to deteriorate.[43] Sharon Houseknecht also lent support to the relationship between childlessness and enhanced marital adjustment, although the differences between the voluntarily childless wives and the mothers in her survey were small in magnitude.[44] This finding led her to suggest that it may not be the presence or absence of children per se but rather education, employment, religion, or some combination of these that has the major impact on marital adjustment. In any case, the available evidence on the consequences of voluntary childlessness to persons or marriages does not appear to be negative.

Is this satisfaction true among involuntarily childless women and among older persons as well? In other words, what about women or couples who want children and can't have them, or older persons who, either by choice or necessity, have no children? As will be evident in later chapters, children serve as an important source of gratification to many married couples and as a source of support to older persons. For both the involuntary childless and the elderly, some limited data indicate less marital or personal satisfaction among those without children. Choice

---

41. Victor J. Callan, "The Impact of the First Birth: Married and Single Women Preferring Childlessness, One Child, or Two Children," *Journal of Marriage and the Family* 48 (May 1986): 261–269.

42. Karen A. Polonko, John Scanzoni, and Jay D. Teachman, "Childlessness and Marital Satisfaction," *Journal of Family Issues* 3 (December 1982): 545–573.

43. Karen S. Renne, "Childlessness, Health, and Marital Satisfaction," *Social Biology* 23 (Fall 1976): 183–197.

44. Sharon K. Houseknecht, "Childlessness and Marital Adjustment," *Journal of Marriage and the Family* 41 (May 1979): 259–265.

may well be one of the most significant determinants of a satisfaction with a particular life-style.

Results from northern Nigeria showed a higher level of marital adjustment among mothers than among *involuntarily* childless women,[45] And four surveys by the National Opinion Research Center of the University of Chicago asked males and females aged sixty-five and over how much satisfaction they get from family life.[46] The findings indicated that childlessness had an overall significant negative effect on family satisfaction, with the effect most pronounced among the oldest age cohort and more pronounced for females than for males. Whether the current cohorts of childless women under ages forty and thirty will be negatively affected by the absence of children when they reach ages sixty-five and seventy-five remains to be seen. Future friendship or formal support systems may alter the effects of childlessness discovered among today's elderly.

Effects of large or small families

There is little doubt that the number of people in a group influences the interaction and behavior of the members of that group. If you have one roommate and you agree, a decision is unanimous. If you have two roommates, both of whom agree with each other but differ from you, you have the unhappy choice of accepting their decision, trying to change the decision of at least one, or going your own way. Clearly, the number of interactions, the probability of dissensus, the attention given to any one person, and the like are influenced by the number of members in the group. The same factors hold true within a family system. One-child families are conducive to certain patterns of life that differ from two-, three-, or four-child families.

One-child families have, in general, not been viewed positively for either the parents or the child. The "only" child has been described as spoiled, selfish, overly dependent, maladjusted, and lonely. Parents have been described as selfish, self-centered, immature, cold, and abnormal. National surveys over the past thirty years have consistently showed a majority of respondents indicating that being an only child is a disadvantage. Very few people say they want to have just one child or that the ideal number of children for a family is one. The popular stereotype of the unhappy, maladjusted only child and the common view that one child is neither a preferred or desirable family size, calls for an empirical look at this "small" family.

---

45. Daniel I. Denga, "Childlessness and Marital Adjustment in Northern Nigeria," *Journal of Marriage and the Family* 44 (August 1982): 799–802.

46. B. Krishna Singh and J. Sherwood Williams, "Childlessness and Family Satisfaction," *Research on Aging* 3 (June 1981): 218–227.

Grandparents only hope for today's only child?

Only children are in again. I keep reading that teachers and shrinks and other double-domes now say that only children are not a disadvantaged minority cursed with multiple neuroses after all. Instead, only children tend to be bright, well-adjusted high-achievers who usually grow up to be self-reliant adults. The secret is out. Too bad.

I feel a special kinship with only children. That's because I am one. Unlike this present crop, however, I grew up at a time when being an only child was definitely out. You were considered odd and a little pathetic. Everybody worried about you, and this made for a splendid life. I am saddened to think that the only children in contemporary society may not enjoy the advantages I had, surrounded by worry worts.

The feeling back when we were hacking McClure Street out of the wilderness of Peoria was that every house ought to have at least three or four kids in it. Most did. Some had five or six. Ours had me.

My parents fretted that because I had no brothers or sisters (or cousins either) I was not growing up with a proper sense of normal family life. If someone had suggested to Mom or Dad that our life was abnormal, there would have been a rhubarb, no doubt. Secretly, however, they felt something was missing from my life.

My parents also fretted that through dearth of siblings I was not learning the all-important concept of sharing. This was nonsense. I had to share chalk and crayons and books and half my lunch with the kids at school. Actually, I didn't have to share my lunch. I just did that so that I could get a banana-flip in trade for my apple. I also learned very quickly in the empty lot that if you don't share your stuff with the other kids, they just cut you out of the game, or they clobber you. Kids work these things out. They never care whether you are an only child or the eighth in a string of 14.

Anyway, the guilt and worry my parents felt whenever somebody said, "Oh, she's an only child, poor thing," worked to my distinct advantage. I got to take tap dance lessons at the YWCA on Saturdays.

I also got to spend one month every summer on a farm. My parents found this family with eight kids and cut some deal so that I could join the

In looking at only children as adults, data from seven U.S. national surveys were used to establish the effects of a number of siblings on eight dimensions of well-being.[47] Without exception, all the effects of having siblings were negative, or stated differently, all were positive effects of being an only child. Only children were more likely to say they were

---

47. Norval D. Glenn and Sue Keir Hoppe, "Only Children as Adults," *Journal of Family Issues* 5 (September 1984): 363–382.

group. I gathered eggs and fed chickens, milked cows (not well), slopped pigs and got to swing on a rope in the hay mow like Tarzan. Yahooo! At night after supper everybody used to gather around the piano in the parlor to sing hymns and hillbilly songs. We did not sing hymns or hillbilly songs at my house. I liked the farm a lot.

None of the kids with brothers and sisters got to do these things. They got to stay home and play with each other which was considered the normal American way. They didn't have my disadvantage. I was pathetic and required special education. Ha!

Grandparents were especially aware of the deprivation of an only child. They were always sure you would be bored and lonely on a rainy day, so they sent lots of toys through the mail even when it wasn't your birthday. They also took you to the circus and the movies or to Forest Park Highlands in St. Louis to ride the roller coaster as many times as you wanted because you were a poor, lonesome, only child. Ha, again!

What nobody noticed back in the olden times was that I had just as many neighborhood playmates as any other kids and did all the same things they did. The only difference I could see was that I had a room of my own while most of my friends shared space with a brother or sister. I didn't see this as a disadvantage.

Still, it was necessary for me to have all of this special attention in order to make up for this terrible deficiency in my life, perceived only by adults. You can see why I feel sorry for all the sprouting only children today. They are not going to be considered unusual. No one is going to consider them pitiful, so they won't get to go to the farm. Born too late, poor babies.

Grandparents may be the only hope. They will still be convinced that an only child is lonely, despite scientific evidence to the contrary.

If today's kids are lucky, one or another of their grandparents will own a farm or know somebody who does. Maybe Granddad will insist that poor, pitiful Pauline will spend half the summer there with an army of farm kids and a flock of chickens. I wonder if farmers still have hay mows and pianos in the parlor. I hope so. Pauline will love it.

Source: Nickie McWhirter, *Detroit Free Press*, October 25, 1978, p. 1-C. Reprinted with the permission of the Detroit Free Press.

very happy, find life exciting, see their health as excellent, get satisfaction from where they live, from their non-working activities, from their family life, from their friendships, and from their physical condition. The evidence most clearly contradicts the popular stereotype of the unhappy, maladjusted only child.

Some research on adult only children in Boston indicated that when compared with first borns of siblings and with individuals of higher birth orders, only children were found to have higher educational levels, higher occupational status, smaller families, and to be more secularly oriented.[48] Female onlies were more likely to be working, to have planned their families before marriage, and to have been more autonomous in deciding to work. All groups were similar in terms of perceived happiness or satisfaction with life, in their social activities, and in the ways their children viewed them as parents. The researchers concludes that onlies, that is, one-child adults, were not emotionally or personally handicapped by their lack of siblings.

Similar results come from Blake,[49] who concludes that research findings on the only child do not support the negative stereotypes that still persist about singletons. She claims they are intellectually superior, have no obvious personality defects, tend to count themselves happy, and are satisfied with important aspects of life, notably jobs and health. In fact, her research goes beyond the only child or small family area to support the "dilution model" that predicts, on average, the more children per family, the lower the quality of each child. "Quality of each child" does not refer to the intrinsic worth of one person over another but to objective measures of human capital such as educational or occupational attainment. Her research shows that even if one is well-off it is not easy to avoid the negative consequences of large familes, whose children were found to have less ability, lower grades, and less academic encouragement from their parents.

To perceive a family as large or small is relative. In the United States four or more children may be viewed as a "large family." In many countries, and perhaps in the United States at the turn of the century, a family of four would lead to a reaction such as "only four?" Irrespective of the cutoff point as to what is a large or small family, a small family is such for one of two primary reasons: either the parents wanted a small family and achieved their desired size or they wanted a large family but were unable to attain it. In both cases, there is a low probability of unwanted children. In contrast, a large family is such because the parents achieved the size they desired or because they had more children than they in fact wanted. The probability is therefore greater that larger families include unwanted or unloved children.

Particularly in large families, last-born children are more likely to be

48. Denise F. Polit, Ronald L. Nuttall, and Ena V. Nuttall, "The Only Child Grows Up: A Look at Some Characteristics of Adult Only Children," *Family Relations* 29 (January 1980): 99–106.

49. Judith Blake, "Family Size and the Quality of Children," *Demography* 18 (November 1981): 421–442; and Judith Blake, "The Only Child in America: Prejudice versus Performance," *Population and Development Review* 7 (March 1981): 43–54.

unwanted than first- or middle-born children. This idea is consistent with what is known of abortion patterns among married women. That is, married women are most likely to resort to abortion when they have achieved the number of children they want or feel they can afford to have.

A substantial body of evidence exists concerning the relationship between family size or number of children and factors such as discipline, achievement, and health. One review of family size effects[50] showed that in larger families, child rearing becomes more rule ridden, less individualized, with corporal punishment and less investment of resources. Persons from smaller families tended to have higher IQs, academic achievement, and occupational performance. Large families produce more delinquents and alcoholics. In regard to health, in large families perinatal (surrounding birth) morbidity and mortality rates are higher, and mothers are at greater risk of several physical diseases. In the words of the authors:

> Women who have many children more frequently develop hypertension, stress symptoms, gall bladder disease, diabetics, and postpartum depression. Women with many children are at higher risk for cancer to the cervix, digestion organs, and peritoneum, but are at less risk for breast cancer.
>
> Fathers of large families are at greater risk of hypertension and peptic ulcers.[51]

While a number of studies revealed no effect, positive or negative, to be associated with family size, very few exist that substantiate positive consequences associated with large families. The consequences of a large family size, as with most social structural variables, will tend to vary by factors such as educational level, social class, or religious subculture.

One prime example of this can be seen in a study of Mormon women who had at least seven children, were all college graduates, and were married to college graduates.[52] In this highly atypical sample, the basis for the mothers' commitment to large families was rooted in religious beliefs such as that the number of children are destined by God, birth control is wrong, and good families have many children. Even in this context, the mothers perceived pressure from relatives to slow down their childbearing and encountered situations of prejudice and discrimination. Most of the mothers had difficulties meeting the various demands of the wife and mother role, had self-doubts, and felt they had many faults and weaknesses. Yet, on balance, they felt the rewards of the struggle were worth the costs. While admitting that rearing a large number of children

---

50. Mazie Earle Wagner, Herman J. P. Schubert, and Daniel S. P. Schubert, "Family Size Effects: A Review," *The Journal of Genetic Psychology* 146 (March 1985): 65–78.

51. Ibid., p. 72.

52. Howard M. Bahr, Spencer J. Condie, and Kristen L. Goodman, *Life in Large Families: Views of Mormon Women* (Washington, D.C.: University Press of America, 1982).

Fallout from excess kids

Since 1968, there has been a dramatic increase in big families. Today 48 percent say 2.1 children is the ideal family.

Where does that leave me? Somewhere between the propagation of the faith, the population explosion and 1.1 surplus kid at my dinner table.

And don't think I haven't paid dearly for my 1.1 overflow. To begin with, he fouled up the family vote. We used to vote even, at two-all, which left some room for persuasion. Since he arrived, my husband and I haven't won a decision in 15 years. Whether it is a vote on a vacation site, what TV show we are going to watch, or whether or not parents are to be impeached, the vote is always the same: Kids, 3—Parents, 2.

I am not being dramatic when I say this is a two-child-geared society. If the Good Lord had meant for people to have more than two children, he would put more than two windows in the back set of the car. We once threatened to put one on the front fender and the other two cried because they each wanted one.

A popsicle can only be divided two ways. There are two pairs of shoelaces in a package, so that one child always goes around with gym shoes that flop off his feet when he walks. There are only four chairs to a dinette set (so that one never matches) and four breakfast sweet rolls to a package.

We always had one too many for a rowboat, and when we rode the Ferris wheel, it was two to a seat and the odd one always rode alone like an only child.

Few people realize this, but did you know that a No. 2 can of fruit cocktail contains only two maraschino cherries? This means when you divide two maraschino cherries between three children, two are happy and the other one runs right out and retains F. Lee Bailey to fight a cherry custody suit.

Chores are geared toward twos—one washes dishes and the other dries, but what does the third child do? He becomes a useless bum and grows up to steal hubcaps.

Bunk beds come in twos. There are two sinks to a bathroom, two Hostess Twinkees to a package and free circus tickets come in pairs.

I mentioned this to the kids the other night and half-kiddingly said, "You know what this means, don't you? One of you has to go. Just for kicks, let's take a vote on it."

When the votes were counted, it was 4—1. I had been phased out of the family.

Somehow, I expected more from a full-grown man who has his own car window.

Source: From *At Wit's End* by Erma Bombeck. Reproduced through the courtesy of Field Newspaper Syndicate.

was no easy task, their religious commitment and a wide repertoire of techniques for coping with stress made them effective mothers.

It should be emphasized that it is not family size per se that creates varied systems of family living. Rather, it is the life factors and personal values that arise in relation to a certain size of group. Large families heighten the complexity of intragroup relations, pose additional problems in the fulfillment of family needs, and are likely to influence the amount of parental comfort or praise available per child.

Birth order and sibling relationships

Birth order (sibling position) has been found to have a major influence on a wide variety of behavioral and attitudinal phenomena. A frequently reported and well-documented lineage is between first-born status and superior intellectual achievement. That family structure and interaction rather than any innate factor explains this relationship is evident in research findings of Pfouts, who found that family socialization shapes first-borns' academic achievement relative to second-borns even when second-borns are more intellectually gifted.[53]

The complexity of the birth order issue is evident in articles such as one which questions whether the consequences of birth order are real, artifactual (produced artificially), or both.[54] Steelman and Powell, in using two nationally representative samples, find no significant relationship between birth order and academic performance but do find a highly positive relationship between birth order and social skills, with later born children being more outgoing, able to get along with others, more popular, and able to make friends easier. Leadership skills were found to contradict the stereotype of the eldest child, with the younger males exhibiting greater leadership skills. Females exhibited no differences in leadership by birth order. They stress the need in birth order research to control for variables such as sex (male or female) and family size (number of siblings).

An additional dimension, beyond sex and family size, that may be important in birth order research is a combination of size and sex. How many siblings are of the same or different sex? For example, one study showed that among male adolescents, first-borns and last-borns perceived their father's educational goals more accurately than did the middle-borns. But female adolescents most likely to perceive their mother's goals accurately

---

53. Jane H. Pfouts, "Birth Order, Age-Spacing, IQ Differences, and Family Relations," *Journal of Marriage and the Family* 42 (August 1980): 517–531.

54. Lala Carr Steelman and Brian Powell, "The Social and Academic Consequences of Birth Order: Real, Artifactual, or Both?" *Journal of Marriage and the Family* 47 (February 1985): 117–124.

Parenting includes those special moments when son can *help* dad. (Photo: ©
Robert Kalman/The Image Works)

were those in families where male children were in the majority. Apparently
the accuracy of paternal educational goals is affected both by the sex
composition of one's siblings as well as birth order.[55]

Returning to the research that is less complex than that which controls
for family size, sibling composition, or interaction effects, most research
has tended to suggest that, in general, first-borns tend to be intellectual
achievers and higher in self-esteem. Female first-borns, in particular, tend
to be more religious, more sexually conservative, more traditionally oriented
toward feminine roles, and more likely to associate with adults. The last-
born or youngest children, like the one-child family, tends to be more
sexually permissive, more likely to engage in social activities, visit with

55. Jeannie S. Kidwell, "The Neglected Birth Order: Middleborns," *Journal of Marriage
and the Family* 44 (February 1982): 225–235.

friends more frequently, make use of the media, and be consistently less traditional. Explanations for these differences often focus on the older child being role models for the younger, having more responsibility for other children, and receiving less attention as siblings enter the scene.

Even middle-borns appear to differ from first-borns and last-borns. An analysis of a national sample of several thousand adolescent males found middle-borns to have a significantly lower self-esteem than the first or last born.[56] A one- or three-year spacing between siblings was more positive for self-esteem than a two-year spacing, as was having siblings who were female as opposed to male or both brother and sister siblings. The explanation of a lower self-assessment of the middle-born may be based on a theory that first- and last-borns have a uniqueness that facilitates status recognition and attention by parents and siblings. The middle child lacks this inherent uniqueness.

The role and significance of siblings is often underrepresented in family textbooks. Yet, it is clear siblings have a major impact on the socialization process (described in the next chapter), on each other as friends and companions, and on parents. Based on a review of research, Ann Goetting illustrates how the sibling bond typically persists over the life cycle.[57] Some sibling relationships are relatively constant, such as companionship and emotional support, while others, such as specific types of caretaking and sibling rivalry, stand out as unique to specific stages in the life cycle. Sibling relationships are unique in their duration, their common genetic and social heritage, and their common early experiences with the family.

Sex control and gender preference

An interesting question to ponder at the end of a chapter dealing with the parental system is "What will be the consequences as parents can increasingly control whether to have a boy or a girl (sex control) and can choose a male or a female (gender preference)?" The day is at hand when parents will be able to choose the sex of their children using either of two basic procedures: (1) by controlling the type of sperm that will fertilize the egg, or (2) by prenatally determining the sex of an embryo and then aborting it if it is of the undesired sex. Amniocentesis and ultrasound photography are becoming low-risk, routine ways to both diagnose the

---

56. Thomas Ewin Smith, "Sex and Sibling Structure: Interaction Effects Upon the Accuracy of Adolescent Perceptions of Parental Orientations," *Journal of Marriage and the Family* 46 (November 1984): 901–907.

57. Ann Goetting, "The Developmental Tasks of Siblingship Over the Life Cycle," *Journal of Marriage and the Family* 48 (November 1986): 703–714.

Choose the sex of your child via new technique

As reported in the *New York Times* (May 29, 1984), a new technique has been developed that enhances the chances of sex determination. It was developed by Dr. Ronald Ericsson, a specialist in reproductive physiology in California. How is this done?

In a laboratory the husband's semen is washed in a tissue medium and the sample then is run through first one, then a second glass column containing an increasingly viscous layer of human serum albumen. Sperm cells containing the Y chromosome, which have the genes for males, are heavier, stronger, and swim faster than sperm containing the X chromosome, but the sperm may contain either X or Y. Since a Y chromosome is necessary for the conception of a male, the chances are enhanced by an artificial concentration of Y's. After the sperm have descended to the bottom of the second glass column they are withdrawn, separated from the liquids that surround them, concentrated, and injected directly into the wife's cervix shortly after ovulation.

Dr. Ericsson said sperm that are immature or abnormal in some other way are almost completely screened out through the use of this procedure, thus, reducing the eventual risk of spontaneous abortion as well as of the birth of babies that are either physically deformed or mentally retarded. In addition, the technique may be used to increase the sperm concentration for men with a low sperm count.

Sex selection for females is more complicated, involving not only the sifting out of X chromosomes but also the use of a drug that both induces ovulation and, for some unknown reason, skews the sex ratio toward females.

The technique is not foolproof, and some specialists have expressed skepticism about claims for its success rate. But a study of about 250 births that involved the procedure shows that it appears to raise the chances of having a child of the desired sex from the ratio that might be expected by chance (about 106 male per 100 females) to more than 75 percent in cases in which a boy is desired.

health of fetuses already conceived and to confirm their sex months before birth occurs. In brief, it is no longer unrealistic to foresee the ability to guarantee the reproduction of offspring of the chosen sex.

How would you react to a number of projected societal consequences of sex control? Will sex control result in an unbalanced sex ratio? It has been estimated that choosing the sex of the child will increase the proportion of male births by 7 to 10 percent. Also, a series of research reports seems to indicate that boys are preferred over girls in much of Africa, Asia, and the Middle East, among the Swiss, Belgians, and Italians in Europe, and among Jews and Catholics in the United States, to mention a few. If this excess of males were to occur, would it increase the number of males who never marry due to a marriage squeeze, delay their age at marriage, force an increase in homosexuality and prostitution, or even force the introduction of polyandry?

Would a consequence of choosing the sex of a child be a reduction in the birth rate because some parents would not have to bear additional children in order to have one or another of a particular sex? Studies indicate that the desire for more children is closely correlated with the number of sons.

Would a consequence be an increased proportion of first-born males? Some of the consequences of birth order have already been shown. Thus, the result may be children who have more friends, are more conservative, or are more eminent scholars.

Finally, would a consequence of choosing a boy or a girl be improved family relationships by avoiding births of the undesired sex, by having fewer resented or rejected children, or by the elimination of gender-role confusion?

We are living in a "biological revolution" of which sex control is one aspect, yet such control is one biological "advancement" that could have a far-reaching social impact on the parental system in the United States and around the world.

SUMMARY

1. The previous chapter examined various aspects of the marital system. Continuing through the life cycle, children follow shortly after the beginning of most marriages. This chapter examines structural factors relating to the parental system: a system of interrelated statuses of parents and children.

2. Parenthood and its consequences cannot be evaluated apart from the society in which it functions. Parenthood has a major impact, particularly for women, on leaving the world of paid employment, and for couples it affects marital stability by decreasing—in the short term at least—the likelihood of separation and divorce.

3. The transition to parenthood requires a major reorganization of statuses, roles, and relationships. Early studies labeled parenthood as a crisis event; however, more recent studies focused on the transition to new responsibilities and duties. Time appears to be a major problem for most mothers. In spite of numerous difficulties, children are found to be a major source of self-fulfillment, esteem, and affection for many parents.

4. Young parenthood and unwed parenthood are issues of specific concern, both in terms of the parents and the children. Parents are often

at a disadvantage in terms of the marriage, education, income, employment, and training in general. Unwed parenthood does appear to make a difference in the child's ability to get started on an equal footing with children born in wedlock and to avoid disadvantages after infancy as well. While the birth rate within marriage is dropping, the number of births outside of marriage is increasing sharply. The greatest increases are not among teenagers but among women who are older.

5. Most couples want, have, or expect to have children. The rate of births varies by wars and periods of economic depression and prosperity. Over the past few decades, women have been delaying their first births with the consequences of having fewer children and being better off economically.

6. Some couples have no children by choice. Less than one couple in five, either by choice or by circumstances, is childless. Many of these women choose a career path and marital style that rejects mothering and parenthood.

7. Family size does make a difference. Research evidence tends to support the "dilution model" that predicts, on average, the more children per family, the lower the quality of the child in terms of their educational or occupational attainment. Most of the negative stereotypes about the small family or single child family find little, if any, support.

8. As with family size, differences exist by order of birth. First-borns appear to be more traditionally oriented, less sexually permissive, more achievement-oriented, and differ from later-born children in a variety of ways. But researchers warn against ignoring sex and family size in these considerations.

9. Some evidence suggests that gender preferences exist within the population of many countries for male children. Perhaps within the near future parents can choose to have a child of one sex or the other. This ability to choose could result in dramatic changes in the sex ratio, in birth rates, and in family relationships in general.

10. This chapter covered a range of topics dealing with parents and parenthood. Some attention was devoted to both young and unwed parenthood and to an examination of factors related to family size. The next chapter continues with the parenthood issue, but focuses more specifically on parent-child interaction, socialization patterns, and gender role differences.

KEY TERMS AND TOPICS

DISCUSSION QUESTIONS

1. Discuss the likely effects of the following structural dimensions on parenthood: age of parents, length of marriage, number of children, spacing of children, and sex of children.

2. In what ways do urbanization and industrialization affect parental roles in U.S. society? Are there advantages for farm families in rearing children?

3. What conditions are likely to increase the probability that parenthood will be a "crisis" event?

4. Why are young parenthood and unwed parenthood considered social problems? If they are social problems, why doesn't society make birth control, abortion, sterilization, and the like available for the unwed teenage males or females?

5. A number of states have passed or are attempting to pass legislation that requires Planned Parenthood clinics to notify parents that their teenage children have requested contraceptive information. What would you predict to be some of the consequences of this type of action?

6. Discuss the myth of the "maternal instinct." How do you explain the widespread acceptance of it? What factors disprove its existence?

7. Examine the birth rate data presented. Explain: (1) why the birth rate dropped sharply in the 1930s, (2) how it was accomplished without the pills, abortions, and sterilizations more prevalent today, and (3) the drop in the birth rate in the 1960s and then its recent upturn.

8. Why are childless marriages not likely to become the norm? Are there advantages to marriage without children?

9. Discuss the implications of the slogan "stop at two" in regard to family size. Why two? What if everyone had two? What means should be used to accomplish this if it is perceived as a desirable goal?

10. Itemize advantages of large and small families. What are the consequences of being an only child? What types of factors are likely to influence the size of a family?

11. Discuss the implications of being an oldest, middle, or youngest child. Does spacing make any differences?

12. If sex of the fetus could be determined accurately within a few weeks following pregnancy, what effect, if any, would this have on birth rates? Would most parents in the United States choose boys, girls, or have no preferences? What about other countries, particularly outside of the Western world?

FURTHER READINGS

Bahr, Howard, M.; Condie, Spencer J.; and Goodman, Kristen, L. *Life in Large Families: Views of Mormon Women.* Washington, D.C.: University Press of America, 1982. A study of large families in the Latter-Day Saint religious subculture: the social pressures, self-perceptions, loneliness, management of a conjugal corporation, stress, and involvement in the church.

Campbell, Elaine. *The Childless Marriage.* New York: Tavistock, 1986. A sympathetic and humanistic account of the childless careers of seventy-eight people in a Scottish city.

Elster, Arthur, B., and Lamb, Michael E. (eds.) *Adolescent Fatherhood.* Hillsdale, N.J.: Lawrence Erlbaum Association, 1986. A compilation of eleven writings on adolescents, including topics such as risking paternity, stresses and coping strategies, parent behavior, and others.

Falbo, Toni (ed.) *The Single Child Family.* New York: Guilford Press, 1984. A collection of papers that dispels traditional notions about the disadvantages of being an only child.

Fox, Greer Litton. *The Childbearing Decision: Fertility Attitudes and Behavior.* Beverly Hills: Sage Publications, 1982. A multidisciplinary collection of eleven articles summarizing connections between fertility decision making and factors such as socialization, sex roles, work, motivational variables, and divorce.

Furstenberg, Frank F., Jr. *Unplanned Parenthood: The Social Consequences of Teenage Childbearing.* New York: The Free Press, 1976. A longitudinal investigation of the social, economic, and psychological consequences of adolescent motherhood from the pregnancy through the first five years of parenthood. Classmates who did not become pregnant were used as a control group.

Gallas, Howard B., ed. "Teenage Parenting: Social Determinants and Consequences." *Journal of Social Issues* 36 (Winter 1980): 1–44. A special issue of seven articles on teenage parenting covering topics such as mother-daughter communication about sexuality, socialization for childbearing, the father's impact on mother and child, and coping with unmarried motherhood.

Hanson, Shirley M. H., and Bozett, Frederick, W. (eds.) *Dimensions of Fatherhood.* Beverly Hills: Sage Publications, 1985. An interdisciplinary compilation of nineteen articles that view fathers and fatherhood in a variety of social roles presented in a life-span perspective.

LaRossa, Ralph. *Becoming a Parent.* Beverly Hills: Sage Publications, 1986. A look at becoming a parent, fertility decision-making, pregnancy, birth, and infant care, with an emphasis on how these experiences differ between the sexes.

LeMasters, E. E., and DeFrain, John. *Parents in Contemporary America: A Sympathetic View.* 4th ed. Homewood, Ill.: Dorsey, 1983. An overview of parents in the United States today, including an analysis of parenthood and folklore, roles, social class, minority groups, parents without partners, social change, and counseling.

Mackey, Wade C. *Fathering Behaviors: The Dynamics of the Man-Child Bond*. New York: Plenum Press, 1985. A cross-cultural observation study of interaction between adults (especially males) and children in public places.

Robinson, Bryan, E., and Barret, Robert L. *The Developing Father: Emerging Roles in Contemporary Society*. New York: Guilford Press, 1986. A comprehensive view of fathers, based on both research and personal accounts of men describing their own fathering experiences.

Photo: (c) David S. Strickler/The Picture Cube

14

Parent-Child Interaction and Socialization

The previous chapter examined selected structural arrangements of the family system: norms and values surrounding parenthood, young parenthood, unwed parenthood, birth rates and birth expectations, effects of large or small families, birth order, and the like. This chapter as well looks at selected social structural patterns such as gender (male-female) differences, but it focuses primary attention on interactional and social psychological patterns in parent-child relationships. Of central concern are theoretical frames of reference that vary in their explanations of the socialization process.

THE SOCIALIZATION OF PARENTS AND CHILDREN

The helplessness of human infants is perhaps unequaled among newborns. They cannot walk, feed themselves, know where danger lies, seek food or shelter, or even roll over. Infants may grow up to be criminals, teachers, or athletic superstars, but first they must learn to care for basic needs, learn to interact with other humans, and learn what behavior is expected and accepted. In short, they must learn to be human.

The process of acquiring these physical and social skills to become a social being and a member of society is called **socialization**. Socialization, the central concept of this chapter, is a never-ending process of developing the self and of learning the ways of a given society and culture. While the focus of attention in the socialization literature is generally upon the newborn and the young child, teenagers, middle-aged, and older people as well are in a continual process of learning skills, developing the self, and becoming a participant in the groups and social systems of society. Parents too need to be socialized to parenthood. Parents not only influence and shape the behavior of children, but children do the same to parents.[1]

Socialization, particularly of the young infant, may be the single

1. Note: John F. Peters, "Adolescents as Socialization Agents to Parents," *Adolescence* 20 (Winter 1985): 920–933.

universal function of the family.[2] There may be others—such as social placement—but every society appears to link people by affinity (marriage) or consanguineous (blood) ties to the nurturant socialization of persons. This does not imply that families do not fulfill other functions, that socialization only occurs among infants, or that the family is the only socializing agent. Rather, the key implication is that the basic function of the family in all societies is nurturant socialization.

Preconditions for socialization

Frederick Elkin and Gerald Handel state that there are three preconditions for adequate socialization:

1.   There must be an ongoing society.
2.   Children must have the requisite biological inheritance.
3.   The child requires human nature.[3]

First, the newborn enters an existing society that has rules, norms, values, attitudes, ways of behaving, and a wide variety of social structures that are highly regular and patterned but in constant change. The unsocialized infant has no knowledge of these changes, structures, or processes. The patterns of thinking, feeling, and acting of that society are what the socializing agents must pass on to the newcomer. This is the task of socialization.

The second precondition for socialization is a biological inheritance that is adequate to permit learning processes to occur. Thus a brain, a digestive system, and a beating heart are clearly prerequisites for socialization. These prerequisites, however, while necessary, are not sufficient. A "perfect" biological system, while influencing the socialization process, will not be the determinant of what is internalized mentally. Factors such as brain damage, deafness, extreme tallness or shortness, shape of nose and chin, or a wide variety of other physical conditions may hinder or influence interaction and socializing processes. But it should be made extremely clear that the biological inheritance, while influencing learning processes and necessary for their occurrence, are never sufficient conditions for socialization. Certain needs such as food, drink, and sleep are basic to survival, but they can be satisfied in a wide variety of ways. And while temperaments and intelligence may be basically biological, the development or direction that they take is influenced and modified by the society in

---

2. Ira L. Reiss, "The Universality of the Family: A Conceptual Analysis," *Journal of Marriage and the Family* 27 (November 1965): 443–453.

3. Frederick Elkin and Gerald Handel, *The Child and Society: The Process of Socialization*, 4th ed. (New York: Random House, 1984): 11.

Sect parents who don't "spare the rod"

The Northeast Community Church, a 400 member religious sect group in Vermont, was under investigation by state officials in the mid-1980s because of child beating. A public meeting was called after the state seized 112 children of church members to have them examined for signs of physical and psychological abuse. They were released within hours after a judge ruled there was not enough evidence to warrant the emergency detention.

Newspaper accounts of the public meeting gave comments of the seven church elders in attendance. One told the angry townspeople that a lost generation would result unless youngsters, even babies, were "properly spanked." When asked at what age children should be spanked, a response was that if you wait until a child is able to reason, you have waited too long. Another said that even little babies have a fallen nature and needed strict discipline.

A Mr. Wiseman, who faced charges that he beat a 13-year-old for seven hours, quoted the Book of Psalms by saying "Serve the Lord with fear." He argued that strict discipline is part of the standard of God. Strict discipline included the use of slender wooden rods for reasons ranging from lying to asking for second helpings at meals.

which the infant exists. In brief, while biological requisites are necessary for adequate socialization, they alone are not determinants of socialization.

The third precondition is human nature. Here *human nature* refers to certain factors that are universal among humans and yet distinctive to humans as compared to other animals. Within the symbolic interaction frame of reference, human nature would include the ability to take the role of the other, the ability to feel as others feel, or in general the ability to symbolize. To symbolize is to give meaning to abstractions, to recognize words, sounds, and gestures, and to attach meaning to them. The wink of an eye, the shake of a fist, or the nod of a head take on meaning in terms of human beings' ability to symbolize. As far as is known, this is a nature unique to humans.

THEORIES OF SOCIALIZATION PROCESSES

As previously defined, *socialization* refers to the process by which the infant and adult learn the ways of a given society and culture and develop into participants capable of operating in that society. A number of relatively comprehensive theories have been developed to explain various aspects of this process. Let's examine a number of these.

A learning-behaviorist frame of reference

Learning theory, also recognized as reinforcement theory, stimulus-response theory, and behaviorism, assumes that the same concepts and principles that apply to lower animals apply to humans. Thus it is logical and rational to spend time in the laboratory experimenting with rats, cats, dogs, pigeons, monkeys, or other animals to learn more about humans. Although there are many variations of learning theory, as with the other theories that follow, basic assumptions and common lines of agreement do exist.

Learning, or socialization as applied to the newborn infant, involves changes in behavior that result from experience. (This is opposed to changes in behavior that result from physiological maturation or biological conditions.) Learning involves conditioning that may include classical conditioning or instrumental (operant) conditioning. *Classical conditioning* links a response to a known stimulus. Most students are already familiar with Pavlov's dog experiment, which provides a good example of classical conditioning. The hungry dog, placed in a soundproof room, heard a tuning fork prior to receiving meat. When repeated on several occasions, the dog salivated upon hearing the tuning fork prior to receiving, or even without receiving, the meat. The tuning fork, a conditioned stimulus, produced the response (salivation). In the classical conditioning experiment, the focus of attention is largely on the stimulus. If this works with dogs, the same principle should hold true with an infant upon hearing his mother's approaching footsteps. The footstep stimulus, with repeated occurrences, should elicit a response from the child.

Instrumental conditioning, or what Skinner calls *operant conditioning*, places the focus of attention on the response. The responses are not related to any known stimuli but rather they function in an instrumental fashion. We learn to make a certain response on the basis of the consequences the response produces. It is the response, rather than the stimulus, that is correlated with reinforcement. Let's return to the example of the hungry dog. Under classical conditioning the dog salivated upon hearing the tuning fork, the stimulus. Under operant conditioning, the hungry dog may sniff, paw, and chew whatever is around. If upon pawing, the dog opens a door behind which is food, the sniffing and chewing will soon decrease and the pawing on the door will occur whenever food is desired. Thus instrumental conditioning is a response followed by a reward (reinforcement).

How does this apply to an infant? Suppose the infant utters sounds like "da-da-da." Father, who is convinced the child is saying daddy, rewards him or her by picking up, feeding, or rocking. As a result, the response (da-da-da) soon becomes used by the infant all day long. The infant has learned to make a certain response on the basis of the consequence or

B. F. Skinner now sees little hope for the world's salvation

CAMBRIDGE, MASS.—For decades, B. F. Skinner has written about and preached his behavioral theory of human psychology. Thoughts, emotions and actions, he contends, are exclusively products of environment; free will, according to the Harvard University psychologist, simply does not exist. He envisioned utopian societies, and described one in his book, "Walden II," that resulted from tightly controlled systems in which people were motivated solely by the manipulation of what he called positive and negative reinforcements.

Now Dr. Skinner is conceding that behavioral psychology may be unable to significantly improve the collective human condition.

He said in an interview at his office that 10 years ago, when his book "Beyond Freedom and Dignity" was published, he believed behavioral psychology provided the "technology" to solve the world's problems. But he hadn't thought through, he says, "the question of whether people would ever have the inclination" to use this tool.

Now he has thought it through. "I'm very pessimistic," he said. "We're not going to solve our problems, really."

At the same time, he has issued what he calls "my answer to sociobiologists." Dr. Skinner says he is proposing that the sociobiologists are wrong to assert that specific genes for specific behaviors, such as altruism, have evolved by natural selection as a means of preserving the species. He acknowledges that genes play a role in behavior but in his scheme their responsibility is much more general. He proposes that human beings are born with a set of genes programmed for operant conditioning, the process by which they learn to behave in response to the rewards and punishments presented by society. Whether or not a person will act to help another in a given situation is dictated by the culture, he says, and not some inborn trait designed to perpetuate and advance the human race.

Some of Dr. Skinner's critics have repeatedly asserted that debates over

result the response will produce; hence it is the response that is correlated with reinforcement.

These same general principles, refined by behaviorists with reference to intermittent reinforcement, partial reinforcement, negative and positive reinforcement, discrimination of stimuli, differentiation of response, and the like are said to apply in the learning of any kind of behavior. Socialization results from stimulus-response conditioning and from positive and negative reinforcements. The conditioning stimuli (classical conditioning) and the consequences of responses (operant conditioning) are both external to the animal or human.

Many of these processes are most readily observed in early childhood when parents use rewards and punishment as deliberate techniques for teaching the child approved forms of behavior. As individuals mature, the controlling of entire societies are academic; psychologists, they argue, simply do not possess the means, for better or worse, to alter substantially the course of the human race.

Now, it seems, Dr. Skinner agrees. "Why do we not act to save our world?"

The answers he offers are complex and bound up in the behavioral theory, which says that people do not initiate action on their own, but act in ways that have been successful in the past. But today's problems of overpopulation, pollution, energy depletion and other environmental hazards cast a pall over the future that promises to make it more unlike the present than perhaps at any other point in modern history, Dr. Skinner suggests. Therefore, solving such potential life-and-death problems through strategies that worked before is little more than a pipedream, according to Dr. Skinner.

The only hope, he says, would be to get people to act on *predictions* of future conditions and thus alter institutions and practices. But a basic tenet of behavioral theory states that the environment shapes people's actions; and since, as Dr. Skinner notes, "the future does not exist, how can it affect contemporary human behavior?" The solution might be somehow to persuade people, through behavioral techniques, that their very survival might depend on their actions right now.

But realistically, Dr. Skinner says, "you can't get four-and-a-half billion people to change. Those few people who do respond to the dire conditions of the future—journalists, environmentalists, behavioral scientists—tend not to be powerful," he said. "So, we go to the powerful people: leaders in religion, government, and industry. But these people are concerned with the present; the Pope is interested in saving souls, the governors in re-election and the industrial tycoons in profits.

"And I suppose if we were powerful, we might not be interested in the future either."

Source: Joel Greenberg, *The New York Times*, September 15, 1981, pp. 21 and 23. Copyright 1981/1982 by The New York Times Company. Reprinted by permission.

sanctioning becomes increasingly complex, and candy, weekly allowances, spanking, or other forms of rewards and punishments lose their ability to either eliminate undesirable behavior or increase desirable behavior.

Within the learning theory–behaviorist framework, symbols, language, reasoning, internalized meanings, and other internal processes play a minimal role. This is in sharp contrast to the symbolic interaction framework (described in Chapter 2 and later in this section) where the socialized being can create his or her own stimuli and responses, can define and categorize, can distinguish between self and nonself, can separate inner and outer sensations, and can take the role of the other. As a result, this basically mechanistic approach to socialization is rejected by most sociologists to whom the self, roles, reference groups, and symbolic processes are viewed as central to an understanding of human behavior. Although learning theory has been extremely illuminating in research with animals and infants, it has been less successful in explaining social situations, group norms, or the learning of language itself.

From the biased perspective of this author, it is largely a waste of time, effort, and expense to attempt to understand the behavior of socialized humanity, capable as we are of dealing with symbolic processes, reasoning, shared meanings, and the like, by studying nonhuman forms. Behaviorism does, however, add greatly to our understanding of the human who (1) has not learned to share meanings—the infant, the isolate, or the severely retarded—or (2) has once learned but no longer has the capacity to share meanings—the more severe cases of aphasia or the extreme cases of schizophrenia where words may exist but the meanings are not shared with others.

This brief, minimal treatment of learning theory may seem unfair to the disciples of behaviorism. The same can be said for the minimal treatment of the psychoanalytic theory that follows. Both are intended to illustrate some contrasting views on the nature of socialization.

A psychoanalytic frame of reference

Classic psychoanalytic theory, developed by Sigmund Freud and his adherents, stresses the importance of biological drives and unconscious processes. This is in sharp contrast to the behaviorist theory just described. The process of socialization, according to this framework, consists of a number of precise though overlapping stages of development. What happens at these stages from birth to age five or six, although unconscious, becomes relatively fixed and permanent. These stages are referred to as the *oral, anal,* and *phallic* stages, followed later by a period of *latency* and a *genital* phase. Attention is focused around three principal erogenous zones: the mouth, the anus, and the genitals, which are the regions of the body where excitatory processes tend to become focalized and where tensions can be removed by some action such as stroking or sucking. Each region is of extreme importance in the socialization process because they are the first important sources of irritating excitations with which the baby has to contend and upon which the first pleasurable experiences occur.

The first stage of development, the *oral stage,* occurs during the first year of the child's life. The earliest erotic gratifications come from the mouth and, as a result, the child forms strong emotional attachments to the mother who supplies the source of food, warmth, and sucking. During the first year, the child is narcissistic with the self-gratification derived via the oral source, namely the mouth. The modes of functioning of the mouth include taking in, holding on, biting, spitting out, and closing, all prototypes for ways of adjusting to painful or disturbing states. They serve as models for adaptations in later life.

The *anal stage* of development follows and overlaps with the oral stage. This phase is so called because the child experiences pleasure in excretion and because toilet training may become a major problem. At this point, two functions become central: retention and elimination. Since the mother is still the predominant figure, her methods of training the child and her attitudes about such matters as defecation, cleanliness, and control are said to determine the impact that toilet training will have upon the development of the person. Carried to the extreme, the mother who praises the child for a large bowel movement may produce an adolescent who will be motivated to produce or create things to please others or to please himself or herself, as he or she once made feces to please mother. On the other hand, if the mother is very strict and punitive, the child may intentionally soil himself or herself and, as an adolescent, be messy, irresponsible, disorderly, wasteful, and extravagant.

The *phallic stage* is the period of growth during which the child is preoccupied with the genitals. Prior to this stage, the first love object of both the boy and girl is the mother. But with the arrival of this stage, the sexual urge increases, the boy's love for his mother becomes more intense, and the result is jealousy of the father who is his rival. The boy's attachment to his parent of the opposite sex is widely known as the *Oedipus complex*. Concurrently, the male becomes fearful that his father will remove his genitals and develops a fear known as *castration anxiety*. This anxiety increases upon observation of the female who has, in his unconscious mind, "already been castrated." A similar or reverse process is in operation for the female. She forms an attachment to her father, the *Electra complex*, but has mixed feelings for him because he possesses something that she does not have. The result is *penis envy*. According to traditional Freudian psychology, penis envy is the key to feminine psychology. Located here are the roots of male dominance and female submissiveness, male superiority and female inferiority.

The oral, anal, and phallic stages taken together are called the *pregenital period* and occupy the first five or six years of one's life. These are the important years when the basic personality patterns are established and fixed. Following this time, for the next six or seven years until the onset of puberty, the male and female egos go through a *latency phase* when the erotic desires of the child are repressed and he or she forms attachments to the parent of the same sex.

Finally, with the arrival of puberty, the *genital phase* of development begins. This period is less a stage than the final working out of the previous stages, particularly the oral, anal, and phallic that occurred during

No hitter can hold a candle to mom

Everybody says motherhood is the toughest game in the world, a grueling physical, psychological contest. Winners and losers shape the entire future of our society, perhaps worldwide. Motherhood makes pro baseball, football and basketball look like child's play.

So, where are the stats? Where's the rule book? Where are the coaches and fans, the amateur and pro leagues, pennants, trophies and those fat TV contracts? Nowhere, and that's a crock.

So far, motherhood is considered a sissy sport, even a non-sport. Not one high school or college has a varsity team. There are only neighborhood pickup games, so to speak. Everybody is an amateur player, all ages, all levels of talent, all unsung. And when their playing days are over, there's no Motherhood Hall of Fame.

Not one aging mother has been hired as a greeter in Las Vegas, or a manufacturer's rep. Oh, some ex-mothers are employed, for sure. Lots of them hold down full-time jobs even while they're playing the game at full potential, which is frequently awesome. But nobody hires any player just because she's a world-class mother. Mothers get hired because they can type or do neurosurgery.

The interest is there, but there's no money and no organization. There's no pro tour to watch on Wide World of Sports. Motherhood is ignored by the International Olympic Committee.

The competition is on

All that has to change. If there's room on the sports pages for the USFL (ho-hum), there has to be room for the National Motherhood League. I can see it now . . .

the pregenital period. At this time, group activities, marriage, establishing a home, developing vocational responsibilities, and "adult" interests become the focus of attention. Given the importance of the early years, one can readily understand why factors such as bottle or breast feeding, nursing on a regular or self-demand time schedule, weaning abruptly or gradually, bowel training early or late, bladder training early or late, punishment or nonpunishment for toilet accidents, or sleeping alone or with one's mother, serve as crucial items of attention to the psychoanalyst.

The claims of the Freudians regarding the importance of infant training to personality adjustment have received mixed empirical support. The support that has been received has, in general, been derived from clinical studies of emotionally disturbed individuals. Other studies show different results. For example, one attempt to test empirically the crucial role of infant discipline in character formation and personality adjustment was

Detroit Matriarch players and fans breathed a collective sign of relief Tuesday night. Mary Smith's elbow is healthy again.

In Detroit's decisive 28–25 victory over the Chicago Mummies, Smith was in top form, high-scorer with 14 points, and voted MVP. All Smith's points came in the critical diapering and burping phase of this best-of-seven preliminary to the conference semifinals. Detroit's D&B specialist, Smith has been plagued with recurring bursitis of the left elbow since spring training, when she attempted to hoist a four-year-old out of a sandbox while simultaneously balancing a two-year-old on her right hip.

"I've done that maneuver a million times,' she said. 'Maybe I tried to do too much too fast."

Coach Crusty McCrea agreed and took Smith out of the lineup until last night. That hasn't been easy for the plucky player from Petoskey. While Smith was out, the Matriarchs barely managed to squeak out victories over the Baltimore Mamas and the Los Angeles Mommie Dearests. But Smith was at the top of her form again on Tuesday.

"I couldn't let the fans down tonight," Smith said after the game in the locker room. "This was one we had to win. I can score from the inside and the outside, and that's what we needed. I gave it everything I had. The elbow felt fine. I'm just glad I had the stuff."

A capacity crowd of 27,325 wildly cheering Matriarch fans were more than glad. They were ecstatic. "Goldang! I wish I had a mother like that 'un!" shouted one enthusiastic Matriarch booster as he tipped over a police car on Michigan Avenue after the game. Don't we all pal? Don't we all!

Source: Nickie McWhirter, *Detroit Free Press*, May 12, 1985, p. 16. Reprinted by permission of the Detroit Free Press.

published approximately thirty-five years ago and has since become a somewhat classic article on the subject.[4] That study set up a series of null hypotheses concerning the relationship of specific infant disciplines to subsequent personality adjustments. The general hypothesis was that the personality adjustment and traits of children who had undergone varying infant training experiences would not differ significantly from each other. These infant training experiences included the self-demand feeding schedule, gradual weaning, late bowel training, and similar factors. The results indicated support for the null hypothesis, that is, there were no significant differences in the personality adjustments of children who had undergone varying infant training experiences. Of 460 Chi-square tests,

---

4. William H. Sewall, "Infant Training and the Personality of the Child." *The American Journal of Sociology* 58 (September 1952): 150–159.

Most child development specialists recognize the importance of imitation and role playing in the socialization of a child to adult roles. (Photo: © Jeffry W. Myers/Freelance Photographer's Guild)

only eighteen were significant at or beyond the .05 level.[5] Of these, eleven were in the expected direction and seven were in the opposite direction from that expected on the basis of psychoanalytic writings. Such practices

---

5. The .05 level means that these relationships would occur simply by chance less than 5 times in 100.

as breast feeding, gradual weaning, demand schedule, bowel training, and bladder training, which have been so emphasized in the psychoanalytic literature, were almost barren in terms of their relationship to personality adjustment.

Child development frames of reference

The ideas of Erik Erikson and of Jean Piaget are of interest in dealing with the socialization issue. Both, like Freud, focus their attention primarily on stages of development. Both, unlike Freud, extended their stages beyond the early years and place more importance on social structure and reasoning.

Erik Erikson's ideas Erikson, one of Freud's students, was a psychoanalyst who saw socialization as a lifelong process, beginning at birth and continuing into old age. He developed and is well-known for his eight stages of human development.[6] Each stage constitutes a crisis brought on by physiological changes, and the constantly changing social situation. In infancy (the first year), the crisis centers around *trust versus mistrust*. Being totally dependent on adults, the feelings of the child are developed in response to the quality of maternal care as dependable or undependable, accepting or rejecting. In early childhood (the first two to three years), the issue centers around *autonomy versus shame and doubt*. Again the feelings of the child are developed in response to the actions of parents who allow the child to accomplish new things and govern himself or herself (autonomy) or receive constant supervision, indicating he or she cannot reach, walk, control bowels, and the like without ridicule and shame.

The play stage (age 4 or 5) involves the issue of *initiative versus guilt*. As children master their own bodies, as they play and fantasize and act out adult roles, they develop feelings of self-worth. Ridicule and disinterest lead to guilt feelings, while encouragement to explore may lead to personal initiative. By school age and up to adolescence, the issue centers around *industry versus inferiority*. Parents become less the focal point as the school and the community take on greater importance. Recognition is received by achieving success in physical and mental skills and producing things (industry), while failure in school, disapproval of race or family background, and inability to achieve may be negative experiences that result in feelings of inferiority.

By adolescence, the issue becomes one of *identity versus role confusion*. Identity, the focal concern of Erikson,[7] is being able to achieve a sense of continuity about one's past, present, and future. An inability to

---

6. Erik K. Erikson, *Childhood and Society* 2d ed. (New York: Norton, 1963), Chapter 7.

7. Erik K. Erikson, *Identity: Youth and Crisis* (New York: Norton, 1968).

Ways that TV affects children

Parents should be concerned about what their children watch on television and how much time they spend watching it, says psychologists and communications specialists.

Although there is some disagreement about just how much and in what way television viewing affects children, the following effects have been established by one or more researchers.

Viewing violent programs fosters aggressive behavior in some children.

Production techniques—such as loud music, fast pacing, rapid changes of scene and special visual and sound effects used in cartoons—may also contribute to aggressive behavior, particularly in small children.

Television viewers often have a distorted view of how much violence there is in the world and thus are more likely to be anxious and insecure.

The stereotypical way blacks and other minority groups, women and the elderly are often portrayed on television contributes to children's prejudices, especially when they do not have models in their own lives to counteract those on television.

Children who watch commercials do pressure their parents to buy the products advertised; they are primarily toys, sugar-coated cereals, fast-food meals, snack foods and candy.

Heavy viewing of television adversely affects the development of language and imagination in young children. It also adversely affects children's reading ability. However, educational television, combined with teacher or parental follow-up, can stimulate some children's imagination and interest in reading and teach some reading skills.

Parents are an important factor in how television viewing affects their children. By watching with children and discussing programs, parents can mediate the effects of violence, stereotypical portrayals and advertising.

Source: The New York Times, July 30, 1981, p. 15. Copyright 1981/1982 by The New York Times Company. Reprinted by permission.

integrate the many and varied roles into a clear identity leads to role confusion. Peers at this point are of prime importance.

Young adulthood, another major turning point in life, involves the issue of *intimacy versus isolation*. Friendship, love affairs, and intimacy require the risk of rejection, losing the friend or lover, and being hurt. Only with a clear sense of ego identity and an ability to trust can one avoid isolation. In young adulthood and middle age the issue centers around *generativity versus stagnation*. People can feel they are making contributions to society, working creatively, rearing children for the next generation, and in general being productive, or they may find life boring, painful, and dull. Childish self-absorption and "early invalidism, physical or psychological, are signs that a person has not found generativity."[8] Old age, the last stage of development is one of reflection and evaluation and focuses on the issue of *integrity versus despair*. Integrity involves coming to terms with life and death. Despair involves seeing life as a series of missed opportunities and realizing it is too late to start over.

Erikson sees the social order as resulting from and in harmony with these eight stages of development. As people work out solutions to these developmental concerns, the solutions become institutionalized in the culture.

Jean Piaget's ideas Piaget, a Swiss social psychologist, spent more than thirty years observing and studying the development of intellectual functions and logic in children.[9] His work has stimulated an interest in maturational stages of development and in the importance of cognition in human development. Differing dramatically from the views of the learning and psychoanalytic frames of reference, Piaget sees development as an ability to reason abstractly, to think about hypothetical situations in a logical way, and to organize rules (which he calls *operations*) into complex, higher order structures. Children invent ideas and behaviors that they have never witnessed or had reinforced.

Piaget believes that there are four major stages of intellectual development: *sensorimotor* (0 to 18 months), *preoperational* (18 months to age 7), *concrete operations* (ages 7 to 12), and finally *formal operations* (ages 12 onward). The stages are continuous and each is built upon and is a derivative of the earlier one.

The *sensorimotor stage*, further differentiated into six developmental stages,[10] involves for the child a physical understanding of himself or herself and his or her world. The unlearned responses such as sucking and closing one's fist become repetitive but with no intent, purpose, or interest in the effect this behavior has on the environment. Later activities in this first stage become more intentional. A child may kick his or her legs to produce a swinging motion in a toy hung on the crib. A child may knock down a pillow to get a toy behind it. A primary cognitive development at this stage is the discovery of object permanence: toys and mother do not dissolve when they are not visible. Early development includes the coordination of simple motor arts with incoming perceptions (sensorimotor arts).

---

8. Erikson, *Childhood and Society*, p. 267.

9. Jean Piaget and Barbara Inhelder, *The Psychology of the Child* (New York: Basic, 1969); and Piaget's theory in P. H. Mussen, ed., *Carmichael's Manual of Child Psychology*, 3d ed. (New York: Wiley, 1970): 703–732.

10. These stages Piaget refers to as *reflexes, primary circular reactions, secondary circular reactions, coordination of secondary reactions, tertiary circular reactions,* and *internal experimentation*. Jean Piaget, *The Construction of Reality in the Child* (New York: Basic, 1954).

Child-rearing in the kibbutz

The kibbutz is extremely child centered. Children represent the future. The manner in which child rearing occurs follows a collective pattern from infancy to adulthood. The infant is born of a kibbutz couple who generally marry just before or soon after the first child is born. This is done in accordance with the laws of Israel and gives the child legal rights. Upon return from the hospital, the infant is placed in the infant house. During the first year of the infant's life, his or her mother comes to this house to breast-feed the infant as long as she physically can. Young fathers participate at this period in bottle-feeding and diapering. In a radical departure from child rearing in most of the world, neither an infant nor any older children live with or are directly supported by the biological father and mother. The socialization and education of kibbutz children are functions of nurses and teachers.

During the first year, the general pattern of child care emerges. Most of the child's time is spent with peers in the children's house. In the afternoon, two or three hours may be spent with parents in their flat or room, meeting with other families or engaging in some joint activity. On the Sabbath, only the essential chores are performed, and children of all ages spend much time with their parents. In addition to these hourly and Sabbath visits, the child frequently sees the parents while they work or by attending this weekly assembly of the kibbutz. Thus parents are extremely important in the life of the child but are, in a sense, junior partners.

Training occurs, for the most part, separate from the residence of the parents. For the first year, the infant is in the nursery. The child is then moved to a toddler's house, each of which has approximately two nurses and eight children. This is where toilet training, learning to feed oneself, and learning to interact with age-mates occur. When the children reach the ages of two or three, a nursery teacher replaces one of the nurses. By the fourth or fifth birthday, the children move into the kindergarten. This involves a different building, sometimes a new nurse and teacher, and an enlargement of the original group to approximately sixteen members. This enlarged group remains together as a unit until age twelve and the completion of sixth grade. At this point they enter high schools where for the first time they encounter male educational teachers and begin to work directly in the kibbutz economy. Their work varies from one to three hours per day, depending on age, and is done in one of the economic branches under the supervision of adults (not parents). Upon completion of high school, the students are expected to live outside the kibbutz for approximately one year. Membership in the kibbutz follows this experience.

While the children do not sleep with, do not have their physical needs cared for, are not taught social, book or economic skills by, and are not—for the most part—disciplined or socialized by their parents, most writers stress the importance of parents in the development of the child. They serve as the object of identification and provide a certain security and love not obtained from others.

The *preoperational stage* involves language and its acquisition. Objects are treated as symbolic of things other than themselves. Dolls may be treated as babies or a stick may be treated as a candle. At this stage, overt actions and the meaning of objects and events are manipulated, but the child has difficulty taking the point of view of another child or adult. Unlike the next (operational) stage, the child does not have a mental representation of a series of actions. For example, a child may be able to walk to a store several blocks away but cannot draw the route on paper. Nor can the child at this stage grasp the notion of relational terms (darker, larger), reason simultaneously about part of the whole and the whole, or arrange objects according to some quantified dimension such as weight or size.

The *operational stage* involves the ability to do things such as those just mentioned. Children learn to manipulate the tools of their culture. They learn that mass remains constant in spite of changes in form. They learn to understand cause and effect, to classify objects, to consider the viewpoints of others, and to differentiate between dreams and real things. By approximately age twelve the child enters the adult world and the stage of formal operations.

The *formal operations stage* includes the ability to think in terms of abstract concepts, theories, and general principles. Alternate solutions to problems can be formulated. Hypothetical propositions can be formulated and answered. Preoccupation with thought is the principal component of this stage of development.

Piaget's insights into cognitive development are unsurpassed. His stages take into account both social and psychological phenomena. Like Freud, Piaget has a specific conception of the goals of maturity and adulthood. Also like Freud, Piaget believes that the child passes through stages. But where Freud emphasized emotional maturity and the unconscious as extremely important, Piaget emphasizes reasoning and consciousness. Whereas Freud focused on bodily zones, Piaget focuses on the quality of reasoning.

The frames of reference covered up to this point can be summarized by suggesting that the learning theorists are concerned with overt behavior, the Freudians with motives and emotions (often unconscious and rooted early in childhood), and the child developmentalists with motor skills, thought, reasoning processes, and conflicts. Let's now turn our attention to a symbolic interaction frame of reference that shares many assumptions of Erikson and Piaget in the importance given to language, reasoning, and societal influences.

A symbolic interaction frame of reference

Contrasting considerably with the learning and psychoanalytic frames of reference is the symbolic interaction frame of reference. Within this framework, although the first five years are important, personality does not become fixed; socialization becomes a lifelong process. Within this framework, although mother is an important figure, so too are fathers, siblings, grandparents, teachers, and many others who are perceived as significant to the child or adult. Although internal needs and drives are important as energy sources and motivating devices, greater significance comes from interactions with others and the internalized definitions and meanings of the world in which one interacts. Although erogenous zones may be sources of pleasure and gratification, the significance of these zones depends on the learned internalized meanings attached to them. Whereas unconscious processes may be at the core of socialization (purely speculative), conscious processes relating to perceptions of self and others take on prime importance. Whereas rewards and punishments influence behavior, these too can only be understood in the light of the meanings attached to them. Whereas conditioning (classical or operant) is significant and basic to learning, internal processes cannot be ignored. To understand socialization as explained within a symbolic interaction frame of reference (*see* Chapter 2), it is necessary to review in more detail the basic assumptions and meaning of key concepts such as "social self," "significant others," and "reference groups."

Basic assumptions of symbolic interactionism   As summarized in Chapter 2, the interactionist frame of reference, when applied to the study of the family and to an understanding of socialization, is based on several **basic assumptions**. Four of these have been delineated by Sheldon Stryker.[11] The initial assumption is that *humans must be studied on their own level*. Symbolic interactionism is anti-reductionistic. If we want to understand socialization, infant development, and parent-child relationships among humans, then we must study humans and not infer their behavior from the study of nonhuman or infrahuman forms of life.

The basic difference between human and infrahuman is not simply a matter of degree but a basic difference of kind. The evolutionary process involves quantitative differences in species, not merely qualitative ones. The human-nonhuman difference centers around language, symbols, meanings, gestures, and related processes.

Thus, to understand a person's social development and behavior, relatively little can be gained by observing chimpanzees, dogs, pigeons, or rats. Social life, unlike biological, physiological life, or any nonhuman

---

11. Sheldon Stryker, "The International and Situational Approaches," in *Handbook of Marriage and the Family,* ed. by Harold T. Christensen (Chicago: Rand McNally, 1964): 134–136; and Sheldon Stryker, "Symbolic Interaction Theory: A Review and Some Suggestions for Comparative Family Research," *Journal of Comparative Family Studies* 3 (Spring 1972): 17–32.

form, involves sharing meanings, communicating symbolically. Due to language and the use of gestures, human beings can respond to one another on the basis of intentions or meanings of gestures. This assumption is in direct contrast with the behaviorist assumption, which suggests that humans can best be understood by studying forms of life other than humans. Psychologists who assume that the difference between human and animal is one of degree have relatively good success in explaining and controlling those who do not share meanings or communicate with one another at a symbolic level: infants, extreme psychotics, isolated children, the severely retarded, the brain damaged, people with more severe forms of aphasia, and the like. To the interactionist, the possession of language has enabled humans alone to deal with events in terms of the past, present, or future and to imagine objects or events that may be remote in space or entirely nonexistent.

The differences between socialized human beings and the lower animals, or between human families and nonhuman families, may be summarized by saying that the lower animals do not have a culture. They have no system of beliefs, values, and ideas that are shared possessions of groups and are symbolically transmitted. They have no familial, educational, religious, political, or economic institutions. They have no sets of moral codes, norms, or ideologies. Much stress and emphasis is placed on similarities between the animal and human worlds, but an equal amount of emphasis needs to be given to understanding and focusing on that which is different in humans. Recognizing these differences, the symbolic interactionists assume that to understand humans one must study humans. Thus very little can be learned about socialization, husbands, wives, children, in-laws, grandparents, or family life-styles of the upper class, native Americans, or the Amish by studying nonhuman forms.

A second assumption is that *the most fruitful approach to social behavior is through an analysis of society*. One can best understand the behavior of a husband, wife, or child through a study and an analysis of the society and subculture of which they are a part. Personal behavior is not exclusively or even primarily an individual phenomenon but is predominantly a social one. The assumption is not made that society is the ultimate reality, that society has some metaphysical priority over the individual, or that cultural determinism explains all behavior. Neither does it exclude biogenic and psychogenic factors as important in explaining or understanding behavior. However, these factors are not salient variables. They are viewed as constants in a social setting and as random variables in a personality system.

Being born into a given society means that the language one speaks, the definitions one gives to situations, and the appropriateness or inappropriateness of any activity are those learned within a social and cultural context. Thus, the behavior of couples from rural areas in the Philippines who would not be seen holding hands in public, or the behavior of a U.S. couple kissing and necking in a public park can only be understood by analyzing the society in which these behaviors take place.

A third assumption is that *the human infant at birth is asocial.* Original nature lacks organization. The infant is neither social nor antisocial (as with original sin in certain religious organizations or the id within the psychoanalytic scheme). The equipment with which the newborn enters life does, however, have the potential for social development.

It is the society and the social context that determine what type of behavior is social or antisocial. A newborn infant does not cry all night to punish or displease his or her parents nor does she or he sleep all night to please them. Only after these expectations become internalized do social or antisocial acts take on meaning. Although the newborn infant has impulses—as does any biological organism—these impulses are not channeled or directed toward any specific ends. But the human infant, having the potential for social development, can, with time and training, organize these impulses and channel them in specific directions. This process, by which the newborn infant becomes a social being, is the main concern of social psychologists, who are interested in the process of socialization, and of family sociologists, who are interested in child rearing.

A fourth assumption is that a *socialized human being,* meaning one who can communicate symbolically and share meanings, *is an actor as well as a reactor.* This does not simply mean that one person acts and another person reacts. The socialized human being does not simply respond to stimuli from the external environment. Rather, humans respond to a symbolic environment that involves responses to interpreted and anticipated stimuli.

That humans are actors as well as reactors suggests that investigators cannot understand behavior simply by studying the external environment and external forces; they must see the world from the viewpoint of the subject of their investigation. Humans not only respond to stimuli but select and interpret them. As a result, it becomes crucial and essential that this interpretation and meaning be known. It is this assumption that most precisely differentiates symbolic interactionists from the positivists in sociology and the behaviorists in psychology.

The assumption that humans are both actor and reactor suggests that humans alone can take the role of the other—that is, they can view the world from the perspective of the other person. Thus we can "put ourselves in the shoes of another person." We feel sad over the misfortune of a friend; we share the joys of our children even though the experience did not happen to us. A professor can take the role of the student and anticipate the response to a three-hour lecture or a certain type of exam without giving either the lecture or the exam. A wife can anticipate the response of her husband to an embrace or inviting friends to dinner. The responses of the professor and the wife may be inaccurate but the perception and the meaning or definition attached to the situation will influence and direct behavior. In short, a person's behavior is not simply a response to others but is a self-stimulating response: a response to internal symbolic productions.

The development of a social self   "Self" is a key concept in understanding socialization and personality. Self, although often seen in psychological and personal terms, is a social phenomenon. It is developed in interaction with others. The process of socialization, a primary concern of child rearing and that which makes humans social beings, is the development of a social self: the organization of internalized roles.

A woman may occupy the statuses of wife, mother, sister, student, executive, Methodist, and many others. Each status has expectations (roles) assigned to it. A person must know how each role is related to the others. All these roles need to be organized and integrated into some reasonable, consistent unity. This organization of internalized roles is the **social self**.

This organization of roles and the internalization of them occurs in interaction with others; the social self is never fixed, static, or in a "final" state. George Herbert Mead used *self* to mean simply that a person is the object of his or her own activities; he or she can act toward him- or herself as he or she acts toward others.[12] Thus, we can talk to ourselves, be proud of ourselves, be ashamed, or feel guilty.

It does not take much imagination to assess the central role a grandparent, parent, spouse, or sibling—that is, family members— play in the development of a social self.[13] Who we are, how we feel, what we want, and so on constitute our social self. The animals, infants, and other forms of life who have neither language nor any internalized role definitions have no social self. They cannot take the position of others and cannot view themselves as objects. Neither can they judge past, present, or prospective behavior. Among humans, where potential exists for sharing meanings, a social self can develop.

The importance of significant others and reference groups   Significant others and reference groups are of central importance in understanding the development of the child and the modification of the social self. Not all persons or groups are of equal importance to us. Certain persons and groups, again in processes of interaction, come to be perceived as more important, as more significant, and as a source of reference. These persons

12. George Herbert Mead, *Mind, Self and Society* (Chicago: University of Chicago Press, 1934).

13. *See,* for example, Viktor Gecas and Michael L. Schwalbe, "Parental Behavior and Adolescent Self-esteem," *Journal of Marriage and the Family* 48 (February 1986): 37—46.

Resocializing the severely deprived: a case example

I could write volumes about this foster child we've raised. When he came to us he was two years and four months old and was really a basket case. I had read about children from deprived backgrounds, but I had never seen one. It was really a cultural shock for all of us.

The child didn't seem to know what people were for. He could ignore a person like he ignored a piece of furniture. He apparently had never had any interpersonal relations with another human. He did not want anybody near him and he was only two years old. Our way was to hold our children, cuddle them, tell them bedtime stories and carry them around. The older children played with him but he had no idea of what they were doing. Everything terrified him. It was a lot more than I miss my mother. In fact, he did not know the words *mama, daddy*. He didn't miss anybody 'cause he didn't know what anybody was for. He had no language in that he didn't understand like our two-year-olds understood everything. He had no understanding of the difference between *yes, go ahead and do it*, or *no, you can't do that*. *No* was a concept he never heard.

Apparently he never sat at a table and ate a meal. He was more like an animal. I really hate using that word when we are talking about humans. But, you could not sit him at a table; he didn't know what it was for. I recall the first breakfast we had—that he had with us. He drank orange juice for as long as I gave it to him. Like he had four or five glasses of orange juice. He gobbled up toast and ate huge bowls of cereal. First I thought, "Gee, the kid is starved." But then I realized that he ate like that probably because that's his pattern. You eat all you could get when you could get it because you didn't know when the next meal was coming from. But we ate three times a day. It was years, and I means years, before he could really sit at the table with us, eat a meal, and then leave without creating a major disturbance. By major, I mean he thought he could get his jollies by just sweeping everything off the table or grabbing the table and making things spill or taking his own food and throwing

and groups with which we psychologically identify are termed respectively, **significant others** and **reference groups**.

To most infants and young children, mother is a significant person, that is, an object of emotional involvement, especially in the child's development. Note that "mother," in terms of interaction and involvement, is a social not a biological concept. As a result, an adoptive foster parent, grandparent, or other person—male or female—can fulfill the expectations (roles) of mother. And mother (socially or biologically) is not the only significant other, as is seen in the influence of the father, siblings, peers, teachers, athletes, or movie stars. These are persons who are important and with whom one psychologically identifies. To identify with them is to it around. You would think that in a few weeks this will all go away. But it didn't and we started bringing him around to psychologists and the agency was very helpful. He was seen by neurologists and psychologists and he had EEGs, intelligence tests, and all of the support that seemed to be available in the community. They would all just say that as far as they could see he had no brain damage; his intelligence was maybe low normal.

For a long time he was as rigid as a door. He would not bend an inch. Like here's an example of what I mean. At our house the children play outside in the summer. We have playground equipment in the backyard and the children have bikes. I raised a bunch of kids who really love the outdoors. But I don't think he had ever been outside his little apartment or whatever it was they lived in. So, I would put him outside in the morning and his hands would go up to his eyes like he couldn't stand the light. I'd stay out there with him, but unless I was holding his hand, he would spin right around and go into the house again. So I'd take him out and put him outside again. We actually had to physically hold him out there. You could not walk him. You couldn't put him in the sandbox. He didn't know what a sandbox was for. He didn't know what toys were for. He had no idea what you did with a toy. We had to very patiently teach him all of this.

Eventually he began to show that it became important to him that he start pleasing us. But now this didn't happen until he was almost school age. Prior to that he couldn't care less whether he pleased us or pleased anybody else. He had not been socialized that way and I think that kind of socialization happens really early. I'm even more aware of it with my own grandchildren. They're sensitive. They cry if they are corrected. He never cried. We still laugh about the time I broke the pingpong paddle on him and he got up and said, "That didn't hurt." He went back and started doing exactly the same thing he was spanked for. I just had to take a deep breath and sit back and let him do it. Or I would have killed him that day, I'm sure I would have.

Source: Personal interview with a mother of a severely damaged foster child.

attempt to conform to the expectations one perceives they have toward oneself. An attempt is made to please and receive approval from those others who are significant.

There are two essential ways in which significant others present themselves: (1) by what they do and (2) by what they say and how they say it. The doing and saying is organized in terms of roles. Mothers (traditionally, at least) change diapers, cook meals, clean houses, offer tenderness, and the like. Fathers leave home for work, read newspapers, complain about bills, watch football games, and so on. As a child or an adult interacts with others, he or she becomes interested in some, attached to others, and shares certain expectations and behaviors with them. Significant others are perceived as role models. Personal behavior and thinking is patterned on the conduct of these persons. Uncle Pete the pilot, Sally the movie star, or Marcia the teacher, as a significant other, may each play a decisive part in the socialization and development of our social self. A sister or brother,[14] a boyfriend or girlfriend,[15] or a television figure may become a role model, a significant other, and a person with whom we psychologically identify.

In addition to persons who are viewed as significant, groups (real or imaginary) are used as a frame of reference with which a person psychologically identifies. These groups are generally termed *reference groups*: any group from which an individual seeks acceptance or uses as a source of comparison. A church, a club, or a company may serve as a point of reference in making comparisons or contrasts, especially in forming judgments about self. In some instances, a person may attempt to gain membership or acceptance in the group, although this is not always the case. These groups, like significant others, serve as standards for conduct, as bases for self-evaluation, and as sources of attitude formation.

To most adolescents, peers rather than parents are said to be key groups of reference. They serve many functions once fulfilled by parents. Peers, who understand the adolescent and share his or her world, become his or her reference set for sizing up problems, strivings, and ambition. Behavior defined as deviant by parents may be given social approval by peers. Drugs, alcohol, premarital sex, interracial dating, political liberalism, and the like may be conforming behavior to peers. The antisocial behavior of adolescents, as viewed by parents, may simply mean that the adolescent is "in step with a different drummer" (peers). In Chapter 10, a reference group framework was used to explain an increase in personal sexual permissiveness when the behavior of friends was viewed as permissive. Wilbur Bock and others[16] use reference group theory to explain the anomaly that exists between sexual morality, socioeconomic status, and religiosity. SES and religiosity are related to each other yet SES is related to liberal sexual attitudes and religiosity is related to conservative sexual attitudes. Specifications of reference group theory help to pinpoint the conditions under which particular choices are made. Thus, reference groups serve

14. *See*, for example, Virginia Adams, "The Sibling Bond: A Lifelong Love/Hate Dialectic," *Psychology Today* 15 (June 1981): 32–47; and Robert B. Stewart, Jr., "Sibling Interaction: The Role of the Older Child as Teacher for the Younger," *Merrill-Palmer Quarterly* 29 (January 1983): 47–68.

15. Luther B. Otto, "Girl Friends as Significant Others: Their Influence on Young Men's Career Aspirations and Achievements," *Sociometry* 40 (September 1977): 287–293.

16. E. Wilbur Bock, Leonard Beeghley, and Anthony J. Mixon, "Religion, Socioeconomic Status, and Sexual Morality: An Application of Reference Group Theory," *The Sociological Quarterly* 24 (Autumn 1983): 545–559.

as sources of comparison, decision making, and as influential sources of behavioral and attitudinal change for children, youths, and adults.

Socialization stages and interaction processes The importance of the early years cannot be denied. Very early experiences provide the infant with his or her first sense of self, other persons, and social relationships. It is usually the mother who becomes the first, primary, and most significant other. But rather than specific priorities such as breast or bottle feeding, or toilet training early or late, the significant dimensions in the socialization process become attention, love, and warmth, or their absence. More important, the nature of the social relationships with mother and others influences the image that the infant or child has of himself or herself. Scolding, slapping, pampering, or praising may not be crucial per se, but their repetitive nature leads to the internalization of a sense of self-worth and an image of one's self. Although mother is crucial in the development of these images, so are father, siblings, other kin, and friends. Although mother carries out most of the infant care functions, the socialization experiences of most infants include interaction with other members of the nuclear family, extended family, and others. Since relationships with different persons signify statuses and roles in relation to kin, each provides a unique and different contribution to the socialization process. Each contributes to what Erikson claims is the first issue facing the helpless newborn: that of trust versus mistrust.[17]

In the development of the self, Mead postulated that children go through three continuous stages of observation: preparatory, play, and game.[18] In the *preparatory stage*, children do not have the ability to view their own behavior. Actions of others are imitated. As described under the learning frame of reference and also under the interaction frame of reference, certain sounds like "da-da-da" bring attention and a response from others. This operant conditioning leads the child to repeat and learn the sounds.

The second stage, overlapping with and a continuation of the preparatory stage, is the *play stage*. At this point, children take roles of others, that is, they play at being the others whom they observe. They may sweep the floor, put on their hat, and pretend to read a book. Elkin and Handle described a four-year-old "playing daddy" who put on his hat and coat, said "goodbye," and walked out the front door only to return a few minutes later because he did not know what to do next.[19]

---

17. Erikson, *Childhood and Society*, pp. 247–251.

18. Mead, *Mind, Self and Society*, p. 150. For a comparison of Piaget and Mead regarding play and games, *see* Norma K. Denzin, "Play, Games and Interaction: The Contexts of Childhood Socialization," *The Sociological Quarterly* 16 (Autumn 1975): 458–478.

19. Elkin and Handel, *The Child and Society*, p. 57.

Later, children enter the *game stage*. At this point, they do not merely play or take the role of another; they now participate in games involving an organization of roles, involving the development of the self. At this point they have to recognize the expected behavior of everyone else. This involves a process of responding to the expectations of several other people at the same time. This is termed the **generalized other**. In Mead's famous example of the baseball game, the child

> must have the responses of each position involved in his own position. He must know what everyone else is going to do in order to carry out his own play. He has to take all of these roles. They do not all have to be present in consciousness at the same time, but at some moments he has to have three or four individuals present in his own attitude, such as the one who is going to throw the ball, the one who is going to catch it, and so on. These responses must be, in some degree, present in his own makeup.[20]

The concept of "generalized other" enables us to understand how given individuals may be consistent in their behavior even though they move in varying social environments. We learn to see ourselves from the standpoint of multiple others who are either physically or symbolically present.

In light of this perspective of socialization, it should be recognized that any behavior results less from drives or needs, less from unconscious processes, and less from biological or innate characteristics than from interaction processes and internalized meanings of self and others. As a result, the behavior appropriate to whites or blacks, royalty or outcasts, Jews or gentiles, or males or females is dependent less upon skin color, genital makeup, or biological facts than upon the internalized meanings and definitions that result from interaction with others. These interactions, viewed in their broadest context, include schools, peers, the mass media, and all involvement of daily living. And these interactions continue beyond early childhood, through adolescence and middle age, into old age.

SOCIALIZATION IN ADOLESCENCE AND AFTER

Most books on socialization, most chapters on child-rearing, and the greatest public interest in both focus generally on the young child. Perhaps this is readily understandable since, to the newborn child, the entire world is new. Even the most common and routine events must be learned. But if socialization is role learning, if socialization refers to learning the ways of a given society and culture, and if socialization means the development of members who are capable of operating in society, then how can anyone

---

20. Mead, *Mind, Self and Society*, p. 151.

argue that socialization is complete after five or six years of life? Particularly in a rapidly changing society such as exists in the United States, persons are newcomers to unfamiliar events almost daily. Without a doubt, early socialization experiences will have a major influence and impact on the type of events and experiences that are acceptable or unacceptable. But socialization is a continuous process, and learning experiences after the early years not only mean incorporating the new but discarding much of the old.

It is a rare society in which the individual can be prepared during childhood for the complex roles that are essential to know at a later time. This in no way denies the fundamental importance of socialization experiences in the childhood years but only asserts that role learning is a continuous process. The emphasis placed on education at the junior high, high school, and college levels represents formalized attempts at changing adolescents' perceptions about the world in which they live.

Studies of adolescents clearly document the extent to which key socializing agents shift from the home to "outsiders." Peers rather than parents become important reference figures for high school youths. During the teen years, the school and the peer group are powerful and pervading socializing forces. Learning processes similar to those in early childhood are in operation. The adolescent is actively engaged in sex-role identification, learning the norms and expectations of the opposite sex, participating in new and different types of social activities, gaining insights and skills for the future occupational world, attempting to become emancipated from parents, and developing a new sense of self-reliance. Many studies indicate clearly the significance of socialization during the adolescent years.[21]

Socialization does not end at adolescence, but when attention shifts from adolescents, the available research data on adult socialization, even at a descriptive level are minimal. From age twenty through sixty a mythical assumption seems to be that socialization to new roles, tasks, and activities either doesn't exist or is unnecessary. The social self, it seems, is believed to be relatively stable or even fixed in these adult years, thus, it is not an exciting or vital area for research. This idea seems to change somewhat at retirement with some literature making reference to the need for re-socialization to the new life-styles associated with aging and the aged (*see* Chapter 15).

Socialization, whether for young children, adolescents, mid-life adults,

---

21. Irving Tallman, Ramona Marotz-Baden, and Pablo Pindas, *Adolescent Socialization in Cross-Cultural Perspective* (New York: Academic Press, 1983); Greer Litton Fox, "The Mother–Adolescent Daughter Relationship as a Sexual Socialization Structure: A Research Review," *Family Relations* 29 (January 1980): 21–28; and Lloyd B. Lueptow, "Social Influence, Social Change and Parental Influence in Adolescent Sex-Role Socialization: 1964–1975," *Journal of Marriage and the Family* 42 (February 1980): 93–103.

or the aged, follows similar interaction processes. The same is true in terms of content: socialization to violence (Chapter 16), sexual socialization (sexualization—Chapter 10), or socialization to gender-sex roles. Our attention turns to this issue of sex-role socialization for the rest of this chapter.

GENDER IDENTITY AND SEX-ROLE SOCIALIZATION

Confusion often exists over concepts such as sex, sex roles, gender roles, and gender identity. But more precisely, one's sex, irrespective of behavior, refers to a biological condition of being male or female. Sex roles, therefore, refer to the expectations associated with being biologically of one sex or the other. Gender, rather than sex, is the umbrella term that refers to the totality of being male or female, masculine or feminine. Gender roles, thus, become the expectations associated with being masculine or feminine and may or may not correspond precisely with one's sex. Doesn't he (biological male) act feminine (gender expectation)? is one example of how sex and gender can be differentiated. **Gender identity** refers to the way one defines or perceives oneself in terms of one's sex, as male or female, and as masculine or feminine.

Roles, differentiated both by sex and gender, are discussed frequently throughout this book, particularly those of male-female and husband-wife. Chapter 1 includes a discussion of the issue of marital and gender role differentiation, including the psychological concept of androgyny. Chapter 2 describes various approaches to roles consistent with a structural-functional and an interactional theoretical orientation. Chapter 3 examines differential treatment given to male and female members of kin groups. The entire fourth chapter focused on family and work, particularly the employment of women and male-female roles in the home. Other chapters look at gender-role differences among the Chinese and blacks, in mate selection, in sexual behavior, in marriage, in child rearing, and throughout the life cycle, with a particular focus on sexual differences in mid-life and old age, in crisis, and in remarriage.

Female-male differences

There is no denying that normatively, attitudinally, behaviorally, and physically, males and females differ.[22] Anthropologists provide clear evidence

---

22. A fascinating accounting of these differences can be found in Cullen Murphy, "Men and Women: A Survey of the Research," *The Wilson Quarterly* 6 (Winter 1982): 63–80.

Writing in *The New York Times* (September 19, 1986) Anna Quindlen argues that women are the superior sex. She claims that she can't think of any jobs that women can't do—or for that matter that women don't do, including lawyers, doctors, editors, interior decorators, or garbage slingers.

Reading about sanitation workers convinced her of the inherent superiority of women. That New York City has finally hired women to pick up the garbage seemed to make sense since she feels that a good bit of being a woman consists of picking up garbage. But of particular interest was the male santitation workers' responses of how women were incapable of doing the job. The comment of one worker was that this wasn't their kind of job since women were designed to do dishes and men were designed to do yard work. This type of comment peeved Ms. Quindlen because personally, not only has she done dishes, yard work and tossed Hefty bags, but because she would fight for a laid-off sanitation worker to work, for example, at a gift-wrap counter "even though any woman knows that men are hormonally incapable of wrapping packages or tying bows."

For men to say that women are the superior sex means they are "too wonderful to enter courtrooms, enjoy sex, or worry our minds about money." For Ms. Quindlen to say that women are the superior sex means that "what passes as a terrific man would only be an adequate woman." She expects men to be polite and clean. But from her female friends she expects unconditional love, their ability and willingness to pour their hearts out to her, and even their ability to inform her why the meat thermometer isn't supposed to touch the bone. Who can doubt which sex is superior?

that in a worldwide perspective, certain activities such as hunting, trapping, herding, and fishing are predominantly the province of men. Other activities such as care of infants and children, grinding grain, carrying water, gathering herbs or sods, and preserving food are predominantly the province of women.

These divisions are found both in the most primitive as well as in the most egalitarian societies. The Tasady, the tribe discovered in the Philippine forests of Mindanao, had a division of labor by sex with women preoccupied with child care and men with hunting. Even in Finland and Sweden where sex roles are deemphasized, wives in the majority of families feed the family, do the cleaning and washing, and serve as primary care-takers for the children.[23] Likewise, in the Israeli kibbutz, which was founded on sex-egalitarian terms, most of the men are in agricultural and industrial roles and most of the women are in service or educational roles. Similar

---

23. Linda Haas, "Domestic Role Sharing in Sweden," *Journal of Marriage and the Family* 43 (November 1981): 957–967.

Basic to gender identity and sex-role socialization are opportunities for both sexes to interact with adults in their daily experiences. (Photo: © Susan Buckler/The Image Works)

household and child care patterns are said to exist today in the Soviet Union and mainland China (*see* Chapter 5) even though the overwhelming majority of the women are employed outside the home.

Beyond these male-female task differences, who would deny that physical differences exist beween males and females? Probably no one. But who among us would argue that differences in the behavior of males and females are rooted in the genes, in the innate, in the hormones, in the biological, or in the anatomy? Probably some would, others wouldn't be so sure, and still others would deny it forcefully. Maybe all three groups are partially correct. For centuries, it was assumed that male-female differences in behavior were inborn or "natural." Females had "maternal instincts" and were submissive; males were aggressive and dominant. More recently, certain social scientists—particularly anthropologists who discovered societies where men are passive and women domineering—have questioned any relevance of biological factors in behavior. They have argued that all behavior is learned. While I tend to lean more toward the latter position, the most accurate answer probably lies between the two positions and is far more complex than suggested by a nature-nurture, biology-culture argument.[24]

The argument for the biological is deeply rooted in a number of theories of socialization, including the psychoanalytic frame of reference discussed earlier in this chapter. It is further enhanced by research into hormones (such as progesterone and estrogen secreted by the ovaries in females and testosterone and the androgens secreted by the testes in males) that initiate sexual differentiation in the fetus and later at puberty activate the reproductive system and the development of secondary sex characteristics. Research has shown that if a female fetus is given testosterone, she will develop male-like genitalia. If a male is castrated (testes removed) prior to puberty, he will not develop secondary sex characteristics such as a beard. But do these chemical substances known generally as hormones determine behavior?

The strength of cultural factors is overwhelming in our understanding of gender identity and sex-role socialization. One prime example comes from cross-cultural data that have shown great diversity in the attitudes, values, and behavior of both men and women. Margaret Mead's classic study of three primitive tribes in New Guinea found both men and women among the Arapesh to be cooperative, mild-mannered, gentle, and unaggressive (sex-typed feminine behavior). Among the Mundugumor, both men and women were hostile, aggressive, combative, individualistic, and unresponsive (sex-typed masculine behavior). Among the Tchambuli, the typical sex roles found in the Western cultures were reversed: women were dominant, powerful, and impersonal; men were emotionally dependent and less responsible.[25] If it can be assumed that the biological makeup and hormonal balance of men and women in these tribes and men and women in the Western world are similar, then how is the difference explained? It is not necessary to go to New Guinea in the 1930s to note the strength of cultural factors in gender differences and sex-role socialization. Data from Utah in the 1980s, for example, show that the attitudes toward appropriate roles for men and women are strongly affected by religious affiliation.[26]

Another, and even more convincing, line of research comes from studies of hermaphrodites, persons who possess complete sets of both male and female genitalia and reproductive organs. Infants who were assigned one sex at birth and were later found to belong biologically to

24. *See*, for example, Lois Wladis Hoffman, "The Changing Genetics/Socialization Balance," *Journal of Social Issues* 41 (1985): 127–148.

25. Margaret Mead, *Sex and Temperament in Three Primitive Societies* (New York: Mentor, 1950). Originally published in 1935 by Morrow.

26. Moshe Hartman and Harriet Hartman, "Sex Role Attitudes for Mormons and Non-Mormons in Utah," *Journal of Marriage and the Family* 45 (November 1983): 897–902.

Brother becomes sister: The alteration of masculine-feminine behavior

A young rural couple took their identical twin boys to a physician to be circumcised. During the first operation, performed with an electric cauterizing needle, a surge of current burned off the baby's penis. Desperate for a way to cope with this tragedy, the parents took the advice of sex experts: "Bring the baby up as a girl." The experiment has apparently succeeded. Aided by plastic surgery and reared as a daughter, the once normal baby boy has grown into a nine-year-old child who is psychologically, at least, a girl.

This dramatic case, cited by Medical Psychologist John Money at the Washington meeting of the American Association for the Advancement of Science, provides strong support for a major contention of women's liberationists: that conventional patterns of masculine and feminine behavior can be altered. It also casts doubt on the theory that major sexual differences, psychological as well as anatomical, are immutably set by the genes at conception. In fact, says Money, there are only four imperative differences: women menstruate, gestate, and lactate; men impregnate. Many scientists believe that crucial psychological imperatives follow from these biological facts, limiting the flexibility of sexual roles. Money, however, is convinced that almost all differences are culturally determined and therefore optional. The Johns Hopkins psychologist further spells out his views on sex-role learning in a book titled: *Man & Woman, Boy & Girl.*

In the normal process of sexual differentiation, Money explains, if the genes order the gonads to become testes and to produce androgen, the embryo develops as a boy; otherwise it becomes a girl. Androgen not only shapes the external genitals but also "programs" parts of the brain, so that some types of behavior may come more naturally to one sex than to the other. For instance, both men and women can mother chidren—the necessary circuits are there in every brain—but the "threshold" for releasing this behavior is higher in males than in females. The same phenomenon is demonstrated by laboratory animals. If a mature female rat is put into a cage with newborn rats, she begins mothering them at once. In a similar situation, a male rat does nothing at first, but after a few days he too begins to display maternal behavior.

Money believes that hormones secreted before and after birth have less

the opposite sex, behaved as they were assigned and taught. Biological females, defined and reared as males, grew up developing fantasies of males, enjoyed sports assigned generally to males, fell in love with girls, and the like. Biological males, defined and reared as females, had the "maternal instinct," preferred marriage over a career, and were oriented toward dolls and domestic tasks.[27] Thus, when socialization contradicts

27. John Money, *Sex Research: New Developments* (New York: Holt, Rinehart and Winston, 1965). *See also* John Money, "Sex Assignment in Anatomically Intersexed Infants," in M. A. Watson, ed., *Readings in Sexology* (Dubuque, Ia.: Kendall/Hunt, 1984).

effect on brain and behavior in human beings than the "sex assignment" that takes place at birth with the announcement: "It's a boy!" or "It's a girl!" This exultant cry tells everyone how to treat the newborn baby, and sets off a chain of events, beginning with the choice of a male or female name, that largely determines whether the child will behave in traditionally masculine or feminine ways.

Money's evidence for this familiar thesis comes largely from cases in which accidents before or after birth made it impossible to raise children according to their genetically determined sex. In each of his examples, youngsters learned to feel, look, and act like members of the opposite sex.

For the little boy who lost his penis, the change began at 17 months with a girl's name and frilly clothes. An operation to make the child's genitals look more feminine was done, and plans were made to build a vagina and administer estrogen at a later age. The parents, counseled at the Johns Hopkins psychohormonal research unit, began to treat the child as if he were a girl. The effects of the parents' changed attitude and behavior were marked. "She doesn't like to be dirty," the mother told the clinic in one of her periodic reports. "My son is quite different. I can't wash his face for anything. She seems to be daintier. Maybe it's because I encourage it. She is very proud of herself when she puts on a new dress, and she just loves to have her hair set."

The experience of two hermaphrodites, from different families, further bolsters Money's view. Each was born with the female chromosome pattern, and each had internal female organs but a penis and empty scrotum outside. One set of parents believed they had a boy and raised their child accordingly; the other set assigned their offspring as a girl. (Surgery and hormones made the youngsters' appearance conform to the chosen sex.) According to Money, the children's "antithetical experiences signified to one that he was a boy and to the other that she was a girl." The girl therefore reached preadolescence expecting to marry a man; in fact, she already had a steady boy friend. The boy, by contrast, had a girl friend and "fitted easily into the stereotype of the male role in marriage,"even though "he and his partner would both have two X chromosomes."

Source: *Time Magazine*, January 8, 1973, p. 34. Reprinted by permission from TIME, The Weekly Newsmagazine. Copyright Time Inc.

the biological, hormonal, or genetic, the learned and interactional experiences prove to be powerful determinants of current gender roles (see "Brother Becomes Sister" panel).

Sex-role socialization

Socialization to sex (female-male) and gender roles follows basic socialization processes described earlier in this chapter. Gender role socialization begins at birth and continues throughout one's lifetime.[28] As Lenore Weitzman indicated, "from the minute a newborn baby girl is wrapped in a pink blanket and her brother in a blue one, the two children are treated differently."[29] From that point on, socialization as to appropriate roles for males and females constitutes one of life's most important learning experiences.

There is little doubt that children learn about gender roles very early in their lives, certainly long before they enter school. One study reported that by the time boys and girls are age four, they realize that the primary feminine role is housekeeping while the primary masculine role is wage earning.[30] Another study indicated that low-income white and black preschool children have a knowledge of conventional adult sex assignment despite father absence and role reversals in their own families.[31] The cost of this knowledge of adult sex assignment was clearly seen in the latter study. That is, discrepancies resulted between the expectations—that father should be the breadwinner—and the reality—that restricted job opportunities prevented the unemployed father from living up to these expectations. This researcher, Joan Aldous, claims that the roots of parent-child and marital conflict in lower-class life lie in the very early socialization learnings of children.

The acquisition of sexual roles follows the same general processes of socialization.[32] In interaction with others, in words, deeds, films, and books, the child is taught what behavior is appropriate for each sex. As one writer indicated:

> We throw boy babies up in the air and roughhouse with them. We coo over girl babies and handle them delicately. We choose sex-related colors and toys for our children from their earliest days. We encourage the energy and physical activity of our sons, just as we expect girls to be quieter and more docile. We love both our sons and daughters with equal fervor, we protest, and yet we are disappointed when there is no male child to carry on the family name.[33]

---

28. Peter I. Rose, ed., *Socialization and the Life Cycle* (New York: St. Martin's Press, 1979); and Rhoda E. Estep, Martha R. Burt, and Herman J. Milligan, "The Socialization of Sexual Identity," *Journal of Marriage and the Family* 39 (February 1977): 99–112.

29. Lenore J. Weitzman, *Sex-Role Socialization* (Palo Alto, Cal.: Mayfield Publishing Co., 1979): 1.

30. Ruth E. Hartley, "Children's Concepts of Male and Female Roles," *Merrill-Palmer Quarterly* 6 (1960): 83–91.

31. Joan Aldous, "Children's Perceptions of Adult Role Assignment: Father-Absence, Class, Race and Sex Influences," *Journal of Marriage and the Family* 34 (February 1972): 55–65.

32. Spencer E. Cahill, "Reexamining the Acquisition of Sex Roles: A Social Interactionist Approach," *Sex Roles* 9 (March 1983): 1–15.

33. Florence Howe, "Sexual Stereotypes Start Early," *Saturday Review* (October 16, 1971): 76.

In regard to relative status, boys are more highly valued than girls. In regard to personality differences, most boys are active and achieving whereas most girls are passive and emotional.

Lenore Weitzman and others concentrated on one aspect of sex-role socialization: the socialization of preschool children through picture books.[34] They chose eighteen children's books identified as "the very best": the winners of the Caldecott medal, given by the Children's Service Committee of the American Library Association for the most distinguished picture book of the year. Their analysis was concentrated on winners and runners-up for a period of five years. To ensure representativeness of the study, the authors examined three other groups of children's books: the Newbery Award winners, the Little Golden Books, and the "prescribed behavior or etiquette books." Their findings make interesting reading. They noted that it would be impossible to discuss the image of females in children's books without first noting that, in fact, women are simply invisible. They found females underrepresented in the titles, central roles, pictures, and stories in every sample of books examined. Most children's books were about boys, men, and male animals, and most dealt exclusively with male adventures. Where there were female characters, they were usually insignificant or inconspicuous.

What were the activities of boys and girls in the world of picture books? Weitzman et al. found that not only were boys presented in more exciting and adventuresome roles, but they engaged in more varied pursuits and demanded more independence.[35] In contrast, most of the girls in the picture books were passive and immobile. Girls were more often found indoors than were boys. The girls in the stories played traditional feminine roles directed toward pleasing and helping their brothers and fathers.

Most books clearly implied that women cannot exist without men. That is, the role of most of the girls was defined primarily in relation to that of the boys and men in their lives and was not defined primarily in relation to girls working or playing together.

What about adult role models? Weitzman's study found the image of the adult women to be stereotyped and limited.[36] Again, the females were passive while the males were active. Men predominated the outside activities and women the inside ones. While inside, the women almost exclusively performed service functions, taking care of the men and children in their families. When men lead, women follow. When men rescue others, women are the rescued.

---

34. Lenore J. Weitzman, Deborah Eitler, Elizabeth Hokada, and Catherine Ross, "Sex-Role Socialization in Picture Books for Preschool Children," *American Journal of Sociology* 77 (May 1972): 1125–1150.

35. Ibid., pp. 1131–1138.

36. Ibid., pp. 1139–1144.

Sex-role differentiation and the draft

How far should we carry the idea that no sex or sex-role differentiaton should exist? We don't have to search long for contemporary issues that confront this question. For example, take the issue of draft registration or the draft itself. Assuming a draft registration is necessary (which many youths have difficulty doing), are there biological, psychological, or social grounds on which to logically include one sex and not the other? Should men be included but not women? Should husbands be included but not wives? Should fathers be included but not mothers?

In July 1980, draft registration for men was revived. All 19- and 20-year-old men were required to register at their local post offices. Failure to register was considered a felony punishable by up to five years in prison and a $10,000 fine. Immediately the American Civil Liberties Union sued to block the plan, alleging sex discrimination.

The ACLU charge was that it is unconstitutional to register men and not women. The suit said that solely because they are not female, the plaintiffs, all men, are burdened with the requirement of registering for the draft. Imposition of this burden on men while exempting women denies men equal protection under the law.

One interesting finding of particular significance for this chapter was that not one woman in the Caldecott sample had a job or profession. Motherhood was presented in the picture books as a full-time, lifetime job, despite the reality that about 90 percent of the women in this country will be in the labor force at sometime in their lives and that the average women has completed the main portion of her child rearing by her mid-thirties. Most of the stories portrayed the woman as a mother or a wife, although she also played the role of fairy, fairy godmother, or underwater maiden. The roles that men played were highly varied: storekeepers, housebuilders, kings, spiders, storytellers, gods, monks, fighters, fisherman, policeman, soldiers, adventurers, fathers, cooks, preachers, judges, and farmers.[37]

You may note that these findings by Lenore Weitzman and others were published in 1972, and understandably predict that with the women's movement and the heightened awareness of sex stereotyping and the changing roles of women, children's books have changed since then. But have they?

A study was reported in 1981[38] that attempted to replicate the Weitzman

---

37. Ibid., pp. 1140–1141.
38. Richard Kolbe and Joseph C. LaVoie, "Sex-Role Stereotyping in Preschool Children's Picture Books," *Social Psychology Quarterly* 44 (December 1981): 369–374.

study of the previous decade. It was found that the number of books containing stories about females had not changed much, although the rates of male to female pictures (human and nonhuman) had changed. Female characters continued to be cast as passive and dependent and placed in traditional nonsignificant and stereotyped roles. The activities engaged in by females continued to consist of service and helping roles. Women continued to be portrayed as engaged in indoor ventures. The stereotyping was as evident in female-authored as it was in male-authored books, suggesting that female writers are not changing the status quo.

If it is assumed that children's books are one influential factor in the sex-role socialization of children and do influence children's attitudes and behavior, we can predict a continuation of sex-role stereotyping in this and the future decades. This is particularly true when it is recognized that these sex-typed portrayals are not confined to children's books or the preschool years. Throughout the school years, the educational system tends to stereotype males and females. Textbooks, achievement tests, athletic emphases, vocational counseling, parental and peer pressures, all tend to reinforce stereotypical expectations and behaviors. Beyond the school, the mass media, the religious and work worlds, and most of our social institutions tend quite consistently to put men in selected occupations, to put women in others, and to stress "appropriate" behavior for women that is not identical to that stressed for men.

In the socialization of males and females, empirical evidence suggests a continuation of sex-role stereotyping and gender segregation in spite of tremendous shifts in sex-role attitudes.[39] Current conceptions of femaleness and maleness have marked similarities to earlier conceptions. A contemporary view of men as aggressive, work minded, and capable of leadership resembles characteristics similar to those attributed to men in earlier research. Current conceptions of femaleness as stressing sensitivity, affection, and consciousness of appearance are also similar to earlier stereotypes of women.[40] Socialization to sex-gender roles, in spite of shifts in attitudes, continues to emphasize a differentiation between males and females, with a heavy concentration on the perpetuation of traditional expectations and behaviors for each sex.

---

39. Barrie Thorne and Zella Luria, "Sexuality and Gender in Children's Daily Worlds," *Social Problems* 33 (February 1986): 176–190; Andrew Cherlin and Pamela Barnhause Walters, "Trends in United States Men's and Women's Sex-Role Attitudes: 1972 to 1978," *American Sociological Review* 46 (August 1981); 453–460; and Raymond J. Adamek and Mike Miller, "Changes in Coeds' Sex Role Concepts: 1969 and 1980," *Sociological Spectrum* 4 (1984): 71–87.

40. Patricia A. Smith and Elizabeth Midlarsky, *Sex Roles* 12 (1985): 313–328.

SUMMARY

1. The central concept in dealing with parent-child relationships is socialization—the process by which the infant and adult learn the ways of a given society and culture and develop into participants capable of operating in that society. Socialization of the young infant may be the single universal function of the family. Preconditions for socialization include an ongoing society, biological inheritance, and human nature.

2. Several frames of reference were examined to explain various aspects of socialization: learning-behaviorist, a psychoanalytic, two of child development, and a symbolic interactionist. Learning or reinforcement theory assumes that the same concepts and principles that apply to lower animal forms apply to humans. The conditioning processes may be classical or operant. The former links a response to a known stimulus, the latter links a response of the consequence produced by the response. Child-rearing and socialization processes result from conditioning and positive or negative reinforcements.

3. Classic psychoanalytic theory contrasts sharply with the behaviorist theory. Internal drives and unconscious processes are of central importance. Socialization takes place according to precise, though overlapping, stages of development. These include the oral, anal, and phallic, followed later by a period of latency and a genital phase. What happens in these early stages from birth to age five or six, although unconscious, becomes relatively fixed and permanent, serving as the basis for responses in later life.

4. Child development theories focus on the individual and the manner in which motor skills, thought, and reasoning develop. Erikson described eight stages of human development, each constituting a crisis brought on by changing social situations as the individual moves from infancy through old age. Piaget focused more on the cognitive development of the child and described four major stages of intellectual development.

5. Symbolic interaction theory contrasts considerably with the theories already described. Infants, who are not born social, develop through interaction with other persons. As interaction occurs, meanings are internalized and organized and the self develops. The social self enables a person to consciously and purposively represent to him- or herself what he or she wishes to represent to others.

6. A social being can take the role of others, can interpret and define, and can have and use symbols. In interaction with others, the child learns to define him- or herself and the world in certain ways. These definitions and meanings in turn predispose him or her to behave

in ways consistent with these self-concepts. Interaction, the social self, significant others, reference groups, and the generalized other are concepts basic to the socialization process.

7. Socialization does not end at any given age but is a lifelong process. For teens, school and peer groups serve as important sources of reference, interaction and identity. Minimal research exists on adult socialization with an increased amount focusing on resocialization for the elderly.

8. Gender identity and gender roles refer to one's identity and the expectations associated with being masculine or feminine. Male-female and masculine-feminine differences are universal. Debate continues over the extent to which sex and gender roles have their roots in biology, culture, or a combination of the two.

9. Sex role socialization follows the principles of any type of socialization. In interaction with others, children learn about gender-sex roles very early in their lives. This is heavily reinforced in schools, particularly through childrens' books. While some change in sex role attitudes has taken place, current conceptions of femaleness and maleness fit earlier stereotypes and highly traditional expectations.

10. The previous chapter on the parental system and this one on parent-child interaction follow a life course sequence that generally, but not always, follows marriage. The next chapter continues this time sequence by turning to families in the middle and later years.

KEY TERMS AND TOPICS

DISCUSSION QUESTIONS

1. Discuss ways in which parents need to be socialized. What role does the infant play in this process?

2. Review the preconditions for adequate socialization. What would happen if any of them were absent? Would socialization be possible? Why or why not?

3. What do you perceive to be the most important factors in producing stable, healthy adults?

4. Contrast the learning-behaviorist, the psychoanalytic, the child development, and the symbolic interaction frames of reference in regard to socialization. What are the contributions each makes? What are some of the drawbacks of each?

5. Take a pencil and paper to a nearby park, a preschool setting, or somewhere where you can observe the interaction between adults (preferably a parent) and children. Record what is said and done for a five- or ten-minute period. What inferences can you draw about social class, language patterns, child-rearing practices, discipline, and the like?

6. Interview three mothers of preschool children. Find out whether the arrival of their first child was a crisis; whether they toilet-trained their babies early, breast-fed or bottle-fed them, etc., and whether they believe it makes any difference; what means of punishment they use; what role the father plays in child-rearing; how other children assist or hinder the socialization process; and so forth.

7. In what ways and areas are you being socialized? To what extent are you a victim of early childhood experiences, a father-absent family, a lower-class background, or a home with marital conflict? When will you be ''fully'' socialized?

8. What influence did early adolescence, dating, friendship relationships, siblings, or teenage experiences have on your personality? To what extent is your personality today a product of your early, as opposed to more recent, socialization experiences?

9. Is a marriage with no sex or gender role differentiation (androgyny) possible? Explain and give examples.

10. To what extent does your biological sex determine your behavior? Do you believe that you could be socialized to think and act like the opposite sex?

11. In spite of women's movements, an increasing number of women entering the paid work force, decreasing family size, and so forth, why do school materials, the mass media, the work world, etc. continue to differentiate and segregate people by sex?

FURTHER READINGS

Belsky, Jay; Lerner, Richard M.; and Spanier, Graham B. *The Child in the Family.* Reading, Mass.: Addison-Wesley Publishing Company, 1984. A life-span and ecological perspective of the reciprocal relations between infant, child, and adolescent development and changes in the family.

Davis, Kingsley. "The Sociology of Parent-Child Conflict." *American Sociological*

Review 5 (August 1940): 523–535. Although published several decades ago, this classic paper on parent-child conflict is still widely reprinted today.

Elkin, Frederick, and Handel, Gerald. *The Child and Society: The Process of Socialization.* 4th ed. New York: Random House, 1984. A coherent treatment, from a sociological standpoint, of how children are socialized in modern society.

Eshleman, J. Ross, and Clarke, Juanne N. *Intimacy, Commitments, and Marriage: Development of Relationships.* Boston: Allyn and Bacon, 1978. Part II—"Becoming a Human Being"—includes chapters on gender identity and development, sex-role socialization, and socialization and child-rearing patterns.

Gecas, Viktor. "The Influence of Social Class on Socialization." *Contemporary Theories About the Family* Vol. 1. Edited by Wesley R. Burr et al. New York: The Free Press, 1979, pp. 365–404. An attempt to establish interrelated propositions explaining socialization.

Huber, Joan, and Spitze, Glenna. *Sex Stratification: Children, Housework and Jobs.* New York: Academic Press, 1983. Based on an evolutionary theory of sex stratification, a test is made of the effects of social factors on the division of household labor, marital stability, and sex-role attributes.

Lewis, Robert A., and Salt, Robert E., eds. *Men in Families.* Beverly Hills: Sage Publications, 1986. A collection of sixteen writings, several of which deal with men's involvement as fathers and socializing agents.

Lipman-Blumen, Jean. *Gender Roles and Power.* Englewood Cliffs, N.J.: Prentice-Hall, 1984. An extensive examination of sex and gender roles with Chapters 8 and 9 focusing on the family.

Robinson, Bryan E., Rowland, Bobby H., and Coleman, Mike. *Latchkey Kids: Unlocking Doors for the Children and Their Families.* Lexington, Mass.: Lexington Books, 1986. An exploration of children ages five to thirteen, involved in self-care before and after school.

Rossi, Alice A. *Gender and the Life Course.* Hawthorne, N.Y.: Aldine Pub. Co., 1985. An interdisciplinary collection of original essays on the lives of men and women as they are affected by processes that attend maturation and aging.

Tallman, Irving; Marotz-Baden, Ramona; and Pindas, Pablo. *Adolescent Socialization in Cross-Cultural Perspective.* New York: Academic Press, 1983. The authors provide a theory of socialization and an empirical examination of how families and adolescents in Mexico and the United States deal with the social changes in their countries.

Walters, James, and Walters, Lynda Henly. "Parent-Child Relationships: A Review, 1970–1979." *Journal of Marriage and the Family* 42 (November 1980): 807–822. A decade review article that identifies ten emerging and re-emerging substantive issues dealing with parent-child relationships.

Weitzman, Lenore J., *Sex Role Socialization.* Palo Alto, Cal.: Mayfield Publishing, 1979. A brief easy-reading paperback covering socialization to sex roles from early childhood through the school and college years, with a concluding chapter on where socialization fails to help women to achieve.

15

Marriage and the Family in the Middle and Later Years

Chapters 13 and 14 examined some selected aspects of the family with children. But marriage and family life do not end when children enter adolescence or, in later adolescence, when the children leave home for marriage, employment, school, or some other reason. Family structure, interactions, and life-styles change considerably at this period of the family life cycle: the second half. A prime example of this change was shown in Chapter 12 in dealing with marital satisfaction over the life cycle. Studies indicated a process of disenchantment and a decrease in satisfaction at this time, followed by increases in the later years.

It is the intent of this chapter to examine two major periods in the life cycle: the middle years from approximately age forty to retirement and the later years from approximately age sixty or sixty-five. This includes general descriptions of families at these periods plus a consideration of grandparents, retirement, socialization of the aged, and social conditions and problems surrounding the aged.

THE POSTPARENTAL PERIOD: THE MIDDLE YEARS

In order to capture the experience of the period after children leave home, a number of phases have been used. Among others are the *stage of the empty nest*, the *launching stage*, the period of *contracting family size*, and the term used here, the **postparental**. Technically, the term post-parental is a misnomer, for parents do not stop being parents or become ex-parents. Postparental suggests that the children are now legally and socially recognized as adults and assume a greater independence from their parents and greater personal autonomy and responsibility. While the "launching" stage entails periods of child "reentry" into the parental home for many families, it involves the return of the conjugal family to a two-person, married-couple household and many nuclear one-parent units to a one-person household. The periods of family life from this point until the death of one or both parents include: (1) families launching their oldest children: ages 45–54; (2) families of preretirement: ages 55–64; (3) the "young-old" retired families: ages 65–74; and (4) the "old-old"

TABLE 15–1
Marital status of men and women, ages 45–64, March 1985 (percentage distribution)

	Age of men		Age of women	
Marital status	*45–54*	*55–64*	*45–54*	*55–64*
Single	6.3%	6.1%	4.6%	3.7%
Married	79.9	81.2	72.3	67.0
Separated	4.1	2.8	4.0	3.0
Widowed	1.2	3.7	7.0	17.4
Divorced	8.7	6.2	12.1	8.9
Total	100.0	100.0	100.0	100.0

Source: U.S. Bureau of the Census, *Current Population Reports*, Series P-20, no. 410, "Marital Status and Living Arrangements, March 1985" (Washington, D.C.: U.S. Government Printing Office, 1986), Table 1, p. 17.

families in the later years: age 75 and after. This section examines families in the middle years as they launch their children and approach retirement, the age period of approximately 45–65.

Marital status and the length of the middle years

In 1985, of those persons in this age period, about 80 percent of the men and 69 percent of the women were married (*see* Table 15–1). Compared with other age categories, the percentage married is high with relatively low percentages of single, separated, widowed, or divorced. For women, the percentage who are widowed begins to climb sharply at ten-year intervals after age 54. The figures change from 7 percent (ages 45–54) to 17 percent (ages 55–64), to 39 percent (ages 65–74), to 68 percent (age 75 and over).[1]

The period after the children leave home lasts longer than any other stage in the marital life cycle. Interestingly, this factor is unique to the twentieth century. At the turn of the century, men married at age 26, had their last child at age 36, saw their last child marry at age 59, but lost their spouses at age 57. Women married at age 22, had their last child at 32, saw their last child married at 55, and lost their spouses at 53.[2]

---

1. The first two figures are taken from Table 15–1. The last two are taken from Table 15–3 presented later in the chapter.

2. Figures taken from Paul C. Glick, "The Life Cycle of the Family," *Marriage and Family Living* 17 (1955): 3–9.

The result for both sexes was no postparental period, since the typical or average couple survived two years short of the time their last child (which on the average was their fifth) was expected to marry.

In contrast, today both sexes marry in their early or mid-twenties, have their last child in their late twenties, see their last child launched in their mid-to-late forties, but do not lose their spouse until the early or mid-seventies. The result is a postparental period of twenty to twenty-five years. Although marriage occurs at a similar age, children are fewer in number and parents gain an earlier release from child rearing. These factors, combined with a longer life expectancy for both sexes, give the average couple several decades together prior to retirement or the death of one spouse.

There are, of course, many exceptions to parents gaining an early release from child rearing. Recent demographic indicators show that more young adults now than a few years ago are residing with their parents.[3] Most young adults leave their parental homes during their late teens or early twenties, some linger while they continue schooling or hold jobs, while others return to their parents following a job loss, a disrupted marriage, unwed motherhood, or when hardships arise.

There are as well many exceptions to a return to the two-person husband-wife family even if all children are "launched." In addition to the return of children, some evidence suggests an increase in extended households due to the taking in of aged parents.[4] Traditionally, the common pattern was adult children moving into the homes of parents. The situation today is usually reversed with the aged parents moving into the home of adult children. The effect of either children or parents returning to the family in the middle years is to modify the nature of the postparental period as one that returns to the two-person marital unit.

The significance of the middle years

What is the significance of being a quadragenarian (age 40 or more but less than 50)? To many couples, the middle years are the "prime of life." Business and professional men in particular are likely to hold their top positions and family total income is at its peak. For example, in 1985, the median family income for householders of ages 45–54 was $36,653

---

3. Paul C. Glick and Sung-Ling Lin, "More Young Adults are Living with Their Parents: Who are They?" *Journal of Marriage and the Family* 48 (February 1986): 107–112; and David M. Heer, Robert W. Hodge, and Marcus Felson, "The Cluttered Nest: Evidence That Young Adults are More Likely to Live at Home Now Than in the Recent Past," *Sociology and Social Research* 69 (April 1985): 436–441.

4. Scott H. Beck and Rubye W. Beck, "The Formation of Extended Households During Middle Age," *Journal of Marriage and the Family* 46 (May 1984): 227–287.

compared to $19,162 for those 65 and over and $15,282 for those of ages 18–24.[5]

Debate exists over whether the middle years are depressing and strain-filled or whether they are the prime time as family income data suggest. The one argument suggests that, combined with the physical processes and changes, it is the time when men are pressured to "get ahead." For many, "it's now or never." The prestigious position they were going to attain, the book they were going to write, or the stardom they were going to achieve may become a reality or may become a dream never to be fulfilled. A man's "handsome ladies' man" image of ten to twenty years earlier may turn into a need to convince himself of his virility. The expenses of weddings or college and the departure of the child may produce restless nights. This argument suggests, then, that the middle years are rough—physically, socially, and emotionally.

The opposite argument suggests that this is a period of life when things are brightest. Income is highest, leisure time is the greatest, child-bearing responsibility is past, and opportunities exist as never before. Which view is correct—or is it possible that both are?

Contrary to their expectations, Farrell and Rosenberg, in comparing 300 men entering middle age to men in their late twenties, did not find evidence for a universal midlife crisis or of signs of increased alienation or social disconnection.[6] The exception was among men in the lowest socioeconomic class. Men who were unskilled laborers gave evidence of personal disorganization and psychopathology as they approached middle age. Lower-middle-class men (skilled workers, clerical workers, small businessmen) showed a remarkable ability to ignore, distort, or deny information that challenged their world views. Professionals and middle-class executives exhibited neither denial patterns nor identity problems but reported satisfaction with work, family, and their positions in the community.

Some psychologists refer to a **mid-life transition** for men around age forty. This transition may go relatively smoothly or may involve considerable turmoil. The transition involves a sense of disparity between "what I've reached at this point" and "what it is I really want." It is a matter of the goodness of fit between the life structure and the self. A man may do extremely well in achieving his goals and yet find his success hollow and bittersweet. The issues involved in this mid-life transition include: (1) the sense of bodily decline and the more vivid recognition of one's mortality, (2) the sense of aging, which means to be old rather than young, and (3)

---

5. U.S. Bureau of the Census, *Current Population Reports*, Series P-60, no. 154 "Money Income and Poverty Status of Families and Persons in the United States: 1985" (Washington, D.C.: U.S. Government Printing Office, 1986), Table 6, p. 12.

6. Michael P. Farrell and Stanly D. Rosenberg, *Men at Midlife* (Boston: Auburn House, 1981).

Empty nest syndrome must have flown the coop

We can forget all about the empty nest syndrome. What a relief!

The empty nest syndrome was in the news a lot about 10 years ago. It was said to be the inescapable scourge of women in their tragic middle years. Husbands were advised to be especially understanding of and sympathetic to their wives' symptoms. Shrinks everywhere stood ready to help with counsel and advice, at $75 an hour and up.

Empty nest syndrome symptoms were alleged to include depression, restlessness, loss of identity, loss of self-confidence and a general feeling of being worthless. It was awful, worse than menopause. (No one had invented Herpes II yet.)

Women whose children had grown up and left home were supposed to be victims of the syndrome. Without babies to burp, women were supposed to feel they had no useful function. Without kids at home to mess up the kitchen, throw wet towels around the bathroom, or have tomato fights in the garage, women were supposed to become lumps of quivering insecurity.

Some of these suffering women just couldn't stand it and went ahead and got pregnant all over again, at age 45. That's what the magazine articles said. Some of them had nervous breakdowns, got divorces, looked for jobs or otherwise behaved peculiarly. The magazine articles said that, too.

Altogether, the empty nest syndrome was something dreadful, greatly to be feared. I kept looking for symptoms in myself as soon as all my kids were in college. I was still looking when they graduated, when Sue got married, when the boys moved into their own house and apartment. Nothing.

I figured even if I had no immediate symptoms, the empty nest syndrome was only delayed. It would get me. It would strike as soon as I reached my tragic middle years.

I asked local experts, such as my friends, to pinpoint the tragic middle years of a woman's life. They couldn't agree. Men said somewhere around age 27. Women said it was closer to age 82. I developed my own guidelines, based on maturation, not years.

the polarity of masculine and feminine including changing relationships to women and an integration of the more feminine aspects of the self.

It has been suggested that a mid-life crisis for males may be negatively affected by the sex-role socialization that most males have received since childhood. The "male mystique" requires men to be strong, aggressive, unemotional, and tough—all characteristics that may be called into question during the decades from forty to sixty, when the male is confronted with the beginnings of bodily decline, career stagnation, and drastic changes within his family unit.[7]

7. Jessica Field Cohen, "Male Roles in Mid-Life," *The Family Coordinator* 28 (October 1979): 469.

I decided the tragic middle years of a woman's life must occur when . . .

the cellulite spreading in all directions from her thighs finally reaches her dewlap

she can no longer remember the last time she wore a bikini bathing suit, or if she ever wore a bikini bathing suit

she has no interest in frisbee games, beach parties, roller skating, wind surfing, or becoming a Pepper

she thinks Willie Nelson is cute

she gives up saying, "I'll have whatever you have, Darling," to her dinner partners in restaurants, shamelessly puts on her coke bottle glasses, reads the menu, and orders for herself—liver and onions!

There were some other things. Anyway I figured I had just about reached the perigee of my tragic middle years, and I hadn't recognized a single symptom of the empty nest syndrome yet. I was obviously in for it, any day now. Then, deliverance!

I read about a recent survey of more than 200 women, aged 35 to 55. Grace Baruch and Rosalind Barnett, a couple of Wellesley College psychologists, did it. They called these women middle aged, although they didn't mention cellulite or Willie Nelson testing. Anyway, Baruch and Barnett found that 74 percent of the women whose children had grown up and left home were not depressed at all. There was no tragedy in their middle years. In fact, they were relieved, happy, even delighted.

The women said such things as, "I've never felt better," and "I'd never go back to being 20 again!" The researchers found that these women also had greater feelings of self-worth now than they ever had when they were younger with houses full of children to tend.

Baruch and Barnett labeled the empty nest syndrome a cruel myth and hoax. I wouldn't count on such good luck with Herpes II.

Source: Nickie McWhirter, *Detroit Free Press*, June 6, 1982, p. C-1. Reprinted with the permission of the Detroit Free Press.

What about women? Is the "empty nest" or postparental stage of the family life cycle a traumatic and unhappy period? According to data from six U.S. national surveys, middle-aged women whose children have left home report, as a whole, somewhat greater happiness and enjoyment of life than women of similar age with a child (or children) living at home, and the former also report substantially greater marital happiness than the latter.[8] Thus, the children's leaving home does not typically lead to

---

8. Norval D. Glenn, "Psychological Well-Being in the Postparental Stage: Some Evidence from National Surveys," *Journal of Marriage and the Family* 37 (February 1975): 105–110.

For many couples, the middle and later years are a time of life when they can
enjoy doing things together, without the daily responsibilities of child care.
(Photo: © Mark Antman/The Image Works)

an enduring decline in the psychological well-being of middle-aged mothers.
Rather, on balance, the effects seem to be moderately positive.
Similar effects were reported in a study of North Carolina mothers.[9]

---

9. Elizabeth Bates Hawkins, "Effects of Empty Nest Transition on Self-Report of Psy-

The empty nest transition was not a particularly stressful period in most women's lives, and there was no significant effect from either age or menopausal status on either psychological or physical well-being. It was suggested that the only threat to well-being may be in having a child who does not become successfully independent when it is expected.

For females, the notion of the **empty-nest syndrome** as a period of depression, identity crisis, role loss, and a lowered sense of well-being that occurs when the last child leaves the parental home has little research support. The extent of its existence is likely to vary by factors such as socioeconomic level or employment status. Dolores Borland hypothesizes that if the empty-nest syndrome occurs, it may occur to a greater degree in a particular cohort of white middle-class women because of a unique set of social circumstances in which they live and a unique set of family values and social norms concerning women's "proper" roles.[10] These are women who dedicate their lives selflessly to their families' needs and believe that to be feminine and happy is to be married and mothers. Lower- and upper-socioeconomic status women, she argues, are less likely to experience this syndrome because the former have had to work throughout their lives to help support the family and the latter have developed other community roles, have resources to find parental role substitutes, and have smaller families, which leads them to the empty-nest stage at a younger age.

The absence of children symbolizes the children's new independence. Since the children are gone, many mothers form new nonfamilial relationships to fill the void. Many women in this age category become more active in civic and religious affairs, an increasing number of wives and mothers become employed (*see* Chapter 4), and this is the time period when mothers become grandmothers and fathers gain the status of grandfather.

THE GRANDPARENT STATUS

Grandparenting has become a middle-age in addition to an old-age phenomenon with the potential of spanning three or four decades of life. With the majority of men and women in U.S. society marrying in their early or mid-twenties, and with many of these having children within the first year or two of marriage, parents are becoming grandparents in their

---

chological and Physical Well-Being," *Journal of Marriage and the Family* 40 (August 1978): 549–556.

10. Dolores Cabic Borland, "A Cohort Analysis Approach to the Empty-nest Syndrome Among Three Ethnic Groups of Women: A Theoretical Position," *Journal of Marriage and the Family* 44 (February 1982): 117–129.

forties. The rocking-chair and the cane-carrying grandfather images seem grossly inappropriate.

After prolonged neglect, grandparenthood is now receiving greater attention in the literature on adulthood, family development, and intergenerational relations.[11] Two key demographic changes have shaped modern grandparenthood in U.S. society: increased life expectancy and changed fertility patterns. With more people reaching old age, more people experience grandparenthood as well as great- and great-great-grandparenthood. And the reduction in family size, closer spacing of children, and women having their last child at a younger age leads to the transition into grandparenthood as a distinct status of the middle years, separate from and with less overlap with one's own parenting.

Marion Crawford suggests that the role of grandparent can be seen as instrumental for the family as a social institution.[12] First, it can bring together the two adult generations that may tend to drift apart during the postparental phase of the family life cycle. Grandchildren provide a common focus of interest, activity, and affection. Second, the family can benefit materially from grandparents, both in terms of financial and other services while the grandparents are alive and also in terms of capital and property after their deaths. In the transfer of property, children and grandchildren are expected to receive first priority. Third, while the role of grandparent has been seen by some writers as an essentially maternal or feminine role, it may also ease the transition into retirement for men. She suggests that in these three ways, grandparenthood, while not occurring in old age, may be a useful preparation for both sexes for old age by re-integrating the middle-aged person into the family unit and by anticipatory socialization into the role of retired persons.

Perhaps the role of grandparent, like that of parent, differs considerably by social class. It has been suggested that the middle-class grandparent role is one which is "ideological" rather than "real." That is, there is a kinship position of grandparent, but there are no normative rights and obligations attached to it, so grandparenthood could be described as a "roleless role."[13] Thus, middle-class parents, on becoming grandparents, must construct a role for themselves as babysitter, surrogate parent, gift giver, crisis intervenor, and the like. In contrast, the lower-class grandparent is one who is far more integrated into ongoing daily family life. The lower-class maternal grandmother frequently socializes and nurtures her grand-

11. Gunhild O. Hagestad, "Grandparenthood, Life Context, and Family Development," *American Behavioral Scientist* 29 (March/April 1986): 471–484.

12. Marion Crawford, "Not Disengaged: Grandparents in Literature and Reality, An Empirical Study in Role Satisfaction," *The Sociological Review* 29 (1981): 499–519.

13. Sylvia Clavan, "The Impact of Social Class and Social Trends on the Role of Grandparent," *The Family Coordinator* 27 (October 1978): 351–357.

On Sunday, George and Catherine Layton plan to pick up their 6-year-old grandson, Mark Foster, and take him to the nearby Oakdale Mall. They want to visit a toy store, watch the fountain, then cap off the afternoon at Burger King or the Friendly Ice Cream Shop.

For Mr. and Mrs. Layton, however, this is not just an ordinary weekend outing. It is the first time they have been allowed to see their grandson in more than two years, and it marks the culmination of a bitter court battle that began shortly after Mark's parents were divorced.

Last week, the state's highest court ruled, over the objections of the boy's mother, and adoptive father, that the Laytons had a right under state law to visit their grandson. In effect, the court granted the Laytons visiting rights no longer enjoyed by their son, Mark's natural father. The Layton case is the most recent example of how, as the divorce rate and human longevity have increased, courts in New York State and elsewhere have had to grapple with the special bond between grandparent and grandchild.

It is a bond that, while relatively new to the law, was captured long ago in an Italian adage the Laytons quoted in court papers.

"Si niente va bene, chiama nonno e nonna," it states. "If nothing else is going well, call your grandfather and grandmother."

According to Harry D. Krause, a family law expert at the University of Illinois Law School, at least 42 states, including New York, now have laws that protect the rights of grandparents in the event of a parent's death or divorce.

Under these statutes, family law authorities say, courts have held that the rights of grandparents and grandchildren can limit the autonomy traditionally given to parents in the rearing of children.

Put another way, the laws mark the legal system's growing commitment to the preservation of the extended family where it is in a child's best interests.

"We've had men's lib, women's lib, and now we have kid's lib," said Doris Jonas Freed, a New York lawyer and an authority on family law. "Even little children have rights that cannot be abrogated. They're not chattels anymore."

For the Layton's who live here in Binghamton, only a few miles from their grandson, the decision means the end of years of anguish spent looking for "Marky" wherever they went and sending birthday cards that were never acknowledged. It is also a second chance of sorts.

In the last three years, the Laytons have seen their grandson for only a few seconds. In December 1981, Mr. Layton saw him briefly when he tried, without success, to take him to the General Electric Christmas party. Several months later, Mrs. Layton ran into the boy, with the Fosters, at the meat counter of a local supermarket. She says he waved to her before the Fosters whisked him out to the car.

The Laytons are now preparing themselves for Mark's visit, retrieving all of his favorite pictures and toys.

"If he reaches for my hand, that will be great," said Mr. Layton. "But if I ask him to go with us and he says 'no,' I'm going to have a broken heart. Why should I make a little boy suffer?"

Source: David Margolick, *The New York Times*, January 27, 1984, pp. 1 and 12. Copyright 1983/1984 by The New York Times Company. Reprinted by permission.

children, engages in more regular interaction, and feels a sense of obligation far more than simple contact between generations.

Grandparenthood appears to have different meanings for grandmothers and grandfathers. Sometimes the grandparent role is depicted as a maternal role with women feeling greater responsibility to and intimate involvement with their grandchildren. One study, for example, concluded that the grandfather role was perceived by older men as less important than other social roles, such as worker, church participant, and leisure user. A second conclusion pointed to the moderate to low levels of interaction and mutual assistance between grandfathers and grandchildren.[14] Both these conclusions appear to be more salient at older ages, making grandparenthood a more important role in middle age than in later or old age.

Joan Robertson found that grandmotherhood is a role actively enjoyed by 80 percent of the respondents and, for many, it is more enjoyable than parenting because it provides easy joy and pleasure without the responsibilities associated with parenthood.[15] With grandparenting as a positive life experience, it is little wonder that, given the frequency of divorce/remarriage patterns, many grandparents experience frustration in maintaining contact and frequent interaction with their grandchildren. This is particularly true when the grandchildren reside with the son- or daughter-in-law rather than the son or daughter. A relatively new and increasingly frequent phenomenon are the legal and court cases involving grandparent-grandchild visitation rights (note the panel example).

With the changes described in the life cycle, great-grandparenthood rather than grandparenthood, is emerging as the familial status associated with old age. It is likely that this status, like the described middle-class grandparent status, is more "ideological" than "real" and that great-grandparents need to construct the type of role they wish to perform in their ascribed great-grandparent status.

THE FAMILY OF LATER LIFE

Since the turn of the century, one of the more significant changes in family and marital relationships has related to life expectancy. People are living longer and more people are living, both of which increase the number of older persons (*see* Figure 15–1). An early age at marriage, the absence of divorce, and a longer life combine to increase the length of marriage, the number of generations of family members living, and

---

14. Vira R. Kivett, "Grandfathers and Grandchildren: Patterns of Associations, Helping, and Psychological Closeness," *Family Relations* 34 (October 1985): 565–571.

15. Joan F. Robertson, "Grandmotherhood: A Study of Role Conceptions," *Journal of Marriage and the Family* 39 (February 1977): 165–174.

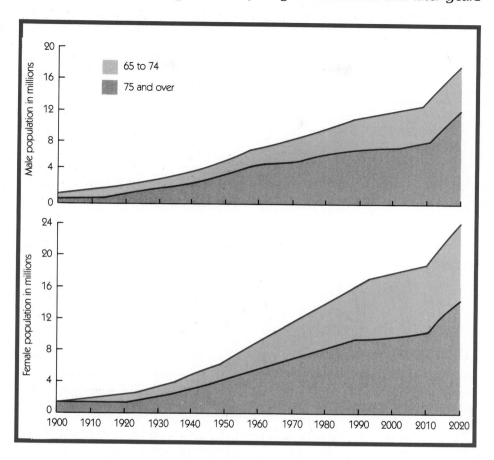

FIGURE 15-1

The growth of the population 65 years and over, 1900-2020. (*Source:* U.S. Bureau of the Census, *Current Population Reports.*)

the extension of the kin network. In 1983, at birth the infant could expect to live 74.6 years. For white males, this figure was 71.7 years and for white females, 78.8 years (*see* Table 15-2). Those who reach age 65 can expect to live 16.7 more years (14.5 for white men; 18.7 for white women; 13.4 for black men; and 17.3 for black women).

There has been relatively little increase in the life expectancy of older persons since the turn of the century. In 1900, the person who reached age 65 could expect to live until age 76.9. In 1983, the person who reached age 65 could expect to live until age 81.7 or slightly less than five years longer than his or her counterpart of more than eighty years earlier. More people are living, however, as fewer people are dying in infancy or childhood. In 1983, approximately 74 percent of the men and

TABLE 15–2
Life table: Life expectancy, by race, age, and sex, United States, 1983

		White		Black	
Age	Total	Male	Female	Male	Female
At birth	74.6	71.7	78.8	65.4	73.6
5	70.6	67.6	74.5	61.5	70.1
10	65.7	62.7	69.6	57.2	65.2
15	60.8	57.8	64.6	52.3	60.3
20	56.0	53.1	59.8	47.6	55.4
25	51.3	48.5	54.9	43.1	50.6
30	46.6	43.9	50.1	38.7	45.9
35	41.9	39.2	45.2	34.4	41.2
40	37.2	34.6	40.4	30.2	36.7
45	32.7	30.0	35.7	26.2	32.2
50	28.3	25.7	31.2	22.5	28.1
55	24.1	21.6	26.8	19.1	24.1
60	20.3	17.9	22.6	16.0	20.5
65	16.7	14.5	18.7	13.4	17.3
70	13.5	11.5	15.1	10.9	14.1
75	10.7	9.0	11.8	9.0	11.5
80	8.1	6.9	8.8	7.1	9.0
85 and over	6.1	5.2	6.5	6.0	7.4

Source: U.S. Bureau of the Census, *Statistical Abstract of the United States: 1987,* 107th ed. (Washington, D.C.: U.S. Government Printing Office, 1986), no. 108, p. 71.

85 percent of the women reached age 65.[16] In 1900, only 39 percent of the men and 44 percent of the women reached age 65. Thus, although a much higher percentage of people are living longer, there has been a relatively small increase in the life expectancy of older persons.

In 1985 there were approximately 28.5 million U.S. citizens age 65 and over.[17] This number makes up about 12 percent of the population of the United States, and the rates have been expanding far more rapidly than the nation's population as a whole. Whereas the number of U.S. citizens has increased by 17.7 percent since 1970 (203 million to 239 million), the number of people age 65 and over has increased by 43 percent (20 million to 28.5 million) in fifteen years. The increase in these figures is not due to an increase in the life span (the biological age limit) or due to the fact that older individuals are living much longer but rather

16. U.S. Bureau of the Census, *Statistical Abstract of the United States, 1986,* 106th ed. (Washington, D.C.: U.S. Government Printing Office, 1985), no. 107, p. 68.
17. Ibid., no. 20, p. 18.

to the larger number of people living. With birth rates declining or remaining stable, the aged will likely constitute an even larger proportion of the population for decades to come.

Throughout history older persons have played significant roles, particularly men who, with increasing age, often received increasing status, prestige, and deference. In the United States, and apparently in modernized societies in general, old age does not bring increased prestige and status but rather brings negative perceptions and definitions.[18] Frequently, old age is defined as a time of dependency and declining productivity and vitality. The socioeconomic status held is generally determined by the achievement of earlier periods of life; if the achievements were limited and provisions for these years were inadequate, opportunities for a full, meaningful life are limited.

It is not difficult to remain sensitive to the older person and aging. In tomorrow's community newspapers will be pictures of couples who are celebrating their fiftieth wedding anniversaries, announcements of community and business leaders who are retiring, polls showing attitudinal differences beween the old and the young, and of course the obituary notices. All these serve as reminders of the social dimension of aging and of the position of the older person in society.

Social gerontology, the study of older persons and the aging process, as well as the closely related field, the sociology of aging, have both been concerned with the social definition of who is thought to be old, their interaction patterns and behaviors, the expectations that are imposed upon them, the age, sex, place of residence, and other demographic factors about them, as well as the problems and needs that older members within a society face. Within this framework, the family of later life has come to take on a particular significance in dealing with, and understanding, these other factors of concern to the aged.

Marriage and family in the later years

In 1985, there were an estimated 11.5 million men and 17 million women in the United States who were 65 years old and over. Seventy-nine percent of the men and 49 percent of the women aged 65–74 were married. At age 75 and over, 67 percent of the men and 23 percent of the women were married (*see* Table 15–3).

Relatively few men and women in these age categories are divorced,

---

18. Donald O. Cowgill, "Aging in Comparative Cultural Perspective," *Mid-American Review of Sociology* 6 (1981): 1–28; and Carol Seefeldt, "Children's Attitudes Toward the Elderly: A Cross-Cultural Comparison," *International Journal of Aging and Human Development* 19 (1984): 319–328.

TABLE 15–3
Marital status of men and women, aged 65 and over, March 1985 (percentage distribution)

| | Men | | Women | |
| | Aged 65–74 | Aged 75 and over | Aged 65–74 | Aged 75 and over |
Marital status				
Single	5.2%	5.3%	4.4%	6.2%
Married	78.9	67.4	49.1	22.8
Separated	2.4	1.9	2.0	0.9
Widowed	9.3	22.7	38.9	67.7
Divorced	4.2	2.7	5.6	2.4
Total	100.0	100.0	100.0	100.0

Source: U.S. Bureau of the Census, Current Population Reports, Series P-20, no. 401, "Marital Status and Living Arrangements, March 1985" (Washington, D.C.: U.S. Government Printing Office, 1986), Table 1, p. 17.

separated, or single. This is a time when the widowed status becomes increasingly frequent. Whereas less than one in ten men aged 65–74 and slightly more than one in five of the men aged 75 and over are widowers, about four in ten women aged 65–74 and seven in ten aged 75 and over are widows. This factor will be discussed later in this chapter.

Married couples in this over-sixty-five group comprise a high proportion who have been married a long time. Of those in first marriages, most of them previously celebrated silver wedding anniversaries, and many have or will celebrate their golden anniversaries. Over the years they have shared many joys and weathered many crises. Although it exists, rarely does one read about divorce or incompatibility among these couples. Even when unhappy in their marriage, the experiences of their years, the lives and activities of their children, and perhaps the lack of realistic alternatives to the marriage keep the couple together.

Marital and family relationships are often proclaimed to be the primary sources of social involvement, companionship, fulfillment, and happiness for the elderly. Existing studies suggest that marriage has a positive effect on psychological well-being among the elderly (particularly when compared to the divorced and widowed)[19] and, as shown earlier, that marital satisfaction may be higher for the elderly than for married people in the intermediate stages of the family life cycle. Gary Lee found that marital

19. *See,* for example, Wayne C. Seelbach and Charles J. Hansen, "Satisfaction with Family Relations Among the Elderly," *Family Relations* 29 (January 1980): 91–96; and Colleen Leahy Johnson, "The Impact of Illness on Late-life Marriages," *Journal of Marriage and the Family* 47 (February 1985): 165–172.

Many elderly experience the loneliness of living alone and the problems associated with shopping, preparing meals, and housework while a number of elderly are simply alone. (Photo: © Victor Aleman/Freelance Photographer's Guild)

satisfaction has a positive effect on morale, which he suggests supports the more general proposition that satisfying primary relations are crucial to the psychological well-being of older people.[20] The positive effects of marital satisfaction on morale were greater for women than for men, consistent with the typically greater involvement of women in marital and family affairs over the course of the life cycle.

What about the childless elderly? The value of children to their elderly parents in providing emotional, material, financial, and other support is widely asserted and empirically supported. However, one study of the childless elderly demonstrated levels of well-being that match and sometimes exceed those of parent elderly.[21] The childless were more financially

20. Gary R. Lee, "Marriage and Morale in Later Life," *Journal of Marriage and the Family* 40 (February 1978): 131–139.

21. Judith Rempel, "Childless Elderly: What Are They Missing," *Journal of Marriage and the Family* 47 (May 1985): 343–348.

secure (*see* Chapter 13 on the childless as well) and in better health, while parents tended to be surrounded by a greater number of friends and have more general satisfaction with life. But by and large, this study and others show that the elderly, whether parent or childless, are very satisfied with family, friendships, and life, while less satisfied with health and income, two problems discussed in the pages that follow.

What about the unmarried elderly who never married, are divorced, or widowed? These groups comprise a sizable proportion of the aged population. How important are families to them? One study showed that geographic proximity to siblings, particularly same sex siblings, exerted a positive influence on life satisfaction.[22] Another study based on two national samples concluded that men and women were more isolated from neighbors and friends than from family. Men were somewhat more likely to be isolated from family than were women.[23] Women were more likely than men to see relatives and maintain contacts with them by phone.

Interestingly, one hedge against loneliness for the unmarried was found to be dating.[24] While older women were said to derive increased prestige from dating, older men stressed the importance of dating as a means for self-disclosure. For most persons, greater emphasis was placed on the companionate nature of such relationships. As one 73-year-old woman stated:

> It was a lot harder when my boyfriend, Ted, died than when my husband of 40 years passed away. I needed Ted in a way I never needed my husband. Ted and I spent so much time together; he was all I had. And at my age I know it will be hard to find someone else. . . but, well, let's face it; how many men want a 73-year-old woman?[25]

Living arrangements among the elderly

As persons reach age sixty-five and over, an increasing number retire, suffer decreases in income, and experience the loss by death of spouses and siblings. Where do people of this age category live? Are they institutionalized? Do they live with children? Do they live alone? The answer to this will greatly depend on the sex to which you are referring.

In 1985, three-fourths of the men were living with their spouses

---

22. Jerrie L. McGhee, "The Effects of Siblings on the Life Satisfaction of the Rural Elderly," *Journal of Marriage and the Family* 47 (February 1985): 85–91.

23. Pat M. Keith, "Isolation of the Unmarried in Later Life," *Family Relations* 35 (July 1986): 389–395.

24. Kris Bulcroft and Margaret O'Connor, "The Importance of Dating Relationships on Quality of Life for Older Persons," *Family Relations* 35 (July 1986): 397–401.

25. Ibid., p. 401.

TABLE 15–4

Characteristics of persons 65 years and over, by sex, 1970 and 1985

Characteristics	1970		1985	
	Male	Female	Male	Female
Total (in millions)	8.3	11.5	11.0	15.8
Percent of population	8.5%	11.1%	9.7%	13.1%
Percent below poverty level				
Family householders	16.6%	23.5%	6.0%	13.0%
Unrelated individuals	40.0	49.9	20.8	25.2
Family Status (by percent)				
In families	79.2%	58.5%	82.4%	56.7%
Non-family householders	14.9	35.2	15.4	42.1
Secondary individuals	2.4	1.9	2.2	1.2
Residents of institutions	3.6	4.4	(n/a)	(n/a)
Years of school completed				
8 years or less	61.5%	56.1%	37.2%	34.1%
1–4 years of high school	25.0	32.0	42.2	47.6
1 or more years of college	13.5	11.9	20.6	18.3
Labor-force participation (by percent)				
Employed	25.9%	9.4%	15.3%	7.0%
Not in labor force	74.1	90.6	84.7	93.0
Living arrangements (by percent)				
Living in household	95.5%	95.0%	99.5%	99.6%
Living alone	14.1	33.8	14.7	41.1
Spouse present	69.9	33.9	75.0	38.3
Living with someone else	11.5	27.4	9.8	20.2
Not in household	4.5	5.0	.5	.4

Source: U.S. Bureau of the Census, *Statistical Abstract of the United States: 1987,* 107th ed. (Washington, D.C.: U.S. Government Printing Office, 1986), no. 38, p. 34.

compared to less than 40 percent of the women (*see* Table 15–4). Women were far more likely than men to be living alone (41 percent versus 15 percent) or to be living with someone other than their spouse (20 percent versus 10 percent). Many of these people were living with children or other relatives. A situation of this nature may be a matter of choice or of necessity. Where both parents and children elect to live together, the arrangements frequently work out to the satisfaction of both the older members and the children. If a wife is employed, the mother or mother-in-law is likely to assume much of the major responsibility of the household. Babysitting, lawn care, cooking, and fulfilling the daily needs of the home are often functions that older persons can satisfactorily perform. If, however, the arrangement is not one of choice but of necessity, the probability of difficulty is likely to increase. Frequently the relationship is unsatisfactory both for the aging parents and for the children, and in some instances the grandchildren.

Another living arrangement that is frequently satisfactory is for the aging parents and the married children to have separate but geographically close residences where they can maintain close relationsips. Many parents like to be independent and want their children to allow them to remain so. This permits both generations to give favors or suggestions with fewer threatening feelings. In addition, it permits both to share interests and life-styles without the constant physical presence of the other. Unfortunately, census data are not available on the number or percentage of persons in the later years who maintain residences separate from their children but live close to them.

The men and women 65 years of age and over who live in long-term care institutions, primarily nursing homes, represent an estimated 5 percent of the population. This would total 1.4 million persons, a relatively small proportion of the total aged population. About 20 percent of all persons 85 years of age or older live in institutions and it is suggested that, over a lifetime, about one in four older persons will spend some time in an institution.[26] As a result of differing mortality between the sexes, women not only greatly outnumber men among the older population generally, but among the population living in institutions particularly, at a ratio of about two to one.

These figures tend to lend support to the ideas that: (1) most of the elderly are not in nursing homes or in long-term care institutions, and (2) most elderly are not abandoned by their families. Even those who are institutionalized are disporportionately drawn from those who are childless, widowed, and living alone. Gordon Streib argues for alternative living arrangements for older persons which include, for many, living in their own homes, in families with a spouse, with children, or with other relatives. But an increasing number of elderly people encounter problems in these arrangements. For these, he suggests a continuum of living arrangements from living independently to a full-care institution with twenty-four-hour nursing care. These arrangements may include retirement communities, retirement hotels, cooperative housing arrangements, or "Share-A-Home."[27] The latter involves a "family" of nonrelated senior adults who share their own household, employ a manager, and share expenses. A board of

---

26. James E. Montgomery, "The Economics of Supportive Services for Families with Disabled and Aging Members," *Family Relations* 31 (January 1982): 21.

27. Gordon F. Streib, "An Alternative Family Form for Older Persons: Need and Social Context," *The Family Coordinator* 27 (October 1978): 413–420.

directors of community citizens provides leadership and guidance. This concept blends in one location both familial and bureaucratic functions.

Other alternatives that could be considered include a partial institutionalization plan in which the member could participate in group recreational or work activities during the day and sleep at home or a night institutional plan where persons would sleep at the institution but be free to participate in community programs and activities during the day. Or older persons could live in "foster homes" in which they would be given the opportunity to actively participate in the activities of the host family. Thereby, a person could maintain healthy social interactions, gain a feeling of usefulness, and have physical needs provided for as well. The host family would be paid for the services they provided, either by the person or by the state (as is frequently done with young children).

PROBLEMS FACING THE AGED

As already suggested, the problems facing the aged are many. It is a time of life when a disproportionate number are isolated, disabled, sick, or poor. For example, some type of health problem almost invariably accompanies old age. Sometimes hospitalization is required, which raises a range of issues involving medical payments, visiting patterns, care for the residence of the hospitalized, and, on occasion, legal matters. Yet, in a nationwide sample of the noninstitutionalized elderly over age 65, Shanas[28] found there were twice as many old people who were housebound and bedfast at home (10 percent of the elderly) as were living in all kinds of institutions (approximately 5 percent). She found the majority of the frail and sick were taken care of at home, with the main source of help for the homebound invalid to be the spouse or an immediate family member. Wives took care of the men who were ill while women, more apt to be widows, were cared for by their children. Family members not only assumed the care of the bedfast but prepared meals and did the housework and shopping.

Other research as well confirms the preference for and the importance of family members and adult children, particularly daughters, as caregivers for the impaired noninstitutionalized elderly. It is widely believed that families are becoming less willing than families were historically to care for their elderly impaired family member at home. This belief, referred to as the "myth of abandonment," has little scientific evidence to support it, and, indeed, much evidence to the contrary. National surveys show that informal care-giving by families is currently the dominant mode, by

28. Ethel Shanas, *National Survey of the Elderly,* Report to the Administration on Aging (Washington, D.C.: Department of Health and Human Services, 1979).

far, of providing care services to the aged in general and the functionally disabled more specifically.[29] These functionally disabled may require assistance with personal care (bathing, eating, toileting), mobility (from room to room or in and out of chairs or beds), or daily living tasks (shopping, cleaning, cooking).

In economic terms, the aged remain a sizable segment of the nation's poor. As of 1985, the median total money income of all families with a householder age 65 or over was $19,162.[30] This compared with a total median family income of $27,735 for all families and $32,669 for householders aged 45–54. Persons age 65 and over who were unrelated individuals, that is, not living in or with families, had median incomes of $7,568. One in eight persons age 65 and over (12.6 percent) were below the poverty level. As can be seen in Figure 15–2, the poverty rate varies dramatically by race and sex. Black females in particular, while having a poverty rate nearly four times that of white males or white females in the 60–70 age category, show the largest increase in the percentage in poverty after age 70.

In spite of these figures and the decline in income after age 60 and 70, the quality of life of the elderly in the United States had improved dramatically. A report in *Family Planning Perspectives* (July/August 1984:186) in reference to an address of demographer Samuel H. Preston noted that a growing number of elderly are demanding and getting what they need, whereas the needs of many children are being ignored. As a result, the incidence of poverty among children under 14 in 1982 was 56 percent greater than that of the elderly. In 1970, the opposite was the case. This switch in economic well-being was attributed to the expansion of social security and noncash benefits such as medicare. Preston claimed that federal expenditures for the elderly in 1983 equaled $7,700 per person, while expenditures for all the major child-oriented programs combined (AFDC, Head Start, food stamps, and education) were approximately $700 per child. The politics of this major switch reveals the power of special interest groups determined by wealth and size. Children don't vote nor do they have much financial clout.

David Cheal, as well, reminds us that old people in the United States are, overall, not as deficient in economic resources as the image generally

---

29. Pamela Doty, "Family Care of the Elderly: The Role of Public Policy," *The Milbank Quarterly* 64 (1986): 34–75; and Kathryn Beckham and Jeffrey A. Giordano, "Illness and Impairment in Elderly Couples: Implications for Marital Therapy," *Family Relations* 35 (April 1986): 257–264.

30. U.S. Bureau of the Census, *Current Population Reports*, Series P-60, no. 154, "Money Income and Poverty Status of Families and Persons in the United States: 1985" (Washington, D.C.: U.S. Government Printing Office, 1986), Table 6, p. 12 and Table B, p. 3.

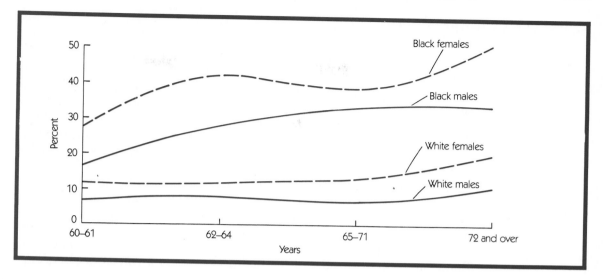

FIGURE 15–2
Poverty rate in 1981 of persons 60 years and over, by age, race, and sex. (*Source:* U.S. Bureau of the Census, *Current Population Reports,* Series P-23, no. 128, "America in Transition: An Aging Society" [Washington, D.C.: U.S. Government Printing Office, 1983], Figure 14, p. 11.)

presented would suggest.[31] While average income declines sharply, so do average expenditures. The ownership of domestic assets, such as the family home, makes it possible to enjoy a certain standard of living with a lower income than would otherwise be required. In fact, he suggests that young adults are major beneficiaries of familial transactions, that gift giving by old people is more significant than might be expected, and that financial aid is given by the elderly to relatives more freqeuntly than received.

A third problem facing the elderly is that of abuse and neglect. This may be one of our "newest" social problems in that little or no information prior to the late 1970s was published about domestic mistreatment of the elderly in their homes by relatives or other domestic caregivers. This issue is examined more thoroughly in the next chapter.

Extreme caution must be taken in the categorization of the aged as a homogeneous population. Although dependency, sickness, isolation, and abuse are frequent, a sizable proportion of these people have few health problems, carry on active lives with families and friends, and continue to make major economic and social contributions to their communities and society.

31. David J. Cheal, "Intergenerational Family Transfers," *Journal of Marriage and the Family* 45 (November 1983): 805–813.

Socialization of the aged

The tremendous emphasis given to children and youth in socialization literature largely ignores and overshadows the resocialization needs of the aged. In contrast to the aged, children receive much of their socialization within the family, from peers, schools, jobs, or the community. But what socializing agents exist to direct the aged from one life stage to another? Where is the training for retirement? Where is the training for widowhood? Where is the training or preparation for illness or death? Where is the training for the narrowing of social relationships?

In many ways U.S. society overlooks the fact that persons over sixty-five are social beings, that their world is maintained and meaning is found through interaction with others. As should have become very clear in the previous chapter, of primary importance to the socialization process and to the defining and redefining of the self is the extent and nature of friendship ties, association with significant others, involvement in groups of reference, and social interaction in general. Why should these factors be less important to persons over age sixty-five than to those under age twenty? It could be argued that these social relationships take on increased importance as persons move outside of their occupational spheres and as they experience the deaths of their age-peers.

When compared with younger adults, older persons as a group are removed from primary social roles. Society has provided few role definitions for older persons that would attach them to or keep them active in the social system. Whereas students, parents, and persons in the business or professional world speak with glee of the day when they will be relieved of social responsibility, older persons often find their new "freedom" carries with it grave consequences. Simply providing a variety of recreational activities does not serve as an adequate functional substitute for the responsibilities of gainful employment. For many, the later years bring with them a feeling of uselessness, not with the past but with the present.

Intimacy and familiarity characterize the family system and make it highly suitable to fulfill many of the needs, services, and interaction patterns of the individual members. However, it should be noted that family factors do not operate independently of the culture in which families operate. To avoid having the aged become "socially disabled," there needs to be a congruity between the cultural goals and structural opportunities that a society provides. The effectiveness of the family as a resource is largely contingent upon the values and services of the larger society: job opportunities, leisure time activities, health care, clarity of role, perception of the aged as fulfilling valuable functions, and socializing and resocializing opportunities appropriate to the later stage of the life cycle.

RETIREMENT

The problem of retirement involves the resocialization of men and women to new roles and life-styles. Traditionally, men assumed the major economic responsibility for their families and men's lives revolved heavily around work-employment roles. Thus it could be expected that the literature on retirement would focus heavily on the husband. Women's retirement was less studied because it was not perceived to constitute a salient social issue. With the dramatic increase in the labor force employment of women and the growing proportion of women retirees, studies of the preparation for and effect of retirement on both sexes are appearing with increasing frequency.

Robert Atchley suggests that the retirement process involves three major periods: preretirement, the retirement transition, and postretirement.[32] The first, *preretirement*, looks ahead to retirement: when to retire, what to expect, and the like. The *retirement transition* involves leaving one's job and taking up the role of retired person. The *postretirement* period involves life without the job or employment that occupied a major focus of time and attention in the preceding years. Retirement is thus viewed as a process that can occur over many years rather than a time-specific event.

To see what happens in the retirement process, Atchley received responses to mailed questionnaires in 1975 from more than 1,100 persons of both sexes in a small town near a large metropolitan area. These respondents were resurveyed again in 1977, 1979, and 1981. About 350 respondents were in the preretirement period and employed full-time. About 50 of these did not plan to retire, due to self-employment, good health, and for women, an unmarried status. Those who planned to retire gave a mean planned retirement age of sixty-four. Women were much more likely than men to plan to retire before age sixty as well as at age seventy or after. The early retirees tended to have high social status and to be married while the late retirees tended to have low social status and to be unmarried. This reinforces the notion of important class differences in retirement and cautions against relying too heavily on general statements about women's retirement. Less than 1 percent of either sex in this pre-retirement period had negative attitudes toward retirement.

The retirement transition period included about 170 persons who retired between 1975 and 1979. Those who had a negative attitude toward retirement (17 percent of the women and 11 percent of the men) were more likely to have poorer health and a low social status and to see their

---

32. Robert C. Atchley, "The Process of Retirement: Comparing Men and Women," in Maximiliane Szinovacz, *Women's Retirement: Policy Implications of Recent Research* (Beverly Hills: Sage Publications, 1982): 153–168.

income as inadequate. But retirement turned out better than expected and attitude scores went up significantly following retirement. For both men and women in the total sample, retirement tended to improve life satisfaction slightly, irrespective of marital status, health, income adequacy, social status, or living arrangements. Retirement reduced the activity level for both sexes, although the reduction was much greater for women than for men due to their much higher level of activity before retirement.

The postretirement period included nearly 300 persons who were retired in 1975. Attitudes toward their retirement were very positive, activity levels were relatively high, and life satisfaction scores were positive for both sexes. Activity level was a strong predictor of morale among retired men and health was more important among retired women. Interestingly, the older the retired woman, the more positive her attitude toward retirement was likely to be. It should be noted that the findings reported in this particular study occurred with generally healthy people in one small community that offered many opportunities for participation. In this context at least, people look forward to retirement, go through the transition smoothly, and find life in retirement satisfying.

Studies on the effects of retirement on marriage have tended to focus on the reactions of wives, changes in role differentiation, and the sharing of household tasks. Satisfaction of wives in retirement was highly related to joint decision-making by husbands and wives.[33] Brubaker and Hennon, in comparing household tasks between dual-earner and dual-retired marriages, found few differences.[34] Husbands had the primary responsibility for lawn work, car maintenance, and earning money. Wives were responsible for cooking, washing clothes and dishes, writing letters, and cleaning house. The only differences in task allocation were in shopping (retired couples were more likely to share) and earning money (retired couples were more likely to assign responsibility to the husband).

As indicated previously, with the increased employment of women, retirement for women is likely to take on increased significance and in many ways parallel the experiences and issues traditionally faced by men. This seems to be true already. One study of 1530 retired residents of Washington state found that retirement is not materially different for women than for men.[35] No support was found for the idea that retirement is a

33. Lorraine T. Dorfman and Elizabeth A. Hill, "Rural Housewives and Retirement: Joint Decision-Making Matters," *Family Relations* 35 (October 1986): 507–514.

34. Timothy H. Brubaker and Charles B. Hennon, "Responsibility for Household Tasks: Comparing Dual-Earner and Dual-Retired Marriages," in Maximiliane Szinovacz, *Women's Retirement*, pp. 205–219.

35. Karen Seccombe and Gary L. Lee, "Gender Differences in Retirement Satisfaction and its Antecedents," *Research on Aging* 8 (September 1986): 426–440. *See also* Fred C. Pample and Sookja Park, "Cross-National Patterns and Determinants of Female Retirement," *American Journal of Sociology* 91 (January 1986): 932–955.

less stressful event for women. In fact, women reported somewhat lower levels of satisfaction with retirement than men. Reasons given for this included their lower incomes and, to a lesser degree, their lower probability of being married. Regardless of gender, those in better health and those with higher incomes were most likely to express satisfaction with retirement.

Irrespective of the reasons for retirement, it seems likely that major role readjustments will be necessary for both sexes. Health, income, status, and feelings of self-worth often tend to decrease at the time of retirement, with the problems compounded upon the death of a spouse.

HOW FAMILIES DEAL WITH DYING AND DEATH

Two adages that come to mind in relation to death are "Two things are certain in life: Taxes and Death," and "Don't love and you won't get hurt." In the application of these to the family, the first would suggest that, pleasant or unpleasant, death is an inescapable event that will occur within all family or kin networks. The second suggests that the loss of those one loves most intensely is likely to cause tremendous pain. For most family members, while death may be certain, the loss of a parent, spouse, child, or other family member is a painful experience. Few relationships are more intimate and few groups more primary than those of marriages and families.

Terminal illness, dying, and death are separate but interrelated events or processes. The application of interaction theory to these events would suggest that definitions and meanings attached to illness and death would greatly influence the ability to accept, cope, or adjust to them. A recognition of significant others may help explain why many persons choose to endure illness and death at home rather than in a hospital or institutional setting. An understanding of reference groups may help us understand the relevance of the church, friends, or the kin network as support systems in facing these circumstances. While death may be a physical process, it is the cultural, social, and interpersonal processes that influence and affect it. To mourn, to wear black, to commit suicide by burning following the death of a spouse, to build mausoleums, or to bury in air-tight vaults are dependent upon cultural, class, and other social conditions.

An examination of the attitudes of college students toward the terminally ill and the dying suggests that health is associated with the young while illness and dying are associated with old age.[36] The dying are viewed in more negative terms, stigmatized, which often leads to isolation from others and a loss of resources. The authors suggest that if one wants to

---

36. Rita J. Epley and Charles H. McCaghy, "The Stigma of Dying: Attitudes Toward the Terminally Ill," *Omega* 8 (1977–78): 379–393.

be viewed positively by others, stay healthy, or if necessary become ill, but never run the risk of being labeled as dying.

Widows and widowers, described in the section that follows, were said to be a group that suffers because they are perceived to be carriers and transmitters of the realities of death.[37] The word *widow* itself forces persons with this social status to respond as if they have an infectious disease. People want to know when—if ever—they will "get over it." They want to know if anyone ever "completely recovers." The death of a spouse is consistently seen as a major source of stress requiring more readjustment than any other event in life. The loss of any loved one is likely to result in consequences that include grief, loneliness, depression, and economic difficulties. The economic difficulties may not be associated solely with the loss of income but from illness and funeral expenses as well.

In the United States as well as in most cultures, in times of illness, the immediate family and the immediate kin network has been found to be a major social support. Among the elderly, the presence of relatives makes it possible for bedridden persons to live outside institutions. Elderly people turn first to their families for help, then to neighbors, and, finally, to the bureaucratic replacements for families. Thus, it is not surprising that surveys indicate most people say they would like to die at home. In spite of this, medical attention, nursing care, and social-work help for the dying is hospital-based. And while four people would prefer to die at home for every one who would like to die in a hospital, in actual practice the ratio is reversed.[38]

Movements seem to be in process to make family-kin interaction with the terminally ill or dying patient more possible. One plan, called *hospice*, is a therapeutic environment designed from the patients' point of view. Unlike a regular hospital, which stresses privacy, hospice programs deemphasize this, emphasizing instead space for interaction with staff, family, and friends. Instead of subordinating the patient to the needs of the institution with families waiting in the hall, hospice programs are designed to provide as much care in the patient's home as possible; when medical facilities are needed, they involve a team of medical, nursing, psychiatric, and religious people, social workers, and family members as the need indicates. The concern is on increasing the quality of the last days of life and on making humane care synonymous with good medical practice. As a result, the family of the institutionalized patient is encouraged to be involved: bring in "home cooking," bathe the patient, supply medication,

37. Carol J. Barrett, "Women in Widowhood," *Signs: Journal of Women in Culture and Society* 2 (Summer 1977): 856.

38. Virginia H. Hine, "Dying at Home: Can Families Cope?" *Omega* 10 (1979–80): 175.

or bring along the family dog. Hours or visits are unlimited and interaction is permitted with young children or grandchildren.

The significance of family ties takes on an added dimension when one looks at the relationship between marital status and mortality. Mortality is lower for married persons with children than for those without children, and lower for nonmarried persons who are household heads than for those who are not heads.[39] These findings tend to suggest that protection against death itself may be afforded by different kinds of social ties, particularly marital, parental, and kin ties. These same ties, or severance of them, may explain some of the difficulties of the widow or widower.

THE POSTMARITAL FAMILY: THE WIDOW AND WIDOWER

The postmarital family, consisting of the widow or widower, is not unique to the aged family but is disproportionately represented after age 65 (*see* Figure 15–3). In 1985, there were 11.4 million widows and 2.1 million widowers, with 70 percent of them age 65 and over.[40] Facing the loss of a spouse and making the shift from a married to a widowed status may present extreme emotional and financial difficulties.

Society compounds the difficulty of adjusting to the widowed status by placing an unstated taboo on the discussion of death between husband and wife or parents and children while they are alive. As a result, the widow or widower is often unprepared for the decisions that need to be made. Even if discussions preceded the death, the likelihood is great that loneliness, social isolation, and a need for major readjustments in living patterns will result. There is probably no other period in one's life when there is a greater effort at self-awareness. Feelings of inadequacy and guilt, which lead to depression, are frequent occurrences after the death of a spouse.

Readjustment processes may be less difficult if widowhood follows a major illness or some type of major role change on the part of the spouse. Widowhood is often surmounted best when a person has already built some autonomy of personality, close continuing friendships, a realistic philosophy of life, economic security, and some meaningful personal interests.

While studies indicate a high degree of contact between older people

---

39. Frances E. Kobrin and Gerry E. Hendershot, "So Family Ties Reduce Mortality? Evidence from the United States, 1966–1968," *Journal of Marriage and the Family* 39 (November 1977): 737–745.

40. U.S. Bureau of the Census, *Current Population Reports*, Series P-20, no. 410, "Marital Status and Living Arrangements, March 1985" (Washington, D.C.: U.S. Government Printing Office, 1986), Table 1, p. 17.

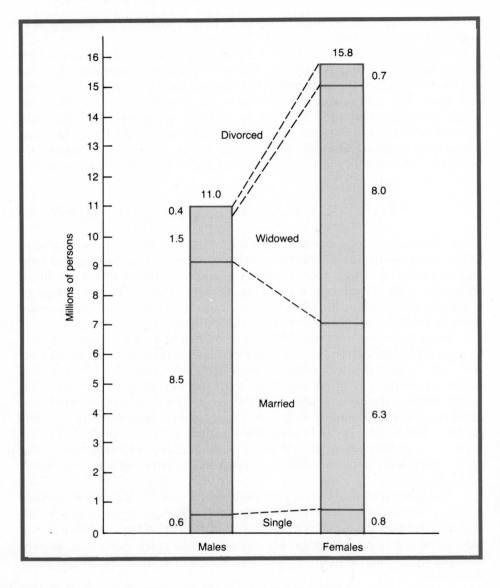

FIGURE 15–3
Number of males and females over age 65 by marital status, 1985. (*Source:*
Adapted from U.S. Bureau of the Census, *Current Population Reports*, Series
P-20, no. 410, "Marital Status and Living Arrangements, March 1985"
[Washington, D.C.: U.S. Government Printing Office, 1986], Table 1, p. 17).

and younger family members, especially adult children, this contact is
not directly associated with higher morale or greater personal satisfaction.[41]

41. Norval D. Glenn and Sara McLanahan, "The Effects of Offspring on the Psychological

Casserole women

The *Wall Street Journal* (April 22, 1986) reported that in South Florida's retirement communities, the women in pursuit of husbands are called "casserole women" because they descend on newly eligible men bearing food and sympathy. Men who live to an old age and want to date have little trouble finding partners.

One 75-year-old retired speechwriter said he has lots of fun and to prove it pulled from his wallet photographs of a woman leaning on his shoulder and another of a blond woman talking on the telephone. A 78-year-old ex-chef spurns women his own age and says he doesn't take to the old because they have no pep, no sex life.

Yet, the intense shortage of unmarried older men is not without its difficulties. Unattached men report periods of intense loneliness whereas women often find a supportive community of other women in similar situations. The chairman of a governing board of one of the retirement communities says that there are two basic social units in retirement communities — couples and widows. The single men aren't a viable entity as a group. Widowers are so scarce that the single man becomes the odd man out in retired life.

An attorney who often draws up pre-nuptial agreements to preserve the separation of assets, says the aged date and marry with few illusions. They come in holding hands, saying, "Dearie this" and "Dolly that" — but "Don't touch my money."

In contrast to family members, friendship-neighboring is clearly related to less loneliness and worry, to a feeling of "usefulness," and to individual respect within the community. Friendship relationships are voluntary and are often based upon common interests and a common life-style, while family ties are often marked by dissimilar concerns, different interests, formal obligations, and a role reversal between the elderly parent and the adult children. Certain intergenerational difficulties may be inevitable and be increased by factors such as ill heath and economic dependency.

One problem, believed to be widespread among elderly persons in general but particularly among the widowed, is that of social isolation and loneliness.[42] Social isolation is the objective condition of having few contacts with family, friends, or both. Loneliness is a subjective condition

Well-Being of Older Adults," *Journal of Marriage and the Family* 43 (May 1981): 409–421; and Elizabeth A. Bankoff, "Social Support and Adaptation to Widowhood," *Journal of Marriage the the Family* 45 (November 1983): 827–839.

42. Helena Znaniecki Lopata, *Widowhood in an American City* (Cambridge, Mass.: Schenkman, 1973): Philip G. Clark, Robert W. Siviski, and Ruth Weiner, "Coping Strategies of Widowers in the First Year," *Family Relations* 35 (July 1986): 425–430; and Marilyn J. Essex and Sunghee Nam, "Marital Status and Loneliness Among Older Women: The Differentiated Importance of Close Family and Friends," *Journal of Marriage and the Family* 49 (February 1987): 93–106.

which includes feelings of emptiness, aimlessness, and lack of companionship and involves a dissatisfaction with the present level of social interaction. One study of widows found that loneliness was listed by almost half of the respondents as their most serious difficulty; another third listed it as second.[43] Social norms for the United States and numerous other countries stress independence, but independence apart from frequent social interaction, marriage, employment, or adequate income leads to an increased vulnerability toward loneliness and low levels of mental and physical health.

The extreme outcome of conditions such as those just mentioned can be seen in examining the frequency of suicides. Within a given age group, the suicide rates of the widowed are consistently higher than those of the married, and the rate of completed suicides is significantly higher for males than for females. A study of aged persons in Florida reported the following major findings:

> (1) The widowed exhibit higher suicide rates than the married; (2) this differential is partially explained by the greater social isolation of the widowed, particularly the widowers; (3) the widowed can find in other types of relationships meaningful alternatives to marriage which help prevent suicidal behavior; (4) widowers have greater difficulty than widows in making effective substitutions for the loss of spouse; and (5) there appear to be limits to the effective mitigation of these alternatives for the widowed, especially the widower.[44]

These problems do not exist independently of retirement—discussed previously—and may be aggravated by it. The widow and widower are removed from their major sources of self-identity: job and the relationships with co-workers. The result of losing a spouse in old age, particularly among males, is therefore characterized by unhappiness, low morale, mental disorders, high death rates, and high suicide rates. All these seem to be related to the social isolation the widower faces. Not only has he lost a significant other in his spouse, but he becomes isolated from other persons significant to him: friends, neighbors, kin, and those connected with formal organizations. On the other hand, the widow has a greater opportunity for role continuity: housekeeping, interacting with relatives, going to church, and participating in various other kinds of formal and informal relationships.

Some widows and widowers remarry, but the chances of remarriage are, of course, higher for widowers than for widows. With women outliving men, the sex ratio (about 67) is very unbalanced in the later years. Of

---

43. Lopata, *Widowhood in an American City*, p. 70.

44. E. Wilbur Bock and Irving L. Webber, "Suicide Among the Elderly: Isolating Widowhood and Mitigating Alternatives," *Journal of Marriage and the Family* 34 (February 1972): 24.

those not married, the ratio is even more unbalanced. In 1985, the ratio of unmarried males over age 65 to unmarried females over age 65 was 26 to 100 (*see* Figure 15–3 and note 2.5 million unmarried men versus 9.5 million unmarried women). Programs to encourage remarriage among widows and widowers could not be successful, at least in a monogamous system. The problem is further compounded in our society by the norm that suggests that women should marry men of their own age or older. The remarriage problem for widowers is less severe since there is both an excess of women their own age as well as a social approval given to marrying women younger than themselves.

The questions centering around the remarriage of widows and widowers are often different from the questions centering around the remarriage of divorced persons. The persons are generally older and face different circumstances surrounding the ending of the previous marriage. A remarriage after the death of a spouse is likely to lead to a comparison of the new spouse with the memory of the deceased. It has been suggested that the perceived quality of marriage improves after the death of a spouse; the tendency is to recall the pleasant experiences and be keenly aware of the spouse's absence. Lopata's sample of Chicago widows showed a strong tendency to idealize the late husband and life with him, often to the point of sanctification.[45] This was less likely to happen among young and black women, those with a lower education and income, and those who had a difficult time in marriage. Older white widows in particular were apt to sanctify their husbands. Perhaps it is not accidental that saints exist primarily among the deceased.

SUMMARY

1. This chapter included an examination of two major periods of the life cycle: the middle years from approximately age forty to retirement, and the later years from approximately age sixty or sixty-five until the end of the life span.
2. The middle years, after the departure of children and prior to retirement, is a period when most men and women are married, with small percentages of single, widowed, or divorced people. It is one of the longest periods of the marital life cycle, covering a span of twenty to twenty-five years.
3. The significance of the middle years appears to differ somewhat for men and women. While family income approaches its peak, mixed

45. Helena Znaniecki Lopata, "Widowhood and Husband Sanctification," *Journal of Marriage and the Family* 43 (May 1981): 439–450.

evidence exists as to the extent to which this period of life for men and women is bright or difficult. Writers talk of a mid-life crisis or transition for men and an empty-nest syndrome for women. It appears likely that family-work changes lessen the negative impact of this period for both sexes.

4. Grandparenting has become a middle-age in addition to an old-age phenomenon. It may be an instrumental role for family systems in linking generations, in financial and service support functions, and in assisting the transition to other life-cycle stages. It appears to be a positive status for most respondents, although the roles vary considerably by social class and cultural context.

5. In the United States, later life is often viewed as an undesirable period, accented by dependency relationships and declining productivity. This stands in contrast to much of the world where older persons receive increasing status, prestige, and deference.

6. In the United States, nearly 80 percent of the men but less than one-half of the women aged 65–74 are married. After age 75, more than two-thirds of the men but less than one-fourth of the women are married. Marriages that do exist are perceived as favorable when compared to preceding periods of the life cycle. Most of the men and women of this age are living in families or living in geographical proximity to their children. Relatively few are in long-term care institutions such as nursing homes.

7. The problems facing the aged population are many, but this chapter focused briefly on three: health, money, and abuse. Most health problems are handled in the home rather than hospitals, with primary care coming from spouses or children. Money income drops sharply in old age but most families cope quite well and even give more than they receive.

8. Retirement, widowhood, changing relationships, and the like create a need for resocialization to new roles and definitions of self in relation to society.

9. Retirement has been described as a process involving periods of preretirement, the retirement transition, and postretirement. For both sexes it appears to be positive. Marital and household roles appear to change relatively little in retirement over the traditional patterns established during years of employment. The increased employment of women appears to be lessening the difference between the sexes in significance of retirement.

10. Dying and death are processes and events of major importance and significance to family members. Family members have been found to be major support systems both to the dying persons as well as to one another following death. The recognition of this seems to be encouraging movements in treating terminally ill and dying patients in home settings or in family-focused medical settings.

11. The postmarital family, particularly as represented by the widow or widower, while not unique to the aged family is disproportionately represented after age sixty-five: more women occupy a widow status than any other marital status. With the unbalanced sex ratio, remarriage is out of the question for a large number of women. For men, although the availability of a new spouse is less of a problem, the problems may be equally severe. Suicides are high among this marital status group, particularly among the very old.

12. The family life cycle, while ending for a particular nuclear family grouping, continues for the multigenerational extended family. Each stage or category of the life cycle has circumstances that are both unique to, and different from, the other stages. This chapter examined selected factors relating to the postparental periods: middle years, retirement, and old age. Conflict, crisis, and marital disorganization, although present at these periods of the life cycle, are not confined to them. The next chapter explores social patterns surrounding crisis and disorganization.

KEY TERMS AND TOPICS

DISCUSSION QUESTIONS

1. What is unique about the middle years or the empty-nest period? How is the period of adjustment different for women and for men?

2. Discuss the mid-life transition and the empty-nest syndrome. Do they exist and, if so, how serious are they? How might sex-role socialization patterns affect the middle years for both sexes?

3. Indicate changes in the grandparent role over the last thirty years. How might this role affect generational relationships? How might the grandparent status differ by class and subculture?

4. How true is the argument "you can't teach an old dog new tricks" when applied to the middle-aged or aged couple?

5.   Health, money, and abuse were stated as problems facing the aged. What other problems exist? How might a society establish programs, tax structures, and social policies that lessen the negative impact of these problems?

6.   Discuss changes in husband-wife roles that are likely to accompany illness, retirement, grandparenthood, remarriage, and so forth. How can resocialization be facilitated?

7.   What are the implications of retirement at age seventy, sixty, or fifty? Note marital status and male-female differences in adjustment patterns after retirement.

8.   What advantages or disadvantages exist to the widow or widower: if living alone, if living with kin, if living in a private home with other than kin, if living in an institution? What types of conditions make one more favorable than another?

9.   Explain the incidence of suicide among widowers versus widows, and single versus married persons.

10.   Invite several persons over age seventy-five to your class or to a "bull-session" to discuss such topics as the empty-nest syndrome, grandparenthood, retirement, widowhood, or facing death. Examine the significance of having children and their importance as systems of support.

FURTHER READINGS

Blau, Zena Smith ed. *Current Perspectives on Aging and The Life Cycle*. Greenwich, Conn.: JAI Press, Inc., 1985. This volume, the first in an ongoing series, focuses on work, retirement, and social policy viewed from a life course perspective.

Brubaker, Timothy H. *Later-Life Families*. Beverly Hills: Sage Publications, 1986. An intensive look at marriages, generational relationships, widowhood, and the future of persons and families in later life.

Brubaker, Timothy H. *Married for Fifty Years*. Lexington, Mass.: Lexington Books, 1986. Interviews with fifty couples who were married for fifty years reveal how they view marriage, mortality, and themselves.

Cherlin, Andrew, and Furstenberg, Frank F., Jr. *The New American Grandparent*. New York: Basic Books, 1986. Based on a nationwide study, two family sociologists provide a portrait of grandparenthood in U.S. society.

Farrell, Michael P., and Rosenberg, Stanley D. *Men at Midlife*. Boston: Auburn House, 1981. A study comparing men in their late twenties to men in their late thirties and early forties to determine what happens to men as they experience middle age.

Giele, Janet Zollinger. *Women in the Middle Years*, New York: John Wiley and Sons, 1982. A look at women in adulthood: their health, development, work, and family roles. The book includes an appendix that summarizes longitudinal and cross-sectional data sources on this age-grouping of women.

Lopata, Helena Znaniecki. *Women as Widows*. New York: Elsevier North Holland, 1979. A theoretical and descriptive study of widows that focuses on the societal, community, family, and personal resources available to them.

Markson, Elizabeth W., ed. *Older Women: Issues and Prospects*. Lexington, Mass.: Lexington Books, 1983. A collection of original contributions on older women, including a section on variations in life-styles without and within the family.

Peterson, Warren, A., and Quadagno, Jill, eds. *Social Bonds in Life: Aging and Interdependence*. Beverly Hills: Sage Publications, 1985. Twenty readings dealing with the interdependence of intimate relationships, social support systems, and health and social services.

Streib, Gordon, F., and Beck, Rubye Wilkerson. "Older Families: A Decade Review." *Journal of Marriage and the Family* 42 (November 1980): 937–956. One of the decade review articles dealing with intergenerational and family relations, marital satisfaction, widowhood, and older ethnic families.

Szinovacz, Maximiliane, ed. *Women's Retirement: Policy Implications of Recent Research*. Beverly Hills: Sage Publications, 1982. A compilation of fifteen original publications of research specifically devoted to women's retirement.

U.S. Bureau of the Census. "America in Transition: An Aging Society," *Current Population Reports*. Series P-23, no. 128. Washington D.C.: U.S. Government Printing Office, 1983. One of the special studies published by the Bureau of the Census, giving a wide variety of statistics covering the numerical growth, income and poverty, health status, and social characteristics of older persons.

VI

MARITAL CRISIS, DIVORCE, AND FAMILY POLICIES

Photo: © Camerique Stock Photos/E.P. Jones, Co.

16

Family Crisis and Domestic Violence

Marriages and families have been examined throughout the life cycle. No period in life is without the potential for **marital crisis**. You may recall references to parenthood as crisis, low levels of marital satisfaction ten to fifteen years after marriage, role conflicts, and the like. Each refers to some event or process that produces or produced stress, conflict, crisis, or reorganization to the marital or family unit.

If eyewitnesses to the family in the United States are to be believed, this institution and the interpersonal relationships within it have been in a state of decline for the past several hundred years. Preachers, teachers, philosophers, political leaders, commentators, and others have recorded their beliefs, irrespective of the generation in which they lived, that parental authority was becoming more lax, sexual taboos were weakening, spouses were rebelling against one another, and so forth. This was usually contrasted to the "old days" when authority was respected, sexual taboos were observed, and spouses were more understanding and tolerant. That each generation makes reference to weakness and decline may indicate dissatisfaction with present events, whatever these events may be, and sentimentality over the past, or it may indicate that actual conditions are never equal to the ideal. In either case, marital and family life is seldom "perfect" either for a given marriage or family as it covers the life cycle or for the marital and family system at any given time within a society. Stressor events produce crisis and a need for family reorganization. Let's examine some of these social stresses on the family.

SOCIAL STRESSES ON THE FAMILY

In a widely quoted article, now more than thirty years old. Reuben Hill speaks of *stressor* or crisis-provoking events.[1] These are situations for

----

1. Reuben Hill, "Social Stresses on the Family," *Social Casework* 39 (February/March 1958): 139–150; *see also* Donald A. Hansen and Reuben Hill, "Families Under Stress," in *Handbook of Marriage and the Family*, ed. by Harold T. Christensen (Chicago: Rand McNally, 1964): 782–819.

which the family has had little or no prior preparation. They are never the same for any given family but vary in striking power by the hardships that accompany them. Hardships are those complications in a crisis-precipitating event that demand competencies from the family that the event itself may have temporarily paralyzed or made unavailable.

Closely related to this idea is Jean Lipman-Blumen's usage of *crisis* to mean "any situation which the participants of a social system recognize as posing a threat to the status quo, well-being, or survival of the system or any of its parts, whose ordinary coping mechanisms and resources are stressed or inadequate for meeting the threat."[2] Note that both writers extend their definitions beyond events or situations per se. The event or situation need be one in which the family is ill prepared, demands competencies, is recognized as posing a threat, and stresses the available resources or coping mechanisms.

It is interesting that different families with similar competencies and resources respond very differently to similar events. The key appears to be at the "meaning" dimension. That is, to transform a stressor event into a crisis requires an intervening variable that has been variously termed "meaning of the event" or "definition of the event." This produces a formula as follows: A (the event) → interacting with B (the family's crisis-meeting resources) → interacting with C (the definition the family makes of the event) → produces X (the crisis).[3] Let's examine this ABCX formulation more closely.

Stressor events (A) may come from a wide variety of sources both within and outside the family. The consequences are likely to differ considerably depending on the source. For example, a general principle in sociology indicates that certain events outside a group such as war, flood, or depression tend to solidify the group. Thus, although stressful, certain external events may tend to unify the family into a more cohesive unit rather than lead or contribute to its breakdown. These same events may not be defined as critically stressful because other persons are in the same situation or worse. For example, it is disappointing to professional researchers to have their writings rejected by editors of journals. The pain may be less severe if it is recognized that a given publication has a 90 percent rejection rate. To know that many others submitted articles and were rejected, did not get their research funded, lost their homes, had premature births, or were unemployed often makes the event appear less critical. That is, others share similar misfortunes.

Events within the family that are defined as stressful may be more

---

2. Jean Lipman-Blumen, "A Crisis Framework Applied to Macrosociological Family Changes: Marriage, Divorce and Occupational Trends Associated with World War II," *Journal of Marriage and the Family* 37 (November 1975): 890.

3. Hill, "Social Stresses on the Family," p. 141.

disruptive because they arise from troubles that reflect poorly on the family's internal adequacy. These events may be nonsupport, mental breakdown, violence, suicide, or alcoholism, among others. The range of events, either within or outside the family, that disturb the family's role patterns is numerous. Not only do they involve losses of persons, jobs, or incomes, but additions as well. The arrival of a child, grandmother, or mother-in-law may be as disruptive as the loss of any of those three. Sudden fame or fortune may be as disruptive as loss of either. Any sudden change in family status or conflict among family members in the conceptions of their roles may further produce family crisis.

The dimensions that characterize any given stressor or crisis-provoking event extend far beyond whether it occurs internally or externally to the family. A crisis-producing event may affect the entire system or only a limited part, may occur gradually or suddenly, may be intense or mild, may be a short- or long-term problem, may be expected and predicted or random, may arise from natural conditions or artificial and technological man-made effects, may represent a shortage or overabundance of vital commodities, may be perceived to be solvable or insolvable, and may vary in substantive content.[4] The nature of the crisis event will influence the specific response of an individual or family system.

Again, what factors make for crisis proneness and freedom from crisis proneness? The explanation lies in B and C in the formula presented earlier. That is, to what extent do families have resources to meet the event (factor B) and to what extent do families define the event as a crisis (factor C)? Crisis-meeting resources (factor B) may include many factors: family adaptability, family roles, kin support systems, money income, insurance, friends, religious beliefs, education, good health, and the like. Problem families are often those without adequate resources to meet the stressor events. The extent to which families define the event as a crisis (factor C) reflects the value system of the family and previous experience in meeting crisis. Crisis proneness (X) is therefore a function of both a deficiency in family organization resources (factor B) and the tendency to define hardships as crisis producing (factor C). These two factors are combined into one concept of family inadequacy or family adequacy.

McCubbin and others, in an attempt to build on Hill's **ABCX model**, have proposed a **double ABCX model** that differentiates the precrisis and postcrisis variables.[5] The model now becomes a longitudinal one and the factor of time differentiates the precrisis from the postcrisis situation. The initial stressor event becomes a double "A" by separating the changes

4. Lipman-Blumen, "A Crisis Framework," p. 890.

5. Hamilton I. McCubbin and Joan M. Patterson, "Family Adaptation to Crisis," *Family Stress, Coping, and Social Support*, ed. by Hamilton I. McCubbin et al. (Springfield, Ill.: Charles C Thomas, 1982): 44–46.

that occur irrespective of the initial stressor from those changes that are consequences of the family's efforts to cope with the hardships of the situation. The resources become a double "B" by differentiating those resources already available to the family from those coping resources strengthened or developed in response to the crisis situation. The perception and meaning becomes a double "C" by likewise differentiating the definition prior to the event of how stressful it may be from the postcrisis perceptions of the level of stress. Combining the pre- and postcrisis ABC factors leads to family adaptation (or maladaptation) as a possible outcome. This double model was put to an empirical test using data on army families' adaptation to the crisis of relocation.[6]

Alexis Walker makes a case for expanding the ABCX model of stress and crisis to incorporate new dimensions.[7] These include a recognition that (1) all levels of the social system are interdependent and (2) stress occurs in a unique and influential sociocultural context. The interdependence of levels incorporates individual factors with dyadic, family, non-family, and community ones. That is, levels more macro than individuals and families need to be incorporated into the model.

Individual resources may be very different from family, community, or societal ones. Definitions or perceptions may vary for multiple members of a family. Whose definition is more important? If members don't agree, will the crisis be unresolvable?

The sociohistorical context recognizes how perceptions of stressful circumstances and resources available vary considerably over time. The differing contexts, and the unique perspectives and resources related to a given context, need to be recognized. In brief, in examining the process of adjustment to stress, it becomes necessary to focus, over time, on individual changes, dyadic changes, social network changes, and developments in the wider society that influence the ability of an individual, dyad, or family to respond effectively.

One example of a contextual analysis and the incorporation of the larger society (macroanalysis) into research comes from Kersti Yllo.[8] She attempts to understand violence against wives by looking at the balance of power in marital relationships as they are shaped by women's aggregate economic, political, legal, and educational status. Interpersonal interaction, including stress and violence, does not occur within a social vacuum and

---

6. Yoav Lavee, Hamilton I. McCubbin, and Joan M. Patterson, "The Double ABCX Model of Family Stress and Adaptation: An Empirical Test by Analysis of Structural Equations with Latent Variables," *Journal of Marriage and the Family* 47 (November 1985): 811–825.

7. Alexis J. Walker, "Reconceptualizing Family Stress," *Journal of Marriage and the Family* 47 (November 1985): 827–837.

8. Kersti Yllo, "The Status of Women, Marital Equality, and Violence Against Wives," *Journal of Family Issues* 5 (September 1984): 307–320.

needs to incorporate factors such as patriarchal social structures and social inequalities built into marriages.

While the list of stressor events, family problems, or conflict situations in marriages and families may seem infinite, this chapter focuses only on a selected one: violence. Other potentially stressful events such as mobility, commuter marriages, dual-career situations, sexual or racial inequality, poverty, intermarriage, sexual inadequacies, incest, conjugal decision making, parenthood, father-mother absence, mid-life crisis, widowhood, death, and aging were discussed in some detail in prior chapters. Other issues, like separation, divorce, and stepchildren, are discussed in the next chapter.

FAMILY VIOLENCE

Each year in the United States, at least six million men, women, and children are victims of severe physical attacks at the hands of their spouses

The frequency of husband-wife conflict and domestic fights including hitting and beating dispels the myth of the family as nonviolent. (Photo: © Jean Broughton/The Picture Cube)

or parents—that is twice the population of the city of Los Angeles.[9] It is claimed that in our society people are more likely to be hit, beat up, physically injured, or even killed in their own homes by another family member than anywhere else or by anyone else. Nearly one out of every four murder victims in the United States is killed by a member of his or her own family, and this is also the case in Africa, Great Britain, and Denmark.[10]

As is so often the case in matters defined as personal, private, and internal to the family, precise data on conjugal and parental abuse and violence are difficult to obtain. Not only are they behind closed doors, but they may not be perceived as improper. Behaviors such as spouse shoving, child spanking, and sibling fighting may be defined as normative, appropriate, and even necessary marital and family behaviors. Given this type of situation, one can only infer and speculate about how much intrafamily violence and/or abuse exists. What is no longer speculative is the idea that violence is a pervasive and common feature between spouses and among family members.

The myth of the family as nonviolent

Richard Gelles and Murray Straus suggest that intraviolence may be more common to the institution of the family than love.[11] Their suggestion is based on their own research and a review of other studies. The data indicate that:

1. Between 84 and 97 percent of all parents use physical punishment at some point in the child's life.
2. Conservative estimates of child abuse run to between 200,000 and 500,000 cases per year in the United States.
3. Twenty to 40 percent of all homicides involve domestic relationships.
4. Family fights are the largest single category of police calls.
5. A study of applicants for divorce found that 23 percent of middle-class couples and 40 percent of working-class couples gave "physical abuse" as a major complaint.
6. A national cross section of the population revealed that one in four

9. Murray A. Straus, Richard J. Gelles, and Suzanne K. Steinmetz, *Behind Closed Doors: Violence in the American Family* (New York: Doubleday/Anchor, 1979).

10. Richard J. Gelles, *Family Violence* (Beverly Hills: Sage Publications, 1979): 11. For a look at violence throughout the world, *see International Perspectives on Family Violence,* ed. by Richard J. Gelles and Claire Pedrick Cornell (Lexington, Mass.: Lexington Books, 1983).

11. Richard J. Gelles and Murray A. Straus, "Determinants of Violence in the Family: Toward a Theoretical Integration," in *Contemporary Theories About the Family. Vol. 1,* ed. by Wesley R. Burr et al. (New York: The Free Press, 1979): 550–552.

men and one in six women would approve of slapping a wife under certain conditions, and 26 percent of the men and 19 percent of the women would approve of slapping a husband.

7.   Within a single year, 62 percent of high school seniors studied had used physical force on a brother or sister, and 16 percent of their parents had used physical force on each other.

These types of data offer a persuasive counterargument to the widespread view that violence within families is a rare phenomenon found in scattered families. Suzanne Steinmetz and Straus suggest that part of the misperception is due to an unconscious commitment to the myth of the family as being nonviolent. This creates perceptual blindness on the part of the public and "selective inattention" on the part of social scientists.[12] That a marriage license is unconsciously accepted as a hitting license is well illustrated by Gelles and Straus who wrote:

> Although some want to reverse our figures and say that 80 percent of the spouses studied by Gelles did not have a regular pattern of hitting each other, and that 44 percent of the spouses studied by Gelles *never* hit each other . . . imagine the same statistics for a factory, a church, or a university. Would it be taken as nonviolence if the studies showed that 44 percent of the workers, faculty, or members of a congregation never hit each other, and 80 percent did not do so on a regular basis?[13]

Why so much violence in the family? Again drawing upon the work of Gelles and Straus, they suggest that the family has unique characteristics as a social group which contribute to making it a violence-prone setting. The irony of these characteristics is that they also have the potential for making the family a warm, supportive, and intimate environment. These characteristics include: the intense time spent interacting with other family members; the wide range of activities and interests of families; the intensity of involvement; the impinging activities of multiple members wanting differing things at the same time; the right to influence and attempt to change the behavior of others; the sexual and age differences which make the family an arena of cultural conflict; the assignment of roles based on ascription rather than on interest and competence; the privacy and insulation of the family from both social controls and assistance with conflict; the difficulty in terminating long-term marriage commitments and the impossibility of terminating birth relationships; the high levels of stress brought on by continual family changes associated with births, jobs, aging, and the like; and the social norms which provide parents with the right to use physical violence.[14]

---

12. Suzanne K. Steinmetz and Murray A. Straus, eds., *Violence in the Family* (New York: Harper and Row, 1974): 6–17.

13. Gelles and Straus, "Determinants of Violence in the Family," p. 552.

14. Ibid., pp. 552–554.

Spanking illegal

According to a report in *Parade Magazine* (August 19, 1979), Sweden has outlawed the old adage "spare the rod and spoil the child." On July 1, it became illegal for Swedish parents to spank their children or treat them in a humiliating way. A member of the justice ministry in Stockholm said that this new law is an attempt to change people's attitudes toward the physical punishment of their children and to show them that society does not approve of this sort of behavior. It is based on the belief that the reaction of children when hit by parents is one of revenge, not one of respect, and that physical punishment of children stimulates fear instead of love.

Many theories have been advanced to explain interpersonal violence in general and family violence more specifically.[15] Some theories place the explanation within the individual in the form of psychopathologies, alcohol, or drugs. Other theories are social-psychological in nature, with the explanations rooted in social learning, exchange, or social interaction. A third grouping of theories is sociocultural, with the explanations found in societal resources, conflict systems, or the larger culture. Irrespective of cause, let's examine selected forms of family abuse and violence.

Child abuse and violence

The history of the western world reveals that children have been subject to a range of abuses and cruelties, including the abandonment of infants left to die. While today only isolated incidents of such action are heard, physical punishment of children is legal in every state in the United States. While most of the physical and mental cruelty that children experience is behind closed doors of the home, most of us have personally witnessed in public places instances of children being hit or verbally abused.

One study of a nationally representative sample of 2,143 families in the United States included 1,146 with at least one child between the ages of three and seventeen living at home.[16] Violence was defined as an act

15. Fifteen of these theories and conceptual frameworks can be seen in ibid., pp. 560–568. Theories dealing with child maltreatment can be seen in Jerry J. Sweet and Patricia A. Resick, "The Maltreatment of Children: A Review of Theories and Research," *Journal of Social Issues* 35 (Spring 1979): 40–59. A review of the literature, including theories of violence, can be seen in Suzanne K. Steinmetz, "Violence Between Family Members," *Marriage and Family Review* 1 (May/June 1978): 1–16. The use of a systems theory approach can be seen in Jean Giles-Sims, *Wife Battering: A Systems Theory Approach* (New York: The Guilford Press, 1983).

16. Richard J. Gelles, "Violence Toward Children in the United States," *American*

carried out with the intention, or perceived intention, of physically injuring another person. The injury could range from a slap to murder, with motives ranging from concern for a child's safety to hostility desiring the death of the child. The results indicated that nearly two-thirds of these families mentioned at least one violent episode during the survey year. The milder forms of violence, as expected, were the most common: slaps, spankings, pushing, or shoving. Twenty percent of the parents reported hitting, and 10 percent reported throwing, as having ever taken place. Least frequent were the most dangerous types of violence. Eight percent reported kicking, biting, or hitting their child with a fist at some point in the raising of the child. Four percent reported "beating up" the child, and three percent said that they had at some time threatened their child with a gun or knife.

The researchers, extrapolating the above data to the 46 million children between the ages of 3 and 17 who lived with both parents during the year of the study, suggested that between 3.1 and 4.0 million of these children had been kicked, bitten, or punched by their parent at some time, between 1.4 and 2.3 million children had been "beaten up," and between 900,000 and 1.8 million had experienced their parents using a gun or knife on them. These forms of violence, with the exception of the use of a gun or knife, were found to be a pattern of parent-child relations rather than an isolated event. Since the data come from self-reports of "intact" families and from only one of the two parents, they are seen as quite conservative and low estimates of the true level of violence toward children in the United States.

What seems to be happening with time? Is there an epidemic of child abuse that is increasing each year? Apparently not. Murray Straus and Richard Gelles compared the rate of physical abuse of children from a 1975 study with the rates from a 1985 replication.[17] Both studies showed an extremely high incidence of severe physical violence against children; however, the 1985 physical child abuse rate (as measured by the number of children who were kicked, punched, bitten, beaten up, or attacked with a knife or gun) was 47 percent lower than the rate ten years earlier.

They argue that the lower rates are not due to differences in the methodology used. Thus, it must be due to a greater reluctance on the part of the respondents to report violence or an actual decrease in child abuse. Obviously, the desirable interpretation would be the latter one of an actual decrease. But they state that even if the former (greater reluctance to report) were true, this suggests an important, if not remarkable, degree

---

Journal of Orthopsychiatry 48 (October 1978): 585–586; and Richard J. Gelles and Murray A. Strauss, "Violence in the Family," *Journal of Social Issues* 35 (Spring 1979): 22–26.

    17. Murray A. Straus and Richard J. Gelles, "Societal Change and Change in Family Violence from 1975 to 1985 as Revealed by Two National Surveys," *Journal of Marriage and the Family* 48 (August 1986): 465–479.

of success in a change in public attitudes and standards concerning violence. The authors use their findings as a basis for believing that when a national effort is made about some aspects of intrafamily violence (as with child abuse programs), a national accomplishment can result. But they remind us even with the reduction in child abuse, that still leaves a minimum estimate of over a million abused children aged three through seventeen in two-parent households.

Who are these abusive parents? In general, it appears that mothers are slightly more likely than fathers to use violence in parent-child relations. However, male children are more likely to be victims.[18] The first finding may be related to the likelihood of mothers spending more time with children than the fathers, but factors other than time are likely to be operative. The second finding may be explained from a sex-differentiation perspective in which parents may see physical acts toward boys as helping them grow up but a less important character builder for girls. Young children seem to be more frequent victims of parental violence, perhaps suggesting greater interference in parents' activities and a lesser ability to use reason as punishment.

The issue of child abuse, maltreatment, and violence is extremely complex. Concerns relate not merely to the frequency of their occurrence and the types of abuse and the abusers, but extend to neglect, to the availability of services, and to the forms of legal intervention including the questions of custody and placement, decision making, and program coordination. Case identification lags considerably behind the actual rates of abuse, and the increasing levels of reporting place strains upon the limited levels of services available. Listed in the footnotes are other sources for a more extensive treatment of this issue.[19]

Wife abuse and violence

Following the concern over the abuse of children is the abuse of wives. It was previously stated that one in six women expressed the belief that their husbands had the right to slap them under certain conditions. And as women learn that husbands have the right to slap, so do men learn that violence against their wives is acceptable. Data from a national probability sample of about 2,000 men and women revealed that men are more likely to approve of violence against women if they observed their

---

18. Gelles, "Violence Toward Children in the United States," pp. 588–589.

19. Harriet D. Watkins and Marilyn R. Bradbard, "Child Maltreatment: An Overview with Suggestions for Intervention and Research," *Family Relations* 31 (July 1982): 323–333; and Michael J. Martin and James Walters, "Familial Correlates of Selected Types of Child Abuse and Neglect," *Journal of Marriage and the Family* 44 (May 1982): 267–276.

Abused wives: why do they stay?

Richard Gelles in a series of papers has addressed the issue of violence in the home: physical aggression between husbands and wives, wife abuse, child abuse, pregnancy beatings, and the like. One article attempts to answer the question as to why physically abused wives stay with their husbands.

He found that: (1) the less severe and the less frequent the violence, the more a woman will remain with her spouse and not seek outside aid, (2) the more a wife was struck by her parents, which apparently raises her tolerance for violence, the more inclined she is to stay with her abusive husband, (3) wives who stay with an abusive husband are less likely to have completed high school and are more likely to be unemployed, i.e., they have less power and fewer resources, and (4) the actions of the wife are influenced by external constraints in the form of police and agency and court lack of understanding about marital violence.

Gelles found some spouses who suffered repeated severe beatings or even stabbings without so much as calling a neighbor. Some spouses reported that it is acceptable for a husband to beat his wife "every once in a while." Divorce appears to be a solution only after a history of conflict and reconciliation, when the wife can no longer believe her husband's promise of no more violence nor forgive past episodes of violence, when the violence is severe and frequent, and when women recognize and have the needed resources for this type of action.

Source: Richard J. Gelles, "Abused Wives: Why Do They Stay?" *Journal of Marriage and the Family* 38 (November 1976): 659–668.

fathers hitting their mothers.[20] Violence begets violence and the cycle of violence continues from one generation to the next.

That violence against women, like much family violence, is not always viewed as improper or deviant has historical precedence. As recently as the late nineteenth century in Great Britain and the United States, it was considered a necessary aspect of a husband's marital obligation to control and chastise his wife through the use of physical force. Violence against wives can be viewed as a logical extension of a patriarchal family system in which the husband, as the dominant ruler and head, uses whatever means necessary to obtain obedience and control. And considerable evidence suggests that irrespective of whether violence toward wives is a carryover of an historical pattern, whether it is a logical extension of a

---

20. Patricia Ulbrich and Joan Huber, "Observing Parental Violence: Distribution and Effects," *Journal of Marriage and the Family* 43 (August 1981): 623–631; and Debra Kalmuss, "The Intergenerational Transmission of Marital Aggression," *Journal of Marriage and the Family* 46 (February 1984): 11–19.

patriarchal system, or whether it is granted a level of acceptability for some other reason, the practice is common.

Marital conflict is an established and well-known pattern. How these conflicts are resolved takes a wide variety of forms including silence, screaming, withholding services, leaving, throwing objects, homicide, or others. In a review of research in the 1970s that included studies of the extent of violence between marital partners. Gelles noted that 16 percent of those surveyed reported some kind of physical violence between spouses during the past year; 28 percent reported marital violence at some point in their marriage; and a national study revealed that 3.8 percent of U.S. women were victims of abusive violence during the preceding 12 months.[21] Steinmetz as well noted reports of 17,000 wife-abuse complaints brought to New York family courts, 1,125 cases of wife beating reported to Salt Lake City police per year; 2,000 cases of wife beating in Fairfax County, Virginia (estimated to be under-reported by 40 percent); and numerous other reports each testifying to the commonality of violence toward women of a nature extreme enough to come to the attention of the police and the courts.[22] Steinmetz's own research in a Delaware sample revealed severe physical abuse received by 7 percent of wives (and 6 percent of husbands). And extrapolating from a national sample to the total population, as was done with the child abuse data, Steinmetz indicated that 3.3 million wives have experienced severe beatings from their spouses.

The question raised about changes in child abuse will be raised about wife or spouse abuse. Is there an epidemic of wife abuse that is increasing each year? And again the answer is, apparently not. The same Straus-Gelles study mentioned earlier comparing violence rates in 1975 and 1985 showed that wife beating (as measured by the number who were kicked, punched, hit with an object, bitten, beaten up, or attacked with a knife or gun) decreased by 27 percent.[23] Interestingly, similar severe assaults by wives on husbands (*see* next section) decreased only 4.3 percent. Again, even if these rates indicate actual reductions, that still leaves over a million and a half beaten wives each year in the United States.

Most abuse and violence toward wives does not take the form of beating, but rather it takes the form of throwing things, shoving, pushing, grabbing, slapping, or hitting. These events appear to be more common at selected times such as during a wife's pregnancy or following the husband's drinking, although the exact extent is an unanswered question. Sexual abuse as well, including marital rape, appears to be a relatively

---

21. Richard J. Gelles, "Violence in the Family: A Review of Research in the Seventies," *Journal of Marriage and the Family* 42 (November 1980): 877.

22. Steinmetz, "Violence Between Family Members," p. 4.

23. Straus and Gelles, "Societal Change and Change in Family Violence," pp. 465–479.

common form of violence sustained by wives. As noted in Chapter 11, the forcing of sexual intercourse by a husband, technically marital rape although legally not recognized as such, is seldom viewed as rape by wives, who often blame themselves for the incident. That wives blame themselves or learn to accept forced sexual intercourse may be why so little attention has been devoted to this topic in spite of what may be a widespread occurrence.

Whereas abused children cannot readily choose to leave family members who abuse them, wives, it seems, have this choice. Thus a logical question is, Why do abused wives stay? Some answers to this question appear in the panel on abused wives. Other answers stem from two separate research studies that both emphasize economic dependency.[24] Wives who are highly dependent on marriage were less able to discourage, avoid, leave, or put an end to abuse than women in marriages where the balance of resources between husband and wife was more nearly equal. Dependent wives lacked both alternatives to marriage and resources within marriage to negotiate change.

Of those abused wives who do leave, a number turn to shelters: short term refuges from violent relationships. It is estimated that over 700 of these shelters exist in the United States alone and represent the result of an international movement that began in England. The emphasis of shelters is placed on separating the victim from the assailant, providing alternate room and board, and providing support services. The effects seem to depend upon the attributes of the victim. For women who actively take control of their lives, a shelter stay was found to dramatically reduce the likelihood of new violence. For others, shelters were found to have no impact or even trigger retaliation or disobedience.[25] Within the context of the ABCX model, shelters represent an important community resource for many physically abused wives.

Another community resource that appears to be effective in wife-battery incidents is that of police response with a follow-up arrest. For over two years in one county in California, researchers explored the deterrent effect of arrests (made in 26 percent of wife-battery incidents) and concluded that (1) on the average, arrests deter new wife-battery incidents, and (2) reductions in wife-battery are greatest and especially effective for batterers

---

24. Debra S. Kalmuss and Murray A. Straus, "Wife's Marital Dependency and Wife Abuse," *Journal of Marriage and the Family* 44 (May 1982): 277–286; and Michael J. Strube and Linda S. Barbour, "The Decision to Leave an Abusive Relationship: Economic Dependence and Psychological Commitment," *Journal of Marriage and the Family* 45 (November 1983): 785–793.

25. Richard A. Berk, Phyllis J. Newton, and Sarah Fenstermaker, "What a Difference a Day Makes: An Empirical Study of the Impact of Shelters for Battered Women," *Journal of Marriage and the Family* 48 (August 1986): 481–490.

whom police would ordinarily be inclined to arrest.[26] This is no guarantee that simply increasing the number of arrests would have the same deterrent effect, but with the more serious incidents where arrest did occur, it had the desired deterrent effect.

Husband abuse and violence

Existing research data tend to focus attention on child abuse and wife abuse. But overlooked aspects of family violence include the abused husband, abused siblings, and abused elderly.

It has already been stated that many men and women grant social approval to slapping husbands. In addition some general surveys indicate that wives often exceed their husbands in the use of physical violence during a marital conflict and in the frequency with which these acts occur. Murray Straus stated that one of the cruel ironies of marriage is that, although husband-wife relationships are largely male dominant, the use of physical violence seems to be one of the few aspects of marriage that approach equality between spouses.[27] It should be noted, however, that the *effects* of this violence are far from equal, for the husbands generally cast the last and most damaging blows. The high rate of violence by women, Straus claims, can be accounted for by: (1) retaliatory violence which increases the probability of initiating family violence; (2) implicit cultural norms that make the marriage license also a hitting license; (3) childhood training in the use of violence within the family; (4) child care in U.S. society that involves role practice in violence since over 90 percent of parents use physical punishment; and (5) the high degree of frustration involved in marriage, with wives relatively powerless in comparison with their husbands.

Wife abuse and husband abuse are treated separately here. Yet, it needs to be emphasized that mutual abuse is more common than either alone. Likewise, disparity between husbands and wives in recall of violence is evident. Whereby husbands tend to view their marital relationships as mutually violent, wives view the husbands as violent.[28] Both spouses report more violence for their partner than they are willing to acknowledge for

---

26. Richard A. Berk and Phyllis J. Newton, "Does Arrest Really Deter Wife Battery? An Effort to Replicate the Findings of the Minneapolis Spouse Abuse Experiment," *American Sociological Review* 50 (April 1985): 253–262.

27. Murray Straus, "Victims and Aggressors in Marital Violence," *American Behavioral Scientist* 23 (May/June 1980): 681–704.

28. James Browning and Donald Dutton, "Assessment of Wife Assault with the Conflict Tactics Scale: Using Couple Data to Quantify the Differential Reporting Effect," *Journal of Marriage and the Family* 48 (May 1986): 376–379.

Quaker families and marital violence

Among Judeo-Christian religions, perhaps none is better known for their stand against violence and for peace than are the Quakers, known formally as the Religious Society of Friends. They are noted for their emphasis on peaceful means of resolving conflict, on the deep respect for each person's right to conscience, and on their identification as conscientious objectors and participants in peace movements.

Do these principles that operate at the international level carry into Quaker homes as well? Judith Brutz and Craig Allen (*Journal of Marriage and the Family*, August 1986) received questionnaire returns from 159 Quaker wives and 131 Quaker husbands. For both wives and husbands, and for both communication violence and ordinary physical violence, lower levels of marital violence were associated with high levels of religious participation. But they found important gender-related differences in the meanings attached to religious experience and violence. For wives, high levels of peace activism were associated with low levels of marital violence. For husbands, high levels of peace activism were associated with high levels of marital violence. The authors suggest that commitment to Quaker principles is confounded with traditional norms of non-aggressiveness for Quaker wives and aggressiveness for Quaker husbands.

themselves. Also, each spouse tends to be more likely to report their own victimization than their own use of violence.

The effects of family structure on both spouse and child abuse are evident from data on stepfamilies and remarriages. Findings show that spouse and child abuse is more likely in stepfamilies and families in which one or both spouses have been divorced (remarried and reconstituted) than in never-divorced (intact) families.[29] Explanations for this occurrence may relate to carrying on previously learned behavior patterns, to stepparents not having the strong bonding and blood ties, to selecting spouses who dominate or can be dominated, to higher levels of stress in remarried families, or to other reasons. In any case, there is a continuity of abuse in reconstituted families.

The effects of marital violence extend to persons beyond those who are directly abused or battered. Specifically, children who witness a parent being abused may be vulnerable to a variety of behavioral and emotional difficulties, including psychosomatic disorders and aggression. Results of students who had viewed parental violence were found to be significantly

---

29. Debra Kalmuss and Judith A. Seltzer, "Continuity of Marital Behavior in Remarriage: The Case of Spouse Abuse," *Journal of Marriage and the Family* 48 (February 1986): 113–120; and Jean Giles-Sims and David Finkelhor, "Child Abuse in Stepfamilies," *Family Relations* 33 (July 1984): 403–413.

The impact of negative family experiences such as neglect and/or abuse is often difficult to assess but a feeling of loneliness, low self-esteem, and depression are probable outcomes. (Photo: © Smolan/Stock, Boston)

more anxious than those from satisfactory relationships. Females, in addition, showed elevated levels of depression and aggression.[30] This finding is consistent with a "learned helplessness" model of wife abuse that suggests seeing one's mother in a helpless situation transmits the message that women are helpless to control their own lives. This promotes depression in women most likely to identify with the victim-mother. In contrast, men who witness parental violence might be more likely to identify with the aggressor-father than with the victim, thus avoiding depression. These men in turn are more likely to be abusive husbands themselves.

Sibling abuse and violence

It seems that the most frequent and acceptable form of violence within families occurs between siblings. Available evidence fom the Straus and

---

30. Barbara Forsstrom-Cohen and Alan Rosenbaum, "The Effects of Parental Marital Violence on Young Adults: An Exploratory Investigation," *Journal of Marriage and the Family* 47 (May 1985): 467–472.

Gelles studies mentioned previously revealed that 40 percent of children whose parents they interviewed had hit a brother or sister with an object during the preceding year and 82 percent had engaged in some form of violence against a sibling.

This is a form of violence granted a high degree of tolerance. Identical acts between parent and child or husband and wife might well result in possible criminal charges and social service intervention. It appears that although male sibling pairs outdo female sibling pairs in throwing things, pushing, and hitting, the greatest amount of physical violence occurs between boy-girl pairs.

This type of activity is usually explained in terms of sibling rivalry or jealousy. Supposedly, each sibling resents something the other has: parental attention, privileges, clothes, objects, and the like, or centers around differences over limited resources: use of the bathroom or telephone, what TV show to watch, or who gets the remaining candy bar. These resentments and differences may become aggravated when greater powers (parents) intervene and insist they share or make a decision that favors one over the other. Reacting abusively toward a sibling who is more one's equal in size and age is both more equitable as well as more acceptable than acting abusively toward parents, although as noted later, this does occur as well.

Sometimes sibling discord revolves around the division of labor in the family. Siblings compete in avoiding undesirable tasks or chores: dishes, cleaning rooms, sweeping walks, etc. Age differences may aggravate the situation if younger children are assigned fewer chores. In short, exchange theory is operative and perceived inequalities lead to conflict. While obviously not all inequity leads to abuse or violence, fighting or throwing objects are resources available to most children. And even when one child is outmatched, parental intervention in stopping the fight, protecting the younger sibling, or punishing the older siblings is a realistic possibility.

It is factors such as these that help to explain the common occurrence of sibling abuse and violence. Recognizing the importance of socialization experiences and social contexts would lead us to expect that even among siblings, differences in abuse would exist by sex, ethnicity, and social class.

Elderly abuse and violence

The battered elderly parent, as noted in the previous chapter, is the subject of recent investigation. A number of investigators agree that a substantial problem exists, with estimates ranging between 500,000 and 2.5 million cases per year.[31] The variety and severity of mistreatment ranges from passive neglect (unintentionally ignored, forgotten) to active neglect (financial exploitation, withholding of medicine, food, assistance) and from verbal or emotional abuse (calling names, threatening, humiliation) to physical abuse (slapping, pushing, injuring). Abuse may take the form of tying the elderly parent to a bed or chair, excessive use of medication or drugs to keep the parent more manageable, battering with fists or objects to enforce particular behaviors, or nearly any conceivable activity.

The victims are generally the older elderly persons who are frail, mentally or physically disabled, female, and living with the person responsible for mistreatment. A commonly cited "cause" of the abuse includes becoming over-taxed by the requirements of caring for the elderly adult. This burden for caring often leads to despair, anger, resentment, or violence. In some instances the abuse is clearly malicious and intentional, while other instances involve caretakers with more serious emotional and dependency problems who do not deliberately intend to abuse, but are less able to control their behavior.

Research suggests that the typical abused elder, rather than being a dependent, may be an older women supporting a dependent child or, to a lesser extent, a physically or mentally disabled spouse.[32] The powerlessness of the abuser who is dependent on an elderly parent may be a critical factor in understanding elderly abuse. This contradicts the common notion that the dependency of the elderly victim on the abuser is a primary cause of abuse. From an exchange perspective, the victims perceived themselves as being on the losing end, or giving much and receiving little. Most did not leave the situation but felt trapped by a sense of family obligation.

The application of the ABCX formula to marital and family violence suggests that the various types of hitting, throwing, biting, and the like that take place within a family may or may not represent crisis events depending upon the resources available and meanings attached to them. It has been clearly shown that many acts between siblings, between parents and children, or between partners are perceived as expected and normal behaviors. While resources have not been covered in detail per se, strength, withholding of money or services, friends and other kin, police, crisis intervention centers, and the like may all be essential resources.

---

31. Richard L. Douglass, "Domestic Neglect and Abuse of the Elderly: Implications for Research and Service," *Family Relations* 32 (July 1983); and Claire Pedrick-Cornell and Richard J. Gelles, "Elder Abuse: The Status of Current Knowledge," *Family Relations* 31 (July 1982): 457–465.

32. Karl Pillemer, "The Dangers of Dependency: New Findings on Domestic Violence Against the Elderly," *Social Problems* 33 (December 1985): 146–158.

Violence among other intimates

Abuse and violence may have its origin long before husbands, wives, children, and siblings enter the scene. One key example centers around friendships and intimates involved in the mate selection-courtship process. Most studies that deal with the courtship processes of dating, going steady, or engagement tend to portray these events in a context of love, attraction, affection, mutual disclosure, and increasing closeness and commitment as the courtship process moves toward marriage. Laner and Thompson,[33] in a study of abusive and aggressive premarital relationships, inform us that violence is more likely to occur in more involved relationships than in less involved ones.

Exploratory studies of college students were completed by James Makepeace in an attempt to estimate the incidence of courtship violence and gender differences in victimization.[34] As expected, the incidence of courtship violence "known of" by the students in the study greatly exceeded what was directly experienced. Also, as expected, more extreme forms of violence, such as assault with an object or weapon, were less common than the milder forms, such as pushing or slapping. Nearly two-fifths of the students knew of instances of threats, pushing, or slapping. Overall, males and females were about equal in initiating, committing, and sustaining violence. Females, being the principal victims, more often reported serious forms of violence done to them; they also more often report sustaining sexual assault, physical injury, and emotional trauma. Yet, males rarely reported that sexual assault was attempted or occurred and did not perceive that females sustained greater physical or emotional harm. Attempts to explain these disparities included for males denial, the nonrecognition or recall of details of experiences, and the minimization of the frequency and intensity of the males' abuse.

Results from Oregon students indicated that nearly all of them had been involved in some conflict, including heated discussion, crying, sulking, stomping away, or getting drunk or stoned during dating and courtship.[35] About two-thirds had been involved in some type of abuse including insulting, swearing, spiteful acts, or threats to hit or throw something. Sexuality was an important source of violence in dating and courtship, with males more likely to inflict a variety of forms of sexual aggression and females more likely to experience sexual victimization.

---

33. Mary Riege Laner and Jeanine Thompson, "Abuse and Aggression in Courting Couples," *Deviant Behavior: An Interdisciplinary Journal* 3 (1982): 229–244.

34. James M. Makepeace, "Courtship Violence Among College Students," *Family Relations* 30 (January 1981): 97–102; and "Gender Differences in Courtship Victimization," *Family Relations* 35 (July 1986): 383–388.

35. Katherine E. Lane and Patricia A. Gwartney-Gibbs, "Violence in the Context of Dating and Sex," *Journal of Family Issues* 6 (March 1985): 45–59.

It appears that violence among high-school couples is similar to that found in college couples, with the only difference in that it occurs to a lesser degree. A study of high-school juniors and seniors in Michigan showed that one sudent in ten had a direct personal experience of dating violence, and three in ten knew someone who did.[36] The authors, in comparing their results of high-school students with studies of college students, suggest that the main causes of violence are the same (jealousy and alcohol), as well as where it occurs (places of residence and vehicles), how it is interpreted (anger, confusion, and love), and its effects on the relationship (ranging from termination to improvement). Adolescents who experience violent interaction in dating may be establishing patterns that will continue into subsequent relationships and ultimately into marriage.

A final form of violence among intimates to be mentioned is that of teenage violence directed toward parents. The overall incidence of this type of violence was found to be relatively low (from 7 to 11 percent toward either parent).[37] Fathers were more likely than mothers to be the target. Youth-to-parent violence was higher where parental violence was displayed toward them and lower where family cohesion was greater.

The occurrence of violence during adolescence, whether exhibited toward parents or in the courtship process, seems to be a foundation for marital and parental violence. The experience of violence between spouses or toward children is seldom the perpetrator's first experience.

SUMMARY

1.   The central issues of this chapter, marital and family crisis and violence, are not unique to any given stage of the family life cycle or any particular family structure.
2.   Stressor or crisis-provoking events refer to any situation that threatens the status quo and well-being of the system or its members. These events may come from sources both within and outside the family. Certain events may solidify the unit, while others may be very disruptive.
3.   The ABCX model refers to some event (A) interacting with the family's crisis-meeting resources (B) and the definition or meaning given to the event (C), resulting in the level or degree of crisis (X). When and if B and C are adequate, the level of stress and crisis will be minimal. If they are inadequate, the level of stress and crisis will be high.
4.   Since the original ABCX model was proposed, other writers have

36. Bruce Roscoe and John E. Callahan, "Adolescents' Self-Report of Violence in Families and Dating Relations," *Adolescence* 20 (Fall 1985): 545–553.
37. Charles W. Peek, Judith L. Fischer, and Jeannie S. Kidwell, "Teenage Violence Toward Parents: A Neglected Dimension of Family Violence," *Journal of Marriage and the Family* 47 (November 1985): 1051–1058.

expanded it to include a double ABCX model and recommended the incorporation of new dimensions, such as interrelating the levels of various systems and recognizing the sociohistorical context.

5. One common event within families is abuse and violence. Unique characteristics of the family as a social group make it a violent-prone setting for both spouses, for the children, and the interpersonal relationships among them. The prevalence of violence offers a persuasive counterargument against the myth of the family as nonviolent.

6. Considerable attention is focused on the abuse of children. Traditional modes of discipline grant legitimacy to the spanking and physical punishment of children. Since most of it occurs behind closed doors, most abuse never comes to the attention of the public. Recent data suggest an increasing awareness of this as an important issue and an actual decrease in child abuse.

7. Wife abuse, like child abuse, is not always viewed as inappropriate, particularly in contexts of male authority and dominance. Marital conflict is a well-established phenomenon, and this conflict is often acted out in verbally and physically abusive ways. Like child abuse, we may have witnessed an actual decrease in abusive acts such as wife beating. Many wives do not or cannot leave their violent husband due to economic dependency or lack of alternatives, while others turn to shelters.

8. Husband abuse is granted far less attention than the abuse of children and wives; however, physical violence seems to be one aspect of a marriage that approaches equality between the spouses. Marital violence extends beyond the spouses to children in a way that often has both short- and long-term negative consequences.

9. Sibling abuse is the most frequent and acceptable form of violence within families. Explanations often center around sibling rivalry and jealousy. Supposedly each sibling resents something the other has, or the tensions center around differences over availability of limited resources. Sibling discord often involves the family division of labor as well.

10. Elderly abuse frequently centers around aging parents, particularly the mother. The typical abused adult, rather than being a dependent, may be an older person supporting a dependent child. The mistreatment ranges from passive or active neglect to verbal and physical abuse.

11. Other forms of violence among intimates include that of adolescents in the dating-courtship process and adolescents toward parents.

12. While this chapter focused on marital and family stress and violence, the next chapter turns to the termination of marriages, particularly via divorce and the subsequent pattern of remarriage.

DISCUSSION QUESTIONS

1. Itemize a list of "stressor events." What ways exist to prepare for events such as these? How is it possible that certain events "strengthen" families whereas others tend to "tear them apart"?

2. What factors make for crisis-proneness and freedom-from-crisis-proneness? Using the formula given in the chapter, show how "resources" and "meanings" lead to family adequacy or family inadequacy in facing potential crisis situations.

3. Select any personal or family problem. How could or does the availability of resources affect the problem? What are these resources? How does your definition of the problem affect the level of stress?

4. Explain the myth of the family as nonviolent. Why are behaviors involving abuse and violence so common and so acceptable within families that would be punishable and unacceptable among nonfamily members?

5. Discuss the likely differences in frequency and type of child abuse based on characteristics of the child: age, sex, retarded, or handicapped. What is the impact of ethnicity or sociohistorical context in explaining differences?

6. Is not marriage an interpersonal private relationship? If so, should the community or state get involved in what husbands and wives do to each other? Why or why not? What actions should "outsiders" take?

7. Why don't abused wives leave?

8. Is it necessary to pay attention to or do research on violence toward husbands or between siblings? Can not husbands take care of themselves? Are not fights "natural" among children?

9. Think of personal childhood and sibling experiences of violence. Did they occur? With whom? For what reason?

10. Discuss various forms of abuse that exist within families toward elderly parents. What type of action or programs might lessen the problem or the severity of it?

11. Are you aware of abuse or violence in dating or in nonmarital heterosexual interactions? What form did or does it take? How do you explain its prevalence?

12.   What is the relationship of factors such as alcoholism, drug addiction, unemployment, lack of money, and the like to violence and abuse? How might a pregnancy, birthday, or holiday affect the likelihood of violence?

FURTHER READINGS

Finkelhor, David, and Associates. *A Sourcebook on Child Sexual Abuse*. Beverly Hills: Sage Publications, 1986. A consideration of the prevalence of sexual abuse, children at high risk, offenders, effects, and prevention.

Gelles, Richard J. "Violence in the Family: A Review of Research in the Seventies." *Journal of Marriage and the Family* 42 (November 1980): 873–885. A decade review of research findings on violence including its extent, factors associated with violence, and theoretical approaches.

Gelles, Richard, J., and Cornell, Claire Pedrick. *Intimate Violence in Families*. Beverly Hills: Sage Publications, 1985. A comprehensive overview of family violence covering child, courtship, spouse, sibling, parent, and elder abuse with a concluding chapter on prevention and treatment.

Gelles, Richard J., and Cornell, Claire Pedrick. *International Perspectives on Family Violence*. Lexington, Mass.: Lexington Books, 1983. A collection of eleven articles on child abuse, spouse abuse, and family violence around the world.

Hansen, Donald A., and Johnson, Vicky A. "Rethinking Family Stress Theory: Definitional Aspects." *Contemporary Theories About The Family, Vol. 1*. Edited by Wesley R. Burr et al. New York: The Free Press, 1979, pp. 582–603. A focus on the "definitional aspects" of the ABCX model of stress.

Klein, David, M., and Hill, Reuben. "Determinants of Family Problem-Solving Effectiveness." *Contemporary Theories About the Family, Vol. 1*. Edited by Wesley R. Burr et al. New York: The Free Press, pp. 493–548. An extensive analysis of family problem solving, including conceptualization, partial theories, and an effort at an integrated formal theory.

Lystad, M., ed. *Violence in the Home*. New York: Brunner/Mazel, 1986. A compilation of twelve writings covering violence and U.S. society, causes of family violence, and clinical and community intervention programs.

McCubbin, Hamilton I.; Cauble, A. Elizabeth; and Patterson, Joan M. eds. *Family Stress, Coping, and Social Support*. Springfield, Ill.: Charles C. Thomas, 1982. An anthology of thirteen articles divided into two sections, one dealing with stress and crisis theory and the other dealing with stressors, coping, and social support.

McCubbin, Hamilton, I., et al. "Family Stress and Coping: A Decade Review." *Journal of Marriage and the Family* 42 (November 1980): 855–871. A decade review article revealing the concerted effort made to identify which families, under what conditions, and with what resources are able to endure the hardships of family life.

Quinn, Mary Joy, and Tomita, Susan K. *Elder Abuse and Neglect*. N. Y.: Springer Publishing Co., 1986. An investigation of the phenomenon of elder abuse, including diagnosis and intervention.

Sonkin, Daniel Jay; Martin, Del; and Walker, Lenore E. Auerback. *The Male Batterer:*

A Treatment Approach. The first chapter focuses on a sociological perspective of domestic violence, the second on an overview of the male batterer, and the rest of the book on treatment.

Straus, Murray A.; Gelles, Richard J.; and Steinmetz, Suzanne K. *Behind Closed Doors: Violence in the American Family.* New York: Anchor Books, 1980. A report on the experiences of 2,143 families as to the extent, breadth, and meaning of violence within families in the United States.

COURT WAITING

304
DISTRICT COURT
WAITING ROOM

17

Divorce and Remarriage

All societies have one or more ways for husbands, wives, or both to deal with unsatisfactory marital relationships. Highly patriarchal, male-dominant societies are likely to permit men mistresses or concubines to co-exist with their marriage. In many societies, including the United States, marriage may be regarded as a civil contract with the state specifying how old people have to be to get married, how many spouses they may have, and the conditions under which marriages can be dissolved.

In some countries, often in conformity with the Canon Law of the Roman Catholic Church, marriage was, until recently, indissolvable except by death. These included countries such as Argentina, Brazil, Chile, and Colombia in Latin America; the Philippines in Southeast Asia; and Italy, Ireland, and Spain in Western Europe. In some countries, such as the United States, France, Switzerland, Russia, Poland, and the Scandinavian countries, a divorce is granted if one or both parties has been guilty of a grave violation of marital obligations or if it is shown that the marriage is completely broken in fact. Finally, the official law of Islam and of Judaism grants free power of the husband to terminate his marriage by repudiation of his wife. In reality, this occurs infrequently and movements exist to provide power to wives to bring about a dissolution of the marriage as well.

In the United States, divorce is the best known and most common means of ending an unsatisfactory marital relationship; thus, most attention in this chapter will be devoted to it. Desertions, legal separations, informally agreed upon separations, and annulments are other means that people use to get out of, at least temporarily if not permanently, a marriage.

DESERTION AND MARITAL SEPARATION

Desertion refers to the willful abandonment, without legal justification, of one's spouse, children, or both. Compared to divorce, little is known about desertion, and few studies exist on this issue. Traditionally, it has been assumed that desertion applied only to men. More recently, reports exist on "runaway wives." Unlike men who may want out of a marriage, deserting women are more likely to seek escape from childrearing and home responsibilities that become unbearable. For both sexes it appears that desertion is one response or solution to dealing with an issue they define as incapable of being handled: children, marital conflicts, alcoholism, infidelity, inability to support a family, and the like.

Unlike divorce, desertion is not institutionalized, no registration takes place with the courts or any other official body, the deserting and nondeserting spouse cannot remarry, and little clarity exists as to exactly what constitutes desertion and what roles are appropriate in legal, economic, or social situations. For example, how many days' absence constitutes desertion? When a spouse leaves and returns on multiple occasions, do marital and parental role patterns resemble those of the one- or two-parent family? Is one spouse legally responsible for the expenses and activities of the other? Because of the lack of institutionalized norms and the ambiguity of events surrounding desertion, it is believed that desertion has far more negative effects than divorce.

The Bureau of the Census uses the term *marital separations* in reference to married persons living apart. In 1985, 4.3 million persons or 3.2 percent of the U.S. population were so classified (*see* Tables 15–1 and 15–3 for differences by sex and selected age categories).[1] In some cases such separations are legalized. In cases of **legal separations** the husband and wife are authorized to live apart, and formal agreements specify visiting patterns, support, and so forth. These are sometimes referred to as limited divorce, partial dissolution, or divorce from bed and board.

The majority of separations are not legalized. These **informal separations** are often arrangements between husband and wife where one or both decide to live separately. Unlike desertion, each knows the whereabouts of the other and unlike divorce, the couple is legally married and cannot remarry. These couples seem to be overrepresented among low-income families and have been referred to in literature as the "poor man's divorce."

One of the few recent studies of marital separations was done in the metropolitan Cleveland area with a random sample of over 1,100 residents.[2] It was found that one in six couples was likely to separate for at least forty-eight hours at some point in their relationship because of arguments or disagreements. Some separations were a step on the way to permanent separation or divorce. Others were used as a conflict resolution technique

---

1. U.S. Bureau of the Census, *Current Population Reports,* Series P-20, no. 410, "Marital Status and Living Arrangements, March 1985," (Washington, D.C.: U.S. Government Printing Office, 1986), Table 1, p. 17.

2. Gay C. Kitson, "Marital Discord and Marital Separation: A County Survey," *Journal of Marriage and the Family* 47 (August 1985): 693–700.

or a dramatic gesture to force some action on the part of the spouse. Some separated persons remained in relationships because of psychological restraints, such as physical abuse, or structural restraints, such as low income or the presence of minor children. Those most likely to separate were blacks, women, and those with low income and minor children. For most, separations were associated with a high sense of emotional distress.

ANNULMENT

The word *annul,* legally defined, means to reduce to nothing, to obliterate, to make void and of no effect, to abolish, to do away with, to eradicate. To say a marriage has been annulled is to say that a court, acting under the law of the state, found that cases existed *prior* to the marriage that render the marriage contract void. The court is saying that the marriage, when performed, was in fact no marriage at all, and is annulling it as though it had never existed.

Generally, the distinction between divorce and **annulment** revolves around the time of the cause or the time in which certain actions occurred. Divorce generally involves an action that occurred *after* the date of marriage—adultery, incompatibility, cruelty, desertion, nonsupport, alcoholism, and the like. Annulment generally involves an action that occurred *before* the date of marriage—being under age, another existing marriage, incurable impotence, incestuous relationship, and the like. While the marriage was a social and psychological reality, legally it never existed. If there are children, the "husband who never existed" may be required by the court to support minor children. Socially, relatives and friends are well aware of the once-existing marriage. Psychologically, both the male and female involved are well aware of once "being married" and the mate selection processes that preceded it.

DIVORCE

Attitudes toward separation and divorce have changed over the past few decades with a definite trend toward approval. Interviews with mothers over an eighteen-year-period show that by 1980 three-fifths believed that divorce is usually the best solution when marital problems cannot be solved.[3] The shift in marital dissolution and attitudes was, however, primarily unidirectional. That is, attitudes toward separations had very little influence

---

3. Arland Thornton, "Changing Attitudes toward Separation and Divorce: Causes and Consequences," *American Journal of Sociology,* 90 (January 1985): 856–872.

on subsequent divorce but virtually all women who had been separated or divorced expressed approval.

Divorce is permitted in every state in the United States. With each state having its own divorce code, with each marriage sharing difficulties of other marriages and having a few unique unto itself, it could be expected that the grounds for divorce would vary widely. An examination of these grounds follows.

Legal grounds for divorce   The legal **grounds for divorce** vary somewhat for each state.[4] Apart from "no-fault" divorce, the most widely accepted legal grounds for divorce are breakdown of marriage, incompatibility, cruelty, and desertion. In all states adultery is either grounds for divorce or evidence of incompatibility, irreconcilable differences, or a breakdown of the marriage. Other legal grounds in at least one state include nonsupport, alcohol and/or drug addiction, felony, impotence, insanity, joining a religious order, disbelieving in marriage, treatment that injures health or endangers reason, pregnancy at marriage, fraudulent contract, gross neglect of duty, bigamy, attempted homicide, and the like. California, Colorado, and Oregon have procedures whereby a couple can obtain a divorce without an attorney and without appearing in court provided certain requirements (such as being married less than two years, having no children, no real estate, and few debts) are met.

As one might well surmise, the majority of grounds are never used, and those that are can be defined or interpreted in a wide variety of ways. For example, cruelty—the most popular legal ground prior to no-fault—may include physical abuse, quarreling, name calling, and the like. One wife might claim cruelty because her husband talks constantly, giving her no peace of mind, while the next wife might claim cruelty because the husband never talks to her. Whereas cruelty once meant physical cruelty or an attack upon the spouse's life, today it may mean little more than "incompatibility," thus covering almost any reasons available to the imagination.

Under a "fault" or "guilt" system, the wife brings suit in about seven of ten divorce actions. The social norm favors the wife in terms of cruelty, adultery, drunkenness, physical threat, and the like, which makes the entire process easier to finalize. It is also more socially acceptable for the husband to accept the blame even though common sense alone would attest to the infrequency and unlikelihood of one spouse guilty and the other spouse innocent. Under a "no-fault" system, the sex of the filer for divorce shifts drastically. Figures from California, Florida, and Georgia

---

4. These can be seen in *The World Almanac and Book of Facts* (New York: Newspaper Enterprise Association, 1986): 86.

The legal "revolution" in divorce procedures

"In little more than a decade, divorce in the 50 states has been revolutionized," says Dr. Doris Jonas Freed, a family law scholar. Following are some of the major changes:

No-fault divorce. Only two states, Illinois and South Dakota, still limit divorce to traditional fault grounds. All others have some form of no-fault divorce grounds, such as mutual consent, incompatibility, living apart for a specified period or irretrievable breakdown of the marriage.

Property division. Most state laws now have specified guidelines designed to promote a fair distribution of the couple's wealth at the time of divorce. Exceptions are the three remaining "title" states, South Carolina, Mississippi, and West Virginia, where property is awarded on the basis of the name or names on the title. Four community property states—California, Idaho, Louisiana, and New Mexico—provide for an equal division of property, while all others provide formulas for an "equitable," but not necessarily equal, division.

Homemaker's contribution. Laws in 31 states, including New York, require courts to view such contributions as marital assets in distributing property.

Rights to retirement benefits. In all community property states and most equitable distribution states, pensions earned during a marriage are deferred compensation and should be divided as marital property.

Spousal support. Formerly known as alimony, it is now commonly called maintenance and is payable to either a husband or a wife. As in property division, many states provide specific guidelines to the courts on maintenance. The emphasis is on the need of the recipient and the ability of the other spouse to pay. Maintenance is often awarded for a limited period to allow the recipient to become self-supporting, unless he or she is incapable of self-support. Usually it may be modified by the court if there is a substantial change in economic circumstances.

following no-fault show a dramatic increase in the percentage of men who filed for divorces.[5] Men can now proceed without the fear that their wives will contest the divorce or file damaging countercharges leading to protracted court battles.

The adversary divorce system in the United States, in which one party must be innocent and the other guilty, has led numerous states to **no-fault divorce.** The present no-fault trend first reached fruition

---

5. Ruth B. Dixon and Lenore J. Weitzman, "When Husbands File for Divorce," *Journal of Marriage and the Family* 44 (February 1982): 103–114; and B. G. Gunter and Doyle P. Johnson, "Divorce Filing as Role Behavior: Effect of No-Fault on Divorce Filing Patterns," *Journal of Marriage and the Family* 40 (August 1978): 571–574.

Child support. Once the primary obligation of the father, child support in most states has become the duty of both parents, according to their ability to pay. In New York and some other states, visitation rights and child support may be linked. A few states impose support obligations on stepparents.

Child custody. The drive for equal custody rights for fathers has led to the decline of the old presumption favoring mothers. Laws in 28 states either permit joint custody or give priority to it when in the child's best interests. Some states allow a lawyer or guardian to represent the child in custody disputes, and two states, Wisconsin and New Hampshire, require this.

Grandparents' rights. Laws in 42 states now permit grandparents to seek visitation rights when denied them by the parent who has custody of the children. In some states, the trend is to extend the law to cover other close relatives, such as aunts, uncles and siblings.

Custody enforcement. Except for Massachusetts and Texas, all states have adopted the Uniform Child Custody Jurisdiction Act, designed to discourage taking children to other states in search of more favorable custody rulings. Also, many states have either enacted laws making "child snatching" by parents a crime or strengthened existing laws.

Support enforcement. When a parent fails to pay court-ordered child support, many states now provide for payment directly to the court clerk or for garnishment or assignment of wages, or for contempt proceedings that may result in the jailing of the delinquent parent. Some states have agreements with the computerized Federal Parent Locator, allowing them to track missing parents and enforce support judgments across state lines. In addition, a new Federal law permits the Internal Revenue Service to withhold tax refunds of parents in arrears on child support, and a number of states have similar laws.

Source: The New York Times, February 7, 1983, p. 12. Copyright © 1983/1984 by The New York Times Company. Reprinted by permission.

in California, where traditional fault grounds were abolished January 1, 1970 in favor of dissolution of marriage based on "irreconcilable differences which have caused the irremedial breakdown of the marriage" and incurable insanity. Irreconcilable differences are defined as any grounds that are determined by the court to be substantial reasons for not continuing the marriage and that make it appear that the marriage should be dissolved. In California, the term *divorce* was replaced with *dissolution of marriage.* Community property was to be *substantially* equally divided. Alimony was to be determined by considering a woman's earning ability and the duration of the marriage. The one-year residence requirement was cut to six months.

Since the first no-fault divorce law was instituted, all states have displaced the traditional grounds for fault (adultery, desertion, cruelty) with the more subjective standards of "irreconcilable differences." Did the no-fault law changes accomplish its intended goals? Regrettably, studies of property settlements have suggested consistently that divorcing mothers are faring more poorly under the no-fault system than they did under the former adversary system. Welch and Price-Bonham, in replicating earlier studies, found that with no-fault divorce, alimony was rarely awarded; child custody was customarily awarded to the mothers; child-support awards had not diminished in value; and assets and liabilities tended to be shared equally.[6]

Divorce proceedings under the no-fault system are relatively routine. Where cases are contested, they can become drawn-out affairs with much bitterness, fighting, and expense resulting. Attempts to decrease this conflict have led to divorce *mediation*. Mediation is a conflict resolution process where the divorcing couple meets with a neutral third-party intervenor (mediator) who helps them negotiate an agreement about property distribution, support, and child custody. The emphasis is on direct communication, openness, attention to emotional issues and the underlying causes of the disputes, and avoidance of blame. Proponents of mediation stress that it relieves court dockets clogged with matrimonial actions, reduces the alienation couples experience in court, inspires durable consensual agreements, helps couples resume workable relationships to jointly rear their children, and translates into savings in time and money. Research findings in general tend to support these claims.[7] The mediation process works on building and strengthening relationships, while the adversarial process tends to weaken and destroy them.

Social grounds for divorce   If the legal grounds for divorce do not reflect the reality of the divorce conflict, what then are the marital difficulties that cause divorce? This answer is far more complex than it may appear at first sight. Are "real" reasons "really real"? That is, if the wife's frigidity is the "real" reason for the husband wanting to end the marriage, could his response to her not have contributed to her frigidity? If the husband drinks too much, and alcoholism is the "real" reason for the wife wanting to end the marriage, could she not have contributed to his drinking in many ways?

---

6. Charles E. Welch, III, and Sharon Price-Bonham, "A Decade of No-Fault Divorce Revisited: California, Georgia, and Washington," *Journal of Marriage and the Family* 45 (May 1983): 441–418.

7. Lois Vanderkooi and Jessica Pearson, "Mediating Divorce Disputes: Mediator Behaviors, Styles and Roles," *Family Relations* 32 (October 1983): 557–566.

Family law changes in Greece

In 1983, the Greek parliament in Athens approved changes in the country's family law, making divorce easier, guaranteeing equality between spouses, and ending official discrimination against illegitimate children.

The new law also abolished the dowry, a centuries-old tradition, as a legal requirement in marriage.

Couples are now allowed to divorce by consent. Under the old system, one partner had to show that the other was responsible for the marriage's breakdown on strictly defined grounds, including bigamy, adultery, and desertion.

These examples are not meant to imply that reasons given are unreal, that all reasons simply serve as rationalizations, or that stated reasons should be ignored. On the contrary, "that which is defined as real is real." Marital complaints in a sample of divorcing men and women in metropolitan Cleveland revealed considerable differences by sex, with women making significantly more complaints than men.[8] Women were more likely to make complaints about personality, authority, drinking, "being out with the boys," sex problems, non-support, the husband's infidelity and money management. Men were more likely to mention the wife's infidelity and complaints concerning relatives. Men were more likely than women to be unsure about what caused the breakup of the marriage. Respondents were more likely to blame their partners (71 percent) than themselves (7 percent) for the breakup.

Most disagreements and divorce conflicts extend over a period of years. Although conflict is often depicted as resulting from a single event (adultery, pregnancy, drunkenness), most divorces result from a series of minor maladjustments or difficulties, none of which can be singularly listed as the "cause" or "reason." Levinger claims that people stay in relationships because they are attracted to them and/or they are barred from leaving them and that, consciously or not, people compare their current relationships with alternative ones.[9] If internal attraction and barrier

---

8. Gay C. Kitson and Marvin B. Sussman, "Marital Complaints, Demographic Characteristics, and Symptoms of Mental Distress in Divorce," *Journal of Marriage and the Family* 44 (February 1982): 87–101. *See also* Gay C. Kitson, Karen Benson Babri, and Mary Joan Roach, "Who Divorces and Why: A Review," *Journal of Family Issues* 6 (September 1985): 255–293.

9. George Levinger, "A Social Psychological Perspective on Marital Dissolution," *Journal of Social Issues* 32 (Winter 1976): 43; *see also* John N. Edwards and Janice M. Saunders, "Coming Apart: A Model of the Marital Dissolution Decision," *Journal of Marriage and the Family* 43 (May 1981): 379–389; and Stan L. Albrecht and Phillip R. Kunz. "The Decision to Divorce: A Social Exchange Perspective," *Journal of Divorce* 3 (Summer 1980): 319–337.

forces become distinctly weaker than those from a viable alternative, the consequence is breakup.

While this approach is somewhat different from that adopted by exchange theorists, the decision to divorce still contains important reward-cost considerations. The rewards (attractions) may include love, goods, services, security, joint possessions, children, sexual enjoyment, and so forth while the costs (barriers) may include feelings of obligation or inadequacy, fears of family/friend reactions, religious prohibitions, financial costs, and the like. The key implication is that the probabilities for divorce increase as alternatives are perceived that provide greater rewards or lower costs than exist in marriage.

In the Western world, divorce is generally viewed as an unfortunate event for the persons involved and as a clear index of failure of the family system. But in addition to divorce being seen as a personal misfortune or as an index of failure, it may also be viewed as an escape valve, a way out of the tensions of marriage itself. William Goode claims that divorce is permitted in nearly all the world's nations (Spain and Ireland are still exceptions), and has been common in most tribal societies.[10] In addition, a few nations have had higher divorce rates than the United States at different times in the past, such as Japan in the period 1887–1919; Algeria, 1887–1940; and Egypt, 1935–1954. At present, the United States may have the highest divorce rate in the world. In 1984, the U.S. rate of divorce per 1,000 persons in the population was 5.0 compared to 3.4 in the U.S.S.R., 3.0 in Germany, 2.9 in Cuba, 2.7 in Canada, 2.5 in Sweden, 1.5 in Japan, 1.3 in Poland, 1.2 in Israel, and 0.3 in Italy.[11] Divorce rates are not available, or perhaps even computed, for a number of the highly Catholic countries (Philippines, Spain, Mexico, and others). Take note of some of the different meanings attached to the use of this rate versus others.

Divorce rates

Divorce rates are likely to be calculated in one of three ways: by the number of divorces that take place per 1,000 persons in the total population, by the number of divorces per 1,000 married females aged 15 and over, and by the ratio of divorces granted in a given year to the number of marriages contracted in that same year. Note the difference in rate depending on the figures used.

---

10. William J. Goode, *The Family*, 2nd ed. (Englewood Cliffs, N.J.: Prentice-Hall, 1982): 150.

11. United Nations, *Demographic Yearbook, 1984* (New York, 1986), Table 25, pp. 499–501.

The number of divorces that took place *per 1,000 persons in the total population* in the United States in 1984 was 5.0. This means that for every 1,000 persons in the population (men, women, children, adults, married, single, etc.), 10.0 persons obtained or 5.0 marriages ended in divorce or annulment. Said another way, if you come from a city of 100,000 population where 500 divorces were granted in 1984, the divorce rate was 5.0. Since our system is monogamous (two persons per divorce), 1,000 individuals in a city of 100,000 persons were divorced last year. Note how this divorce rate can be influenced by factors such as the age distribution or the proportion of the married or single population. A country or city with a large family size, a low life expectancy, a late age at marriage, a sizable proportion of the population being children or single teenagers, and a disproportionate number of the population unmarried, could have a sizable percentage of those married getting divorces and yet have a seemingly "low" divorce rate.

The number of divorces, again including annulments, that took place *per 1,000 married women aged 15 and over* in the United States in 1984 was 21.5.[12] This means that there were 21.5 divorces per 1,000 (215 per 10,000) married females of age 15 and over. Of the three rates mentioned this one is probably the most accurate. Unlike the first rate described, men, single persons, children, and the like are excluded. It is figured on the basis of the legally married women who constitute the group that is susceptible to divorce. This figure could be used to compare the divorce rate cross-culturally without being influenced by the number, age, or marital status of the total population.

The ratio of *divorces granted in a given year to the number of marriages in that year* was close to 46 in 1984. This is the rate used to best illustrate the "breakdown in the U.S. family." See for yourself. Nearly one out of two marriages end in divorce—or does it? Let's assume that your city of 100,000 population issued 1,000 marriage licenses in 1987. The same year, 500 divorces were granted. This would result in a divorce-marriage ratio of 1 in 2 or 50 divorces per 100 marriages. Thus, there was one divorce for every two marriages in your community in the year 1987. Suppose your state modified its divorce law that year and instead of 500 divorces, 2,000 divorces took place while the number of marriages remained constant at 1,000. Now, according to this rate, we have two divorces for every marriage or a divorce rate of 200.

While it may be accurate to speak of twice as many divorces as marriages in a given year, it is not accurate to say that of all marriages one-half will end in divorce. The inaccuracy is due to at least three reasons.

---

12. National Center for Health Statistics, "Advance Report of Divorce Statistics, 1984," *Monthly Vital Statistics Report,* vol. 35, no. 6 (Public Health Service, Hyattsville, Md., September 25, 1986), Table 1, p. 5.

It was the big d-ivorce for 108 Texas couples

DALLAS—(UPI)—They don't call this town "Big D" for nothing, but dissolving 108 marriages at one mass divorce hearing is large even by Texas standards.

The 20-minute ceremony was the idea of attorney Averil Schweitzer, who claims to be the leading divorce lawyer in Dallas and says his firm handles about 3,000 divorces a year, at $75 a pop.

At the appointed time, Schweitzer entered the auditorium, announced, "I'm your lawyer," and started the show.

Family court Judge Linda Thomas asked the multitude to rise and swear in unison that their papers were truthful, and then she said: "I grant your divorce per your decree."

Schweitzer than closed the proceeding by warning his clients that the divorce isn't final until the county mails the papers.

The ceremony ended with a collective burst of laughter when Schweitzer said, "Wait 30 days before getting married."

Patty Marriot, 19, said the mass ceremony seemed the quickest end for her marriage, which lasted 2½ months.

"They change after you marry them," she said.

Source: Detroit Free Press, August 21, 1983, p. 7-B. Reprinted with the permission of the Detroit Free Press.

First, the divorces ended marriages that began over a lengthy time period, not the marriages that began in any specific year. These divorces, the marriages of which began one, eight, or thirty years ago, are all compared with the number of marriages in 1987. Second, approximately 40 percent of all marriages that are remarriages of one or both spouses are not taken into account. Persons who divorce and remarry in the same year contribute to both the number of marriages and the number of divorces giving a ratio of 1 to 1:as many divorces as marriages. To redivorce the same year would again produce the impossible result of more divorces than are marriages from which to divorce. The third reason, like the example just shown, results in a number of marriages that is smaller than the number of marriage dissolutions. Note an example using 1984 census figures. In 1984, there were 2.49 million marriages. The same year there were 1.17 million marriages that ended in divorce (46 percent). Also that year there were approximately 2.05 million deaths, giving a ratio of deaths to marriages of 82 (82 percent). Since the majority of these deaths occurred among married persons, the sum of marriages that ended in death or divorce was 128 percent—28 percent more marriages ending than existing.

Irrespective of the manner of calculation, you should be aware that statistics on divorce are not perfect.[13] Even national data reported by the National Vital Statistics Division (NVSD) are based on estimates obtained from states participating in the divorce-registration area (DRA). As of 1985, thirty-one states and the Virgin Islands participated in the DRA.[14] Thus, actual data from all fifty states are not available. Second, sampling rates vary among the DRA states, depending on the size of their annual divorce totals. All statistics estimated from probability samples have a sampling error. Third, completeness of reporting individual demographic items on divorce records varies considerably among DRA states. For example, some states do not require the reporting of race and others do not require the reporting of the number of this marriage. Fourth, often many items are left blank. This is particularly true of personal characteristics of husband and wife—age, race, and number of this marriage. Although the accuracy of divorce rates and statistics is improving, the divorce data are not perfect. The best available information is presented with the recognition that the figures are based on estimates from selected available data.

Trends in divorce rates in the United States

The number of divorces and annulments granted in the United States increased from the pre–World War II figure of 264,000 in 1940, to the post–World War II figure of 379,000 in 1954, to 708,000 in 1970, to a peak of 1,213,000 in 1981. The number declined since then to the 1985 figure of 1,187,000. The rate per 1,000 population increased from 2 in 1940, to 2.4 in 1954, to 3.5 in 1970, to 5.3 in 1981 with a decline to 5.0 in 1985. The increase was not as steady as it appears from the selected figures given (*see* Table 17–1 and Figure 17–1).

The 1981 figure of 1,213,000 divorce decrees—that is, more than 2.42 million divorced persons—was the highest national total ever observed for the United States. Over the past decade until that year, the number of divorces increased more rapidly than the total population and the married population of the United States. The 1982 figures, however, show the first annual decrease in several decades. By 1985, an estimated 1.19 million couples divorced, 2 percent fewer than in 1981.

Generally, divorce rates have declined in times of economic depression and risen during times of prosperity (*see* Figure 17–1). The Depression years between 1932–1933 had the lowest rate of divorce per 1,000 married

---

13. A clear overview of divorce statistics and their meanings can be seen in John F. Crosby, "A Critique of Divorce Statistics and Their Interpetation," *Famly Relations* 29 (January 1980): 51–58.

14. U.S. Bureau of the Census, *Statistical Abstract of the United States: 1987*, p. 56.

TABLE 17-1
Number of divorces and divorce rates: United States, 1945-1985

		Rate per 1,000				Rate per 1,000	
Year	Number of decrees	Total population	Married women	Year	Number of decrees	Total population	Married women
1985	1,187,000	5.0	—				
1984	1,169,000	5.0	21.5	1970	708,000	3.5	14.9
1983	1,158,000	4.9	21.3	1968	584,000	2.9	12.4
1982	1,170,000	5.0	21.7	1966	499,000	2.5	10.9
1981	1,213,000	5.3	22.6	1964	450,000	2.4	10.0
1980	1,189,000	5.2	22.6	1962	413,000	2.2	9.4
1979	1,181,000	5.3	22.8	1960	393,000	2.2	9.2
1978	1,130,000	5.1	21.9	1958	368,000	2.1	8.9
1977	1,091,000	5.0	21.1	1956	382,000	2.3	9.4
1976	1,083,000	5.0	21.1	1954	379,000	2.4	9.5
1975	1,036,000	4.9	20.3	1952	392,000	2.5	10.1
1974	977,000	4.6	19.3	1950	385,000	2.6	10.3
1973	915,000	4.4	18.2	1948	408,000	2.8	11.2
1972	845,000	4.1	17.0	1946	610,000	4.3	17.9
1971	773,000	3.7	15.8	1945	485,000	3.5	14.4

Source: National Center for Health Statistics, "Advance Report of Divorce Statistics, 1984," *Monthly Vital Statistics Reports,* vol. 35, no. 6 (Public Health Service, Hyattsville, Md., September 25, 1986), Table 1, p. 5; and *Statistical Abstract, 1987,* no. 80, p. 58.

women in the last fifty-five years. Following the Depression, the rate of divorce moved upward almost steadily until the first postwar year, 1946. After 1946, the rate dropped sharply until 1950. For about fifteen years, until 1965, the divorce rate showed considerable stability, increasing slightly some years and decreasing during the mini-recession years of 1954 and 1958. Since 1965, the divorce trend has again climbed relatively sharply, reaching the highest rate in the history of the United States in 1981. The recessionary period of the early 1980s has again proven to be effective in reducing the number and rate of divorces.

Scott South agrees that the relationship between economic conditions and the divorce rate has changed over time. However, it is his contention that substantially stronger influences on the divorce rate are changes in age structure and the labor-force participation of women.[15] In regard to age structure, the suggestion is that the rise in divorce rates over the

15. Scott J. South, "Economic Conditions and the Divorce Rate: A Time-Series Analysis of the Postwar United States," *Journal of Marriage and the Family* 47 (February 1985): 31–41.

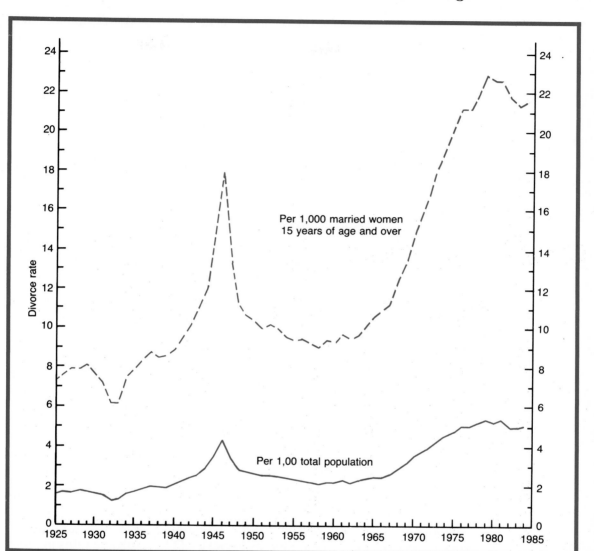

FIGURE 17–1

Divorce rates: United States, 1925–1985. *Source:* National Center for Health Statistics, "Advance Report of Divorce Statistics, 1984," *Monthly Vital Statistics Report,* vol. 35, no. 6 [Public Health Service, Hyattsville, Md., September 25, 1986], Figure 1, p. 2.)

past several decades is at least partially attributable to the economic pressures faced by the large cohort of the baby boom generation. With the abundance of younger workers, their incomes fall relative to older workers, and their prospects for marital dissolution are increased. In regard to the labor-force participation of women, the suggestion follows that made at several other places in this chapter. As economic opportunities for women expand, wives become less dependent on husbands (or marriage) for financial support. Wives whose earnings are high relative to their husbands' have a particularly increased probability of experiencing marital dissolution.

Variations in divorce rates

Divorce rates vary widely by geographic, demographic, and social characteristics. Let's examine several variations and seek explanations for higher or lower rates according to the selected characteristics.

Geographic distribution   The geographic distribution of divorce rates in the United States indicates a general trend toward an increase as one moves from east to west. This appears to have been true since the nineteenth century. The divorce rate is highest in western states, followed by the south, the midwest, and the northeast.

Major variations exist by individual states as well. The divorce rate per 1,000 population in 1984 was lowest in Massachusetts (rate of 2.9) and highest in Nevada (a rate of 13.7). States with a rate of 3.6 or less per 1,000 population in 1984 included Connecticut, Maryland, Massachusetts, Minnesota, North and South Dakota, New York, Pennsylvania, Wisconsin, and Iowa. States with rates of 6.5 or more included Alaska, Arizona, Arkansas, Florida, Nevada, New Mexico, Oklahoma, Tennessee, and Wyoming.[16] Note how the lowest rates generally occur in the Northeast and the highest rates in the South and West.

How can these geographical variations be explained? It is likely that different factors operate in different areas, but it is believed that divorce rates will be lower in culturally homogeneous rather than heterogeneous communities, and in communities with primary face-to-face interactions in contrast to communities with anonymous relationships, segmentalized relationships, or both. In traditional Durkheimian social structural terms, this refers to a social integration hypothesis of lower divorce rates in areas with high consensus on rules of behavior (norms) and effective social controls to ensure conformity. Communities or areas (regions, states) that are highly integrated socially would tend to exert stronger social pressures against "deviant" behaviors (as divorce is often perceived to be) and exert both formal and informal pressure for conformity to community norms.

---

16. National Center for Health Statistics, *Monthly Vital Statistics Report*, vol. 35, no. 6, September 25, 1986, Table 2, pp. 6–7. Specific divorce rates by state can be found as well in U.S. Bureau of the Census, *Statistical Abstract of the United States: 1987*, no. 124, p. 81.

The level of social integration and pressure toward conformity are likely to be influenced by residential mobility as well. High levels of residential movement are related both to higher levels of divorce and lower levels of social integration. Norval Glenn and Beth Ann Shelton state that the very high level of marital dissolution in the U.S. "divorce belt" (the West South Central, Mountain, and Pacific census divisions) can be accounted for by a very high level of residential mobility there.[17] Residential mobility and other variables associated with lower levels of social integration would effect variations in divorce rates not only by region of the country and by state but would result in lower levels of divorce in rural than in urban areas as well.

Unique circumstances like those that exist in Nevada are greatly influenced by legal requirements. While Nevada may produce a small fraction of the total divorces granted nationally (about 1 percent), the divorce rate per 1,000 population within that state can be affected significantly by relatively few couples who come into the state from another state. Except for Nevada and a few other states, it is unlikely that migratory divorce has a major effect on divorce rates.

Age of husband and wife   The divorce rate is very high among young marriages. Spanier and Glick, analyzing census material, report that women who marry at ages 14 to 17 are three times as likely to divorce and women married at ages 18 and 19 are twice as likely to divorce as women who married in their twenties. Men who marry in their teens are twice as likely to divorce as men who marry in their twenties.[18] Explanations for this high rate may include emotional immaturity, inability to assume marital responsibilities, greater incidences of early marriage in lower socioeconomic statuses where divorce is more likely, a longer time period in which to get divorced, more premarital pregnancies (also related to higher incidences of divorce), and similar factors.

Young marriages are not, however, responsible for the dramatic increases in family dissolution witnessed in the United States over the past twenty years.[19] While they manifest higher rates of marital disruption, the typical ages at divorce after the first marriage are 25–29. More than half of all divorces occur among persons in their late twenties, and the largest increase in the divorce rate exists among those of ages 25–39. In 1984,

---

17. Norval D. Glenn and Beth Ann Shelton, "Regional Differences in Divorce in the United States," *Journal of Marriage and the Family* 47 (August 1985): 641–652.

18. Graham B. Spanier and Paul C. Glick, "Marital Instability in the United States: Some Correlates and Recent Changes," *Family Relations* 30 (July 1981): 333.

19. A. Wade Smith and Jane E. G. Meitz, "Cohorts, Education, and the Decline in Undisrupted Marriages," *Journal of Marriage and the Family* 45 (August 1983): 613–622.

the median age for divorce after the first marriage was 34.3 for men and 31.7 for women.[20]

Although divorce rates are highest in young marriages and occur most frequently in the first few years following a marriage, these factors should not blind us to the reality that divorce is a common occurrence at any age or stage of the family life cycle. It is only recently that any attention at all has been focused on divorce among the elderly, for example.[21] Yet, the increasing numbers of older persons, the changes in the perceptions of the roles of women, a shifting social acceptability of divorce, and so forth, present a realistic potential for dramatic increases in the number of divorced older persons.

Duration of marriage   The largest number of divorce decrees are granted one to three years after marriage and the number declines relatively consistently with increasing duration. In 1984, 4.2 percent of the divorcing couples had been married less than one year. One-third of divorcing couples (33.6 percent) were married one to four years, and about one-fourth (25.7 percent) were married five to nine years. The remaining third of divorcing couples had been married ten years or more with 15 percent married ten to fourteen years and 21 percent married fifteen years or more.[22] Without doubt, the breakup of marriages in all ways except the legal begins well before the actual divorce. Although more divorces occur during the second and third year of marriage (the mode) than at any other time, the first and second year may be the modal ones for marital breakups. Divorces that occur in the seventh or fourteenth year of marriage may simply be a legal break of a marriage broken years earlier.

In 1982, the median interval between the first marriage and divorce was 7.0 years. For those who remarried and got another divorce, the median interval between the second marriage and redivorce was approximately 5 years. For the third marriage, the median interval was about 3.5 years. It would appear that the median length of each succeeding marriage that ends in divorce is shorter than the previous one. Some support seems to exist for the idea that the first divorce experience is the most difficult one. Having been through a divorce, accepting the divorce status, and later remarrying may tend to make divorce a more acceptable

20. National Center for Health Statistics, "Advance Report of Divorce Statistics, 1984," *Monthly Vital Statistics Report* vol. 35, no. 6 (Public Health Service, Hyattsville, Md., September 25, 1986), Table 7, p. 11.

21. Michael R. DeShane and Keren Brown-Wilson, "Divorce in Late Life: A Call for Research," *Journal of Divorce* 4 (Summer 1981): 81–91; and Peter Uhlenberg and Mary Anne P. Myers, "Divorce and the Elderly," *The Gerontologist* 21 (1981): 276–282.

22. *Monthly Vital Statistics Report*, vol. 35, no. 6 (September 25, 1986), Table 11, p. 14.

solution to an unsuccessful second, third, or fourth marital relationship.[23] Perhaps remarriages involve all kinds of relationships that are not covered by norms: ex-spouses, ex-inlaws, stepchildren, and so on. Perhaps remarriages are comprised of people who have problems that make stable marriages difficult: alcoholic, abusive, or unstable persons. Whatever the reason (and this issue is discussed further in this chapter), the time span of remarriages that end in divorce is shorter than in first marriages.

As indicated at the beginning of this section, the number of divorces declines relatively consistently with increasing duration. In other words, after the peak years for divorce (years two, three, and four) have been passed, the proportion of divorces by length of marriage gradually diminishes. I know of no evidence that supports an increase in divorce "after the children have grown up." That phase of the life cycle of the family is reached at quite varied lengths of time after marriage.

Readers need to be cautioned about differentiating divorce at mid-life and later based on age at divorce versus duration of the marriage.[24] The dissolution of a three-year marriage at age fifty is probably quite different from the dissolution of a 25-year marriage at the same age.

Many marriages that never end in divorce are broken in fact except for the legal decree. This leads to a point indicated at various times throughout the book: that length of marriage is not necessarily an index of success or adjustment and that divorce is not necessarily a good index of marital breakdown. Divorce may simply provide an indication of the greater willingness or acceptance to acknowledge a legal ending of a previously ended meaningful marital relationship. It is possible that higher divorce rates indicate greater success, greater adjustment, and higher levels of satisfaction among existing marriages in the United States. In other words, the ending of more of the "poor" marriages raises the overall quality level of exisiting marriages.

Race, religion, and socioeconomic status   The success of interracial and interfaith marriages was discussed in Chapter 8. At this point, rather than looking at the success or divorce rate of mixed marriages, the question becomes how rates differ by race, religion, or socioeconomic level in nonmixed or endogamous marriages. Are divorce rates different for blacks or whites, Protestants or Catholics, and lower or higher socioeconomic levels?

Divorce rates by race usually differ within a state as well as for the

23. Frank F. Furstenberg, Jr. and Graham B. Spanier, "The Risk of Dissolution in Remarriage: An Examination of Cherlin's Hypothesis of Incomplete Institutionalization," *Family Relations* 33 (July 1984): 433–441.

24. Sally A. Lloyd and Cathleen D. Zick, "Divorce at Mid and Later Life: Does the Empirical Evidence Support the Theory?" *Journal of Divorce* 9 (Spring 1986): 89–102.

same racial groupings in different states. For example, for the United States as a whole in 1985, white males had a divorce rate per 1,000 persons in the population of 9.8 compared to 17.9 for black males. The rate for white females was 14.2 compared to 32.6 for black females.[25] Racial differences may be partly explained by urban residence, mobility patterns, social-class differences, or by differing accessibility to various types of social and economic resources. Generally, the greater the accessibility to these resources, the lower the incidence of divorce.

What about religion? What divorce differentials exist by major religious affiliation? Data from seven U.S. national surveys by Glenn and Supancic showed that marital dissolution is moderately higher for Protestants, considered as a whole, than for Catholics, and is lower for Jews than for Catholics.[26] The highest rates are for persons with no religion. This is consistent with the data on frequency of attendance of religious services; religiosity is an important deterrent to divorce and separation.

Contrary to what one might expect, the Glenn and Supancic study as well as others show that Protestant fundamentalists, the most conservative Protestant denominations (Nazarene, Pentecostal, Baptist), have relatively high dissolution rates in spite of their strong disapproval of divorce. Factors associated with conversion to these fundamentalist denominations were found to be important in producing the higher dissolution rate.[27] Conversion may signify the cultural conflict that results from the radical transition from one context to another. It may indicate a lack of normative integration in the anti-separation–divorce doctrine on the one hand, while urging acceptance and tolerance of the converted "sinner" on the other. This higher divorce-separation rate may also reflect the lower than average socioeconomic status of persons in these denominations; the strong demands these groups make on the time, energy, and money of their adherents (which may negatively affect marriages); the inflexibility or rigidity of their theological position; or even the focus and emphasis on the next life rather than the current one.

What about socioeconomic level? The increased incidence of divorce has been occurring at all socioeconomic levels; yet, the proportion of persons ever-divorced remains the highest for relatively disadvantaged

25. U.S. Bureau of the Census, *Statistical Abstract of the United States: 1986,* no. 52, p. 41.

26. Norval D. Glenn and Michael Supancic, "The Social and Demographic Correlates of Divorce and Separation in the United States: An Update and Reconsideration," *Journal of Marriage and the Family* 46 (August 1984): 563–575. *See also* Jay Y. Brodbar-Nemzer, "Divorce and Group Commitment: The Case of the Jews," *Journal of Marriage and the Family* 48 (May 1986): 329–340.

27. S. Kenneth Chi and Sharon K. Houseknecht, "Protestant Fundamentalism and Marital Success: A Comparative Approach," *Sociology and Social Research* 69 (April 1985): 351–375.

Is there ever a winner in a divorce?

WASHINGTON—It was an old story, one I've heard many times before. The woman sitting across the table from me had just been told by her husband that their marriage was over. He wanted out after 15 years.

True to the standards for women of her generation, she had worked his way through college and medical school, carving out no career for herself other than that of wife and mother. In her eyes, she had done everything right. In his, she had gotten boring. Now, in tears, she tried to figure out what would happen next. He had it all figured out—a sensible settlement, then out the door. She was apprehensive about her financial future. What, she asked me, did he owe her? Hadn't she helped make him what he was?

I didn't have the heart to tell her what she would learn soon enough: Parceling out property after divorce is sticky enough; allowing for the intangible investments either partner has made in a marriage is just about impossible.

Now comes a Stanford University study confirming something most divorced women have known for years: After divorce, men in general get richer; women get poorer.

Men often earn high incomes later in life after their wives worked as switchboard operators and filing clerks to launch their husbands' careers; and some courts are beginning to ask what, indeed, is owed beyond a division of tangible property. The answer may well be revolutionary: a piece of the husband's financial future.

That means that a woman could be compensated for the investments of work and energy she makes in a joint future that falls apart. After having lived on a struggling doctor's salary, a woman would get part of what he earns when he becomes a high-paid surgeon—even if she's been replaced.

Stories abound of rapacious women who clean out their husbands at divorce proceedings, but the truth is that most divorced women get very little money. Alimony is rare. And at least half of all divorced men stop supporting their children within a few years.

The Stanford study takes note of the fact that even in equal-property-division states such as California, men get richer and women poorer after divorce. The reason is simple: When judges are forced to divide everything 50-50, that usually means selling the family home. A man who goes on to make more money can reestablish his life-style in a few years. But a woman without the same opportunity gets stuck with the kids in rental housing.

The fact that the courts are taking a harder look at the realities of divorce settlements is heartening. But it doesn't change a basic lesson for women who hope never to be left financially helpless. It's a lesson learned often only through experience, which is why I believe women should teach it to their daughters in the cradle. It is this: Married or single, a woman should have a way of supporting herself.

As my friend who sat across from me will learn, putting a price tag on a marriage is still a no-win game.

Source: Patricia O'Brien, *Detroit Free Press*, June 6, 1982, p. 9-A. Reprinted with the permission of the Detroit Free Press.

groups. Whether education, occupation, or income is used as an index of socioeconomic level, the divorce rate goes up as socioeconomic level goes down. One exception to this relationship exists among professional women who have five or more years of college education. Their rate of marital disruption is surpassed only by women who have not graduated from high school. Houseknecht et al. conclude that marital disruption among highly educated women is caused, at least partly, by the strain resulting from their efforts to balance both work and family roles.[28]

The greater marital instability and higher divorce rates at the lower socioeconomic levels may stem from a number of factors. First, the frustrations involved in the great difficulty in meeting expenses and the lesser income may affect other areas of marital life. Second, at higher social strata, satisfaction in work and sexual spheres may less necessitate an escape from marriage. Third, the upper strata are more tied in to long-term investment expenditures that are less easily stopped or ended in contrast to the immediate daily need expenditures of the lower strata. Fourth, although the income is insufficient at the lower strata for the type of car, house, or fur coat of the higher strata, the desire for them remains. The purchase of these goods is the responsibility of the husband, and failure to obtain them is the failure of the husband. Fifth, the kin and friend network of the upper strata is larger and more tightly knit, making divorce more difficult and giving it far greater consequences.

The alert reader may note what appears to be a contradiction in the data. For example, it was shown in Figure 17–1 and mentioned in the text that divorce rates tend to decrease during an economic depression and rise during times of prosperity. Also, it was just mentioned that the incidence of divorce increases as socioeconomic level goes down. How is it possible that divorce rates decrease during depressions when "times are hard," and increase among the lower strata where "times are also hard"?

Several factors are involved. During depressions, divorce rates drop at all classes levels. The lower classes during the Great Depression of the 1930s still had the highest divorce rate. Many of the marriages that "survived" the 1930s contributed to the divorce rate of the 1940s. Also, the total life-style, the sense of loyalty, the linkages with kin, the occupational and income security, and the group support in general affect rates of divorce. These factors were different for Depression families and are different for lower-class families. Once again we note the powerful influence of the social network in something perceived to be so "individualistic and personal" as divorce.

---

28. Sharon K. Houseknecht, Suzanne Vaughan, and Anne S. Macke, "Marital Disruption Among Professional Women: The Timing of Career and Family Events," *Social Problems* 31 (February 1984): 273–284.

These variables that show differences in divorce rates do not vary much over the marital life course. Variables such as race, wife's labor-force participation, husband's employment, and urban residence were found to influence the probability of divorce irrespective of the duration of marriage.[29] The principal exception was the effect of the wife's education. With time, wives with a higher level of education had higher probabilities of marital dissolution. This is consistent with the socioeconomic material just presented. Increasing the status of women and, thus, decreasing their dependence on husbands, heightens the likelihood of divorce. Findings such as this suggest that societies desiring both family stability and sexual equality face a serious dilemma.

Children of divorced parents

The existence of children of divorced parents is increasingly common. Data from a national survey discovered that nearly a third of all children have experienced family disruption by the time they reach the age of fifteen. When children of never-married parents and those not currently living with a biological parent are included, the authors expect "that close to half of all children living in the United States today will reach age eighteen without having lived continuously with both biological parents."[30]

The number of children involved in divorce has exceeded 1 million every year since 1971. The average number of children per decree granted has generally been falling since 1964 when it peaked at 1.36. By 1984, this measure had fallen to 0.92 children per decree, meaning that today there are more divorces than children involved (*see* Figure 17–2). One reason for the decline is the drop in the birth rate. Other reasons include a slight increase in the proportion of childlessness at divorce and a decline in the estimated interval between marriage and divorce.

Approximately three of every five divorces involve children. Are children a deterrent to divorce? The answer appears to be both yes and no. Data show that children serve as a deterrent to both separation and divorce only when they are at the preschool ages. Once all the children in a family are in school, they do not seem to influence the probability of separation and divorce.[31]

29. Scott J. South and Glenna Spitze, "Determinants of Divorce over the Marital Life Course," *American Sociological Review* 51 (August 1986): 583–590. *See also* Tim B. Heaton, Stan L. Albrecht, and Thomas K. Martin, "The Timing of Divorce," *Journal of Marriage and the Family* 47 (August 1985): 631–639.

30. Frank F. Furstenberg, Jr., Christine Winquist Nord, James L. Peterson, and Nicholas Zill, "The Life Course of Children of Divorce: Marital Disruption and Parental Contact," *American Sociological Review* 48 (October 1983): 667.

31. Andrew Cherlin, "The Effect of Children on Marital Dissolution," *Demography* 14 (August 1977): 265–272.

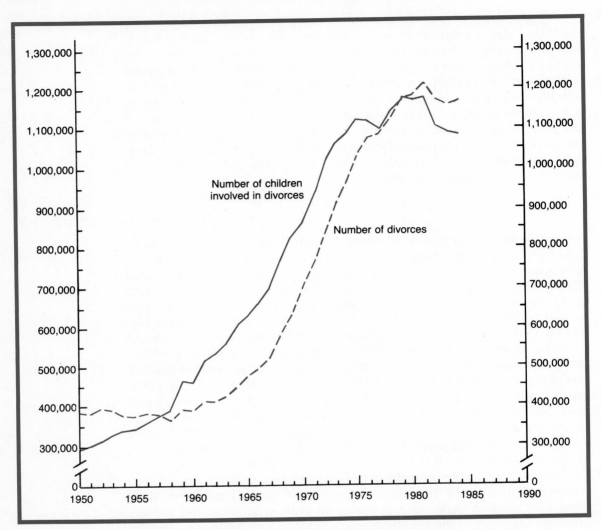

FIGURE 17–2

Divorces and children involved: United States, 1950–1984. (*Source:* National
Center for Health Statistics, "Advance Report of Divorce Statistics, 1984,"
Monthly Vital Statistics Reports, vol. 35, no. 6 [Public Health Service,
Hyattsville, Md., September 25, 1986], Figure 2, p. 3.)

Data from over 11,000 divorcing families in northern California clearly
support the relationship between the length or duration of marriage and
the presence of children.[32] Explanations for children delaying (not pre-

32. Robert P. Rankin and Jerry S. Maneker, "The Duration of Marriage in a Divorcing
Population: The Impact of Children," *Journal of Marriage and the Family* 47 (February 1985):
43–52.

venting) divorce include the presence of children making divorce more costly than continuation in the marriage, the cost in having the wife confined to the home and less free to take employment, the articulation of older children about their feelings, the possibility that people who have children may be more secure in the marriage than their childless counterparts, the stigma couples may feel toward parents who divorce, or anticipated complications attending divorce action: child custody, co-parenting, or single-parent problems. Note that all the couples in this study got divorced, thus, it provides no support for the myth that "children prevent divorce." What it supports is the notion of a longer duration of marriage before a divorce with the presence of children.

Given that there are more than 1 million children each year involved with divorced parents, the question of greater concern is, What are the effects or consequences on these children? Should couples, although unhappily married, stay together for the sake of the children? The presumed effect of divorce on children is usually negative. That is, the assumption is that divorce is always traumatic for the children, who will suffer psychologically, socially, and economically.

Very few of us would quarrel with the notion that children are better off in happy, stable families than in divorced or unhappy, unstable families. For example, one study found that whether black, white, male, or female, respondents from parental homes that were disrupted by death or divorce during their own childhood had higher rates of divorce or separation in their own first marriages.[33] Research findings such as this confirm the popular notion that divorce is bad for children. This belief is further supported by research results such as those by Rankin, who shows that children from broken homes are more highly associated with family-related offenses such as running away and truancy.[34] He concludes that studies that suggest that broken homes are not an important causal factor are misleading because of their inadequate operational definition of both family context and delinquency.

In spite of findings such as these, rarely do research results suggest or support the idea that, for the sake of the children, partners in unhappy marriages should stay together, that is, not divorce or separate. For example, one national sample of 1,400 children aged 12–16 showed that conflict in intact homes, especially if persistent, was as harmful as disruption itself.[35] Thus, we are faced with two "less than optimal" choices. Both the

---

33. Hallowell Pope and Charles W. Mueller, "The Intergenerational Transmission of Marital Instability: Comparisons by Race and Sex," *Journal of Social Issues* 32 (Winter 1976): 49–65.

34. Joseph H. Rankin, "The Family Context of Delinquency," *Social Problems* 30 (April 1983): 466–479.

35. James L. Peterson and Nicholas Zill, "Marital Disruption, Parent-Child Relationships, and Behavior Problems in Children," *Journal of Marriage and the Family* 48 (May 1986): 295–307.

intact home with persistent conflict and the divorced home are likely to result in varying degrees of stress, pain, and difficulties. The impact of divorce on children will probably vary considerably according to the age of the children and many other factors.

One of these factors relates to custody and the level of economic support. Joint custody is generally perceived to be the most ideal arrangement, and research does show joint-custody fathers to be more involved in parental decision making, shared responsibility, and making contact and participating in activities with their children than non-custodial fathers.[36] However, most custody is not joint. It is estimated that in about 90 percent of divorces that involve minor children, the mothers gain custody. The impact of being a female-headed single parent and the likelihood of being at a poverty level is very great (review Chapter 7).

One primary reason for this poverty status following divorce is the father's non-compliance with child support awards. The severity of this problem is well documented by U.S. census and other reports that show only about one-half of all children for whom child support has been decreed actually receive it. Another one-fourth of the children receive less than the specified amount, and the remaining one-fourth receive no support at all. Reasons for this non-support extend well beyond court enforcement or even ability to pay to interpersonal reasons, such as the level of attachment between former spouses and the quality of their relationship.[37] But the inescapable conclusion is that poverty, in general, and nonsupport, more specifically, have effects on the welfare of children.

An in-depth study of sixty families in California concluded that divorce produces not a single pattern in childrens' lives but at least three patterns with many variations.[38] Five years after the marriage breakup, 34 percent of the kids were said to be happy and thriving. Their self-esteem was high, and they were coping competently with the tasks of school, playground, and home. Twenty-nine percent were doing reasonably well: considered average by teachers, learning at grade level, and scoring in the middle range of psychological health. Nevertheless, islands of unhappiness and diminished self-esteem or anger continued to demand significant portions of these children's attention and energy. The final 37 percent were found to be consciously and intensely unhappy and dissatisfied with their lives,

---

36. Madonna E. Bowman and Constance R. Ahrons, "Impact of Legal Custody Status on Fathers' Parenting Postdivorce," *Journal of Marriage and the Family* 47 (May 1985): 481–488.

37. David W. Wright and Sharon J. Price, "Court-Ordered Child Support Payment: The Effect of the Former Spouse Relationship on Compliance," *Journal of Marriage and the Family* 48 (November 1986): 869–874.

38. Judith Wallerstein and Joan B. Kelly, "California's Children of Divorce," *Psychology Today* 13 (January 1980): 67–76.

experienced moderate to severe depression, felt intense loneliness, and complained of coming home to empty houses. Many of these children expressed defensive anger which reflected underlying fear, sorrow, and a sense of powerlessness.

Perhaps it is understandable that research has shown very mixed results on the consequences of divorce on children. Clearly many structural variations such as custody arrangements, remarriage of parent, presence of grandparents or other kin, age of children, educational and neighborhood influences, economic resources, presence of siblings, and the like tend to influence the consequences of a shift from a marital to a divorced parental status. Thus, taken alone, findings comparing the adjustment of children from broken homes with children from unhappy, unbroken homes do not produce results that are nearly as detrimental as is often believed to occur. One of the few differences that emerged in a study comparing college students with intact and separated/divorced families was a more favorable attitude toward divorce among the latter.[39] And as indicated previously, data do reveal that children from disrupted marriages have a higher rate of divorce than children from intact marriages. Thus resides one partial clue to the intergenerational transmission of divorce.

Consequences of divorce for adults

Consequences of divorce are evident at both the individual and interpersonal (micro) levels as well as at the organizational and societal (macro) levels. Most research focuses on the former. But one macro-level finding in both the United States and Canada, supports the proposition of a direct relationship between high rates of divorce and high rates of suicide. This is consistent with the work on suicide originally published in 1897 by Emile Durkheim, who theorized that societies with lower degrees of social integration typically share higher rates of suicide. With divorce used as one indicator of a lower level of social integration, research supports a heightened risk of suicide in provinces or areas where divorce rates are higher as well.[40]

A consequence of divorce is its influence on psychological well-being. Do changes occur in levels of mental health or feelings of depression

39. Ellen F. Greenberg and W. Robert Hay, "The Intergenerational Transmission of Marital Instability Reconsidered," *Journal of Marriage and the Family* 44 (May 1982): 335–347.

40. Frank Trovato, "The Relationship between Marital Dissolution and Suicide: The Canadian Case," *Journal of Marriage and the Family* 48 (May 1986): 341–348; and Ira M. Wasserman, "A Longitudinal Analysis of the Linkage Between Suicide, Unemployment, and Marital Dissolution," *Journal of Marriage and the Family* 46 (May 1984): 853–859.

A portfolio to prepare for a marital bear market

Last week I heard about two marriages of many decades that are heading for the divorce shredder. In both cases the husbands asked out, and the wives were dumbfounded.

Ready or not, however, the women now have to hire lawyers and set about the serious business of dividing up the pots and pans, equitably. They're scared almost speechless.

What is your husband's income? What are the sources of his income, all sources, all income? How is it disbursed, invested?

How much did the house cost? The cottage? The furnishings? Are there any rental properties? What and where? What is fair market value today for all of the above?

Stocks, bonds, trusts, foreign accounts, real property, personal property, coin collections, artworks, retirement funds, pension benefits, who, what, where, when, how, how much? Stop!

Both women said many of the same things: "I never thought it would happen to me." "My husband took care of everything. I don't even know what the gas bill is at our house."

Get your disaster plan going

The moral of this story is that even the most happily married woman should not pack her brains away with her wedding gown.

In this era of profligate divorce—a little over 50 percent at present—I would suggest all wives formulate divorce plans right now. Just as we buy car insurance and home-and-contents insurance, praying we'll never need them, women should put together divorce survival insurance, praying they'll never need that either.

Some basics:

following a change in marital status from married to divorced? It is clear that a change does occur. Data from a large metropolitan Chicago sample showed that the newly divorced became significantly more depressed.[41] This increase in depression following divorce closely reflected their greater economic problems, the perception that one's standard of living had deteriorated, and the lesser availability of close, confiding relationships.

The consequences, particularly economic ones, differ dramatically for female and males. The economic situation improves for men and declines for women. California data show a radical change in the standard

41. Elizabeth G. Menaghan and Morton A. Lieberman, "Changes in Depression Following Divorce: A Panel Study," *Journal of Marriage and the Family* 48 (May 1986): 319–328.

Know what your separate and joint assets are, where they are, how they are accessed and by whom. How do you find out? I guess you'll have to ask your spouse. Tough. Do it anyway.

Know what your living expenses are. Some women don't even know if the family home has a second mortgage, if the car or cars are paid for, if husband has personal or home-improvement loans outstanding, all kinds of things.

A woman who does not work outside her home should seriously think about a paying job she would enjoy. Prepare for it. Study for it. Work at it, if possible—part-time, perhaps, or as a volunteer. You may never need or want to do this work for a living, but if you must, you can.

Choose a highly qualified divorce lawyer based on experience and track record, not personal friendship or because he's your cousin. You don't have to contact him or her at all. Sober, cool-headed research in advance of need is all that is required. It's like knowing the name and phone number of a fine doctor, all the while you hope never to need the doctor's services.

Consider where you might live should you be unable to live in the family home after a divorce. Do you know a qualified real estate broker? Find one. Consult. Think of temporary and permanent locations, neighborhoods, housing types. What are the advantages or disadvantages of each? What do they cost? Are you sure, or guessing?

Imagine yourself divorced and you will know what other information to put into your survival insurance portfolio. It's the same information any widow needs and often doesn't have.

A wise person is not caught in the rain without an umbrella. You have to think about that in advance, too. Sensible. Prudent, and a comfort.

Source: Nickie McWhirter, *Detroit Free Press* September 8, 1986, p. 1-C. Reprinted with the permission of The Detroit Free Press.

of living just one year after a legal divorce. Men experienced a 42 percent improvement in their postdivorce standard of living while women experienced a 73 percent loss.[42] Little wonder that more divorced women report that they are in constant financial crisis, are perpetually worried

42. Lenore J. Weitzman, "The Economics of Divorce: Social and Economic Consequences of Property, Alimony, and Child Support Awards," *UCLA Law Review* 28 (August 1981): 1251. The economic impact of divorce and separation on women can be seen in Robert S. Weiss, "The Impact of Marital Dissolution on Income and Consumption in Single-Parent Households," *Journal of Marriage and the Family* 46 (February 1984): 115–127; and Randal D. Day and Stephen J. Bahr, "Income Changes Following Divorce and Remarriage," *Journal of Divorce* 9 (Spring 1986): 75–88.

about not being able to pay their bills, have more stress, and feel less satisfied with their lives than any other group in the United States. In contrast, men who divorce or separate are immediately better off. They retain most of their labor incomes, typically do not pay large amounts of alimony and child support to their ex-wives, and no longer have to provide for the level of needs associated with their former families.[43]

These findings are highly consistent with others that show trauma and stress to be significantly greater for the female than for the male. The Wallerstein longitudinal study of sixty divorcing families referred to earlier shows significant differences between former spouses in the quality of their lives.[44] Among women, persistence of anger and widespread loneliness was prevalent. This was particularly true among women over age forty. Even ten years after the divorce, many of these women felt angry, lonely, and rejected and were living in economic, social, and psychological conditions well below that which they had achieved during their marriage. Younger women were more likely to exhibit greater economic and emotional progress. Wallerstein indicates that the capacity to replace failed relationships is neither a psychological nor social given. In two-thirds of the families, only one of the former spouses was able to make use of the divorce to significantly improve the quality of his or her life. In only 10 percent of the couples did both former spouses do so. Apparently there are few victimless divorces even among adults and fewer still when children are involved.

In reviewing the literature on the possible long-term effects of divorce on the adults involved, Ann Goetting suggests that physical and mental health are best among the happily married, worst among the unhappily married, and between the two extremes are the divorced.[45]

REMARRIAGE AND RECONSTITUTED FAMILIES

The United States is recognized as practicing monogamy. Yet it is likely that a greater number, as well as proportion, of people in the United States experience a multiple number of spouses than in many, if not most, countries recognized as polygamous. This would be especially true for women since polyandry occurs rarely. Whereas the marriage of one man to several women is common, the marriage of one woman to several men is infrequent. Thus, it is possible that in the United States, more

---

43. Greg J. Duncan and Saul D. Hoffman, "A Reconsideration of the Economic Consequences of Marital Dissolution," *Demography* 22 (November 1985): 485–497.

44. Judith S. Wallerstein, "Women After Divorce: Preliminary Report from a Ten Year Follow-up," *American Journal of Orthopsychiatry* 56 (January 1986): 65–77.

45. Ann Goetting, "Divorce Outcome Research: Issues and Perspectives," *Journal of Family Issues* 2 (September 1981): 350–378.

Remarriage, especially for widowers among the elderly population, is a common occurrence. (Photo: © David S. Strickler/The Picture Cube)

than anywhere in the world, women are likely to experience multiple husbands. As of 1980, about one out of five households maintained by a married couple included one or both spouses who had been divorced and one-sixth of all children under eighteen in the United States lived in these households.[46] Remarriages and reconstituted families are common.

---

46. Andrew Cherlin and James McCarthy, "Remarried Couple Households: Data from the June 1980 Current Population Survey," *Journal of Marriage and the Family* 47 (February 1985): 23–30. Readers interested in this topic may wish to consider Kay Pasley and Marilyn

Like first marriages, couples are likely to marry for reasons of love, be monogamous, and expect the marriage to last until death. Yet the remarried couple faces life experiences and engages in life-styles that in many ways differentiate them from a couple in their first marriage. Those who remarry are older on the average than those marrying for the first time, presumably more mature, and more likely to have a child upon entering the marriage.

Remarriage is different enough to lead some sociologists to refer to it as an "incomplete institution"[47] or a "noninstitution."[48] Andrew Cherlin, for one, argues that the higher divorce rate for remarriages than for first marriages is due to the incomplete institutionalization of remarriage after divorce. Persons who remarry, particularly those with children from a previous marriage, face problems unlike those encountered in first marriages. The institution of the family provides no standard solutions to many of these problems. In contrast, first marriages are supported by effective institutional controls, as is evidenced in both language and the law. How does a child address a stepparent? Does a husband or wife introduce their spouse as "new" or "second"? Likewise, the law assumes the marriage in question is a first one. Few provisions exist for selected problems of remarriage, such as balancing the financial obligation of husbands or wives to their spouses and children from current and previous marriages, or defining incest and consanguineal marriage (for example, sexual relations or marriage between a stepmother and stepson or between two stepchildren). This lack of institutional support and control for the remarried makes the unity of families of remarriage precarious, resulting in higher divorce rates.

Remarriage rates

As indicated earlier, more than one million divorces occur each year. This has been true since 1975. Persons whose marriages end in divorce are more likely to renounce a particular marriage partner rather than the institution of marriage. An estimated two-thirds of all divorced persons remarry. A life course analysis of divorce and remarriage revealed that at least 60 percent of women and 70 percent of men who became divorced were subsequently remarried.[49] The chance of remarrying following wid-

Ihinger-Tallman (guest editors), "Remarriage and Stepparenting," *Family Relations* 33 (July 1983), and Paul C. Glick and Sung-Ling Lin, "Remarriage After Divorce: Recent Changes and Demographic Variations," *Sociological Perspectives* 30 (April 1987): 162–179.

47. Andrew Cherlin, "Remarriage as an Incomplete Institution," *American Journal of Sociology* 84 (November 1978): 634–650.

48. Sharon Price-Bonham and Jack O. Balswick. "The Noninstitutions: Divorce, Desertion and Remarriage," *Journal of Marriage and the Family* 42 (November 1980): 959–972.

49. Thomas J. Espenshade and Rachel Eisenberg Braun, "Life Course Analysis and

owhood was substantially smaller, especially for women, for whom the probability was less than 15 percent. Interestingly, the mean age at remarriage after widowhood for women was ten years *less* than the mean age at widowhood. This paradox suggests that, even though the probability of remarriage following widowhood is small for females, it is the youngest widows who are most likely to remarry. Remarriage among older widows is compounded by the declining supply of potential husbands due to higher male mortality rates.

As suggested, remarriage rates are higher for men than for women among both the divorced and the widowed in all age groups. The likelihood of remarriage varies depending on social and demographic characteristics.[50] By race, remarriage is both more likely and more quickly experienced for white than for black women. By age, remarriage is more likely for those who are married at a relatively young age and for those who are under age thirty at the time of divorce. By children, remarriage is more likely for those who have no children or only a small number of children in their first marriage. By education, remarriage is greater for those who have less than a college education. By employment, remarriage is more likely if the woman is not in the labor force. By income, remarriage is more likely for women with lower income.

In analyzing remarriage according to the financial condition of women, Anne-Marie Ambert suggests that financially secure women display behavior that is dysfunctional on the remarriage market.[51] While they have more opportunities to meet men, have more dates, and have more steady relationships, they are also more likely to break up relationships that do not suit them, are less likely to tolerate abusive male behavior towards them, and are less likely to flatter a man's ego. In brief, consistent with an exchange theory model, high status women have less to gain from remarriage than lower status women.

It would appear that for all remarriages, the time span following divorce is about two years. The 1983 census data show the median age at divorce after the first marriage to be 32.3 for males and 29.8 for females.[52] The median age at remarriage is listed as 36.2 for males and

Multistate Demography: An Application to Marriage, Divorce and Remarriage," *Journal of Marriage and the Family* 44 (November 1982): 1032.

50. Paul C. Glick, "Remarriage: Some Recent Changes and Variations, *Journal of Family Issues* 1 (December 1980): 455–478; and Paul C. Glick and Sung-Ling Lin, "Recent Changes in Divorce and Remarriage," *Journal of Marriage and the Family* 48 (November 1986): 737–747.

51. Anne-Marie Ambert, "Separated Women and Remarriage Behavior: A Comparison of Financially Secure Women and Financially Insecure Women," *Journal of Divorce* 6 (Spring 1983): 43–54.

52. U.S. Bureau of the Census, *Statistical Abstract of the United States: 1986,* no. 123, p. 80.

32.9 for females. Accordingly, the time lapse between the median age of divorce and the median age of remarriage is 3.9 years for males and 3.1 years for females. Thus, while remarriage rates are higher for men than for women, the women who do remarry do so more quickly than the men. Useful predictors of early remarriage for women include not being employed and, to a lesser extent, not having any children.[53]

Marriage among the remarried

Earlier in this chapter it was stated that the length of remarriages that end in divorce is less than that of first marriages. Various explanations for this were presented. One that was not given has to do with the presence of stepchildren. Data from a national probability sample of married persons show that the higher divorce rate among remarriages is limited to the most complex form of remarriage: where both spouses have been previously married and there are stepchildren in the household.[54] Respondents with stepchildren reported significantly less satisfaction with their family life than those with biological children. In addition, stepfamilies moved teenagers out of the home and emptied the nest faster than biological families.

Does a somewhat higher rate of divorce, the presence of stepchildren, or both mean that remarriages are more conflict-ridden and unsuccessful than first marriages? One test of this is to compare the present marriage of remarried persons with their own first marriage. In a study of 369 remarried persons living in eight western states, respondents rated their marriages as much better than their previous marriages, as better than the marriages of others they knew, and better than they had anticipated them to be prior to their occurrence.[55]

Helen Weingarten compared remarried adults with first-married and currently divorced adults.[56] When comparing the remarried with the divorced, similarities existed in levels of self-esteem, perceived internal control, levels of dissatisfaction, perceived shortcomings, worry, anxiety, immobilization, physical health symptoms, and substance use. But the divorced were significantly more likely to report that they are "not too happy," less likely to report that the present is the happiest time of life, and more likely to view the past as much happier than the present. When comparing

53. Frank L. Mott and Sylvia F. Moore, "The Tempo of Remarriage Among Young American Women," *Journal of Marriage and the Family* 45 (May 1983): 427–435.

54. Lynn K. White and Alan Booth, "The Quality and Stability of Remarriages: The Role of Stepchildren," *American Sociological Review* 50 (October 1985): 689–698.

55. Stan L. Albrecht, "Correlates of Marital Happiness Among the Remarried," *Journal of Marriage and the Family* 41 (November 1979): 857–867.

56. Helen R. Weingarten, "Marital Status and Well-Being: A National Study Comparing First-Married, Currently Divorced, and Remarried Adults," *Journal of Marriage and the Family* 47 (August 1985): 653–662.

the remarried with the currently married, similarities existed in reporting they feel "very happy," consider the present to be the happiest time of their lives, and are optimistic about the future. But the remarried were more likely to answer "a lot" when asked how frequently difficult events have occurred in their lives, more frequently reported feelings of having a nervous breakdown, and were more likely to report ill health and use of alcohol and medicine, measures sensitive to chronic stress. It does appear that first marriage, divorce, and remarriage are distinctive "institutions" with both similarities and significant differences between them.

The prospects for divorced males to enter into satisfactory marriages apparently are somewhat better than for divorced females. This sexual difference is explained by Lynn White in two ways.[57] The first is that remarriage is differentially selective of men and women so that differences in happiness are a result of recruitment. She hypothesized that remarriage would attract the least financially secure divorced women and the most financially secure divorced men. Her data showed that women in second marriages reported both lower levels of education and lower family incomes than women in first marriages, whereas the men in second marriages reported both higher levels of education and higher family incomes than divorced men or those in first marriages. To the extent that socioeconomic status is associated with happiness (and evidence for this is substantial), this recruitment process would tend to produce this sexual difference. The second explanation is that the experience of remarriage is different for men and women. Remarried women are less well off with regard to factors which prompt happiness: marital satisfaction, general satisfaction with the quality of their life, and affiliation with friends, relatives, and organizations. Yet, irrespective of these male-female differences, it can be said that remarriage remains a satisfactory "solution" to divorce for a large percentage of divorced persons.

Furstenberg and Spanier found that among those who do remarry, individual well-being is greatest for those whose marriages are well adjusted. They concluded that remarriage per se was not found to enhance a person's well-being but when the second marriage was successful and rewarding, individuals typically fared better than they would if they remained divorced.[58]

Remarried couples with stepchildren

Traditionally, remarriages and stepfamilies were formed primarily as a result of the death of a spouse; today the formation results primarily from

---

57. Lynn K. White, "Sex Differentials in the Effect of Remarriage on Global Happiness," *Journal of Marriage and the Family* 41 (November 1979): 869–876.

58. Frank F. Furstenberg, Jr. and Graham B. Spanier, *Recycling the Family: Remarriage after Divorce* (Beverly Hills, Cal.: Sage Publications, 1984): 176–177. Chapters 8 and 9 examine remarriage and well-being and the risk of dissolution in remarriage.

divorce. These "remarried," "reconstituted," "binuclear," "blended," and "stepparent" families constitute significant nontraditional marital and family arrangements that present unique circumstances and relationships. Step-families may include a stepfather, mother, and her children; a stepmother, father, and his children; or a mother and father joining two sets of children. Unique circumstances arise when the stepparent couple is not married but live together, when two separated parents living in separate households both attempt to provide financial and emotional support to their children, or when the children visit as opposed to live with the stepparent.

This latter circumstance, for example, whether living or visiting the stepparent, was found to be an important one in stepparent and step-children's relationships.[59] The stepparenting experience, particularly for stepmothers, was more positive with live-in stepchildren. Most research suggests the role of stepmother is a more difficult one than that of stepfather, and this difficulty seems to stem in large part from the fact that most stepmothers do not have live-in stepchildren. In contrast, most stepfathers do. When stepchildren visit, it is usually the stepmothers and not the children's fathers who have the extra housecleaning, shopping for food, and cooking. This work is often perceived as a burden because they receive little benefit emotionally from the visits. And like stepparenting, stepsiblings' relations were found to be more positive when they lived together rather than visited.

Stepfamilies differ structurally from first families in a number of ways. First, there is one biological parent not presently living in the household. Second, the parent and child relationship predates the new marriage. And third, while a legal relationship binds the remarriage, no legal relationship binds the stepchildren and stepparents. In fact, Sarah Ramsey reports that only 14 states have statutes that even obligate the stepparent to support stepchildren, and typically even in those instances, the obligation is more limited than that imposed on a natural parent.[60]

These structural elements have been found to alter parenting practices in a major way. One national sample of children between the ages of seven and eleven revealed that in a majority of families, marital disruption effectively destroyed the relationship between children and the biological parent living outside the home.[61] Nearly half of all children had not seen their nonresident fathers in the past year. Unlike that suggested in the

---

59. Anne-Marie Ambert, "Being a Stepparent: Live-in and Visiting Stepchildren," *Journal of Marriage and the Family* 48 (November 1986): 795–804.

60. Sarah H. Ramsey, "Stepparent Support of Stepchildren: The Changing Legal Context and the Need for Empirical Policy Research," *Family Relations* 35 (July 1986): 363–369.

61. Frank F. Furstenberg, Jr. and Christine Winquist Nord, "Parenting Apart: Patterns of Childrearing After Marital Disruption," *Journal of Marriage and the Family* 47 (November 1985): 893–904.

Remarriage often involves a ceremony that includes the presence of children and stepchildren from a first or earlier marriage. (Photo: © Donald Dietz/Stock, Boston)

media, children of divorce rarely have two homes and only a minority have ever slept over at their fathers' houses. It was suggested that perhaps a majority have never set foot into the houses of their non-resident fathers. In addition, the contact that does exist with the outside parent tends to be a social rather than an instrumental exchange. That is, the non-resident parent may take the children to dinner or on trips but rarely helps with schoolwork or daily projects.

The unique structural elements of stepfamilies raise a variety of questions and problem situations not likely to be found in the traditional nuclear unit. For example: How does the "ex-spouse" affect the relationship with the "new" spouse? Which parent "gets" the child for birthdays, holidays, and special events? Do parents compete in giving the more expensive gift? Does the gift come equally from the parents and stepparents? Is discipline likely to be equal and consistent coming from a mother and stepmother or father and stepfather? Do incestuous relationships become frequent issues of concern, particularly between stepfathers and step-daughters? Are children the messengers or communication link between the mother and father who may or may not be on cordial terms? How is the spending of one parent controlled or influenced by the other parent? What socialization difficulties occur in the process of stepparenting? Clearly the list could be extended considerably.

SUMMARY

1. All societies have some mechanism to cope with marital discord or to terminate marital relationships. In some countries divorce is not permitted, but particularly for men, other types of relationships may co-exist with a marriage.

2. In the United States, divorce is the best known and most common means of ending an unsatisfactory marital relationship but desertion, marital separation, and annulments exist as well. Desertion shares with marital separation the condition that the spouses are married and cannot remarry. Separation may be formally and legally arranged or informally agreed upon. Annulment, due to conditions existing prior to the marriage, eradicates it so that in theory, at least, it never existed.

3. The legal grounds for divorce vary somewhat for each state, with the most widely accepted grounds being marital incompatibility or evidence of irreconcilable differences. In the past decade, no-fault divorce has been adopted in most states to resolve many of the difficulties associated with proving "fault." Studies suggest, however, that women are faring more poorly under no-fault than under the former adversary system.

4. Social grounds for divorce often differ considerably from the legal grounds. Divorce mediation as a conflict resolution process has grown rapidly as a means of diminishing the bitterness and divisiveness that accompanies divorce. Reasons for staying in or leaving a marriage are viewed as attractions (rewards) and barriers (costs) and take on significance in light of alternatives available.

5. The rate of divorce is likely to be calculated in a number of ways such as per 1,000 persons in the total populaton, per 1,000 women age 15 and over, or the ratio of divorces to the number of marriages in a given year. Irrespective of how the rate is calculated, the trend has been upward with a leveling off or slight decrease in the last few years.

6. Within the United States, divorce rates vary by a wide range of geographic, demographic, and social characteristics. Rates vary consid-

erably by state as well as by metropolitan areas within the state. Teenage marriages have higher divorce rates than marriages begun when the couple were in their twenties. The duration of a marriage is related to the incidence of divorce. Persons who are married more than once have a higher likelihood of divorce than those married only once. By race, divorce rates are higher for blacks than for whites; by religion, divorce rates are higher for Protestants than for Jews and Catholics; and by socioeconomic level, divorce rates tend to go up as educational level, income, or occupational positions go down. One exception to this relationship exists among educated professional women.

7. Children are a primary concern to those interested in divorce. While research would not lend support to the idea that unhappy or unsuccessful marriages should remain intact for the sake of the children, neither does it lend support to the idea that children of divorced parents do not go through periods of stress and periods of major readjustment. Mothers tend to get custody of children and the underpayment or nonpayment of child support creates hardships for many women and children.

8. The consequences of divorce for adults are evident at both macro- and micro-levels, as reflected in factors such as higher rates of suicide and depression. The economic consequences differ dramatically for males and females, with men doing better and women much worse following divorce.

9. Most persons who end one marriage enter another. The remarriage rate climbs as the divorce rate climbs. Men are more likely to remarry than women, divorcees are more likely to remarry than widows, and younger persons are more likely to remarry than older persons. Although people may have failed in their first marriage, the remarriage was generally perceived to be better than the former.

10. The complexities of remarriage are compounded by the presence of children. The stepparenting experience is most difficult for the stepmother but is more positive with live-in stepchildren. Structural elements such as one biological parent not living in the home, the child predating the new marriage, and the lack of legal, binding relationships between stepchildren and stepparents alter parenting in dramatic ways—even to the extent of destroying many relationships between children and the biological parent living outside the parental home.

11. This chapter focused on divorce and remarriage. To have "strong" families and to offer programs and establish policies that lend support to marriages and families is, at least in terms of rhetoric, the goal of governmental and community units. Our attention in the final chapter is directed to this issue of the family and social policy.

KEY TERMS AND TOPICS

DISCUSSION QUESTIONS

1. What are some of the reasons for desertion, separation, or annulment rather than divorce? How does each affect husbands, wives, or children?

2. Visit a local court that handles divorce cases. Arrange to meet with the judge to discuss the legal process, the legal grounds for divorce compared to the nonlegal reasons for divorce, and his or her views on divorce mediators, joint custody, grandparents' rights, and other legal issues. What legal changes does he or she view as necessary?

3. Discuss the implications and consequences of no-fault divorce. What are its pros and cons? What effect is it likely to have on rates, long-term trends, and the like?

4. What do you define as the primary reasons that marriages end? Are these reasons that can be predetermined or influenced prior to marriage? Why do many "poor" marriages not end?

5. How are divorce rates determined? In this chapter, three different divorce rates were given for the same year. How is this possible? What does each mean? What factors influence rates even when the number of divorces remains constant?

6. Summarize the trend in divorce rates in the United States. Indicate conditions that are likely to increase or lower the rate of divorce.

7. Divorce rates were found to differ by duration of marriage, race, religion, socioeconomic status, and the like. What were the differences and how are these variations explained?

8. In regard to religion, explain why conservative or fundamentalist Protestant religious groups that oppose divorce tend to have high divorce rates.

9. Discuss the relationship between the presence or absence of children, the number of children, and divorce. What are the consequences of divorce on children? Compare with children from unbroken but unhappy homes.

10. Examine some of the consequences of divorce for adults. Why are the consequences so different for males and females?

11. How do remarriages differ from first marriages? Is remarriage an incomplete institution or a noninstitution? Explain.

12. How do stepchildren affect a marriage? Discuss some advantages and difficulties that accompany reconstituted or binuclear families.

FURTHER READINGS

Cherlin, Andrew J. *Marriage, Divorce, Remarriage.* Cambridge, Mass.: Harvard University Press, 1981. An examination of the trends in marriage, divorce, and remarriage; explanations for these trends; and the consequences.

Furstenberg, Frank, Jr., ed. "Remarriage." *Journal of Family Issues* 1 (December 1980). A special issue that examines social and demographic variations, historical aspects, transitions to, and adjustments associated with remarriage.

Furstenberg, Frank F., Jr., and Spanier, Graham B. *Recycling the Family: Remarriage After Divorce.* Beverly Hills, Cal.: Sage Publications, 1984. The results of an eight-year study examining aspects of adjustment unique to the marriage-divorce-remarriage transition.

Jacobson, Gerald F. *The Multiple Crisis of Marital Separation and Divorce.* N.Y.: Grune and Stratton, Inc., 1983. One of the volumes in the "Seminars and Psychiatry Series," this book bridges the gap between clinical phenomena and statistically oriented research.

Kitson, Gay C., and Raschke, Helen J. "Divorce Research: What We Know; What We Need to Know." *Journal of Divorce* 4 (Spring 1981): 1–37. A very readable overview of the research on the antecedents and consequences of divorce for adults.

Little, Marilyn. *Family Breakup: Understanding Marital Problems and the Mediating of Child Custody Decisions.* San Francisco: Jossey-Bass, 1982. A study of how families approach separation and cope with divorce.

Messinger, Lillian. *Remarriage: A Family Affair.* N.Y.: Plenum Press, 1984. A reporting of "remarrieds'" experiences, including the separation, custody dilemmas, the group experience, and remarriage.

Spanier, Graham B., and Thompson, Linda. *Parting: The Aftermath of Separation and Divorce.* Beverly Hills, Cal.: Sage Publications, 1984. A comparison volume to *Recycling the Family* that examines the complex transition from marriage to divorce.

Walczak Yvette, with Burns, Sheila. *Divorce: The Child's Point of View.* N.Y.: Harper and Row, 1984. A brief paperback about children and divorce based on "conversations" with children of divorced parents.

Photo: © Carolyn Hine/The Picture Cube

18

Family and Social Policy

Few persons, married or single, are willing to dismiss the family as insignificant and unimportant to their own lives or to the lives of others. In fact, one could make an argument for the value-laden position that, across cultures and throughout history, no single institution has had a greater influence in shaping the lives of persons, in affecting interpersonal relationships, or even in determining national stature. Yet the United States has no explicit national policy (or policies) for families. The United States, with all its agencies overseeing education, health, commerce, labor, energy, transportation, defense, agriculture, and the like, has no agency devoting its attention directly to families. The government, while professing the importance of the family, in many ways provides negative tax incentives for marriage, is disruptive of kin networks in programs related to labor and defense, and punishes persons or groups who don't conform to a particular marital and family life-style.

Perhaps a "national family policy" is both unnecessary and unwanted. First, United States citizens have gotten along without an explicit family policy for centuries; thus, why now? Second, a family policy is an unrealistic goal since no one family policy could meet the needs of the many family life-styles in the United States (*see* Chapters 4–7). And no single policy would be able to deal with premarital, nonmarital, and marital interactions ranging from mate selection to sexual relationships (*see* Chapters 8–11). Nor could one policy be made equally relevant to families at all stages of the marital and family life cycle (*see* Chapters 12–15). Thus, no one policy could answer questions that affect everything from crisis to abuse to divorce (*see* Chapters 16–17). For these reasons we should begin with an examination of what is meant by "family policy" and how this concept can profitably be explored in this chapter.

THE MEANING AND USE OF FAMILY AND SOCIAL POLICY

Family policy has been defined as that set of support programs created by the larger society to supplement functions once performed by the

The re-creation of family policy includes those who advocate the status quo or even a return to some earlier imagined family life-style as well as those who desire pluralistic and newly-emerging life styles. (Photo: © Mark Antman/The Image Works)

family.[1] Certain programs support the *nurturance* function: child care, health care, services to the elderly or handicapped. Other programs support the *economic* functions of the family by providing welfare benefits or stimulating employment. The *ecological* or social function is served by programs that promote helping arrangements, social networks and the exchange of services. Finally, certain aspects of family law and social policy clarify the boundaries and strengthen the identity of the family as a *legal and cultural* entity.

    Social policy, as used in this chapter, will refer to a definite course or method of action (including support programs) to guide, influence, or determine present and future social organization, social behaviors, or social decisions. *Family policy,* like *social policy,* refers to a course or method of action directed at the family (including marriage and kin) with

---

    1. Janet Zollinger Giele, *Women and the Future* (New York: The Free Press, 1978): 189–190.

the intent of guiding, influencing, or determining the *structures* it assumes, the *functions* it performs, *processes* of change, or the *behavior* (including ideas and values) of its members. Examples of policy related to the legal status of family structure may include whether and under what conditions persons might have more than one spouse, whether the spouse can be of the same sex, or whether fathers must be absent for mothers to receive welfare assistance. Examples of policys related to family functions may include the use or provision of day care centers in addition to, or as a substitute for the parents for the socialization of children, the possession of guns for protection, or the legitimacy of sterilization, abortion, or chemicals in controlling reproduction. Examples of policy related to family behavior may include the kinds of support granted to househusbands, the employment of women, or the endorsement of corporal punishment.

The intent here is to deal with family policy in general terms. This would include policies directed specifically at families as well as more general social policies that have a direct impact upon and social consequences for families. This includes research that evaluates existing policies and programs as well as research that provides direction to or influences new policies and programs. Our attention is directed first at family policy research.

FAMILY POLICY RESEARCH

Within the social sciences, an issue that frequently emerges is the extent to which social research can or should be value-free. This issue becomes particularly acute when dealing with family policy research. One side of the issue argues for value neutrality, objectivity, and basic research apart from any policy objective. The opposite side of the issue argues that value-free research is impossible even if desired and that trained social researchers need to provide their expertise in constructive ways. One solution to these dichotomous positions is to do both by "wearing two hats": one of researcher and one of citizen. The researcher provides empirical evidence of what *is*, the citizen works for goals she or he deems important. Nye and McDonald,[2] for example, distinguish between **family policy research** and **family policy advocacy.** The researcher attempts to maintain objectivity throughout the research endeavor. The advocate endorses and actively works for a course of action that improves family life and hopefully enhances the well-being of its members. They argue that individuals who

---

2. F. Ivan Nye and Gerald W. McDonald, "Family Policy Research: Emergent Models and Some Theoretical Issues," in F. Ivan Nye, ed., *Family Relationships: Rewards and Costs* (Beverly Hills: Sage Publications, 1982): 195.

choose to be both researcher and advocate need to state which role they are performing at any given time.

Scanzoni makes a case for both positions.[3] His research and theory in *Shaping Tomorrow's Families* is basically positivistic because it describes and analyzes *what is.* Yet it is stimulated by policy and normative considerations of *what should be.* His position is that research itself be conducted under the strictest positivist procedural canons possible. Yet researchers should not be deluded into thinking they have no vested interest in the outcome of the investigations any less than a medical researcher has an interest in finding some cure or solution to a sickness or disease. That empirical research must simultaneously be kept distinct from and yet connected with practical applications, Scanzoni recognizes as a difficult tightrope to walk. Yet this sort of "balancing art" is required because family *research* has often been devoid of practical application on the one hand and because family *policy* has been devoid of basic research and organizing principles on the other.

Family evaluation research

In dealing with family policy research, a number of types can be identified and differentiated. Nye and McDonald note three emerging models.[4] One of these is **family evaluation research.** Evaluation research is conducted at a programmatic level to determine the degree to which social programs have achieved or are achieving the stated goals of a public policy or resultant program. For example, Aid to Families with Dependent Children (AFDC) policy is intended to encourage the care of dependent children in their own homes or those of relatives in ways that maintain and strengthen family life, retain personal independence, and provide parental care and protection. Family evaluation research would attempt to determine if these basic goals are being met and address such issues as whether eligible families are being serviced, whether the financial aid contributes to greater family stability, or whether the level of assistance is greater than necessary or inadequate to achieve the goals.

Shirley Zimmerman, using a family perspective, examined research findings and other data dealing with government policies and programs to determine their effectiveness or lack thereof.[5] Effectiveness was viewed as a fit between the goals or objectives of a program and their actual

---

3. John Scanzoni, *Shaping Tomorrow's Family: Theory and Policy for the 21st Century* (Beverly Hills, Cal.: Sage Publications, 1983).

4. Nye and McDonald, "Family Policy Research," pp. 185–191.

5. Shirley L. Zimmerman, "Public Policies and Family Outcomes: Empirical Evidence or Ideology?" *Social Casework* 64 (March 1983): 138–146.

outcomes. Drawing upon other studies as the source of her evaluation attempts, she assessed the effectiveness of income guarantee experiments, AFDC, Supplementary Security Income (SSI) and social security, deinstitutionalization policies in relation to the mentally ill and retarded family members, compensatory preschool education, and abortion services. While her conclusions cannot be considered definitive given the limited number of studies and the various interpretations of different criteria, she claims that from a family perspective, government programs seem to have promoted family well-being under conditions that take family variables into account. When programs do run counter to family interests, the negative effects of such policies and programs on affected families tend to reflect the absence, rather than the presence, of supportive service policies and programs. Her evaluation research provides evidence that changes or reductions in public programs and government's involvement in them cannot be justified on the basis of ineffectiveness. Those changes rest more on idiological grounds than on empirical evidence.

Family impact analysis

A second type of family policy research is **family impact analysis.** Here the attempt of the research is to assess the intended and unintended consequences of public policy and social programs. Unlike evaluation research that is focused on whether the goals or objectives are being met, family impact analysis looks at how families are affected beyond the explicit intentions or goals of the policy or program. As a result, evaluation research may show the intended goals are being met but impact analysis may show the goals are counterproductive by having negative consequences for families in unintended ways. In our previous example of AFDC families, evaluation research may show the level of funding is adequate to feed, clothe, and house the dependent children, yet an impact analysis may show the funding and support has negative consequences as well.

In fact, Patricia Spakes examined the impact of the AFDC mandatory work registration policy on AFDC clients.[6] The mandatory work registration requirement is intended to insure that AFDC recipients register to work through the Work Incentive Program (WIN). The purpose was to move families off welfare through employment, thus reducing welfare dependency, enhancing clients' self-esteem, and establishing the parent as a positive working role model for children in order to break the welfare cycle. In studying 102 welfare clients in Wisconsin, the data suggested that the

---

6. Patricia Spakes, "Mandatory Work Registration for Welfare Parents: A Family Impact Analysis," *Journal of Marriage and the Family* 44 (August 1982): 685–699.

mandatory work registration requirement had no effect on the majority of individuals or their families. However, 28 percent reported negative individual effects and 24 percent reported negative family effects (compared to 5 percent who reported positive effects).

Negative individual impacts were most often described in terms of the strain of having to look for work in addition to performing other duties, lowered self-concept as a result of failure to obtain employment, and disappointment with the failure to get training or a better job. Negative family consequences included expensive and inadequate child care, behavior problems of unsupervised children, and concern regarding children left at home to care for themselves. In brief, a family impact analysis of the policy that required welfare parents to register for work showed negative consequences for adults and children alike and an increase in family problems. These findings lead to questioning whether the psychological benefit to society in seeing welfare mothers work is worth the millions of dollars it costs to implement the program and the negative social psychological consequences to its recipients.

Research for family policy

The third type of family policy research that Nye and McDonald identify they term **research for family policy.** Research for family policy typically starts with a general hypothesis that some kind of social actions may be desirable. It does not assume a problem exists, does not evaluate an existing policy or program, and does not assess the consequences of a policy or program. Rather, given some "nontraditional" life-style (cohabitation, dual-career marriages, female-headed households, reconstituted families, never-married parents, and so forth) research for family policy examines certain categories of persons who have a particular structural arrangement or life-style and seeks to discover the outcome of that way of life for the individuals involved as well as for society as a whole. The result of the research for family policy may be that all is well and nothing needs to be done, or it may be that laws need to be changed, programs developed, or action taken to fulfill specific needs.

An example of research for family policy can be seen in a study aimed to determine the socioeconomic processes that determine the use of welfare and its accompanying dependency, and the impact of labor market conditions on the determinants of dependency.[7] The life-style at issue was low-income female-headed households dependent on welfare. Data were gathered from more than 300 of these women in New Jersey

---

7. Robert F. Kelly, "Welfare Dependency Under Depressed Labor Market Conditions: Lessons from the 1970s for the 1980s," *Journal of Urban Affairs* 5 (Fall 1983): 331–348.

at three different time periods. One of the hypotheses was that the most immediate economic trade-off faced by low-income single female parents was between the expected return from labor supplied to the formal labor market, and the need for her at home. Findings provided basic support to the idea that welfare can be reduced by making the expected value of work outside the home greater than home-related work. The policy implication is not to merely expand jobs or provide work of any kind, but to provide jobs that maximize the potential for financial independence. In other words, producing fewer, but relatively better, jobs may be a more useful strategy than producing poor jobs for a broad cross-section of the low-income population. The research suggests that welfare dependency among low-income women can be reduced by jobs that possess internal job ladders, the possibility of advancement, on-the-job training, and the job protection afforded by unionization. Unfortunately, federal support has largely been withdrawn for these types of training and job experiences. And workfare, as this research suggests, if it is only an administrative requirement that some job be found regardless of the job's quality, is unlikely to have a long-term positive impact.

Of the three types of family policy research, this third type of research for public policy should ideally be undertaken first to determine if programs or policies are necessary. If they are necessary and are put into effect, then family evaluation research and impact analysis can be conducted to assess their effectiveness and consequences.

In a highly pluralistic society such as exists in the United States, a wide variety of value positions are evident. Some value a minimum level of income for all families while others value independence and self-achievement, thus opposing programs such as AFDC and welfare. Some value the right of a woman to determine if she desires to abort a pregnancy while others value a pregnancy as a life and abortion as contrary to the will of God. The establishment of family policies demands a recognition of divergent value positions and divergent views that exist on this matter. Let's note some key issues, presented again in ideal-type terms, that surround the formulation and enforcement of policies directed toward or affecting families.

ISSUES SURROUNDING FAMILY POLICY

Policy matters seldom exist without a divergence of ideas, conflicts over positions, or opposing recommendations. Policy matters seldom satisfy all interest groups or get the endorsement of all social and political organizations. At times these differences relate to basic philosophies of life, perceptions of the role of government, or images of what the family is or should be. Following is an examination of several of these differences.

While they are presented in dichotomous or "either/or" terms and often as polar extremes, both views do exist simultaneously. Rarely can they be resolved into either/or positions.

Policy for the status quo or as a force for change?

The first issue addresses questions related to the type of family or families desired and the goals or objectives of family policy. Should policy be directed toward "*the* family" or toward a diversity of families? Is policy directed at preventing the family from change and maintaining the status quo or at supporting change, flexibility, and creativity? This issue is at the heart of Scanzoni's differentiation of conventionals from progressives.[8]

Conventionals are those that believe the normal family is conjugal. A male as husband is head of the household and the sole economic provider. A female as wife and mother is a helpmate to the husband and a homemaker who is responsible for household duties, domestic care, and the socialization of the children. Children are helpless and dependent. Conventionals, represented by political and religious conservatives, want to save this traditional image of what families should be. Groups like the New Right and the Moral Majority view family change as a breakdown of morality and disintegration of *the* family. They have demonstrated substantial political power in crippling sex education programs, halting the Equal Rights Amendment, and electing persons who oppose abortion. They have influenced legislation such as the Family Protection Act that provides that parents be notified when an unmarried minor receives contraceptive devices or abortion services from a federally supported organization, restricts the federal government from interfering with state statutes pertaining to child abuse, and changes the definition of abuse to exclude corporal punishment (spanking), prohibits funds for abortion, legal services for homosexuals, or education materials that do not reflect differences in ways women and men live and "do not contribute to the American way of life as it has been historically understood" (Family Protection Act, Section 301). The function of policy from the perspective of conventionals is to maintain the status quo or return to some idealized image of what the family once was and should be.

Progressives are those that believe a normal family can take many forms. The view is not of *the* family but of families. A progressive model is a pluralistic one that allows many options. At the core of this model is

---

8. Scanzoni, *Shaping Tomorrow's Family,* and John Scanzoni, "Reconsidering Family Policy: Status Quo or Force for Change?" *Journal of Family Issues* 3 (September 1982): 277–300.

the notion that involved adults should strive to become equal partners and should seek to achieve equity among family members. Scanzoni states that "given their pluralistic view of society, progressives accept the notion that alternative views of family should be allowed to 'compete' in the marketplace, with nonaligned persons being allowed to gravitate toward those patterns suiting them best."[9] Conservatives cannot accept this notion.

Theoretically, Scanzoni links the functionalist approach with the conventionals. The emphasis is on structure and stability. Thus couples who stay together are successful and those who divorce are failures and represent breakdown. Out-of-wedlock births and female-headed households represent disorganization. In contrast, progressives are linked more closely with the conflict approach. Here the emphasis is on process and change. A wide variety of goals are legitimate and result from complex negotiations between interest groups, each with preferred family patterns. Thus, childless marriages, equalitarian family patterns, divorce, marriage in middle or old age, diverse family forms among minorities or the poor, cohabitation without marriage, homosexual relationships, abortion, wives in the employed labor force, or husbands as housekeepers and childrearers all become acceptable marital and family life-styles.

Scanzoni notes that in spite of the unified and influential efforts of the conventionals, the major weakness of their model is that it is out of sync with the times. It does not conform to what is actually happening on the current scene. Society is not static, families are not uniform, and goals are not unanimous. As Scanzoni states:

> To be sure, the progressive vision includes order, but the order is not maintenance of the status quo. Instead, order emerges out of the ongoing development of satisfactory equity as well as intimacy: Creativity replaces conformity and flexibility supersedes fixed duties.[10]

From the progressive perspective, marriage is not entered to carry out predictable, predetermined duties where husbands do certain things and wives do others but is entered as a context for the facilitation of interests held by both spouses. Children are not helpless and dependent but effectively trained in the dynamics of equitable decision making. Individuals may choose not to marry, to cohabit, to have no children, and to find employment that was traditionally defined as inconsistent with their gender. The fundamental issue is not, as claimed by conservatives, responsibility versus irresponsibility, but instead the preferred image of marriage and family. Policy is aimed not at maintaining past traditions or the status quo that the majority of citizens has already discarded, but at looking ahead and coming up with fresh ideas molded around an equal-

---

9. Ibid., p. 153.
10. Ibid., p. 159.

partner framework. The function of policy is first to recognize and accept the reality of changes already becoming apparent in Western society. A second function is to implement further change in a fashion that is responsive both to the question of social order as well as to the preferences of the persons involved. Other related issues surround this task.

The family as a public or private institution?

A second issue revolves around the extent to which the family is a **public** or a **private** institution. Strong arguments exist for a separation of church and state. Should not there be a separation of family and state as well? Is the family not a matter of personal concern, a haven for privacy, a place of unconditional affection and love, a network for sharing fears, anxieties, or joys, and a source of protection and security free from "big brother" and public dominance? Should interpersonal relationships within the family and decisions made by its members be free of societal dictates or laws? Cannot husbands and wives decide for themselves when, where, and how they desire to "make love," the number of children they want or don't want, the manner in which they control that number, and how they discipline, educate, clothe, or feed these children? Or does the state (the public) have the right (or obligation) to establish boundaries on each of the above marital-parental activities?

Advocates of the privacy position might argue for minimal intervention of the state into family matters. Advocates of the public position might argue that laws must be written and enforced to protect all family members and enhance equal rights and opportunities for all citizens. Interestingly, advocates of the privacy position on certain issues such as child care and a minimum family income often take a public position on governmental intervention on the prohibition or the passage of rigid requirements for divorce. For example, the right-wing groups mentioned previously led organized efforts in the 1970s and early 1980s against child and family legislation and against the Equal Rights Amendment, but for anti-abortion laws.

Alvin Schorr sees the resistance to government intervention in private affairs of individuals to be one of the key factors against ever seeing an explicit family policy in the United States. In his words:

> As citizens, we are profoundly suspicious of and opposed to government. Despite all the power that government has come to have, we perennially oppose its spread—and, most particularly, where we believe it to be interfering in matters private, sentimental, or sexual.[11]

---

11. Alvin L. Schorr, "Views of Family Policy," *Journal of Marriage and the Family* 41 (August 1979): 465.

How about tests for marriage and parenthood—renewable if passed?

Anyone who has attended school is familiar with tests. They follow a course of training and are intended to measure familiarity and competence in that area. If you pass them, you get certain rewards such as higher grades, course or class advancement, degrees, and the like. If you fail them, some alternatives may be to drop out, take them again, or find some substitute for the course or exam. Anyone who drives an automobile at one time received instructions, took a driving test, a written exam or both, and if passed, received a license. Anyone who has a life-saving certificate received it after a period of training and evidence of knowledge and competence. Are marriage and parenthood less important? Do persons who marry and become parents have no need for training? Should couples receive licenses or endorsements for marriage or parenthood only following the passing of a test showing competence?

Evidence surrounding divorce, abuse, alcoholism, crime, or mental illness suggests that many persons should not marry, or if married, should not have children. Evidence shows that many married couples and parents say they were not fully aware of what they were getting into, had no formal and explicit training, and were not prepared financially or emotionally to cope adequately. Some would not have married or have had children at all. Others would have delayed both marriage and parenthood.

As a possible remedy, one suggestion could be to require training for marriage and parenthood and require the passing of tests (other than age and blood) for entrance into these new status positions. A more radical suggestion could be to require periodic retesting. These ideas are not suggested as cure-alls to marital and family problems, but they could be considered a service to many would-be spouses and parents and might serve as a deterrent to or constraint on certain persons who are not prepared for or equipped to handle these situations. What are the implications of such suggestions? Everyone has heard cases of couples who decided to end "serious" premarital relationships after one or both became aware that a marriage with that particular individual couldn't work. Should this situation be established into a more formal process? Should training and testing be required for obtaining a marriage license, for entrance into parenthood, or both? Who would write the requirements? What do you think?

The fact that no explicit national or governmental family policy exists should not lead you to believe that the government is totally uninvolved in or neutral to families. A wide range of public policies deal with social security, health and medical care, child welfare, education, day care, and most areas of interest to family members. In the opinion of Sidney Johnson, III, the government is up to its eyeballs in programs that affect families intimately. He invites us to consider the effects on the family of the following policies: the financial incentive in medicare for institutional care for the aged as opposed to home health care; a welfare law that still permits half the states in this country to withhold federal aid to mothers and children unless the father is absent from the home; and the so-called anti-grand-mother provision in the day-care deduction. This last policy basically says that you can get a deduction for paying someone to care for your children where both parents or one parent are working, providing that the person who cares for your children is not a relative closer than a cousin. Under this ruling, if it's the child's grandmother who is claimed as a dependent, it's not a deductible expense: if it's the neighbor's grandmother, it is.[12]

The lack of a coherent plan, set of services, or national policy may be testimony to the fact that families have no organized or powerful lobby groups to influence family legislation and oversee the impact of any leg-islative matters on marriages and families. By contrast, business, religious, and medical groups have many organized efforts to protect their vested interests.

The difficulty of family policy formulation may also reflect the wide range of nontraditional forms, functions, and processes of United States families. As indicated previously, perhaps a first step in the formation of family policies relates to the need to recognize that families do not all fit one monolithic stereotype with a husband as wage earner, a wife as homemaker, and two children (one girl and one boy, of course) as future replicants of their parents. This is one component of the next issue as well.

Policy for all families, or just for families with problems?

Assuming certain family policies are necessary, a third issue is whether these policies should be directed toward families in general or toward those families with "problems," toward families with any life-style or toward families with "pathologies." The former position focuses on issues that affect all families: employment, health, minimum wages, housing, sexual and racial equality, tax equity, and the like. The latter position focuses on "problem" areas: unwed parenthood, abortion, abuse, single parents, divorce, and the like. Perhaps a medical analogy is relevant. Traditionally, medical care in the United States was directed toward the sick. Physicians were to be seen only when colds, disease, or broken bones "created" the need. An emerging view is directed at prevention, as a holistic orientation to care, or toward an emphasis on health and how to maintain it.

Advocates of the families-in-general position might argue that to

12. A. Sidney Johnson, III, "Public Policies and Families," in *The American Family: Dying or Developing?* ed. by David Reiss and Howard A. Hoffman (New York: Plenum Press, 1979): 207.

focus on family problems may alert the public to a policy need and may be a logical starting point. But the prevention of future problems would mean a focus on the family generally and from the very beginning would encompass all families, including the "problem" ones. Advocates of the families-with-problems position might argue that policies should be directed to specific needs and concerns, with the assumption that most families don't need, or perhaps want, either assistance or restrictions. To focus on problems directs energy and funds to where it is most needed.

To label specific types of families as *problems, pathological,* or *ill* may in itself affect the type of policy directed toward that form of family. Consider single parenthood as an example. If this form of family—one parent with children—is "pathological," then policy is likely to be couched in terms of preventing the formation of single-parent family structures and providing services designed to facilitate reconstitution of these "less than complete" families. On the other hand, if one-parent families are one of many accepted family life-styles, the policy is likely to be couched in terms of what is necessary for all families: minimum incomes, adequate housing, inexpensive child care, employment opportunities, support services, and the like. Issues change focus drastically if, in the words of Alvin Schorr and Phyllis Moen, "one views single parenthood as a normal and permanent feature of our social landscape."[13]

This issue of single parenthood, like most others, is not an either/or situation. But it may focus attention on three related questions. One is the key issue just described of whether we focus on all families or families with problems. The second is the issue of how the definition of a particular behavior or family structure may affect the type of policies suggested. The third issue is the question of what effect any specific policy may have for families. It seems safe to assume that policies are rarely established in response to this question, but rather they seem to be directed at some specific "problem" areas of concern, either in general social policy or in solving some problematic aspect of family policy. In illustration of this, Sidney Johnson observed that there was only one issue he could remember in the years he had worked in the Senate on which some part of the decision was based on an explicit debate of what it meant to families: that was the decision to revoke year-round daylight saving time.[14] The intent of the new policy was directed at energy conservation. But parents around the country would not stand for sending their children to a bus stop in the early morning darkness. The correctness of that daylight saving time decision can always be debated, but the point is that the impact of this decision on families, and more specifically on children, became for

---

13. Alvin L. Schorr and Phyllis Moen, "The Single Parent and Public Policy," *Social Policy* 9 (March/April 1979): 20.

14. Johnson, "Public Policies and Families," p. 209.

once the key item of concern. This question, What does a given policy mean to families? is one that needs to be asked continually if the family is to be an institution of importance and concern to our policy making.

Policy for families or for individuals?

The fourth issue is whether family policy should be directed at *families* or at *individuals*. This involves a difference between one perception of the family unit as a system in which all parts (statuses) are interrelated and interdependent, versus another perception of the family unit as a collection of separate and isolated individuals. The individual perspective focuses on the person as the unit of analysis, with little attention devoted to the family unit of which that individual is a part. Today, a heavy emphasis appears to be toward individuals and specific persons. To deal with a marital problem, counsel the husband or the wife. To deal with the elderly, the ill, unwed mothers, the mentally retarded, delinquent youths, abused children, and the like, provide housing (or institutionalization), personal counseling, and individual attention. In contrast, the family-system perspective recognizes the marriage, the nuclear family, or the extended family as a composite unit, rather than as collections of individuals. In dealing with marital or family problems, the system focus would be directed toward the whole system or unit, recognizing that all components of that unit affect all other components.

The advocates of the individualistic position might argue that the sick person, the unwed mother, or the mentally retarded person is the one with the problem and needs the "treatment" and the attention. They may also argue that one is never sure of exactly what comprises the family unit. Advocates of the family-system position might argue that persons never exist in isolation of a larger social order and society. According to a system view, statuses are reciprocal. Husbands only exist in relation to wives, children in relation to parents, and brothers and sisters in relation to other siblings. Thus, the proponents of a system approach will argue that social policy needs to include a recognition that all social beings are parts of, and are affected by, other parts, and that the welfare of any given individual is greatly affected by the persons, groups, and community with which that individual identifies. While the family unit may not consist of one mother, one father, and two children, various organizational structures fulfill similar familial functions.

From a system viewpoint, policies directed at families are not anti-individual—nor are they intended to be. The needs of children, husbands, wives, adolescents, or the elderly may be equally important to the needs of the families. A system approach suggests that individuals are components of social networks, and that those individuals can be served best by a

How about divorce insurance?

In the United States people are encouraged to protect themselves against future difficulties by insuring themselves. We buy automobile insurance to protect us from the economic loss of the automobile and the possibility of suit against loss of life and property. We buy health insurance to protect us from the possibility of major medical bills. We buy dental insurance to protect us from major costs associated with tooth decay, removal, or correction. We buy property insurance to protect us from destruction or loss of our homes. We buy disability insurance to protect us from an inability to work and maintain an income. We pay dues or taxes to cover unemployment compensation as protection against the loss of a job. We pay into a social security system to (hopefully) provide income for our retirement years. Should we not be covered by divorce insurance?

As shown in Chapter 17, more than one million divorces occur annually. An overwhelming number of female-headed households and some male-headed households face a serious problem of inadequate income. While welfare and child support payments are available to many persons, it can be argued that a welfare dollar is different from an insurance dollar and child support payments are different from social security payments. Divorce insurance, involving largely the private sector of the economy, may for many parents, provide them with the freedom and autonomy to plan for their own lives and those of their children with assurance and certainty.

Let's consider how such a system might work: Divorce insurance premiums, unlike most health and life insurance premiums, could be large during the early years of the policy and decrease with the length of time married. Benefits could work inversely: small benefits for brief marriages and increasingly larger benefits for longer-term marriages. If the benefits are paid over time rather than in one lump sum, divorce for the purpose of insurance collection could be minimized. The basic principle behind this type of insurance, like any other insurance, would be to provide guaranteed financial resources to the single parent, particularly those with children. Would newly married couples be motivated to invest in such insurance? If not, how would the insurance be funded? What do you think?

recognition of one of the most important of these networks, the family. It also suggests a recognition of the family as a singular unit rather than as a collection of separated and isolated individuals.

Policy at a micro- or a macro-level?

A fifth issue, somewhat related to the fourth, is whether family policy should operate at primarily a **micro-level** or **macro-level.** Micro-level policy focuses on patterns of personal interactions that characterize everyday life. Macro-level policy focuses on the social patterns and forms of social organization that shape an entire society. These patterns are beyond the control of any given individual, yet they play a powerful role in affecting families and influencing personal lives.

Many social policies at a macro-level are related to areas such as taxation, medical care, employment, housing, education, or leisure. While policies in these areas may not be established directly for the benefit of families, they affect them greatly. If poverty status is characterized by lowered levels of commitment to marriage, and if high rates of marital dissolution are related to frequency of unwed parenthood, child abuse, and low levels of mental and marital health, then it seems imperative that social policy be directed not merely at counseling the mother or the abused wife or child, but at the conditions maintaining poverty. If welfare policies force men to live separately from their mate and children, or if federal tax laws or social security requirements impose penalties on marriage, then these policies, operating at a macro-level, need to be reexamined. If sexual or racial inequality in society prevents wives from establishing credit or owning property and black families from living in certain neighborhoods or attending certain schools, then these practices and conditions need to be addressed at a level beyond any given individual or family.

One example of this can be seen in a paper dealing with the consequences of unemployment for families in the 1980s.[15] Phyllis Moen, using data from several depression periods, notes that: (1) most families of the unemployed who suffered financial hardship received no government income support; (2) unemployment benefits are an important coping mechanism for families of the long-term unemployed; (3) limiting the duration of unemployment appears to be as important a strategy for preventing financial hardship as is the availability of income support; and (4) families with more than a single wage earner are much more able to avoid economic privation. The differential distribution and unequal sharing of the costs of unemployment across families highlights the plight of black families, single parents, and parents of young children, and highlights how unemployment and its financial repercussions are shaped by broad social, economic, and political forces operating at a macro-level. Even with a healthy economy with "full employment," some portion of the labor force remains jobless. With major cutbacks in social programs plus the lag in governmental response, the financial toll on families experiencing unemployment can be traumatic. Note how events at a macro-level increase or decrease the level of unemployment and how macro-level policies lessen or heighten the negative impact of being unemployed.

Moen suggests as well that public policies facilitating the employment

15. Phyllis Moen, "Unemployment, Public Policy, and Families: Forecasts for the 1980s," *Journal of Marriage and the Family* 45 (November 1983): 751–760.

of women (flexible work patterning, day care, nondiscriminatory hiring and wage practices) could help both two-earner families and single-parent women make ends meet.[16] The policies are, however, slow in being developed and implemented.

Scanzoni[17] presents the argument that macro-level family-related objectives have rarely addressed fundamental issues, since it is impossible to define a family in concrete terms and not exclude many of the non-traditional forms as described throughout this text. Likewise, micro-level responses have been inadequate because a gap often exists between the demands of contemporary society and the capabilities of conventional families and individuals to grapple with those demands. Thus he argues for policy at a **meso** level, an alternative model that supplies a fit between the macro- and micro-levels. The meso-level involves "mediating structures," that is, groups and organizations that extend beyond the person or family but don't encompass an entire state or nation. These include community groups, agencies, churches, local chapters of national organizations such as the National Organization for Women (NOW), the American Civil Liberties Union (ACLU), Planned Parenthood, Family Service Associations, veterans' associations, unions, political action groups, and so forth. These groups could mediate, provide training, and offer support to the diverse range of family structures and concerns found in our pluralistic society. This is closely linked to the next issue of who has the responsibility for establishing family policies.

Policy at a federal or local level?

A sixth issue is whether federal, state, or local units should assume responsibility in the formulation and enforcement of family policy. Under the Reagan administration this issue was central to funding activities. The federal government position has been that states, in the form of block grants from the federal government, should determine how and for what purposes the money should be spent. Opponents of this position argue that family-related concerns will be ignored even more than at present and that policies that are established will reflect the views of the most conservative segments of the population. Evidence does suggest that the thrust of state family laws continues to support the conventional family model described in the first issue.

As indicated elsewhere, the United States has no federal family policy as such. As noted in Chapters 8 and 17, for example, the legal control of marriage and divorce in the United States currently resides with the

---

16. Ibid., p. 758.
17. Scanzoni, *Shaping Tomorrow's Family*, pp. 97–118 and 225–227.

How about a tax-free family lunch?

Those familar with our basic social institutions are well aware of the tax breaks afforded them. All church property and religious holdings, amounting to billions of dollars, are free of federal and state taxation. Educational expenses relating to employment such as books, supplies, professional meetings, or additional training to improve skills in a current position are tax-deductible items. Gifts to politicians, their travel expenses, postage costs, office space and supplies, and entertaining costs are at the taxpayers' expense. Business expenses such as food, lodging, travel, supplies, labor, gifts, or entertainment done on behalf of a business become legitimate pre-profit expenses and are not subject to taxation.

Is marriage and the family of lesser social importance? Can dinner with a wife be considered as worthwhile as a dinner with a business associate? Is taking a son or daughter to one baseball game not as valid for society as the block of season tickets the company writes off as an expense? Is the home and shelter provided for families not as important to society as the elaborate churches, synagogues, and cathedrals of religious groups? Is a family vacation not equal in importance to the political junkets of a small town official or a U.S. Congressman or -woman? Should the husband pay taxes at a higher rate because his wife takes on a part-time job to supplement the family income? How about a tax-free family lunch? What do you think?

states rather than the federal government.[18] All states designate the husband as the head of the family and require him to support his family. While no state permits polygamy per se, the states differ considerably as to grounds for divorce and ease of remarriage. While no state permits the marriage of pre-teenage children, states vary as to the age that youth may legally marry. Involvement at the federal level becomes evident when one notes how certain restrictions set at the state level, such as the prohibition of miscegenation (marriage between members of different races), abortion, and the distribution of contraceptives, were ruled unconstitutional by the Supreme Court. So, while marriage laws are formulated and enforced by the state, federal courts have at times declared various practices to be unconstitutional. Also at the federal level, the United States Congress has established both explicit and implicit civil rights policies that have an impact on every facet of marriage and family life.

For decades, the federal government held White House conferences

---

18. For an overview of many of these state laws, *see* Doris Jonas Freed and Timothy B. Walker, "Family Law in the Fifty States: An Overview," *Family Law Quarterly* 19 (Winter 1986): 331–441.

on children. In the latter part of the 1970s, the president of the United States called for a White House conference on the family. Immediately steeped in controversy, the conference was postponed, and in 1980 a series of conferences on families were held throughout the country. Among other consequences, these conferences, which were initiated at the federal level, focused attention on American families and sought to establish social policies that would lend support and strength to this social institution.

This issue, like all others, is not an either/or question. There are both advantages and disadvantages to the establishment of family policies at either a national or a state level. Robert Leik and Reuben Hill[19] illustrate advantages of family policy at the federal level as including:

1. The family per se would not be lost in local obscurity but would become visible as the major unit of concern, which may be as much a symbolic advantage as a practical one.
2. Many major influences on families, such as the military, labor, business, or agriculture, occur primarily at the national level and only at this level can significant power be obtained for families.
3. Standards can be set at a national level which minimize local prejudices, indifference, or economy-minded legislative concerns.
4. Large-scale funding and the establishment of priorities are possible at a national level, but impossible at a state or local level.
5. Only at the national level can a vision for families be created which transcends regions and localities.

While there are distinct advantages of family policy at the federal level, there are also inherent problems. One problem centers around how policies can be maximally adapted to the special needs of racial, ethnic, regional, or other cultural groups. A second problem centers around how to make policies maximally responsive and accountable to clients. This requires local control. A third problem centers around assessing the adequacy of monitoring services provided. Leik and Hill suggest that there are appropriate roles for the participation of the national government, state or regional government, local government, and the private sector in an overall set of policies aimed at helping and strengthening families.[20] According to this view, money alone cannot do the job; nor can one level of government.

THE FUTURE OF THE FAMILY SYSTEM

The underlying issue in this chapter dealing with family policy related issues is that of the future of the family system. Will it survive? What types

---

19. Robert K. Leik and Reuben Hill, "What Price National Policy for Families?" *Journal of Marriage and the Family* 41 (August 1979): 458–459.
20. Ibid., p. 459.

It is expected that in the future most Americans will continue to seek marriage, children, and some type of family involvement in their lives. (Photo: © Camerique Stock Photos/E. P. Jones, Co.)

of families and societies will exist in the next ten, fifty, or one hundred years? How do we prepare for them? What type of training do we need to provide for our children and grandchildren (assuming they will be "our" children)? What types of family structures will exist? What functions will the family perform? Will the family be necessary? Will marriage exist? Will women have equal status with men? Will heterosexual partners be necessary for marriage or for children? These are a sampling of the questions that can be raised. The answers may depend on who gives them, the basis or theory on which the projection is based, the length of time projected, the types of family and social policies instituted, and, perhaps, the personal wishes of the projector.

That the family is changing and will continue to change is perhaps, although not necessarily, a definitive statement and one on which we could find widespread agreement. But comments on decay and breakdown or on progress and advancement must be approached cautiously. The following observations are made in relation to predicting the future. First, changes that take place and will take place in the society or family are not necessarily pleasing or regrettable, good or bad, or constructive or destructive per se. Changes are likely to be welcomed or rejected depending largely on one's own frame of reference, the groups with which one identifies, and the value orientations to which one adheres. Rising divorce rates can be viewed either as a problem or as a solution to other problems. Homosexuality may be viewed as an illness or as a right to love whomever one chooses. War may be viewed as vital to national defense or as an immoral destruction of life and property. This is not meant to imply that there are not changes that are disruptive to the social order, but it is meant to imply that social matters must be seen in the context in which they occur. It is a rare issue that cannot be interpreted in various ways.

Second, although many people see the family at the core of society and as the most basic of all institutions, it should be made clear what has been stated time and again: the family cannot be understood as an isolated phenomenon. It must be viewed in relation to economic, educational, religious, and political institutions. In addition, factors such as population density, mobility patterns, and stratification divisions must be taken into account. It is not by chance that agricultural societies will tend to emphasize extended families, parental involvement in mate selection, and, often, plural marriage. Neither is it by chance that the United States places an emphasis on romantic love, separate households, and monogamous marriages. The central point is that, if accurate family predictions are to be made, it is essential to have an understanding of what is going to take place in other social systems. A change in any element of a social system will likely lead to changes in other elements, including the family.

Third, the family is not a uniform entity. That change will occur is almost without question. But to speak of the changing family, or even of families in the United States, as if they were uniform entities can be misleading. From the very beginnings of U.S. society, the cultural base of its population was diverse and varied. Then, as today, one could expect to find variations in family patterns by factors such as rural-urban residence, region of the country, religious affiliation, racial and ethnic identity, social-class background, or age. And yet, despite the diversity that comprises family life in the United States, one significant change has been the assimilation of quite different cultural heritages. One must recognize the manifest differences that exist in social class, race, and religious background and at the same time recognize that within this diversity there are strands of unity that belie heterogeneous origins.

Fourth, any type of social projection into the future is hazardous. Some trends are short-term ones, tied to the economic climate of prosperity that so drastically affects marriage, birth, and divorce rates. Some trends are not necessarily linear or even directional and may be highly or basically unpredictable. Other changes may be internal to the system or external to it, accidental or planned, behavioral or attitudinal, material or nonmaterial, actual or ideal, patterned or nonpatterned, peaceful or violent, continuous or spasmodic, rapid or slow, due to single causes or many causes. This suggests that predictions should be made cautiously—no one can predict the future without error.

Having provided all these qualifications—that change is not equal to decay, breakdown, or destruction; that what happens to the larger social order and other systems affects the family; that the family itself is extremely diverse; and that projection into the future is hazardous—permit me to brave this hazard and state, unequivocally, that as long as a society exists, *the family system will survive.* More difficult to state with equal conviction are the forms the family will take, the meaning it will have for its members, the structure of relationships, and how or what specific functions it will perform.

There is little doubt that the passing of the conventional family has left a great many traumas, a great deal of suffering, and a great many loose ends. As Jessie Bernard suggests:

> It will take considerable re-thinking, searching and re-searching, and balancing of costs and benefits before these problems can be dealt with optimally. It will take much painful re-evaluation of the pursuit of happiness. If the 1970s were a time of crisis, revolution, and moral political issues, the 1980s will be a time of putting the pieces together to develop family structures suitable for this time and place, this day and age.[21]

Whatever those re-assembled pieces will be, we can be assured that the family will continue to perform various major functions. Most Americans will continue to find marriage and family interaction as a basic source of emotional and psychic stability. Families will continue to be primary sources of socialization, primary sources of security and affection, and primary sources of meaning. Partners within the marriage may change, the expectations of men and women may change, the sexual codes and practices may change, the general family life-styles may be vastly different. These changes are not necessarily to be equated with decay, immorality, or a general deterioration of U.S. families. If our society is destroyed and the family has a hand in this destruction, it is not likely to be because of change but rather because of an inability to change.

SUMMARY

1. All areas of marriage and family life are affected by certain economic, political, or other social policies. It seems safe to assume that while

---

21. Jessie Bernard, "Facing the Future," *Society* 18 (January/February 1981): 59.

most social policies have an effect on families, few of these policies were developed or formulated with marriages and families in mind. As used in this chapter, *family policy* refers to definite methods of action directed at marriages, families, or kin groups with the intent of guiding, influencing, or determining their form, their functions, or the behavior, ideas, or values of their members.

2.   This chapter deals with three family and change topics. First, family policy research is examined and three specific types are presented. Second, six issues that surround family policy are discussed. Third, the chapter concludes with some comments on the future of the family.

3.   Family policy research, perhaps even more than most, is confronted with the issue of whether or not the researcher permits a personal value stance or policy objective to influence the research. It raises anew the research issue of focusing on what is as opposed to what should be.

4.   Three types of family policy research are discussed. Family evaluation research attempts to determine the degree to which social programs achieve the stated goals. Family impact analysis assesses the intended and unintended consequences of public policy and social programs. Research for public policy examines some particular family structure or life-style to determine if certain policies or programs are necessary and make recommendations as to what they should be.

5.   Policy matters seldom exist without a divergence of ideas, conflicts over positions, or opposing recommendations. At a general level of analysis, six of these issues or differences are examined. These include:

a.   The extent to which policies are aimed at maintaining the status quo or serve as forces for change. Conventionals seek the status quo as idealized in *the* traditional conjugal family while progressives seek change and multiple family forms more consistent with a pluralistic society.

b.   The extent to which the family is a *public* or *private* institution, meaning basically the extent to which there should be a separation of family and governmental or legal intervention.

c.   The extent to which policies should be directed toward *families in general* or toward *families with problems*—that is, toward all families irrespective of life-style or toward families with "pathologies."

d.   The extent to which policies should be directed at *families* or at *individuals*—that is focusing on the social unit or system or focusing on persons as our unit of attention.

e.   The extent to which policies should operate at primarily a *micro-level* or *macro-level*—that is, focusing on small-group or interpersonal relationships or focusing on social patterns or forms of social organization that shape entire societies.

   f. The extent to which policies should be established or controlled at the *federal, state,* or *local* level—that is, national in scope and control or in the hands of regional, state, or local communities.

6.   What about the future of the family? Our social policies will, without doubt, affect the future directions the family and its members take. The family is changing and will continue to change. We should take note that, first, these changes are not good or bad, per se. Second, the future of the family cannot be understood separate from other institutions and systems. Third, the family of the future will not be a uniform entity. And, fourth, any type of social projection into the future must be made cautiously. Given these qualifications, I predict unequivocally that as long as a society exists, the family system will survive. It will have many differing structural arrangements, perform a variety of functions, and fulfill a range of personal and social needs. Whether your interest in the family is at a professional level of teaching, research, or social action or at a personal level of dating, child rearing, or caring for aged parents, it will be impossible not to affect or be affected by families.

KEY TERMS AND TOPICS

DISCUSSION QUESTIONS

1.   How would you differentiate among policy, social policy, and family policy? Can you think of examples of social policy that exist independently of or have no impact on families?

2.   Can, or should, family policy research be value-free? Can, or should, policy research be separated from policy advocacy? How can family policy researchers

integrate or combine finding out what *is* with a concern over *what should be?*

3. Describe the different goals or intents of family evaluation research, family impact analysis, and research for public policy.

4. What arguments exist for establishing policy to maintain the status quo as opposed to policy that permits or forces change and diversity? Is it possible to talk about *the* family in the Western world? Why or why not?

5. Contrast the stances taken by conventionals and progressives. How do these stances translate into policy directives on issues such as teenage sexual behavior and contraceptive usage, sex education, abortion, day care facilities, cohabitation, divorce, remarriage, the employment of mothers of young children, and so forth?

6. Discuss some of the arguments for or against the separation of family and state. List areas in which the government clearly has no "right" to get involved and areas in which its involvement is mandatory.

7. One issue differentiated policy directed at all families from policy issues directed at families with problems. Explain. What are some effects of labeling certain family life-styles or structural arrangements as "problems"?

8. How might family policies for children, unwed mothers, the terminally ill, or the elderly differ depending on whether they are directed at individuals or directed at marital, family, or kinship units?

9. Do you believe effective family change can occur within a society by directing programs and policies exclusively at individuals or interpersonal relationships, that is, at a micro-level? Explain.

10. List some arguments for family policy to be established at a federal as opposed to a state or local level. What are arguments against this idea? Is a national family policy possible or realistic? Why or why not?

11. Examine the three panels, all of which end with "What do you think?" What do you think about tests for marriage and parenthood, divorce insurance, or a tax-free family lunch? Explain.

12. What predictions can you make about families and marital life-styles in the twenty-first century? Describe their structures, functions, the impact of new technologies, changing parent-child relationships, the division of marital roles and tasks, the status of women, and sexual norms. What areas are most likely to remain static, stable, and relatively unchanged?

FURTHER READINGS

Bane, Mary Jo. *Here to Stay: American Families in the Twentieth Century.* New York: Basic Books, 1976. A book divided into two distinct parts: the first deals with contemporary U.S. families in the perspectives of change during this century; the second explores policy areas illuminated by data presented in Part I.

Dempsey, John J. *The Family and Public Policy.* Baltimore: Paul H. Brooks, 1981. An historical overview of developments leading to the emergence of the family as a public policy issue.

Giraldo, Zaida I. *Public Policy and the Family: Wives and Mothers in the Labor Force.* Lexington, Mass.: D. C. Heath, 1980. An examination of the impacts of employment on family life, tax policy on employed women, and the Equal Rights Amendment on families.

Hannan, Michael T.; Tuma, Nancy Brandon; and Groeneveld, Lyle P. "Income and Marital Events: Evidence from an Income-Maintenance Experiment." *American Journal of Sociology* 82 (May 1977): 1186–1211. A report on the impacts of Seattle and Denver income-maintenance experiments on marital dissolution and remarriage, showing how changes in economic situation do affect marital events in low-income populations.

Huttman, Elizabeth Dickerson. *Introduction to Social Policy.* New York: McGraw-Hill, 1981. An introduction to social policy issues. Chapter 8 deals with AFDC and the poor, Chapter 9 with child welfare services, and Chapter 10 with the aged.

Moroney, Robert M. *Shared Responsibility: Families and Social Policy.* Hawthorne, N.Y.: De Gruyter Aldine, 1986. A development of the notion of shared responsibility between the family and the state in the delivery of social care through social services.

Nye, F. Ivan, and McDonald, Gerald. "Special Issue: Family Policy." *Journal of Marriage and the Family* 41 (August 1979): 453–664. A special issue on family policy covering a wide range of issues including the need for an explicit family policy, policy research, European and United States political contexts, and the effects of welfare and recession on families and others.

Scanzoni, John. *Shaping Tomorrow's Family: Theory and Policy for the 21st Century.* Beverly Hills: Sage Publications, 1983. An insightful analysis of the struggle between "conventionals" and "progressives" in determining the type of family or families appropriate for U.S. society.

Steiner, Gilbert Y. *The Futility of Family Policy.* Washington, D.C.: Brookings Institution, 1981. A commentary on the family policy developments of the 1970s, with the central theme that not only is a comprehensive family policy futile, it simply does not exist.

Glossary

Achieved status A social position that is obtained through one's own efforts, such as husband or teacher.

Affiliated families A variation of an extended family in which a nonrelative (often an older person) becomes recognized as a part of the nuclear family network.

Androgyny A society with no sex-role differentiation. Androgynous individuals are those who are capable of expressing both or either masculine or feminine behavior.

Annulment The ending of a marriage because of conditions that existed prior to the marriage. The result makes the marriage nonexistent.

Arranged marriage When marital partners are selected by persons (parents, matchmakers, etc.) other than the couple themselves.

Ascribed status A social position that is assigned to persons by society or by birth such as age, race, or sex.

Behaviorism A theory of learning that focuses on actual behavior believed to be the result of conditioning through rewards and punishments.

Bigamy The marriage of one person to two persons of the opposite sex (like polygamy but restricted to two).

Bilateral system A family system that traces descent and inheritance through both the male and female lines.

Birth order Sibling position based on the order of birth.

Blue-collar families The "working class" or the upper-lower class of semiskilled, service, and other workers with some sort of manual skill.

Bourgeoisie   The "class" or grouping of people who control the means of production and use capital, natural resources, and labor for profit.

Cohabitation   An arrangement where an unmarried male and female share a common dwelling.

Commune   A group of people holding collective ownership and use of property.

Complementary marriage   A traditional type of marriage where the husband and wife perform interdependent but different tasks: he is employed outside the home and she does the domestic tasks.

Complementary needs   A theory of mate selection based on the idea that people marry those who provide the maximum need gratification. Needs tend to be complementary rather than similar.

Concept   Tools or symbols by which one can share meanings and enable a phenomenon to be perceived in a certain way.

Conceptual frameworks   A cluster of interrelated concepts used to describe and classify phenomena.

Conflict frame of reference   A perspective of society that views conflict as natural, permanent, and inevitable and as a significant source of social change.

Conjugal family   A nuclear family which always has a husband and wife (the conjugal unit) and may or may not include children.

Consanguine families   Extended families based on blood relationships as the basis of descent from the same ancestors.

Conventionals   Groups and persons who want to maintain the status quo and adhere to a traditional image of what families should be.

Dependent variable   A variable that is changed or influenced by the effect of another variable (termed the **independent variable**).

Developmental frame of reference   A perspective that emphasizes the life cycle and various stages of transition with specific tasks to be accomplished at each stage.

Double standard   The use of one set of norms and values for females and a different set for males.

Dual-career marriages   Employment by both husband and wife in careers with levels of commitment and continuous developmental sequences.

Ecology   The relationships between the physical environment and the human population that lives in that environment.

Egalitarian family   Equal authority of husband and wife in family matters.

Electra complex   The unconscious desire of the female to marry her father.

Endogamy   A marriage pattern requiring persons to marry someone within their own social group.

Evaluation research   As applied to families and family policy, evaluation research is conducted at a pragmatic level to determine the extent to which the stated goals are being achieved.

Exchange frame of reference   A perspective that seeks to explain personal and social behaviors based on a reciprocity of rewards and costs.

Exogamy   A marriage pattern requiring individuals to marry outside their own group.

Extended family   A family in which two or more generations of the same kin live together (extension beyond the nuclear family).

Extramarital coitus   Nonmarital sexual intercourse between a man and a woman, at least one of whom is married to someone else.

Family   A kinship-structural group of persons related by blood, marriage, or adoption, usually related to the marital unit and including the rights and duties of parenthood.

Family life cycle   The social sequence of events such as marriage, children, empty nest, retirement, and death that are repeated by successive generations of families.

Family networks or clusters   A circle of families who live separately but meet regularly to share ideas, services, and supports.

Family of orientation   The nuclear family into which one was born and reared (consists of self, siblings, and parents).

Family of procreation   The nuclear family formed by marriage (consists of self, spouse, and children).

Fecundity   The biological potential of a woman to bear children (in contrast to fertility, the actual number of births).

Fertility   The actual number of births to women of childbearing age.

Fraternal polyandry   The marriage of one woman to two or more men all of whom are brothers.

Function   As related to a structural-functional frame of reference refers to what a [family] system does (the functions it performs) or the consequences of a given form of structure.

Gender   The cultural concepts of masculinity and femininity that society creates around sex (the biological fact of being male or female).

Gender identity (sexual identity)   The sex of which one considers one's self to be a member.

Group marriage   The marriage of two or more women to two or more men.

Heterosexuality   Sexual acts or feelings directed toward members of the opposite sex.

Homogamy   Marriage to a person with similar social characteristics.

Homosexuality   Sexual acts or feelings directed toward members of the same sex.

Horizontal mobility   A change from one social status to another that is roughly equivalent.

Household   The persons who occupy a housing unit.

Hypergamy   Marriage wherein the female marries upward into a higher social stratum (male marries down).

Hypogamy Marriage wherein the female marries downward into a lower social stratum (male marries up).

Hypothesis A statement of a relationship between variables that can be put to an empirical test.

Ideal-type constructs Hypothetical models of polar extremes which provide contrasting (opposite) points with which to compare any social phenomenon.

Illegitimacy The birth of a child to an unmarried woman.

Impact analysis Research aimed at an assessment of the intended and unintended consequence of family policy and programs.

Incest Socially forbidden sexual relationships or marriage with certain close relatives.

Independent variable A variable that causes a change or variation in another variable (termed the **dependent variable**).

Institution A stable cluster of values, norms, statuses, and roles that develop around a basic need of society.

Intergenerational mobility A change in the social status of family members from one generation to the next.

Internalization The process by which one makes the society's values part of one's personality.

Joint family One type of extended family in which brothers share property but do not always live in a single household.

Kin A network of persons who are related by common ancestry (birth), adoption, or marriage.

Legitimate birth Birth to parents who are married to each other.

Levirate The marriage of a widow to the brother of her deceased husband.

Life expectancy The average number of years that a person in a given population can expect to live.

Lifespan The maximum length of life possible in a given society.

Life-style As related to families, the shared patterns of marital and family relationships, childbearing, dress, eating, recreation, etc.

Macro-level policy Policies that focus on large-scale units such as social categories, systems, and forms of social organization that affect families: taxation, medical care, employment, housing, education, laws, and so forth.

Marriage A socially approved sexual union of some permanence between two or more persons.

Marriage squeeze The effects of an imbalance between the number of males and females in the prime marriage ages due to rising or falling birth rates and the median age difference at marriage.

Mating gradient The tendency for high-status women and low-status men to be less likely to date and marry.

Matriarchal family A family in which the wife rules or has dominance over the husband.

Matrilineal system   A family system that traces descent and inheritance through the mother's line.

Matrilocal residence   A family system in which a newly married couple is expected to live with the wife's family.

Mediation   A conflict resolution process where a divorcing couple meets with a third-party intervenor who helps them negotiate an agreement on property settlement, child support and custody, and other important matters.

Mésalliance   Marriage with a person of an inferior position.

Meso-level policy   Policies that focus on groups and organizations as mediating structures between the large-scale macro units and the small-scale micro units.

Micro-level policy   Policies that focus on small-scale units such as individuals and small-group interaction.

Minority group   Any group that is subordinate to another group.

Miscegenation   Marriage and interbreeding between members of different races, as in the United States between blacks and whites.

Modified-nuclear, modified-extended family   Nuclear families which retain considerable autonomy and yet maintain a coalition with other nuclear families where they exchange goods and services.

Monogamy   The marriage of one male to one female.

Neolocal residence   A family system in which a newly married couple is expected to establish a new place of residence separate from either parent.

No-fault divorce   The dissolution of marriage based on irreconcilable differences where neither party is "at fault."

Norm   A rule that tells members of a society how to behave in particular situations.

Nuclear family   Any two or more persons of the same or adjoining generation related by blood, marriage, or adoption sharing a common residence.

Oedipus complex   The unconscious desire of the male to marry his mother.

Orderly replacement   The idea of having successive generations being duplicates or similar to the preceding generation.

Parallel marriages   A type of marriage where the husband and wife perform similar tasks on an equitable basis: both are employed and both share child care and domestic tasks.

Patriarchal family   A family in which the husband rules or has dominance over the wife.

Patrilineal system   A family system that traces descent and inheritance through the father's line.

Patrilocal residence   A family system in which a newly married couple is expected to live with the husband's family.

Peer group   A group of people with similar or equal status and usually of similar age.

Policy   In reference to families, these are definite courses or methods of action with the intent of influencing or determining present and future forms of family organization, behaviors, or decisions.

Polyandry   The marriage of a woman to more than one husband.

Polygamy   The marriage of one man or one woman to more than one wife or more than one husband at the same time.

Polygyny   The marriage of one man to more than one wife at the same time.

Power   The ability to control or influence the behavior of others, even in the absence of their consent.

Primary group   A small group of people who interact in a personal, direct, and intimate way.

Progressives   Groups and persons who view families as pluralistic and accept change and nontraditional life styles as legitimate.

Proletariat   The "class" or grouping of people who labor and serve as the instrument of production for the bourgeoisie.

Propinquity   The marriage of persons who live close to one another.

Proposition   A statement of the relationship between two or more concepts or variables.

Random sample   A selection of persons in a way in which every member of the population has an equal chance of being chosen.

Reciprocity   Two-way exchange of goods and services. Basic to a social exchange frame of reference.

Reference group   A group with which persons psychologically identify and to whom people refer when making evaluations of themselves and their behavior.

Remarriage   Marriage by anyone who has previously been married.

Role   The social expectations or behaviors that accompany a particular status.

Role conflict   The situation in which incompatible expectations or behaviors accompany a given status or set of statuses.

Role taking   The ability to assume the status of persons with whom one interacts and see the world from their perspective.

Secondary group   A group whose members interact in an impersonal manner, have few emotional ties, and come together for a specific, practical purpose.

Separation   Individuals who are legally married but are not sharing a common household or residence.

Sequential monogamy   Marriage to a succession of partners but always to only one at a time.

Sex   The biological fact of being male or female.

Sex ratio   The number of males per one hundred females in a population.

Sex role Learned patterns of behavior expected of males and females in society.

Sexualization Sexual socialization. The process by which individuals acquire their sexual self-concepts, values, attitudes, and behaviors.

Sexual scripts A learned designation of the who, what, when, where, and why of sexuality.

Sibling One's brother or sister.

Significant other A person with whom one psychologically identifies and whose opinions are important.

Single parent Generally used in reference to a mother-child or father-child nuclear family unit.

Social class An aggregate of individuals who occupy broadly similar positions on the scale of prestige.

Socialization The process of learning the rules of and expectations for behavior for a given society.

Social self The organization of internalized roles which were developed in interaction with others.

Social system A set of interrelated social statuses (positions) and the accompanying expectations that accompany these positions.

Society A group of interacting individuals sharing the same territory and participating in a common culture.

Sociology The study of human society and social behavior.

Sororal polygyny The marriage of one man to two or more women all of whom are sisters.

Sororate The marriage of a widower to the sister of his deceased wife.

Status A socially defined position that a person occupies which may be ascribed (age, race, sex and so forth) or achieved (husband, father, teacher and so forth).

Stepchildren The children by a former marriage of one's husband or wife (stepmother, wife of one's father by remarriage; stepbrother, son of one's stepparent by a former marriage; etc.).

Stratification The differential ranking of people into horizontal layers (strata) of equality and inequality.

Structural-functional frame of reference A perspective that emphasizes the units of organization plus the consequences of that particular structural arrangement.

Subculture A group of persons who share in the overall culture of a society but also has its own distinctive values, norms, and life-styles.

Swinging A type of extramarital coitus in which the couple openly and willingly engages in sexual relationships with other married persons. Sometimes referred to as *co-marital sexual mate sharing* or *consensual adultery*.

Symbolic interaction frame of reference A perspective that stresses interaction between people as well as the social processes that occur within individuals made possible by language and internalized meanings.

Symmetrical family   Families as consumption units rather than production units where marital roles based on gender are eliminated.

Theory   A set of logically and systematically interrelated propositions that explain some particular process.

Underclass   Families within the poverty population that are characterized by persistent poverty and a variety of associated problems such as welfare dependency and crime.

Unilineal system   A family system that traces descent and inheritance through either the male line *or* the female line.

Universal permanent availability   The idea that any individual is a potential mate or available for marriage with any other individual.

Variable   A characteristic such as age, class, or income that can vary from one person or context to another.

Vertical mobility   Social mobility that involves movement toward a higher or lower social status.

Widowhood   The loss of a spouse by death.

NAME INDEX

SUBJECT INDEX